Lecture Notes in Computer Science 6402

Commenced Publication in 1973
Founding and Former Series Editors:
Gerhard Goos, Juris Hartmanis, and Jan van Leeuwen

Swee-Huay Heng   Kaoru Kurosawa (Eds.)

Provable Security

4th International Conference, ProvSec 2010
Malacca, Malaysia, October 13-15, 2010
Proceedings

 Springer

Volume Editors

Swee-Huay Heng
Multimedia University
Faculty of Information Science and Technology
Jalan Ayer Keroh Lama, 75450 Malacca, Malaysia
E-mail: shheng@mmu.edu.my

Kaoru Kurosawa
Ibaraki University
Department of Computer and Information Sciences
4-12-1 Nakanarusawa, Hitachi, Ibaraki, 316-8511, Japan
E-mail: kurosawa@mx.ibaraki.ac.jp

Library of Congress Control Number: 2010935665

CR Subject Classification (1998): E.3, C.2, K.6.5, D.4.6, J.1, E.4

LNCS Sublibrary: SL 4 – Security and Cryptology

ISSN	0302-9743
ISBN-10	3-642-16279-7 Springer Berlin Heidelberg New York
ISBN-13	978-3-642-16279-4 Springer Berlin Heidelberg New York

springer.com

© Springer-Verlag Berlin Heidelberg 2010
Printed in Germany

Typesetting: Camera-ready by author, data conversion by Scientific Publishing Services, Chennai, India
Printed on acid-free paper   06/3180

Preface

ProvSec 2010 was held in Malacca, Malaysia, October 13–15, 2010. This was the 4th Provable Security conference in the series aimed at stimulating the exchange of ideas in the emerging areas of provable security. This conference was organized by the Faculty of Information Science and Technology, Multimedia University, Malaysia, and co-organized by the Malaysian Society for Cryptology Research (MSCR).

The conference received a total of 47 submissions. Each submission was reviewed by at least three members of the Program Committee, and submissions co-authored by members of the Program Committee were reviewed by at least five members. The review process was a challenging task, 17 papers were accepted for presentation at the conference (with 1 conditionally accepted) after almost two months of review process, and some good submissions had to be rejected. This proceedings contains the revised versions of the accepted papers, which were not subject to editorial review, and the authors bear full responsibility for their contents. The conference also featured an invited lecture by Eike Kiltz entitled "Cryptographic Protocols from Lattices."

There were many parties who contributed in one way or another to the success of ProvSec 2010. We would like to thank all of the authors from many different countries for submitting their work. We are deeply grateful to the Program Committee for their hard work and effort in ensuring that each submission received a fair and thorough review. We also gratefully acknowledge the effort and expertise of the external reviewers. Lastly, we would like to record our appreciation to the General Chair, Bok-Min Goi, and the local Organizing Committee, for their dedication and commitment in organizing the conference, and to Shai Halevi, for granting us the permission to use the user-friendly Web-Submission-and-Review system.

October 2010

Swee-Huay Heng
Kaoru Kurosawa

ProvSec 2010

The Fourth International Conference on Provable Security

Malacca, Malaysia
October 13–15, 2010

Organized by Multimedia University, Malaysia
Co-organized by Malaysian Society for Cryptology Research (MSCR)

Supported by INSPEM, Universiti Putra Malaysia

General Chair

Bok-Min Goi   Universiti Tunku Abdul Rahman, Malaysia

Program Co-chairs

Swee-Huay Heng   Multimedia University, Malaysia
Kaoru Kurosawa   Ibaraki University, Japan

Program Committee

Alexandra Boldyreva   Georgia Institute of Technology, USA
Xavier Boyen   Stanford University, USA
David Cash   University of California, San Diego, USA
Dario Catalano   Universit di Catania, Italy
Alexander W. Dent   Royal Holloway, University of London, UK
Eiichiro Fujisaki   NTT, Japan
Jun Furukawa   NEC Corporation, Japan
Matthew Green   The Johns Hopkins University, USA
Vipul Goyal   Microsoft Research, India
Goichiro Hanaoka   AIST, Japan
Swee-Huay Heng   Multimedia University, Malaysia (Co-chair)
Takeshi Koshiba   Saitama University, Japan
Noboru Kunihiro   University of Tokyo, Japan
Kaoru Kurosawa   Ibaraki University, Japan (Co-chair)
Benoit Libert   Université catholique de Louvain, Belgium
David Naccache   École normale supérieure, France
Gregory Neven   IBM Research, Switzerland
Jesper Buus Nielsen   University of Aarhus, Denmark

Tatsuaki Okamoto   NTT, Japan
Josef Pieprzyk   Macquarie University, Australia
Palash Sarkar   Indian Statistical Institute, India
Berry Schoenmakers   TU Eindhoven, The Netherlands
Gil Segev   Weizmann Institute of Science, Israel
Willy Susilo   University of Wollongong, Australia
Keisuke Tanaka   Tokyo Institute of Technology, Japan

Steering Committee

Feng Bao   Institute for Infocomm Research, Singapore
Xavier Boyen   Stanford University, USA
Yi Mu   University of Wollongong, Australia
Josef Pieprzyk   Macquarie University, Australia
Willy Susilo   University of Wollongong, Australia

Organizing Committee

Ji-Jian Chin   Multimedia University
Michael Goh   Multimedia University
Hailiza Kamarulhaili   MSCR/Universiti Sains Malaysia
Muhammad Rezal K.A.   MSCR/Universiti Putra Malaysia
Huo-Chong Ling   Multimedia University
Chu-Kiong Loo   Multimedia University
Thian-Song Ong   Multimedia University
Shing-Chiang Tan   Multimedia University
Connie Tee   Multimedia University
Wei-Chuen Yau   Multimedia University

External Reviewers

Tadashi Araragi   Xinyi Huang   Palash Sarkar
Man Ho Au   Jae Ahn Hyun   Thomas Shrimpton
Zvika Brakerski   Toshiyuki Isshiki   Martijn Stam
Pierre-Louis Cayrel   Akinori Kawachi   S. Sree Vivek
André Chailloux   Yutaka Kawai   Bogdan Warinschi
Sanjit Chatterjee   Virendra Kumar   Kan Yasuda
Dario Fiore   Daisuke Moriyama   Kenji Yasunaga
Fuchun Guo   Ryo Nishimaki   Kazuki Yoneyama
Vanishree H   David Nowak   Maki Yoshida
Satoshi Hada   Adam O'Neill   Tsz Hon Yuen
Yoshikazu Hanatani   Somindu C. Ramanna   Wei Zhang
Qiong Huang   Thomas Ristenpart

Table of Contents

Improved Zero-Knowledge Identification with Lattices

Pierre-Louis Cayrel[1], Richard Lindner[2], Markus Rückert[2],
and Rosemberg Silva[3],[*]

[1] CASED – Center for Advanced Security Research Darmstadt,
Mornewegstrasse, 32, 64293 Darmstadt, Germany
pierre-louis.cayrel@cased.de
[2] Technische Universität Darmstadt, Fachbereich Informatik,
Kryptographie und Computeralgebra, Hochschulstraße 10,
64289 Darmstadt, Germany
{rlindner,rueckert}@cdc.informatik.tu-darmstadt.de
[3] State University of Campinas (UNICAMP), Institute of Computing,
P.O. Box 6176, 13084-971 Campinas, Brazil
rasilva@ic.unicamp.br

Abstract. Zero-knowledge identification schemes solve the problem of authenticating one party to another via an insecure channel without disclosing any additional information that might be used by an impersonator. In this paper we propose a scheme whose security relies on the existence of a commitment scheme and on the hardness of worst-case lattice problems. We adapt a code-based identification scheme devised by Cayrel and Véron, which constitutes an improvement of Stern's construction. Our solution sports analogous improvements over the lattice adaption of Stern's scheme which Kawachi *et al.* presented at ASIACRYPT 2008. Specifically, due to a smaller cheating probability close to $1/2$ and a similar communication cost, any desired level of security will be achieved in fewer rounds. Compared to Lyubashevsky's scheme presented at ASIACRYPT 2009, our proposal, like Kawachi's, offers a much milder security assumption: namely, the hardness of SIS for trinary solutions. The same assumption was used for the SWIFFT hash function, which is secure for much smaller parameters than those proposed by Lyubashevsky.

Keywords: Lattice-based cryptography, identification scheme, hash function, SIS problem, zero-knowledge.

1 Introduction

One of the main objectives in cryptography is to provide means of access control, and identification (ID) schemes are typically applied in order to reach this goal. These schemes describe interactive protocols between a designated prover and

---

[*] Supported by The State of São Paulo Research Foundation under grant 2008/07949-8.

S.-H. Heng and K. Kurosawa (Eds.): ProvSec 2010, LNCS 6402, pp. 1–17, 2010.

verifier with the purpose of demonstrating that the prover knows a secret that is associated with his identity. In zero-knowledge schemes, no information about this secret is revealed, except the fact that the prover knows it. Besides, using hard lattice problems as security basis allows for very mild assumptions in the sense that they are worst-case instead of average-case and provide resistance against quantum adversaries.

There is an efficient generic construction due to Fiat and Shamir that transforms any ID scheme into a signature scheme, in the random oracle model [7]. Therefore, having an efficient ID solution from lattices gives rise to a similarly efficient signature construction, keeping the same hardness assumption. One of the main hardness assumption for ID schemes based on lattices is the short integer solution (SIS) problem. One is given an average case instance $\mathbf{A} \in \mathbb{Z}_q^{n \times m}$, $m = \Omega(n \log(n))$, and a norm bound b. Then, the task is to find a non-zero vector $\mathbf{v} \in \mathbb{Z}^m$ such that $\mathbf{A}\mathbf{v} \equiv \mathbf{0} \pmod{q}$ and $\|\mathbf{v}\|_\infty \leq b$. This is hard to accomplish as long as there is at least one single n-dimensional lattice, where solving the approximate shortest vector problem is hard for approximation factors $\gamma \geq b \cdot \tilde{O}(1)$. Hence, it is desirable to build an ID scheme based on SIS with the least possible norm bound b, which is $b = 1$.

The most relevant ID schemes based on number theoretic problems, e.g., [7] and [5], do not resist quantum attacks that use Shor's algorithm [22]. One of the first schemes to resist such kind of attack was proposed by Stern [23]. It relies on the syndrome decoding problem and uses of a 3-pass zero-knowledge proof of knowledge (ZK-PoK) with a soundness error of $2/3$ and perfect completeness. Recently, Kawachi, Tanaka, and Xagawa [11] were able to change the security assumption of Stern's scheme to SIS with norm bound 1. With their work, Kawachi et al. provide a more efficient alternative to Lyubashevsky's ID scheme [13,16], which uses a stronger assumption, SIS with norm bound $O(n^2 \log(n))$. In contrast to typical zero-knowledge schemes, Lyubashevsky's construction is based on a witness-indistinguishable (not zero-knowledge) proof of knowledge. Furthermore, it has no soundness error. However, it a completeness error of $1 - 1/e$, which leads to increased communication costs and the undesirable scenario of having an honest prover being rejected by the verifier.

In code-based cryptography, there is also the scheme proposed by Cayrel and Véron [4] that improves the Stern's scheme by reducing the soundness error to $q/(2(q-1)) \approx 1/2$. This improvement leads to lower the communication cost, when comparing both schemes for a given security level. Currently, in terms of efficiency, there is no practical lattice-based construction that is comparable to that put forward by Cayrel and Véron.

We propose such a scheme with a soundness error of $(q+1)/2q \approx 1/2$ and perfect completeness[1]. It is based on the same efficient version of the SIS problem that is used by Kawachi et al. or by the SWIFFT compression function [17]. Both the small soundness error and the mild assumption make our scheme more efficient than previous lattice-based ones. Moreover, by transferring code-based

---

[1] We conjecture that Cayrel and Véron's scheme has the same soundness error by the arguments given in Section 3.2.

Table 1. Comparison of lattice-based identification schemes

Scheme	Secret key [Kbyte]	Public key [Kbyte]	Rounds	Total communication [Kbyte]	SIS norm bound
Lyubashevsky [16]	0,25	2,00	11	110,00	$\tilde{O}(n^2)$
Kawachi et al. [11]	0,25	0,06	27	58,67	1
Section 3	0,25	0,06	17	37,50	1

constructions to lattices, we can exploit efficiency improvements using ideal lattices without losing provable security. As a result, our scheme has smaller public keys and more efficient operations than those associated with the current code-based ID schemes.

For a comparison with the most recent lattice-based ID schemes, see Table 1, which assumes that the parameters listed in Table 2 are used, and that a soundness error of 2^{-16} (one of the values recommended in the norm ISO/IEC 9798) is specified. We computed that Lyubashevsky's scheme takes 11 rounds to reach a completeness error below 1%, when it is using the most efficient parameters listed in [14].

The content of this paper is organized as follows. We present the concepts that are used in the construction of the identification scheme in Section 2, as well as the original schemes by Stern, Cayrel and Véron, whose key aspects were combined in the current work. Later, we give a detailed description of the algorithms that comprise the new scheme, and discuss the decisions that were made from a performance and security point of view in Section 3. Then, we analyze potential attacks and show how they affect the choice of parameters in Section 4.

2   Preliminaries

Notation. We write vectors and matrices in boldface, while one-dimensional variables such as integers and reals will be regular. All vectors are columnvectors unless otherwise stated. We use || to signify that multiple inputs of a function are concatenated. For example, let $h\colon \{0,1\}^* \to \{0,1\}^m$ be a hash function, and $\mathbf{a}, \mathbf{b}$ be vectors, then we write $h(\mathbf{a}||\mathbf{b})$ to denote the evaluation of h on some implicit binary encoding of $\mathbf{a}$ concatenated with an implicit encoding of $\mathbf{b}$. For the scope of this work, the actual encoding used is assumed to be efficient, and generally not discussed since it has no relevance for the results.

Security Model. We apply in the current work a string commitment scheme in the trusted setup model, according to which a trusted party honestly sets up the system parameters for the sender and the receiver.

For security model, we use impersonation under concurrent attacks. This implies that we allow the adversary to play the role of a cheating verifier prior to impersonation, possibly interacting with many different prover clones concurrently. Such clones share the same secret key, but have independent coins and keep their own state. As stated in [3], security against this kind of attack implies security against impersonation under active attack.

In the security proofs along this text we use the concept of zero-knowledge interactive proof of knowledge system. In such context, an entity called prover P has as goal to convince a probabilistic polynomial-time (PPT) verifier V that a given string x belongs to a language L, without revealing any other information. This kind of proof satisfies three properties:

- Completeness: any true theorem can be proven. That is, $\forall x \in L \operatorname{Prob}[(P, V)[x] = \text{YES}] \geq 1 - \text{negligible}(k)$. Where, (P, V) denotes the protocol describing the interaction between prover and verifier, and negligible(k) is a negligible function on some security parameter k.
- Soundness: no false theorem can be proven. That is, $\forall x \notin L \; \forall P' \operatorname{Prob}[(P', V)[x] = \text{YES}] \leq 1/2$
- Zero-Knowledge: anything one could learn by listening to P, one could also have simulated by oneself. That is, $\forall V'_{PPT} \; \exists S_{PPT} \; \forall x \in L \; \text{VIEW}_{P,V'}(x)$ close to $S(x)$. Where, VIEW represents the distribution of the transcript of the communication between prover and verifier, and $S(x)$ represents the distribution of the simulation of such interaction. Depending on the proximity of $\text{VIEW}_{P,V'}(x)$ and $S(x)$, as defined in [10], one can have:
  - Perfect Zero-knowledge: if the distributions produced by the simulator and the proof protocol are exactly the same.
  - Statistical Zero-knowledge: if the statistical difference between the distributions produced by the simulator and the proof protocol is a negligible function.
  - Computational Zero-knowledge: if the distributions produced by the simulator and the proof protocol are indistinguishable to any efficient algorithm.

Lattices. Lattices are regular pointsets in a finite real vector space. They are formally defined as discrete additive subgroups of $\mathbb{R}^m$. They are typically represented by a basis $\mathbf{B}$ comprised of $n \leq m$ linear independent vectors in $\mathbb{R}^m$. In this case the lattice is the set of all combinations of vectors in $\mathbf{B}$ with integral coefficients, i.e. $L = \mathbf{B}\mathbb{Z}^n$. In cryptography, we usually consider exclusively integral lattices, i.e. subgroups of $\mathbb{Z}^m$.

There are some lattice-based computational problems whose hardness can be used as security assumption when building cryptographic applications. We will give definitions of all the problems relevant for this article now. We will use an unspecified norm in these definition, but for the scope of our article this will always be the max-norm.

Definition 1 (SVP). *Given a lattice basis $\mathbf{B} \in \mathbb{Z}^{m \times n}$, the shortest vector problem (SVP) consists in finding a non-zero lattice vector $\mathbf{B}x$ such that $\|\mathbf{B}x\| \leq \|\mathbf{B}y\|$ for any other $y \in \mathbb{Z}^n \setminus \{0\}$.*

SVP admits formulations as approximation, as well as promise (or gap) problems. For these versions, the hardness can be proved under suitable approximation factors, such as constants, as seen for example in [19].

Definition 2 (SIS). *Given a matrix* $\mathbf{A} \in \mathbb{Z}_q^{n \times m}$, *the short integer solution (SIS) problem consists in finding a non-zero vector* $\mathbf{x} \in \mathbb{Z}^m$ *that satisfies the equation* $\mathbf{Ax} = \mathbf{0}$ (mod q) *and that has length* $\|\mathbf{x}\| \leq b$.

There are lattice-based cryptographic hash function families for which it can be shown that breaking a randomly chosen instance is at least as hard as finding solutions for worst-case instances of lattice problems. In [1] and [2], Ajtai first showed how to use computationally intractable worst-case lattice problems as building blocks for cryptosystems. The parameter sizes involved, however, are not small enough to enable practical implementations.

Using cyclic lattices, Micciancio showed that it is possible to represent a basis, and thus public keys, with space that grows quasilinearly in the lattice dimension [18]. Together with Lyubashevsky, he improved this initial result, achieving compression functions that are both efficient and provably secure assuming the hardness of worst-case lattice problems for a special type of lattices, namely ideal lattices [15]. We will talk in more detail about ideal lattices later on.

A variety of hard problems associated with lattices has been used as security basis in a number of cryptographic schemes. For example, Lyubashevsky's identification scheme is secure under active attacks, assuming the hardness of approximating SVP in all lattices of dimension n to within a factor of $\tilde{O}(n^2)$. By weakening the security assumption, on the other hand, one can achieve parameters small enough to make a practical implementation feasible, as seen in the identification scheme proposed by Kawachi et al. in [11]. In this later work, the authors suggest to use approximate Gap-SVP or SVP within factors $\tilde{O}(n)$.

Ideal Lattices. Lattices are additive groups. However, there is a particular class of lattices that are also closed under (properly defined) ring multiplications. They correspond to the ideals of some polynomial quotient ring and are defined below. In the definition, we implicitly identify polynomials with their vector of coefficients.

Definition 3 (Ideal lattices). *Let* f *be some monic polynomial of degree* n. *Then, L is an* ideal lattice *if it corresponds to an ideal I in the ring* $\mathbb{Z}[x]/\langle f \rangle$.

The concept of ideal lattices is very general. So, often lattice classes resulting from specific choices of f have their own names. For example, $f(x) = x^n - 1$ corresponds to cyclic lattices, and $f(x) = x^n + 1$ to anticyclic lattices. We also have the class of cyclotomic lattices resulting from all cyclotomic polynomials f. The later class is the only one relevant for practical applications at the moment.

Whereas, for general lattices of full rank n and entries of bitsize q, one needs $n^2 \log(q)$ bits to represent a basis, for ideal lattices only $n \log(q)$ bits suffice. This property addresses one of the major drawbacks usually associated with lattice-based cryptosystems: the large key sizes. Another good characteristic of the subclass of cyclotomic lattices is that associated matrix/vector multiplications can be performed in time $O(n \log(n))$ using discrete FFTs.

Lyubashevsky and Micciancio found that it is possible to restrict both SIS and SVP to the class of ideal lattices and keep the worst-case to average-case connection (for a fixed polynomial f that is irreducible over the integers) discovered by Ajtai. The corresponding problems are denoted with the prefix "Ideal-". As is customary, we again identify polynomials with their vectors of coefficients.

Definition 4 (Ideal-SIS). *Let f be some monic polynomial of degree n, and R_f be the ring $\mathbb{Z}[x]/\langle f \rangle$. Given m elements $a_1, \ldots, a_m \in R_f/qR_f$, the* Ideal-SIS *problem consists in finding $x_1, \ldots, x_m \in R_f$ such that $\sum_{i=1}^m a_i x_i = 0 \pmod{q}$ and $0 < \|(x_1, \ldots, x_m)\| \leq b$.*

Switching between the ideal and general lattice setting for schemes based on SIS happens by replacing the randomly chosen matrix $\mathbf{A}$ for the general SIS setting with

$$\mathbf{A}' = [a_1, a_1 x, \ldots, a_1 x^{n-1} | a_2, a_2 x, \ldots, a_2 x^{n-1} | \cdots | a_m, a_m x, \ldots, a_m x^{n-1}],$$

where $a_1, \ldots, a_m \in R_f/qR_f$ is chosen uniformly at random.

Identification Scheme. An identification scheme is a collection of algorithms (Setup, Key Generation, Prover, Verifier) meant to provide a proof of identity for a given part. The Setup algorithm takes as input a security parameter and generates structures (such as lattice or code basis) to be used by the other algorithms. The Key Generation algorithm takes as input the parameters generated by the Setup algorithm and derives key pairs (private, public) to be associated with a set of users. The Prover and Verifier algorithms correspond to a protocol that is executed by entities A and B, respectively, such that the first convinces the latter about its identity authenticity, by proving to have knowledge of a solution to a hard problem, which establishes the relation between the components of A's key pair (private, public).

Stern's Identification Scheme. The first practical code-based identification scheme was proposed by Stern [23]. Its basic algorithm uses a hash function h, a pair of keys $(\mathbf{i}, \mathbf{s})$ related by $\mathbf{i} = \mathbf{H}^T \mathbf{s}$, where $\mathbf{H}$ is a public parity check matrix of a given code, $\mathbf{s}$ is a private binary vector of Hamming weight p, and $\mathbf{i}$ is its public syndrome. In a given round, $\mathbf{y}$ is chosen uniformly at random from the same space as $\mathbf{s}$, a permutation σ of the integers $\{1, \ldots, \dim(\mathbf{y})\}$ is similarly chosen, and the commitments are calculated by the prover as follows

$$
\begin{aligned}
c_1 &= h(\sigma \| \mathbf{H}^T \mathbf{y}) \\
c_2 &= h(\sigma(\mathbf{y})) \\
c_3 &= h(\sigma(\mathbf{y} \oplus \mathbf{s})).
\end{aligned}
$$

Upon receipt of a challenge b chosen uniformly at random from $\{0, 1, 2\}$, the prover reveals the information that enables the verifier to check the correctness of the commitments as below:

$b = 0$: Reveal $\mathbf{y}$ and σ. Check c_1 and c_2.
$b = 1$: Reveal $\mathbf{y} \oplus \mathbf{s}$ and σ. Check c_1 and c_3.
$b = 2$: Reveal $\sigma(\mathbf{y})$ and $\sigma(\mathbf{s})$. Check c_2, c_3, and $\mathrm{wt}(\sigma(\mathbf{s})) = p$

This scheme has a soundness error of $2/3$. In order to reach a confidence level L on the authenticity of the prover, it has to be repeated a number r of times, so that $1 - (2/3)^r \geq L$.

In the same work Stern also proposed a few variants of the basic scheme focusing on specific goals, such as: minimize computing load, minimize number of rounds, apply identity-based construction, and employ an analogy of modular knapsacks. For the minimization of number of rounds, he suggested the following solution:

1. The private key $\mathbf{s}$ is replaced by the generators $\{\mathbf{s}_1, \ldots, \mathbf{s}_m\}$ of a simplex code.
2. Only two commitments $c_1 = h(\sigma \| \mathbf{H}^T \mathbf{y})$ and $c_2 = h(\sigma(\mathbf{y}) \| \sigma(\mathbf{s}_1) \| \ldots \| \sigma(\mathbf{s}_n))$ are used.
3. The prover computes $z = \sigma(\mathbf{y} \oplus \bigoplus_{j=1}^m b_j \mathbf{s}_j)$ using a binary vector $\{b_1, \ldots, b_m\}$ received from the verifier.
4. Upon challenge 0, the prover reveals σ, and the verifier checks c_1.
5. Upon challenge 1, the prover discloses $\{\sigma(\mathbf{s}_1), \ldots, \sigma(\mathbf{s}_m)\}$, and the verifier checks that c_2 is correct and that the code generated by $\{\mathbf{s}_1, \ldots, \mathbf{s}_m\}$ is simplex with the required weight.

This solution replaces the 3-pass approach by a 5-pass one, but it is not effective as far as communication costs are regarded. A more efficient solution is shown in the following paragraph. It also corresponds to the underlying approach for our lattice-based solution.

Cayrel and Véron's Identification Scheme. The identification scheme proposed by Stern [23] was based on the hardness of the syndrome decoding problem. An improvement over this scheme, using the dual construction, was proposed by Véron [24], achieving lower communication costs and better efficiency. Like the basic Stern construct, however, a dishonest prover can have success with probability up to $2/3$ in any given round.

By modifying the way the commitments are calculated, incorporating a value chosen at random by the verifier, Cayrel and Véron [4] were able to bound the cheating probability within a given round close to $1/2$, with similar communication costs. The approach followed will be outlined later for the case of our scheme in Algorithm 2, where the syndrome decoding problem is replaced by the shortest vector problem as hardness assumption. It involves a 5-pass solution, similar to Stern's construction. It avoids the heavy payload associated with transmitting the whole basis of a simplex code (or of a lattice), though.

Another scheme suggested by Gaborit requires smaller storage for public data [8]. Given that the schemes we have seen are dealing with codes, this usually implies that a generator matrix or a parity check matrix is needed to fully characterize them. The idea applied by Gaborit was to use double-circulant matrices for a compact representation.

In our work, we point out that a combination of these two approaches can be used in the lattice context, namely ideal lattices (which allow a very compact representation, as efficient as double-circulant matrices) for an identification scheme structure with soundness error of $1/2$. With this, we manage to have the lowest communication costs and lowest public data storage needs.

3 Identification Scheme

Taking Cayrel and Véron's scheme [4] as basis and changing the main security assumption from the syndrome decoding problem (code-based) to the short integer solution problem (lattice-based), we obtain a new identification scheme. The transformation is non-trivial since low-weight codewords that are required in one setting are not necessarily short vectors as required in the other and vice versa.

We begin by describing the new identification scheme and then give arguments regarding all major properties such as completeness, soundness, and zero-knowledge as well as performance.

3.1 Description

The scheme consists of two main parts: a key generation algorithm (Figure 1) and an interactive identification protocol (Figure 2).

KEYGEN:

$\mathbf{x} \xleftarrow{\$} \{0,1\}^m$, s.t. $\mathrm{wt}(\mathbf{x}) = m/2$

$\mathbf{A} \xleftarrow{\$} \mathbb{Z}_q^{n \times m}$

$\mathbf{y} \longleftarrow \mathbf{A}\mathbf{x} \bmod q$

COM $\xleftarrow{\$} \mathcal{F}$, suitable family of commitment functions

Output $(\mathrm{sk}, \mathrm{pk}) = (\mathbf{x}, (\mathbf{y}, \mathbf{A}, \mathrm{COM}))$

Fig. 1. Key generation algorithm, parameters n, m, q are public

The key generation algorithm receives as input a set of parameters (n, m, q), e.g., $(64, 2048, 257)$ (see Section 4.1 for a discussion on why this is a sensible choice). It chooses a matrix $\mathbf{A} \in \mathbb{Z}_q^{n \times m}$ uniformly at random and selects as private key a binary vector $\mathbf{x} \in \{0,1\}^m$ of Hamming weight $m/2$. The public key consists of an n-dimensional vector $\mathbf{y} = \mathbf{A}\mathbf{x} \bmod q$, the random matrix $\mathbf{A}$, and a commitment function COM. To instantiate the algorithm, we need to select a family of statistically hiding and computationally binding commitment functions $\mathcal{F}$.

For the time being we recommend the commitment functions used by Kawachi *et al.* since they merely require a lattice-based collision resistant, regular hash function, in our case SWIFFT, which allows us to have a single security assumption. The commitment functions COM that we use are deterministic algorithms,

$$\begin{array}{ll}
\textbf{Prover } \mathcal{P}(\text{sk}, \text{pk}) & \textbf{Verifier } \mathcal{V}(\text{pk}) \\
\end{array}$$

Prover $\mathcal{P}(\text{sk}, \text{pk})$ Verifier $\mathcal{V}(\text{pk})$

$(\text{sk}, \text{pk}) = (\mathbf{x}, (\mathbf{y}, \mathbf{A}, \text{COM})) \longleftarrow \text{KEYGEN}$

$\mathbf{u} \xleftarrow{\$} \mathbb{Z}_q^m, \sigma \xleftarrow{\$} S_m, \mathbf{z} \longleftarrow \mathbf{P}_\sigma \mathbf{x}$

$\mathbf{r}_0 \xleftarrow{\$} \{0,1\}^n, \mathbf{r}_1 \xleftarrow{\$} \{0,1\}^n$

$c_0 \longleftarrow \text{COM}(\sigma \,\|\, \mathbf{A}\mathbf{u}; \mathbf{r}_0)$

$c_1 \longleftarrow \text{COM}(\mathbf{z} \,\|\, \mathbf{P}_\sigma \mathbf{u}; \mathbf{r}_1)$

$\xrightarrow{\quad c_0, c_1 \quad}$

$\xleftarrow{\quad \alpha \quad} \quad \alpha \xleftarrow{\$} \mathbb{Z}_q$

$\beta \longleftarrow \mathbf{P}_\sigma(\mathbf{u} + \alpha \mathbf{x}) \qquad \xrightarrow{\quad \beta \quad}$

$\xleftarrow{\quad \text{Challenge } b \quad} \quad b \xleftarrow{\$} \{0,1\}$

If $b = 0$: $\qquad \xrightarrow{\quad \sigma, \mathbf{r}_0 \quad}$ Check $c_0 \overset{?}{=} \text{COM}(\sigma \,\|\, \mathbf{A}\mathbf{P}_\sigma^{-1}\beta - \alpha\mathbf{y}; \mathbf{r}_0)$

$\sigma \overset{?}{\in} S_m$

Else: $\qquad \xrightarrow{\quad \mathbf{z}, \mathbf{r}_1 \quad}$ Check $c_1 \overset{?}{=} \text{COM}(\mathbf{z} \,\|\, \beta - \alpha\mathbf{z}; \mathbf{r}_1)$

$\mathbf{z} \overset{?}{\in} \{0,1\}^m, \text{wt}(\mathbf{z}) \overset{?}{=} m/2$

Fig. 2. Identification protocol

which get as second input a nonce r that is assumed to be chosen uniformly at random from a set big enough to guarantee the hiding property of the commitment.

The identification protocol in Figure 2 describes the interaction between prover and verifier in order to convince the second party about the identity of the first. All computation in the protocol is performed modulo q, and we use the following notations. The set of all permutations on m elements is S_m. Any permutation $\sigma \in S_m$ is a linear operation and the associated $m \times m$ binary matrix is $\mathbf{P}_\sigma$.

The protocol is an adaption of the code-based identification scheme [4] which represents a major improvement to Véron's [24] and Stern's [23] schemes. In the same way our protocol represents an improvement over the lattice adaptions of Stern's scheme by Kawachi *et al.* [11]. Like Kawachi's, our adaptation to the lattice setting is non-trivial, since we need to ensure that a binary secret key is used (regardless of the Hamming weight). This needs to be guaranteed throughout the protocol which entails some change in the β that is used. Similarly to the coding-based scheme, a cheating prover, not knowing the secret key, can lead a verifier to believe that he actually knows that secret value with a probability up to $1/2$ in an individual round of execution. Therefore, in order to diminish the success rate of such an impersonation, the protocol has to be repeated a number of times, which is a function of the degree of confidence requested by the application that is using the scheme. This will be discussed further in Section 3.2, where we argue the soundness.

In the commitment phase, the prover commits to two values c_0, c_1, where c_0 is comprised of the random choices he made and c_1 contains information about his secret key. An adversary that can also correctly compute them with overwhelming probability either is able to break the commitment or to solve the hard problem that makes it possible to obtain a private key from its public counterpart. Those commitments are sent to the verifier, who responds in the second phase with value α taken uniformly at random from $\mathbb{Z}_q$. Upon receipt of the this value, the prover is supposed to multiply it by the private key, add to a permuted masking value u (uniformly chosen at random from $\mathbb{Z}_q^m$) and make a permutation over the sum. Since $\mathbf{u}$ was random, β can be seen as a random variable with uniform distribution over $\mathbb{Z}_q^m$, leaking no information about the private key x.

Upon receipt of this value, the verifier makes a challenge to the prover, picking a value uniformly at random from the set $\{0, 1\}$. The prover responds to it by revealing some piece of information that allows the verifier to compute and check the commitments. An honest prover will always be able to respond either challenge. Besides checking the correctness of the commitments, the verifier must also check that the values disclosed by the prover are well-formed, although in practice this would be solved by defining a suitable encoding for the data.

We will see in Section 3.3 how an impersonator can always cheat with a success probability of $1/2$, and that no better strategy is possible under our hardness assumptions. So in order to reach a prescribed level of security the interaction proposed here must be repeated an appropriate number of times.

Ideal lattices. The present construction makes no assumptions about the structure of the SIS matrix $\mathbf{A}$. Therefore, the space necessary for storing this matrix is $\tilde{O}(n^2)$, which is too big for practical purposes. Using ideal lattices, one can reduce such space requirements to $\tilde{O}(n)$ and simultaneously increase computation speed of matrix vector products in the form $\mathbf{A}\mathbf{x}$ to $\tilde{O}(n)$ operations. This has been proposed and performed many times, perhaps most elegantly in the case of the SWIFFT compression function [17].

3.2   Security

In this section we show that the protocol in Figure 2 corresponds to a zero-knowledge interactive proof of knowledge of the predicate defined below. Let $I = \{\mathbf{A}, \mathbf{y}, m, q\}$ be public data shared by the parties A and B. Consider the predicate $P(I, \mathbf{x})$ as "$\mathbf{x}$ is a binary vector of Hamming weight $m/2$ satisfying the equation $\mathbf{A}\mathbf{x} = \mathbf{y} \bmod q$".

We provide below proofs for the completeness, soundness and zero-knowledge properties of the identification scheme described in Figure 2. In particular, soundness holds even against concurrent attacks, i.e., an adversary may try to impersonate a given identity after having access to polynomially many verifier instances in parallel. Each of the verifier instances has the same secret key but is run with a different random tape. The challenge is to simulate the environment of the attacker during these interactions *and* still being able to extract "useful" information from the adversary during the impersonation phase. The required assumptions are that COM is a statistically hiding and computationally binding commitment scheme, e.g., based on SIS (cf. [11]), and the hardness of the SIS problem.

Completeness. Given that an honest prover has knowledge of the private key $\mathbf{x}$, the blending mask $\mathbf{u}$ and the permutations $\mathbf{P}_\sigma$, he will always be able to derive the commitments c_0 and c_1, and reveal to the verifier the information necessary to verify that they are correct. He can also show that the private key in his possession has the appropriate Hamming weight. So, the verifier will always accept the honest prover's identity in any given round. This implies perfect completeness.

Zero-Knowledge. We give a demonstration of the zero-knowledge property for the identification protocol shown in Figure 2. Here, we require the commitment function COM to be statistically hiding, i.e., $\text{COM}(x; r)$ is indistinguishable from uniform for a uniform $r \in \{0, 1\}^n$.

Theorem 1. *Let q be prime. The described protocol is a statistically zero-knowledge proof of knowledge if the employed commitment scheme is statistically-hiding.*

Proof. To prove the zero-knowledge property of our protocol, we construct a simulator S that output a protocol view $V = (c_0, c_1, \alpha, \beta, b, (\sigma, r_0), (\mathbf{z}, r_1))$ without knowing the secret $\mathbf{x}$, such that V is indistinguishable from an the interaction of an honest prover with an honest verifier. It has access to a cheating verifier V^*, which contributes α and b. Therefore, S generates r_1, r_2 according to protocol and it gets $(\mathbf{A}, \mathbf{y}, \text{COM})$ as input. The simulator has to guess b before talking to V^*. For the moment, let us assume the guess is correct.

If $b = 0$, the simulator selects $\mathbf{u}$ and σ as per protocol and solves the equation $\mathbf{Ax} \equiv \mathbf{y} \pmod{q}$ for $\mathbf{x}$, which does not need to be short. With this pseudo secret key, the simulator computes c_0 and c_1 according to the protocol. The deviation in c_1 is not recognized because COM is statistically hiding. Then, S computes $\beta \longleftarrow \mathbf{P}_\sigma(\mathbf{u} + \alpha\mathbf{x})$ after obtaining α from $V^*(c_1, c_2)$. The result is uniform because $\mathbf{u}$ is chosen uniformly at random. As a result, S can reveal (σ, r_0), which passes the verification for $b = 0$.

If $b = 1$, the simulator needs to play against the second verification branch. It selects a binary $\mathbf{x}$ with Hamming weight $m/2$ and selects σ as per protocol. It computes c_1, c_2 and obtains $\alpha \longleftarrow V^*(c_1, c_2)$. Then, it computes $\beta \longleftarrow \mathbf{P}_\sigma(\mathbf{u} + \alpha\mathbf{x})$. As a result, S can reveal $\mathbf{P}_\sigma\mathbf{x}$ that passes verification.

In consequence, the simulator outputs a correct view with probability $1/2$. Since the simulator has access to V^*, it can restart the verifier whenever the guess b was incorrect. The result is a statistically close simulation if COM is statistically hiding. □

Soundness. We now show that a dishonest prover is able to cheat a verifier to accept his identity with a probability limited by $(q + 1)/2q \approx 1/2$. The number of possible queries sent by the verifier to a prover is given by all combinations of challenge bits $b \in \{0, 1\}$ and $\alpha \in \{0, \ldots, q - 1\}$ Hence, there are $2q$ possible queries. Say, the dishonest prover wants to answer all challenges where $b = 0$, then he computes an alternate secret key $\mathbf{x}'$ with large entries such that $\mathbf{Ax}' = \mathbf{y}$.

This is can be done with Gaussian elimination, for example. At the same time, when $\alpha = 0$ he can also answer in the case $b = 1$ by sending a random $\mathbf{z}$. Since $\alpha = 0$ this is not checked in the commitment.

Note that the $\alpha = 0$ query issue cannot be resolved by removing 0 from the set that α is drawn from, because the dishonest verifier can effectively shift the values of α by changing his protocol. Say he wants some fix α_0 to take the place of 0 in the unmodified scheme, then he changes both the computations of the commitments and β to:

$$c_0 \longleftarrow \text{COM}(\sigma \parallel \mathbf{A}\mathbf{u} - \alpha_0\mathbf{y}; r_0), \qquad \beta \longleftarrow \mathbf{P}_\sigma(\mathbf{u} + (\alpha - \alpha_0)\mathbf{x}),$$
$$c_1 \longleftarrow \text{COM}(\mathbf{z} \parallel \mathbf{P}_\sigma\mathbf{u} - \alpha_0\mathbf{z}; r_1).$$

In effect, he can answer both challenges bits $b = 0, 1$ for $\alpha = \alpha_0$ now.

Thus, in total, the adversary can answer correctly for $q + 1$ out of $2q$ queries. In the proof, we show that if an adversary is able to answer more queries, it is also able to break one of the underlying assumptions, i.e. solve SIS or break the commitment.

Theorem 2. *If an honest verifier accepts a dishonest prover with probability* $Pr \geq (q+1)/2q + \epsilon(n)$, *with* $\epsilon(n)$ *non-negligible, then there exists a polynomial time probabilistic machine M which breaks the binding property of the commitment* COM *or solves the SIS problem with non-negligible probability.*

Proof. On input $(n, m, q, \mathbf{A})$ (the SIS problem instance) and a challenge commitment function COM, we need to simulate the adversary's environment in two phases: a verification phase and an impersonation phase. In order to correctly prove knowledge of a valid secret key $\mathbf{x}$ during the verification phase, we choose $\mathbf{x}$ and $\mathbf{y}$ as in the key generation protocol and run the adversary $\mathcal{A}$ on public parameters (as per protocol).

Therefore, in the verification phase, we can perfectly simulate the prover. Since the protocol is statistically zero-knowledge, the adversary does not learn any information about $\mathbf{x}$ and the output distribution is the same as for all alternative secret keys $\mathbf{x}' \neq \mathbf{x}$.

After the first phase, we let $\mathcal{A}$ play the role of the cheating prover. First, we receive the commitments c_0, c_1. Then, because q is polynomial in n, we challenge the adversary with all $2q$ challenge pairs (α, b) and record successes as "1" and failures as "0" in a table with column labels "$b = 0$", "$b = 1$" and row labels "$\alpha = 0$", ..., "$\alpha = q-1$". This is done by rewinding the adversary appropriately.

For the moment, let us assume that there exist two rows, for α and α', such that both columns contain "1". Let $(\beta, \sigma, \mathbf{r}_0)$ and $(\beta', \sigma', \mathbf{r}_0')$ be the outcomes for challenge $(\alpha, 0)$ and $(\alpha', 0)$, respectively. Furthermore, let $(\beta, \mathbf{z}, r_1)$ and $(\beta', \mathbf{z}', r_1')$ be the outcomes for challenges $(\alpha, 1)$ respectively $(\alpha', 1)$.

Since the commitment COM is binding, we infer that $r_0 = r_0'$, $r_1 = r_1'$, and

$$\sigma \parallel \mathbf{A}P_\sigma^{-1}\beta - \alpha\mathbf{y} = \sigma' \parallel \mathbf{A}P_{\sigma'}^{-1}\beta' - \alpha'\mathbf{y}, \tag{1}$$
$$\mathbf{z} \parallel \beta - \alpha\mathbf{z} = \mathbf{z}' \parallel \beta' - \alpha'\mathbf{z}'. \tag{2}$$

Equation (1) implies $\sigma = \sigma'$. Similarly, (2) shows that the binary vectors $\mathbf{z}, \mathbf{z}'$ of weight $m/2$ are equal. Now, we turn to extracting $\mathcal{A}$'s secret key by rearranging parts of (1) and (2), we get

$$\mathbf{A}P_\sigma^{-1}(\beta - \beta')(\alpha - \alpha')^{-1} \equiv \mathbf{y} \pmod{q}, \tag{3}$$

$$(\beta - \beta')(\alpha - \alpha')^{-1} \equiv \mathbf{z} \pmod{q}. \tag{4}$$

This proves that $\mathbf{x}' := P_\sigma^{-1}\mathbf{z}$ is a valid secret key and the reduction outputs the short lattice vector $\mathbf{v} = \mathbf{x} - \mathbf{x}'$. Notice that $\beta \neq \beta'$ because we have (1), $\alpha \neq \alpha'$, and $\sigma = \sigma'$. The extracted secret key is also different from the one of the simulator because the function $\mathbf{A}\mathbf{x} \bmod q$ compresses the set of valid secret keys and statistically hides them in the sense that the protocol is also witness indistinguishable. Hence, the adversary cannot learn the simulator's key but with probability $\leq 1/2 + n^{-\omega(1)}$

What is left to show is that such a pair (α, α') exists. To see this, we apply a simple counting argument [21]. We know that $\mathcal{A}$ can answer correctly for $> q+1$ challenges. W.l.o.g., assume that it succeeds $\geq c$ times for $b = 0$ and $> q+1-c$ times for $b = 1$. Thus, there are $\geq c$ "1" entries in column "$b = 0$" and $> q+1-c$ "1" entries in column "$b = 1$".

Towards contradiction, assume that there is no such pair (α, α') for which $\mathcal{A}$ succeeds for the challenges $(\alpha, 0)$, $(\alpha, 1)$, $(\alpha', 0)$, and $(\alpha', 1)$. In other words, assume that the above extraction procedure breaks down. Then, there must be at least $c - 1$ zeros in column "$b = 0$". In consequence, the total number of entries in the second column is $> c - 1 + q + 1 - c$. Since this is $> q$, we arrive at the desired contradiction and conclude that the knowledge extractor succeeds with non-negligible probability if $\epsilon(n)$ is non-negligible.   □

Given that the scheme is a zero-knowledge proof of knowledge, it is also witness indistinguishable with respect to the secret $\mathbf{x}$. Fortunately, witness-indistinguishability is preserved under parallel composition. Thus, our scheme can be run many, i.e., $\omega(\log(n))$, times in parallel to achieve a negligible soundness error but without increasing the number of rounds.

3.3   Security Considerations

The code-based identification scheme proposed by Cayrel and Véron and that serves as starting point for this work has very good performance characteristics. Its security is based on the assumption that selecting a a random generator or parity check matrix will result in hard instances of the q-ary syndrome decoding problem, though. When adapting this scheme to use lattices, on the other hand, one achieves a construct based on the hardness of the SIS problem, and that has an worst-case/average-case reduction.

As pointed out in the description of the algorithms, ideal lattices can also be used in the scheme to improve performance and reduce the amount of public data. The precautions regarding the (a) irreducibility of the polynomial that characterizes the ring upon which the lattice is defined and (b) its expansion factor must be observed, as recommended in [15]. This ensures that finding short vectors in such lattice is still hard to perform.

The present scheme is also secure against active attacks. Thus, an attacker is allowed to interact with a prover prior to attempting to impersonate him to a verifier. As consequence of the zero-knowledge property, however, no adversary that interacts with a real prover is able to obtain any knowledge that can be used later on to impersonate the prover.

We now prove that our scheme is secure against concurrent attacks, by showing that a public key corresponds to multiple secret keys and that the protocol is witness indistinguishable. It is a standard procedure, as seen in [6].

First, the existence of multiple secret keys associated with a given public key is assured by the parameter choice (See inequation 5). Second, given that our protocol is a zero-knowledge interactive proof, it is also witness indistinguishable [12].

4   Attacks

The most efficient way to attack this scheme, but probably the most difficult one, consists in solving the inhomogeneous short integer solution (ISIS) problem that is defined by the public key $\mathbf{y}$ and the public matrix $\mathbf{A}$, expressed as $\mathbf{A}\mathbf{x} = \mathbf{y} \bmod q$, where $\mathbf{x}$ is expected to be binary, with dimension m and Hamming weight $m/2$. This equation can be re-written as $\mathbf{A}'\mathbf{x}' = 0 \bmod q$, with $\mathbf{A}' = [\mathbf{A}|\mathbf{y}]$ and $\mathbf{x}' = [\mathbf{x}|-1]^T$. Lattice basis calculation and reduction can then be applied in this second lattice to try to find a solution. The approximation factor, however, is $\tilde{O}(n)$, making the task hard.

4.1   Parameters

In order to guarantee with overwhelming probability that there are other solutions to $\mathbf{A}\mathbf{x} = \mathbf{y} \bmod q$, besides the private key possessed by the prover (which is pivotal in the demonstration of security against concurrent attacks), one can make q and m satisfy the relation below

$$q^n \ll card\{\mathbf{x} \in \mathbb{Z}_2^m : weight(\mathbf{x}) = m/2\}. \tag{5}$$

Besides, q is bounded by the following theorem, which Micciancio and Regev proved in [20].

Theorem 3. *For any polynomially bounded functions $\beta(n), m(n), q(n) = n^{O(1)}$, with $q(n) \geq 4\sqrt{m(n)}n^{1.5}\beta(n)$ and $\gamma(n) = 14\pi\sqrt{n}\beta(n)$, there is a probabilistic polynomial time reduction from solving $GapCVP_\gamma$ in the worst-case to solving $SIS_{q,m,\gamma}$ on the average with non-negligible probability. In particular, for any $m = \Theta(n \log n)$, there exists $q(n) = O(n^{2.5} \log n)$ and $\gamma = O(n\sqrt{\log n})$, such that solving $SIS_{q,m}$ on the average is at least as hard as solving $GapSVP_\gamma$ in the worst case.*

Taking as reference the state-of-the-art lattice reduction algorithms studied in [9], the length of the shortest vector that can currently be found by the reduction algorithms is given by ($\delta \approx 1.011$):

$$length = \min\{q, q^{n/m}\delta^m\} \tag{6}$$

We propose the set of parameters below, in Table 2, which are comparable to those used by the SWIFFT hash function. The best combinatorial attack for finding short lattice vectors [25] has a computational complexity above 2^{100} (generalized birthday attack, dividing in 16 groups at each turn). This means that our security level is 100 bits. In addition to that, the best lattice reduction algorithms return vectors with euclidean norm above 42, taking into account our set of parameters. Given that the private keys resulting from our parameters have euclidean norm 32, the choice made is safe. Besides, we can also see that the selected parameters satisfy both Theorem 3 and the restriction given by equation 5.

Table 2. Concrete Parameter

Bit-security	n	m	q	Commitment Length (bits)
100	64	2048	257	256

5 Conclusion and Further Work

In this work we derived a lattice-based identification scheme from a code-based one. By shifting from one domain area to the other, we were able to provide stronger security evidences, given that the security arguments are now based on worst-case hardness instead of average-case. By using ideal lattices and suitable approximation factors, we were also able to obtain parameters that allow practical implementations for reasonable levels of security. We have also shown that it has better performance than all other lattice-based identification schemes.

A natural extension of the approach followed in the present work consists in adapting the structure of other cryptographic schemes and changing the hard problem upon which their security relies. By shifting between code and lattice domains and assessing which kind of gains such change provides, stronger security properties or more efficient implementations can be obtained.

Another extension consists in deriving a signature scheme from the current work. As we pointed out in Section 5.1, the present identification scheme has some characteristics that can result in efficient signature constructs, when its parameters are conveniently selected. In this context, it may be worthwhile to construct a "dual" ID scheme in the sense that it has a completeness error of $1/2$ and no soundness error as using the Fiat-Shamir transform on this "dual" scheme would result in very short signatures.

5.1 Signature via Fiat-Shamir Heuristics

If the verifier is replaced by a random oracle, one can derive signature schemes from identification counterparts. As pointed out by Lyubashevsky when comparing his lattice-based identification scheme [14] with Kawachi's solution [11], the latter does not result in an efficient signature scheme due to the fact that every bit of the challenge (thus, each bit of a message digest when we consider a signature application) results in a reasonable amount of data sent by the prover. For a 240-bit message digest, for example, Kawachi's scheme would result in a signature of over two million bits, when applying Fiat-Shamir heuristics.

Our identification scheme, however, has some characteristics of Lyubashevsky's, in the sense that we can relate a message digest with the variable α that the verifier sends to the prover in "pass 2" of Algorithm 2, instead of doing it with the challenge bits. Thus, we can make the field from which such a variable is defined to have a width that better suits the signature scheme needs, circumventing the drawback pointed out above. At the same time, we need to ensure that the total number of rounds we run the scheme is bigger than the desired bit-security level of the resulting signature. This is because an attacker who can correctly guess the challenge bits for each round can generate a signature.

Acknowledgments

We are grateful to Daniele Micciancio for his advice on the soundness proof and signature discussion, and we thank the anonymous referees for their useful suggestions. This work was supported by CASED (www.cased.de).

References

1. Ajtai, M.: Generating hard instances of lattice problems. Electronic Colloquium on Computational Complexity (ECCC) 3(7) (1996)
2. Ajtai, M., Dwork, C.: A public-key cryptosystem with worst-case/average-case equivalence. Electronic Colloquium on Computational Complexity (ECCC) 3(65) (1996)
3. Bellare, M., Palacio, A.: GQ and Schnorr identification schemes: Proofs of security against impersonation under active and concurrent attacks. In: Yung, M. (ed.) CRYPTO 2002. LNCS, vol. 2442, pp. 162–162. Springer, Heidelberg (2002)
4. Cayrel, P.-L., Véron, P.: Improved code-based identification scheme (2010), http://arxiv.org/abs/1001.3017v1
5. Feige, U., Fiat, A., Shamir, A.: Zero knowledge proofs of identity. In: STOC 1987, pp. 210–217. ACM, New York (1987)
6. Feige, U., Shamir, A.: Witness indistinguishable and witness hiding protocols. In: STOC 1990, pp. 416–426. ACM, New York (1990)
7. Fiat, A., Shamir, A.: How to prove yourself: Practical solutions to identification and signature problems. In: Odlyzko, A.M. (ed.) CRYPTO 1986. LNCS, vol. 263, pp. 186–194. Springer, Heidelberg (1987)
8. Gaborit, P., Girault, M.: Lightweight code-based identification and signature. IEEE Transactions on Information Theory (ISIT), 186–194 (2007)
9. Gama, N., Nguyen, P.Q.: Predicting lattice reduction. In: Smart, N.P. (ed.) EUROCRYPT 2008. LNCS, vol. 4965, pp. 31–51. Springer, Heidelberg (2008)
10. Goldwasser, S., Micali, S., Rackoff, C.: The knowledge complexity of interactive proof-systems. In: Proceedings of the Seventeenth Annual ACM Symposium on Theory of Computing, p. 304. ACM, New York (1985)

11. Kawachi, A., Tanaka, K., Xagawa, K.: Concurrently secure identification schemes based on the worst-case hardness of lattice problems. In: Pieprzyk, J. (ed.) ASI-ACRYPT 2008. LNCS, vol. 5350, pp. 372–389. Springer, Heidelberg (2008)
12. Kilian, J., Petrank, E.: Concurrent and resettable zero-knowledge in polyloalgorithm rounds. In: STOC 2001: Proceedings of the Thirty-Third Annual ACM Symposium on Theory of Computing, pp. 560–569. ACM, New York (2001)
13. Lyubashevsky, V.: Lattice-based identification schemes secure under active attacks. In: Cramer, R. (ed.) PKC 2008. LNCS, vol. 4939, pp. 162–179. Springer, Heidelberg (2008)
14. Lyubashevsky, V.: Fiat-shamir with aborts: Applications to lattice and factoring-based signatures. In: Matsui, M. (ed.) ASIACRYPT 2009. LNCS, vol. 5912, pp. 598–616. Springer, Heidelberg (2009)
15. Lyubashevsky, V., Micciancio, D.: Generalized compact knapsacks are collision resistant. In: Bugliesi, M., Preneel, B., Sassone, V., Wegener, I. (eds.) ICALP 2006. LNCS, vol. 4052, pp. 144–155. Springer, Heidelberg (2006)
16. Lyubashevsky, V., Micciancio, D.: Asymptotically efficient lattice-based digital signatures. In: Canetti, R. (ed.) TCC 2008. LNCS, vol. 4948, pp. 37–54. Springer, Heidelberg (2008)
17. Lyubashevsky, V., Micciancio, D., Peikert, C., Rosen, A.: Swifft: A modest proposal for fft hashing. In: Nyberg, K. (ed.) FSE 2008. LNCS, vol. 5086, pp. 54–72. Springer, Heidelberg (2008)
18. Micciancio, D.: Generalized compact knapsacks, cyclic lattices, and efficient one-way functions. In: Computational Complexity. Springer, Heidelberg (2007)
19. Micciancio, D., Goldwasser, S.: Complexity of Lattice Problems: a cryptographic perspective. The Kluwer International Series in Engineering and Computer Science, vol. 671. Kluwer Academic Publishers, Boston (March 2002)
20. Micciancio, D., Regev, O.: Worst-case to average-case reductions based on gaussian measures. SIAM J. Comput. 37(1), 267–302 (2007)
21. Ohta, K., Okamoto, T.: On concrete security treatment of signatures derived from identification. In: Krawczyk, H. (ed.) CRYPTO 1998. LNCS, vol. 1462, pp. 354–369. Springer, Heidelberg (1998)
22. Shor, P.W.: Polynominal time algorithms for discrete logarithms and factoring on a quantum computer. In: Huang, M.-D.A., Adleman, L.M. (eds.) ANTS 1994. LNCS, vol. 877, p. 289. Springer, Heidelberg (1994)
23. Stern, J.: A new identification scheme based on syndrome decoding. In: Stinson, D.R. (ed.) CRYPTO 1993. LNCS, vol. 773, pp. 13–21. Springer, Heidelberg (1994)
24. Véron, P.: Improved identification schemes based on error-correcting codes. Appl. Algebra Eng. Commun. Comput. 8(1), 57–69 (1996)
25. Wagner, D.: A generalized birthday problem. In: Yung, M. (ed.) CRYPTO 2002. LNCS, vol. 2442, pp. 288–303. Springer, Heidelberg (2002)

Identification Schemes of Proofs of Ability Secure against Concurrent Man-in-the-Middle Attacks

Hiroaki Anada and Seiko Arita

Institute of Information Security, Yokohama, Japan
hiroaki.anada@gmail.com, arita@iisec.ac.jp

Abstract. We give a series of three identification schemes. All of them are basically 2-round interactive proofs of ability to complete Diffie-Hellman tuples. Despite their simple protocols, the second and the third schemes are proven secure against concurrent man-in-the-middle attacks based on tight reduction to the Gap Computational Diffie-Hellman Assumption without the random oracle. In addition, they are more efficient than challenge-and-response 2-round identification schemes from previously known EUF-CMA signature schemes in the standard model.

Our first scheme is similar to half the operation of Diffie-Hellman Key-Exchange. The first scheme is secure only against two-phase attacks based on strong assumptions. Applying the tag framework, and employing a strong one-time signature for the third scheme, we get the preferable schemes above.

Keywords: Identification Scheme, Concurrent Man-in-the-Middle Attack, the Gap Computational Diffie-Hellman Assumption, Tight Reduction.

1 Introduction

An identification (ID) scheme enables a prover to convince a verifier that the prover is certainly itself by proving possession of some secret identifying information. In public key framework the prover holds a secret key and the verifier refers to a matching public key. They interact for some rounds doing necessary computations until the verifier feels certain.

Most of ID schemes, such as the Guillou-Quisquater scheme [14] and the Schnorr scheme [21], are proofs of knowledge which belong to a class called Σ-protocols [8]. A Σ-protocol consists of 3-round interaction and satisfies the special soundness property. By the property it is possible to extract witness of the prover via its adversary (the Reset Lemma [5]). But when we depend on the property we must give up tight reduction to computational hardness assumptions in its security proofs.

As for attacks on ID schemes, if someone malicious can impersonate a prover then the ID scheme collapses. So the prime requirement for ID schemes is robustness against impersonation by adversaries who attack various cheating ways. Among attacks a concurrent man-in-the-middle attack is one of the strongest

S.-H. Heng and K. Kurosawa (Eds.): ProvSec 2010, LNCS 6402, pp. 18–34, 2010.

threat. In concurrent man-in-the-middle composition, while trying to impersonate a prover, an adversary may interacts with prover clones in arbitrarily interleaved order of messages.

1.1 Our Contribution

This paper addresses to the problem to construct ID schemes secure against concurrent man-in-the-middle attacks. Unlike the known schemes, our principle is neither Σ-protocols nor proofs of knowledge, but are proofs of ability ([13]) to complete Diffie-Hellman tuples.

The first scheme is like half the operation of Diffie-Hellman Key-Exchange and consists of 2-round interaction. Three exponentiations and one multiplication are build into the first scheme along the idea for the tag-based encryption scheme of Kiltz [17]. A string "tag" is assumed to be given to a prover and a verifier by the first round. To leave the tag framework, the CHK transformation [9] is applied to the second scheme; a strong one-time signature is build in to get the third scheme. The second and the third schemes are proven secure against concurrent man-in-the-middle attacks based on tight reduction to the Gap Computational Diffie-Hellman (Gap-CDH) Assumption in the standard model.

As for efficiency, our schemes need less computational amount than that of EUF-CMA signature schemes in the standard model. More precisely, using EUF-CMA signature schemes or IND-CCA encryption schemes, we can construct challenge-and-response 2-round ID schemes secure against concurrent man-in-the-middle attacks ([3]). However, note that known efficient such schemes are proven secure only in the random oracle model, or, in the standard model, they need heavy exponentiations or pairing computations under some artificial number theoretic assumptions, such as the Strong Diffie-Hellman (SDH) Assumption ([2,24,18]).

Though each technique is already known, the second and the third schemes are so secure and efficient that we establish them in this paper.

1.2 Related Works

Our first, prototype scheme is similar to the scheme of Stinson and Wu [22,23]. They proved it secure in the random oracle model under the CDH and the Knowledge-of-Exponent Assumption (KEA) [11]. Unlike theirs, we provide a security proof in the standard model. Although the assumptions utilized, the KEA and the Gap Discrete Logarithm (Gap-DL) Assumption, are fairly strong, we stress that the first scheme is a steppingstone towards the second and the third schemes.

Concerning man-in-the-middle attacks, Katz [15] constructed a non-malleable proof of knowledge. It is basically a Σ protocol. It utilizes the so-called OR-Proof technique and is rather complicated.

Gennaro [12] constructed a concurrently non-malleable proof of knowledge. It is also a Σ protocol. The security proof is based on "strong-type" assumption (the SDH or the Strong RSA).

Concerning tight reduction to computational hardness assumptions, Arita and Kawashima [1] proposed an ID scheme whose security proof is based on tight reduction to the One More Discrete Log (OMDL) [5] type assumption and the KEA. Here the KEA is considered a strong assumption and our first scheme also depends on the KEA. But our second and third schemes succeed in leaving the KEA.

1.3   Organization of This Paper

In the next section we fix some notations. We briefly review the model of attacks on ID schemes, then we describe computational hardness assumptions. In Section 3 we discuss the first, prototype ID scheme. Our main results, the second and the third schemes and their security, are presented in Section 4 and 5, respectively. In Section 6 we conclude our work.

2   Preliminaries

The empty string is denoted ϕ. The security parameter is denoted k. On input 1^k a group parameter generator $\mathtt{Grp}$ runs and outputs (q, g), where q is a prime of bit length k and g is a base element of order q in a multiplicative cyclic group G_q. G_q is a general cyclic group of order q throughout this paper. The ring of exponent domain of G_q, which consists of integers from 0 to $q - 1$ with modulo q operation, is denoted $\mathbf{Z}_q$.

When an algorithm A on input a outputs z we denote it as $z \leftarrow A(a)$. When A on input a and B on input b interact and B outputs z we denote it as $\langle A(a), B(b) \rangle = z$. When A does oracle-access to an oracle $\mathcal{O}$ we denote it as $A^{\mathcal{O}}$. When A does concurrent oracle-access to n oracles $\mathcal{O}_1, \ldots, \mathcal{O}_n$ we denote it as $A^{\mathcal{O}_1 | \cdots | \mathcal{O}_n}$. Here concurrent means that A accesses to oracles in arbitrarily interleaved order of messages.

A probability of an event X is denoted $\Pr[\mathrm{X}]$. A probability of an event X on conditions $\mathrm{Y}_1, \ldots, \mathrm{Y}_m$ is denoted $\Pr[\mathrm{Y}_1; \cdots ; \mathrm{Y}_m : \mathrm{X}]$.

2.1   ID Schemes

An *ID scheme ID* is a triple of probabilistic polynomial time (PPT) algorithms $(\mathtt{K}, \mathtt{P}, \mathtt{V})$. $\mathtt{K}$ is a key generator which outputs a pair of a public key and a matching secret key $(\mathtt{pk}, \mathtt{sk})$ on input 1^k. $\mathtt{P}$ and $\mathtt{V}$ implement a prover and a verifier, recpectively. We require $\mathtt{ID}$ to satisfy the completeness condition that boolean decision output by $\mathtt{V}(\mathtt{pk})$ after interaction with $\mathtt{P}(\mathtt{sk})$ is one with probability one. We say that $\mathtt{V}(\mathtt{pk})$ *accepts* if its boolean decision is one.

2.2   Attacks on ID Schemes

The aim of an adversary $\mathcal{A}$ on an ID scheme $\mathtt{ID}$ is impersonation. We say that $\mathcal{A}$ *wins* when $\mathcal{A}(\mathtt{pk})$ succeeds in making $\mathtt{V}(\mathtt{pk})$ accept.

Attacks on ID schemes are divided into two kinds. One is passive and the other is active. We are concentrating on active attacks. Active attacks are divided into four patterns according to whether they are serial or concurrent and whether they are two-phase or man-in-the-middle.

Firstly a concurrent attack ([3,5]) means that an adversary $\mathcal{A}(\text{pk})$ interacts with polynomially many clones $P_i(\text{sk})$s of the prover $P(\text{sk})$ in arbitrarily interleaved order of messages. Here all prover clones $P_i(\text{sk})$s are given independent random tapes and independent inner states. A serial attack is a special case that an adversary $\mathcal{A}(\text{pk})$ interacts with the prover clone $P(\text{sk})$ arbitrary times, but with only one clone at a time. So concurrent attacks are stronger than serial attacks.

Secondly a two-phase attack ([3,5]) means that an adversary $\mathcal{A}$ consists of two algorithms $(\mathcal{A}_1, \mathcal{A}_2)$. In the first phase, the learning phase, $\mathcal{A}_1$ starts with input pk, interacts with prover clones $P_i(\text{sk})$s and outputs its inner state. In the second phase, the impersonation phase, $\mathcal{A}_2$ starts with input the state, interacts with the verifier $V(\text{pk})$ and tries to make $V(\text{pk})$ accept. On the other hand, a man-in-the-middle attack means that an adversary $\mathcal{A}$ starts with input pk, interacts with both $P_i(\text{sk})$s and $V(\text{pk})$ simultaneously in arbitrarily interleaved order of messages. So man-in-the-middle attacks are stronger than two-phase attacks.

Note that man-in-the-middle adversary $\mathcal{A}$ is prohibited from relaying a transcript of a whole interaction. This is the standard and natural rule when we consider a man-in-the-middle attack. Denote the set of transcripts between $P_i(\text{sk})$s and $\mathcal{A}(\text{pk})$ as Π and a transcript between $\mathcal{A}(\text{pk})$ and $V(\text{pk})$ as π, then the rule is described as $\pi \notin \Pi$.

We define *imp-2pc (impersonation by two-phase concurrent attack) advantage of* $\mathcal{A} = (\mathcal{A}_1, \mathcal{A}_2)$ *over ID* as;

$$\mathbf{Adv}_{\text{ID},\mathcal{A}}^{\text{imp-2pc}}(k) \overset{\text{def}}{=} \Pr[(\text{pk}, \text{sk}) \leftarrow \text{K}(1^k); st \leftarrow \mathcal{A}_1^{P_1(\text{sk})|\cdots|P_n(\text{sk})}(\text{pk})$$
$$: \langle \mathcal{A}_2(st), V(\text{pk}) \rangle = 1].$$

We say that ID is secure against two-phase concurrent attacks if, for any PPT algorithm $\mathcal{A}$, $\mathbf{Adv}_{\text{ID},\mathcal{A}}^{\text{imp-2pc}}(k)$ is negligible in k.

In an analogous way, we define *imp-cmim (impersonation by concurrent man-in-the-middle (cmim) attack) advantage of* $\mathcal{A}$ *over ID* as;

$$\mathbf{Adv}_{\text{ID},\mathcal{A}}^{\text{imp-cmim}}(k) \overset{\text{def}}{=} \Pr[(\text{pk}, \text{sk}) \leftarrow \text{K}(1^k)$$
$$: \langle \mathcal{A}^{P_1(\text{sk})|\cdots|P_n(\text{sk})}(\text{pk}), V(\text{pk}) \rangle = 1 \wedge \pi \notin \Pi].$$

We say that an ID is secure against concurrent man-in-the-middle attacks if, for any PPT algorithm $\mathcal{A}$, $\mathbf{Adv}_{\text{ID},\mathcal{A}}^{\text{imp-cmim}}(k)$ is negligible in k.

2.3   Tag-Based ID Schemes

A tag-based ID scheme TagID works in the same way as an ordinary scheme ID except that a string *tag* t is a priori given to P and V by the first round. An interaction depends on the given tag t.

As for attacks, the selective-tag attack is considered in this paper, referring to the line of Kiltz [17]. That is, an attack on TagID by an adversary $\mathcal{A}$ is modeled in the same way as on ID except that, an adversary $\mathcal{A}$ designates a *target tag* t^* firstly, and then $\mathcal{A}$ gets a public key pk. $\mathcal{A}$ gives a tag $t_i(\neq t^*)$ to each $P_i(sk)$ and t^* to $V(pk)$

We define *selective-tag imp-cmim advantage* of $\mathcal{A}$ over *TagID* as;

$$\mathbf{Adv}_{\mathtt{TagID},\mathcal{A}}^{\text{stag-imp-cmim}}(k) \overset{\text{def}}{=} \Pr[(pk, sk) \leftarrow K(1^k); t^* \leftarrow \mathcal{A}(1^k)$$
$$: \langle \mathcal{A}^{P_1(t_1, sk)| \cdots |P_n(t_n, sk)}(pk), V(t^*, pk) \rangle = 1 \wedge (t_i \neq t^*, \forall i)].$$

We say that TagID is secure against selective-tag concurrent man-in-the-middle attacks if, for any PPT algorithm $\mathcal{A}$, $\mathbf{Adv}_{\mathtt{TagID},\mathcal{A}}^{\text{stag-imp-cmim}}(k)$ is negligible in k.

2.4   Computational Hardness Assumptions

We say a solver $\mathcal{S}$, an algorithm, *wins* when $\mathcal{S}$ succeeds in solving a computational problem instance.

The Gap-CDH Assumption. A quadruple (g, X, Y, Z) of elements in G_q is called a Diffie-Hellman (DH) tuple if (g, X, Y, Z) is written as (g, g^x, g^y, g^{xy}) for some elements x and $y \in \mathbf{Z}_q$. A CDH problem instance consists of $(q, g, X = g^x, Y = g^y)$, where the exponents x and y are hidden. The CDH oracle $\mathcal{CDH}$ is an oracle which, queried about a CDH problem instance (q, g, X, Y), answers $Z = g^{xy}$. A DDH problem instance consists of (q, g, X, Y, Z). The DDH oracle $\mathcal{DDH}$ is an oracle which, queried about a DDH problem instance (q, g, X, Y, Z), answers a boolean decision whether (g, X, Y, Z) is a DH-tuple or not. A CDH problem solver is a PPT algorithm which, given a random CDH problem instance (q, g, X, Y) as input, tries to return $Z = g^{xy}$. A CDH problem solver $\mathcal{S}$ that is allowed to access $\mathcal{DDH}$ arbitrary times is called a Gap-CDH problem solver. We consider the following experiment.

Experiment$_{\mathtt{Grp},\mathcal{S}}^{\text{gap-cdh}}(1^k)$

   $(q, g) \leftarrow \mathtt{Grp}(1^k), x, y \leftarrow \mathbf{Z}_q, X := g^x, Y := g^y$

   If $\mathcal{S}^{\mathcal{DDH}}(q, g, X, Y)$ outputs $Z = g^{xy}$ then return WIN else LOSE.

Then we define *Gap-CDH advantage* of $\mathcal{S}$ over *Grp* as;

$$\mathbf{Adv}_{\mathtt{Grp},\mathcal{S}}^{\text{gap-cdh}}(k) \overset{\text{def}}{=} \Pr[\mathbf{Experiment}_{\mathtt{Grp},\mathcal{S}}^{\text{gap-cdh}}(1^k) \text{ returns WIN}].$$

We say that the Gap-CDH assumption [20] holds when, for any PPT algorithm $\mathcal{S}$, $\mathbf{Adv}_{\mathtt{Grp},\mathcal{S}}^{\text{gap-cdh}}(k)$ is negligible in k.

The Gap-DL Assumption. A discrete log (DL) problem instance consists of $(q, g, X = g^x)$, where the exponent x is hidden. A DL problem solver is a PPT algorithm which, given a random DL problem instance (q, g, X) as input, tries to return x. A DL problem solver $\mathcal{S}$ that is allowed to access $\mathcal{CDH}$ arbitrary times is called a Gap-DL problem solver. We consider the following experiment.

Experiment$_{\mathtt{Grp},\mathcal{S}}^{\text{gap-dl}}(1^k)$

$(q,g) \leftarrow \mathtt{Grp}(1^k), x \leftarrow \mathbf{Z}_q, X := g^x$

If $\mathcal{S}^{\mathcal{CDH}}(q,g,X)$ outputs x^* and $g^{x^*} = X$ then return WIN else LOSE.

Then we define *Gap-DL advantage of $\mathcal{S}$ over $\mathtt{Grp}$* as;

$$\mathbf{Adv}_{\mathtt{Grp},\mathcal{S}}^{\text{gap-dl}}(k) \stackrel{\text{def}}{=} \Pr[\mathbf{Experiment}_{\mathtt{Grp},\mathcal{S}}^{\text{gap-dl}}(1^k) \text{ returns WIN}].$$

We say that the Gap-DL assumption holds when, for any PPT algorithm $\mathcal{S}$, $\mathbf{Adv}_{\mathtt{Grp},\mathcal{S}}^{\text{gap-dl}}(k)$ is negligible in k.

Though the Gap-DL assumption is considered fairly strong, it is believed to hold for a certain class of cyclic groups [19].

The Knowledge-of-Exponent Assumption. Bellare and Palacio [6] and Canetti and Dakdouk [7,10] discussed the Knowledge-of-Exponent Assumption (KEA) [11]. Informally, the KEA says that, given a randomly chosen $h \in G_q$ as input, a PPT algorithm $\mathcal{H}$ can extend (g,h) as a DH-tuple (g,h,X,D) *only when $\mathcal{H}$ knows the exponent x of $X = g^x$.* The formal definition is as follows.

Let $\mathcal{H}$ and $\mathcal{H}'$ be any PPT algorithms and W be any distribution. $\mathcal{H}$ and $\mathcal{H}'$ take input of the form (g,h,w). Here g is any fixed base and h is a randomly chosen element in G_q. w is a string in $\{0,1\}^*$ output by W called an auxiliary input [7,10]. We consider the following experiment.

Experiment$_{\mathtt{Grp},\mathcal{H},\mathcal{H}'}^{\text{kea-indaux}}(1^k)$

$(q,g) \leftarrow \mathtt{Grp}(1^k), w \leftarrow W, a \leftarrow \mathbf{Z}_q, h := g^a$

$(X,D) \leftarrow \mathcal{H}(g,h,w), x' \leftarrow \mathcal{H}'(g,h,w)$

If$(X^a = D$ and $g^{x'} \neq X)$ then return WIN else LOSE.

Note that w is independent auxiliary input with respect to h in our experiment above. This independency is crucial ([7,10]).

Then we define *KEA advantage of $\mathcal{H}$ over $\mathtt{Grp}$ and $\mathcal{H}'$* as;

$$\mathbf{Adv}_{\mathtt{Grp},\mathcal{H},\mathcal{H}'}^{\text{kea-indaux}}(k) \stackrel{\text{def}}{=} \Pr[\mathbf{Experiment}_{\mathtt{Grp},\mathcal{H},\mathcal{H}'}^{\text{kea-indaux}}(1^k) \text{ returns WIN}].$$

Here an algorithm $\mathcal{H}'$ is called the *KEA extractor*. We say that the KEA holds when, for any PPT algorithm $\mathcal{H}$, there exists a PPT algorithm $\mathcal{H}'$ such that for any distribution W $\mathbf{Adv}_{\mathtt{Grp},\mathcal{H},\mathcal{H}'}^{\text{kea-indaux}}(k)$ is negligible in k.

3 A Prototype ID Scheme Secure against Two-Phase Concurrent Attacks

In this section we construct and discuss a prototype ID scheme IDproto.

3.1   IDproto and Its Security

IDproto consists of a triple (K, P, V) as shown in the Fig.1. On input 1^k, a key generator K runs as follows. A group parameter generator Grp outputs (q, g) on input 1^k. Then K chooses $x \in \mathbf{Z}_q$, puts $X = g^x$ and sets $pk = (q, g, X)$ and $sk = (q, g, x)$. Then K returns (pk, sk).

P and V interact as follows. In the first round, V is given pk as input, chooses $a \in \mathbf{Z}_q$ randomly and computes $h = g^a$. Then V sends h to P. In the second round, P is given sk as input and receives h as input message, computes $D = h^x$. Then P sends D to V. Receiving D as input message, V verifies whether (g, X, h, D) is a DH-tuple. For this sake, V checks whether $D = X^a$ holds. If so, then V returns 1 and if not, then 0.

Key Generation
- K: given 1^k as input;
  - $(q, g) \leftarrow Grp(1^k), x \leftarrow \mathbf{Z}_q, X := g^x$
  - $pk := (q, g, X), sk := (q, g, x)$, return (pk, sk)

Interaction
- V: given pk as input;
  - $a \leftarrow \mathbf{Z}_q, h := g^a$, send h to P
- P: given sk as input and receiving h as input message;
  - $D := h^x$, send D to V
- V: receiving D as input message;
  - If $D = X^a$ then return 1 else return 0

Fig. 1. A Prototype ID Scheme IDproto

Theorem 1. *IDproto is secure against two-phase concurrent attacks under the Gap-DL assumption and the KEA; for any PPT two-phase concurrent adversary $\mathcal{A} = (\mathcal{A}_1, \mathcal{A}_2)$, there exists a PPT Gap-DL problem solver $\mathcal{S}$ which satisfies the following tight reduction;*

$$\mathbf{Adv}^{\text{imp-2pc}}_{\text{IDproto}, \mathcal{A}}(k) \leqslant \mathbf{Adv}^{\text{gap-dl}}_{\text{Grp}, \mathcal{S}}(k) + \mathbf{Adv}^{\text{kea-indaux}}_{\text{Grp}, \mathcal{H}, \mathcal{H}'}(k).$$

3.2   Proof of Theorem 1

Let $\mathcal{A} = (\mathcal{A}_1, \mathcal{A}_2)$ be as in Theorem 1. Using $\mathcal{A}$ as subroutine, we construct a Gap-DL problem solver $\mathcal{S}$. The construction is illustrated in Fig.2.

$\mathcal{S}$ is given $q, g, X = g^x$ as a DL problem instance, where x is random and hidden. $\mathcal{S}$ initializes inner state, sets $pk = (q, g, X)$ and invokes $\mathcal{A}_1$ on pk.

In the first phase $\mathcal{S}$ replies in answer to $\mathcal{A}_1$'s queries as follows. In case that $\mathcal{A}_1$ sends h_i to the i-th prover clone $P_i(sk)$, $\mathcal{S}$ queries its CDH oracle $\mathcal{CDH}$ for the answer of a CDH problem instance (q, g, X, h_i) and gets D_i. Then $\mathcal{S}$ sends D_i to $\mathcal{A}$. In case that $\mathcal{A}_1$ outputs its inner state st, $\mathcal{S}$ stops $\mathcal{A}_1$ and invokes $\mathcal{A}_2$ on st.

In the second phase S replies in answer to A_2's query as follows. In case that A_2 queries $V(pk)$ for the first message by an empty string ϕ, S chooses $a^* \in \mathbf{Z}_q$ randomly and computes $h^* = g^{a^*}$. Then S sends h^* to A_2. In case that A_2 sends D^* to $V(pk)$, S verifies whether (g, X, h^*, D^*) is a DH-tuple. For this sake, S checks whether $D^* = X^{a^*}$ holds. If it does not hold then S returns a random element $z \in \mathbf{Z}_q$. If it holds then S invokes the KEA extractor $\mathcal{H}'$ on (g, h^*, st). Here $\mathcal{H}'$ is the one associated with the $\mathcal{H}$ below;

$$\mathcal{H}(g, h^*, st)\{D^* \leftarrow A_2(st, h^*), \mathrm{return}(X, D^*)\}.$$

Note that (g, h^*, X, D^*) is a DH-tuple because (g, X, h^*, D^*) is a DH-tuple. Note also that a distribution W is A_1 here. An auxiliary input st output by A_1 satisfies independency with respect to h^*.

When $\mathcal{H}'$ outputs x^* S checks whether x^* is the discrete log of X on base g. If so, S outputs $z = x^*$ and if not, a random element $z \in \mathbf{Z}_q$.

It is obvious that S simulates both concurrent $P_i(sk)s$ and $V(pk)$ perfectly. Now we evaluate Gap-DL advantage of S. A wins iff $X^{a^*} = D^*$. If $X^{a^*} = D^*$ then x^* is output by $\mathcal{H}'$. If $g^{x^*} = X$ then S wins. Therefore;

$$\Pr[S \text{ wins}] \geqslant \Pr[A \text{ wins} \wedge g^{x^*} = X]$$
$$= \Pr[A \text{ wins}] - \Pr[A \text{ wins} \wedge g^{x^*} \neq X].$$

So $\qquad \Pr[S \text{ wins}] \geqslant \Pr[A \text{ wins}] - \Pr[X^{a^*} = D^* \wedge g^{x^*} \neq X].$

That is; $\quad \mathbf{Adv}^{\mathrm{gap\text{-}dl}}_{\mathrm{Grp}, S}(k) \geqslant \mathbf{Adv}^{\mathrm{imp\text{-}2pc}}_{\mathrm{IDproto}, A}(k) - \mathbf{Adv}^{\mathrm{kea\text{-}indaux}}_{\mathrm{Grp}, \mathcal{H}, \mathcal{H}'}(k).$ (Q.E.D.)

Given (q, g, X) as input;
Initial Setting
– Initialize inner state, $pk := (q, g, X)$, invoke A_1 on pk
The First phase : Answering A_1's Queries
– In case that A_1 sends h_i to $P_i(sk)$;
     • $D_i \leftarrow \mathcal{CDH}(g, X, h_i)$, send D_i to A_1
– In case that A_1 outputs its inner state st;
     • Stop A_1, invoke A_2 on st
The Second phase : Answering A_2's Query
– In case that A_2 queries $V(pk)$ for the first message;
     • $a^* \leftarrow \mathbf{Z}_q$, $h^* := g^{a^*}$, send h^* to A_2
– In case that A_2 sends D^* to $V(pk)$;
     • If $X^{a^*} \neq D^*$ then return random element $z \in \mathbf{Z}_q$
     • else invoke $\mathcal{H}'$ on (g, h^*, st) and get x^* from $\mathcal{H}'$
If $g^{x^*} = X$ then return $z := x^*$
else return random element $z \in \mathbf{Z}_q$

Fig. 2. A Gap-DL Problem Solver S for the Proof of Theorem 1

3.3   Discussion

Though the Gap-DL and the KEA are fairly strong assumptions, the fact that
IDproto is proven secure against two-phase concurrent attacks is rather surprising, because it is obvious that IDproto is insecure under man-in-the-middle attacks. To see it just recall the typical man-in-the-middle attack on Diffie-Hellman
Key-Exchange.

Analogous phenomenon also occurs, for example, for the Schnorr ID scheme
[5]. It seems that the security against two-phase concurrent attacks is somewhat
artificial. In Section 4 and Section 5 we modify IDproto to strengthen its security
up to (concurrent) man-in-the-middle level.

4   A Tag-Based ID Scheme Secure against CMIM Attacks

In this section we construct an ID scheme TagIDcmim. Referring to the idea of
the tag-based encryption scheme of Kiltz [17], we apply the tag framework to
IDproto to get TagIDcmim.

4.1   TagIDcmim and Its Security

TagIDcmim consists of a triple (K, P, V). The construction is as shown in the Fig.3.
A string tag t is a priori given to P and V by the first round. In our composition
we set t in $\mathbf{Z}_q$.

On input 1^k, a key generator K runs as follows. A group parameter generator
Grp outputs (q, g) on input 1^k. Then K chooses $x, y \in \mathbf{Z}_q$, puts $X = g^x$ and
$Y = g^y$, and sets $pk = (q, g, X, Y)$ and $sk = (q, g, x, y)$. K returns (pk, sk).

P and V interact as follows. In the first round, V is given pk as input. V chooses
$a \in \mathbf{Z}_q$ randomly and computes $h = g^a$ and $d = (X^t Y)^a$. Then V sends (h, d) to
P. In the second round, P is given sk as input and receives (h, d) as input message.
P verifies whether $(g, X^t Y, h, d)$ is a DH-tuple. For this sake, P checks whether

---

Tag-Receiving
- P and V receive a tag $t \in \mathbf{Z}_q$ by the first round

Key Generation
- K: given 1^k as input;
  - $(q, g) \leftarrow \text{Grp}(1^k), x, y \leftarrow \mathbf{Z}_q, X := g^x, Y := g^y$
  - $pk := (q, g, X, Y), sk := (q, g, x, y)$, return (pk, sk)

Interaction
- V: given pk as input;
  - $a \leftarrow \mathbf{Z}_q, h := g^a, d := (X^t Y)^a$, send (h, d) to P
- P: given sk as input and receiving (h, d) as input message;
  - If $h^{tx+y} \neq d$ then $D := \perp$ else $D := h^x$, send D to V
- V: receiving D as input message;
  - If $X^a = D$ then return 1 else return 0

Fig. 3. A Tag-Based ID Scheme TagIDcmim

$h^{tx+y} = d$ holds. If it does not hold then P puts $D = \perp$. Otherwise P computes $D = h^x$. Then P sends D to V. Receiving D as input message, V verifies whether (g, X, h, D) is a DH-tuple. For this sake, V checks whether $X^a = D$ holds. If so, then V returns 1 and if not, then 0.

Theorem 2. *TagIDcmim is secure against selectiev-tag concurrent man-in-the-middle attacks under the Gap-CDH assumption; for any PPT selectiev-tag concurrent man-in-the-middle adversary $\mathcal{A}$ there exists a PPT Gap-CDH problem solver $\mathcal{S}$ which satisfies the following tight reduction;*

$$\mathbf{Adv}^{\text{stag-imp-cmim}}_{\text{TagIDcmim},\mathcal{A}}(k) \leqslant \mathbf{Adv}^{\text{gap-cdh}}_{\text{Grp},\mathcal{S}}(k).$$

4.2   Proof of Theorem 2

Let $\mathcal{A}$ be as in Theorem 2. Using $\mathcal{A}$ as subroutine, we construct a Gap-CDH problem solver $\mathcal{S}$. The construction is illustrated in Fig.4.

$\mathcal{S}$ is given $q, g, X_1 = g^{x_1}, X_2 = g^{x_2}$ as a CDH problem instance, where x_1 and x_2 are random and hidden. $\mathcal{S}$ initializes inner state. $\mathcal{S}$ invokes $\mathcal{A}$ on input 1^k and gets the target tag t^* from $\mathcal{A}$. $\mathcal{S}$ chooses $r \in \mathbf{Z}_q$ randomly. $\mathcal{S}$ puts $Y = X_1^{-\mathsf{t}^*} g^r$, sets $\mathsf{pk} = (q, g, X_1, Y)$ and inputs pk into $\mathcal{A}$. Note that $\mathcal{S}$ knows neither x_1 nor y, where y is the discrete log of Y;

$$y = \log_g(Y) = -\mathsf{t}^* x_1 + r.$$

$\mathcal{S}$ replies in answer to $\mathcal{A}$'s queries as follows.

In case that $\mathcal{A}$ queries V(pk) for the first message by ϕ, $\mathcal{S}$ chooses $a^* \in \mathbf{Z}_q$ randomly and $\mathcal{S}$ puts $h^* = X_2 g^{a^*}$ and $d^* = (h^*)^r$. Then $\mathcal{S}$ sends (h^*, d^*) to $\mathcal{A}$ (Call this case SIM-V).

In case that $\mathcal{A}$ gives a tag t_i and sends (h_i, d_i) to the i-th prover clone $\mathsf{P}_i(\mathsf{sk})$, $\mathcal{S}$ verifies whether $(g, X_1^{\mathsf{t}_i} Y, h_i, d_i)$ is a DH-tuple. For this sake, $\mathcal{S}$ queries its DDH oracle $\mathcal{DDH}$ for the answer. If it is not satisfied then $\mathcal{S}$ puts $D_i = \perp$. Otherwise $\mathcal{S}$ puts $D_i = (d_i/h_i^r)^{1/(\mathsf{t}_i - \mathsf{t}^*)}$ (Call this case SIM-P). $\mathcal{S}$ sends D_i to $\mathcal{A}$. Note that, in the selective-tag framework, $\mathcal{A}$ is prohibited from using t^* as t_i (i.e. $\mathsf{t}^* \neq \mathsf{t}_i$ for any i).

In case that $\mathcal{A}$ outputs D^* to V(pk), $\mathcal{S}$ verifies whether (g, X_1, h^*, D^*) is a DH-tuple. For this sake, $\mathcal{S}$ queries $\mathcal{DDH}$ for the answer. If so, then $\mathcal{S}$ returns $Z = D^*/X_1^{a^*}$ and if not, $\mathcal{S}$ returns random element $Z \in G_q$.

In the case SIM-V, $\mathcal{S}$ simulates V(pk) perfectly. This is because the distribution of (h^*, d^*) is equal to that of (h, d). To see it, note that (h^*, d^*) corresponds to (h, d) when $x_2 + a^*$ is substituted for a;

$$h^* = g^{x_2+a^*}, \quad d^* = (g^{x_2+a^*})^r = (g^r)^{x_2+a^*} = (X_1^{\mathsf{t}^*} Y)^{x_2+a^*}.$$

In the case SIM-P, $\mathcal{S}$ simulates concurrent $\mathsf{P}_i(\mathsf{sk})$s perfectly. This is because D_i is equal to $h_i^{x_1}$ by the following equalities;

$$d_i/h_i^r = h_i^{\mathsf{t}_i x_1 + y - r} = h_i^{(\mathsf{t}_i - \mathsf{t}^*)x_1 + (\mathsf{t}^* x_1 + y - r)} = h_i^{(\mathsf{t}_i - \mathsf{t}^*)x_1}.$$

As a whole $\mathcal{S}$ simulates both $\mathtt{V}(\mathtt{pk})$ and $\mathtt{P}_i(\mathtt{sk})$s perfectly. Now we evaluate Gap-CDH advantage of $\mathcal{S}$. When $\mathcal{A}$ wins (g, X_1, h^*, D^*) is a DH-tuple and the followings hold;

$$D^* = (g^{x_1})^{x_2 + a^*} = g^{x_1 x_2} X_1^{a^*}.$$

So $\mathcal{S}$ wins because its output Z is $g^{x_1 x_2}$. Therefore the probability that $\mathcal{S}$ wins is lower bounded by the probability that $\mathcal{A}$ wins;

$$\Pr[\mathcal{S} \text{ wins}] \geqslant \Pr[\mathcal{A} \text{ wins}].$$

That is; $\mathbf{Adv}_{\mathtt{Grp}, \mathcal{S}}^{\text{gap-cdh}}(k) \geqslant \mathbf{Adv}_{\mathtt{TagIDcmim}, \mathcal{A}}^{\text{stag-imp-cmim}}(k).$ (Q.E.D.)

Given (q, g, X_1, X_2) as input;
Initial Setting
– Initialize inner state, invoke $\mathcal{A}$ on input 1^k, get the target tag $\mathtt{t}^*$ from $\mathcal{A}$
– $r \leftarrow \mathbf{Z}_q, Y := X_1^{-\mathtt{t}^*} g^r$, $\mathtt{pk} := (q, g, X_1, Y)$, input $\mathtt{pk}$ into $\mathcal{A}$
Answering $\mathcal{A}$'s Queries
– In case that $\mathcal{A}$ queries $\mathtt{V}(\mathtt{pk})$ for the first message (the case SIM-V);
  • $a^* \leftarrow \mathbf{Z}_q, h^* := X_2 g^{a^*}, d^* := (h^*)^r$, send (h^*, d^*) to $\mathcal{A}$
– In case that $\mathcal{A}$ gives $\mathtt{t}_i$ and sends (h_i, d_i) to $\mathtt{P}_i(\mathtt{sk})$;
  • If $\mathcal{DDH}(g, X_1^{\mathtt{t}_i} Y, h_i, d_i) \neq 1$ then $D_i := \perp$
  • else $D_i := (d_i / h_i^r)^{1/(\mathtt{t}_i - \mathtt{t}^*)}$ (the case SIM-P)
  • Send D_i to $\mathcal{A}$
– In case that $\mathcal{A}$ sends D^* to $\mathtt{V}(\mathtt{pk})$;
  • If $\mathcal{DDH}(g, X_1, h^*, D^*) = 1$ then return $Z := D^* / X_1^{a^*}$
  • else return random element $Z \in G_q$

Fig. 4. A Gap-CDH Problem Solver $\mathcal{S}$ for the Proof of Theorem 2

4.3   Discussion

By virtue of the tag framework, the solver $\mathcal{S}$ can simulate concurrent prover clones ($\mathtt{P}_i(\mathtt{sk})$s) perfectly in the interaction with a selective-tag adversary $\mathcal{A}$. Moreover, $\mathcal{S}$ embeds a portion of CDH problem instance (X_2) simulating a verifier ($\mathtt{V}(\mathtt{pk})$) perfectly, and succeeds in extracting the answer ($X_1^{a^*}$ times $g^{x_1 x_2}$).

5   An ID Scheme Secure against CMIM Attacks

In this section we construct an ID scheme $\mathtt{IDcmim}$. We apply the CHK transformation [9] to $\mathtt{TagIDcmim}$. That is, to leave the tag framework, we add a one-time signature $\mathtt{OTS}$ to $\mathtt{TagIDcmim}$ and replace the tag $\mathtt{t}$ by a verification key $\mathtt{vk}$.

5.1   IDcmim and Its Security

$\mathtt{IDcmim}$ consists of a triple $(\mathtt{K}, \mathtt{P}, \mathtt{V})$. $\mathtt{IDcmim}$ employs a strong one-time signature $\mathtt{OTS} = (\mathtt{SGK}, \mathtt{Sign}, \mathtt{Vrfy})$ such that the verification key $\mathtt{vk}$ is in $\mathbf{Z}_q$. The definition and security of strong one-time signatures is noted in Appendix A.

The construction is as shown in the Fig.5. On input 1^k a key generator K runs as follows. A group parameter generator Grp outputs (q, g) on input 1^k. Then K chooses $x, y \in \mathbf{Z}_q$, puts $X = g^x$ and $Y = g^y$, and sets $\mathtt{pk} = (q, g, X, Y)$ and $\mathtt{sk} = (q, g, x, y)$. Then K returns $(\mathtt{pk}, \mathtt{sk})$.

P and V interact as follows. In the first round, V is given pk as input. V runs signing key generator SGK on input 1^k to get $(\mathtt{vk}, \mathtt{sgk})$. V chooses $a \in \mathbf{Z}_q$ randomly and computes $h = g^a$ and $d = (X^{\mathtt{vk}}Y)^a$. V runs $\mathtt{Sign}_{\mathtt{sgk}}$ on message (h, d) to get a signature σ. Then V sends $\mathtt{vk}, (h, d), \sigma$ to P. In the second round, P is given sk as input and receives $\mathtt{vk}, (h, d), \sigma$ as input message. P verifies whether the signature σ for the message (h, d) is valid under vk and whether $(g, X^{\mathtt{vk}}Y, h, d)$ is a DH-tuple. For the latter sake, P checks whether $h^{(\mathtt{vk})x+y} = d$ holds. If at least one of them does not hold then P puts $D = \perp$. Otherwise P computes $D = h^x$. Then P sends D to V. Receiving D as input message, V verifies whether (g, X, h, D) is a DH-tuple. For this sake, V checks whether $X^a = D$ holds. If so, then V returns 1 and if not, then 0.

Key Generation
- K: given 1^k as input;
    - $(q, g) \leftarrow \mathtt{Grp}(1^k), x, y \leftarrow \mathbf{Z}_q, X := g^x, Y := g^y$
    - $\mathtt{pk} := (q, g, X, Y), \mathtt{sk} := (q, g, x, y)$, return $(\mathtt{pk}, \mathtt{sk})$

Interaction
- V: given pk as input;
    - $(\mathtt{vk}, \mathtt{sgk}) \leftarrow \mathtt{SGK}(1^k), a \leftarrow \mathbf{Z}_q, h := g^a, d := (X^{\mathtt{vk}}Y)^a, \sigma \leftarrow \mathtt{Sign}_{\mathtt{sgk}}((h, d))$
    - Send $\mathtt{vk}, (h, d), \sigma$ to P
- P: given sk as input and receiving $\mathtt{vk}, (h, d), \sigma$ as input message;
    - If $\mathtt{Vrfy}_{\mathtt{vk}}((h, d), \sigma) \neq 1$ or $h^{(\mathtt{vk})x+y} \neq d$ then $D := \perp$ else $D := h^x$
    - Send D to V
- V: receiving D as input message;
    - If $X^a = D$ then return 1 else return 0

Fig. 5. An ID Scheme IDcmim

Theorem 3. *IDcmim is secure against concurrent man-in-the-middle attacks under the Gap-CDH assumption and the one-time security in the strong sence of OTS; for any PPT concurrent man-in-the-middle adversary $\mathcal{A}$ there exist a PPT Gap-CDH problem solver $\mathcal{S}$ and a PPT forger $\mathcal{F}$ on OTS which satisfies the following tight reduction;*

$$\mathbf{Adv}_{\mathtt{IDcmim}, \mathcal{A}}^{\mathrm{imp\text{-}cmim}}(k) \leqslant \mathbf{Adv}_{\mathtt{Grp}, \mathcal{S}}^{\mathrm{gap\text{-}cdh}}(k) + \mathbf{Adv}_{\mathtt{OTS}, \mathcal{F}}^{\mathrm{ef\text{-}cma}}(k).$$

The detailed proof of Theorem 3 is provided in Appendix B.

6 Conclusion

We have presented three ID schemes which are basically proofs of ability to complete Diffie-Hellman tuples. By virtue of the tag framework, simulation went well in the security reduction for Theorem 2. At the same time, embed-and-extract technique worked for CDH problem instance. As a result, the second scheme got security against selective-tag concurrent man-in-the-middle attacks based on tight reduction to the Gap-CDH Assumption. Applying the CHK transformation to the second scheme, We left the tag-framework to get the third scheme.

Acknowledgements

We appreciate thoughtful comments offered by the anonymous reviewers.

References

1. Arita, S., Kawashima, N.: An Identification Scheme with Tight Reduction. IEICE Transactions on Fundamentals of Electronics, Communications and Computer Sciences E90-A(9), 1949–1955 (2007)
2. Boneh, D., Boyen, X.: Short Signatures without Random Oracles. In: Cachin, C., Camenisch, J.L. (eds.) EUROCRYPT 2004. LNCS, vol. 3027, pp. 56–73. Springer, Heidelberg (2004)
3. Bellare, M., Fischlin, M., Goldwasser, S., Micali, S.: Identification Protocols Secure against Reset Attacks. In: Pfitzmann, B. (ed.) EUROCRYPT 2001. LNCS, vol. 2045, pp. 495–511. Springer, Heidelberg (2001)
4. Bleichenbacher, D., Maurer, U.: On the Efficiency of One-time Digital Signatures. In: Kim, K.-c., Matsumoto, T. (eds.) ASIACRYPT 1996. LNCS, vol. 1163, pp. 196–209. Springer, Heidelberg (1996)
5. Bellare, M., Palacio, A.: GQ and Schnorr Identification Schemes: Proofs of Security against Impersonation under Active and Concurrent Attacks. In: Yung, M. (ed.) CRYPTO 2002. LNCS, vol. 2442, pp. 162–177. Springer, Heidelberg (2002)
6. Bellare, M., Palacio, A.: The Knowledge-of-Exponent Assumptions and 3-Round Zero-Knowledge Protocols. In: Franklin, M. (ed.) CRYPTO 2004. LNCS, vol. 3152, pp. 273–289. Springer, Heidelberg (2004)
7. Canetti, R., Dakdouk, R.R.: Extractable Perfectly One-way Functions. In: Aceto, L., Damgård, I., Goldberg, L.A., Halldórsson, M.M., Ingólfsdóttir, A., Walukiewicz, I. (eds.) ICALP 2008, Part II. LNCS, vol. 5126, pp. 449–460. Springer, Heidelberg (2008)
8. Crame, R., Damgård, I., Nielsen, J.B.: Multiparty Computation from Threshold Homomorphic Encryption. In: Pfitzmann, B. (ed.) EUROCRYPT 2001. LNCS, vol. 2045, pp. 280–300. Springer, Heidelberg (2001)
9. Canetti, R., Halevi, S., Katz, J.: Chosen-Ciphertext Security from Identity-Based Encryption. In: Cachin, C., Camenisch, J.L. (eds.) EUROCRYPT 2004. LNCS, vol. 3027, pp. 207–222. Springer, Heidelberg (2004)
10. Dakdouk, R.R.: Theory and Application of Extractable Functions. Doctor of Philosophy Dissertation, Yale University, USA (2009)
11. Damgård, I.: Towards Practical Public Key Systems Secure against Chosen Ciphertext Attacks. In: Feigenbaum, J. (ed.) CRYPTO 1991. LNCS, vol. 576, pp. 445–456. Springer, Heidelberg (1992)
12. Gennaro, R.: Multi-trapdoor Commitments and their Applications to Non-Malleable Protocols. In: Franklin, M. (ed.) CRYPTO 2004. LNCS, vol. 3152, pp. 220–236. Springer, Heidelberg (2004)

13. Goldreich, O.: Foundations of Cryptography: Basic Tools. Cambridge University Press, Cambridge (2001)
14. Guillou, L., Quisquater, J.J.: A Paradoxical Identity-Based Signature Scheme Resulting from Zero-Knowledge. In: Goldwasser, S. (ed.) CRYPTO 1988. LNCS, vol. 403, pp. 216–231. Springer, Heidelberg (1990)
15. Katz, J.: Efficient Cryptographic Protocols Preventing "Man-in-the-Middle" Attacks. Doctor of Philosophy Dissertation, Columbia University, USA (2002)
16. Katz, J.: Efficient and Non-Malleable Proofs of Plaintext Knowledge and Applications. In: Biham, E. (ed.) EUROCRYPT 2003. LNCS, vol. 2656, pp. 211–228. Springer, Heidelberg (2003)
17. Kiltz, E.: Chosen-Ciphertext Security from Tag-Based Encryption. In: Halevi, S., Rabin, T. (eds.) TCC 2006. LNCS, vol. 3876, pp. 581–600. Springer, Heidelberg (2006)
18. Kurosawa, K., Desmedt, Y.: A New Paradigm of Hybrid Encryption Scheme. In: Franklin, M. (ed.) CRYPTO 2004. LNCS, vol. 3152, pp. 426–442. Springer, Heidelberg (2004)
19. Maurer, U., Wolf, S.: Lower Bounds on Generic Algorithms in Groups. In: Nyberg, K. (ed.) EUROCRYPT 1998. LNCS, vol. 1403, pp. 72–84. Springer, Heidelberg (1998)
20. Okamoto, T., Pointcheval, D.: The Gap-Problems: A New Class of Problems for the Security of Cryptographic Schemes. In: Kim, K.-c. (ed.) PKC 2001. LNCS, vol. 1992, pp. 104–118. Springer, Heidelberg (2001)
21. Schnorr, C.P.: Efficient Signature Generation by Smart Cards. Journal of Cryptology 4(3), 161–174 (1991)
22. Stinson, D.R., Wu, J.: An Efficient and Secure Two-flow Zero-Knowledge Identification Protocol. Journal of Mathematical Cryptology 1(3), 201–220 (2007)
23. Wu, J., Stinson, D.R.: An Efficient Identification Protocol and the Knowledge of Exponent Assumption. Cryptology ePrint Archive, 2007/479, http://eprint.iacr.org/
24. Waters, B.: Dual System Encryption: Realizing Fully Secure IBE and HIBE under Simple Assumptions. In: Halevi, S. (ed.) CRYPTO 2009. LNCS, vol. 5677, pp. 619–636. Springer, Heidelberg (2009)

A   One-Time Signatures

A *one-time signature* OTS is a triple of PPT algorithms ($\mathtt{SGK}, \mathtt{Sign}, \mathtt{Vrfy}$). $\mathtt{SGK}$ is a signing key generator which outputs a pair of a verification key and a matching signing key ($\mathtt{vk}, \mathtt{sgk}$) on input 1^k. $\mathtt{Sign}$ and $\mathtt{Vrfy}$ are a signing algorithm and a verification algorithm, respectively. We say that (m, σ) is *valid* if $\mathtt{Vrfy}_{\mathtt{vk}}(m, \sigma)$ outputs one. We require OTS to satisfy the standard completeness condition. We also require OTS to be existentially unforgeable against chosen message attack (EUF-CMA) by any PPT forger $\mathcal{F}$. The following experiment is the strong one.

Experiment$_{OTS, \mathcal{F}}^{\text{ef-cma}}(1^k)$

$(\mathtt{vk}, \mathtt{sgk}) \leftarrow \mathtt{SGK}(1^k), m \leftarrow \mathcal{F}(\mathtt{vk}), \sigma \leftarrow \mathtt{Sign}_{\mathtt{sgk}}(m), (m', \sigma') \leftarrow \mathcal{F}(\mathtt{vk}, (m, \sigma))$

If $\mathtt{Vrfy}_{\mathtt{vk}}(m', \sigma') = 1 \wedge (m', \sigma') \neq (m, \sigma)$ then return WIN else LOSE.

Then we define *advantage of existential forgery by chosen message attack of* $\mathcal{F}$ over OTS as;

$$\mathbf{Adv}_{OTS,\mathcal{F}}^{\text{ef-cma}}(k) \stackrel{\text{def}}{=} \Pr[\mathbf{Experiment}_{OTS,\mathcal{F}}^{\text{ef-cma}}(1^k) \text{ returns WIN}].$$

We say that a OTS is EUF-CMA (or, has *one-time security*) in the strong sence when, for any PPT algorithm $\mathcal{F}$, $\mathbf{Adv}_{OTS,\mathcal{F}}^{\text{ef-cma}}(k)$ is negligible in k (and then we say that OTS is a strong one-time signature).

B   Proof of Theorem 3

Let $\mathcal{A}$ be as in Theorem 3. Using $\mathcal{A}$ as subroutine, we construct a Gap-CDH problem solver $\mathcal{S}$. The construction is illustrated in Fig.6.

$\mathcal{S}$ is given $q, g, X_1 = g^{x_1}, X_2 = g^{x_2}$ as a CDH problem instance, where x_1 and x_2 are random and hidden. $\mathcal{S}$ initializes inner state. $\mathcal{S}$ gets $(\text{vk}^*, \text{sgk}^*)$ from $\text{SGK}(1^k)$ and chooses $r \in \mathbf{Z}_q$ randomly. $\mathcal{S}$ puts $Y = X_1^{-\text{vk}^*} g^r$, sets $\text{pk} = (q, g, X_1, Y)$ and invokes $\mathcal{A}$ on input pk. Note that $\mathcal{S}$ knows neither x_1 nor y, where y is the discrete log of Y;

$$y = \log_g(Y) = -\text{vk}^* x_1 + r.$$

$\mathcal{S}$ replies in answer to $\mathcal{A}$'s queries as follows.

In case that $\mathcal{A}$ queries $\text{V}(\text{pk})$ for the first message by ϕ, $\mathcal{S}$ chooses $a^* \in \mathbf{Z}_q$ randomly and $\mathcal{S}$ puts $h^* = X_2 g^{a^*}$ and $d^* = (h^*)^r$. $\mathcal{S}$ gets a signature σ^* from $\text{Sign}_{\text{sgk}^*}((h^*, d^*))$. Then $\mathcal{S}$ sends $\text{vk}^*, (h^*, d^*), \sigma^*$ to $\mathcal{A}$ (Call this case SIM-V).

Given (q, g, X_1, X_2) as input;
Initial Setting
– Initialize inner state, $(\text{vk}^*, \text{sgk}^*) \leftarrow \text{SGK}(1^k)$
– $r \leftarrow \mathbf{Z}_q, Y := X_1^{-\text{vk}^*} g^r$, $\text{pk} := (q, g, X_1, Y)$, invoke $\mathcal{A}$ on pk
Answering $\mathcal{A}$'s Queries
– In case that $\mathcal{A}$ queries $\text{V}(\text{pk})$ for the first message (the case SIM-V);
    • $a^* \leftarrow \mathbf{Z}_q, h^* := X_2 g^{a^*}, d^* := (h^*)^r$, $\sigma^* \leftarrow \text{Sign}_{\text{sgk}^*}((h^*, d^*))$
    • Send $\text{vk}^*, (h^*, d^*), \sigma^*$ to $\mathcal{A}$
– In case that $\mathcal{A}$ sends $\text{vk}_i, (h_i, d_i), \sigma_i$ to $\text{P}_i(\text{sk})$;
    • If $\text{Vrfy}_{\text{vk}_i}((h_i, d_i), \sigma_i) \neq 1$ or $\mathcal{DDH}(g, X_1^{\text{vk}_i} Y, h_i, d_i) \neq 1$ then $D_i := \perp$
    • else
        If $\text{vk}_i \neq \text{vk}^*$ then $D_i := (d_i/h_i^r)^{1/(\text{vk}_i - \text{vk}^*)}$ (the case SIM-P)
        else abort (the case ABORT)
    • Send D_i to $\mathcal{A}$
– In case that $\mathcal{A}$ sends D^* to $\text{V}(\text{pk})$;
    • If $\mathcal{DDH}(g, X_1, h^*, D^*) = 1$ then return $Z := D^*/X_1^{a^*}$
    • else return random element $Z \in G_q$

Fig. 6. A Gap-CDH Problem Solver $\mathcal{S}$ for the Proof of Theorem 3

In case that $\mathcal{A}$ sends $\mathrm{vk}_i, (h_i, d_i), \sigma_i$ to the i-th prover clone $\mathrm{P}_i(\mathrm{sk})$, $\mathcal{S}$ verifies whether $((h_i, d_i), \sigma_i)$ is valid under vk_i and whether $(g, X_1^{\mathrm{vk}_i} Y, h_i, d_i)$ is a DH-tuple. For the latter sake, $\mathcal{S}$ queries its DDH oracle $\mathcal{DDH}$ for the answer. If at least one of them is not satisfied then $\mathcal{S}$ puts $D_i = \perp$. Otherwise, if $\mathrm{vk}_i \neq \mathrm{vk}^*$ then $\mathcal{S}$ puts $D_i = (d_i/h_i^r)^{1/(\mathrm{vk}_i - \mathrm{vk}^*)}$ (Call this case SIM-P). If $\mathrm{vk}_i = \mathrm{vk}^*$, $\mathcal{S}$ aborts (Call this case ABORT). $\mathcal{S}$ sends D_i to $\mathcal{A}$ except the case ABORT.

In case that $\mathcal{A}$ outputs D^* to $\mathrm{V}(\mathrm{pk})$, $\mathcal{S}$ verifies whether (g, X_1, h^*, D^*) is a DH-tuple. For the latter sake, $\mathcal{S}$ queries $\mathcal{DDH}$. If so, then $\mathcal{S}$ returns $Z = D^*/X_1^{a^*}$ and if not, $\mathcal{S}$ returns random element $Z \in G_q$.

In the case SIM-V, $\mathcal{S}$ simulates $\mathrm{V}(\mathrm{pk})$ perfectly. This is because the distribution of (h^*, d^*) is equal to that of (h, d). To see it, note that (h^*, d^*) corresponds to (h, d) when $x_2 + a^*$ is substituted for a;

$$h^* = g^{x_2 + a^*}, \quad d^* = (g^{x_2 + a^*})^r = (g^r)^{x_2 + a^*} = (X_1^{\mathrm{vk}^*} Y)^{x_2 + a^*}.$$

In the case SIM-P, $\mathcal{S}$ simulates concurrent $\mathrm{P}_i(\mathrm{sk})$s perfectly. This is because D_i is equal to $h_i^{x_1}$ by the following equalities;

$$d_i/h_i^r = h_i^{\mathrm{vk}_i x_1 + y - r} = h_i^{(\mathrm{vk}_i - \mathrm{vk}^*) x_1 + (\mathrm{vk}^* x_1 + y - r)} = h_i^{(\mathrm{vk}_i - \mathrm{vk}^*) x_1}.$$

As a whole $\mathcal{S}$ simulates both $\mathrm{V}(\mathrm{pk})$ and $\mathrm{P}_i(\mathrm{sk})$s perfectly except the case ABORT. Now we evaluate Gap-CDH advantage of $\mathcal{S}$. When $\mathcal{A}$ wins (g, X_1, h^*, D^*) is a DH-tuple and the followings hold;

$$D^* = (g^{x_1})^{x_2 + a^*} = g^{x_1 x_2} X_1^{a^*}.$$

So $\mathcal{S}$ wins because its output Z is $g^{x_1 x_2}$. Therefore the probability that $\mathcal{S}$ wins is lower bounded by the probability that $\mathcal{A}$ wins and the case ABORT does not happen;

$$\Pr[\mathcal{S} \text{ wins}] \geqslant \Pr[\mathcal{A} \text{ wins} \wedge \neg \text{ABORT}]$$
$$\geqslant \Pr[\mathcal{A} \text{ wins}] - \Pr[\text{ABORT}].$$

That is; $\mathbf{Adv}_{\mathrm{Grp}, \mathcal{S}}^{\mathrm{gap\text{-}cdh}}(k) \geqslant \mathbf{Adv}_{\mathrm{IDcmim}, \mathcal{A}}^{\mathrm{imp\text{-}cmim}}(k) - \Pr[\text{ABORT}].$

Claim. *The probability that the case ABORT occurs is negligible in k.*

Proof of the Claim. Using $\mathcal{A}$ as subroutine, we construct a signature forger $\mathcal{F}$ on OTS as follows. Given vk^* as input, $\mathcal{F}$ initializes inner state, chooses $x_1, x_2 \in \mathbf{Z}_q$ randomly and puts $X_1 = g^{x_1}, X_2 = g^{x_2}$. Similarly to $\mathcal{S}$, $\mathcal{F}$ generates r, Y, pk and invokes $\mathcal{A}$ on pk.

In case that $\mathcal{A}$ queries $\mathrm{V}(\mathrm{pk})$ for the first message, $\mathcal{F}$ generates a^*, h^*, d^* and sends $\mathrm{vk}^*, (h^*, d^*), \sigma^*$ to $\mathcal{A}$ in a similar way to $\mathcal{S}$ except querying its signing oracle $\mathcal{SIGN}_{\mathrm{sgk}^*}$ for a signature σ^* on (h^*, d^*).

In case that $\mathcal{A}$ sends $\mathrm{vk}_i, (h_i, d_i), \sigma_i$ to the i-th prover clone $\mathrm{P}_i(\mathrm{sk})$, $\mathcal{F}$ verifies whether the signature is valid and whether $(g, X_1^{\mathrm{vk}_i} Y, h_i, d_i)$ is a DH-tuple. For the latter sake, $\mathcal{F}$ checks whether the following holds;

$$h_i^{(\mathrm{vk}_i - \mathrm{vk}^*) x_1 + r} = d_i.$$

Then, if $\mathrm{vk}_i \neq \mathrm{vk}^*$ then $\mathcal{F}$ sends D_i to $\mathcal{A}$ in a similar way to $\mathcal{S}$. If $\mathrm{vk}_i = \mathrm{vk}^*$ then $\mathcal{S}$ returns $((h_i, d_i), \sigma_i)$ and stops (Call this case FORGE).

Note that the view of $\mathcal{A}$ in $\mathcal{F}$ is the same as the view of $\mathcal{A}$ in $\mathcal{S}$. So;

$$\Pr[\text{FORGE}] = \Pr[\text{ABORT}].$$

Now in the case FORGE the followings hold;

$$\mathrm{vk}_i = \mathrm{vk}^*, ((h_i, d_i), \sigma_i) \neq ((h^*, d^*), \sigma^*).$$

This is because if $((h_i, d_i), \sigma_i)$ were equal to $((h^*, d^*), \sigma^*)$ then the transcript of a whole interaction would be relayed by $\mathcal{A}$. This is ruled out.

So in the case FORGE, $\mathcal{F}$ succeeds in making up an existential forgery and we have $\mathbf{Adv}_{\text{OTS},\mathcal{F}}^{\text{ef-cma}}(k) = \Pr[\text{FORGE}](= \Pr[\text{ABORT}])$. But the advantage is negligible in k by the assumption in Theorem 3. (Q.E.D.)

A Calculus for Game-Based Security Proofs

David Nowak[1] and Yu Zhang[2]

[1] Research Center for Information Security, AIST, Japan
[2] Institute of Software, Chinese Academy of Sciences, China

Abstract. The game-based approach to security proofs in cryptography is a widely-used methodology for writing proofs rigorously. However a unifying language for writing games is still missing. In this paper we show how CSLR, a probabilistic lambda-calculus with a type system that guarantees that computations are probabilistic polynomial time, can be equipped with a notion of game indistinguishability. This allows us to define cryptographic constructions, effective adversaries, security notions, computational assumptions, game transformations, and game-based security proofs in the unified framework provided by CSLR. Our code for cryptographic constructions is close to implementation in the sense that we do not assume arbitrary uniform distributions but use a realistic algorithm to approximate them. We illustrate our calculus on cryptographic constructions for public-key encryption and pseudorandom bit generation.

Keywords: game-based proofs, implicit complexity, computational indistinguishability.

1 Introduction

Cryptographic constructions are fundamental components for information security. A cryptographic construction must come with a security proof. But those proofs can be subtle and tedious, and thus not easy to check. Bellare and Rogaway even claim in [9] that:

> "*Many proofs in cryptography have become essentially unverifiable. Our field may be approaching a crisis of rigor.*"

With Shoup [27], they advocate game-based proofs as a remedy. This is a methodology for writing security proofs that makes them easier to read and check. In this approach, a security property is modeled as a probabilistic program implementing a game to be solved by the adversary. The adversary itself is modeled as an external probabilistic procedure interfaced with the game. Proving security amounts to proving that any adversary has at most a negligible advantage over a random player. An adversary is assumed to be efficient i.e., it is modeled as a probabilistic polynomial-time (for short, PPT) function.

However a unifying language for writing games is still missing. In this paper we show how Computational SLR [29] (for short, CSLR), a probabilistic lambda-calculus with a type system that guarantees that computations are probabilistic

S.-H. Heng and K. Kurosawa (Eds.): ProvSec 2010, LNCS 6402, pp. 35–52, 2010.

polynomial time, can be equipped with a notion of game indistinguishability. This allows us to define cryptographic constructions, effective adversaries, security notions, computational assumptions, game transformations, and game-based security proofs in the unified framework provided by CSLR.

Related work. Nowak has given a formal account of the game-based approach, and formalized it in the proof assistant Coq [24,25]. He follows Shoup by modeling games directly as probability distributions, without going through a programming language. With this approach, he can machine-check game transformations, but not the complexity bound on the adversary. Previously, Corin and den Hartog had proposed a probabilistic Hoare logic in [10] to formalize game-based proofs but they suffer from the same limitation. This issue is addressed in [3] where the authors mention that their implementation includes tactics that can help establishing that a program is PPT. Their approach is direct in the sense that polynomial-time computation is characterized by explicitly counting the number of computation steps. Backes et al. [2] are also working on a similar approach with the addition of higher-order aimed at reasoning about oracles.

The above approaches are limited to the verification of cryptographic algorithms, and cannot deal with their implementations. This issue has been tackled by Affeldt et al. in [1] where, by adding a new kind of game transformation (so-called implementation steps), game-based security proofs can be conducted directly on implementations in assembly language. They have applied their approach to the verification of an implementation in assembly language of a pseudo-random bit generator (PRBG). However they do not address the issue of uniform distributions. Indeed, because computers are based on binary digits, the cardinal of the support of a uniform distribution has to be a power of 2. Even at a theoretical level, probabilistic Turing machines used in the definition of PPT choose random numbers only among sets of cardinal a power of 2 [14]. In the case of another cardinal, the uniform distribution can only either be approximated or rely on code that is not guaranteed to terminate, although it will terminate with a probability arbitrarily close to 1 [18]. With arbitrary random choices, one can define more distributions than those allowed by the definition of PPT. This raises a fundamental concern that is usually overlooked by cryptographers.

Mitchell et al. have proposed a process calculus with bounded replications and messages to guarantee that those processes are computable in polynomial time [22]. Messages can be terms of OSLR — SLR with a random oracle [21]. Their calculus aim at being general enough to deal with cryptographic protocols, whereas we aim at a simpler calculus able to deal with cryptographic constructions. Blanchet and Pointcheval have implemented CryptoVerif, a semi-automatic tool for making game-based security proofs, also based on a process calculus. Courant et al. have proposed a specialized Hoare logic for analyzing generic asymmetric encryption schemes in the random oracle model [11]. In our work, we do not want to restrict ourselves to *generic* schemes. Impagliazzo and Kapron have proposed two logics for reasoning about cryptographic constructions [19]. The first one is based on a non-standard arithmetic model, which they prove, captures probabilistic polynomial-time computations. The second one is built on top of the first one, with rules justifying computational indistinguishability. More recently Zhang has developed a logic for computational indistinguishability on top of Hofmann's SLR [29].

Contributions. We propose to use CSLR [29] to conduct game-based security proofs. Because the only basic type in CSLR is the type for bits, our code for cryptographic constructions is closer to implementation than the code in related work: in particular, we address the issue of uniform distributions by using an algorithm that approximates them.

CSLR does not allow superpolynomial-time computations (i.e., computations that are not bounded above by any polynomial) nor arbitrary uniform choices. Although this restriction makes sense for the cryptographic constructions and the adversary, the game-based approach to cryptographic proofs does not preclude the possibility of introducing games that perform superpolynomial-time computations or that use arbitrary uniform distributions. They are just idealized constructions that are used to define security notions but are not meant to make their way into implementations. We thus extend CSLR into CSLR+ that allows for superpolynomial-time computations and arbitrary uniform choices. However the cryptographic constructions and the adversary will be constrained to be terms of CSLR.

We propose a notion of game indistinguishability. Although, it is not stronger than the notion of computational indistinguishability of [29], it is simpler to prove and well-suited for formalizing game-based security proofs. We indeed show that this notion allows to easily model security definitions and computational assumptions. Moreover we show that computational indistinguishability implies game indistinguishability, so that we can reuse as it is the equational proof system of [29]. We illustrate the usability of our approach by: proving formally in our proof system for CSLR that an implementation in CSLR of the public-key encryption scheme ElGamal is semantically secure; and by formalizing the pseudorandom bit generator of Blum, Blum and Shub with the related security definition and computational assumption.

Compared with [2] and [3], our approach has the advantage that it can automatically prove (by type inference [16]) that a program is PPT [17].

2   Computational SLR

Bellantoni and Cook have proposed to replace the model of Turing machines by their *safe recursion* scheme which defines exactly functions that are computable in polynomial time on a Turing-machine [4]. This is an intrinsic, purely syntactic mechanism: variables are divided into safe variables and normal variables, and safe variables must be instantiated by values that are computed using only safe variables; recursion must take place on normal variables and intermediate recursion results are never sent to normal variables. When higher-order recursors are concerned, it is also required that step functions must be linear, i.e., intermediate recursive results can be used only once in each step. Thanks to those syntactic restrictions, exponential-time computations are avoided. This is an elegant approach in the sense that polynomial-time computation is characterized without explicitly counting the number of computation steps.

Hofmann later developed a functional language called *SLR* to implement safe recursion [16,17]. It provides a complete characterization through typing of the complexity class of probabilistic polynomial-time computations. He introduces a type system with modality to distinguish between normal variables and safe variables, and linearity to distinguish normal functions and linear functions. He proves that well-typed functions of a proper type are exactly polynomial-time computable functions. Moreover there is a type-inference algorithm that can automatically determine the type of any expression [16]. Mitchell et al. have extended SLR by adding a random bit oracle to simulate the oracle tape in probabilistic Turing-machines [21].

More recently, Zhang has introduced CSLR, a non-polymorphic version of SLR extended with probabilistic computations and a primitive notion of bit-strings [29]. His use of monadic types [23], allows for an explicit distinction in CSLR between probabilistic and purely deterministic functions. It was not possible with the extension by Mitchell et al. [21]. We recall below the definition of CSLR and its main property.

Types. Types are defined by:

$$\tau, \tau', \ldots ::= \mathsf{Bits} \mid \tau \times \tau' \mid \Box \tau \to \tau' \mid \tau \to \tau' \mid \tau \multimap \tau' \mid \mathsf{T}\tau$$

Bits is the base type for bitstrings. The monadic types $\mathsf{T}\tau$ capture probabilistic computations that produce a result of type τ. All other types are from Hofmann's SLR [17]. $\tau \times \tau'$ are cartesian product types. There are three kinds of functions: $\Box \tau \to \tau'$ are types for modal functions with no restriction on the use of their argument; $\tau \to \tau'$ are types for non-modal functions where the argument must be a safe value; $\tau \multimap \tau'$ are types for linear functions where the argument can only be used once. Note that linear types are not necessary when we do not have higher-order recursors, which are themselves not necessary for characterizing PTIME computations but can ease and simplify the programming of certain functions (such as defining the Blum-Blum-Shub pseudorandom bit generator in Section 3).

SLR also has a sub-typing relation $<:$ between types. In particular, the sub-typing relation between the three kinds of functions is: $\tau \multimap \tau' <: \tau \to \tau' <: \Box \tau \to \tau'$. We also have $\mathsf{Bits} \to \tau <: \mathsf{Bits} \multimap \tau$, stating that bitstrings can be duplicated without violating linearity. The subtyping relation is inherited from CSLR, with an additional rule saying that the constructor T preserves sub-typing [29].

Expressions. Expressions of CSLR are defined by the following grammar:

$$e_1, e_2, \ldots ::= x \mid \mathsf{nil} \mid \mathsf{B}_0 \mid \mathsf{B}_1 \mid \mathsf{case}_\tau \mid \mathsf{rec}_\tau \mid \lambda x.e \mid e_1 e_2$$
$$\mid \langle e_1, e_2 \rangle \mid \mathsf{proj}_1 e \mid \mathsf{proj}_2 e \mid \mathsf{rand} \mid \mathsf{return}(e) \mid \mathsf{bind}\ x \leftarrow e_1\ \mathsf{in}\ e_2$$

B_0 and B_1 are two constants for constructing bitstrings: if u is a bitstring, $\mathsf{B}_0 u$ (respectively, $\mathsf{B}_1 u$) is the new bitstring with a bit 0 (respectively, 1) added at the left end of u. case_τ is the constant for case distinction: $\mathsf{case}_\tau(n, \langle e, f_0, f_1 \rangle)$

tests the bitstring n and returns e if n is an empty bitstring, $f_0(n)$ if the first bit of n is 0 and $f_1(n)$ if the first bit of n is 1. rec_τ is the constant for recursion on bitstrings: $\mathrm{rec}_\tau(e, f, n)$ returns e if n is empty, and $f(n, \mathrm{rec}_\tau(e, f, n'))$ otherwise, where n' is the part of the bitstring n with its first bit cut off. rand returns a random bit 0 or 1, each with the probability $\frac{1}{2}$. $\mathrm{return}(e)$ is the trivial (deterministic) computation which returns e with probability 1. $\mathrm{bind}\ x \leftarrow e_1\ \mathrm{in}\ e_2$ is the sequential computation which first computes the probabilistic computation e_1, binds its result to the variable x, then computes e_2. All other expressions are from Hoffman's SLR [17].

To ease the reading of CSLR terms, we shall use some syntactic sugar and abbreviations in the rest of the paper:

- $\lambda_-.e$ represents $\lambda x.e$ when x does not occur as a free variable in e;
- $x \overset{\$}{\leftarrow} e_1; e_2$ represents the probabilistic sequential computation
  $\mathrm{bind}\ x \leftarrow e_1\ \mathrm{in}\ e_2$;
- $x \leftarrow e_1; e_2$ represents the deterministic sequential (call-by-value) computation $(\lambda x.e_2)e_1$;
- if e then e_1 else e_2 represents a simple case distinction
  $\mathrm{case}(e, \langle e_2, \lambda_-.e_2, \lambda_-.e_1 \rangle)$, which tests the first bit of e: if it is 1 then e_1 is executed, otherwise e_2 is executed;
- when a program F is defined recursively by $\lambda n.\mathrm{rec}_\tau(e_1, e_2, n)$, we often write the definition as:

$$F \overset{\mathrm{def}}{=} \lambda n.\mathrm{if}\ n \overset{?}{=} \mathrm{nil}\ \mathrm{then}\ e_1\ \mathrm{else}\ e_2(n, F(\boldsymbol{tail}(n))),$$

where $\overset{?}{=}$ and $\boldsymbol{tail}$ are respectively the equality test between two bitstrings and the function that remove the left-most bit from a bitstring. These functions can be defined in CSLR [29].

Type system and semantics for CSLR are given in [29]. The main property of CSLR [21,29] is:

Theorem 1. *The set-theoretic interpretations of closed terms of type $\Box \mathsf{Bits} \to \mathsf{TBits}$ in CSLR are exactly the functions that can be computed by a probabilistic Turing machine in polynomial time.*

This theorem implies that CSLR is expressive enough to model an adversary and to implement cryptographic constructions, as they both are probabilistic polynomial-time functions. We remark that adversaries can return values of types other than Bits (e.g., tuples of bitstrings), but we can always define adversaries as a PPT function of type $\Box \mathsf{Bits} \to \mathsf{TBits}$ by adopting some encoding of different types of values into bitstrings, so the theorem still applies. The same is true in case of functions with multiple arguments: we can uncurrify them and then adopt some encoding so that the theorem still applies.

An example of PPT function. The random bitstring generation is defined as follows:

$$\boldsymbol{rs} \overset{\mathrm{def}}{=} \lambda n.\mathrm{if}\ (n \overset{?}{=} \mathrm{nil})\ \mathrm{then}\ \mathrm{return}(\mathrm{nil})$$
$$\mathrm{else}\ b \overset{\$}{\leftarrow} \mathrm{rand};\ u \overset{\$}{\leftarrow} \boldsymbol{rs}(\boldsymbol{tail}(n));\ \mathrm{return}(b \bullet u)$$

where $\bullet$ denotes the concatenation operation of bitstrings, which can be programmed and typed in CSLR [29]. $\mathbf{rs}$ receives a bitstring and returns a uniformly random bitstring of the same length. It can be checked that $\vdash \mathbf{rs} : \Box\mathsf{Bits} \to \mathsf{TBits}$.

3   Cryptographic Constructions in CSLR

Uniform distributions are ubiquitous in cryptography. However modern computers are based on binary digits, and thus in implementations the cardinal of the support of a uniform distribution has to be a power of 2. In case of a different cardinal, such a distribution can be approximated by repeatedly selecting a random value in a larger distribution whose cardinal is a power of 2, until one obtain a value in the desired range or reach the maximal number of allowed attempts (*timeout*, which determines the precision of the approximation). In the latter case a default value is returned. We implement this pseudo-uniform sampling in CSLR as follows:

$$\mathbf{zrand} \stackrel{\text{def}}{=} \lambda n\,.\,\lambda t\,.\,\texttt{if } t \stackrel{?}{=} \texttt{nil then return}(0^{|n|})$$
$$\texttt{else } v \stackrel{\$}{\leftarrow} \mathbf{rs}(n);\ \texttt{if } v \geq n \texttt{ then } \mathbf{zrand}(n, \mathbf{tail}(t))$$
$$\texttt{else return}(v)$$

The program takes two arguments: the sampling range (represented by the value $\widehat{n}$) and the timeout (represented by $|t|$). The test $\geq$ can be programmed in CSLR. The timeout is represented by the length of the bitstring t for the sake of simplicity and readability of the program, but an alternative representation of using $\widehat{t}$ as the timeout is certainly acceptable.

The program $\mathbf{zrand}$ uses $u = 2^{\lceil \log_2 \widehat{n} \rceil}$ as the cardinal of the larger distribution and makes samplings in this distribution. The probability that one sampling falls outside the desired range is $\frac{u-\widehat{n}}{u}$, thus probability that $|t|$ consecutive attempts fail is $\left(\frac{u-\widehat{n}}{u}\right)^{|t|}$. $\mathbf{zrand}$ will return $0^{|n|}$ as the default value after $|t|$ consecutive failures, so the probability that a value smaller than $\widehat{n}$ but other than $0^{|n|}$ is returned is $\frac{1-\left(\frac{u-\widehat{n}}{u}\right)^{|t|}}{\widehat{n}}$, and the probability that $0^{|n|}$ is returned is $\frac{1+(\widehat{n}-1)\cdot\left(\frac{u-\widehat{n}}{u}\right)^{|t|}}{\widehat{n}}$.

Similarly, a finite group can be encoded in CSLR and multiplication and group exponentiation can be programmed (as implied by Theorem 1). In the sequel, we shall write $\mathbb{Z}_q$ (q a bitstring) for the set of bitstrings (of the same length than q) of $\{0, 1, \ldots, \widehat{q} - 1\}$, and $\mathbb{Z}_q^{\$}$ for the truly uniform distribution from $\mathbb{Z}_q$.

The public-key encryption scheme ElGamal. Let G be a finite cyclic group of order q (depending on the security parameter η) and $\gamma \in G$ be a generator. The ElGamal encryption scheme [13] can be implemented in CSLR by the following programs:

– Key generation:

$$\mathbf{KG} \stackrel{\text{def}}{=} \lambda\eta\,.\,x \stackrel{\$}{\leftarrow} \mathbf{zrand}(q, \eta);\ \texttt{return}(\gamma^x, x)$$

$\mathbf{KG}$ is of type $\Box\mathsf{Bits} \to \mathsf{T}(\mathsf{Bits} \times \mathsf{Bits})$.

– Encryption:

$$\boldsymbol{Enc} \stackrel{\mathrm{def}}{=} \lambda\eta \,.\, \lambda pk \,.\, \lambda m \,.\, y \stackrel{\$}{\leftarrow} \boldsymbol{zrand}(q,\eta);\ \mathtt{return}(\gamma^y, pk^y * m)$$

$\boldsymbol{Enc}$ is of type $\Box\mathsf{Bits} \to \mathsf{Bits} \to \mathsf{Bits} \to \mathsf{T}(\mathsf{Bits} \times \mathsf{Bits})$.
– Decryption:

$$\boldsymbol{Dec} \stackrel{\mathrm{def}}{=} \lambda\eta \,.\, \lambda sk \,.\, \lambda c \,.\, \mathtt{proj}_2(c) * (\mathtt{proj}_1(c)^{sk})^{-1}$$

$\boldsymbol{Dec}$ is of type $\Box\mathsf{Bits} \to \mathsf{Bits} \to \mathsf{Bits} \to \mathsf{Bits}$, which does not involve monadic type because decryption is deterministic.

Note that when encoding cryptographic constructions in CSLR, we put the security parameter η explicitly as the argument of the programs. However, as we work on bitstrings in CSLR, the security parameter in traditional cryptographic contexts actually corresponds to $|\eta|$ here. In the case of ElGamal encryption, the group order q will be determined by η. Particularly, for the encryption scheme to be semantically secure, we must choose a suitable group such that the DDH assumption holds, and its order will be necessarily exponential in $|\eta|$. There are efficient algorithms which computes a suitable DDH group given η, hence can be programmed in CSLR [8].

In the implementation of $\boldsymbol{KG}$ and $\boldsymbol{Enc}$, the security parameter η is used directly as the timeout of $\boldsymbol{zrand}$. A more general implementation would instantiate the timeout by a polynomial of $|\eta|$, i.e., $\boldsymbol{zrand}(q, p(\eta))$ where p is a well-typed SLR function of type $\Box\mathsf{Bits} \to \mathsf{Bits}$. The choice of p will affect the final distribution of the program and consequently the advantage of adversaries in security games or experiments, but that remains negligible. It is possible to use CSLR to deal with exact security and the exact timeout with p is necessary in that case. In this paper, we use the specific timeout for the sake of clarity.

The Blum-Blum-Shub pseudorandom bit generator. The BBS generator defined in [7] is a deterministic function and can be programmed in CSLR as follows:

$$\boldsymbol{BBS} \stackrel{\mathrm{def}}{=} \lambda\eta \,.\, \lambda l \,.\, \lambda s \,.\, \boldsymbol{bbsrec}(\eta, l, s^2 \mathrm{mod}\ n)$$

where $\boldsymbol{bbsrec}$ is defined recursively as

$$\boldsymbol{bbsrec} \stackrel{\mathrm{def}}{=}$$
$$\lambda\eta \,.\, \lambda l \,.\, \lambda x \,.\, \mathtt{if}\ l \stackrel{?}{=} \mathtt{nil}\ \mathtt{then}\ \mathtt{nil}\ \mathtt{else}\ \boldsymbol{parity}(x) \bullet \boldsymbol{bbsrec}(\eta, \boldsymbol{tail}(l), x^2 \mathrm{mod}\ n)$$

where n is determined by the security parameter η. $\boldsymbol{BBS}$ is a well typed SLR-function of type $\Box\mathsf{Bits} \to \mathsf{Bits} \to \mathsf{Bits} \to \mathsf{Bits}$, with the second argument being the length of the resulted pseudo-random bitstring and the third argument being the seed.

4   Game Indistinguishability

In game-based proofs, an adversary involved in a game can be an arbitrary probabilistic polynomial-time program, hence it can be encoded as a CSLR program of type $\Box\mathsf{Bits} \to \mathsf{T}\tau$, where the security parameter will bound its running time, and τ is the type of messages returned by the adversary. A *game* is encoded as a closed higher-order CSLR function of type $\Box\mathsf{Bits} \to (\Box\mathsf{Bits} \to \mathsf{T}\tau) \to \mathsf{TBits}$ that takes the security parameter and the adversary as arguments and returns one bit denoting whether the adversary wins the game. We say two games are indistinguishable if no adversary can win one of the game with significantly larger probability than in the other.

Definition 1 (Game indistinguishability). *Two CSLR games g_1 and g_2 are game indistinguishable (written as $g_1 \approx g_2$) if for every term A such that $\vdash A : \Box\mathsf{Bits} \to \mathsf{T}\tau$, and every positive polynomial P, there exists some $N \in \mathbb{N}$ such that for all bitstring η with $|\eta| \geq N$,*

$$|\mathbf{Pr}[[\![g_1(\eta, A)]\!] \rightsquigarrow 1] - \mathbf{Pr}[[\![g_2(\eta, A)]\!] \rightsquigarrow 1]| < \frac{1}{P(|\eta|)}$$

The above definition formalizes the idea that the change between the two games g_1 and g_2 cannot be noticed by an adversary. A more general notion of *computational indistinguishability* in cryptography has been defined in the original CSLR system [29].

Definition 2 (Computational indistinguishability [29]). *Two CSLR terms f_1 and f_2, both of type $\Box\mathsf{Bits} \to \tau$, are computationally indistinguishable (written as $f_1 \simeq f_2$) if for every closed CSLR term A of type $\Box\mathsf{Bits} \to \tau \to \mathsf{TBits}$ and every positive polynomial P, there exists some $N \in \mathbb{N}$ such that for all bitstring η with $|\eta| \geq N$*

$$|\mathbf{Pr}[[\![A(\eta, f_1(\eta))]\!] \rightsquigarrow 1] - \mathbf{Pr}[[\![A(\eta, f_2(\eta))]\!] \rightsquigarrow 1]| < \frac{1}{P(|\eta|)}$$

This definition is a reformulation of Definition 3.2.2 of [14] in CSLR. In particular, a CSLR term of type $\Box\mathsf{Bits} \to \mathsf{T}\tau$ defines a so-called probabilistic *ensemble*.

Intuitively, the difference between the two notions of indistinguishability is that, computational indistinguishability allows for any arbitrary use of the compared terms by the adversary, while the game indistinguishability provides more control over the adversary as it is usual in game-based security definitions. Hence, game indistinguishability is no stronger than computational indistinguishability as proved in the following proposition. This is why we can sometimes use the CSLR proof system, which is designed for proving computational indistinguishability, for proving game indistinguishability.

Proposition 1. *Computational indistinguishability implies game indistinguishability.*

Proof. Let g_1 and g_2 be two arbitrary games of type $\Box\mathsf{Bits} \to (\Box\mathsf{Bits} \to \mathsf{T}\tau) \to \mathsf{TBits}$. For every adversary A of type $\Box\mathsf{Bits} \to \mathsf{T}\tau$, construct the following adversary A':

$$\lambda\eta . \lambda g . b \overset{\$}{\leftarrow} g(A);$$
$$\text{if } b \overset{?}{=} 1 \text{ then return(nil) else return}(0).$$

Clearly, $\mathbf{Pr}[\llbracket \mathcal{A}'(\eta, g_i(\eta)) \rrbracket = \mathtt{nil}] = \mathbf{Pr}[\llbracket g_i(\eta, \mathcal{A}) \rrbracket = 1]$, and because g_1 and g_2 are computationally indistinguishable, $\mathbf{Pr}[\llbracket \mathcal{A}'(\eta, g_1(\eta)) \rrbracket = \mathtt{nil}] - \mathbf{Pr}[\llbracket \mathcal{A}'(\eta, g_2(\eta)) \rrbracket = \mathtt{nil}]$ is negligible. □

We will also use the program equivalence defined in [29]. Roughly speaking, two terms e_1 and e_2 are equivalent (written $e_1 \equiv e_2$) if they have the same denotational semantics in any environment.

Our further development in CSLR also relies on the following lemma about **zrand**:

Lemma 1. *Let q be a CSLR bitstring. The probabilistic ensemble $\llbracket \lambda \eta \, . \, \mathbf{zrand}(q, \eta) \rrbracket$ and the ensemble of truly uniform distributions $\mathbb{Z}_q^\$$ are computationally indistinguishable, i.e., for every closed CSLR term $\mathcal{A}$ of type $\Box\mathsf{Bits} \to \tau \to \mathsf{TBits}$ and every positive polynomial P, there exists some $N \in \mathbb{N}$ such that for all bitstring η with $|\eta| \geq N$*

$$\left| \mathbf{Pr}[\llbracket \mathcal{A}(\eta, \mathbf{zrand}(q, \eta)) \rrbracket \rightsquigarrow 1] - \mathbf{Pr}[\llbracket \mathcal{A}(\eta) \rrbracket (\mathbb{Z}_q^\$) \rightsquigarrow 1] \right| < \frac{1}{P(|\eta|)}.$$

Proof. We show that the two ensembles are *statistically close*:

$$\frac{1}{2} \cdot \Sigma_{v \in \mathbb{Z}_q} \left| \mathbf{Pr}[\llbracket \mathbf{zrand}(q, \eta) \rrbracket \rightsquigarrow v] - \mathbf{Pr}[\mathbb{Z}_q^\$ \rightsquigarrow v] \right|$$

$$= \frac{1}{2} \cdot \left(\left| \frac{1 + (\widehat{q} - 1) \cdot \varepsilon}{\widehat{q}} - \frac{1}{\widehat{q}} \right| + (\widehat{q} - 1) \cdot \left| \frac{1 - \varepsilon}{\widehat{q}} - \frac{1}{\widehat{q}} \right| \right)$$

$$= \frac{\widehat{q} - 1}{\widehat{q}} \cdot \varepsilon$$

is negligible with respect to $|\eta|$, where $\varepsilon = \left(\frac{u - \widehat{q}}{u} \right)^{|\eta|}$ and $u = 2^{\lceil \log_2 \widehat{n} \rceil}$. We can then conclude because statistical closeness implies computational indistinguishability (cf. Section 3.2.2 of [14]). □

4.1   Security Notions

Security notions can be defined in term of game indistinguishability. We show how to use it to define some common security notions in cryptography.

Semantic security. An public-key encryption scheme $(\textbf{\textit{KG}}, \textbf{\textit{Enc}}, \textbf{\textit{Dec}})$ is said to be *semantically secure* [15] if:

$$\begin{aligned}
&\lambda \eta \, . \, \lambda \mathcal{A} \, . \, (pk, sk) \xleftarrow{\$} \textbf{\textit{KG}}(\eta); \\
&\qquad (m_0, m_1, \mathcal{A}') \xleftarrow{\$} \mathcal{A}(\eta, pk); \\
&\qquad b \xleftarrow{\$} \mathtt{rand}; \\
&\qquad c \xleftarrow{\$} \textbf{\textit{Enc}}(\eta, m_b, pk); \qquad \approx \lambda \eta \, . \, \lambda \mathcal{A} \, . \, \mathtt{rand} \\
&\qquad b' \xleftarrow{\$} \mathcal{A}'(c); \\
&\qquad \mathtt{return}(b' \stackrel{?}{=} b)
\end{aligned}$$

where $\mathcal{A}$ and $\mathcal{A}'$ are functions of respective types $\Box\mathsf{Bits} \to \tau_k \to \mathsf{T}(\tau_m \times \tau_m \times (\tau_e \to \mathsf{TBits}))$ and $\tau_e \to \mathsf{TBits}$. Note that τ_k, τ_e and τ_m are the respective types of public keys, cipher-texts and plain-texts, which can be tuples of bitstrings that are distinguished in the language. Roughly speaking, it means that any adversary $\mathcal{A}$ playing the semantic security game (left-side game) cannot do significantly better than a random player (right-side game). The semantic security game is to be read as follows: A pair (pk, sk) of public and secret keys is generated; the public key pk is passed to the adversary $\mathcal{A}$ which returns two messages m_1, m_2 and a function $\mathcal{A}'$, which can be seen as the continuation of the adversary $\mathcal{A}$ and contains necessary information that $\mathcal{A}$ has already obtained; one of the messages m_b, is selected at random and encrypted with the public key pk; the obtained cipher-text c is then passed to the function $\mathcal{A}'$, which returns its guess b' for the selected message; the result of the game is whether the adversary is right or not.

Left-bit unpredictability. An SLR-function F is *left-bit unpredictable* if:

$$\lambda\eta . \lambda\mathcal{A} . s \xleftarrow{\$} \boldsymbol{zrand}(q, \eta); \; u \leftarrow F(\eta, s); \atop b \xleftarrow{\$} \mathcal{A}(\eta, \boldsymbol{tail}(u)); \; \mathtt{return}(b \overset{?}{=} \boldsymbol{head}(u)) \qquad \approx \; \lambda\eta . \lambda\mathcal{A} . \mathtt{rand} \qquad (1)$$

where $\mathcal{A}$ is of type $\Box\mathsf{Bits} \to \mathsf{Bits} \to \mathsf{Bits}$. Roughly speaking, it means that any adversary $\mathcal{A}$ playing the unpredictability game (left-side game) cannot do significantly better than a random player (right-side game). The left-bit unpredictability game is to be read as follows: a seed s is selected at random in a set of cardinal q; the function F is then used to compute a pseudorandom sequence of bits u of size $l(|q|) > |q|$ where l is a polynomial; the sequence u minus its first bit is passed to the adversary $\mathcal{A}$ which returns its guess b for the first bit; the result of the game is whether the adversary is right or not. It was proved by Yao in [28] that left-bit unpredictability is equivalent to passing all polynomial-time statistical tests.

4.2   Game Transformations

Game transformation will consist in rewriting modulo the game indistinguishability relation or the computational indistinguishability. In particular, we will reuse as it is the equational proof system of [29] for game transformations.

We will also need some intermediate lemmas. Those lemmas state basic game transformations used in almost all game-based proofs. The first one states that an expression e which does not depend on a random bit b cannot guess this bit b.

Lemma 2. *If $\Gamma \vdash e : \mathsf{TBits}$ and, for all definable $\rho \in [\![\Gamma]\!]$, the domain of the distribution $[\![e]\!]_\rho$ is $\{0, 1\}$, then*

$$b \xleftarrow{\$} \mathtt{rand}; \; x \xleftarrow{\$} e; \; \mathtt{return}(x \overset{?}{=} b) \equiv \mathtt{rand}$$

where $x, b \notin \mathrm{dom}(\Gamma)$.

Proof. We denote by e' the program on the left-hand side. For every definable $\rho \in \Gamma$, $[\![e']\!]_\rho = \{(0, p_0), (1, p_1)\}$, where

$$p_0 = \mathbf{Pr}[[\![\mathrm{rand}]\!]_\rho \neq [\![e]\!]_\rho] = \frac{1}{2} \cdot \mathbf{Pr}[[\![e]\!]_\rho \neq 0] + \frac{1}{2} \cdot \mathbf{Pr}[[\![e]\!]_\rho \neq 1] = \frac{1}{2}$$

$$p_1 = \mathbf{Pr}[[\![\mathrm{rand}]\!]_\rho = [\![e]\!]_\rho] = \frac{1}{2} \cdot \mathbf{Pr}[[\![e]\!]_\rho = 0] + \frac{1}{2} \cdot \mathbf{Pr}[[\![e]\!]_\rho = 1] = \frac{1}{2}$$

hence $e' \equiv \mathrm{rand}$.   □

The second lemma allows for a simplification when the semantics of a subexpression is a permutation.

Lemma 3. *Let* f, f' *be two closed CSLR terms of type* $\Box\mathsf{Bits} \to \mathsf{Bits}$ *such that* $[\![f]\!]$ *is a permutation over* $\mathbb{B}$, *and, for every bitstring* q, $[\![f']\!]$ *is a permutation over* $\{[\![f]\!](v) \mid v \in \mathbb{Z}_q\}$. *It holds that*

$$\lambda\eta . x \xleftarrow{\$} \mathbf{zrand}(q, \eta); \ \mathrm{return}(fx) \simeq \lambda\eta . x \xleftarrow{\$} \mathbf{zrand}(q, \eta); \ \mathrm{return}(f'(fx))$$

Proof. Let e_1, e_2 denote the two programs on the left-hand and right-hand side respectively. Then for a given bitstring η, $[\![e_i]\!](\eta)$ are two distributions over bitstrings, and $\mathrm{dom}([\![e_2]\!](\eta)) = \{[\![f]\!](v) \mid v \in \mathbb{Z}_q\} = \mathrm{dom}([\![e_1]\!](\eta))$ since $[\![f']\!]$ is a permutation over $\mathrm{dom}([\![e_1]\!](\eta))$. For every CSLR adversary $\mathcal{A}$ of type $\Box\mathsf{Bits} \to \mathsf{TBits} \to \mathsf{TBits}$, define two new adversaries

$$\mathcal{A}_1 \overset{\mathrm{def}}{=} \lambda\eta . \lambda w . \mathcal{A}(\eta, x \xleftarrow{\$} w; \ \mathrm{return}(fx))$$

$$\mathcal{A}_2 \overset{\mathrm{def}}{=} \lambda\eta . \lambda w . \mathcal{A}(\eta, x \xleftarrow{\$} w; \ \mathrm{return}(f'(fx))).$$

Clearly, both $\mathcal{A}_1$ and $\mathcal{A}_2$ are well-typed CSLR adversaries, and $[\![\mathcal{A}(\eta, e_i(\eta))]\!] = [\![\mathcal{A}_i(\eta, \mathbf{zrand}(q, \eta))]\!]$ $(i = 1, 2)$. According to Lemma 1,

$$\varepsilon_i = |\mathbf{Pr}[[\![\mathcal{A}_i(\eta, \mathbf{zrand}(q, \eta))]\!] \rightsquigarrow 1] - \mathbf{Pr}[[\![\mathcal{A}_i(\eta)]\!](\mathbb{Z}_q^{\$}) \rightsquigarrow 1]|$$

$(i = 1, 2)$ are negligible. Also, by Lemma 3.1 of [25], $[\![\mathcal{A}_1(\eta)]\!](\mathbb{Z}_q^{\$}) = [\![\mathcal{A}_2(\eta)]\!](\mathbb{Z}_q^{\$})$ as $[\![f']\!]$ is a permutation. Hence,

$$\begin{aligned}
&|\mathbf{Pr}[[\![\mathcal{A}(\eta, e_1\eta)]\!] \rightsquigarrow 1] - \mathbf{Pr}[[\![\mathcal{A}(\eta, e_2\eta)]\!] \rightsquigarrow 1]| \\
&= |\mathbf{Pr}[[\![\mathcal{A}_1(\eta, \mathbf{zrand}(q, \eta))]\!] \rightsquigarrow 1] - \mathbf{Pr}[[\![\mathcal{A}_1(\eta)]\!](\mathbb{Z}_q^{\$}) \rightsquigarrow 1] \\
&\quad - (\mathbf{Pr}[[\![\mathcal{A}_2(\eta, \mathbf{zrand}(q, \eta))]\!] \rightsquigarrow 1] - \mathbf{Pr}[[\![\mathcal{A}_2(\eta)]\!](\mathbb{Z}_q^{\$}) \rightsquigarrow 1])| \\
&\leq \varepsilon_1 + \varepsilon_2
\end{aligned}$$

is still negligible.   □

5   Applications

5.1   Computational Assumptions

Computational assumptions can be defined in CSLR too. As in the case of defining El-Gamal encryption scheme in CSLR, we have to replace all occurrences of uniform distributions by calls to the function $\mathbf{zrand}$.

Decisional Diffie-Hellman assumption. Let q be a bitstring depending on the security parameter η, G be a finite cyclic group of order $\hat{q}$ and $\gamma \in G$ be a generator. The Decisional Diffie-Hellman (DDH) assumption [12] states that, roughly speaking, no efficient algorithm can distinguish between triples of the form $(\gamma^x, \gamma^y, \gamma^{xy})$ and $(\gamma^x, \gamma^y, \gamma^z)$ where x, y and z are random number such that $0 \leq x, y, z < \hat{q}$[1]. DDH cannot be written directly in CSLR because it involves arbitrary uniform distributions. Instead we write the following assumption that we call *DDH-Bits*:

$$DDHBL \simeq DDHBR$$

where

$$DDHBL \overset{\text{def}}{=} \lambda\eta \,.\, x \overset{\$}{\leftarrow} \mathbf{zrand}(q, \eta); \; y \overset{\$}{\leftarrow} \mathbf{zrand}(q, \eta);$$
$$\texttt{return}(\gamma^x, \gamma^y, \gamma^{xy})$$

$$DDHBR \overset{\text{def}}{=} \lambda\eta \,.\, x \overset{\$}{\leftarrow} \mathbf{zrand}(q, \eta); \; y \overset{\$}{\leftarrow} \mathbf{zrand}(q, \eta); \; z \overset{\$}{\leftarrow} \mathbf{zrand}(q, \eta);$$
$$\texttt{return}(\gamma^x, \gamma^y, \gamma^z)$$

Proposition 2. *DDH-bits holds when the DDH assumption holds.*

Proof. Let e_1, e_2 denote the two programs on the left-hand and right-hand side respectively. Then for a given bitstring η, $[\![e_i]\!](\eta)$ are two distributions over bitstrings, and $\text{dom}([\![e_2]\!](\eta)) = \{[\![f]\!](v) \mid v \in \mathbb{Z}_q\} = \text{dom}([\![e_1]\!](\eta))$ since $[\![f']\!]$ is a permutation over $\text{dom}([\![e_1]\!](\eta))$. For every CSLR adversary $\mathcal{A}$ of type $\square$Bits $\to$ TBits $\to$ TBits, define two new adversaries

$$\mathcal{A}_1 \overset{\text{def}}{=} \lambda\eta \,.\, \lambda w \,.\, \mathcal{A}(\eta, x \overset{\$}{\leftarrow} w; \; \texttt{return}(fx))$$
$$\mathcal{A}_2 \overset{\text{def}}{=} \lambda\eta \,.\, \lambda w \,.\, \mathcal{A}(\eta, x \overset{\$}{\leftarrow} w; \; \texttt{return}(f'(fx))).$$

Clearly, both $\mathcal{A}_1$ and $\mathcal{A}_2$ are well-typed CSLR adversaries, and $[\![\mathcal{A}(\eta, e_i(\eta))]\!] = [\![\mathcal{A}_i(\eta, \mathbf{zrand}(q, \eta))]\!]$ $(i = 1, 2)$. According to Lemma 1,

$$\varepsilon_i = |\mathbf{Pr}[[\![\mathcal{A}_i(\eta, \mathbf{zrand}(q, \eta))]\!] \rightsquigarrow 1] - \mathbf{Pr}[[\![\mathcal{A}_i(\eta)]\!](\mathbb{Z}_q^\$) \rightsquigarrow 1]|$$

$(i = 1, 2)$ are negligible. Also, by Lemma 3.1 of [25], $[\![\mathcal{A}_1(\eta)]\!](\mathbb{Z}_q^\$) = [\![\mathcal{A}_2(\eta)]\!](\mathbb{Z}_q^\$)$ as $[\![f']\!]$ is a permutation. Hence,

$$|\mathbf{Pr}[[\![\mathcal{A}(\eta, e_1\eta)]\!] \rightsquigarrow 1] - \mathbf{Pr}[[\![\mathcal{A}(\eta, e_2\eta)]\!] \rightsquigarrow 1]|$$
$$= |\mathbf{Pr}[[\![\mathcal{A}_1(\eta, \mathbf{zrand}(q, \eta))]\!] \rightsquigarrow 1] - \mathbf{Pr}[[\![\mathcal{A}_1(\eta)]\!](\mathbb{Z}_q^\$) \rightsquigarrow 1]$$
$$-(\mathbf{Pr}[[\![\mathcal{A}_2(\eta, \mathbf{zrand}(q, \eta))]\!] \rightsquigarrow 1] - \mathbf{Pr}[[\![\mathcal{A}_2(\eta)]\!](\mathbb{Z}_q^\$) \rightsquigarrow 1])|$$
$$\leq \varepsilon_1 + \varepsilon_2$$

is still negligible. $\qquad\square$

---

[1] We do not assume that $\hat{q}$ is prime. However most groups in which DDH is believed to be true have prime order [8].

5.2   Semantic Security of El-Gamal Encryption Scheme

In this section, we illustrate our proof system by proving the semantic security of El-Gamal encryption scheme in Fig. 1. The proof follows the same structure as the one in [24], but here the type system of CSLR guarantees that the adversary is probabilistic polynomial-time. This was not dealt with in [24]. Moreover here all transformations are purely syntactic (thus allowing the immediate prospect of being implemented in a tool), while in [24] they were done at the semantics level.

Note that by using Lemma 3, we assume that the adversary $\mathcal{A}$ will not send any junk messages, i.e., bitstrings that are not elements of the group $\mathcal{G}_\eta$. This is considered as a trivial case in cryptography proofs because the El-Gamal encryption procedure will automatically reject the junk messages. But in practice, in more complex crypto-systems, this may not be trivial at all. In our proof system, we can also consider the case where adversaries may send junk messages. It suffices to provide the corresponding code in the program *Enc* which tests the validity of incoming messages, and we can still prove semantic security in the CSLR proof system. Another possibility would be to use a richer type system to reject adversaries returning junk.

6   Extending CSLR

The discussion in the previous sections was limited to the setting of CSLR with bitstrings. In particular, it does not allow superpolynomial-time computations nor arbitrary uniform sampling. Although these restrictions make sense for the cryptographic constructions and the adversary, the game-based approach to cryptographic proofs does not preclude the possibility of introducing games that perform superpolynomial-time computations or that use arbitrary uniform distributions. They are just idealized constructions that are used to define security notions but are not meant to make their way into implementations.

In this section, we extend CSLR into CSLR+ so that we can manipulate games with superpolynomial-time computations and arbitrary uniform choices.

6.1   CSLR+

CSLR+ extends CSLR with a uniform sampling primitive sample of type Bits $\multimap$ TBits and constants for primitive (and possibly superpolynomial-time) computations. sample receives a bitstring as argument and returns uniformly a random bitstring of the same length whose integer value is strictly smaller than that of the argument. For instance, the distribution produced by sample(101) is $[\![\texttt{sample}(101)]\!] = \{(000, \frac{1}{5}), \ldots, (100, \frac{1}{5})\}$. We can program a sampling from an arbitrary finite set (of CSLR definable elements, usually just bitstrings in cryptography) using sample, assuming that there is an index function over the set, but we shall omit the implementation details and write $x \xleftarrow{\$} A$; for assigning to x a uniformly sampled value from set A.

$$\lambda\eta \triangleright \lambda\mathcal{A} \triangleright \langle pk\,\varsigma\,sk\rangle \xleftarrow{\$} \mathbf{KG}(\eta);\ \langle m_0\,\varsigma\,m_1\,\varsigma\,\mathcal{A}'\rangle \xleftarrow{\$} \mathcal{A}(\eta\,\varsigma\,pk);$$
$$b \xleftarrow{\$} \mathrm{rand};\ c \xleftarrow{\$} \mathbf{Enc}(\eta\,\varsigma\,pk\,\varsigma\,m_b);\ b' \xleftarrow{\$} \mathcal{A}'(c);$$
$$\mathrm{return}(b \overset{?}{=} b')$$

$$\equiv \lambda\eta \triangleright \lambda\mathcal{A} \triangleright \langle pk\,\varsigma\,sk\rangle \xleftarrow{\$} \begin{array}{l} x \xleftarrow{\$} \mathbf{zrand}(q\,\varsigma\,\eta); \\ \mathrm{return}(\gamma^x\,\varsigma\,x) \end{array} ;\ \langle m_0\,\varsigma\,m_1\,\varsigma\,\mathcal{A}'\rangle \xleftarrow{\$} \mathcal{A}(\eta\,\varsigma\,pk);$$
$$b \xleftarrow{\$} \mathrm{rand};\ c \xleftarrow{\$} \begin{array}{l} y \xleftarrow{\$} \mathbf{zrand}(q\,\varsigma\,\eta); \\ \mathrm{return}(\gamma^y\,\varsigma\,pk^y * m_b) \end{array} ;\ b' \xleftarrow{\$} \mathcal{A}'(c);$$
$$\mathrm{return}(b \overset{?}{=} b')$$
(Inline of definition of $\mathbf{KG}$ and $\mathbf{Enc}$)

$$\equiv \lambda\eta \triangleright \lambda\mathcal{A} \triangleright x \xleftarrow{\$} \mathbf{zrand}(q\,\varsigma\,\eta);\ y \xleftarrow{\$} \mathbf{zrand}(q\,\varsigma\,\eta);\ b \xleftarrow{\$} \mathrm{rand};$$
$$\langle m_0\,\varsigma\,m_1\,\varsigma\,\mathcal{A}'\rangle \xleftarrow{\$} \mathcal{A}(\eta\,\varsigma\,\gamma^x);\ b' \xleftarrow{\$} \mathcal{A}'(\gamma^y\,\varsigma\,(\gamma^x)^y * m_b);$$
$$\mathrm{return}(b \overset{?}{=} b')$$
(By the equivalence rules *AX-BIND-3* and *AX-BIND-1* in [29])

$$\equiv \lambda\eta \triangleright \lambda\mathcal{A} \triangleright v \xleftarrow{\$} \mathbf{DDHBL}(\eta);\ b \xleftarrow{\$} \mathrm{rand};\ \langle m_0\,\varsigma\,m_1\,\varsigma\,\mathcal{A}'\rangle \xleftarrow{\$} \mathcal{A}(\eta\,\varsigma\,\mathrm{proj}_1(v));$$
$$b' \xleftarrow{\$} \mathcal{A}'(\mathrm{proj}_2(v)\,\varsigma\,\mathrm{proj}_3(v) * m_b);$$
$$\mathrm{return}(b \overset{?}{=} b')$$
(Inline of $\mathbf{DDHBL}$)

$$\approx \lambda\eta \triangleright \lambda\mathcal{A} \triangleright v \xleftarrow{\$} \mathbf{DDHBR}(\eta);\ b \xleftarrow{\$} \mathrm{rand};\ \langle m_0\,\varsigma\,m_1\,\varsigma\,\mathcal{A}'\rangle \xleftarrow{\$} \mathcal{A}(\eta\,\varsigma\,\mathrm{proj}_1(v));$$
$$b' \xleftarrow{\$} \mathcal{A}'(\mathrm{proj}_2(v)\,\varsigma\,\mathrm{proj}_3(v) * m_b);$$
$$\mathrm{return}(b \overset{?}{=} b')$$
(By DDH-Bits assumption and *SUB*)

$$\equiv \lambda\eta \triangleright \lambda\mathcal{A} \triangleright x \xleftarrow{\$} \mathbf{zrand}(q\,\varsigma\,\eta);\ y \xleftarrow{\$} \mathbf{zrand}(q\,\varsigma\,\eta);\ z \xleftarrow{\$} \mathbf{zrand}(q\,\varsigma\,\eta);\ b \xleftarrow{\$} \mathrm{rand};$$
$$\langle m_0\,\varsigma\,m_1\,\varsigma\,\mathcal{A}'\rangle \xleftarrow{\$} \mathcal{A}(\eta\,\varsigma\,\gamma^x);\ b' \xleftarrow{\$} \mathcal{A}'(\gamma^y\,\varsigma\,\gamma^z * m_b);$$
$$\mathrm{return}(b \overset{?}{=} b')$$
(Inline of $\mathbf{DDHBR}$)

$$\equiv \lambda\eta \triangleright \lambda\mathcal{A} \triangleright x \xleftarrow{\$} \mathbf{zrand}(q\,\varsigma\,\eta);\ y \xleftarrow{\$} \mathbf{zrand}(q\,\varsigma\,\eta);\ b \xleftarrow{\$} \mathrm{rand};\ \langle m_0\,\varsigma\,m_1\,\varsigma\,\mathcal{A}'\rangle \xleftarrow{\$} \mathcal{A}(\eta\,\varsigma\,\gamma^x);$$
$$v' \xleftarrow{\$} \begin{array}{l} z \xleftarrow{\$} \mathbf{zrand}(q\,\varsigma\,\eta); \\ \mathrm{return}(\gamma^z * m_b) \end{array} ;\ b' \xleftarrow{\$} \mathcal{A}'(\gamma^y\,\varsigma\,v');$$
$$\mathrm{return}(b \overset{?}{=} b')$$
(By the equivalence rules *AX-BIND-3* and *AX-BIND-1* in [29])

$$\approx \lambda\eta \triangleright \lambda\mathcal{A} \triangleright x \xleftarrow{\$} \mathbf{zrand}(q\,\varsigma\,\eta);\ y \xleftarrow{\$} \mathbf{zrand}(q\,\varsigma\,\eta);\ b \xleftarrow{\$} \mathrm{rand};\ \langle m_0\,\varsigma\,m_1\,\varsigma\,\mathcal{A}'\rangle \xleftarrow{\$} \mathcal{A}(\eta\,\varsigma\,\gamma^x);$$
$$v' \xleftarrow{\$} \begin{array}{l} z \xleftarrow{\$} \mathbf{zrand}(q\,\varsigma\,\eta); \\ \mathrm{return}(\gamma^z) \end{array} ;\ b' \xleftarrow{\$} \mathcal{A}'(\gamma^y\,\varsigma\,v');$$
$$\mathrm{return}(b \overset{?}{=} b')$$
(By Lemma 3 as $(\_ * m_b)$ is a permutation over the group when m_b is also from the group)

$$\equiv \lambda\eta \triangleright \lambda\mathcal{A} \triangleright b \xleftarrow{\$} \mathrm{rand};\ x \xleftarrow{\$} \mathbf{zrand}(q\,\varsigma\,\eta);\ y \xleftarrow{\$} \mathbf{zrand}(q\,\varsigma\,\eta);\ z \xleftarrow{\$} \mathbf{zrand}(q\,\varsigma\,\eta);$$
$$\langle m_0\,\varsigma\,m_1\,\varsigma\,\mathcal{A}'\rangle \xleftarrow{\$} \mathcal{A}(\eta\,\varsigma\,\gamma^x);\ b' \xleftarrow{\$} \mathcal{A}'(\gamma^y\,\varsigma\,\gamma^z);$$
$$\mathrm{return}(b \overset{?}{=} b')$$
(By the equivalence rules *AX-BIND-3* and *AX-BIND-1* in [29])

$$\equiv \lambda\eta \triangleright \lambda\mathcal{A} \triangleright \mathrm{rand}$$
(By Lemma 2)

Fig. 1. Proof of semantic security of ElGamal

The type system of CSLR+ is extended with only the proper rules for `sample` and constants. Note that the type of `sample` is Bits $\multimap$ TBits so that it can accept arguments that are defined using linear resources. In fact, in CSLR+ we do not care any more about the complexity class that can be characterized using the type system[2] — CSLR+ is the language for describing games, not adversaries.

The definitions of *computational indistinguishability* and *game indistinguishability* are almost the same as before, except that we are now considering distributions that are produced by CSLR+ programs:

Definition 3 (Game indistinguishability in CSLR+). *Two closed CSLR+ programs g_1 and g_2, both of type $\Box$Bits $\rightarrow$ ($\Box$Bits $\rightarrow$ Tτ) $\rightarrow$ TBits, are* game indistinguishable *(written as $g_1 \approx_+ g_2$) if for every closed CSLR term $\mathcal{A}$ of type $\Box$Bits $\rightarrow$ Tτ, and every positive polynomial P, there exists some $N \in \mathbb{N}$ such that for all bitstring η with $|\eta| \geq N$,*

$$|\mathbf{Pr}[\llbracket g_1(\eta, \mathcal{A}) \rrbracket = 1] - \mathbf{Pr}[\llbracket g_2(\eta, \mathcal{A}) \rrbracket = 1]| < \frac{1}{P(|\eta|)}$$

Definition 4 (Comput. indistinguishability in CSLR+). *Two CSLR+ terms f_1 and f_2, both of type $\Box$Bits $\rightarrow \tau$, are* computationally indistinguishable *(written as $f_1 \simeq_+ f_2$) if for every closed CSLR term $\mathcal{A}$ of type $\Box$Bits $\rightarrow \tau \rightarrow$ TBits and every positive polynomial P, there exists some $N \in \mathbb{N}$ such that for all bitstring η with $|\eta| \geq N$*

$$|\mathbf{Pr}[\llbracket \mathcal{A}(\eta, f_1(\eta)) \rrbracket = 1] - \mathbf{Pr}[\llbracket \mathcal{A}(\eta, f_2(\eta)) \rrbracket = 1]| < \frac{1}{P(|\eta|)}$$

CSLR+ inherits most of the equational proof system of CSLR. All the rules for program equivalence in CSLR can be used directly in CSLR+. No extra rules are needed for the primitive `sample`, but we can add rules for constants if necessary. The four rules for proving computational indistinguishability remain the same as in CSLR (Figure 2) except that in the rule *SUB*, a new premise enforces that the substitution context (the term e) must be definable in CSLR, i.e., a program that does not contain `sample` or any CSLR+ constant. The soundness of the system still holds and the proof just goes as for CSLR [29]. In particular, the proof for the rule *SUB* contains a construction of a new adversary with the context, which remains a CSLR term (i.e., a PPT adversary) thanks to the new premise enforcing that the context must be definable in CSLR.

Note that the rule *H-IND* is not used throughout this paper, but it is an important rule representing the hybrid proof technique that is frequently used in cryptography. Interested readers can find more detailed explanation and examples in [29].

---

[2] One might expect that the complexity class characterized by CSLR+ is PPT^X, where X is the smallest complexity class in which additional constants can be defined, but the exact relation between CSLR+ and the complexity classes remains to be clarified — the addition of the primitive `sample` alone allows for defining more distributions than in PPT.

$$\frac{\vdash e_i : \Box\mathsf{Bits} \to \tau \ (i = 1\lessdot 2) \quad e_1 \equiv_+ e_2}{e_1 \simeq_+ e_2} \ EQUIV$$

$$\frac{\vdash e_i : \Box\mathsf{Bits} \to \tau \ (i = 1\lessdot 2\lessdot 3) \quad e_1 \simeq_+ e_2 \quad e_2 \simeq_+ e_3}{e_1 \simeq_+ e_3} \ TRANS\text{-}INDIST$$

$$\frac{x :^n \mathsf{Bits}\lessdot y :^n \tau \vdash e : \tau' \quad e \text{ is definable in CSLR} \quad \vdash e_i : \Box\mathsf{Bits} \to \tau \ (i = 1\lessdot 2) \quad e_1 \simeq_+ e_2}{\lambda x \triangleright \{e_1(x)\lhd y] \simeq_+ \lambda x \triangleright \{e_2(x)\lhd y]} \ SUB$$

$$\frac{x :^n \mathsf{Bits}\lessdot n :^n \mathsf{Bits} \vdash e : \tau \quad \lambda n \triangleright \{u \lhd x] \text{ is numerical for all bitstring } u}{\lambda x \triangleright \{i(x)\lhd n] \simeq_+ \lambda x \triangleright \{B_1 i(x)\lhd n] \text{ for all canonical polynomial } i \text{ such that } \clubsuit\!\!\clubsuit\!\!\lessdot \ \clubsuit\!\!\clubsuit}{\lambda x \triangleright \{nil\lhd n] \simeq_+ \lambda x \triangleright \{p(x)\lhd n]} \ H\text{-}IND$$

Fig. 2. Rules for computational indistinguishability in CSLR+

6.2   Applications

This extension of CSLR+ allows us to express directly DDH in the formalism and thus does not require to go through the non-standard computational assumption introduced in Section 5. We can reproduce almost as such the proof of semantic security for ElGamal given in [24]. The difference is that now we can check automatically that the adversary built in the proof is PPT, and all transformations are purely syntactic.

We can also reproduce the proof of unpredictability for the pseudorandom bit generator of Blum, Blum and Shub given in [25]. The proof requires a test for quadratic residuosity which is a superpolynomial-time computation — it can be introduced into CSLR+ as a constant. Moreover this proof is based on the Quadratic Residuosity Assumption that uses arbitrary uniform choices.

Quadratic Residuosity Assumption. Let n be a positive number and $\mathbb{Z}_n$ be the set of integers modulo n. The multiplicative group of $\mathbb{Z}_n$ is written $\mathbb{Z}_n^*$ and consists of the subset of integers modulo n which are coprime with n. An integer $x \in \mathbb{Z}_n^*$ is a quadratic residue modulo n iff there exists a $y \in \mathbb{Z}_n^*$ such that $y^2 = x \pmod{n}$. Such a y is called a square root of x modulo n. We write $\mathbb{Z}_n^*(+1)$ for the subset of integers in $\mathbb{Z}_n^*$ with Jacobi symbol equal to 1. The quadratic residuosity problem is the following: given an odd composite integer n, decide whether or not an $x \in \mathbb{Z}_n^*(+1)$ is a quadratic residue modulo n. The quadratic residuosity assumption (QRA) states that the above problem is intractable when n is the product of two distinct odd primes [20]. We reformulate the assumption in CSLR+:

$$\lambda\eta \,.\, \lambda\mathcal{A} \,.\, x \xleftarrow{\$} \mathbb{Z}_n^*(+1); \ b \xleftarrow{\$} \mathcal{A}(\eta, n, x); \ \mathtt{return}(b \overset{?}{=} \boldsymbol{qr}(x)) \quad \approx_+ \quad \lambda\eta \,.\, \lambda\mathcal{A} \,.\, \mathtt{rand}$$

where $\mathcal{A}$ must be definable in CSLR of type $\Box\mathsf{Bits} \to \mathsf{Bits} \to \mathsf{Bits} \to \mathsf{TBits}$, $\boldsymbol{qr}(x)$ is the quadratic residuosity test of the element x of $\mathbb{Z}_n^*$ in our encoding, and n is an expression that depends on the security parameter η.

Blum-Blum-Shub. CSLR+ is expressive enough to encode the proof of [25] that BBS is left-bit unpredictable: for every positive integer l,

$$\lambda \eta \, . \, \lambda \mathcal{A} \, . \, s \xleftarrow{\$} \mathbb{Z}_q^*; \; u \leftarrow \textit{BBS}(\eta, l+1, s); \atop b \xleftarrow{\$} \mathcal{A}(\eta, q, \textit{tail}(u)); \; \texttt{return}(b \stackrel{?}{=} \textit{head}(u)) \quad \approx_+ \; \lambda \eta \, . \, \lambda \mathcal{A} \, . \, \texttt{rand}$$

where $\mathcal{A}$ is must be definable in CSLR of type $\Box$Bits $\rightarrow$ Bits $\rightarrow$ Bits $\rightarrow$ TBits.

References

1. Affeldt, R., Nowak, D., Yamada, K.: Certifying assembly with formal cryptographic proofs: the case of BBS. In: Proceedings of the 9th International Workshop on Automated Verification of Critical Systems, AVoCS 2009 (2009)
2. Backes, M., Berg, M., Unruh, D.: A formal language for cryptographic pseudocode. In: Cervesato, I., Veith, H., Voronkov, A. (eds.) LPAR 2008. LNCS (LNAI), vol. 5330, pp. 353–376. Springer, Heidelberg (2008)
3. Barthe, G., Grégoire, B., Zanella Béguelin, S.: Formal certification of code-based cryptographic proofs. In: Proceedings of the 36th ACM SIGPLAN- SIGACT Symposium on Principles of Programming Languages (POPL 2009), pp. 90–101. ACM Press, New York (2009)
4. Bellantoni, S., Cook, S.A.: A new recursion-theoretic characterization of the polytime functions. In: Computational Complexity, vol. 2, pp. 97–110 (1992)
5. Bellare, M., Namprempre, C.: Authenticated Encryption: Relations among Notions and Analysis of the Generic Composition Paradigm. Journal of Cryptology 21, 469–491 (2008)
6. Blanchet, B., Pointcheval, D.: Automated security proofs with sequences of games. In: Dwork, C. (ed.) CRYPTO 2006. LNCS, vol. 4117, pp. 537–554. Springer, Heidelberg (2006)
7. Blum, L., Blum, M., Shub, M.: A simple unpredictable pseudo random number generator. SIAM Journal on Computing. Society for Industrial and Applied Mathematics 15(2), 364–383 (1986)
8. Boneh, D.: The Decision Diffie-Hellman problem. In: Buhler, J.P. (ed.) ANTS 1998. LNCS, vol. 1423, pp. 48–83. Springer, Heidelberg (1998)
9. Bellare, M., Rogaway, P.: Code-based game-playing proofs and the security of triple encryption. Cryptology ePrint Archive, Report 2004/331 (2004)
10. Corin, R., den Hartog, J.: A probabilistic Hoare-style logic for game-based cryptographic proofs. In: Bugliesi, M., Preneel, B., Sassone, V., Wegener, I. (eds.) ICALP 2006. LNCS, vol. 4052, pp. 252–263. Springer, Heidelberg (2006)
11. Courant, J., Daubignard, M., Ene, C., Lafourcade, P., Lakhnech, Y.: Towards automated proofs for asymmetric encryption schemes in the random oracle model. In: Proceedings of the 15th ACM Conference Computer and Communications Security, CCS 2008, pp. 371–380. ACM Press, New York (2008)
12. Diffie, W., Hellman, M.E.: New directions in cryptography. IEEE Transactions on Information Theory 22(6), 644–654 (1976)
13. Elgamal, T.: A public key cryptosystem and a signature scheme based on discrete logarithms. IEEE Transactions on Information Theory 31(4), 469–472 (1985)
14. Goldreich, O.: The Foundations of Cryptography: Basic Tools. Cambridge University Press, Cambridge (2001)

15. Goldwasser, S., Micali, S.: Probabilistic encryption. Journal of Computer and System Sciences (JCSS) 28(2), 270–299 (1984) (An earlier version appeared in proceedings of STOC 1982)
16. Hofmann, M.: A Mixed Modal/Linear Lambda Calculus with Applications to Bellantoni-Cook Safe Recursion. In: Nielsen, M. (ed.) CSL 1997. LNCS, vol. 1414, pp. 275–294. Springer, Heidelberg (1998)
17. Hofmann, M.: Safe recursion with higher types and BCK-algebra. In: Annals of Pure and Applied Logic, vol. 1414, 104(1-3), pp. 113–166 (2000)
18. Hurd, J.: A formal approach to probabilistic termination. In: Carreño, V.A., Muñoz, C.A., Tahar, S. (eds.) TPHOLs 2002. LNCS, vol. 2410, pp. 230–245. Springer, Heidelberg (2002)
19. Impagliazzo, R., Kapron, B.M.: Logics for reasoning about cryptographic constructions. Journal of Computer and System Sciences 72(2), 286–320 (2006)
20. Menezes, A.J., van Oorschot, P.C., Vanstone, S.A.: Handbook of Applied Cryptography. CRC Press, Boca Raton (1996)
21. Mitchell, J.C., Mitchell, M., Scedrov, A.: A linguistic characterization of bounded oracle computation and probabilistic polynomial time. In: Proceedings of the 39th Annual Symposium on Foundations of Computer Science (FOCS 1998), pp. 725–733 (1998)
22. Mitchell, J.C., Ramanathan, A., Scedrov, A., Teague, V.: A probabilistic polynomial-time process calculus for the analysis of cryptographic protocols. Theoretical Computer Science 353(1-3), 118–164 (2006)
23. Moggi, E.: Notions of computation and monads. Information and Computation 93(1), 55–92 (1991)
24. Nowak, D.: A framework for game-based security proofs. In: Qing, S., Imai, H., Wang, G. (eds.) ICICS 2007. LNCS, vol. 4861, pp. 319–333. Springer, Heidelberg (2007)
25. Nowak, D.: On formal verification of arithmetic-based cryptographic primitives. In: Lee, P.J., Cheon, J.H. (eds.) ICISC 2008. LNCS, vol. 5461, pp. 368–382. Springer, Heidelberg (2009)
26. Ramsey, N., Pfeffer, A.: Stochastic lambda calculus and monads of probability distributions. In: Proceedings of the 29th SIGPLAN-SIGACT Symposium on Principles of Programming Languages (POPL 2002), pp. 154–165 (2002)
27. Shoup, V.: Sequences of games: a tool for taming complexity in security proofs. Cryptology ePrint Archive, Report 2004/332 (2004)
28. Yao, A.C.: Theory and applications of trapdoor functions. In: Proceedings of the IEEE 23rd Annual Symposium on Foundations of Computer Science (FOCS 1982), pp. 80–91. IEEE, Los Alamitos (1982)
29. Zhang, Y.: The Computational SLR: A Logic for Reasoning about Computational Indistinguishability. In: Curien, P.-L. (ed.) TLCA 2009. LNCS, vol. 5608, pp. 401–415. Springer, Heidelberg (2009)

Automating Computational Proofs for Public-Key-Based Key Exchange[*]

Long Ngo, Colin Boyd, and Juan González Nieto

Information Security Institute, Queensland University Of Technology,
GPO Box 2434, Brisbane QLD 4001, Australia
{lt.ngo,c.boyd,j.gonzaleznieto}@qut.edu.au

Abstract. We present an approach to automating computationally sound proofs of key exchange protocols based on public-key encryption. We show that satisfying the property called *occultness* in the Dolev–Yao model guarantees the security of a related key exchange protocol in a simple computational model. Security in this simpler model has been shown to imply security in a Bellare–Rogaway-like model. Furthermore, the occultness in the Dolev–Yao model can be searched automatically by a mechanisable procedure. Thus automated proofs for key exchange protocols in the computational model can be achieved. We illustrate the method using the well-known Lowe–Needham–Schroeder protocol.

1 Introduction

Proving security of cryptographic protocols and verifying those proofs is a hard, time-consuming and error-prone task when done by hand. Many flaws in security proofs were found after the proofs have been accepted and published [11,10]. As a consequence, automated proofs have been considered a promising solution.

Research on automated proofs in Dolev–Yao models [16] has a long history thanks to the model's simplicity. Although this simplicity means sacrificing the faithfulness of the model, such automated tools have brought many significant successes in finding flaws. A well-known example is the Needham–Schroeder public-key protocol that was believed to be secure for many years until an attack was found by Lowe [19]. On the other hand, such tools cannot guarantee security in a computational sense, since Dolev–Yao models do not capture computational attacks defined in the usual cryptographic models.

Some automatic approaches for more realistic computational models have been proposed recently, shedding some light on this problem. However, the number of approaches and the types of protocol they can be applied on is still limited.

Contribution. This paper shows how we can automate the verification of security of key exchange protocols based on public key encryption. The security proofs achieved are computationally sound. The basic idea is as follows.

---

[*] Research partially funded by the Australian Research Council through Discovery Project DP0773348.

S.-H. Heng and K. Kurosawa (Eds.): ProvSec 2010, LNCS 6402, pp. 53–69, 2010.
© Springer-Verlag Berlin Heidelberg 2010

- Kudla and Paterson proposed a modular way to prove security of key agreement protocols [18]. According to their approach, a security proof in the BR2000 model [2] is reduced to the hardness of a *gap* problem if we can show that the security of a simpler protocol in a simpler (computational) model is reduced to hardness of the related *computational* problem.
- Cortier et al. showed that we can automate secrecy proofs of public-key-based protocols [12]. Their idea results in a mechanisable search procedure for a property called *occultness*. However, their work is based on Dolev-Yao model.
- Our contribution provides a link between these two results. We show that security of a public-key-based protocol which has been checked to be occult in the simpler computational model is reduced to the hardness of a computational problem, which we construct using an IND-CCA encryption scheme. Therefore, to check the security proof in the BR2000 model, we can use the automatic tool by Cortier et al. [12] to check occultness.

Related work. Research on computationally sound automated proofs for cryptographic systems falls into two broad directions: direct proofs on computational models and indirect proofs via Dolev–Yao models.

Direct approaches. Direct approaches reason on protocol specifications often written in a programming language that has a computational semantics. Courant et al. [14] designed a Hoare-style logic to verify computational invariants, e.g. indistinguishability. However, this work can verify IND-CCA security only of an encryption scheme that is constructed from a trapdoor permutation. Later, Gagné et al. [17] extended this work to symmetric block ciphers. Blanchet [5] designed a variant of π-calculus to formalise games, and developed CryptoVerif, a tool that can automatically transform games using game-hopping techniques, thereby freeing the human from the mundane parts of the proof. CryptoVerif can be potentially extended to cover many types of protocols, but it is hard to make it fully automated, i.e. manual guidance is required in non-trivial situations. Datta et al. [15] tuned the Computational Protocol Composition Logic for verifying key exchange protocols, resulting in security proofs in the Bellare-Rogaway model [3]. However, their work is limited to Diffie–Hellman-based protocols and although they claimed the work is mechanisable, they have not shown how to do it in details or provided an actual tool.

Indirect approaches. In contrast, indirect approaches exploit automated tools designed for verifying properties in Dolev–Yao models by showing in which cases symbolic properties imply computational ones. Cortier and Warinschi [13] proved the computational soundness of a Dolev–Yao model, by showing how to map between symbolic and computational traces. They also tested their idea by using Casrul [9], a Dolev–Yao-based tool to make a Dolev–Yao security proof. That work differs from ours in the models used. The Dolev-Yao model they used is the model for Carsul, a protocol verifier for a fixed number of sessions, while the Dolev–Yao model we use is the model for

Securify [12], a tool that gives proofs for an unbounded number of sessions and adversarial operations. In the other side, the computational model they designed is a more general and simpler, e.g. no session corruption, but the one we use, the BR2000 model [2], which is designed specifically for key exchanges.

Canetti and Herzog [6] used ProVerif [4] to automatically verify some symbolic criteria and showed that a protocol satisfying such criteria realises an ideal functionality for key exchange protocols. This work focuses on public-key-based key exchange protocols like our work, but the two results are not strictly comparable. Canetti and Herzog use the universal composability (UC) model with a UC-secure public-key encryption scheme which is a stronger security than we use since it allows security under composability. At the same time their model is weaker than ours because they do not model adaptive corruptions and session key reveals. We also note that Canetti and Krawczyk [8] have shown that universal composability can be obtained for 'free' for a slightly weaker functionality. Canetti and Herzog [6] proved that *strong secrecy* (an equivalence property), or *observational equivalence* between processes that have different values for a secret variable, implies UC-security. We prove that occultness, which means *standard secrecy* (a trace property and a less strong notion), implies security in the Bellare–Rogaway model.

Later, Canetti and Gajek extended the work [7] to deal with key exchange based on key encapsulation and signature schemes. With this type of protocols, they consider adaptive corruptions, session key reveals, and forward secrecy in the model. The authors also showed that the plain Diffie-Hellman protocol realizes their key encapsulation functionality, thus the result is widely applicable on a number of Diffie-Hellman based key exchange protocols.

2 Preliminaries

2.1 Gap Problem

Gap problems were first mentioned by Okamoto and Pointcheval [22]. We summarize the idea here. Let $f : X \times Y \rightarrow \{0, 1\}$ be any relation on sets X and Y.

- The *computational* problem of f is: given $x \in X$, find any $y \in Y$ such that $f(x, y) = 1$ if such a y exists, otherwise return Fail.
- The *decisional* problem of f is: given $(x, y) \in X \times Y$, to decide if $f(x, y) = 1$ or not.

Definition 1. *The gap problem of f is: given the decisional oracle of f, to solve the computational problem.*

2.2 A Modular Proof for Key Agreement

Kudla and Paterson proposed a modular way to prove security of key exchange protocols in a modified Bellare-Rogaway (mBR) model [18]. We use their idea in this work with a little simplification, in that we do not consider any corrupted oracle to be a *fresh* one because we do not model key compromise impersonation attacks. We call our mode mBR' model to differentiate it from Kudla and Paterson's.

The mBR' Game. Denote the set of participants IDs as $\mathcal{U}$ and assume each participant $U \in \mathcal{U}$ has a public key P_U and a private key S_U. We use Π_U^i to denote the oracle of the *ith* instance of U. An oracle Π_U^i may accept once at any time. After that it holds a role *role* $\in \{initiator, responder\}$, a partner ID *pid*, a session ID *sid* and a session key *seskey*. Each oracle follows the protocol rules and responds to input messages from the adversary. Each oracle Π_U^i also stores a public transcript $T_{\Pi_U^i}$ that records all messages sent and received by that oracle.

The game is played between a challenger C and an adversary E. C runs a Setup algorithm on security parameter k, generating public parameters, a set of participants $\mathcal{U}$ and oracles $\{\Pi_U^i\}$, distributing long-term keys to participants, and selecting a bit b. E is also given all public keys and access to all oracles, including random oracles.

Adversarial Queries. The adversary can make the following queries.

- **Send**(U, i, M): E gives the oracle Π_U^i a message M. If this oracle's *pid* $= U'$, then Π_U^i assumes that M is from U' and acts according to the protocol. For initiating oracles, E can make a special **Send** query λ, which tells Π_U^i to set *role*$_U$ = *initiator*. If Π_U^i did not receive a message λ as the first message, *role*$_U$ will be *responder*.
- **Reveal**(U, i): E uses this query to obtain the session key of Π_U^i (if any).
- **Corrupt**(U): This allows E to learn U's long-term key.

Oracle States. An oracle Π_U^i can be in the following states.

- **Accepted**: An oracle is in this state if it has received a properly constructed messages to make a session key and the oracle accepts the key.
- **Rejected**: An oracle is in this state if it decides not to establish a session key and abort the protocol.
- **Revealed**: An oracle is in this state if it has answered a Reveal query.
- **Corrupted**: An oracle is in this state if U has answered a Corrupt query.

Partnership. Two oracles Π_U^i, holding $(seskey, sid, pid)$ and $\Pi_{U'}^j$, holding $(seskey', sid', pid')$ are said to be *partners* if they have accepted and:

1. $sid = sid'$, $seskey = seskey'$, $pid = U'$, $pid' = U$;
2. $role_U = initiator$ and $role_{U'} = responder$ or vice versa;
3. no other oracle has accepted with session ID equals sid.

Freshness. An oracle Π_U^i is *fresh* if it and its partner $\Pi_{U'}^j$ (if any) are not revealed and neither U nor U' is corrupted.

Test Query. After E has made a polynomial number of queries in k, E can make a **Test** query to an oracle Π_U^i, which must be accepted and fresh. If $b = 0$ then Π_U^i outputs a randomly chosen session key $seskey_{random}$, otherwise it outputs its real session key $seskey_{\Pi_U^i}$.

After that, E can continue querying, but not reveal or corrupt the test oracle or its partner. Finally, E outputs his guess b' for b. E's advantage, denoted $Advantage^E(k)$, is $|1/2 - \Pr[b' = b]|$.

Definition of Security. A *benign adversary* is one who just relays messages between parties without any modification. Then the security definition for authenticated key exchange (AKE) is defined as follows.

Definition 2. *A protocol is an mBR'-secure AKE protocol if:*

1. *in the presence of a benign adversary, two oracles running the protocol accept and hold the same session key and session ID, and the session key is distributed uniformly at random on $\{0,1\}^k$; and*
2. *for any adversary E, $Advantage^E(k)$ is negligible.*

The cNR-mBR' Model. The cNR-mBR' model is the same as mBR', except:

- the adversary cannot make any **Reveal** query;
- instead of a normal **Test** query, the adversary selects an accepted and fresh oracle Π_U^i and outputs a guess $seskey$ for the oracle's session key $seskey_{\Pi_U^i}$. Then $Advantage^E(k) = \Pr[seskey = seskey_{\Pi_U^i}]$.

Following the technique of Kudla and Paterson [18], a protocol Π defined in the mBR' model can be first proven secure in the cNR-mBR' model, which is simpler. We will define a compiler to promote such a protocol to one secure in the mBR' model as long as the protocol Π produces a *session string* ss_Π and uses a hash function, which is modelled as a random oracle, to finally compute a *hashed session key*. We also use Kudla and Paterson's notion of strong partnering.

If a protocol has strong partnering, the adversary cannot trivially win the game by making two oracles, which are not partners, have the same session key and then using the **Reveal** query. Strong partnering can always be achieved by including partnering information in the session string; specifically we add the session identifier and the identity of the initiator and responder to the session string.

Definition 3 ([18]). *If Π is a key exchange protocol and there exists an adversary E, who plays the mBR' game with Π, and with non-negligible probability (in security parameter k) can make any two oracles Π_U^i and $\Pi_{U'}^j$ accept and hold the same session key when they are not partners, then we say that Π has weak partnering. Otherwise Π has* strong partnering.

Definition 4. *Suppose Π is a key exchange protocol. The session string decisional problem for protocol Π is: given an oracle Π_U^i and its transcript T_U^i in the mBR' model, public keys P_U and $P_{U'}$ (where $pid_U^i = U'$) and s, to decide whether s is the session string of Π_U^i or not.*

In order to use the cNR-mBR′ model, given a protocol Π, we define a protocol π to be the same as Π, except that the session key of π is the session string of Π.

Theorem 1. *Suppose that a key exchange protocol Π uses a hash function H to compute a hashed session key on completion of the protocol and Π has strong partnering. If the cNR-mBR′ security of the related protocol π is probabilistic polynomial time reducible to the hardness of the computational problem of some relation f, and the session string decisional problem for Π is polynomial time reducible to the decisional problem of f, then the mBR′ security of Π is probabilistic polynomial time reducible to the hardness of the gap problem of f, assuming that H is a random oracle.*

Proof. The proof for the original mBR model is given by Kudla and Paterson [18]. The proof for mBR′ is essentially the same. The idea of the proof is simple. Assume that there is an adversary A, given an algorithm E that can win cNR-mBR game, can solve the computational problem. Now we have to show that we can construct an algorithm B, given the decisional problem oracle and an adversary D that can win mBR game, can solve the computational problem. Thus, the heart of the idea is to use D and the decisional problem oracle to simulate E, and make A solve the computational problem for B.

Notice that in our model mBR′ (hence in cNR-mBR′ also) we do not consider a corrupted oracle to be a fresh one. However, while simulating E, B passes all **Corrupt** queries from D to A blindly, therefore this difference does not matter.

2.3   Chosen Ciphertext Security in the Multi-user Setting

For the simulation in our proof (see Section 3.3), we need an encryption scheme that is secure even if the adversary can ask for more than one challenging ciphertext encrypted by more than one public key. This is call indistinguishability under chosen ciphertext attack in the multi-user setting (IND-CCA-M) [1]. Fortunately, adaptive CCA security also implies such kind of security.

Definition 5 (IND-CCA-M).
   For all equal-length strings m_0, m_1 and any $b \in \{0, 1\}$, the left or right selector LR is defined as

$$LR(m_0, m_1, b) = m_b.$$

For a bit b that is unknown to the adversary, a LR encryption oracle $\mathcal{E}_{pk}LR$ $(\cdot, \cdot, b)$, given query (m_0, m_1) where m_0, m_1 are two equal-length plaintexts, first sets $m_b \leftarrow LR(m_0, m_1, b)$, then outputs the encryption of m_b using the public key pk.

A decryption oracle $\mathcal{D}_{sk}(\cdot)$, given a valid ciphertext c, outputs the corresponding decryption of c using the secret key sk.

We have the following experiment. Let $\mathcal{PE} = (\mathcal{K}, \mathcal{E}, \mathcal{D})$ be a public-key encryption scheme. The adversary, A_{cca}, has access to n LR encryption oracles $\mathcal{E}_{pk_i}LR(\cdot, \cdot, b)$ and n corresponding decryption oracles $\mathcal{D}_{sk_i}(\cdot)$, where A_{cca} is not *allowed to query* $\mathcal{D}_{sk_i}(\cdot)$ *on an output of* $\mathcal{E}_{pk_i}\mathrm{LR}(\cdot,\cdot,b)$. *Let* I *be some initial information string. For* $b \in \{0,1\}$, *we have*

$$\mathbf{Exp}_{\mathcal{PE},I}^{n-cca}(A_{cca},b)$$
$$\quad \mathbf{For}\ i = 1,\ \ldots,\ n\ \mathbf{do}\ (pk_i, sk_i) \leftarrow \mathcal{K}(I)\ \mathbf{EndFor}$$
$$\quad d \leftarrow A_{cca}^{\mathcal{E}_{pk_1}\mathrm{LR}(\cdot,\cdot,b),\ldots,\mathcal{E}_{pk_n}\mathrm{LR}(\cdot,\cdot,b),\mathcal{D}_{sk_1}(\cdot),\ldots,\mathcal{D}_{sk_n}(\cdot)}(I, pk_1, \ldots, pk_n)$$
$$\quad \mathbf{Return}\ d$$

The advantage of A_{cca} *is defined as*

$$\mathsf{Adv}_{\mathcal{PE},I}^{n-cca}(A_{cca}) = \Pr[\mathbf{Exp}_{\mathcal{PE},I}^{n-cca}(A_{cca},0) = 0] - \Pr[\mathbf{Exp}_{\mathcal{PE},I}^{n-cca}(A_{cca},1) = 0]$$

We say that $\mathcal{PE}$ *is secure against* chosen ciphertext attack *in the multi-user setting if for all* A_{cca} *and polynomial* n, $\{\mathsf{Adv}_{\mathcal{PE},I}^{n-cca}(A_{cca})\}$ *is negligible.*

Lemma 1 ([1]). *If an encryption scheme is IND-CCA secure then it is IND-CCA-M secure.*

2.4 An Automatic Search Procedure in Dolev Yao Model

Cortier et al. [12] proposed an automatic procedure that checks whether or not a protocol has the property called *occult*, which has been proved to imply secrecy in the Dolev–Yao model. We will briefly introduce the idea here.

Message Fields. *Fields* is the set of messages, which can be either primitive or compound fields. A primitive field's type can be one of *Agent, Key, Nonce*. *Key* and *Nonce* make the set *Basic*, the only set in which a field can be designated as secret. As a notational convention, variables A, B and variants denote agents; K and variants denotes keys.

Each agent A has a public key $\mathsf{pub}(A)$ and the related private-key $\mathsf{prv}(A)$. Each key K has an inverse key K^{-1}, i.e. $\mathsf{pub}(A)^{-1} = \mathsf{prv}(A)$ and $\mathsf{prv}(A)^{-1} = \mathsf{pub}(A)$.

Events and Global States. The system state is represented by a set of ordered events. There are three kinds of events: *messages*, *spells* and *states*.

- A message event is just a field that is the content of a sent message.
- A spell event $C = (S, L) \in Spells$ where the book $Book(C) = S$, is a set of basic secrets shared among a set of agents $Cabal(C) = L$.
- A state event is of the form $\mathsf{A}_n(X)$ where A is a role, n is the protocol step of role A and X is the concatenated field in memory held by the state. The set of *basic secrets* of a spell is made up by its book and long-term (private) keys of its cabal.

$$Sec(C) = Book(C) \cup ltk(Cabal(C))$$

A *global state* is a set of events. The *content* of a global state H is its set of messages

$$Cont(H) \stackrel{\mathrm{def}}{=} H \cap Fields$$

A basic field is *unused* in H if it is neither a part of any field in $Cont(H)$ nor $Sec(H)$.

$$unused(H) \stackrel{\text{def}}{=} \{X \in Basic | X \notin \mathsf{parts}(Cont(H)), X \notin (Sec(H))\}$$

where $\mathsf{parts}(.)$ is defined in the following paragraph.

Inductive Relations.

- $\mathsf{parts}(S)$ is the set of all sub-fields of fields in S (not including keys of encryptions).
- $\mathsf{analz}(S)$ is the subset of $\mathsf{parts}(S)$ having only subfields that are accessible to adversary.
- $\mathsf{synth}(S)$ is the set of all fields constructible from S by concatenation and encryption using fields and keys in S.
- $\mathsf{fake}(S) \stackrel{\text{def}}{=} \mathsf{synth}(\mathsf{analz}(S))$.

Ideals and Coideals.

- An *ideal* $\mathcal{I}$ is the set of fields that must be protected in order to protect secrets in S. It is the smallest superset of S such that the concatenation $[X, Y] \in \mathcal{I}(S)$ if $X \in \mathcal{I}(S)$ and $Y \in \mathcal{I}(S)$, and $\{X\}_K \in \mathcal{I}(S)$ if $X \in \mathcal{I}(S)$ and $K^{-1} \notin \mathcal{I}(S)$.
- The coideal $\mathcal{C}(S)$ is the complement of $\mathcal{I}(S)$.

Protocols. A protocol specification is made up by a set of transitions. A transition is of the form $Pre(t) \stackrel{New(t)}{\longrightarrow} Post(t)$, where $Pre(t)$ and $Post(t)$ are sets of events and $New(t)$ is a new set of nonces.

Except for the initialisation transition, a transition t shows a state change of one role. A message or post spell (but not both) may be introduced in $Post(t)$.

One restriction is that secrets in a post spell must be in $New(t)$. One condition for protocol security is *regularity*, implying that there is no long-term key introduced into a post message.

Global State Transitions. Given a protocol P and a set of initial knowledge I of the adversary, the *global succession* relation defines how a state H is transformed to a new state H' as follows.

- H' is an *honest* successor of H, if there is an applicable transition t in P such that $H' = (H \backslash (Pre(t) \cap States)) \cup Post(t)$. A transition t is *applicable* in H if $Pre(t) \subseteq H$ and $New(t) \subseteq unused(H)$
- H' is a *fake* successor of H, if there exists a field $X \in \mathsf{fake}(Cont(H) \cup I)$ such that $H' = H \cup \{X\}$.

The set of reachable states from P and I is denoted by $reachable(P, I)$.

Requirement for Secrecy. A spell is *compatible* with initial knowledge I if I does not have any of its basic secrets.

$$compatible(I) \stackrel{\text{def}}{=} \{C | Sec(C) \cap \mathsf{parts}(I) = \emptyset\}$$

Given adversarial initial knowledge I, a global state H is called *I-discreet* if $Cont(H) \subseteq \mathcal{C}(Sec(C))$ for any *I-compatible* spell $C \in H$.

Definition 6. *A P-configuration is a tuple (I, H, C) in which $H \in reachable$ (P, I), H is I-discreet, $C \in compatible(I)$, and $C \in H$. A protocol P is occult if for all P-configuration(I, H, C) and for every transition $t \in P$,*

$$Cont(Post(t)) \subseteq \mathcal{C}(Sec(C)).$$

Millen et al. [21] give a secrecy theorem saying that if a protocol is *occult* then it provides secrecy (in a Dolev–Yao style model). More importantly, Cortier et al. [12] proposed an automatic search procedure to check if a protocol has *occultness*. This result is very important for our work, because later we will show that if a protocol has occultness and passes some simple checks, that protocol is also secure in the cNR-mBR′ model.

3   Security in the cNR-mBR′ Model

In this section, we show that the property *occultness* also implies security in the cNR-mBR model under a condition that both initiator and responder provide nonces for building the session key. We consider only protocols that are based on public-key encryption, i.e. every message includes only fields that can be nonces, party IDs, concatenation or encryption of other fields.

Definition 7. *A two-party protocol is said to be based on public-key encryption if every message m is constructed by the following syntax:*

$$m ::= \mathsf{nonce} \mid \mathsf{partyID} \mid \mathsf{Enc}_{pk}(m) \mid \mathsf{concat}(m, m),$$

where nonce *is a random number,* partyID *is a party ID number,* $\mathsf{Enc}_k(.)$ *is encryption under the public key pk and* concat$(., .)$ *is concatenation of two fields.*

3.1   Occultness Property in cNR-mBR′ Model

In this section we link Dolev-Yao occultness property with some property in our computational models. Those computational properties will be useful for establishing security proofs in the cNR-mBR′ model later.

Lemma 2. *If a protocol π has the occult property, then any secret nonce sent between parties is always encrypted.*

Proof. Informally, *occultness* implies secrecy (in Dolev-Yao models), therefore it must also imply that no secret nonce is sent in the plain form (otherwise the adversary can learn it easily).

Assume that there is transition t, where $Post(t)$ contains a message event whose fields include a nonce r (in the plain form). Because r must be kept secret, there must be a spell event C where $r \in Sec(C)$. This means $r \in \mathcal{I}(Sec(C))$, i.e. $r \notin \mathcal{C}(Sec(C))$. Therefore, $Post(t) \notin \mathcal{C}(Sec(C))$, i.e. $Cont(Post(t)) \notin \mathcal{C}(Sec(C))$. But this means the protocol is not occult.

Lemma 3. *Suppose a protocol π has the occult property in the Dolev-Yao model, and the underlying public key encryption scheme is IND-CCA secure. Consider any oracle Π_Z^i in the cNR-mBR' model, whose pid is V, where Z and V have not been corrupted. Then with a negligible probability a ciphertext of a nonce created by Π_Z^i appears (in a transcript), where that ciphertext is not made either by an oracle of Z whose pid is V or by an oracle of V whose pid is Z.*

Proof (Sketch). Because of the scope of this paper, we will explain the outline of the proof. This lemma is only for a specific case of linking two trace properties, which are enough for our work, between Dolev-Yao and computational models. The idea of proof is based on the trace mapping technique, which has been fully demonstrated by Micciancio and Warinschi [20] for the general case (the models they used are very similar our models here). The intuitive idea behind the proof is: if the adversary is the first to make such a ciphertext, then we can break IND-CCA security; on the other hand, if any party oracle is the first to make such a ciphertext, then the protocol is not occult.

Assume the Lemma is false, then let c be the first such ciphertext. There are two cases: c is created by the adversary or c is created by a party oracle.

First we examine the former case, i.e. there is an adversary A who plays the cNR-mBR' can make c with a non-negligible probability. Now we show that we can construct an algorithm G that can have non-negligible advantage in the experiment $\mathbf{Exp}_{\mathcal{PE},I}^{2-cca}(A_{cca}, b)$ (see Section 2.3) as follows.

- G creates a cNR-mBR' game, and choose two parties Z and V to replace their public keys with the public keys from the experiment $\mathbf{Exp}_{\mathcal{PE},I}^{2-cca}(A_{cca}, b)$.
- Because G has public keys and decryption oracles of Z and V and all of public and secret keys of other parties, the cNR-mBR' game can be simulated perfectly except for either an oracle of Z, whose *pid* is V or an oracle of V, whose *pid* is Z.
- For such an oracle, G prepares two sets of nonces. While simulating it, G always uses the corresponding encryption oracle $\mathcal{E}_{pk_i}\mathrm{LR}(\cdot, \cdot, b)$ whenever G needs encrypting. Notice that G never has to encrypt any of those nonces under a public key not of Z and V, because we are assuming the adversary is the first one to do it. In addition, G never has to use a plain nonce, but its encryption, according to Lemma 2. Therefore, even G does not know which set of nonce is actually used, but the simulation is still perfect, until c appears.
- A can still corrupt any party but not Z and V.

– When c appears, G submits it to the decryption oracle of Z, then G can guess the bit b correctly.

Second, lets examine the latter case, i.e. a party oracle Π_Y^j, whose pid is X, is the first to break the property by creating c under the public key of X, where $\{Y, X\}$ is not $\{Z, V\}$ or $\{V, Z\}$. Notice that Y must be either Z or V, because before Π_Y^j makes c, Π_Y^j must have received another encryption from Z or V^1. We show that it is possible to construct a situation in the Dolev-Yao model, in which the protocol is not occult. First, for every bitstring value, including nonces and party IDs, we map it to a symbolic value. Now, in the Dolev-Yao model, we start with a situation when all parties are corrupted but Z, V. The Dolev-Yao adversary has to make the same transcripts as he did in the computational model, but now with symbolic values. We have to make sure that he is able to do that. Obviously, there is no problem for creating transcripts between Z or V with another party, because that party is corrupted. For any thing in any transcript between Z and V, if that is related to any nonce created by Z and V, then the Dolev-Yao adversary must be able to make the symbolic version, because he has corrupted all other parties except Z and V. In the other case, if that thing is related to a nonce created by an oracle of Z, whose pid is V and vice versa, we argue that the Dolev-Yao adversary is also able to create the symbolic version. Assume the contrary, then there is a bitstring that the Dolev-Yao adversary can not make the symbolic version. Then, in the experiment $\mathbf{Exp}_{\mathcal{PE},I}^{2-cca}(A_{cca}, b)$ above, given that bistring we can always use the decryption oracles to recursively decrypt ciphertexts. For any ciphertext that is not allowed to be decrypted by the decryption oracles, we skip it. There must be a ciphertext, that can be decrypted by the decryption oracles, giving us the hidden nonce in $\mathbf{Exp}_{\mathcal{PE},I}^{2-cca}(A_{cca}, b)$ (if there is no such a ciphertext, there would not be any problem for the Dolev-Yao adversary to make symbolic versions of transcript).

Now we have a situation in the Dolev-Yao model, where we have an instance of party Y sends out a ciphertext of a nonce, which has been created by Z, under the public key of X (where X is not Z). But this means the protocol is not occult.

3.2   Hard Problems Used for Security Proofs

According to the modular approach [18] that we are following, we need a set of computational, decisional and gap problems, which must be hard. Now we define the following problems and show that IND-CCA implies the hardness of them.

Informally, the computational problem we are going to define is based on the encryption property one-wayness under adaptively chosen ciphertext attack in the multi-user setting (OW-CCA-M). In this attack, we ask the adversary to find the plaintext of a random ciphertext, while allowing him to get the ciphertext of any message related to the hidden message, in a two-user setting. And, because

---

[1] Otherwise Π_Y^j has no information about nonces in c, because the adversary has not faked any such an encryption

IND-CCA implies IND-CCA-M, we just have to show that IND-CCA-M implies OW-CCA-M. Then the decisional and gap problems are defined accordingly.

Definition 8. *Given a public-key encryption scheme $\mathcal{PE}$ with plaintext and ciphertext spaces $M_{\mathcal{PE}}$ and $C_{\mathcal{PE}}$, and a pair of public and secret keys (pk_z, sk_z), we define the following relation f:*

$$f : (M_{\mathcal{PE}} \times C_{\mathcal{PE}}) \to \{0,1\},$$

$$\text{where } f(m, c) = \begin{cases} 1 \text{ if } \mathcal{D}_{sk_z}(c) = m \\ 0 \text{ otherwise} \end{cases}$$

Now we can define our problems.

Let $\mathcal{E}_{pk_z}\mathrm{I}(\cdot,\cdot,\cdot)$ be an "inserting" encryption oracle of pk_z, which on input $(m_1, \mathcal{E}_{pk_z}(m_2), m_3)$, outputs $\mathcal{E}_{pk_z}(m_1, m_2, m_3)$; and $\mathcal{E}_{pk_z}^{pk_v}\mathrm{C}(\cdot)$ be a "converting" encryption oracle from pk_z to pk_v, which on input $\mathcal{E}_{pk_v}(m)$, outputs $\mathcal{E}_{pk_z}(m)$.

The adversary is given the public key pk_z, an additional public key pk_v and all corresponding decryption, inserting and converting oracles of pk_z and pk_v, where the decryption oracles never answer if input is from the inserting or converting oracles. We have the following problems of $\mathcal{PE}$.

- **Computational problem:** *The adversary is given c to compute m such that $f(m, c) = 1$.*
- **Decisional problem:** *The adversary is given c and m to determine if $f(m, c) = 1$ or not.*
- **Gap problem:** *Given an oracle that can solve the decisional problem above and c, to compute m such that $f(m, c) = 1$.*

Here the decryption oracle $\mathcal{D}_{sk_z}(\cdot)$ never decrypts c or any ciphertext from any oracles.

Lemma 4. *If the underlying encryption scheme is IND-CCA, the problems in Definition 8 are hard.*

Proof. We have shown that IND-CCA implies IND-CCA-M (see Section 2.3). Therefore, what we have to show is that solving any of the problems above is at least as hard as winning the IND-CCA-M game.

Given an algorithm E that can solve one of the problems above, we construct an algorithm F that can have non-negligible advantage in the experiment $\mathbf{Exp}_{\mathcal{PE},I}^{2-cca}(A_{cca}, b)$ (see Section 2.3).

The construction is as follows. F picks a pair of messages (m_0, m_1) randomly, then submits them to $\mathcal{E}_{pk_1}\mathrm{LR}(\cdot, \cdot, b)$ and then forwards the output c as the challenge ciphertext to E. Now, F has to simulate all necessary oracles that E needs. For any decryption request, F just forwards it to the decryption oracle in the experiment. For requests to inserting and converting oracles, because F can submit any message to oracles $\mathcal{E}_{pk_z}\mathrm{LR}$ and $\mathcal{E}_{pk_v}\mathrm{LR}$, F can also simulate those oracles.

We examine each case as follows.

- If E can solve the computational problem, i.e. output m_b, F can see m_b to guess b correctly.
- If E can solve the decisional problem, F just asks E if m_0 or m_1 is actually encrypted. Therefore F can guess b correctly.
- If E can solve the gap problem, F must simulate the decisional oracle. Given a request to the decisional oracle including a ciphertext c and a plaintext m, if c is not an output of any oracle $\mathcal{E}_{pk_z}\mathrm{LR}$, F can use $\mathcal{D}_{sk_z}(\cdot)$ to check the plaintext. Otherwise, if m is one of the two possible plaintexts of c (F must know them), F just outputs Yes. In this latter case, the probability that F simulates the decisional oracle wrongly is negligible, i.e. m is m_{1-b}, because c contains no information of m_{1-b}.

Finally, F can see the output of E to guess b correctly.

3.3   Our Main Theorem

Theorem 2. *Suppose a protocol π is occult and based on an IND-CCA public-key encryption scheme, each side sends out at least one nonce, and the session key includes all exchanged nonces. Then the security of π in the cNR-mBR' model is probabilistic polynomial time reducible to the hardness of the corresponding computational problem (according to Definition 8).*

Proof. Assume that there is an adversary A that participates in π in the cNR-mBR' model and outputs the session key with a non-negligible probability ϵ_A in a time τ_A, where k is the security parameter. We will show that we can build an adversary B who solves the computational problem, i.e. given a ciphertext c, output the plaintext m of c using some oracles, with some probability $g(\epsilon_A)$ and in time $h(\tau_A)$ where g and h are polynomial functions.

The idea behind the reduction is as follows. B will try to make a session key of an oracle of Z, whose pid is V, to contain m. Without knowing m and the secret key used to decrypt c, B can still do that by using inserting and converting oracles to simulate the transcript of that oracle, as long as the oracle and its partner have not been corrupted. Fortunately, according to Lemma 3, B never has to simulate a ciphertext of m under another key except P_Z and P_V (otherwise the simulation fails because B does not know m). Finally, if A chooses that oracle to test, then the guess of the session key from A will help B to output m.

Now we formally describe how B works. As we have defined the computational problem of f, B is given the public key pk_z, which has been used to make c, an additional public key pk_v and all corresponding decryption, inserting and converting oracles. B makes the cNR-mBR' game as follows.

- **Setting up:** B runs a $\mathsf{Setup}(k)$ algorithm to set up a set of participants $\{U\}$, their oracles and long-term keys for each participant as defined in Section 2.2. Then B chooses randomly two parties Z and V, replaces their public keys with pk_z and pk_v respectively. After that, B picks randomly a party oracle Π_Z^j, whose pid is V.

  Finally B gives all public keys to A.

- **Answering queries:**
  - Send(U, i, M):
    * If this is the query for Π_Z^j, i.e. $U = Z$ and $i = j$, where after that Π_Z^j has to reply the first message containing a nonce (in an encrypted form, see Lemma 8), then Π_Z^j considers the hidden m as his first nonce and starts using corresponding inserting and converting oracles to make valid replies.
      Notice that if Π_Z^j has not been required to use any nonce, then the inserting and converting oracles have not been used any time.
    * If no ciphertext inside M is from any inserting or converting oracles that B has been given (to solve the computational problem), then B can parse all the content M by using relevant secret keys or decryption oracles.
      Now there are two cases:
      · When B is parsing M, if there is a nonce that is supposed to be the hidden m, then B puts the party oracle Π_U^i in the state **Rejected**, because according to Lemma 3, M is an invalid message with an overwhelming probability.
      · Otherwise, B keeps simulating according to the protocol specification.
    * If there is at least one ciphertext inside M that is from any inserting or converting oracles that B has been given, then certainly B knows what is the next state of Π_U^i (B knows m is inside, B just does not know what m is). But it maybe a problem if Π_U^i has to reply something containing m.
      Now, according to Lemma 3, B never have to make a ciphertext of m under a key different from P_Z or P_V. And to make a ciphertext of m under P_Z or P_V, B uses relevant inserting and converting oracles.
  - Corrupt(U):
    * If $U = Z$ or $U = V$, then B stops using A and output randomly one bit b'.
    * Otherwise B just gives A the corresponding private key.
- Finally, A must choose an accepted and fresh oracle and output his guess for the session key.
  Suppose the number of participants is n_{par} and each party may have n_{ses} sessions, where n_{par} and n_{ses} are polynomial functions of k.
  With a non-negligible probability $\frac{1}{n_{par}.n_{ses}}$, Π_Z^j is the oracle chosen by A. In this case, B just extracts all nonces from the session key outputted by A and outputs the nonce which is supposed to be m (Since the session key is made of nonces from both sides, it must contains m). Therefore, if Π_Z^j is chosen, the probability that B wins is $\eta_1 = \epsilon_A$.
  Otherwise, B just stops using A and outputs a random guess. Therefore, if Π_Z^j is not chosen, the probability that B wins is η_2 and negligible.
  Therefore, the probability that B wins is $\eta = \frac{1}{n_{par}.n_{ses}}.\eta_1 + (1 - \frac{1}{n_{par}.n_{ses}}).\eta_2 \geq \epsilon_A.\frac{1}{n_{par}.n_{ses}}$, in a time $h(\tau_A)$ where $h(.)$ is a polynomial function.

4   Automated Proofs in the mBR′ Model

4.1   The Session String Decisional Problem

In order to establish security in the mBR′ model from security in the cNR-mBR′ model, we need to show that while we are making a reduction from the gap problem to mBR′-security, we must be able to solve the session string decisional problem [18]. The following lemma shows that we can do it with any public-key-based protocol.

Lemma 5. *Given all the public and private keys used in an mBR′ game, except the private key of an arbitrary party Z, and the oracle for the decisional problem of f based on public and private key of Z, there exists a polynomial time algorithm S to solve the session string decisional problem in the mBR′ game.*

Proof. Since S has all public and private keys except the secret key of Z, S can open all ciphertexts with the exception of any ciphertext made under the public key of Z. However, for such a ciphertext, S can always use the decisional problem of f to check if a nonce is the plaintext or not. Therefore, S can always solve the session string decisional problem in the mBR′ game in polynomial time.

4.2   How to Automate Proofs

According to the Theorem 1, in order to show the mBR′ security of a key exchange protocol Π that is based on an IND-CCA public-key encryption scheme and computes a session key by hashing, we have to do the following.

- Show that in the case of a benign adversary the protocol completes correctly with a random key (see Section 2.2).
- Show that Π has strong partnering. We can always have this property if we add partnering information into the *session string* (see Section 2.2).
- Show that the cNR-mBR′ security of the related *"no-hashing"* protocol π is probabilistic polynomial time reducible to the hardness of the computational problem. First we check if both sides contribute nonces (very easily checked) and then we use the automatic tool by Cortier et al [12] to check occultness.

We do not have to show that given the decisional problem oracle of f, we can solve the session string decisional problem, because it is done by Lemma 5. Although there a number of steps, they can be done quickly or automatically. Checking the *occultness* property is the only difficult step but it can be automated.

Example 1. Suppose we want to prove the following key exchange protocol Π, which is based on Needham-Schroeder-Lowe protocol. There are parties A and B communicating as follows.

1. A → B: $\mathsf{Enc}_{P_B}(\mathsf{concat}(N_A, A))$
2. B → A: $\mathsf{Enc}_{P_A}(\mathsf{concat}(N_A, N_B, B))$

3. $A \rightarrow B$: $\mathsf{Enc}_{P_B}(\mathsf{concat}(N_B))$

After that, A and B compute $sid = \{N_A, A\}_{P_B}, \{N_A, N_B, B\}_{P_A}, \{N_B\}_{P_B}$ and the session key $seskey_\Pi = hash(N_A, N_B, sid, A, B)$, where $hash(\cdot)$ is a hash function.

Π has mBR′ security because of the following.

- It is trivial to see that the protocol is functional. And because the session key is computed by hashing the concatenation of some uniformly chosen nonces, the session key is distributed uniformly.
- Π has strong partnering because we add (sid, A, B) into the session string according to the technique mentioned in Section 2.2.
- In the related protocol π, both parties contribute nonces. Furthermore, there is a mechanised proof of occultness for π by Cortier et al. [12].

5 Conclusion and Future Work

We have shown an approach of using an automatic technique designed originally for Dolev–Yao models to verify security of public-key-based key exchange protocols in a computational model. The full computational model is reduced to a simpler one first, before we apply a mechanisable technique to establish a security proof. Although the technique was first designed for checking a property in the Dolev–Yao model, we have shown that property also implies security in our simpler computational model. Therefore, the automatic technique proposed by Cortier et al. [12] can be used here to achieve a computationally sound security proof.

This work can be extended in some directions. Firstly, we want to know how the computational model can be extended, for example to modelling symmetric key encryption, while our approach remains applicable. Secondly, it may be possible to design an automatic technique to establish a security proof directly in the cNR-mBR′ model, e.g. using Hoare logic. This may allow us to treat more types of protocols than using the indirect method in this paper. Thirdly, because it is always hard to apply automatic techniques on full computational models, it would be interesting to find more modular approaches, e.g. reducing the complexity of models, and then designing automated proofs in the simpler models.

References

1. Bellare, M., Boldyreva, A., Micali, S.: Public-key encryption in a multi-user setting: Security proofs and improvements. In: Preneel, B. (ed.) EUROCRYPT 2000. LNCS, vol. 1807, pp. 259–274. Springer, Heidelberg (2000)
2. Bellare, M., Pointcheval, D., Rogaway, P.: Authenticated key exchange secure against dictionary attacks. LNCS, pp. 139–155. Springer, Heidelberg (2000)
3. Bellare, M., Rogaway, P.: Entity authentication and key distribution. In: Stinson, D.R. (ed.) CRYPTO 1993. LNCS, vol. 773, pp. 232–249. Springer, Heidelberg (1994)

4. Blanchet, B.: Automatic proof of strong secrecy for security protocols. In: Proceedings of IEEE Symposium on Security and Privacy, 86–100 (2004)
5. Blanchet, B.: A computationally sound mechanized prover for security protocols. IEEE Transactions on Dependable and Secure Computing 5(4), 193–207 (2008)
6. Canetti, R., Herzog, J.: Universally composable symbolic analysis of mutual authentication and key-exchange protocols. In: Halevi, S., Rabin, T. (eds.) TCC 2006. LNCS, vol. 3876, pp. 380–403. Springer, Heidelberg (2006)
7. Canetti, R., Gajek, S.: Universally composable symbolic analysis of Diffie–Hellman based key exchange. Cryptology ePrint Archive, Report 2010/303 (2010), http://eprint.iacr.org/
8. Canetti, R., Krawczyk, H.: Universally composable notions of key exchange and secure channels. In: Knudsen, L.R. (ed.) EUROCRYPT 2002. LNCS, vol. 2332, pp. 337–351. Springer, Heidelberg (2002)
9. Chevalier, Y., Vigneron, L.: A tool for lazy verification of security protocols. In: Proceedings of ASE, vol. 1, pp. 373–376 (2001)
10. Choo, K.K., Boyd, C., Hitchcock, Y.: Errors in computational complexity proofs for protocols. In: Roy, B. (ed.) ASIACRYPT 2005. LNCS, vol. 3788, pp. 624–643. Springer, Heidelberg (2005)
11. Choo, K.K.R., Boyd, C., Hitchcock, Y., Maitland, G.: On session identifiers in provably secure protocols. Security in Communication Networks, 351–366 (2004)
12. Cortier, V., Millen, J., Rueß, H.: Proving secrecy is easy enough. In: Proceedings of the 14th IEEE workshop on Computer Security Foundations, p. 97. IEEE Computer Society, Los Alamitos (2001)
13. Cortier, V., Warinschi, B.: Computationally sound, automated proofs for security protocols. In: Programming Languages and Systems, pp. 157–171
14. Courant, J., Daubignard, M., Ene, C., Lafourcade, P., Lakhnech, Y.: Towards automated proofs for asymmetric encryption schemes in the random oracle model. In: Proceedings of the 15th ACM Conference on Computer and Communications Security, pp. 371–380. ACM, New York (2008)
15. Datta, A., Derek, A., Mitchell, J.C., Warinschi, B.: Computationally sound compositional logic for key exchange protocols. In: 19th IEEE Computer Security Foundations Workshop, p. 14 (2006)
16. Dolev, D., Yao, A.: On the security of public key protocols. IEEE Transactions on Information Theory 29(2), 198–208 (1983)
17. Gagné, M., Lafourcade, P., Lakhnech, Y., Safavi-Naini, R.: Automated security proof for symmetric encryption modes. In: Advances in Computer Science-ASIAN 2009. Information Security and Privacy, pp. 39–53 (2009)
18. Kudla, C., Paterson, K.: Modular security proofs for key agreement protocols. In: Roy, B. (ed.) ASIACRYPT 2005. LNCS, vol. 3788, pp. 549–565. Springer, Heidelberg (2005)
19. Lowe, G.: Breaking and fixing the Needham-Schroeder public-key protocol using FDR. In: Tools and Algorithms for the Construction and Analysis of Systems, pp. 147–166 (1996)
20. Micciancio, D., Warinschi, B.: Soundness of formal encryption in the presence of active adversaries. Theory of Cryptography, 133–151 (2004)
21. Millen, J., Rueß, H.: Protocol-independent secrecy. In: 2000 IEEE Symposium on Security and Privacy, IEEE Computer Society, Los Alamitos (2000)
22. Okamoto, T., Pointcheval, D.: The gap-problems: A new class of problems for the security of cryptographic schemes. In: Kim, K.-c. (ed.) PKC 2001. LNCS, vol. 1992, pp. 104–118. Springer, Heidelberg (2001)

A Framework for Constructing Convertible Undeniable Signatures

Ryo Kikuchi[1], Le Trieu Phong[2], and Wakaha Ogata[3]

[1] NTT
kikuchi.ryo@lab.ntt.co.jp
[2] NICT
phong@nict.go.jp
[3] Tokyo Institute of Technology
wakaha@mot.titech.ac.jp

Abstract. In this paper, we propose a framework for constructing convertible undeniable signatures from *weakly-secure* standard signatures. We then present a concrete instantiation employing a standard signature scheme recently proposed at Eurocrypt '09. The instantiation is the first (convertible) undeniable signature scheme whose unforgeability relies on the well-known RSA assumption.

Keywords: Convertible undeniable signatures, RSA assumption.

1 Introduction

1.1 Background

The concept of undeniable signatures (US) was introduced by Chaum and Antwerpen [7]. Certainly, signatures aim at preserving undeniability, so the term "undeniable signatures" may deserve some more explanation. Namely, while ordinary signatures definitely ensure undeniability, *undeniable* signatures still has the property *even when* the signer takes control of the verifiability. In undeniable signature schemes, a verifier cannot verify the validity of a message-signature pair by himself. Only if the signer agrees to have the pair verified, the verifier is able to be convinced whether the signature is valid or invalid, through executing an interactive protocol with the signer. Main applications of undeniable signatures are in licensing software [6], electronic cash [3,8,30], confidential business agreement [4], and generally, in cases where verification of signatures leads to some benefit for the verifier. Departing from the work of Chaum and Antwerpen [7], there is a considerable effort in the community to construct better undeniable signature schemes, among which are [5,6,17,18,23,24,28] to list just a few.

A subsequent line of research is to add more properties to undeniable signature schemes to enhance its usefulness. Along the line, *convertible* undeniable signature schemes were introduced by Boyar et al. [4]. In such schemes, undeniable signatures can be converted into ordinary self-verifiable ones by having the signer publishing additional pieces of information called *converters*. There

S.-H. Heng and K. Kurosawa (Eds.): ProvSec 2010, LNCS 6402, pp. 70–86, 2010.

are two types of converters. The signer can issue either a "selective converter" which converts a single undeniable signature, or "all converter" which converts all signatures the signer has produced so far.

Many convertible undeniable signature schemes (CUSs) were proposed in the literature, and yet many were broken as well. Boyar et al. [4] originally prove that CUSs exist if one-way functions exist, but the result is purely theoretical. Realizing the fact, Boyar et al. in the same paper proposed another scheme with practical efficiency, but unfortunately was later broken [27]. After that, Damgard and Pedersen [10] suggested some efficient schemes, but they could not prove the security formally; and yet it was recently found by El Aimani [14] that one of the schemes [10] did not satisfy invisibility as conjectured. El Aimani [14] also showed how to fix the scheme in the random oracle model. Using pairings, Yuen et al. [34] showed a CUS scheme in the standard model, but the scheme turned out insecure as showed in [31]. Also with pairings, Huang and Wong [22] suggested a scheme in the standard model, but was showed flawed in [33]. The short history just mentioned shows that constructing CUSs (and US in general) is a highly delicate task, in which a rough intuition seems not enough, and one should works with concrete details.

In this paper, we will work in the RSA group, so let us focus on some CUS schemes in the setting. In ROM, one can even rely on the factoring assumption for unforgeability, as in the work of Galbraith and Mao [17]. However, in the standard model, what we currently have are schemes based on relatively strong assumptions such as the strong RSA assumption for unforgeability, as in [32], or even stronger assumptions as in [26].

1.2 Our Contribution

In this paper, we first show a general construction of CUS, composing from a weakly-secure ordinary signature scheme, a chameleon hash function, and a public key encryption (PKE) scheme with some additional properties but fulfilled by well-known schemes in the literature.

We then show a concrete instantiation derived from our proposed construction. The concrete scheme utilizes the RSA-based ordinal signature/chameleon hash/PKE. Its unforgeability relies on the RSA assumption, which is the weakest assumption used in factoring-based CUS schemes so far in the standard model.

2 Convertible Undeniable Signatures

Throughout this paper, λ denotes the security parameter and PPT algorithm denotes a probabilistic polynomial-time algorithm. For probabilistic algorithm $\mathcal{A}$, $y \xleftarrow{\$} \mathcal{A}(x)$ means that $\mathcal{A}$ with input x takes randomness uniformly at random and outputs y. For finite set $\mathcal{B}$, $y \xleftarrow{\$} \mathcal{B}$ denotes picking y from $\mathcal{B}$ uniformly at random.

A convertible undeniable signature scheme CUS consists of a tuple (CUS.KGen, CUS.USign, CUS.sConvert, CUS.aConvert, CUS.Vrf, CUS.UVrf, CUS.Confirmation, CUS.Disavowal) as follows.

- CUS.KGen: On input 1^λ, this algorithm outputs a pair of public and secret keys, (pk, sk).
- CUS.USign: On input secret key sk and message m, the signing algorithm outputs an element σ, which is the undeniable signature on m.
- CUS.sConvert: On input secret key sk, message m, and signature σ, this algorithm outputs a (selective) converter, cvt, if (m, σ) is a valid pair, that is, $\sigma \in \{x \mid x \leftarrow \text{CUS.USign}(sk, m)\}$. Otherwise, outputs $\perp$.[1]
- CUS.aConvert: On input secret key sk, this algorithm outputs $Acvt$, which is the all converter.
- CUS.Vrf: On input public key pk, message m, signature σ, and converter cvt, this algorithm outputs 1 if (m, σ) is a valid pair for pk and cvt is a converter of σ. Otherwise, outputs 0.
- CUS.UVrf: On input public key pk, message m, signature σ, and all converter $Acvt$, this algorithm outputs 1 if (m, σ) is a valid pair for pk. Otherwise, outputs 0.
- CUS.Confirmation: A protocol between a signer and a verifier such that, given a message m, signature σ, and public key pk, it allows the signer to convince the verifier that σ is indeed a valid signature on m for pk, with the knowledge of the secret key. If (m, σ) is invalid, then no signer can prove the pair as valid with non-negligible probability.
- CUS.Disavowal: A protocol between a signer and a verifier such that, given a message m, a signature σ and a public key pk, it allows the signer to convince the verifier that σ is an invalid signature on m for pk, with the knowledge of the secret key sk. If (m, σ) is valid, then no signer can prove the pair as invalid with non-negligible probability.

Note that "(m, σ) is valid for pk" means $\sigma \in \{x \mid x \leftarrow \text{CUS.USign}(sk, m)\}$ for sk which corresponds to pk.

The following definitions describe securities that a convertible undeniable signature scheme should meet.

2.1   Unforgeability

The unforgeability against chosen message attack (UF-CMA) is defined by using UF-CMA game executed by a forger, $\mathcal{F}$, described as follows.

1. $\mathcal{F}$ is given public key pk.
2. $\mathcal{F}$ is permitted to issue a series of queries to some oracles. ($\mathcal{F}$ is allowed to make adaptive queries here – subsequent queries are made based on the answers of previous queries.)
   - Signing queries: $\mathcal{F}$ submits message m and receives a signature, σ, on m.
   - Convert queries: $\mathcal{F}$ submits message-signature pair (m, σ), and receives a converter, cvt, or $\perp$.

---

[1] We note that converting only valid signatures are sufficient for applications like [3]. However, our construction can even convert invalid signatures, as seen later.

- Confirmation/disavowal queries: $\mathcal{F}$ submits message-signature pair (m, σ) to the oracle. We will consider active attack, where the oracle first checks whether (m, σ) is valid. If (m, σ) is valid, the oracle returns 1 and executes the confirmation protocol with $\mathcal{F}$. Otherwise, the oracle returns 0 and executes the disavowal protocol with $\mathcal{F}$.

3. At the end of this game, $\mathcal{F}$ outputs message-signature pair (m^*, σ^*) such that $\mathcal{F}$ has never queried m^* to the signing oracle.

$\mathcal{F}$ wins UF-CMA game if σ^* is a valid signature on m^*, and its advantage in this game is defined by $\mathbf{Adv}_{\mathsf{CUS}}^{\mathrm{UF-CMA}}(\mathcal{F}) = \Pr[\mathcal{F} \text{ wins UF-CMA game}]$.

Definition 1. *A convertible undeniable signature scheme is UF-CMA secure if no PPT forger $\mathcal{F}$ has non-negligible advantage $\mathbf{Adv}_{\mathsf{CUS}}^{\mathrm{UF-CMA}}(\mathcal{F})$.*

A more strong notion, the strong unforgeability against chosen message attack (sUF-CMA), is defined by using sUF-CMA game. The game is the same as UF-CMA game except that at the end of the game, $\mathcal{F}$ must output (m^*, σ^*) such that it has never received (m^*, σ^*) from the signing oracle. Again, $\mathcal{F}$ wins the game if σ^* is a valid signature on m^* and define the advantage $\mathbf{Adv}_{\mathsf{CUS}}^{\mathrm{sUF-CMA}}(\mathcal{F}) = \Pr[\mathcal{F} \text{ wins sUF-CMA game}]$.

Definition 2. *A convertible undeniable signature scheme is sUF-CMA secure if no PPT forger $\mathcal{F}$ has non-negligible advantage $\mathbf{Adv}_{\mathsf{CUS}}^{\mathrm{sUF-CMA}}(\mathcal{F})$.*

2.2 Invisibility

The invisibility against chosen message attack (IV-CMA) is defined by the following IV-CMA game executed by a distinguisher, $\mathcal{D}$.

1. $\mathcal{D}$ is given public key pk.
2. $\mathcal{D}$ is permitted to issue a series of queries: signing queries, convert queries, confirmation/disavowal queries, as in UF-CMA game.
3. At some point, $\mathcal{D}$ outputs message m^* which has never been queried to the signing oracle, and receives a challenge signature, σ^*, which depends on hidden bit b. If $b = 0$, σ^* is generated from m^* using the signing algorithm. Otherwise, σ^* is chosen randomly from the signature space of the scheme.
4. $\mathcal{D}$ is permitted to issue a series of queries similarly except the restriction that no convert and confirmation/disavowal query (m^*, σ^*) is allowed.
5. At the end of this game, $\mathcal{D}$ outputs a bit, b', as a guess for b.

We say that $\mathcal{D}$ wins IV-CMA game if $b' = b$. The advantage of $\mathcal{D}$ is defined by $\mathbf{Adv}_{\mathsf{CUS}}^{\mathrm{IV-CMA}}(\mathcal{D}) = |\Pr[\mathcal{D} \text{ wins IV-CMA game}] - 1/2|$.

Definition 3. *A convertible undeniable signature scheme is IV-CMA secure if no PPT distinguisher $\mathcal{D}$ has non-negligible advantage $\mathbf{Adv}_{\mathsf{CUS}}^{\mathrm{IV-CMA}}(\mathcal{D})$.*

3 Primitives and Security Notions

In this section, we review some building blocks and slightly extend conventional definitions.

3.1 Standard Signature Scheme

A (standard) signature scheme SIG is a tuple (SIG.KGen, SIG.Sign, SIG.Vrf) as follows. On input 1^λ, key generation algorithm SIG.KGen produces a pair of public and secret keys (pk, sk). On input sk and message m, signing algorithm SIG.Sign produces a signature, σ, which is publicly verifiable using verification algorithm SIG.Vrf on input pk and (m, σ).

Definition 4. *A standard signature scheme is said to be sUF-CMA secure if no PPT forger has a non-negligible advantage in the game which is the same as sUF-CMA game for convertible undeniable signature schemes, except a forger issues only signing queries.*

Definition 5. *A standard signature scheme is said to be sUF-wCMA secure if no PPT forger has a non-negligible advantage in the game which is the same as the game for sUF-CMA security, except a forger issues signing queries at the beginning of the game only, i.e., a forger submits all messages $(m_1, m_2, \ldots, m_q)$ at first, then she gets pk and corresponded signatures $(\sigma_1, \sigma_2, \ldots, \sigma_q)$.*

3.2 Chameleon Hash

Chameleon hash $\mathcal{H}$, introduced in [25], is a family of (H, τ), where $H : \{0, 1\}^* \times \mathbb{R}_H \to \mathbb{G}_H$ is a two-input hash function and τ is a trapdoor for H. The family $\mathcal{H}$ has several properties defined as follows.

- **Collision resistance[2]:** No PPT adversary $\mathcal{A}$ has the non-negligible advantage:

$$\mathbf{Adv}_{\mathcal{H}}^{\mathrm{CR}}(\mathcal{A}) = \Pr\left[(H, \tau) \overset{\$}{\leftarrow} \mathcal{H}; (m, s, m', s') \leftarrow \mathcal{A}(H) : \begin{matrix} H(m, s) = H(m', s'), \\ (m, s) \neq (m', s') \end{matrix}\right].$$

- **Trapdoor collisions:** There is an efficient algorithm which takes τ, m, s, m', and outputs s' such that $H(m, s) = H(m', s')$.
- **Uniformity:** All messages m induce the same probability distribution on $H(m, s)$ for randomly chosen s.

3.3 Enhanced Public Key Encryption Scheme

A public key encryption scheme is a tuple of algorithms as follows. On input 1^λ, key generation algorithm PKE.KGen produces a pair of public and secret keys (pk, sk). On input pk and message m, encryption algorithm PKE.Enc produces ciphertext c, and it can be decrypted by decryption algorithm PKE.Dec on input sk and c. For semantic security, the encryption algorithm is probabilistic, that is, a random number r is used to encrypt.

We consider some additional algorithms and functions.

---

[2] Strictly speaking, the definition of collision resistance is not the same as in [25] (which did not care about the randomness), but it is usually used in later works. In particular, the concrete RSA-based chameleon hash function used in this paper fulfills the definition.

- (f, F): Function f, on input (pk, r), encapsulates the random number r used in encryption, and the value $f(pk, r)$ can be extracted from the value $c = \mathsf{PKE.Enc}(pk, m; r)$ by computing $F(pk, c)$. That is, $f(pk, r) = F(pk, c)$ holds. $f(pk, \cdot)$ must have collision resistance property. i.e., it is intractable to find (r_0, r_1) such that $f(pk, r_0) = f(pk, r_1)$.
- $\mathsf{PKE.Ext}$: On input secret key sk and ciphertext c, the *extraction algorithm* outputs random number(s) r which had been used in encryption.
- $\mathsf{PKE.Dec2}$: On input pk, r, and c, the *alternative decryption algorithm* outputs plaintext m such that $c = \mathsf{PKE.Enc}(pk, m; r)$.

We say that a public key encryption scheme $(\mathsf{PKE.KGen}, \mathsf{PKE.Enc}, \mathsf{PKE.Dec})$ is an enhanced public key encryption scheme if there exist additional (polytime computable) algorithms and functions $(\mathsf{PKE.Ext}, \mathsf{PKE.Dec2}, (f, F))$ with the above properties.

We define new security notion of public key encryption as IV-CPA. It is same to well-known notion IND-CPA except the challenge query. The invisibility against chosen plaintext attack (IV-CPA) is defined by using the following IV-CPA game executed by a distinguisher, $\mathcal{D}$.

1. $\mathcal{D}$ is given public key pk.
2. $\mathcal{D}$ outputs message m^* and receives a challenge ciphertext, c^*, which depends on hidden bit b as follows. If $b = 0$, c^* is a ciphertext of m^*. Otherwise, c^* is chosen uniformly at random from the ciphertext space defined by the public key.
3. At the end of this game, $\mathcal{D}$ outputs bit b' as a guess for b.

$\mathcal{D}$ wins the game if $b' = b$, and its advantage is defined as $\mathbf{Adv}_{\mathsf{PKE}}^{\mathrm{IV-CPA}}(\mathcal{D}) = |\Pr[\mathcal{D} \text{ wins}] - 1/2|$.

Definition 6. *A (enhanced) public key encryption scheme is IV-CPA secure if no PPT distinguisher $\mathcal{D}$ has non-negligible advantage $\mathbf{Adv}_{\mathsf{PKE}}^{\mathrm{IV-CPA}}(\mathcal{D})$.*

It is clear that IV-CPA implies IND-CPA, but the other way does not. Intuitively, it is because IND-CPA does not guarantee that a ciphertext is uniformly distributed over the ciphertext space even if a random number is chosen randomly. Still, we believe this the gap is quite small, because most IND-CPA secure schemes, e.g. ElGamal, Paillier, satisfy IV-CPA under reasonable assumptions. (ElGamal is IV-CPA as a normal PKE, while Paillier is IV-CPA as an enhanced PKE.)

4   Convertible Undeniable Signatures from Weakly-Secure Signatures

In this section, we will show a general and efficient construction of CUS scheme. The scheme is constructed from a weak-secure signature scheme wSIG, combined with a chameleon hash $\mathcal{H}$, an enhanced public key encryption PKE, and some zero-knowledge protocols.

Our approach intuitively follows the sign-then-encrypt paradigm [10], in which a standard signature is encrypted by an IND-CPA-secure PKE scheme. Therefore, the decryption has the role of converting undeniable signatures to ordinary ones. To efficiently realize selective conversion, we require the extraction property of the PKE scheme.

To ensure (strong) unforgeablity, we encrypt *both* the standard signature and the randomness used in encryption. To see why this is necessary, imagine an adversary generating a valid signature-message pair (m, σ') from (m, σ) honestly produced by the signer, which is expectedly an easy task since the PKE is just IND-CPA-secure (and hence malleable). Now the adversary can learn the validity of (m, σ) by simply executing confirmation/disavowal protocol with (m, σ').

However the above method induces a problem: the encrypted message now depends on the randomness used in encryption. Usually, IND-CPA security notion is guaranteed only if the encrypted message and the randomness are chosen independently. Fortunately, the chameleon hash function comes to rescue us from this situation, making the encrypted message independent of the randomness.

It is interesting to ask why IND-CCA-secure PKE schemes are not used to ensure unforgeability. Certainly, with an IND-CCA-secure scheme, it is hard for the adversary to create σ' from σ with a relation as above. However, IND-CCA schemes are quite complex, and it seems hard to construct efficient confirmation and disavowal protocols with such ingredients.

It is worth noting that El Aimani in [12], also with the sign-then-encrypt approach, gives a general construction of designated confirmer signatures. El Aimani makes no use of chameleon hash functions and weakly-secure signature schemes, but instead uses key encapsulation mechanisms and data encapsulation mechanisms (as in [11]). In turn, the conditions required for the ingredients are different, and so are the designs of the confirmation and disavowal protocols. No scheme whose unforgeability relies on the RSA assumption is presented in [12]. Besides the sign-then-encrypt paradigm, another interesting general approach can be found in [13].

4.1 Construction

Let $\mathbb{R}_{\text{PKE}}$ be a set of random numbers used in PKE.Enc. Our proposed scheme is described as follows.

- CUS.KGen(1^λ): Run $(pk_1, sk_1) \overset{\$}{\leftarrow} \text{PKE.KGen}(1^\lambda)$, $(pk_2, sk_2) \overset{\$}{\leftarrow} \text{wSIG.KGen}(1^\lambda)$, and pick $(H, \tau) \overset{\$}{\in} \mathcal{H}$. Output $(pk, sk) = ((pk_1, pk_2, H), (sk_1, sk_2, H))$.
- CUS.USign(sk, m): Pick $r \overset{\$}{\in} \mathbb{R}_{\text{PKE}}$ and $s \overset{\$}{\in} \mathbb{R}_H$. Compute the weakly-secure signature $\rho \leftarrow \text{wSIG.Sign}(sk_2, H(m \| f(pk_1, r), s))$, and $c \leftarrow \text{PKE.Enc}(pk_1, \rho; r)$. Output $\sigma = (s, c)$.
- CUS.sConvert($sk, m, \sigma = (s, c)$): Compute $r = \text{PKE.Ext}(sk_1, c)$ and $\rho = \text{PKE.Dec2}(pk_1, c, r)$. Return $cvt = r$ if $\text{wSIG.Vrf}(pk_2, H(m \| F(pk_1, c), s), \rho) = 1$. Otherwise return $\bot$.
- CUS.aConvert(sk): Output $Acvt = sk_1$.

- CUS.Vrf $(pk, m, \sigma = (s, c), cvt)$: Compute

$$h = H(m\|F(pk_1, c), s), \rho = \mathsf{PKE.Dec2}(pk_1, c, cvt),$$

and return 1 if wSIG.Vrf $(pk_2, h, \rho) = 1$.

- CUS.UVrf $(pk, m, \sigma = (s, c), Acvt)$: Compute $h = H(m\|F(pk_1, c), s), \rho = \mathsf{PKE.Dec}(Acvt, c)$. Return 1 if wSIG.Vrf $(pk_2, h, \rho) = 1$.

- CUS.Confirmation: Given common input $(pk, m, \sigma = (s, c))$, the signer computes $r = \mathsf{PKE.Ext}(sk_1, c)$ and $\rho = \mathsf{PKE.Dec}(sk_1, c)$, and executes the zero-knowledge proof of knowledge (PoK) protocol

$$\mathrm{PoK}\left\{(\rho, r) : \begin{array}{l} c = \mathsf{PKE.Enc}(pk_1, \rho; r) \\ \wedge \quad \mathsf{wSIG.Vrf}(pk_2, H(m\|F(pk_1, c), s), \rho) = 1 \end{array}\right\}.$$

- CUS.Disavowal: Similarly to confirmation protocol, the signer executes the zero-knowledge proof of knowledge protocol

$$\mathrm{PoK}\left\{(\rho, r) : \begin{array}{l} c = \mathsf{PKE.Enc}(pk_1, \rho; r) \\ \wedge \quad \mathsf{wSIG.Vrf}(pk_2, H(m\|F(pk_1, c), s), \rho) \neq 1 \end{array}\right\}.$$

We can replace the above PoK with the following, if the standard signature scheme is deterministic.

$$\mathrm{PoK}\left\{(\rho_1, \rho_2, r) : \begin{array}{l} \rho_1 \neq \rho_2 \wedge c = \mathsf{PKE.Enc}(pk_1, \rho_1; r) \\ \wedge \quad \mathsf{wSIG.Vrf}(pk_2, H(m\|F(pk_1, c), s), \rho_2) = 1 \end{array}\right\}.$$

Remark. In selective conversion, we mainly deal with valid signatures, which is sufficient for applications such as [3]. The reasoning behind is that in such applications, the confirmation protocol is always run before the selective conversion step. The above treatment is usually used in most papers in the literature.

However, with our construction, we can even convert invalid signatures. Namely, in CUS.sConvert, the value $r = \mathsf{PKE.Ext}(sk_1, c)$ is simply published. When verifying, one first checks $F(pk_1, c) = f(pk_1, r)$, and announces that the converter is incorrect if the equation does not hold; otherwise return the bit wSIG.Vrf $(pk_2, H(m\|F(pk_1, c), s), \rho)$ indicating valid or invalid (m, σ).

4.2 Properties of Our Construction

On-line/Off-line. The proposed framework has the on-line/off-line property which is very useful when the signer can use only poor computational power (e.g., smart-card). In our scheme, the signer generates the value c for random message m' (off-line), and when a real message m is given, she generates the value s only with the computation of the trapdoor collision algorithm (on-line), which executes just simple arithmetic operations.

Convertible Undeniable Signatures with Delegation. In a convertible undeniable signature scheme *with delegation*, recently highlighted by [33], signers can delegate the confirmation and disavowal protocol to a third party.

In our proposed scheme, the signer (prover) in the confirmation/disavowal protocol needs only the secret key of the underlying PKE scheme, and the key is useless in the signing algorithm. Therefore, the signer may give it to the third party who performs, say, the confirmation protocol as in [3].

Convertible Undeniable Proxy Signatures. Our proposed scheme also can be treated as a convertible undeniable proxy signature scheme [35], in which a proxy can convert standard signatures (even previously-generated ones) to undeniable signatures. In our proposed scheme, the signer gives the secret key of the PKE scheme to the proxy, allowing him to convert standard signatures to undeniable ones. Readers may refer to [35] for details of such scheme.

4.3   Security

Theorem 1. *Suppose the underlying standard signature scheme, wSIG, is sUF-wCMA secure. Then our proposed scheme CUS is sUF-CMA secure.*

Proof. Assume that there exists forger $\mathcal{F}$ against sUF-CMA security of CUS. Let $(m_i, (s_i, c_i))$ be the i-th signing query and its answer, $(m^*, (s^*, c^*))$ be the forgery output by $\mathcal{F}$. Define $h_i = H(m_i \| F(pk_1, c_i), s_i)$, $\rho_i = \mathsf{PKE.Dec}(sk_1, c_i)$, $r_i = \mathsf{PKE.Ext}(sk_1, c_i)$. Similarly, define h^*, ρ^*, r^* from (m^*, s^*, c^*). When $\mathcal{F}$ wins sUF-CMA game, then $\mathsf{wSIG.Vrf}(pk_2, h^*, \rho^*) = 1$ and (m^*, s^*, c^*) is different from any (m_i, s_i, c_i). There are four cases in which $\mathcal{F}$ wins.

[Case 1]: $h^* \neq h_i$ holds for all i.
[Case 2]: $h^* = h_i$ holds for some i, and $(m^* \| F(pk_1, c^*), s^*) \neq (m_i \| F(pk_1, c_i), s_i)$ holds for such i.
[Case 3]: $h^* = h_i$, $m^* \| F(pk_1, c^*) = m_i \| F(pk_1, c_i)$, and $s^* = s_i$ hold for some i. In this case $c^* \neq c_i$ also holds, because $(m^*, s^*) = (m_i, s_i)$.
[Case 3-1]: For such i, $r^* = r_i$ holds. In this case, we have $\rho^* \neq \rho_i$. (If $\rho^* = \rho_i$, then $c^* = \mathsf{PKE.Enc}(pk_1, \rho^*, r^*) = \mathsf{PKE.Enc}(pk_1, \rho_i, r_i) = c_i$.)
[Case 3-2]: For such i, $r^* \neq r_i$ holds.
If the probability of Case 2 is non-negligible, we can construct an adversary which efficiently finds a collision of H (without the trapdoor). If the probability of Case 3-2 is non-negligible, we can construct an adversary which efficiently finds a collision of f. (Note that $f(pk_1, r^*) = F(pk_1, c^*) = F(pk_1, c_i) = f(pk_1, r_i)$.)

Below, we show that we can construct a forger $\mathcal{A}$ against sUF-wCMA security of wSIG, if the probability of Case 1 or Case 3-1 is non-negligible. Let q be the number of signing queries $\mathcal{F}$ issues. On input 1^λ, $\mathcal{A}$ runs as follows.

Setup: $\mathcal{A}$ chooses $(H, \tau) \overset{\$}{\in} \mathcal{H}$ and $s_i' \overset{\$}{\in} \mathbb{R}_H$, and computes $h_i = H(1, s_i')$ for all $i \in \{1, \ldots, q\}$. It then submits $(h_1, \ldots, h_q)$ and receives $(pk_2, \rho_1, \ldots, \rho_q)$. $\mathcal{A}$ runs $(pk_1, sk_1) \overset{\$}{\leftarrow} \mathsf{PKE.KGen}(1^\lambda)$ and gives (pk_1, pk_2, H) to $\mathcal{F}$.

Signing queries: Suppose $\mathcal{F}$ issues m_i as the i-th query. $\mathcal{A}$ chooses $r_i \overset{\$}{\in} \mathbb{R}_{\text{PKE}}$ and computes s_i such that $H(m_i \| f(pk_1, r_i), s_i) = H(1, s_i')(= h_i)$ holds by using a trapdoor collision algorithm with trapdoor τ. Then $\mathcal{A}$ computes $c_i = \text{PKE.Enc}(pk_1, \rho_i; r_i)$ and returns $\sigma_i = (s_i, c_i)$ to $\mathcal{F}$.

Convert queries: $\mathcal{F}$ issues $(m, \sigma = (s, c))$. If

$$\text{wSIG.Vrf}\big(pk_2, H(m \| F(pk_1, c), s), \text{PKE.Dec}(sk_1, c)\big) = 1,$$

then $\mathcal{A}$ returns $r = \text{PKE.Ext}(sk_1, c)$ to $\mathcal{F}$. Otherwise, returns $\bot$.

Confirmation/disavowal queries: When $\mathcal{F}$ issues $(m, \sigma = (s, c))$, $\mathcal{A}$ computes values $h = H(m \| F(pk_1, c), s)$ and $\rho = \text{PKE.Dec}(sk_1, c)$. If the equation $\text{wSIG.Vrf}(pk_2, h, \rho) = 1$ holds, then returns 1 and executes the confirmation protocol with $\mathcal{F}$. Otherwise, returns 0 and executes the disavowal protocol with $\mathcal{F}$. The confirmation/disavowal protocol is simulatable using rewinding technique [19], since it is zero-knowledge.

Output: Finally, $\mathcal{F}$ outputs $(m^*, (s^*, c^*))$. $\mathcal{A}$ outputs (h^*, ρ^*) as a forged pair, where $h^* = H(m^* \| F(pk_1, c^*), s^*)$ and $\rho^* = \text{PKE.Dec}(sk_1, c^*)$.

These simulations are done well because chameleon hash $\mathcal{H}$ has uniformity.

If $\mathcal{F}$ wins in Case 1, $\mathcal{A}$ wins since h^* is a new message. If $\mathcal{F}$ wins in Case 3-1, $\mathcal{A}$ wins since ρ^* is a new signature for message $h^* = h_i$.   □

Theorem 2. *Suppose the underlying enhanced public key encryption scheme, PKE, is IV-CPA secure and our proposed scheme CUS is sUF-CMA secure. Then CUS is IV-CMA secure.*

The proof will be shown in Appendix A.

5   RSA-Based Convertible Undeniable Signatures

For a concrete example of the proposed construction, we show an RSA-based convertible undeniable signature scheme, named RSA-CUS. It uses the RSA-based signature [21], the RSA-based chameleon hash [20], and the Paillier encryption [30] (as an enhanced public key encryption) and some efficient established zero-knowledge protocols [2, 9, 15, 16]. To our knowledge, it is the first (convertible) undeniable signature scheme whose unforgeability relies on the RSA assumption.

Let us first recap the building blocks.

RSA-based signature [21]:

- wSIG.KGen(1^λ): Setup the RSA-modulus $N_2 = pq$ such that $2^\ell < \phi(N_2) < 2^{\ell+2}$ (ℓ is the another parameter derived from λ) and choose $h \overset{\$}{\leftarrow} \mathbb{Z}_{N_2}^*$. Next, choose a key K of pseudo-random function $P : \{0, 1\}^* \to \{0, 1\}^\ell$, $k \overset{\$}{\in} \{0, 1\}^\ell$ and define the function G as follows.

$$G_{K,k}(z) = P_K(i, z) \oplus k,$$

where i is the minimum number such that $P_K(i, z) \oplus k$ is an odd prime. Set $pk = (N_2, h, k, K)$ and $sk = (pk, p, q)$ then return (pk, sk).

- wSIG.Sign(sk, m): Let m be n-bit message, and $m^{(i)}$ be the first i bits of m. Compute

$$e_i = G_{K,k}(m^{(i)}) \tag{1}$$

for $i = 1$ to n. Return the signature ρ computed by

$$\rho = h^{\prod_{i=1}^n e_i^{-1}} \bmod N_2.$$

- wSIG.Vrf(pk, m, ρ): Compute $e_i = G_{K,k}(m^{(i)})$ for $i = 1$ to n. Return 1 if the following equation holds.

$$h = \rho^{\prod_{i=1}^n e_i} \bmod N_2$$

Proposition 1. [21] *Suppose P is a secure pseudo-random function and the RSA assumption holds. Then the above standard signature scheme is sUF-wCMA.*

RSA-based chameleon hash [20]: Let N_2 be the RSA modulus defined above. Let e be a ℓ bits number which is relatively prime to $\phi(N_2)$, J be $J \xleftarrow{\$} \mathbb{Z}_{N_2}$. The hashing algorithm H, parametrized by (J, e, N_2), is described as follows.

$$H(m, s) = J^{H'(m)} s^e \bmod N_2,$$

where H' is a regular collision-resistant hash function whose range is $\{0, 1\}^{\frac{2\ell}{3}}$, and s is chosen from $\mathbb{Z}_{N_2}$. As a trapdoor τ, uses a factor of N_2 and d such that $ed = 1 \bmod \phi(N_2)$ holds.

Proposition 2. [20] *Suppose the RSA assumption holds. Then the above chameleon hash signature scheme satisfies properties noted in Section 3.2.*

The DNR assumption and Paillier encryption scheme: Let $\mathcal{K}_{dnr}(1^\lambda)$ be the DNR key generator which outputs (N_1, p_1, q_1) where $|N_1| = \lambda$, $N_1 = p_1 \times q_1$ and p_1, q_1 are distinct primes of same length.

The Paillier encryption scheme consists of following algorithms. PKE.KGen(1^λ) runs $\mathcal{K}_{dnr}(1^\lambda)$ and outputs $(pk_1 = N_1, sk_1 = (p_1, p_2))$. PKE.Enc$(pk, m \in \mathbb{Z}_{N_1})$ chooses $r \xleftarrow{\$} \mathbb{Z}_{N_1}^*$ and encrypts as

$$\mathsf{PKE.Enc}(pk, m; r) = r^{N_1}(1 + mN_1) \bmod N_1^2.$$

PKE.Dec(sk_1, c) first solves $c = r^{N_1} \bmod N_1$ for $r \in \mathbb{Z}_{N_1}^*$ and then computes m as $((c(r^{-1})^{N_1} \bmod N_1^2) - 1)/N_1$ over the integers.

In addition to above algorithms, we offer some functions and algorithms for an enhanced public key encryption. The functions (f, F) are defined as $f(N_1, r) = r^{N_1} \bmod N_1$, $F(N_1, c) = c \bmod N_1$, respectively. Extraction algorithm PKE.Ext(sk, c) outputs r where $c \bmod N_1 = r^{N_1} \bmod N_1$. Alternative decryption algorithm PKE.Dec2(pk, c, r) computes m as $((r^{-1})^{N_1}c - 1 \bmod N_1^2)/N_1 = m \bmod N_1$ in the same way of the decryption algorithm. We remark that the function $f(pk_1, \cdot)$ has the collision resistance property since it is bijective.

We now describe the DNR assumption. For distinguisher $\mathcal{D}$ against $\mathcal{K}_{dnr}$, the advantage is defined as follows.

$$
\mathbf{Adv}^{\mathrm{DNR}}(\mathcal{D}) = \left| \Pr \left[\begin{array}{c} (N_1, p_1, q_1) \leftarrow \mathcal{K}_{dnr}(1^\lambda); r^* \xleftarrow{\$} \mathbb{Z}^*_{N_1}; \\ Y_0 \leftarrow (r^*)^{N_1} \bmod N_1^2; Y_1 \xleftarrow{\$} \mathbb{Z}^*_{N_1^2}; \quad : b' = b \\ b \xleftarrow{\$} \{0,1\}; b' \leftarrow \mathcal{D}(1^\lambda, N_1, Y_b) \end{array} \right] - \frac{1}{2} \right|.
$$

Definition 7. *The DNR assumption asserts that the above advantage is negligible in λ for every PPT distinguisher $\mathcal{D}$.*

Since $\mathsf{PKE.Enc}(pk_1, \cdot; \cdot)$ is bijective, c is uniformly at random in its space where c is the encryption of $m \xleftarrow{\$} \mathbb{Z}_{N_1}$ and $r \xleftarrow{\$} \mathbb{Z}^*_{N_1}$. Therefore, we can show the next theorem.

Theorem 3. *The above enhanced public key encryption scheme is IV-CPA secure under the DNR assumption.*

Implementation of confirmation/disavowal protocol: The confirmation and disavowal protocol make use of the following ingredients. (See Appendix B for detail.)

- Fujisaki-Okamoto commitment scheme [9, 15]. We denote a commitment of x by $\mathsf{Com}(x)$.
- Proof of modular polynomial relation [15], which allows the signer to convince the verifier that committed $x_1, \ldots, x_t$ satisfy $poly(x_1, \ldots, x_t) \bmod n = 0$.
- Proof of interval [2], which ensures that committed x is in a certain interval $[a, b]$.

Confirmation protocol.
The common input is $(pk, m, \sigma = (s, c))$, and the (signer's) witness is (r, ρ). The signer first commits the witness by sending $E_0 = \mathsf{Com}(r)$ and $E_1 = \mathsf{Com}(\rho)$. Then the signer executes following proofs of knowledge protocols.

1. $\mathrm{PoK}\{(r) : E_0 = \mathsf{Com}(r) \wedge r \in [1, N_1 - 1]\}$
2. $\mathrm{PoK}\{(\rho) : E_1 = \mathsf{Com}(\rho) \wedge \rho \in [1, N_2 - 1]\}$
3. $\mathrm{PoK}\{(r, \rho) : E_0 = \mathsf{Com}(r) \wedge E_1 = \mathsf{Com}(\rho) \wedge c = r^{N_1}(1 + \rho N_1) \bmod N_1^2\}$
4. $\mathrm{PoK}\{(\rho) : E_1 = \mathsf{Com}(\rho) \wedge h = \rho^{\prod_{i=1}^n e_i} \bmod N_2\}$ (for primes e_i computed by $\mathsf{wSIG.Sign}$ as used in $\mathsf{CUS.USign}$)

Disavowal protocol.
The common input is $(pk, m, \sigma = (s, c))$. The witness is $(r, \rho_1, \rho_2, \widehat{\rho})$, where ρ_1 is decryption of c, ρ_2 is a signature of m, and $\widehat{\rho} = \rho_1 - \rho_2$. The signer sends commitments of the witness similar to the confirmation protocol. Then the signer executes following proofs of knowledge protocols (employing the second way of disavowal since we are using a deterministic standard signature scheme).

1. $\mathrm{PoK}\{(r) : E_0 = \mathsf{Com}(r) \wedge r \in [1, N_1 - 1]\}$
2. $\mathrm{PoK}\{(\rho_1) : E_1 = \mathsf{Com}(\rho_1) \wedge \rho_1 \in [1, N_2 - 1]\}$
3. $\mathrm{PoK}\{(\rho_2) : E_2 = \mathsf{Com}(\rho_2) \wedge \rho_2 \in [1, N_2 - 1]\}$

4. $\mathrm{PoK}\{(\widehat{\rho}) : E_3 = \mathrm{Com}(\widehat{\rho}) \wedge \widehat{\rho} \in [1, N_2 - 1]\}$
5. $\mathrm{PoK}\{(r, \rho_1) : E_0 = \mathrm{Com}(r) \wedge E_1 = \mathrm{Com}(\rho_1) \wedge c = r^{N_1}(1 + \rho_1 N_1) \bmod N_1^2\}$
6. $\mathrm{PoK}\{(\rho_2) : E_2 = \mathrm{Com}(\rho_2) \wedge h = \rho_2^{\prod_{i=1}^{n} e_i} \bmod N_2\}$
7. $\mathrm{PoK}\{(\rho_1, \rho_2, \widehat{\rho}) : E_1 = \mathrm{Com}(\rho_1) \wedge E_2 = \mathrm{Com}(\rho_2) \wedge E_3 = \mathrm{Com}(\widehat{\rho}) \wedge \widehat{\rho} = \rho_1 - \rho_2 \bmod N_2\}$

Using the ingredients described above, the costs of the protocols are at most $\mathcal{O}(\lambda^3)$ with respect to both computation (in term of modular multiplications) and communication (in term of bits).

Combining the above building blocks with the proposed framework, we obtain a concrete scheme, RSA-CUS. From Theorems 1 and 2, we have the following result.

Theorem 4. *If the RSA assumption holds, then RSA-CUS is sUF-CMA secure. If the DNR assumption holds, then RSA-CUS is IV-CMA secure.*

Acknowledgment

The second author thanks Laila El Aimani for fruitful discussions. Thanks also go to the anonymous reviewers for feedback and comments, to which we have also given responses in this proceedings version.

References

1. Ateniese, G., Medeiros, B.: Identity-based chameleon hash and applications. In: Juels, A. (ed.) FC 2004. LNCS, vol. 3110, pp. 164–180. Springer, Heidelberg (2004)
2. Boudot, F.: Efficient Proofs that a Committed Number Lies in an Interval. In: Preneel, B. (ed.) EUROCRYPT 2000. LNCS, vol. 1807, pp. 431–444. Springer, Heidelberg (2000)
3. Boyd, C., Foo, E.: Off-line fair payment protocols using convertible signatures. In: Ohta, K., Pei, D. (eds.) ASIACRYPT 1998. LNCS, vol. 1514, pp. 271–285. Springer, Heidelberg (1998)
4. Boyar, J., Chaum, D., Damgard, I., Pedersen, T.: Convertible undeniable signatures. In: Menezes, A., Vanstone, S.A. (eds.) CRYPTO 1990. LNCS, vol. 537, pp. 189–208. Springer, Heidelberg (1991)
5. Chaum, D.: Zero-knowledge undeniable signatures. In: De Santis, A. (ed.) EUROCRYPT 1994. LNCS, vol. 950, pp. 458–464. Springer, Heidelberg (1995)
6. Chaum, D., van Heijst, E., Pfitzmann, B.: Crypto-graphically strong undeniable signatures, unconditionally secure for the signer. In: Feigenbaum, J. (ed.) CRYPTO 1991. LNCS, vol. 576, pp. 470–484. Springer, Heidelberg (1992)
7. Chaum, D., Antwerpen, H.V.: Undeniable signatures. In: Brassard, G. (ed.) CRYPTO 1989. LNCS, vol. 435, pp. 212–216. Springer, Heidelberg (1990)
8. Chaum, T., Pedersen, T.P.: Wallet databases with observers. In: Brickell, E.F. (ed.) CRYPTO 1992. LNCS, vol. 740, pp. 89–105. Springer, Heidelberg (1993)
9. Damgård, I., Fujisaki, E.: A Statistically-Hiding Integer Commitment Scheme Based on Groups with Hidden Order. In: Zheng, Y. (ed.) ASIACRYPT 2002. LNCS, vol. 2501, pp. 125–142. Springer, Heidelberg (2002)

10. Damgård, I., Pedersen, T.: New convertible undeniable signature schemes. In: Maurer, U.M. (ed.) EUROCRYPT 1996. LNCS, vol. 1070, pp. 372–386. Springer, Heidelberg (1996)
11. El Aimani, L.: Toward a generic construction of universally convertible undeniable signatures from pairing-based signatures. In: Chowdhury, D.R., Rijmen, V., Das, A. (eds.) INDOCRYPT 2008. LNCS, vol. 5365, pp. 145–157. Springer, Heidelberg (2008)
12. El Aimani, L.: On Generic Constructions of Designated Confirmer Signatures. In: Roy, B., Sendrier, N. (eds.) INDOCRYPT 2009. LNCS, vol. 5922, pp. 343–362. Springer, Heidelberg (2009), http://eprint.iacr.org/2009/403
13. El Aimani, L.: Efficient Confirmer Signatures from the Signature of a Commitment Paradigm, Cryptology ePrint Archive, Report 2009/435 (2009), http://eprint.iacr.org/, (accepted to ProvSec 2010)
14. El Aimani, L.: Anonymity from Public Key Encryption to Undeniable Signatures. In: Preneel, B. (ed.) AFRICACRYPT 2009. LNCS, vol. 5580, pp. 217–234. Springer, Heidelberg (2009)
15. Fujisaki, E., Okamoto, T.: Statistical Zero Knowledge Protocols to Prove Modular Polynomial Relations. In: Kaliski Jr., B.S. (ed.) CRYPTO 1997. LNCS, vol. 1294, pp. 16–30. Springer, Heidelberg (1997)
16. Fujisaki, E., Okamoto, T.: Statistical Zero Knowledge Protocols to Prove Modular Polynomial Relations. IEICE Trans. Fundamental E82-A(1), 81–92 (1999)
17. Galbraith, S.D., Mao, W.: Invisibility and Anonymity of Undeniable and Confirmer Signatures. In: Joye, M. (ed.) CT-RSA 2003. LNCS, vol. 2612, pp. 80–97. Springer, Heidelberg (2003)
18. Gennaro, R., Krawczyk, H., Rabin, T.: RSA based undeniable signatures. In: Kaliski Jr., B.S. (ed.) CRYPTO 1997. LNCS, vol. 1294, pp. 132–149. Springer, Heidelberg (1997)
19. Goldreich, O., Oren, Y.: Definitions and properties of zero-knowledge proof systems. Journal of Cryptology 7(1), 1–32 (1994)
20. Hohenberger, S., Waters, B.: Realizing hash-and-sign signatures under standard assumptions. In: Joux, A. (ed.) EUROCRYPT 2009. LNCS, vol. 5479, pp. 333–350. Springer, Heidelberg (2010)
21. Hohenberger, S., Waters, B.: Short and Stateless Signatures from the RSA Assumption. In: Halevi, S. (ed.) Advances in Cryptology - CRYPTO 2009. LNCS, vol. 5677, pp. 654–670. Springer, Heidelberg (2009)
22. Huang, Q., Wong, D.S.: New constructions of convertible undeniable signature schemes without random oracles. Cryptology ePrint Archive, Report 2009/517 (2009), http://eprint.iacr.org/
23. Jakobsson, M., Sako, K., Impagliazzo, R.: Designated verifier proofs and their applications. In: Maurer, U.M. (ed.) EUROCRYPT 1996. LNCS, vol. 1070, pp. 143–154. Springer, Heidelberg (1996)
24. Kurosawa, K., Heng, S.H.: Relations among security notions for undeniable signature schemes. In: De Prisco, R., Yung, M. (eds.) SCN 2006. LNCS, vol. 4116, pp. 34–48. Springer, Heidelberg (2006)
25. Krawczyk, H., Rabin, T.: Chameleon signatures. In: Proc. of Network and Distributed System Security Symposium 2000, pp. 143–154 (2000)
26. Kurosawa, K., Takagi, T.: New approach for selectively convertible undeniable signature schemes. In: Lai, X., Chen, K. (eds.) ASIACRYPT 2006. LNCS, vol. 4284, pp. 428–443. Springer, Heidelberg (2006)
27. Michels, M., Petersen, H., Horster, P.: Breaking and Repairing a Convertible Undeniable Signature Scheme. In: ACM CCS 1996, pp. 148–152 (1996)

28. Ogata, W., Kurosawa, K., Heng, S.-H.: The security of the FDH variant of Chaum's undeniable signature scheme. IEEE Transactions on Information Theory 52(5), 2006–2017 (2006)
29. Paillier, P.: Public-key cryptosystems based on composite degree residuosity classes. In: Stern, J. (ed.) EUROCRYPT 1999. LNCS, vol. 1592, pp. 223–238. Springer, Heidelberg (1999)
30. Pointcheval, D.: Self-scrambling anonymizers. In: Frankel, Y. (ed.) FC 2000. LNCS, vol. 1962, pp. 259–275. Springer, Heidelberg (2001)
31. Phong, L.T., Kurosawa, K., Ogata, W.: New dlog-based convertible undeniable signature schemes in the standard model, Cryptology ePrint Archive, Report 2009/394 (2009), http://eprint.iacr.org/
32. Phong, L.T., Kurosawa, K., Ogata, W.: New RSA-based (selectively) Convertible Undeniable Signature Schemes. IEICE Trans. Fundamental E93-A(1), 63–75 (2010)
33. Jacob, C., Schuldt, N., Matsuura, K.: An Efficient Convertible Undeniable Signature Scheme with Delegatable Verification, Cryptology ePrint Archive, Report 2009/454 (2009), http://eprint.iacr.org/ (to appear in ISPEC 2010)
34. Yuen, T.H., Au, M.H., Liu, J.K., Susilo, W. (Convertible) undeniable signatures without random oracles. In: Qing, S., Imai, H., Wang, G. (eds.) ICICS 2007. LNCS, vol. 4861, pp. 83–97. Springer, Heidelberg (2007)
35. Wu, W., Mu, Y., Susilo, W., Huang, X.: Convertible Undeniable Proxy Signatures: Security Models and Efficient Construction. In: Kim, S., Yung, M., Lee, H.-W. (eds.) WISA 2007. LNCS, vol. 4867, pp. 16–29. Springer, Heidelberg (2008)

A   Proof of Theorem 2

Assume that there exists distinguisher $\mathcal{D}$ against the IV-CMA security of CUS. In IV-CMA game, we define Forge as the event that $\mathcal{D}$ issues a valid pair to the confirmation/disavowal or convert oracle, and it is not a query-answer pair of the signing oracle. Then

$$\Pr[\mathcal{D} \text{ wins IV-CMA game}] - 1/2$$
$$= \Pr[\mathcal{D} \text{ wins} \wedge \text{Forge occurs}] + \Pr[\mathcal{D} \text{ wins} \wedge \text{Forge does not occur}] - 1/2$$
$$\leq \Pr[\text{Forge occurs}] + \Pr[\mathcal{D} \text{ wins} \mid \text{Forge does not occur}] - 1/2.$$

We will show that

(1) if $\epsilon_1 = \Pr[\text{Forge occurs}]$ is not negligible, we can construct a forger, $\mathcal{F}$, which breaks the sUF-CMA security of CUS with probability ϵ_1 by using $\mathcal{D}$ as a subroutine,

(2) if $\epsilon_2 = |\Pr[\mathcal{D} \text{ wins} \mid \text{Forge does not occur}] - 1/2|$ is not negligible, we can construct a distinguisher, $\mathcal{A}$, whose advantage is $\mathbf{Adv}_{\mathsf{PKE}}^{\mathrm{IV-CPA}}(\mathcal{A}) = \epsilon_2$.

(1) We construct $\mathcal{F}$ as follows. At first $\mathcal{F}$ obtains pk, which is inputted to $\mathcal{D}$. When $\mathcal{D}$ makes an oracle query, $\mathcal{F}$ passes the query to own oracle, obtains the answer, and returns it to $\mathcal{D}$. When Forge occurs, i.e., $\mathcal{D}$ issues (m, σ) to the convert or confirmation/disavowal oracle and $\mathcal{F}$'s oracle tells that it is a valid pair, then $\mathcal{F}$ outputs (m, σ) as a forged pair. If $\mathcal{F}$ issues challenge query m^* before $\mathcal{F}$ outputs

a forged pair, then $\mathcal{F}$ flips a coin b. If $b = 0$, $\mathcal{F}$ makes a signing query m^*, and returns its answer σ^* to $\mathcal{F}$. If $b = 1$, returns a random signature to $\mathcal{F}$.

Until Forge occurs, this simulation is perfect. Further, $\mathcal{F}$ wins sUF-CMA game if Forge occurs before $\mathcal{D}$ halts. Therefore,

$$\Pr[\mathcal{F} \text{ wins sUF-CMA game}] = \Pr[\text{Forge occurs}].$$

(2) Next, we construct $\mathcal{A}$ against the IV-CPA security of PKE. $\mathcal{A}$'s input is pk_1.

Setup: $\mathcal{A}$ runs $(pk_2, sk_2) \xleftarrow{\$} \text{wSIG.KGen}(1^\lambda)$, chooses $(H, \tau) \xleftarrow{\$} \mathcal{H}$ and gives (pk_1, pk_2, H) to $\mathcal{D}$. Furthermore, $\mathcal{A}$ initializes a list $Q = \phi$.

Signing queries: When $\mathcal{D}$ issues message m, $\mathcal{A}$ computes a signature, σ, by using the signing algorithm. Returns σ to $\mathcal{D}$, and sets $Q = Q \cup \{(m, \sigma, r, \rho)\}$, where r and ρ are the values it obtained in the signing algorithm.

Convert queries: When $\mathcal{D}$ issues (m, σ), $\mathcal{A}$ returns r to $\mathcal{D}$ if there exists (r, ρ) such that $(m, \sigma, r, \rho) \in Q$. Otherwise, returns $\bot$.

Confirmation/disavowal queries: $\mathcal{D}$ issues (m, σ). If there exists (r, ρ) such that $(m, \sigma, r, \rho) \in Q$, $\mathcal{A}$ returns 1 and executes the confirmation protocol with $\mathcal{D}$, by using (r, ρ). Otherwise, returns 0 and executes the disavowal protocol by using rewinding technique.

Challenge queries: If $\mathcal{D}$ issues challenge message m^*, $\mathcal{A}$ chooses $s' \xleftarrow{\$} \mathbb{R}_H$, computes $\rho^* \xleftarrow{\$} \text{wSIG.Sign}(sk_2, H(0, s'))$, submits ρ^* to its challenge oracle and obtains a corresponding challenge ciphertext c^*. Next, $\mathcal{A}$ computes s^* such that $H(0, s') = H(m^* \| F(pk_1, c^*), s^*)$ holds by using the trapdoor τ. At last, $\mathcal{A}$ returns $\sigma^* = (s^*, c^*)$ to $\mathcal{D}$.

Output: Finally, $\mathcal{D}$ outputs b' as a guess. $\mathcal{A}$ directly outputs b'

If Forge does not occur, $\mathcal{D}$'s environment is the same as in IV-CMA game. Further, $\mathcal{A}$ wins IV-CPA game iff $\mathcal{D}$ wins under the condition that Forge does not occur. Therefore,

$$\epsilon_2 = |\Pr[\mathcal{D} \text{ wins} \mid \text{Forge does not occur}] - 1/2|$$
$$= |\Pr[\mathcal{A} \text{ wins IV-CPA game}] - 1/2| = \mathbf{Adv}_{\text{PKE}}^{\text{IV}-\text{CPA}}(\mathcal{A}).$$

B   Building Blocks for Confirmation/Disavowal Protocol

Fujisaki-Okamoto commitment scheme [9, 15] : The commitment of $x \in [0, N - 1]$ for $|N| = \lambda$ is defined as $\text{Com}(x; r) = b_0^x b_1^r \bmod N$ where $b_0, b_1 \in \mathbb{Z}_N^*$ and $r \xleftarrow{\$} [0, 2^\lambda N)$. The parameters, (N, b_0, b_1), are set up by the verifier or trusted third party so that the committer does not know the factor of N. Please refer to the papers [9, 15] for precise description of setup. This commitment scheme has statistically hiding and computationally binding under factoring assumption. We will omit r to describe the commitment, and just write $\text{Com}(x)$.

Proof of modular polynomial relation [15] : Fujisaki and Okamoto showed how to efficiently implement

$$\text{PoK}\left\{(x_1, \ldots, x_t) : \begin{array}{l} E_1 = \text{Com}(x_1) \wedge \cdots \wedge E_t = \text{Com}(x_t), \\ poly(x_1, x_2, \ldots, x_t) = 0 \bmod n \end{array}\right\},$$

where *poly* is a polynomial function with degree d. Briefly speaking, the committer and the verifier first agree parameter N, n and function *poly*. Second the committer commits $x_1, \ldots, x_t \in [0, N-1]$ and sends the commitments $E_1 = \text{Com}(x_1), \ldots, E_t = \text{Com}(x_t)$ to the verifier. After that, the committer proves to the verifier that the committed values satisfy the following modular polynomial relation $poly(x_1, \ldots, x_t) = 0 \bmod n$. Remark that n only have to satisfy $|n| = \mathcal{O}(\lambda)$, so may differ from N. The costs of both computation and communication are $\mathcal{O}(\lambda \cdot \log_2 d)$ in term of modular multiplications and bits respectively.

Proof of interval [2] : Boudot showed how to efficiently implement $\text{PoK}\{(x) : E = \text{Com}(x) \wedge x \in [a, b]\}$ [2]. The computation and communication costs are estimated as $\mathcal{O}(\lambda)$.

Efficient Confirmer Signatures from the "Signature of a Commitment" Paradigm*

Laila El Aimani

b-it, Dahlmannstr. 2, Universität Bonn, 53113 Bonn, Germany
elaimani@bit.uni-bonn.de

Abstract. Generic constructions of designated confirmer signatures follow one of the following two strategies; either produce a digital signature on the message to be signed, then encrypt the resulting signature, or produce a commitment on the message, encrypt the string used to generate the commitment and finally sign the latter. We study the second strategy by determining the exact security property needed in the encryption to achieve secure constructions. This study infers the exclusion of a useful type of encryption from the design due to an intrinsic weakness in the paradigm. Next, we propose a simple method to remediate to this weakness and we get efficient constructions which can be used with *any* digital signature.

Keywords: Designated Confirmer signatures, "Signature of a commitment" paradigm, Generic construction, Reduction/meta-reduction, Zero Knowledge.

1 Introduction

Digital signatures were introduced in [12] as an analogous to signatures in the paper world to seize most properties needed in a signature, for instance, the universal verification. However, in some applications, the signer might want to restrain the holder of a signature from convincing other parties of the validity of the signature in question. A typical example is a software vendor willing to embed signatures in his products such that only paying customers are entitled to check the authenticity of these products. Undeniable signatures, introduced in [9], provide a solution to this problem as they are: 1. only verified with the help of the signer, 2. non-transferable, 3. binding in the sense that a signer cannot deny a signature he has actually issued. The only drawback of these signatures is that unavailability of the signer obstructs the entire process. To overcome this problem, designated confirmer signatures were introduced in [7], where the confirmation/denial of a signature is delegated to a *designated confirmer*. With this solution, the signer can confirm only signatures he has just generated, whilst the confirmer can confirm/deny any signature. Actually, in the literature, there

---

* This is an extended abstract. The full version [19] is available at the Cryptology ePrint Archive, Report 2009/435.

S.-H. Heng and K. Kurosawa (Eds.): ProvSec 2010, LNCS 6402, pp. 87–101, 2010.

is a clear separation between confirmer signatures and *directed signatures* [21], which share the same concept as confirmer signatures with the exception of allowing both the signer and the confirmer to confirm/deny signatures. Finally, a desirable property in designated confirmer signatures is the convertibility of the signatures to ordinary ones. Indeed, such a property turned out to play a central role in fair payment protocols or in contract signing [4,16].

1.1   Related Work

Most proposals of confirmer signatures from basic primitives fall into one of the following categories:

"Encryption of a signature" approach. This approach consists in first producing a digital signature on the message to be signed, then encrypting the produced signature using a suitable cryptosystem. The construction was first formally described in [5], and required the components to meet the highest security notions (EUF-CMA signatures and IND-CCA encryption). The main weakness of the construction lies in the resort to concurrent zero knowledge (ZK) protocols of general NP statements in the confirmation/denial protocol. Later, the construction in [16] managed to circumvent the problem by encrypting the digital signature during the confirmation protocol. With this trick, the authors managed to get rid of concurrent ZK proofs of general NP statements in the confirmation protocol (the denial protocol still suffers the recourse to such proofs), but at the expense of the security and the length of the resulting signatures. Another construction implementing this principle is given in [10]; the construction uses cryptosystems with labels and is analyzed in a more elaborate security model. However, it is supplied with only one efficient instantiation as the confirmation/denial protocols still resort to concurrent ZK protocols of general NP statements. Finally, the last proposal in this category is given in [20], where the author proposes a construction using certain cryptosystems that are required to be only IND-CPA secure. As a consequence, the confirmation/denial protocols are rendered efficient in case the construction is instantiated from a specific class of signature schemes (similar to the one considered in [16]). Moreover, the resulting confirmer signatures are very efficient and they enjoy strong security properties. However, although the considered class of signatures includes most proposals that appeared in the literature, there exist some schemes which do not seem to belong to it, e.g., the PSS signature scheme [2].

"Signature of a commitment" approach. This technique consists in generating a commitment on the message to be signed, then signing the produced commitment using a digital signature scheme. The confirmer signature is comprised of both the commitment and the signature. The first proposal that realizes this principle is [22] where a construction of confirmer signatures from digital signatures obtained from the Fiat-Shamir paradigm is presented. Thus, the resulting confirmer signatures can be only proven secure in the random oracle model (ROM), inheriting this property from the use of the Fiat-Shamir paradigm, which constitutes their major shortcoming. Moreover, the construction does not support conversion. In [15] and [24], a construction which supports the conversion of the signatures and applies to *any* digital signature scheme was proposed. The key idea resides in augmenting the confirmer signature (comprised of the commitment and a signature on it) by the encryption of the random string used to generate the commitment. Although the confirmation/denial protocols involve general ZK proofs since the confirmer has to prove in concurrent ZK the knowledge of the decryption of an IND-CCA encryption and of a string used for commitment, the construction accepts an efficient instantiation using Camenisch-Shoup's verifiable encryption scheme [6] and Pedersen's commitment scheme. It is worth mentioning that the idea underlying the constructions in [15] and [24] already existed under the name "Commit then Encrypt then Sign Paradigm", and was used in the context of signcryption in [1].

In this paper, we revisit the second approach. In fact, efficient as the first approach is, it still applies only to a restricted class of signatures. This is clearly manifested in the constructions in [16] or [20] which do not seem to be plausible with the signature PSS [2]. Our goal is to further improve the "commit then sign" method in terms of efficiency and security by allowing more efficient instantiations of the encryption and commitment schemes used as building blocks.

1.2 Contributions

We make three contributions. First, we revisit the constructions implementing the "signature of a commitment" paradigm, i.e., [15,24]. We prove that indistinguishability under a *plaintext checking attack* is a minimal and sufficient requirement on the cryptosystem underlying the construction in order to achieve secure confirmer signatures. We conclude that, although we manage to weaken the assumption on the encryption from IND-CCA (needed in [1,15,24]) to IND-PCA, the construction still cannot allow homomorphic encryption in the design which is unfortunate since such an encryption proved to possess efficient ZK protocols for proving the knowledge of the plaintext underlying a given ciphertext, and such a property is profoundly needed in the confirmation/denial protocols.

Second, we show that using a small trick that consists in producing the digital signature on the commitment *concatenated with the encryption of the string used in the commitment* suffices to make the security needed in the encryption drop drastically to being only IND-CPA secure. The key idea is to remark that the original construction is not strongly unforgeable, i.e., one can produce a valid confirmer signature without the help of the signer, which explains the need for PCA security to handle such signatures. With the small trick, we are able to annihilate this weakness and allow a weak encryption in the design without compromising the overall security. As a result, we achieve better performances and more efficient instantiations of the construction (instead of using only Camenisch-Shoup's encryption and Pedersen's commitment) by allowing homomorphic encryption.

Finally, our last contribution sheds light on a particular sub-case of the "signature of a commitment" paradigm, which consists in using IND-CPA encryption instead of the commitment scheme. In fact, it is well known that IND-CPA encryption yields secure commitment schemes, which makes such an instantiation plausible. However, the bright side of this technique consists in not requiring the encryption of the random string anymore. This method clearly improves the original paradigm, however it necessitates efficient non-interactive proofs of knowledge. This is no longer a problem nowadays due to the progress made recently in this area, e.g., [11,18].

We stress that all our constructions of confirmer signatures in the present paper investigate the invisibility (the hardness of distinguishing signatures based on the underlying messages) of the resulting signatures in the *outsider* security model. I.e., we disallow the adversary to know the private key of the signer, oppositely to the *insider* security model considered in [1,15,24]. However, our constructions contrarily to those in [1,15,24] allow the signer to sign the same message many times without loss of invisibility. This property is deeply needed in liscencing software for instance.

2   Convertible Designated Confirmer Signatures (CDCS)

In this section, we present the model of CDCS we adhere to in our constructions. We refer to the full version [19] for the necessary cryptographic primitives that will come into use, that are, digital signatures, public key encryption schemes, commitment schemes, and finally Σ protocols.

2.1   Syntax

A CDCS scheme consists of the following procedures:

Key generation. Generates probabilistically key pairs $(\mathsf{sk}_S, \mathsf{pk}_S)$ and $(\mathsf{sk}_C, \mathsf{pk}_C)$ for the signer and for the confirmer respectively, consisting of the private and of the public key.

ConfirmedSign. On input sk_S, pk_S, pk_C and a message m, the signer outputs a confirmer signature μ, then he (the signer) interacts with the signature recipient to convince him of the validity of μ.

Confirmation/Denial protocol. These are interactive protocols between the confirmer and a verifier. Their common input consists of, in addition to pk_S and pk_C, the alleged signature μ, and the message m in question. The confirmer uses his private key sk_C to convince the verifier of the validity (invalidity) of the signature μ on m. At the end, the verifier either accepts or rejects the proof.

Selective conversion. This is an algorithm run by the confirmer using sk_C, in addition to pk_C and pk_S. The result is either $\perp$ or a string which allows the signature to be universally verified as a valid digital signature.

Remark 1. Sometimes, we require the confirmer to prove (interactively) the correctness of the conversion. The constructions in the present work extend readily to this model as such a proof consists of a protocol that proves a certain ciphertext to decrypt to a given message.

2.2   Security Model

The above algorithms and protocols must be correct and complete resp. Moreover, a CDCS scheme should meet the following properties:

Security for the verifier. This property informally means that an adversary who compromises the private keys of both the signer and the confirmer cannot convince the verifier of the validity (invalidity) of an invalid (a valid) confirmer signature. That is, the protocols confirmedSign, confirmation and denial are *sound*. We refer to [15,24] for the formal definition of such a requirement.

Non-transferability of the ConfirmedSign/confirmation/denial protocols. This property requires that the transcript resulting from the interaction of the verifier with the signer/confirmer during these protocols is indistinguishable from the transcript resulting from the interaction of the verifier with a simulator (which can be rewound) which does not have the private inputs of the signer/confirmer but is allowed to do one oracle call to learn the validity/invalidity of the alleged signature w.r.t. the message in question. We refer to [5] for the formal definition (after considering the fix proposed by [10], namely, the possibility of rewinding the simulator).

Security for the signer (unforgeability). It is defined through the following game: the adversary $\mathcal{A}$ is given the public parameters of the CDCS scheme, namely pk_S and pk_C, the public key of the signer and of the confirmer resp., in addition to the private key sk_C of the confirmer. $\mathcal{A}$ is further allowed to query the signer on polynomially many messages, say q_s. At the end, $\mathcal{A}$ outputs a pair consisting of a message m, that has not been queried yet, and a string μ. $\mathcal{A}$ wins the game if μ is a valid confirmer signature on m. We say that a CDCS scheme is (t, ϵ, q_s)-EUF-CMA secure if there is no adversary, operating in time t, that wins the above game with probability greater than ϵ, where the probability is taken over the random choices of both $\mathcal{A}$ and his challenger.

Security for the confirmer (invisibility). Invisibility against a chosen message attack (INV-CMA) is defined through the following game between an attacker $\mathcal{A}$ and his challenger $\mathcal{R}$: after $\mathcal{A}$ gets the public parameters of the scheme from $\mathcal{R}$, he starts **Phase 1** where he queries the confirmedSign, confirmation/denial, and selective conversion oracles in an adaptive way. Once $\mathcal{A}$ decides that **Phase 1** is over, he outputs two messages m_0, m_1 and requests a challenge signature $\mu^\star$. $\mathcal{R}$ picks uniformly at random a bit $b \in \{0,1\}$. Then $\mu^\star$ is generated using the confirmedSign oracle on the message m_b. Next, $\mathcal{A}$ starts adaptively querying the previous oracles (**Phase 2**), with the exception of not querying $(m_i, \mu^\star)$, $i = 0, 1$, to the confirmation/denial and selective conversion oracles. At the end, $\mathcal{A}$ outputs a bit b'. He wins the game if $b = b'$. We define $\mathcal{A}$'s advantage as $\mathsf{adv}(\mathcal{A}) = |\Pr[b = b'] - \frac{1}{2}|$, where the probability is taken over the random coins of both $\mathcal{A}$ and his challenger. We say that a CDCS scheme is $(t, \epsilon, q_s, q_v, q_{sc})$-INV-CMA secure if no adversary operating in time t, issuing q_s queries to the confirmedSign oracle, q_v queries to the confirmation/denial oracles and q_{sc} queries to the selective conversion oracle wins the above game with advantage greater that ϵ.

Remark 2. – Our definition of security for the verifier and non-transferability of the confirmedSign, confirmation and denial protocols is the same provided in [5,15,24].

– We consider the *insider security model* in our definition for unforgeability. I.e., the unforgeability adversary has the private key of the confirmer at his disposal. This is justified by the need of preventing the confirmer from impersonating the signer by issuing valid signatures on his behalf.

– Our definition of invisibility, oppositely to the definitions in [5,15,24], is considered in the *outsider security model*. I.e., the adversary does not know the private key of the signer. We justify this by considering the CDCS scheme broken if the signer is corrupted or coerced. Actually, insider security might be needed in situations where we want to protect the invisibility of signatures issued by the genuine signer from an adversary who has stolen this signer's private key. However "outsider security might be all one needs" for invisibility as phrased by the authors in [1].

– Our definition of invisibility, oppositely to the definitions in [15,24], allows the signer to sign the same message many times without loss of invisibility, which is needed in liscencing software.

– In our definition of invisibility (like [5,15,24] and unlike [14]), the confirmer signature might convince the recipient that the signer was involved in the signature of some message. We refer to [15] (Section 3) for techniques that can be used by the signer to camouflage the presence of valid signatures, e.g., the signer can for instance publish a few "dummy" signatures during each time period.

3   The Plain "Signature of a Commitment" Paradigm

This paradigm was first considered in [22], then upgraded in [1] to the "Encrypt then Commit then Sign" method, which consists in first generating a random string, say r and encrypting it in e, then using r to generate a commitment c on the message to be signed, and finally producing a digital signature on the commitment c. This approach was used in the context of signcryption in [1]. Later in [15], the authors used it to build confirmer signatures and provided an efficient instantiation using Camenisch-Shoup [6]'s encryption and and Pedersen's commitment. The resulting construction was shown to be invisible in the insider security model if the underlying commitment is hiding and the underlying encryption is IND-CCA secure. However, the authors in [24] disproved this claim by exhibiting an attack against the invisibility of the construction and proposed a fix using *cryptosystems with labels*.

In the rest of this section, we describe the construction of [24] and we analyze its invisibility in the outsider security model.

3.1   The Construction in [24]

Setup. Consider a digital signature scheme Σ, an encryption scheme Γ with labels and a commitment scheme Ω.

Key generation. The signer key pair consists of $(\Sigma.\mathsf{pk}, \Sigma.\mathsf{sk})$, corresponding to the key pair of the signature scheme Σ, whereas the confirmer key pair consists of $(\Gamma.\mathsf{pk}, \Gamma.\mathsf{sk})$ which corresponds to the key pair related to Γ.

ConfirmedSign. To sign a message m, the signer first computes a commitment c on the message, then encrypts in e, under the label $m\|\Sigma.\mathsf{pk}$, the random string used for the commitment, say r, and finally, signs the commitment c using $\Sigma.\mathsf{sk}$. The confirmer signature consists of the triple $(e, c, \Sigma.\mathsf{sign}_{\Sigma.\mathsf{sk}}(c))$. Next, the signer interacts with the verifier in a protocol where he (the signer) proves in ZK the knowledge of r such that $e = \Gamma.\mathsf{encrypt}_{\Gamma.\mathsf{pk},m\|\Sigma.\mathsf{pk}}(r)$ and $c = \Omega.\mathsf{commit}(m, r)$. Such a proof is plausible to issue using the randomness used to encrypt r in e. In fact, the encryption and commitment algorithms in a cryptosystem and a commitment scheme resp. define an NP language that accepts a zero knowledge proof system.

Confirmation/Denial protocol. To confirm/deny a signature $\mu = (\mu_1, \mu_2, \mu_3)$ on a given message m, the confirmer first checks whether μ_3 is a valid digital signature on μ_2 w.r.t. $\Sigma.\mathsf{pk}$, if so, he provides a concurrent ZK proof (using his private key $\Gamma.\mathsf{sk}$) of the equality/inequality of the decryption of μ_1 and the opening value of the commitment μ_2 w.r.t. m. Again this proof is possible since every NP (co-NP in case of inequality) language accepts a zero knowledge proof system

Selective conversion. Selective conversion of a signature $\mu = (\mu_1, \mu_2, \mu_3)$ is achieved by releasing the decryption of μ_1, in case μ is valid, or the symbol $\perp$ otherwise.

This construction was shown, in [24], to provide security for the verifiers, non-transferability of the involved protocols, security for the signer if it uses an EUF-CMA secure digital signature and a binding commitment scheme, and finally it provides security for the confirmer, in the insider model, if it uses IND-CCA secure encryption with labels and a hiding commitment.

In the rest of this section, we prove that IND-PCA cryptosystems with labels are a minimal and sufficient requirement to obtain outsider security for the confirmer if the underlying commitment scheme is both binding and hiding, and the underlying signature is SEUF-CMA secure.

3.2   The Exact Invisibility of the Construction

In this subsection, we prove that IND-PCA cryptosystems with labels are a minimal and sufficient ingredient to achieve invisible signatures. Our study is similar to the one provided in [20] which analyzes the plain "encryption of a signature" paradigm. Thus, we will first exclude OW-CCA secure cryptosystems with labels from use, which will rule out automatically OW-CPA and OW-PCA cryptosystems. We do this using an efficient algorithm (a *meta-reduction*) which transforms an algorithm (*reduction*), reducing the invisibility of the confirmer signatures to the OW-CCA security of the underlying cryptosystem, to an algorithm breaking the OW-CCA security of the same cryptosystem. Hence, such a result suggests that under the assumption of the underlying cryptosystem being OW-CCA secure, there exists no such a reduction, or if it (the cryptosystem) is not OW-CCA secure, such a reduction will be useless. Next, we exclude similarly NM-CPA cryptosystems from the design, which will rule out IND-CPA encryption. The next security notion that has to be considered is IND-PCA, which turns out to be sufficient to achieve invisibility. Likewise, our impossibility results are in a first stage partial in the sense that they apply only to *key preserving* reductions, i.e., reductions which, trying to attack a property of a cryptosystem given by the public key pk, feed the invisibility adversary with the confirmer public key pk. Next, we extend the result to arbitrary reductions under some complexity assumptions on the cryptosystem in question.

Lemma 1. *Assume there exists a key-preserving reduction $\mathcal{R}$ that converts an INV-CMA adversary $\mathcal{A}$ against the above construction into a OW-CCA adversary against the underlying cryptosystem. Then, there exists a meta-reduction $\mathcal{M}$ that OW-CCA breaks the cryptosystem in question.*

As mentioned in the discussion above, the lemma claims that under the assumption of the underlying cryptosystem being OW-CCA secure, there exists no key-preserving reduction $\mathcal{R}$ that reduces OW-CCA breaking the cryptosystem in question to INV-CMA breaking the construction, or if there exists such an algorithm, the underlying cryptosystem is not OW-CCA secure, thus rendering such a reduction useless.

Proof. Let $\mathcal{R}$ be the key-preserving reduction that reduces the invisibility of the construction to the OW-CCA security of the underlying cryptosystem. We construct an algorithm $\mathcal{M}$ that uses $\mathcal{R}$ to OW-CCA break the same cryptosystem by simulating the INV-CMA adversary $\mathcal{A}$ against the construction.

Let Γ be the cryptosystem $\mathcal{M}$ is trying to attack w.r.t. a public key Γ.pk. $\mathcal{M}$ launches $\mathcal{R}$ over Γ with the same public key Γ.pk. After $\mathcal{M}$ gets the label L on which $\mathcal{R}$ wishes to be challenged, he ($\mathcal{M}$) forwards it to his own challenger. Finally, $\mathcal{M}$ gets a challenge ciphertext c, that he forwards to $\mathcal{R}$. Note that $\mathcal{M}$ is allowed to query the decryption oracle on any pair (ciphertext,label) except on the pair (c, L). Thus, all decryption queries made by $\mathcal{R}$, which are by definition different from the challenge (c, L), can be forwarded to $\mathcal{M}$'s own challenger. At some point, $\mathcal{M}$, acting as an INV-CMA attacker against the construction, will output two messages m_0, m_1 such that $L \notin \{m_0\|\Sigma.\text{pk}, m_1\|\Sigma.\text{pk}\}$, where Σ.pk is the public key of the digital signature underlying the construction. $\mathcal{M}$ gets as response a challenge signature $\mu^\star = (\mu_1^\star, \mu_2^\star, \mu_3^\star)$ which he is required to tell to which message it corresponds. Since the messages m_0 and m_1 were chosen such that the label under which is created the encryption $\mu_1^\star$ (either $m_0\|\Sigma.\text{pk}$ or $m_1\|\Sigma.\text{pk}$) is different from the challenge label L, $\mathcal{M}$ can query his decryption oracle on both pairs $(\mu_1^\star, m_0\|\Sigma.\text{pk})$ or $(\mu_1^\star, m_1\|\Sigma.\text{pk})$. Results of such queries will enable $\mathcal{M}$ to open the commitment $\mu_2^\star$, and thus check the validity of the signature $\mu^\star$ w.r.t. to one of the messages m_0 or m_1. Finally, when $\mathcal{R}$ outputs his answer, $\mathcal{M}$ will simply forward this result to his challenger.   □

Lemma 2. *Assume there exists a key-preserving reduction $\mathcal{R}$ that converts an INV-CMA adversary $\mathcal{A}$ against the above construction to an NM-CPA adversary against the underlying cryptosystem. Then, there exists a meta-reduction $\mathcal{M}$ that NM-CPA breaks the cryptosystem in question.*

We provide the proof in [19].

Thus, when the considered notions are obtained from pairing a security goal $\mathrm{GOAL} \in \{\mathrm{OW}, \mathrm{IND}, \mathrm{NM}\}$ and an attack model $\mathrm{ATK} \in \{\mathrm{CPA}, \mathrm{PCA}, \mathrm{CCA}\}$, we have

Theorem 1. *The cryptosystem underlying the above construction must be at least IND-PCA secure, in case the considered reduction is key-preserving, in order to achieve INV-CMA secure signatures.*

Similarly to the study in [20], we generalize the above theorem to arbitrary reductions if the cryptosystem underlying the construction has a *non malleable key generator* (See the full version [19])

Remark 3. Note that the above impossibility result holds true only when the considered notions are those obtained by pairing a security goal $\mathrm{GOAL} \in \{\mathrm{OW}, \mathrm{IND}, \mathrm{NM}\}$ and an attack model $\mathrm{ATK} \in \{\mathrm{CPA}, \mathrm{PCA}, \mathrm{CCA}\}$. Presence of other notions requires an additional analysis, however Lemmas 1 and 2 will still serve when there is a relation between the new notion and the notions NM-CPA and OW-CCA.

Interpretation. One way to explain the above result is to remark that the above construction is not *strongly unforgeable*. In fact, an adversary $\mathcal{A}$, given a valid signature $\mu = (\mu_1, \mu_2, \mu_3)$ on a message m, can create another valid signature μ' on m without the help of the signer as follows; $\mathcal{A}$ will first request the selective conversion of μ to obtain the decryption of μ_1, say r, which he will re-encrypt in μ_1' under the same label $m\|\Sigma.\mathsf{pk}$ ($\Sigma.\mathsf{pk}$ is the public key of the digital signature underlying the construction). Obviously $\mu' = (\mu_1', \mu_2, \mu_3)$ is also a valid confirmer signature on m that the signer did not produce, and thus cannot confirm/deny or convert without having access to a decryption oracle of the cryptosystem underlying the construction. This explains the insufficiency of notions like IND-CPA. However, we observe that an IND-CCA secure encryption is more than needed in this framework since a query of the type μ' is not completely uncontrolled by the signer. In fact, its first component μ_1' is an encryption of some data already disclosed by the signer, namely r, and thus a plaintext checking oracle is sufficient to deal with such a query if the used digital signature is SEUF-CMA secure.

Theorem 2. *The above construction is $(t, \epsilon, q_s, q_v, q_{sc})$-INV-CMA secure if it uses a (t, ϵ', q_s)-SEUF-CMA secure digital signature, a statistically-binding and (t, ϵ_c)-hiding commitment, and a $(t + (q_s + q_{sc})(q_{sc} + q_v)), \frac{1}{2}(\epsilon + \epsilon_c) \cdot (1 - \epsilon')^{(q_{sc} + q_v)},$ $q_{sc}(q_{sc} + q_v))$-IND-PCA secure cryptosystem with labels.*

We provide the proof in [19].

4   An Efficient Construction from the "Signature of a Commitment" Paradigm

One simple way to eliminate the strong forgeability in signatures from the plain "signature of a commitment" technique consists in producing a digital signature on both the commitment and the encryption of the random string used in it. In this way, the attack discussed before Theorem 2 no longer applies, since an adversary will need to produce a digital signature on the commitment and the re-encryption of the random string used in it. Note that such a fix already appears in the construction of [15]. However it was not exploitable as the invisibility was considered in the insider model.

4.1   Construction

Let Σ be a signature scheme given by Σ.keygen that generates $(\Sigma$.pk, Σ.sk$)$, Σ.sign and Σ.verify. Let further Γ denote a cryptosystem given by Γ.keygen that generates $(\Gamma$.pk, Γ.sk$)$, Γ.encrypt and Γ.decrypt. We note that Γ does not need to support labels in our construction. Finally let Ω denote a commitment scheme given by Ω.commit and Ω.open. We assume that Γ produces ciphertexts of length exactly some n. As a result, the first bit of c will always be at the $(n+1)$-st position in $e\|c$, where e is a ciphertext produced by Γ.

The construction of confirmer signatures from Σ, Γ and Ω is given as follows.

Key generation. The signer key pair is $(\Sigma$.pk, Σ.sk$)$ and the confirmer key pair is $(\Gamma$.pk, Γ.sk$)$.

ConfirmedSign. On input message m, produce a commitment c on m using a random string r, encrypt this string in e and then produce a digital signature $\sigma = \Sigma$.sign$_{\Sigma\text{.sk}}(e\|c)$. Output $\mu = (e, c, \sigma)$ as a confirmer signature on m, and prove in ZK the equality of the decryption of e and the string used for the commitment c. This proof is possible using the randomness used to encrypt r in e.

Confirmation/Denial protocol. On a message m and an alleged signature $\mu = (\mu_1, \mu_2, \mu_3)$, check the validity of μ_3 on $\mu_1\|\mu_2$. In case it is not valid, produce $\perp$. Otherwise, compute the decryption r of μ_1 and check whether $\mu_2 \overset{?}{=} \Omega$.commit$(m, r)$, according to the result give a ZK of the equality/inequality of the decryption of c and the string used to create μ_2.

Selective conversion. Proceed as in the confirmation/denial protocol with the exception of issuing the decryption of μ_1 in case the signature is valid and the symbol $\perp$ otherwise.

4.2   Security Analysis

First we note that the security for the verifier and the non-transferability of the confirmedSign, confirmation and denial protocols are ensured by using ZK proofs of knowledge. Furthermore, the construction is EUF-CMA secure and INV-CMA secure if the underlying components are secure.

Theorem 3. *The construction depicted above is (t, ϵ, q_s)-EUF-CMA secure if it uses a statistically binding commitment scheme and a (t, ϵ, q_s)-EUF-CMA secure digital signature scheme.*

Theorem 4. *The construction depicted above is $(t, \epsilon, q_s, q_v, q_{sc})$-INV-CMA secure if it uses a (t, ϵ', q_s)-SEUF-CMA secure digital signature, a statistically binding and (t, ϵ_c)-hiding commitment and a $(t + q_s(q_v + q_{sc}), \frac{1}{2}(\epsilon + \epsilon_c)(1 - \epsilon')^{q_v + q_{sc}})$-IND-CPA secure cryptosystem.*

We provide the proofs of both theorems in [19].

4.3 Efficiency Analysis

We show in this paragraph that requesting the cryptosystem to be only IND-CPA secure improves the efficiency of constructions from the plain "signature of a commitment" paradigm from many sides. First, it enhances the signature generation, verification and conversion cost as encryption and decryption is usually faster in IND-CPA secure encryption than in IND-CCA secure encryption (e.g., ElGamal vs Cramer-Shoup or Paillier vs Camenisch-Shoup). Next, we achieve also a shorter signature since ciphertexts produced using IND-CPA schemes are standardly shorter than their similars produced using IND-CCA secure cryptosystems. Finally, we allow homomorphic encryption in the design, which will render the confirmedSign/confirmation/denial protocols more efficient. In fact, in [15,24], the signer/confirmer has to prove in ZK the equality/inequality of the decryption of an IND-CCA encryption and an opening value of a commitment scheme. Thus, the only efficient instantiation, that was provided, used Camenisch-Shoup encryption and Pedersen commitment. In the rest of this subsection, we enlarge the category of encryption/commitment schemes that yield efficient instantiations thanks to the allowance of homomorphic encryption in the design.

Definition 1. *(**The class $\mathbb{C}$ of commitments**) $\mathbb{C}$ is the set of all commitment schemes for which there exists an algorithm Compute that on the input: the commitment public key pk, the message m and the commitment c on m, computes a description of a one-way function $f : (\mathbb{G}, *) \to (\mathbb{H}, \circ_s)$:*

- *where $(\mathbb{G}, *)$ is a group and $\mathbb{H}$ is a set equipped with the binary operation $\circ_s$,*

- *$\forall r, r' \in \mathbb{G}: f(r * r') = f(r) \circ_s f(r')$.*

and an $I \in \mathbb{H}$, such that $f(r) = I$, where r is the opening value of c w.r.t. m.

It is easy to check that Pedersen's commitment scheme is in this class. Actually, most commitment schemes have this built-in property because it is often the case that the committer wants to prove efficiently that a commitment is produced on some message. This is possible if the function f is homomorphic as shows Figure 1.

---

1. The prover chooses $r' \xleftarrow{R} \mathbb{G}$, computes and sends $t_1 = I \circ_s f(r')$ to the verifier.
2. The verifier chooses $b \xleftarrow{R} \{0, 1\}$ and sends it to the prover.
3. If $b = 0$, the prover sends r'.
   Otherwise, he sends $r * r'$.
4. If $b = 0$, the verifier checks that t_1 is computed as in Step 1.
   Otherwise, he accepts if $f(r * r') = t_1$.

Fig. 1. Proof system for membership to the language $\{r \colon f(r) = I\}$ Common input: I and Private input : r

Theorem 5. *The protocol depicted in Figure 1 is a Σ protocol.*

The proof is straightforward and is given in [19].

For encryption, we use the same class $\mathbb{E}$ that was defined in [20], with the exception of not requiring the cryptosystems to be derived from the hybrid encryption paradigm.

Definition 2. *(**The class $\mathbb{E}$ of cryptosystems**) $\mathbb{E}$ is the set of encryption schemes Γ that have the following properties:*

1. *The message space is a group $\mathcal{M} = (\mathbb{G}, *)$ and the ciphertext space $\mathcal{C}$ is a set equipped with a binary operation $\circ_e$.*
2. *Let $m \in \mathcal{M}$ be a message and c its encryption with respect to a key* pk*. On the common input m and c, there exists an efficient zero knowledge proof of m being the decryption of c with respect to* pk*. The private input of the prover is either the private key* sk*, corresponding to* pk *or the randomness used to encrypt m in c.*
3. *$\forall m, m' \in \mathcal{M}, \forall$* pk*: $\Gamma.\text{encrypt}_{\text{pk}}(m * m') = \Gamma.\text{encrypt}_{\text{pk}}(m) \circ_e \Gamma.\text{encrypt}_{\text{pk}}(m')$. Moreover, given the randomness used to encrypt m in $\Gamma.\text{encrypt}_{\text{pk}}(m)$ and m' in $\Gamma.\text{encrypt}_{\text{pk}}(m')$, one can deduce (using only the public parameters) the randomness used to encrypt $m * m'$ in $\Gamma.\text{encrypt}_{\text{pk}}(m) \circ_e \Gamma.\text{encrypt}_{\text{pk}}(m')$.*

Examples of cryptosystems in the above class are ElGamal's encryption [13], the cryptosystem defined in [3] which uses the linear Diffie-Hellman KEM or Paillier's [23] cryptosystem. In fact, these cryptosystems are homomorphic and possess an efficient protocol for proving that a ciphertext decrypts to a given plaintext: the proof of equality of two discrete logarithms [8], in case of ElGamal or the cryptosystem in [3], or the proof of knowledge on an N-th root in case of Paillier's encryption.

Theorem 6. *The protocol depicted in Figure 2 is a Σ protocol.*

The proof is similar to the one given in [20].   □

The confirmation/denial protocol. The confirmedSign, confirmation and denial protocols of the construction in Subsection 4.1 are depicted below.

Theorem 7. *The confirmation protocol described in Figure 3 is a Σ protocol.*

1. The prover chooses $r' \xleftarrow{R} \mathbb{G}$, computes and sends $t_2 = \Gamma.\text{encrypt}(r') \circ_e e$ to the verifier
2. The verifier chooses $b \xleftarrow{R} \{0, 1\}$ and sends it to the signer.
3. If $b = 0$, the prover sends r' and the randomness used to encrypt it in $\Gamma.\text{encrypt}(r')$.
   Otherwise, he sends $r' * r$ and proves that t_2 is an encryption of $r' * r$.
4. If $b = 0$, the verifier checks that t_2 is computed as in Step 1.
   Otherwise, he checks the proof of decryption of t_2:
      It it fails, he rejects the proof.

Fig. 2. Proof system for membership to the language $\{e \colon \exists m \,:\, m = \Gamma.\text{decrypt}(e)\}$ Common input: $(e, \Gamma.\text{pk})$ and Private input: $\Gamma.\text{sk}$ or randomness encrypting m in e

Theorem 8. *The denial protocol described in Figure 3 is a Σ protocol if the underlying cryptosystem is IND-CPA-secure.*

The proofs of both theorems are given in [19].

1. The prover and verifier, given the public input, compute I as defined in Definition 1.
2. The prover chooses $r' \xleftarrow{R} \mathbb{G}$, computes and sends $t_1 = f(r') \circ_s I$ and $t_2 = \Gamma.\text{encrypt}(r') \circ_e e$ to the verifier.
3. The verifier chooses $b \xleftarrow{R} \{0, 1\}$ and sends it to the prover.
4. If $b = 0$, the prover sends r' and the randomness used to encrypt it in $\Gamma.\text{encrypt}(r')$.
   Otherwise, he sends $r' * r$ and proves that t_2 is an encryption of $r' * r$.
5. If $b = 0$, the verifier checks that t_1 and t_2 are computed as in Step 1.
   Otherwise, he checks the proof of decryption of t_2:
      It it fails, he rejects the proof.
      Otherwise:
         If the prover is confirming the signature, the verifier accepts if $f(r' * r) = t_1$.
         If the prover is denying the given signature, the verifier accepts the proof if $f(r' * r) \neq t_1$.

Fig. 3. Proof system for membership (non membership) to the language $\{(e, c) \colon \exists r \,:\, r = \Gamma.\text{decrypt}(e) \wedge r = (\neq)\Omega.\text{open}(c, m)\}$ Common input: $(e, c, m, \Gamma.\text{pk}, \Omega.\text{pk})$ and Private input: $\Gamma.\text{sk}$ or randomness encrypting r in e

5   The "Signature of an Encryption" Paradigm

We have seen that confirmer signatures realizing the "signature of a commitment" paradigm are comprised of a commitment on the message to be signed, an encryption of the random string used to produce the commitment, and a digital signature on the commitment. Since IND-CPA encryption can be easily used to get secure commitments, one can use instead of the commitment in the previous constructions an IND-CPA secure cryptosystem. With this choice, there will be no need of encrypting the string used to produce the encryption of the message, since the private key of the cryptosystem is sufficient to check the validity of a ciphertext w.r.t. to a given message. Note that this construction already appeared in [1] in the context of signcryption. The encrypt-then-sign method achieves better performances than all previously cited constructions in terms of signature length, generation/verification and conversion cost. Besides, the proofs underlying the confirmedSign/confirmation/denial protocols are reduced in case of Discrete-Logarithm-based cryptosystems to proofs of equality/inequality of discrete logarithms for which there exist efficient protocols [8,6]. The only problem with this technique is the resort to non-interactive ZK (NIZK) proofs of knowledge. In fact, we know how to produce such proofs from their interactive variants using the Fiat-Shamir paradigm, which is known to provide security only in the ROM. However, the recent results in [11,18,17] exhibit efficient NIZK proofs of knowledge in some settings. We refer to [19] for the efficiency and security analyses of this construction.

Acknowledgments

I thank the anonymous reviewers of ProvSec 2010 for their useful remarks. Thanks go also to anonymous reviewers from TCC 2010 for helpful comments that sharpened my knowledge about the topic. Finally, I thank Joachim von zur Gathen for his support and encouragement in the course of this project. This work is funded by the B-IT Foundation and the Land Nordrhein-Westfalen.

References

1. An, J.H., Dodis, Y., Rabin, T.: On the Security of Joint Signature and Encryption. In: Knudsen, L.R. (ed.) EUROCRYPT 2002. LNCS, vol. 2332, pp. 83–107. Springer, Heidelberg (2002)
2. Bellare, M., Rogaway, P.: The Exact Security of Digital Signatures: How to Sign with RSA and Rabin. In: Maurer, U.M. (ed.) EUROCRYPT 1996. LNCS, vol. 1070, pp. 399–416. Springer, Heidelberg (1996)
3. Boneh, D., Boyen, X., Shacham, H.: Short Group Signatures. In: Franklin, M. (ed.) CRYPTO 2004. LNCS, vol. 3152, pp. 41–55. Springer, Heidelberg (2004)
4. Boyd, C., Foo, E.: Off-line Fair Payment Protocols using Convertible Signatures. In: Ohta, K., Pei, D. (eds.) ASIACRYPT 1998. LNCS, vol. 1514, pp. 271–285. Springer, Heidelberg (1998)
5. Camenisch, J., Michels, M.: Confirmer Signature Schemes Secure against Adaptive Adversaries. In: Preneel, B. (ed.) EUROCRYPT 2000. LNCS, vol. 1807, pp. 243–258. Springer, Heidelberg (2000)
6. Camenisch, J., Shoup, V.: Practical Verifiable Encryption and Decryption of Discrete Logarithms. In: Boneh, D. (ed.) CRYPTO 2003. LNCS, vol. 2729, pp. 126–144. Springer, Heidelberg (2003)
7. Chaum, D.: Designated Confirmer Signatures. In: De Santis, A. (ed.) EUROCRYPT 1994. LNCS, vol. 950, pp. 86–91. Springer, Heidelberg (1995)
8. Chaum, D., Pedersen, T.P.: Wallet Databases with Observers. In: Brickell, E.F. (ed.) CRYPTO 1992. LNCS, vol. 740, pp. 89–105. Springer, Heidelberg (1993)
9. Chaum, D., van Antwerpen, H.: Undeniable Signatures. In: Brassard, G. (ed.) CRYPTO 1989. LNCS, vol. 435, pp. 212–216. Springer, Heidelberg (1990)
10. Wikström, D.: Designated Confirmer Signatures Revisited. In: Vadhan, S.P. (ed.) TCC 2007. LNCS, vol. 4392, pp. 342–361. Springer, Heidelberg (2007)
11. Damgård, I., Fazio, N., Nicolosi, A.: Non-interactive zero-knowledge from homomorphic encryption. In: Halevi, S., Rabin, T. (eds.) TCC 2006. LNCS, vol. 3876, pp. 41–59. Springer, Heidelberg (2006)

12. Diffie, W., Hellman, M.E.: New Directions in Cryptography. IEEE Trans. Inf. Theory 22, 644–654 (1976)
13. El Gamal, T.: A Public Key Cryptosystem and a Signature Scheme based on Discrete Logarithms. IEEE Trans. Inf. Theory 31, 469–472 (1985)
14. Galbraith, S.D., Mao, W.: Invisibility and Anonymity of Undeniable and Confirmer Signatures. In: Joye, M. (ed.) CT-RSA 2003. LNCS, vol. 2612, pp. 80–97. Springer, Heidelberg (2003)
15. Gentry, C., Molnar, D., Ramzan, Z.: Efficient Designated Confirmer Signatures Without Random Oracles or General Zero-Knowledge Proofs. In: Roy, B. (ed.) ASIACRYPT 2005. LNCS, vol. 3788, pp. 662–681. Springer, Heidelberg (2005)
16. Goldwasser, S., Waisbard, E.: Transformation of Digital Signature Schemes into Designated Confirmer Signature Schemes. In: Naor, M. (ed.) TCC 2004. LNCS, vol. 2951, pp. 77–100. Springer, Heidelberg (2004)
17. Camenisch, J., Chandran, N., Shoup, V.: A Public Key Encryption Scheme Secure against Key Dependent Chosen Plaintext and Adaptive Chosen Ciphertext Attacks. In: Joux, A. (ed.) EUROCRYPT 2009. LNCS, vol. 5479, pp. 351–368. Springer, Heidelberg (2010)
18. Groth, J., Sahai, A.: Efficient Non-interactive Proof Systems for Bilinear Groups. In: Smart, N.P. (ed.) EUROCRYPT 2008. LNCS, vol. 4965, pp. 415–432. Springer, Heidelberg (2008)
19. El Aimani, L.: Efficient Confirmer Signatures from the Signature of a Commitment Paradigm, Cryptology ePrint Archive, Report 2009/435 (2009), http://eprint.iacr.org/
20. El Aimani, L.: On Generic Constructions of Designated Confirmer Signatures (The "Encryption of a Signature" Paradigm Revisited), Cryptology ePrint Archive, Report 2009/403 (2009), http://eprint.iacr.org/
21. Lim, C.H., Lee, P.J.: Modified Maurer-Yacobi's scheme and its applications. In: Zheng, Y., Seberry, J. (eds.) AUSCRYPT 1992. LNCS, vol. 718, pp. 308–323. Springer, Heidelberg (1993)
22. Michels, M., Stadler, M.: Generic Constructions for Secure and Efficient Confirmer Signature Schemes. In: Nyberg, K. (ed.) EUROCRYPT 1998. LNCS, vol. 1403, pp. 406–421. Springer, Heidelberg (1998)
23. Paillier, P.: Public-Key Cryptosystems Based on Composite Degree Residuosity Classes. In: Stern, J. (ed.) EUROCRYPT 1999. LNCS, vol. 1592, pp. 223–238. Springer, Heidelberg (1999)
24. Wang, G., Baek, J., Wong, D.S., Bao, F.: On the Generic and Efficient Constructions of Secure Designated Confirmer Signatures. In: Okamoto, T., Wang, X. (eds.) PKC 2007. LNCS, vol. 4450, pp. 43–60. Springer, Heidelberg (2007)

Collision Resistant Double-Length Hashing

Ewan Fleischmann[1], Christian Forler[2], Michael Gorski[1], and Stefan Lucks[1]

[1] Bauhaus-University Weimar, Germany
{ewan.fleischmann,michael.gorski,stefan.lucks}@uni-weimar.de
[2] Sirrix AG, Germany
c.forler@sirrix.com

Abstract. We give collision resistance bounds for blockcipher based, double-call, double-length hash functions using (k, n)-bit blockciphers with $k > n$. Özen and Stam recently proposed a framework[21] for such hash functions that use $3n$-to-$2n$-bit compression functions and two parallel calls to two independent blockciphers with $2n$-bit key and n-bit block size.

We take their analysis one step further. We first relax the requirement of two distinct and independent blockciphers. We then extend this framework and also allow to use the ciphertext of the first call to the blockcipher as an input to the second call of the blockcipher.

As far as we know, our extended framework currently covers any double-length, double-call blockcipher based hash function known in literature using a $(2n, n)$-bit blockcipher as, e.g., ABREAST-DM, TANDEM-DM [15], CYCLIC-DM [9] and Hirose's FSE'06 proposal [13].

Our generic analysis gives a simpler proof as in the FSE'09 analysis of TANDEM-DM by also tightening the security bound. The collision resistance bound for CYCLIC-DM given in [9] diminishes with an increasing cycle length c. We improve this bound for cycle lengths larger than 2^6.

Keywords: Cryptographic hash function, blockcipher based, proof of security, double block length, double length, ideal cipher model.

1 Introduction

A cryptographic hash function is a function which maps an input of arbitrary length to an output of fixed length. It should satisfy at least collision-, preimage- and second-preimage resistance and is one of the most important primitives in cryptography [17]. In recent years, the widely used MD4-family hash functions (e.g., MD4 [24], MD5 [25], RIPEMD [11], SHA-1 [19], SHA-2 [20]) have been successfully attacked in several ways [4, 10, 29, 30] which has stimulated researchers to look for alternatives. blockcipher based constructions seem promising since they are very well known – they in fact predate the MD4-approach [16]. One can easily create a hash function using5, e.g., the Davies-Meyer [31] mode of operation and the Merkle-Damgård transform [3, 18]. Also, many of the SHA-3 designs use blockcipher based instantiations. Another reason for the resurgence of interest in blockcipher based hash functions is due to the rise of resource restricted devices such as RFID tags or smart cards. A hardware designer only

S.-H. Heng and K. Kurosawa (Eds.): ProvSec 2010, LNCS 6402, pp. 102–118, 2010.
© Springer-Verlag Berlin Heidelberg 2010

needs to implement a blockcipher in order to obtain an encryption function as well as a hash function. But due to the short output length of most practical blockciphers, one is mainly interested in sound design principles for *double length* hash functions. Such double length hash functions use a blockcipher with n-bit output as the building block by which it maps possibly long strings to $2n$-bit ones.

In this article we focus on double length constructions using two calls to a blockcipher with $2n$-bit key and n-bit plaintext and ciphertext. For an overview of other variants please refer to the discussion of related work in Appendix A.

Our starting point is the recent framework of double length blockcipher based compression functions given by Özen and Stam [21]. It is a generalization of Stam's framework for single-length blockcipher based compression functions [26]. Stam's framework for these single-length compression function works as follows. Given a message M and a chaining value R and two functions, for preprocessing and postprocessing, C^{PRE} and C^{POST}, the new chaining value V is computed by:

1. Prepare key and plaintext: $(K, X) \leftarrow C^{PRE}(M, R)$.
2. Set $Y \leftarrow E(K, X)$.
3. Output $V \leftarrow C^{POST}(M, R, Y)$.

For example, choosing $|X| = |K| = |M| = |R| = |V| = |Y| = n$ and a blockcipher E with n-bit key and plaintext and ciphertext the PGV-schemes [1] can be derived for appropriate choices of C^{PRE} and C^{POST}. In fact, Stam's analysis also covers more general choices by allowing values larger than the block size n.

Naturally, given its key, a blockcipher is easy to invert. For such inverse queries, a modified postprocessing, $C^{AUX}(K, X, Y) = C^{POST}(C^{-PRE}(K, X), Y)$, is also used. Black et al. [1] and Stam [26] categorized these function into three groups:

Type-I: the compression function is collision- and preimage resistant,
Type-II: the compression function is 'secure' only in the iteration and
Insecure: the compression function is not secure, *i.e.*, there are attacks known.

In order to get a Type-I compression function, Stam proved that it is sufficient to show that C^{PRE} and $C^{POST}(M, R, \cdot)$ are both bijective.

Our Contribution. In Section 2, we generalize the double length framework of Özen and Stam [21] to be able to handle constructions similar to TANDEM-DM that reuse the ciphertext inside the compression function. We also discuss the connection of our framework to the class of CYCLIC-DM [9]. We give two special cases of our generic framework, PARALLEL-DL and SERIAL-DL, that virtually cover any double-length, double-call blockcipher based hash function known in literature employing a $(2n, n)$-bit blockcipher. Instantiations of PARALLEL-DL are, *e.g.*, CYCLIC-DM or ABREAST-DM, an example for SERIAL-DL is TANDEM-DM.

In Section 3, we give a collision resistance bound for compression functions in our framework. Using this result, we can, *e.g.*, easily tighten the FSE'09 collision resistance result of TANDEM-DM [8]. Furthermore, we are able to derive a lower bound of collision resistance for CYCLIC-DM compression functions with a cycle lengths larger than 2^6.

Section 4 discusses some more generic cases. An example is Mix-Tandem-DM in Figure 3 on page 116. We are not aware of well-known examples in literature. The interesting fact is that Mix-Tandem-DM has a considerably lower security guarantee in terms of collision resistance as Tandem-DM.

In Section 5 we discuss our results and conclude the paper. An overview of our results and some comparisons is given in Table 1.

Table 1. Comparison of relevant results for double-length, double-call compression functions. *The threshold value δ is the minimum amount of queries that an adversary must place to the blockcipher in order to find a collision with probability greater than $1/2$. The notion of a *cycle* is defined in Section 2.5.

Cycle length	Threshold δ*	Instances	Reference
2^k ($k \geq 2$)	2^{127-k}	Cyclic-DM (*e.g.* Add/k-DM)	[21]
2^k ($k \geq 2$)	2^{127-k}	Parallel-DL	Section 2.5
k ($k \geq 2$)	$2^{120.66}$	Parallel-DL	Section 3
–	$2^{120.4}$	Tandem-DM	[8]
–	$2^{120.66}$	Tandem-DM (via Serial-DL)	Section 3
–	$2^{120.66}$	Parallel-DL, Serial-DL	Section 3
–	$2^{82.8}$	Mix-Tandem-DM (via Generic-DL)	Section 4

2   Preliminaries

2.1   General Notations

A (k, n)-blockcipher is a keyed family of permutations consisting of two paired algorithms $E : \{0, 1\}^k \times \{0, 1\}^n \to \{0, 1\}^n$ and $E^{-1} : \{0, 1\}^k \times \{0, 1\}^n \to \{0, 1\}^n$ both accepting a key of size k bits and an input block of size n bits for some $n > 0$, $k > n$. For positive n, $Block(k, n)$ is the set of all (k, n)-blockciphers. For any $E \in Block(k, n)$ and any fixed key $K \in \{0, 1\}^k$, decryption $E_K^{-1} := E^{-1}(K, \cdot)$ is the inverse function of encryption $E_K := E(K, \cdot)$, so that $E_K^{-1}(E_K(X)) = X$ holds for any input $X \in \{0, 1\}^n$. In the ideal cipher model [1, 6, 14] E is modeled as a family of random permutations $\{E_K\}$ whereas the random permutations are chosen independently for each key K, i.e., formally E is selected randomly from $Block(k, n)$. The number of extra key-bits is defined as $k' = k - n$. We use the convention to write oracles, that are provided to an algorithm, as superscripts. For example $\mathcal{A}^E$ is a algorithm $\mathcal{A}$ with oracle access to E to which $\mathcal{A}$ can request forward- and backward queries. For ease of presentation, we identify the sets $\{0, 1\}^{a+b}$ and $\{0, 1\}^a \times \{0, 1\}^b$. Similarly for $A \in \{0, 1\}^a$ and $B \in \{0, 1\}^b$, the concatenation of these bit strings is denoted by $A\|B \in \{0, 1\}^{a+b} = \{0, 1\}^a \times \{0, 1\}^b$.

2.2   Blockcipher Based Compression Functions

A compression function is a mapping $H : \{0,1\}^m \times \{0,1\}^r \to \{0,1\}^r$ for some $m, r > 0$. A blockcipher based compression function is a mapping $H^E : \{0,1\}^m \times \{0,1\}^r \to \{0,1\}^r$ that, given an r-bit state R and a m-bit message M, computes $H^E(M, R\|S)$ using oracle access to some oracle $E \in Block(k, n)$.

A blockcipher based compression function H is called *double-length, double-call* (DL) if $m = k' = k - n$, $r = 2n$, $|M| = m$, $|R| = |S| = n$ and the $2n$-bit digest (V, W) is computed using two calls to E as shown in Figure 1. Formally, $(V, W) := H^E(M, R\|S)$ for a given message M and a chaining value $R\|S$ is computed using pre- and postprocessing functions $C_T^{PRE}, C_B^{PRE} : \{0,1\}^{k+n} \to \{0,1\}^{k+n}$ and $C_T^{POST}, C_B^{POST} : \{0,1\}^{k+2n} \to \{0,1\}^n$ as well as a linking function $C^{LNK} : \{0,1\}^{k+2n} \to \{0,1\}^{k+n}$ by:

1. Compute $(K_T, X_T) = C_T^{PRE}(M, R\|S)$.
2. Set $Y_T = E(K_T, X_T)$.
3. Compute $L = C^{LNK}(M, R\|S, Y_T)$.
4. Compute $(K_B, X_B) = C_B^{PRE}(L)$.
5. Set $Y_B = E(K_B, X_B)$.
6. Output $(V, W) = (C_T^{POST}(M, R\|S, Y_T), C_B^{POST}(L, Y_B))$.

The inverse of C_T^{PRE} is denoted by C_T^{-PRE} and C_B^{-PRE}, C_T^{-POST} and C_B^{-POST} are defined likewise. Informally, a query is used in the *top-row* if its plaintext, ciphertext and key are (K_T, X_T, Y_T), otherwise (*i.e.*, if the query is (K_B, X_B, Y_B)) we say that it is used in the *bottom-row*.

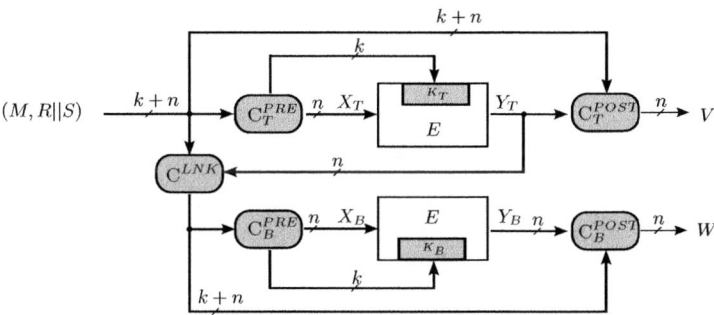

Fig. 1. The double-length compression function H^E where E is a (k, n)-blockcipher. The gray rectangle inside the cipher indicates the key input.

2.3   Classification of Double-Length Compression Functions

GENERIC-DL. The smallest common denominator any double-length compression function shares in our analysis is that, if a top-row query is given, $Q_T = (X_T, K_T, Y_T)$, one can compute the input to the bottom-row forward query (K_B, X_B). We do not require the converse, *i.e.*, we do *not* require that a bottom-row query uniquely determines the top-row query. We call DL compression functions satisfying this generic requirement GENERIC-DL. As an example set $K_B = K_T$ and $X_B = X_T \oplus Y_T$. It follows, that for any given top-row query $Q_T = (K_T, X_T, Y_T)$, the bottom row input to a forward query is uniquely determined. Another example is MIX-TANDEM-DM.

PARALLEL-DL. This is a special case of GENERIC-DL where one can compute (K_T, X_T) uniquely given (K_B, X_B) and vice versa. It is called parallel since the query in the bottom-row does not depend on the ciphertext output of the top row and therefore both can be called in parallel given the input $(M, R||S)$ to the compression function. For ease of presentation, we define a helper function PAR such that $(K_B, X_B) = \text{PAR}(K_T, X_T)$ and $(K_T, X_T) = \text{PAR}^{-1}(K_B, X_B)$. Examples are ABREAST-DM [15] or Hirose's FSE'06 proposal [13].

SERIAL-DL. This is also a special case of GENERIC-DL where one can compute (K_T, Y_T) uniquely given (K_B, X_B). Given $(M, R||S)$, we must call the queries of the top- and bottom row one after another since the bottom-row query depends on the ciphertext-output of the top-row. We again define a helper function SER such that $(K_B, X_B) = \text{SER}(K_T, Y_T)$ and $(K_T, Y_T) = \text{SER}^{-1}(K_B, X_B)$. A prominent example of a SERIAL-DL compression function is TANDEM-DM [15]. It is easy to see that PARALLEL-DL and SERIAL-DL are mutually exclusive.

For our analysis, we assume that the top-row 'is' a Type-I single length (SL) compression function (C_T^{PRE}, C_T^{POST}). Likewise, we assume that the bottom-row (C_B^{PRE}, C_B^{POST}) is Type-I. Therefore, the following three hold [26]:

1. The preprocessings C_T^{PRE} and C_B^{PRE} are both bijective.
2. For all M, R, S, the postprocessings $C_T^{POST}(M, R||S, \cdot)$ and $C_B^{POST}(M, R||S, \cdot)$ are both bijective.
3. For all K, Y, the modified postprocessings $C_T^{AUX}(K, \cdot, Y)$ and $C_B^{AUX}(K, \cdot, Y)$ are both bijective.

In order to give concrete security bounds, we have to make sure, that it is not 'too easy' to use one and the same query in the top row and the bottom row simultaneously. This might essentially render the double-length compression function into a single length compression function. For an adversary this could imply that if she had found a collision in one row, there could automatically be a collision in the other row (depending on the pre- and postprocessing functions). A simple example of such a scenario for a PARALLEL-DL compression function is ignoring the input coming from Y_T and setting C^{LNK} to the identity mapping.

Definition 1 (Independence of top- and bottom row). *Let* $Q_f = (K, X, \mathcal{Y})$ *be a forward query with* $\mathcal{Y} = E(K, X)$. *Now let* $\zeta_1 \in \mathbb{R}$ *be such that*

$$\Pr_{K,X,E}[(K, X) = (C_B^{PRE} \circ C^{LNK})(C_T^{-PRE}(K, X), \mathcal{Y})] \leq \zeta_1.$$

The probability is taken over all K, X, *and blockciphers* E. *Let* $Q_b = (K, \mathcal{X}, Y)$ *be a backward query with* $\mathcal{X} = E^{-1}(K, Y)$. *Let* $\zeta_2 \in \mathbb{R}$ *be such that*

$$\Pr_{K,Y,E}[(K, \mathcal{X}) = (C_B^{PRE} \circ C^{LNK})(C_T^{-PRE}(K, \mathcal{X}), Y)] \leq \zeta_2.$$

Here, the probability is taken over all K, Y, and blockciphers E. The independence ζ of a double-length compression function is now defined as $\zeta := \max(\zeta_1, \zeta_2)$.

2.4   Security Notions

Insecurity is quantified by the success probability of an optimal resource-bounded adversary. The resource is the number of backward and forward queries to the blockcipher E. For a set S, let $z \xleftarrow{R} S$ represent random sampling from S under the uniform distribution. For a probabilistic algorithm $\mathcal{M}$, let $z \xleftarrow{R} \mathcal{M}$ mean that z is an output of $\mathcal{M}$ and its distribution is based on the random choices of $\mathcal{M}$.

An adversary is a computationally unbounded but always-halting collision-finding algorithm $\mathcal{A}$ with access to $E \in Block(k, n)$. We assume that $\mathcal{A}$ is deterministic. The adversary may make a *forward* query $(K, X)_f$ to discover the corresponding value $Y = E(K, X)$, or the adversary may make a *backward* query $(K, Y)_b$, so as to learn the corresponding value $X = E^{-1}(K, Y)$ such that $E(K, X) = Y$. Either way, the result of the query is stored in a triple $(K_i, X_i, Y_i) := (K, X, Y)$ and the *query history* $\mathcal{Q}$ is the tuple $(Q_1, \ldots, Q_q)$ where $Q_i = (K_i, X_i, Y_i)$ and q is the total number of queries made by the adversary. The value $\mathrm{C}^{POST}(\mathrm{C}^{-PRE}(K_i, X_i), Y_i)$ is called the *post-output* of query i. The terms *post-output of a query in the top-row* and *post-output of a query in the bottom row* are defined similarly as $\mathrm{C}_T^{POST}(\mathrm{C}_T^{-PRE}(K_i, X_i), Y_i)$ and $\mathrm{C}_B^{POST}(\mathrm{C}_B^{-PRE}(K_i, X_i), Y_i)$.

Without loss of generality, we assume that $\mathcal{A}$ asks at most once on a triplet of a key K_i, a plaintext X_i and a ciphertext Y_i obtained by a query and the corresponding reply.

The goal of the adversary is to output two different triplets, (M, R, S) and (M', R', S'), such that $H(M, R\|S) = H(M', R'\|S')$. We impose the reasonable condition that the adversary must have made all queries necessary to compute $H(M, R\|S)$ and $H(M', R'\|S')$. We in fact dispense the adversary from having to output these two triplets, and simply determine whether the adversary has been successful or not by examining the query history $\mathcal{Q}$. Formally, we say that $\mathrm{COLL}(\mathcal{Q})$ holds if there is such a collision and $\mathcal{Q}$ contains all the queries necessary to compute it.

Definition 2. (Collision resistance of a DL blockcipher based compression function) *Let $H : \{0, 1\}^{k+2n} \to \{0, 1\}^{2n}$ be a blockcipher based compression function. Fix an adversary $\mathcal{A}$. Then the advantage of $\mathcal{A}$ in finding collisions in H is the real number*

$$\mathbf{Adv}_H^{\mathrm{COLL}}(\mathcal{A}) = \Pr[E \xleftarrow{R} Block(k, n); ((M, R, S), (M', R', S')) \xleftarrow{R} \mathcal{A}^{E, E^{-1}} :$$
$$((M, R, S) \neq (M', R', S')) \wedge H(M, R, S) = H(M', R', S')].$$

For $q \geq 1$ we write

$$\mathbf{Adv}_H^{\mathrm{COLL}}(q) = \max_{\mathcal{A}} \{\mathbf{Adv}_H^{\mathrm{COLL}}(\mathcal{A})\},$$

where the maximum is taken over all adversaries that ask at most q oracle queries, *i.e.*, forward and backward queries to E.

2.5 Parallel-DL and Cyclic-DM

Fleischmann et al. [9] introduced the concept of cyclic double-length blockcipher based compression functions using the Davies-Meyer [31] mode. In short, the idea of cyclic compression functions is that there is a permutation σ such that the input to one row, *e.g.* the top row, determines the input to the bottom row. By applying σ several times again on this new bottom-row input one results again at the initial top-row input. The cycle length c of an input Z is defined as the minimal number such that $\sigma^c(Z) = Z$. The cycle length of a compression function is defined as the maximum cycle length taken over all possible inputs Z.

This idea can also be applied in the more generic setting of PARALLEL-DL. The cycle length of an input $Z = (M, R||S)$ can now be defined as the minimal number c such that $\mathrm{PAR}^c(Z) = Z$. Therefore we define the cycle length of a PARALLEL-DL compression function as the maximum cycle length measured over all possible inputs Z.

This is a generalization of the CYCLIC-DM analysis in [9]. It is easy to see, that the proofs for CYCLIC-DM can be easily applied to our more general case. So we can state bounds for collision resistance of PARALLEL-DL based on the CYCLIC-DM bounds as follows.

Theorem 1. *(Collision Resistance for $c = 2$)* Let H be a PARALLEL-DL compression function with cycle length $c = 2$ and let $N = 2^n$. If $\mathrm{C}_T^{PRE} = \mathrm{C}_B^{PRE}$ and $\mathrm{C}_T^{POST} = \mathrm{C}_B^{POST}$, then $a = 1$, else $a = 2$. Then, for any $q > 1$ and $2q < N$,

$$\mathbf{Adv}_{H^E}^{\mathrm{COLL}}(q) \leq \frac{2aq^2}{(N - 2q)^2} + \frac{2q}{N - 2q}.$$

Theorem 2. *(Collision Resistance for $c > 2$)* Let H be a PARALLEL-DL compression function with cycle length $c > 2$ and let $N = 2^n$. Then, for any $q > 1$ and $cq < N$,

$$\mathbf{Adv}_{H^E}^{\mathrm{COLL}}(q) \leq \frac{c^2}{2}\left(\frac{q}{N - cq}\right)^2.$$

Proof. The proofs are essentially identical to the proofs of Theorems 4 and 5 in [9] and is omitted here.   □

The security bound of Theorem 2 vanishes with an increasing cycle length. *E.g.* for $c = 2^t$ and $n = 128$, no adversary asking less than 2^{127-t} queries can find a collision with probability greater than $1/2$.

2.6 Related Work

An overview of related work can be found in Appendix A.

3   Collision Resistance of Parallel-DL and Serial-DL Compression Functions

3.1   Results Overview

In our analysis, we exclude $c = 1$ for immanent reasons.

Theorem 3. *Let H be a* PARALLEL-DL *or* SERIAL-DL *compression function as given in Section 2.3. Let α, β, κ, n be constants such that $\alpha, \kappa > e$ and let $\tau = N'\alpha/q$, $N = 2^n$, $N' = N - q$. Then*

$$\text{ADV}_{H^E}^{\text{COLL}}(q) \leq q \cdot \left(2\alpha/N' + 2\beta/(N')^2 + q\zeta/N' + 1/N'\right) + L, \tag{1}$$

where

$$L = 2q2^n e^{\tau q(1 - \ln \tau)/N'} + 2q^2/(\beta N') + 2qe^{\kappa(1 + \ln \frac{q}{N'} - \ln \kappa)}.$$

Since similar bounds, *e.g.*, [8, 27, 28], are in their general from rather untransparent, we discuss this bound for $n = 128$. Let $\zeta = 0$, and evaluate expression (1) such that the advantage is equal to $1/2$, thereby maximizing the value of q and numerically optimizing the values of α, β and κ. For $\alpha = 24$, $\beta = 2^{120}$ and $\kappa = 14$ we find that no adversary asking no more than $q = 2^{120.66}$ queries can find a collision with probability greater than $1/2$.

In the full version of the paper [7], we show that Theorem 3 implies the following asymptotic bound.

Theorem 4. *Let $q = 2^{0.93n - \epsilon}$ where $\epsilon \geq 0$ and H a* PARALLEL-DL *or* SERIAL-DL *compression function with $\zeta < 1/N'$. Then $\text{ADV}_{H^E}^{\text{COLL}}(q) \to 0$ as $n \to \infty$.*

3.2   Proof Preliminaries

Overview. We analyze whether the queries to the oracle E made by the adversary *can* be used for constructing a collision of the compression function H^E. We look to see whether there exist four not necessarily distinct queries that form a collision (cf. Figure 2).

To upper bound the probability of the adversary obtaining queries than can be used for a collision, we upper bound the probability of the adversary making a query that can be used as the final query to complete such a collision. Let $\mathcal{Q}_i$ denote the set of the first i queries made by the adversary. We examine the queries of the adversary one at a time (either forward or backward) as they are placed. We denote by the term *last query* the latest query made by the adversary. This query is always given the index i. Therefore, for each i, $1 \leq i \leq q$, we upper bound the probability that the answer to the adversary's i-th query $(K_i, X_i)_f$ or $(K_i, Y_i)_b$ allows the adversary to use this i-th query to complete the collision. In the latter case, the last query is called *successful* and the attack is given to the adversary. As the probability depends on the first $i - 1$ queries, we need to make sure that the adversary hasn't already been too lucky with these. Being

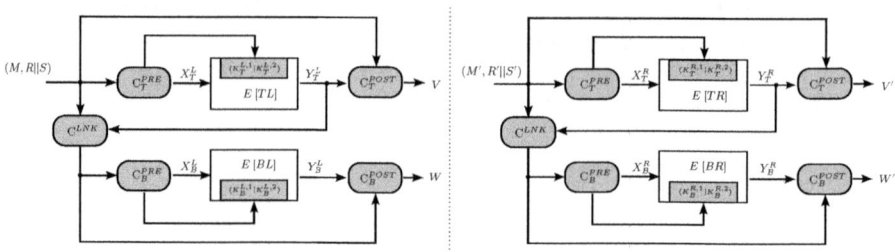

Fig. 2. The double-length compression function H^E using a (k, n)-blockcipher E, the gray rectangle inside the cipher indicates the input used as a key. The four possible positions a query can be used in are denoted by TL, BL, TR, BR.

lucky is explicitly defined in (2), *e.g.* it means – among others – that there exists a large subset of the first $i - 1$ queries that have equal post-output. Our upper bound thus breaks down into two pieces: an upper bound for the probability of the adversary getting lucky and the probability of the adversary ever making a successful i-th query, conditioned on the fact that the adversary has not yet become lucky by its $(i-1)$-th query.

Details. Fix numbers n, q and an adversary $\mathcal{A}$ asking q queries in total to its oracle. We say $\text{COLL}(\mathcal{Q})$ if the adversary wins. Note that winning does not necessarily imply that a collision has been found as is explained now. We upper bound $\Pr[\text{COLL}(\mathcal{Q})]$ by exhibiting the predicates $\text{LUCKY}(\mathcal{Q})$, $\text{WIN}_{TL}(\mathcal{Q})$, $\text{WIN}_{BL}(\mathcal{Q})$, $\text{WIN}_{TL+BL}(\mathcal{Q})$ and $\text{WIN}_{TL+BR}(\mathcal{Q})$ such that

$$\text{COLL}(\mathcal{Q}) \Rightarrow \text{LUCKY}(\mathcal{Q}) \vee \text{WIN}_{TL}(\mathcal{Q}) \vee \text{WIN}_{BL}(\mathcal{Q}) \vee$$
$$\text{WIN}_{TL+BL}(\mathcal{Q}) \vee \text{WIN}_{TL+BR}(\mathcal{Q}).$$

and then by upper bounding separately the probabilities $\text{LUCKY}(\mathcal{Q})$, $\text{WIN}_{TL}(\mathcal{Q})$, $\text{WIN}_{BL}(\mathcal{Q})$, $\text{WIN}_{TL+BL}(\mathcal{Q})$ and $\text{WIN}_{TL+BR}(\mathcal{Q})$. The union bound finally gives

$$\Pr[\text{COLL}(\mathcal{Q})] \leq \Pr[\text{LUCKY}(\mathcal{Q})] + \Pr[\text{WIN}_{TL}(\mathcal{Q})] + \Pr[\text{WIN}_{BL}(\mathcal{Q})] +$$
$$\Pr[\text{WIN}_{TL+BL}(\mathcal{Q})] + \Pr[\text{WIN}_{TL+BR}(\mathcal{Q})].$$

To formally state these predicates, some additional definitions are helpful. Let $\text{NumEqual}_T(\mathcal{Q})$, $\text{NumEqual}_B(\mathcal{Q})$ be functions defined on query sequences $\mathcal{Q}$ of length q as follows:

$$\text{NumEqual}_T(\mathcal{Q}) = \max_{Z \in \{0,1\}^n} |\{i : C_T^{POST}(C_T^{-PRE}(K_i, X_i), Y_i) = Z\}|,$$
$$\text{NumEqual}_B(\mathcal{Q}) = \max_{Z \in \{0,1\}^n} |\{i : C_B^{POST}(C_B^{-PRE}(K_i, X_i), Y_i) = Z\}|.$$

They give the maximum size of a set of queries in $\mathcal{Q}$ whose post outputs are all the same (for the top- and bottom row respectively). Let $\text{NumColl}_T(\mathcal{Q})$,

$\texttt{NumColl}_B(\mathcal{Q})$ be also defined on query sequences $\mathcal{Q}$ of length q as

$$\texttt{NumColl}_T(\mathcal{Q}) = |\{(i,j) \in \{1,\ldots,q\}^2 : i \neq j,$$
$$C_T^{POST}(C_T^{-PRE}(K_i, X_i), Y_i) = C_T^{POST}(C_T^{-PRE}(K_j, X_j), Y_j)\}|,$$
$$\texttt{NumColl}_B(\mathcal{Q}) = |\{(i,j) \in \{1,\ldots,q\}^2 : i \neq j,$$
$$C_B^{POST}(C_B^{-PRE}(K_i, X_i), Y_i) = C_B^{POST}(C_B^{-PRE}(K_j, X_j), Y_j)\}|.$$

They give the number of ordered pairs of distinct queries in $\mathcal{Q}$ which have the same post-outputs. For our analysis we also need to upper bound the number of 'triangle collisions' in the top and bottom row, $\texttt{NumTriangleColl}_T(\mathcal{Q})$ and $\texttt{NumTriangleColl}_B(\mathcal{Q})$. We say a pair of queries (Q_i, Q_j), $i \neq j$, forms a triangle collision in the top-row iff:

1. Q_i is used in TL and BR,
2. Q_j is used in TR and,
3. the post-output of Q_i in TL is equal to the post-output of Q_j in TR.

Similarly, a triangle collision in the bottom-row is defined, only Q_j is then used in BL.

We now define the event $\text{LUCKY}(\mathcal{Q})$ as

$$\begin{aligned}
\text{LUCKY}(\mathcal{Q}) =&(\texttt{NumEqual}_T(\mathcal{Q}) > \alpha) \vee (\texttt{NumEqual}_B(\mathcal{Q}) > \alpha) \vee \\
&(\texttt{NumColl}_T(\mathcal{Q}) > \beta) \vee (\texttt{NumColl}_B(\mathcal{Q}) > \beta) \vee \qquad (2) \\
&(\texttt{NumTriangleColl}_T(\mathcal{Q}) > \kappa) \vee (\texttt{NumTriangleColl}_B(\mathcal{Q}) > \kappa),
\end{aligned}$$

where α, β and κ are the constants from Theorem 3. These constants are chosen depending on n and q by a numerical optimization process. If α, β and κ are chosen larger, $\Pr[\text{LUCKY}(\mathcal{Q})]$ diminishes. The other events consider mutually exclusive configurations on how to find a collision for the compression function. These configurations are formalized by the following four predicates.

Fit$_{TL}$: The last query is used only once in position TL. This is equivalent to the case where the last query is used in position TR.
Fit$_{BL}$: The last query is used only once in position BL or (equivalent) BR.
Fit$_{TL/BL}$: The last query is used twice in a collision, either TL and BL or (equivalent) TR and BR.
Fit$_{TL/BR}$: The last query is used twice in a collision, either TL and BR or (equivalent) TR and BL.

We show in Proposition 1 that these configurations cover all possible cases of a collision. For practical purposes we now define some additional predicates as follows:

$$\begin{aligned}
\text{WIN}_{TL}(\mathcal{Q}) &= \neg\text{LUCKY}(\mathcal{Q}) \wedge \text{FIT}_{TL}(\mathcal{Q}), \\
\text{WIN}_{BL}(\mathcal{Q}) &= \neg(\text{LUCKY}(\mathcal{Q}) \vee \text{FIT}_{TL}(\mathcal{Q})) \wedge \text{FIT}_{BL}(\mathcal{Q}), \\
\text{WIN}_{TL+BL}(\mathcal{Q}) &= \neg(\text{LUCKY}(\mathcal{Q}) \vee \text{FIT}_{TL}(\mathcal{Q}) \vee \text{FIT}_{BL}(\mathcal{Q})) \wedge \text{FIT}_{TL+BL}(\mathcal{Q}), \\
\text{WIN}_{TL+BR}(\mathcal{Q}) &= \neg(\text{LUCKY}(\mathcal{Q}) \vee \text{FIT}_{TL}(\mathcal{Q}) \vee \text{FIT}_{BL}(\mathcal{Q}) \vee \text{FIT}_{TL+BL}(\mathcal{Q})) \\
&\quad \wedge \text{FIT}_{TL+BR}(\mathcal{Q}).
\end{aligned}$$

Proposition 1.

$$\text{COLL}(\mathcal{Q}) \Rightarrow \text{WIN}_{TL}(\mathcal{Q}) \vee \text{WIN}_{BL}(\mathcal{Q}) \vee \text{WIN}_{TL+BL}(\mathcal{Q}) \vee \text{WIN}_{TL+BR}(\mathcal{Q})$$

Proof. We can assume that the adversary has not been lucky, *i.e.*, $\neg\text{LUCKY}(\mathcal{Q})$. Then it is easy to see that

$$\text{FIT}_{TL}(\mathcal{Q}) \vee \text{FIT}_{BL}(\mathcal{Q}) \vee \text{FIT}_{TL+BL}(\mathcal{Q}) \vee \text{FIT}_{TL+BR}(\mathcal{Q}) \Rightarrow \text{WIN}_{TL}(\mathcal{Q})\vee$$
$$\text{WIN}_{BL}(\mathcal{Q}) \vee \text{WIN}_{TL+BL}(\mathcal{Q}) \vee \text{WIN}_{TL+BR}(\mathcal{Q}).$$

So it is sufficient to show that

$$\text{COLL}(\mathcal{Q}) \Rightarrow \text{FIT}_{TL}(\mathcal{Q}) \vee \text{FIT}_{BL}(\mathcal{Q}) \vee \text{FIT}_{TL+BL}(\mathcal{Q}) \vee \text{FIT}_{TL+BR}(\mathcal{Q}).$$

Now, say $\text{COLL}(\mathcal{Q})$ in the adversary's i-th query (meaning that the adversary was not able to find a query prior to its i-th query). Then a collision has been found using queries Q_i, Q_j, Q_k, Q_l from our query history $\mathcal{Q}$, $|\mathcal{Q}| = i$ for some $1 \leq j, k, l \leq i$.

First assume that the last query, *i.e.*, the i-th query, is used once in the collision. If it is used in TL (or TR), then $\text{FIT}_{TL}(\mathcal{Q})$. If it is used in BL (or BR), then $\text{FIT}_{BL}(\mathcal{Q})$. Now assume that the query is used twice in the collision. If it is used in TL and BL (or TR and BR), then $\text{FIT}_{TL+BL}(\mathcal{Q})$. If it is used in TL and BR (or BL and TR), then $\text{FIT}_{TL+BR}(\mathcal{Q})$. We note that a query cannot be used twice in one row (top- or bottom) then no collision occurs since these queries both uniquely determine the bottom-row query and therefore the inputs to the compression function are equal in both cases. The same argument also holds true in the case that the last query is used more than twice. This concludes our analysis as no cases are left. □

The next step is to upper bound $\Pr[\text{LUCKY}(\mathcal{Q})]$, $\Pr[\text{WIN}_{TL}(\mathcal{Q})]$, $\Pr[\text{WIN}_{BL}(\mathcal{Q})]$, $\Pr[\text{WIN}_{TL+BL}(\mathcal{Q})]$, and $\Pr[\text{WIN}_{TL+BR}(\mathcal{Q})]$.

Proposition 2. *Let α, β, κ be as in Theorem 3 and let $\alpha > e$ and $\tau = N'\alpha/q$. Then*

$$\Pr[\text{LUCKY}(\mathcal{Q})] \leq 2 \cdot (q2^n e^{\tau q(1-\ln\tau)/N'} + q^2/(\beta N') + e^{\kappa(1+\ln\frac{q}{N'}-\ln\kappa)}).$$

The proof is given in the full version of the paper [7]. We note that the multiplying factor '2' can be omitted if the post processing functions of the top and bottom-row are equal, *i.e.*, $C_T^{POST} = C_B^{POST}$.

There are two arguments that are used several times in the proof so we state them here in a generic form and reference them later. If the last query is used only once in the configurations we denote the row that the query is used in (*i.e.*, either the top- or the bottom-row) as the *query-row (QR)*; the row the last query is *not* used in is called *other row (OR)*. The function taking the output of the last query and the key and generating the input to the other row is called C^{HLP}(this is either PAR, PAR^{-1}, SER or SER^{-1}).

Argument A. *The input to the last query (i.e., key and plaintext for a forward query or key and ciphertext for a backward query) uniquely determines the input to the query of the other row.* Assume WLOG that the last query is used in position QL. Now, the query in the other row, OL, is now uniquely determined by the *input* of QL via C^{HLP}, we give the query OL to the adversary for free and denote it by $Q = (X_i^O, K_i^O, Y_i^O)$. The post-output of OL is therefore also uniquely determined via C^{AUX} or C^{PRE}. We denote the post output of OL by V_i^O. There are at most α queries that can be used for OR (*i.e.*, that have an equal post-output as OL). For any such matching query in OR, there is at most one query in QR (computed either via C^{HLP}). In total, there are no more than α queries that can possibly be used to find a collision in the query-row. The last query has a chance of succeeding of $\leq \alpha/N'$. In total, for q queries, the chance of ever making a successful query of this type can be upper bounded by $q \cdot \alpha/N'$.

Argument B. *The (randomly determined) result of the last query (either as a forward- or backward query) – and the key input – uniquely determines the input of the query in the other row.* Assume WLOG that the last query is used in position QL. Note that in this case, the *random* output not only determines the post output of the query row, but also is (in conjunction with the query key) responsible for determining the *unique* query in OL.

Sucbase OL = QR. There are at most κ triplets of queries that can be used for OL, OR and QR such that the queries used in OL and QR are the same. So for any single query, the chance of success (only measured in the query row) is $\leq \kappa/N'$.

Sucbase OL ≠ QR. Say OL $\neq$ QR. There are at most β pairs of queries that form a collision in the other row, *i.e.*, OL and OR have equal post output. Since the query in OR uniquely determines the query QR, we have in total β triplets of queries (OL, OR, QR) such that the other row collides. The random output of the last query is relevant for two different places, *i.e.*, in order to use the query QL as a last query for a collision of the compression function. It has to fit with the query in OL and its post output has to be equal to the post output of QR. Since the queries OL, *i.e.*, the key, plaintext and ciphertext and the post output of QR are independent, we can upper bound the success probability of an adversary by $\leq \beta/(N')^2$.

Using the union bound, the chance of ever making a successful query in an attack can be upper bounded by $\leq q \cdot (\alpha/N' + \beta/(N')^2)$.

3.3   Analyzing the Upper Bounds of Success

Proposition 3. $\Pr[\mathrm{WIN}_{TL}(\mathcal{Q})] \leq q \cdot (\alpha/N' + \beta/(N')^2)$.

Proof. The *query-row* QR is the top-row and the *other-row* OR is the bottom-row.   □

Parallel-DL. Assume that the last query is a forward query. In this case Argument A holds. The probability of success is upper bounded by $q \cdot \alpha/N'$.

Now, assume that the last query is a backward query. In this case argument B holds. The total probability of success in this case is therefore upper bounded by $q \cdot (\alpha + \beta)/N'$.

Serial-DL Assume that the last query is a forward query. In this case Argument B holds. Now, we assume that the last query is a backward query. In this case Argument A holds. The total probability of success in this case is therefore upper bounded by $q \cdot (\alpha + \beta)/N'$.   □

Proposition 4. $\Pr[\text{WIN}_{BL}(\mathcal{Q})] \leq q \cdot (\alpha/N' + \beta/(N')^2)$.

Proof. The *query-row* QR is the bottom-row and the *other-row* OR is the top-row. Since the proof is the same as for Proposition 3 we omit it here.   □

Proposition 5. $\Pr[\text{WIN}_{TL+BL}(\mathcal{Q})] \leq q^2 \cdot \zeta/N'$.

Proof. The analysis is the same for forward- and backward queries. The probability that the last query can be used concurrently in the top- and bottom-row (*i.e.*, TL and BL) can be upper bounded by ζ (cf. Definition 1). Trivially, there are at most q queries that can be used for TR and we can upper bound the adversary's success by $\leq q \cdot \zeta/N'$. For a total of q queries, this bound is $q^2 \cdot \zeta/N'$. We note that for PARALLEL-DL, assuming a cycle length $c > 1$, $\zeta = 0$ always.
                                                                                        □

Proposition 6. $\Pr[\text{WIN}_{TL+BR}(\mathcal{Q})] \leq q/N'$.

Proof. **Parallel-DL.** Assume that the last query is a forward query and we use it in TL and BR ($TL = BR$). The queries in BL and TR are uniquely determined by the input to the last query. We assume that the adversary has access to these queries. So the chance of being successful in the top-row is upper-bounded by $1/N'$ and for q queries by q/N'.

Remark: This relatively loose bound takes the possibility of $BL = TR$ into account. In this case $(K_i, X_i) = (C_B^{PRE} \circ (C^{LNK})^2)(C_T^{-PRE}(K_i, X_i), Y_i)$ which would imply a cycle length of two. By assuming a cycle length greater than two, we can tighten this bound to $q/(N')^2$ but we chose not to so since the better bound only has insignificant influence on the final bound.

Now, assume that the last query is a backward query. The randomly determined output of the query in TL, together with the input, *i.e.*, the key, uniquely determines BL. We assume that the adversary has access to a query $Q_j \in \mathcal{Q}$ that can be used in BL. Formally, the following discussion is conditioned on the fact that the adversary has access to a matching Q_j with probability one. Note that this gives the adversary more power than she is likely to have. It follows that the post-output of BL is also uniquely determined. The probability that the post-output of BL matches the randomly determined post-output of BR can therefore be upper bounded by $1/N'$ and for q queries by q/N'.

So, whether we have a forward- or backward query, the total chance of success is $\leq q/N'$.

Serial-DL. Assume that the last query is a forward query and we use it in TL and BR ($TL = BR$). It follows that the query in TR is uniquely determined by the input of the last query. So the chance of success in the top row for q queries is upper bounded by q/N'.

Now assume that the last query is a backward query used again in TL and BR. Since the query in BL is uniquely determined by the input of the last query used in TL, the total chance of success for q queries in the bottom-row is again upper bounded by q/N'. So whether the adversary mounts a forward or backward query, the success probability is bounded by $\leq q/N'$.   □

4   Collision Resistance of Generic-DL Compression Functions

Theorem 3 can not be applied to derive a bound for more generic constructions such as MIX-TANDEM-DM since for PARALLEL-DL or SERIAL-DL compression functions, a query in the bottom-row uniquely determines the query in the top-row.

Theorem 5. *Let H be a* GENERIC-DL *compression function as given in Section 2.3. Let α, β, κ, n and γ be constants such that $\alpha, \kappa > e$ and $\tau = N'\alpha/q$, $N = 2^n$, $N' = N - q$. Let $\Gamma(q, \gamma)$ be a function. Then*

$$\mathrm{ADV}_{H^E}^{\mathrm{COLL}}(q) \leq q\beta(\gamma + 1)/N' + q^2\zeta/N' + q\gamma/N' + L,$$

where

$$L = 2q2^n e^{\tau q(1 - \ln \tau)/N'} + 2q^2/(\beta N') + 2qe^{\kappa(1 + \ln \frac{q}{N'} - \ln \kappa)} + \Gamma(q, \gamma).$$

Proof. The details of the proof can be found in the full version of the paper [7].

The proof of Theorem 5 closely follows the proof of Theorem 3 generalized by a further parameter γ. This parameter gives an upper bound on how many queries can be used in the top-row for a given bottom-row query. Informally, the function $\Gamma(q, \gamma)$ is defined as the probability that a concrete parameter γ is for a specific value of q in fact such an upper bound. We note that the bound for GENERIC-DL is nonetheless considerably worse than for SERIAL-DL or PARALLEL-DL. The main reason for this is that the subtle argumentation of Arguments A and B do not work in this setting and a more generic *Argument C* has to be used.

Application to Mix-Tandem-DM. In the full version of the paper [7], we show that in this case $\zeta = 1/N'$, $\Gamma(q, \gamma) = 0$ and $\gamma = \alpha$. Using a numerical optimization process, it is easy to compute that for $n = 128$ no adversary asking less than $q = 2^{82.8}$ queries can find a collision with probability greater than $1/2$. In this case, the parameters are $\alpha = 5$, $\beta = 2^{39}$ and $\kappa = 15$.

5   Discussion and Conclusion

In this paper we have investigated the security of a very generic form of double-length compression functions. Our security bound tightens the bound of

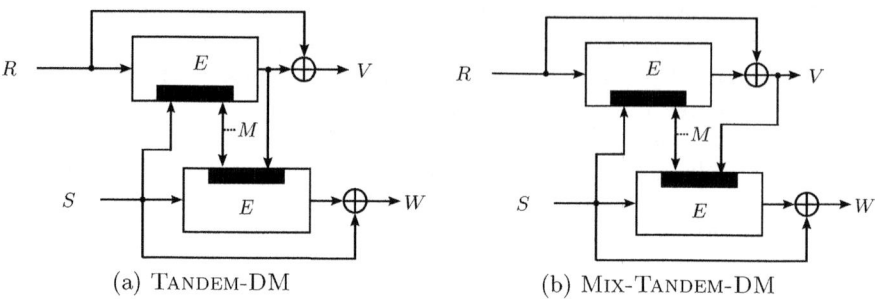

(a) Tandem-DM

(b) Mix-Tandem-DM

Fig. 3. Examples of double-length compression functions with a $(2n, n)$-bit blockcipher E

Tandem-DM given at FSE'09 and also tightens the bound for any Cyclic-DM compression function with cycle length larger than 2^6. We have also stretched the meaning of Davies-Meyer based cyclic compression function to Parallel-DL.

Our proofs not only give better bounds in some important cases, but we also give a better understanding of what ticks inside, for double-length hash functions. This might help finding some security results for , e.g., MDC-4 where similar techniques might be applicable.

We have also discussed the security implication of constructions like Mix-Tandem-DM. The analysis for this type of compression functions is simpler than for Parallel-DL or Serial-DL, but the security bound is also much weaker.

Despite the research that has lately been done in the field of blockcipher based hash functions, there are still a lot of problems that deserve attention. We have not found attacks that show that our bounds are tight. Another open problem is to find good – meaning efficient – double length compression functions that use (n, n)-bit blockciphers. Also, there are other security properties where much less in known, e.g., for preimage resistance or preimage awareness.

References

[1] Black, J., Rogaway, P., Shrimpton, T.: Black-Box Analysis of the Block-Cipher-Based Hash-Function Constructions from PGV. In: Yung, M. (ed.) CRYPTO 2002. LNCS, vol. 2442, pp. 320–335. Springer, Heidelberg (2002)
[2] Brassard, G. (ed.): CRYPTO 1989. LNCS, vol. 435. Springer, Heidelberg (1990)
[3] Damgård, I.: A Design Principle for Hash Functions. In: Brassard [2], pp. 416–427
[4] den Boer, B., Bosselaers, A.: Collisions for the Compression Function of MD-5. In: Helleseth, T. (ed.) EUROCRYPT 1993. LNCS, vol. 765, pp. 293–304. Springer, Heidelberg (1994)
[5] Dunkelman, O. (ed.): Fast Software Encryption. LNCS, vol. 5665. Springer, Heidelberg (2009)
[6] Even, S., Mansour, Y.: A Construction of a Cipher From a Single Pseudorandom Permutation. In: Matsumoto, T., Imai, H., Rivest, R.L. (eds.) ASIACRYPT 1991. LNCS, vol. 739, pp. 210–224. Springer, Heidelberg (1993)

[7] Fleischmann, E., Forler, C., Gorski, M., Lucks, S.: Collision Resistant Double Length Hashing. Cryptology ePrint Archive, Report 2010 (2010), http://eprint.iacr.org/

[8] Fleischmann, E., Gorski, M., Lucks, S.: On the Security of Tandem-DM. In: Dunkelman [5], pp. 84–103

[9] Fleischmann, E., Gorski, M., Lucks, S.: Security of cyclic double block length hash functions. In: Parker [22], pp. 153–175

[10] Dobbertin, H.: The status of MD5 after a recent attack (1996)

[11] Dobbertin, H., Bosselaers, A., Preneel, B.: RIPEMD (RACE integrity primitives evaluation message digest) (1996)

[12] Hirose, S.: Provably Secure Double-Block-Length Hash Functions in a Black-Box Model. In: Park, C.-s., Chee, S. (eds.) ICISC 2004. LNCS, vol. 3506, pp. 330–342. Springer, Heidelberg (2005)

[13] Hirose, S.: Some Plausible Constructions of Double-Block-Length Hash Functions. In: Robshaw, M.J.B. (ed.) FSE 2006. LNCS, vol. 4047, pp. 210–225. Springer, Heidelberg (2006)

[14] Kilian, J., Rogaway, P.: How to Protect DES Against Exhaustive Key Search. In: Koblitz, N. (ed.) CRYPTO 1996. LNCS, vol. 1109, pp. 252–267. Springer, Heidelberg (1996)

[15] Lai, X., Massey, J.L.: Hash Function Based on Block Ciphers. In: Rueppel, R.A. (ed.) EUROCRYPT 1992. LNCS, vol. 658, pp. 55–70. Springer, Heidelberg (1993)

[16] Rabin, M.: Digitalized Signatures. In: DeMillo, R., Dobkin, D., Jones, A., Lipton, R. (eds.) Foundations of Secure Computation, pp. 155–168. Academic Press, London (1978)

[17] Menezes, A., van Oorschot, P.C., Vanstone, S.A.: Handbook of Applied Cryptography. CRC Press, Boca Raton (1996)

[18] Merkle, R.C.: One Way Hash Functions and DES. In: Brassard [2], pp. 428–446

[19] NIST National Institute of Standards and Technology. FIPS 180-1: Secure Hash Standard (April 1995), http://csrc.nist.gov

[20] NIST National Institute of Standards and Technology. FIPS 180-2: Secure Hash Standard (April 1995), http://csrc.nist.gov

[21] Özen, O., Stam, M.: Another glance at double-length hashing. In: Parker [22], pp. 176–201

[22] Parker, M.G. (ed.): Cryptography and Coding. LNCS, vol. 5921. Springer, Heidelberg (2009)

[23] Preneel, B., Govaerts, R., Vandewalle, J.: Hash Functions Based on Block Ciphers: A Synthetic Approach. In: Stinson, D.R. (ed.) CRYPTO 1993. LNCS, vol. 773, pp. 368–378. Springer, Heidelberg (1994)

[24] Rivest, R.L.: The MD4 Message Digest Algorithm. In: Menezes, A., Vanstone, S.A. (eds.) CRYPTO 1990. LNCS, vol. 537, pp. 303–311. Springer, Heidelberg (1991)

[25] Rivest, R.L.: RFC 1321: The MD5 Message-Digest Algorithm. Internet Activities Board (April 1992)

[26] Stam, M.: Blockcipher-based hashing revisited. In: Dunkelman [5], pp. 67–83 (2009)

[27] Steinberger, J.P.: The collision intractability of mdc-2 in the ideal cipher model. Cryptology ePrint Archive, Report 2006/294 (2006), http://eprint.iacr.org/

[28] Steinberger, J.P.: The Collision Intractability of MDC-2 in the Ideal-Cipher Model. In: Naor, M. (ed.) EUROCRYPT 2007. LNCS, vol. 4515, pp. 34–51. Springer, Heidelberg (2007)

[29] Wang, X., Lai, X., Feng, D., Chen, H., Yu, X.: Cryptanalysis of the Hash Functions MD4 and RIPEMD. In: Cramer, R. (ed.) EUROCRYPT 2005. LNCS, vol. 3494, pp. 1–18. Springer, Heidelberg (2005)

[30] Wang, X., Yin, Y.L., Yu, H.: Finding Collisions in the Full SHA-1. In: Shoup, V. (ed.) CRYPTO 2005. LNCS, vol. 3621, pp. 17–36. Springer, Heidelberg (2005)

[31] Winternitz, R.S.: A secure one-way hash function built from des. In: IEEE Symposium on Security and Privacy, pp. 88–90 (1984)

A   Related Work

Preneel *et al.* [23] discussed the security of SL hash functions against several generic attacks. They concluded that 12 out of 64 hash functions are secure against the attacks. However, formal proofs were first given by Black *et al.* [1] about 10 years later. Their most important result is that 20 hash functions – including the 12 mentioned above – are optimally collision resistant. A deeper understanding of these results has been provided by Stam [26].

DL Schemes with non-optimal or unknown collision resistance. These are discussed in the full version of the paper

DL Schemes with Birthday-Type Collision Resistance. Merkle [18] presented three DL hash functions composed of DES with rates of at most 0.276. They are optimally collision resistant in the ideal cipher model. Hirose [12] presented a class of DL hash functions with rate $1/2$ which are composed of two different and independent $(n, 2n)$-blockciphers that have birthday-type collision resistance. Hirose [13] presented a rate $1/2$ and $(n, 2n)$-blockcipher based DL hash function that has birthday-type collision resistance. He essentially stated that for his compression function, no adversary can find a collision with probability greater than $1/2$ if no more than $2^{124.55}$ queries are asked (see [8, App. B] for details on this). Fleischmann et. al. [8] gave a near-birthday collision resistance bound for TANDEM-DM. They also gave at IMACC'09 [9] a bound for ABREAST-DM and a generalization called CYCLIC-DM. ABREAST-DM was shown to have near-birthday collision resistance, CYCLIC-DM has this property only for small cycle lengths.

Interpreting Hash Function Security Proofs

Juraj Šarinay*

EPFL IC LACAL, Station 14, CH-1015 Lausanne, Switzerland
juraj.sarinay@epfl.ch

Abstract. We provide a concrete security treatment of several "provably secure" hash functions. Interpreting arguments behind MQ-HASH, FSB, SWIFFTX and VSH we identify similar lines of reasoning. We aim to formulate the main security claims in a language closer to that of attacks. We evaluate designers' claims of provable security and quantify them more precisely, deriving "second order" bounds on bounds. While the authors of FSB, MQ-HASH and SWIFFT(X) prove existence of non-trivial lower bounds on security, we show that the quantification of the bounds limits the practical significance of the proofs.

Keywords: hash functions, security bounds, provable reducibility.

1   Introduction

A hash function is a mapping that on input a string of arbitrary length outputs a digest of fixed size. Such functions are among the most basic building blocks used in cryptographic schemes. Several traditional hash functions are now considered broken [44, 43, 39] and for a few years there has been an urgent need for new ideas. The NIST search for a new standard attracted over sixty submissions [29]. As the competition entered Round 2 in July 2009, the number of participants was reduced to fifteen.

Confidence in the security of hash functions relies traditionally on cryptanalysis. As an alternative, one may try to prove security properties. With a valid security proof at our disposal, we would not need to consider attacks any more.

Several "provably secure" hash functions appeared recently [8, 12, 31, 11, 26, 1, 16, 15]. The language of the proofs is often incompatible with the view of a practitioner. Cryptanalysts normally speak of rather precise time estimates for programs running on real-world hardware. Security proofs should use similar language to provide lower bounds on the effort needed to break a function. We choose to speak of proofs in "real life" and require security to be quantified. We do not view security as a property, but rather as a measure.

A security proof is a *conditional* statement relying on a hardness assumption. Confidence is "transferred" from the (hopefully more basic) hard problem to the hash function. There needs to be some level of confidence to begin with, such assumptions need to be selected very carefully. Examples of "provably secure" functions based on false assumptions include the Zémor-Tillich, LPS and

---

* Supported by a grant of the Swiss National Science Foundation, 200021-116712.

S.-H. Heng and K. Kurosawa (Eds.): ProvSec 2010, LNCS 6402, pp. 119–132, 2010.

Morgenstern hash functions proposed in [40,11,31,33] and broken in [41,32,20]. This paper only deals with functions believed not to be completely broken. In addition we treat assumptions *literally* as assumptions, i.e. we look at what is implied by them without considering their validity in detail. We concentrate on the structure of proofs and their use in security assessment.

We interpret "provable security" arguments behind MQ-HASH [8], FSB [15], SWIFFTX [1] and VSH [12]. Where possible, we take a concrete viewpoint and carefully follow any comparisons between provable bounds and cost of attacks done by the designers. It turns out that the security is sometimes bounded in a rather complex way, failing to provide a proof.

In case of MQ-HASH and FSB we point out gaps in reasoning. No inconsistencies are discovered in the arguments supporting SWIFFT. We observe that although the improved design of SWIFFTX prevents known attacks, the predecessor is as good in terms of proofs.[1] Very Smooth Hash does provide a concrete lower bound on collision resistance. This is only true of some variants.

Related Work. The general limitations of security proofs in cryptology were discussed by Koblitz and Menezes [22, 21]. A concrete analysis of "provable" claims about a particular stream cipher appeared in [45]. This paper also questions security proofs, looking at hash functions that have not been considered from this perspective.

Block cipher based hash functions enjoy well established provable security properties [34,9,38]. Such constructions assume access to an ideal cryptographic primitive, e.g. an ideal cipher. The hardness assumptions and security claims are thus of a different nature compared to the cases considered in this paper. In addition, the framework normally considers adversaries with oracle access to the idealized building block, hence a straightforward comparison to practical attacks is not possible.

All functions considered in this paper were previously cryptanalyzed. This includes work on FSB [13,7], MQ-HASH [4], SWIFFT [10] and VSH [36]. Interestingly, the papers do not relate attacks to the original security proofs.

2   Preliminaries

The functions considered in this paper follow the Merkle-Damgård construction, or a variant thereof [14]. We limit ourselves to *pre-images* and *collisions*. In our analysis we can therefore stick to fixed-length compression functions. Let $\{H_k\}_{k \in K}$ be a finite family of compression functions $H_k : \{0,1\}^m \rightarrow \{0,1\}^n$. Most basic security properties are tied to the hardness of the following two tasks:

Find a pre-image. Given a random $k \in K$ and an element y in the range of H_k compute x such that $H_k(x) = y$.

Find a collision. Given a random $k \in K$ compute $x \neq x'$ such that $H_k(x) = H_k(x')$.

---

[1] This observation was implicit in [1].

Instead of a single fixed function we work with a family of functions parametrized by k, following the designers of all four functions analyzed in Section 3. This is a standard way towards arguments on collision resistance.[2] Prove the security for *random* members of the function family, then pick a single member at random. Such proofs are believed to provide some confidence in security, although efficient algorithms breaking the fixed function *do* exist.

"Classical" definitions prescribe ideal measures of hardness for the two problems. Due to a generic attack, a pre-image can be found after approximately 2^n evaluations of H_k. By the birthday paradox, collisions can be found after about $2^{n/2}$ evaluations of H_k. Hence the usual requirement is "n bit" pre-image resistance and "$n/2$ bit" collision resistance. Rather than following this ambitious goal, let us look for *any* measure of hardness.

Cost of Attacks. Fix a hash function family $\{H_k\}_{k \in K}$. Let elements of a set S represent computational cost. The precise nature of S will vary between families of functions. There are several ways to measure cost of attacks on a cryptographic primitive. Practical examples include hardware cost, processor cycle count, memory. On the more theoretical side, one can measure advantage as a function of runtime, expected runtime, circuit size, etc. For the functions we examine, choices of S are implicit in the statements of theorems on security. In order to allow different approaches to cost, we only require S to be a partially ordered set, i.e. equipped with a *reflexive, antisymmetric* and *transitive* relation '$\leq$'. This captures the minimal assumption that complexities can be compared and allows a lot of freedom in formalization of cost. While it might appear natural to require the ordering on S to be *linear* as well, it is not necessary for our purposes.[3] Let S contain a least element and a greatest element. The former corresponds to zero cost, the latter to cost that is considered too high to be relevant. In most cases, the elements of S will turn out to be numbers counting some basic operation, such as a bit operation or evaluation of H_k.

Let $\mathcal{A}_{\mathrm{Pr}}$ be the set of all probabilistic algorithms that take as input a random $k \in K$, random n-bit y and with non-zero probability output an m-bit string x, such that $H_k(x) = y$.

Similarly, let $\mathcal{A}_{\mathrm{Col}}$ be the set of all probabilistic algorithms that take as input a random $k \in K$ and with non-zero probability output two different m-bit strings x, x', such that $H_k(x) = H_k(x')$. For $A \in \mathcal{A}_{\mathrm{Pr}} \cup \mathcal{A}_{\mathrm{Col}}$ define $c(A) \in S$ to be the expected cost of A solving the respective challenge.

The sets $\mathcal{A}_{\mathrm{Pr}}$ and $\mathcal{A}_{\mathrm{Col}}$ contain all the possible attacks on the security of $\{H_k\}_{k \in K}$, in particular the respective generic attacks.

Bounding Security. Let $\mathcal{A}$ represent either of $\mathcal{A}_{\mathrm{Pr}}$ or $\mathcal{A}_{\mathrm{Col}}$. Define the following two main *types* of bounds on security:

---

[2] For comments and a different approach to the "foundations-of-hashing" dilemma see [35].

[3] This extra freedom can even be desirable.

- $p \in S$ is a bound of type **L** if for all $A \in \mathcal{A}$ the cost $c(A)$ is at least p.
- $q \in S$ is a bound of type **U** if for every $p \in S$ of type **L** it holds that $p \leq q$.

This captures the fact that every attack leads to an upper bound on security. If p is of type **L** and q of type **U**, then $p \leq q$. Note that we chose to define type **U** bounds with respect to **L** bounds, rather than relating them to attacks directly. It is immediate that $c(A)$ is of type **U** for any $A \in \mathcal{A}$. Yet our definitions allow $q \in S$ to be a **U** bound even if there is no $A \in \mathcal{A}$ such that $q = c(A)$. Similarly, it is possible that $p \in S$ is of type **L** and there is no $A \in \mathcal{A}$ such that $p = c(A)$.

We say $\{H_k\}_{k \in K}$ is *provably secure* if we possess a proof that $p \in S$ is of type **L**. The p is a *lower bound* on security against $\mathcal{A}$. A **U** type bound q is an *upper bound* on provable security.

While type **U** bounds are quite common, as will be shown in Section 3, designers do not often establish bounds of type **L**. To interpret certain results, we shall need the two following auxiliary bound types:

- $r \in S$ is a bound of type **lU**, if $r \leq t$ for t of type **U**. This means r is a lower bound on *some* upper bound on security.
- $s \in S$ is a bound of type **uL**, if $s \geq t$ for t of type **L**, i. e. s is an upper bound on *some* lower bound on security.

Every **L** bound is an **lU** bound and every **U** bound is an **uL** bound. Such implications are trivial, as *any* element of S is of type **lU** and **uL** simultaneously. The "weak" types **uL** and **lU** hence provide no direct useful information on provable security. Both are related to a bound t of one of the "useful" types **U** and **L**. Still the types **uL** and **lU** can carry partial information about the bound t if it is not quantified otherwise. For example, an **uL** bound tied to a particular reduction limits how good the reduction is and an **lU** bound tied to a particular attack algorithm limits how much damage the attack causes.

3   Results on Some Hash Functions

In this section we examine security proofs for hash functions and classify the bounds derived by their designers. To illustrate the proofs we follow a single concrete parameter choice from the original proposals. We follow original cost estimates and comparisons, i.e. adopt the implicit S and $c(\cdot)$.

The hardness assumption necessarily has the form of a lower bound. Ideally, security proofs would transform *any* attack on the function to an attack on the underlying hard problem, thereby establishing an **L** bound on security.

Criteria on Proofs. We evaluate security proofs using two simple conditions:

- Is an **L** bound on security established and quantified?
- Does the security level claimed by designers match the proved **L** bound?

3.1   MQ-HASH

The MQ-HASH is a hash function built on the hardness of solving systems of multivariate quadratic equations over $\mathbb{Z}/2\mathbb{Z}$. It was introduced in [8].

Definition. The compression function maps $m + n$ bit input to n bits. Let $r \geq m+n$, and f be an r-tuple of quadratic polynomials in $m+n$ variables over $\mathbb{Z}/2\mathbb{Z}$. Let g be an n-tuple of quadratic polynomials in r variables over the same field. The precise values proposed are $m = 32$, $n = 160$ and $r = 464$. This means f maps 192 bits to 464 bits and g maps 464 bits to 160 bits. Both f and g are to be selected uniformly at random. The compression function of MQ-HASH is the composition of f and g mapping 192 bits to 160 bits.

Hardness Assumption. The designers assume that inverting random systems (of the type of) f and g is hard. For f, the hardness is quantified at $l_f = 2^{103.88}$ binary operations. By assumption, l_f is of type **L**. Because it is a complexity of an actual attack, it has type **U** as well. The implicitly present type **L** bound tied to g is not quantified. Denote it by l_g.

Security Claims. The designers claim the function pre-image resistant proving the following:

Theorem 1. *Let T_f and T_g denote the time required to evaluate f, resp. g. Let A be an algorithm inverting (a random) $g \circ f$ in time T with probability ε. Then A can be either converted to an algorithm inverting g in time $T + T_f + T_g$ with probability ε or to an algorithm that can invert randomly chosen tuples of 464 quadratic polynomials in 192 variables that runs in time*

$$T' = \frac{128 \times 192^2}{\varepsilon^2} \left(T + T_f + 3T_g + \log\left(\frac{128 \times 192}{\varepsilon^2}\right) + 464 \times 192 + 2 \right)$$

and succeeds with probability $\varepsilon/2$.

The theorem coupled with the hardness assumption(s) does indeed establish a lower bound on cost of any algorithm inverting $g \circ f$. If A inverts g, then $T + T_f + T_g \geq l_g$. This implies a lower bound $l_1 = l_g - T_f - T_g$ on T. If A leads to an algorithm inverting f, then $T' \geq l_f$ and $T \geq l_2$ for some l_2. This leads to a provable **L** bound $l = \min\{l_1, l_2\}$ on T. Because l_g is not known, conclude $l \leq l_2$ and examine l_2. Clearly $T' \geq 128 \times 192^2 \times T$, hence the lower bound l_2 implied by l_f is *at most*

$$\frac{l_f}{128 \times 192^2}.$$

Because the value of l_f is known, we obtain $l_2 \leq 2^{82}$. The theorem thus establishes that 2^{82} is a bound of type **uL**. The authors aim at "80-bit security" and claim the level is consistent with what the theorem implies. While $2^{80} \leq 2^{82}$, the latter quantity is merely an upper bound on l_2. The original proof does not lead to a lower bound on l_2. More information on l_g would have to be known and the connection of T and T' would need to be cleaned up.

The quantity 2^{82} counts bit operations. If we want to translate this to the equivalent of hash function computations, divide by the cost of such an evaluation, estimated to be 2^{24} bit operations.[4] The **uL** bound on pre-image resistance

---

[4] The authors do not comment on how the compression function is to be computed, but their 3 MB memory requirement per evaluation is consistent with our estimate.

then becomes 2^{58} evaluations of the compression function. Existence of a pre-image finding attack with such cost would not contradict the theorem.

Collision resistance. There is no proof of collision resistance in [8]. The authors do however sketch an argument in favor of it. Because f is an injection, collisions can only occur in g. Collisions in g are actually easy to find,[5] but in order to lead to collisions in the complete construction, the colliding inputs would have to be in the range of f and that is unlikely. Even if they were, the f is hard to invert. The argument only considers *one particular attack* on collision resistance, hence would only lead to an **U** type bound. Cost of inverting f is equivalent to around 2^{80} evaluations of the compression function, close to the cost of generic collision search, hence the attack is not a serious threat to collision resistance. A proof, however, would require considering *all attacks*, not only a single one.

Because collisions are no harder than pre-images, we might want to make use of the **uL** bound 2^{58} derived there. A **U** bound tied to pre-images would translate to a **U** bound on the cost of collisions. Type **L** bounds need not be preserved. The **uL** bound 2^{58} on pre-images does transfer to the cost of collisions, but carries little useful information. Such a bound needs to be interpreted in the context of the corresponding security proof. In this case it means that Theorem 1 cannot imply a **L** bound on collision resistance that would exceed 2^{58}.

Conclusion. The lower bound implied by Theorem 1 is not quantified due to unspecified l_g and looseness of the reduction. The "80-bit" security claimed by the designers is not supported by an **L** bound. We have derived an **uL** bound tied to the proof at 2^{58} evaluations of the function. Improved proofs may be possible.

3.2   FSB

The hash function based on problems in coding theory has a rather long history of provably secure variants (several of them broken) [2, 3, 16, 17]. The most recent variant of FSB was submitted to the NIST SHA-3 competition, but did not advance to Round 2 [15].

Definition. The FSB consists of an iterated compression function and a final transformation, that compresses the output further. The compression function is defined as follows: Let H be a $r \times n$ binary matrix, let $s = w \times \lg \frac{n}{w}$ be the input length. Encode the input in a word of length n and weight w, denoted by e. Output the r bits He^T. Denote the compression function by f.

Out of the five FSB variants in [15] we pick FSB_{256} as an example with $n = 2^{21}$, $w = 128$, $r = 1024$ and $s = 1792$. Analogous arguments are possible for the other four variants as well.

Hardness Assumption. Security of the compression function is related to two problems from coding theory:

---

[5] This is why a cascade of two systems is used.

Computational Syndrome Decoding (CSD). Given an $r \times n$ matrix H, an r-bit s and integer $w \leq n$, find $x \in \{0,1\}^n$ such that x has Hamming weight at most w and $Hx^T = s$.

Codeword Finding (CF). Given an $r \times n$ matrix H and integer $w \leq n/2$, find $x \in \{0,1\}^n$ such that x has Hamming weight at most $2w$ and $Hx^T = 0$.

Security Claims. The function is proved pre-image resistant reducing to CSD and collision resistant reducing to CF. Both proofs are immediate. There are no explicit lower bounds tied to the assumptions, hence no lower bounds on security are derived. Security is further assessed looking at attacks only. For FSB_{256}, the instances of CSD can be solved in $2^{261.6}$ operations and instances of CF in 2^{153} operations.[6] Both these bounds are due to attacks. Yet the algorithms are not shown to break the actual function, but the more general underlying problems. The reduction goes only one way. A solution to CF or CSD does not imply a collision or a pre-image, respectively. The bounds are therefore of type **uL**.

A more detailed analysis of attacks is performed in [18], estimating cost of two specific algorithms from below, leading to bounds $2^{245.6}$ on CSD and 2^{153} on CF. Again, the problem considered is more general. Extending our notation, their type would be **luL** (i.e. lower bound on a particular **uL** bound). It is suggested these be adopted as **L** bounds [18].

Security is evaluated making use of the **uL** bounds $2^{261.6}$ and 2^{153}. Output of f is 1024 bits long and the security is deep below the trivial bounds, being 2^{1024} and 2^{512}. A final compression is introduced to "fix" this. The 1024 bits are compressed to yield a 256-bit result using another hash function g, instantiated by Whirlpool [5]. The authors remark that "the complexities of the attacks on the FSB compression function . . . can thus be transposed directly to the whole hash function and are all above the complexities of generic attacks on the whole FSB . . ." Collisions in $g \circ f$ are *no harder* to find than collisions in f. The **uL** bound $2^{261.6}$ thus transfers to $g \circ f$. This is above the trivial **U** bound due to a generic attack. Hence we are left with an **U** bound 2^{256} (that is trivially also an **uL** bound). Such a bound is independent of the hardness assumption.

It might seem that the problem is that the g compresses too much. What if the cost of generic attacks on $g \circ f$ is above the cost of attacks on f? Can the 1024 bits be compressed a little less to maintain some of the provable security? With an output of 320 bits, attacking f might be faster. Still this would only yield an **U** bound, because a collision in $g \circ f$ does not imply a collision in f.

Could lower bounds be preserved? Consider collision resistance. A collision in $g \circ f$ implies a collision in one of the two components. If there were **L** bounds l_f and l_g tied to f and g respectively, the smaller of the two would then be a lower bound on security of the composition. Such proof would be possible if g could be assumed collision resistant in the first place.[7] Although composing the FSB compression function with a provably collision resistant final transformation can preserve the lower bound(s), it would resemble a circular argument

---

[6] Counting evaluations of f.

[7] If g is fixed, the assumption is trivially false.

where a provably collision resistant function is designed given a provably collision resistant function. This trivial observation only appears in [17] and is left out of the submission to NIST [15].

The authors of FSB consider collision resistance of Whirlpool too strong an assumption [15]. For eventual collisions in Whirlpool to extend to the complete FSB_{256} one needs to invert the FSB primitive. However, saying that collisions for Whirlpool do not easily extend to the complete FSB is an argument from the attack perspective and not a proof. Just as in the case of MQ-HASH earlier, this looks at *particular* attacks and thus does not establish **L** bounds.

Conclusion. One claim of the designers in [15] reads as follows:

> The most decisive advantage of FSB is that it comes with a proof of reduction to hard algorithmic problems. An algorithm able to find collisions on FSB or to invert FSB is also able to solve hard problems from coding theory.

No such statement is proved in any of the proposals. The security level claimed by designers is not supported by an **L** bound. This is due to the final compression using Whirlpool. If the step were omitted, **L** bounds on the coding problems would transfer to the compression function. Such bounds were not explicitly provided.

3.3 SWIFFT(X)

SWIFFTX is a SHA-3 proposal based on the simpler primitive SWIFFT [24, 26], not making it to Round 2. It is an example of a generalized knapsack function [27] with security based on hardness of lattice problems.

Definition[8]**.** The SWIFFT compression function takes as input r 64-bit words $x_1, \ldots, x_r$ and outputs 64 elements $z'_0, \ldots, z'_{63} \in \mathbb{Z}_{257}$. The function is indexed by $64r$ fixed elements $a_{1,0}, \ldots, a_{r,63} \in \mathbb{Z}_{257}$ taken to be uniformly random integers modulo 257. Let

$$\mathrm{rev} : \{0, \ldots, 63\} \to \{0, \ldots, 63\}$$

be the "bit-reversal" function on 6-bit binary numbers. Output of SWIFFT can be expressed as follows:

$$z'_i = \sum_{j=1}^{r} a_{j,i} \sum_{k=0}^{63} x_{j,\mathrm{rev}(k)} \cdot \omega^{(2i+1)k}$$

where $\omega = 42$, $x_{j,i}$ is the i-th bit of x_j and arithmetic is performed modulo 257. Within SWIFFTX, r equals either 32 or 25.

---

[8] Copied almost verbatim from [1].

Hardness Assumption. Finding short vectors in lattices isomorphic to ideals of $\mathbb{Z}[\alpha]/(\alpha^d + 1)$ is hard in the worst case as d increases.[9] The assumption is asymptotic and the **L** bound unquantified. In the light of the results in [19] it was pointed out that for the choice $d = 64$ used in SWIFFT variants as above, the lattice problems are actually easy and the lower bound "insignificant" [10].

Security Claims. The SWIFFT function family is proved collision and pre-image resistant [30, 25, 27]. The proof establishes the security properties as the output length increases to infinity.[10] Although asymptotic, the proof does link security of the function for any particular value of d to hardness of a precise lattice problem. We will therefore consider SWIFFT equipped with an **L** bound, yet unknown.

According to the designers in [1]:

> To quantify the exact security of our functions, it is still crucially important to cryptanalyze our specific parameter choices and particular instances of the function.

Instead of finding an **L** bound tied to a proof, the approach chosen is to concentrate on upper bounds due to attacks. While such analysis only establishes bounds of type **U** or **lU**, it does reveal limits of the security proofs provided by the designers of SWIFFT.

The proposal mentions actual attacks on SWIFFT applying the generalized birthday algorithm by Wagner [42]. For $r = 32$, collisions can be found in 2^{106} operations and pre-images in 2^{128} operations. Although the complexities are described as **lU** bounds and estimate the cost of attacks from below, they can be considered good approximations to the actual cost,[11] i.e. bounds of type **U**. Both the bounds are used as such in the proposal to quantify security of the function. Furthermore, the bounds were derived for SWIFFT with $r = 16$ [26]. With $r = 32$ the actual complexities would be lower. While the provable lower bound is not quantified, the two attacks provide **uL** bounds limiting what can be drawn from the proofs available.

For $r = 25$ the authors mention a pre-image finding attack that requires 2^{100} operations. This is an **U** bound, hence also an **uL** bound. Because collisions can be found in at most the same time as pre-images, the same **uL** bound applies to provable collision resistance.

SWIFFTX. Existence of the attacks motivated design of the compression function SWIFFTX. It maps 2048 bits to 520 bits combining four calls to SWIFFT with some extra operations in a way that is believed to make the known attacks inefficient. The precise details of the construction can be found in [1]. Care is taken to preserve the provable collision and pre-image resistance. First the input is compressed using three "parallel" instances of SWIFFT with $r = 32$ to yield

---

[9] Precise statements in [30, 27].

[10] Such arguments have become commonplace in provable security.

[11] Our analysis of the runtime leads to the complexities $2^{106.4}$ and 2^{131}.

1560 bits. A fixed (easily invertible) injection extends this to 1600 bits. Then a single SWIFFT instance with $r = 25$ is applied and 520 bits are output.

The known attacks do not easily extend to SWIFFTX. More precisely, the extended attacks are shown to be more expensive than generic attacks. The construction thus "wipes out" the non-trivial **U** bounds. According to an argument sketched in [1], the construction maintains provable security. A collision in SWIFFTX implies a collision in (at least) one of the four SWIFFT components.[12] Effectively, the *least* of the lower bounds that applied to SWIFFT building blocks is valid for SWIFFTX. We obtain an **uL** bound 2^{100} on provable security for both security properties.

Conclusion. The authors of SWIFFTX rely on attacks and claim pre-image resistance 2^{512} and collision resistance 2^{256}. These are not justified by **L** bounds. While the security proofs would lead to **L** bounds, they are not quantified. The improved function SWIFFTX is no more secure than the original SWIFFT primitive in terms of proofs. The **L** bounds implied by the proof provided cannot exceed 2^{100}. As this is an **uL** bound, improved proofs may be possible.

3.4   VSH

The function VSH was introduced in [12] along with a few variants. Some more appeared in [23]. Security of the hash function is linked to hardness of factoring or discrete logarithms.

Definition. Let M be an n-bit hard to factor modulus,[13] denote the i-th prime number by p_i. Let k be the largest integer such that $\prod_{i=1}^{k} p_i < M$. Let m be a l-bit message to be hashed, consisting of bits $m_1, \ldots, m_l$ and assume $l < 2^k$. The algorithm runs as follows:

1. Let $x_0 = 1$.
2. Let $\mathcal{L} = \lceil \frac{l}{k} \rceil$. Let $m_i = 0$ for $l < i \leq \mathcal{L}k$.
3. Let $l = \sum_{i=1}^{k} l_i 2^{i-1}$ with $l_i \in \{0, 1\}$ be the binary representation of l and define $m_{\mathcal{L}k+i} = l_i$ for $1 \leq i \leq k$.
4. For $j = 0, 1, \ldots, \mathcal{L}$ in succession compute

$$x_{j+1} = x_j^2 \times \prod_{i=1}^{k} p_i^{m_{j \cdot k + i}} \quad \mod M$$

5. Return $x_\mathcal{L}$.

The function iteratively processes blocks of k bits and outputs an n-bit hash. Effectively, it computes a modular k-fold multiexponentiation. The function operates in a variant of the Merkle-Damgård mode processing k bits per iteration. The compression function is not collision resistant, yet the iterated construction is.[14]

---

[12] An analogous argument is possible for pre-image resistance.
[13] Typically a product of two large primes.
[14] Details in [12].

Hardness Assumption. Given a random M it is hard to find $x \in \mathbb{Z}_M^*$ such that $x^2 \equiv \prod_{i=1}^{k} p_i^{e_i} \mod M$ with at least one e_i is odd. The problem is assumed to be k-times easier than the problem of factoring M.

Security Claims. The only security property claimed by the designers is collision resistance. Define the function $L'[M]$ to approximate heuristic running time of the Number Field Sieve algorithm factoring the integer M. Assuming this is an **L** bound on hardness of factoring, finding a collision in VSH takes time at least

$$\frac{L'[M]}{k}$$

This **L** bound is used as the basis for security assessment. As an example, collisions in VSH with $n = 1234$ and $k = 152$ are at least as hard to find as it is to factor a 1024 bit (hard to factor) number [12].

No attack is known that would achieve the lower bound. There is an attack and a (non-trivial) **U** bound on security, though. With the knowledge of $\varphi(M)$, collisions can be created easily. Computing $\varphi(M)$ from M is as hard as factoring the modulus. Factorization of M is essentially a trapdoor in the function.

There is an algorithm that finds collisions in VSH factoring the modulus in time approximately $L'[M]$. This is the least **U** bound known. The security of VSH is somewhere between the **L** bound and the **U** bound. So far, no result has appeared that would get the (provable) lower bound closer to the complexity of factoring the modulus M.

Discrete Logarithm Variant of VSH. If the modulus chosen to be a prime number of the form $2p+1$ for p a large prime and length of input is limited below $k(n-2)$ bits a VSH-DL compression function is obtained. It is computed in the same way as the basic VSH described above. The function is proved collision resistant under a new assumption related to hardness of discrete logarithms in $\mathbb{Z}_M^*$. The assumption is not quantified, hence no lower bound on security of VSH-DL is obtained. Yet an **U** bound is easy to derive, because finding collisions in VSH-DL is no harder than computing discrete logarithms.

Conclusion. Collision resistance of basic VSH is supported by an **L** bound and the designers claim precisely the security that is proved. While the DL variant admits a proof, no measure is associated with its hardness assumption. A proof that does not exceed the known **U** bound may be possible.

4   Summary

While several hash function designs claim provable security, only a few actually link security to the complexity associated with the proof.

We gave examples of **uL** bounds that provide partial information on unknown lower bounds. In this way we limit provable security of MQ-HASH and SWIFFT(X) from above. Such arguments are not due to attacks that would actually break the functions. We can view them as *partial attacks* on proofs. We have demonstrated that such incomplete attacks can provide very concrete and useful information on security levels one can prove. Our bounds speak of *particular* proofs, therefore proofs with higher security levels remain possible.

Three of the functions had the structure of compositions. MQ-HASH composed two functions equipped with **L** bounds on pre-image resistance in a way that leads to an unknown **L** bound on security of the composition. FSB composed a function admitting an **L** bound[15] and a function without such a bound. As a result, the proof disappears, while the complexity of attacks is preserved. Finally, the composition within SWIFFTX preserves the proofs and invalidates (some) attacks. While the approaches appear similar, the outcomes differ significantly. Although some general conclusions could be made, bounds in any provable design need to be carefully examined.

We do advocate the use of proofs (i.e. **L** bounds) in design & analysis of hash functions. We hope to have clarified some very basic features of attacks and proofs in hash function security assessment. If there is both an **L** bound and an **U** bound, the former should be pronounced the security level. We believe the function cannot be considered provably secure otherwise. If more security is claimed, this is based on attacks rather than on proofs, rendering the proofs somewhat useless. If it is believed that security is greater than what the proofs suggest, attempts should be made to raise the **L** bound.

Our results should not be viewed as recommendations against or in favor of any of the functions but rather as suggestions where to look for improvements. A tighter reduction within MQ-HASH and quantified hardness of g might well lead to an **L** bound that exceeds 2^{58}. The FSB may as well have a decent **L** bound if the final transformation is omitted. More conditions on the last step g might even allow an **L** bound to be established for the complete construction. Quantified hardness assumptions behind SWIFFT and VSH-DL would also lead to precise **L** bounds.

Acknowledgements. The author would like to thank Arjen Lenstra, Martijn Stam, Kenny Paterson and the anonymous reviewers for useful comments on the text.

References

1. Arbitman, Y., Dogon, G., Lyubashevsky, V., Micciancio, D., Peikert, C., Rosen, A.: SWIFFTX: A Proposal for the SHA-3 Standard. Submission to NIST (2008)
2. Augot, D., Finiasz, M., Sendrier, N.: A fast provably secure cryptographic hash function. Cryptology ePrint Archive, Report 2003/230 (2003), http://eprint.iacr.org/
3. Augot, D., Finiasz, M., Sendrier, N.: A family of fast syndrome based cryptographic hash functions. In: Dawson, E., Vaudenay, S. (eds.) Mycrypt 2005. LNCS, vol. 3715, pp. 64–83. Springer, Heidelberg (2005)

---

[15] The assumption is not explicitly stated in the proposals.

4. Aumasson, J.-P., Meier, W.: Analysis of multivariate hash functions. In: Nam, K.-H., Rhee, G. (eds.) ICISC 2007. LNCS, vol. 4817, pp. 309–323. Springer, Heidelberg (2007)
5. Barreto, P.S.L.M., Rijmen, V.: The Whirlpool hashing function. Submitted to NESSIE (September 2000) (revised May 2003), http://www.larc.usp.br/~pbarreto/WhirlpoolPage.html
6. Barua, R., Lange, T. (eds.): INDOCRYPT 2006. LNCS, vol. 4329. Springer, Heidelberg (2006)
7. Bernstein, D.J., Lange, T., Niederhagen, R., Peters, C., Schwabe, P.: Implementing Wagner's generalized birthday attack against the SHA-3 round-1 candidate FSB. Cryptology ePrint Archive, Report 2009/292 (2009), http://eprint.iacr.org/
8. Billet, O., Robshaw, M.J.B., Peyrin, T.: On building hash functions from multivariate quadratic equations. In: Pieprzyk, J., Ghodosi, H., Dawson, E. (eds.) ACISP 2007. LNCS, vol. 4586, pp. 82–95. Springer, Heidelberg (2007)
9. Black, J., Rogaway, P., Shrimpton, T.: Black-box analysis of the block-cipher-based hash-function constructions from PGV. In: Yung [46], pp. 320–335
10. Buchmann, J., Lindner, R.: Secure parameters for SWIFFT. In: Roy, B. K., Sendrier, N. (eds.) INDOCRYPT 2009. LNCS, vol. 5922, pp. 1–17. Springer, Heidelberg (2009)
11. Charles, D.X., Lauter, K.E., Goren, E.Z.: Cryptographic hash functions from expander graphs. J. Cryptology 22(1), 93–113 (2009)
12. Contini, S., Lenstra, A.K., Steinfeld, R.: VSH, an efficient and provable collision-resistant hash function. In: Vaudenay, S. (ed.) EUROCRYPT 2006. LNCS, vol. 4004, pp. 165–182. Springer, Heidelberg (2006)
13. Coron, J.-S., Joux, A.: Cryptanalysis of a provably secure cryptographic hash function. Cryptology ePrint Archive, Report 2004/013 (2004)
14. Damgård, I.: A design principle for hash functions. In: Brassard, G. (ed.) CRYPTO 1989. LNCS, vol. 435, pp. 416–427. Springer, Heidelberg (1990)
15. Augot, D., Finiasz, M., Gaborit, P., Manuel, S., Sendrier, N.: SHA-3 proposal: FSB. Submission to NIST (2008)
16. Finiasz, M., Gaborit, P., Sendrier, N.: Improved fast syndrome based cryptographic hash functions. In: ECRYPT Hash Function Workshop 2007 (2007)
17. Finiasz, M.: Syndrome based collision resistant hashing. In: Buchmann, J., Ding, J. (eds.) PQCrypto 2008. LNCS, vol. 5299, pp. 137–147. Springer, Heidelberg (2008)
18. Finiasz, M., Sendrier, N.: Security bounds for the design of code-based cryptosystems. In: Matsui, M. (ed.) ASIACRYPT 2009. LNCS, vol. 5912, pp. 88–105. Springer, Heidelberg (2009)
19. Gama, N., Nguyen, P.Q.: Predicting lattice reduction. In: Smart [37], pp. 31–51
20. Grassl, M., Ilić, I., Magliveras, S., Steinwandt, R.: Cryptanalysis of the Tillich–Zémor Hash Function. Journal of Cryptology (2010)
21. Koblitz, N., Menezes, A.: Another Look at "Provable Security". II. In: Barua, Lange (eds.) [6], pp. 148–175
22. Koblitz, N., Menezes, A.: Another Look at "Provable Security". J. Cryptology 20(1), 3–37 (2007)
23. Lenstra, A.K., Page, D., Stam, M.: Discrete logarithm variants of VSH. In: Nguyen (ed.) [28], pp. 229–242
24. Lyubashevsky, V., Micciancio, D., Peikert, C., Rosen, A.: Provably Secure FFT Hashing. In: 2nd NIST Cryptographic Hash Function Workshop (2006)
25. Lyubashevsky, V., Micciancio, D.: Generalized compact knapsacks are collision resistant. In: Bugliesi, M., Preneel, B., Sassone, V., Wegener, I. (eds.) ICALP 2006. LNCS, vol. 4052, pp. 144–155. Springer, Heidelberg (2006)

26. Lyubashevsky, V., Micciancio, D., Peikert, C., Rosen, A.: SWIFFT: A modest proposal for FFT hashing. In: Nyberg, K. (ed.) FSE 2008. LNCS, vol. 5086, pp. 54–72. Springer, Heidelberg (2008)

27. Micciancio, D.: Generalized compact knapsacks, cyclic lattices, and efficient one-way functions. Computational Complexity 16(4), 365–411 (2007)

28. Nguyên, P.Q. (ed.): VIETCRYPT 2006. LNCS, vol. 4341. Springer, Heidelberg (2006)

29. National Institute of Standards and Technology. Announcing request for candidate algorithm nominations for a new cryptographic hash algorithm (SHA3) family. Federal Register 72(212), 62212–62220 (November 2007)

30. Peikert, C., Rosen, A.: Efficient collision-resistant hashing from worst-case assumptions on cyclic lattices. In: Halevi, S., Rabin, T. (eds.) TCC 2006. LNCS, vol. 3876, pp. 145–166. Springer, Heidelberg (2006)

31. Petit, C., Lauter, K., Quisquater, J.J.: Cayley Hashes: A Class of Efficient Graph-based Hash Functions. Preprint (2007)

32. Petit, C., Lauter, K., Quisquater, J.-J.: Full cryptanalysis of LPS and Morgenstern hash functions. In: Ostrovsky, R., De Prisco, R., Visconti, I. (eds.) SCN 2008. LNCS, vol. 5229, pp. 263–277. Springer, Heidelberg (2008)

33. Petit, C., Quisquater, J.-J., Tillich, J.-P., Zémor, G.: Hard and easy components of collision search in the Zémor-Tillich hash function: New attacks and reduced variants with equivalent security. In: Fischlin, M. (ed.) RSA Conference 2009. LNCS, vol. 5473, pp. 182–194. Springer, Heidelberg (2009)

34. Preneel, B., Govaerts, R., Vandewalle, J.: Hash functions based on block ciphers: A synthetic approach. In: Stinson, D.R. (ed.) CRYPTO 1993. LNCS, vol. 773, pp. 368–378. Springer, Heidelberg (1994)

35. Rogaway, P.: Formalizing human ignorance. In: Nguyen (ed.) [28], pp. 211–228

36. Saarinen, M.-J.O.: Security of VSH in the real world. In: Barua, Lange [6], pp. 95–103

37. Smart, N.P. (ed.): EUROCRYPT 2008. LNCS, vol. 4965. Springer, Heidelberg (2008)

38. Stam, M.: Blockcipher-based hashing revisited. In: Dunkelman, O. (ed.) Fast Software Encryption. LNCS, vol. 5665, pp. 67–83. Springer, Heidelberg (2009)

39. Stevens, M., Lenstra, A.K., de Weger, B.: Chosen-Prefix Collisions for MD5 and Colliding X.509 Certificates for Different Identities. In: Naor, M. (ed.) EURO-CRYPT 2007. LNCS, vol. 4515, pp. 1–22. Springer, Heidelberg (2007)

40. Tillich, J.-P., Zémor, G.: Hashing with SL_2. In: Desmedt, Y.G. (ed.) CRYPTO 1994. LNCS, vol. 839, pp. 40–49. Springer, Heidelberg (1994)

41. Tillich, J.-P., Zémor, G.: Collisions for the LPS expander graph hash function. In: Smart [37], pp. 254–269

42. Wagner, D.: A generalized birthday problem. In: Yung [46], pp. 288–303

43. Wang, X., Yin, Y.L., Yu, H.: Finding collisions in the full SHA-1. In: Shoup, V. (ed.) CRYPTO 2005. LNCS, vol. 3621, pp. 17–36. Springer, Heidelberg (2005)

44. Wang, X., Yu, H.: How to break MD5 and other hash functions. In: Cramer, R. (ed.) EUROCRYPT 2005. LNCS, vol. 3494, pp. 19–35. Springer, Heidelberg (2005)

45. Yang, B.-Y., Chen, C.-H.O., Bernstein, D.J., Chen, J.-M.: Analysis of QUAD. In: Biryukov, A. (ed.) FSE 2007. LNCS, vol. 4593, pp. 290–308. Springer, Heidelberg (2007)

46. Yung, M. (ed.): CRYPTO 2002. LNCS, vol. 2442. Springer, Heidelberg (2002)

Formal and Precise Analysis of Soundness of Several Shuffling Schemes

Kun Peng and Feng Bao

Institute for Infocomm Research
dr.kun.peng@gmail.com

Abstract. Some of the most efficient shuffling schemes employ the same main idea to prove validity of shuffling. However, the principle behind the idea has not been explained in a completely formal and precise way. So formal guarantee of soundness of the shuffling schemes is not complete. Especially, it is unknown exactly how large the probability of failure of soundness is and exactly how strong soundness is. In this paper, why the proof mechanism guarantees validity of shuffling is formally proved to provide a formal guarantee of soundness of those shuffling schemes. Especially, the exact upper bound of the probability of failure of soundness is given to convincingly ensure soundness. Although we do not doubt soundness of most of the shuffling schemes, a formal and precise proof of their soundness is still valuable as it strengthens security guarantee of the schemes and removes a potential obstacle for their application to critical environments requiring formally guaranteed and measurable soundness. Moreover, the formal and precise proof shows that some shuffling scheme has serious problem in soundness.

Keywords: shuffling, soundness, formal proof, precise guarantee.

1 Introduction

Anonymous channel is used to transmit anonymous messages and needed in a wide range of anonymous communication applications like anonymous email [3], anonymous browsing [7] and electronic voting [13,10]. An anonymous channel is publicly verifiable if it can be publicly verified that no message is lost or tampered with in the channel. In applications like e-voting, public verifiability is necessary. Of course, any verification mechanism cannot compromise anonymity of the messages. Shuffling [1,2,6,13,14,10,20,19,12,9,8,17,18] is a very important cryptographic tool to implement publicly verifiable anonymous channels. In shuffling, a shuffling node receives multiple ciphertexts and must shuffle them such that after the shuffling none of the ciphertext can be traced back to its origin. The shuffling node re-encrypts and reorders the ciphertexts before outputting them, such that the messages encrypted in the output ciphertexts is a permutation of the messages encrypted in the input ciphertexts. Repeated shuffling operations by different nodes form a publicly verifiable anonymous channel. If at least one shuffling node conceals the permutation it uses in its shuffling, the

S.-H. Heng and K. Kurosawa (Eds.): ProvSec 2010, LNCS 6402, pp. 133–143, 2010.
© Springer-Verlag Berlin Heidelberg 2010

messages transmitted in the channel are anonymous. The following properties must be satisfied in shuffling.

- Correctness: if the shuffling node follows the shuffling protocol, the plaintexts encrypted in the output ciphertexts are a permutation of the plaintexts encrypted in the input ciphertexts.
- Public verifiability: the shuffling node can publicly prove that he does not deviate from the shuffling protocol.
- Soundness: a successfully verified proof by a shuffling node guarantees that the plaintexts encrypted in the output ciphertexts are a permutation of the plaintexts encrypted in the input ciphertexts.
- Privacy: the permutation used by the shuffling node is not revealed.

In this paper we focus on soundness of shuffling, which is formally and precisely defined as follows.

Definition 1. *In this paper, a proof of soundness is called a formal proof if a complete mathematic deduction from the shuffling operation to the conclusion that the messages encrypted in the output ciphertexts is a permutation of the messages encrypted in the input ciphertexts is provided. A soundness proof is called a precise proof if the concrete probability that soundness fails is found out and clearly demonstrated to be negligible in terms of some concrete security parameters. Intuitive guess that the probability is negligible or the probability that soundness is achieved is overwhelmingly large without a convincing proof based on concrete security parameters is not acceptable.*

A few shuffling schemes [1,2,6,13,14,10,20,19,12,21,9,8,17,18] have been published in recent years. The most difficult and inefficient operation in those schemes is proof and verification of validity of shuffling, while re-encryption is much simpler and efficient. Some of them including the existing most efficient shuffling schemes [10,19,21,9,17,8] employ the same idea to prove validity of shuffling. Suppose input ciphertexts $c_1, c_2, \ldots, c_n$ are shuffled to output ciphertexts $c'_1, c'_2, \ldots, c'_n$. Those shuffling schemes [10,19,21,9,17,8] claim that if

$$RE(\textstyle\prod_{i=1}^{n} c_i^{t_i}) = \prod_{i=1}^{n} c'^{t'_i}_i \tag{1}$$

and t_i for $i = 1, 2, \ldots, n$ are random integers and $t'_1, t'_2, \ldots, t'_n$ is a permutation of $t_1, t_2, \ldots, t_n$ then $D(c'_1), D(c'_2), \ldots, D(c'_n)$ is a permutation of $D(c_1), D(c_2), \ldots, D(c_n)$ with an overwhelmingly large probability where $RE()$ denotes re-encryption function[1] of the employed encryption algorithm. Their claim seems reasonable. However, they do not give a formal proof for this claim. Especially, they do not provide the exact upper bound of the probability of failure of soundness in terms of concrete parameters. Obviously, a precise proof

---

[1] Re-encryption is a probabilistic operation on a ciphertext and output another ciphertext containing the same message. It is supported by various probabilistic encryption algorithms like ElGamal encryption and Paillier encryption. More details can be found in detailed descriptions of those encryption algorithms.

giving an exact upper bound of the probability of failure like 0.0000001 or 2^{-L} where L is a large security parameter is much more convincing in illustrating soundness than an abstract claim that "the probability of failure is negligible" or "soundness is achieved with an overwhelmingly large probability" without giving the exact probability. According to our definition of soundness, their proof of soundness is not formal or precise enough. It is inappropriate to claim that the probability of soundness is overwhelmingly large while no concrete probability of either achievement of soundness or failure of soundness is available. This drawback in provable soundness of the shuffling schemes causes concerns about soundness and reliability of them and limits their application to critical environments requiring formally guaranteed and measurable soundness.

In this paper, it is formally proved why satisfaction of (1) guarantees $D(c'_1), D(c'_2), \ldots, D(c'_n)$ is a permutation of $D(c_1), D(c_2), \ldots, D(c_n)$ and exactly how strong the guarantee is. The probability of failure of soundness while (1) is satisfied is given in terms of concrete parameters. Two formal mathematical theorems are proposed to specify the formal proof respectively with additive homomorphic encryption algorithm and multiplicative homomorphic encryption algorithm (to be defined later). It is clearly shown that with both kinds of encryption algorithms (1) guarantees that the messages encrypted in the output ciphertexts is a permutation of the messages encrypted in the input ciphertexts, the probability of whose failure is definitely demonstrated to be negligible in regard to some concrete security parameters. Instantiating parameters and precise analysis bring another merit: as the probability of soundness is a simple function of the security parameters which also decide the efficiency of the protocols, the parameters can be appropriately chosen to achieve a better trade-off between strength of soundness and efficiency. Thus efficiency of the shuffling protocols can be improved in practical applications. Moreover, it helps to determine what kind of parameter setting and operational cost are necessary to satisfy the concrete soundness requirement of a certain application. In addition, our analysis shows that the shuffling scheme by Wikstrom [21] has a serious problem in soundness as it fails to guarantee that $t'_1, t'_2, \ldots, t'_n$ is a permutation of $t_1, t_2, \ldots, t_n$ in 1, whose importance and necessity have been formally proved in this paper.

2 Formal and Precise Proof of Achievement of Soundness in Shuffling

In the shuffling schemes depending on (1) [10,19,21,9,17,8], several encryption algorithms may be employed. They can be classified into two types: additive homomorphic encryption algorithms and multiplicative homomorphic encryption algorithms. An additive homomorphic encryption algorithm with decryption function $D()$ requires that $D(c_1 c_2) = D(c_1) + D(c_2)$ for any ciphertexts c_1 and c_2. A typical example of additive homomorphic encryption algorithm is Paillier encryption [16]. A multiplicative homomorphic encryption algorithm with decryption function $D()$ requires that $D(c_1 c_2) = D(c_1)D(c_2)$ for any ciphertexts c_1 and c_2. A typical example of multiplicative homomorphic encryption algorithm is ElGamal encryption. All the shuffling schemes depending on (1) support both ElGamal encryption and Paillier encryption. Proof of soundness based on (1) is given in two theorems respectively handling shuffling with ElGamal encryption and shuffling with Paillier encryption. Our analysis demonstrates that complete formal and precise proof of soundness of shuffling needs instantiated parameter setting. In description of the new proof technique, $Pr\left[\ \mu_1, \mu_2, \ldots, \mu_n \in S \mid F\ \right]$ denotes the probability that condition F is satisfied with variables $\mu_1, \mu_2, \ldots, \mu_n$ uniformly distributed over S.

2.1 Shuffling Employing Multiplicative Homomorphic Encryption Algorithm

Let's recall the parameter setting of shuffling schemes employing ElGamal encryption.

- G_1 is a cyclic group with order q and multiplication modulus p where $p-1 = 2q$ and p, q are large primes. More generally, $p-1$ is a multiple of q and $(p-1)/q$ may be larger than 2. For simplicity and without losing generality, the most usual setting in shuffling with ElGamal encryption is adopted: $p-1 = 2q$.
- Let g_1 be a generator of G_1. Private key x is chosen (usually generated and shared by multiple parties) from Z_q and public key $y = g_1^x$ is published.
- The message space is G_1. A message m is encrypted into $E(m) = (g_1^r, my^r)$ where r is randomly chosen from Z_q.
- A ciphertext $c = (a, b)$ can be re-encrypted into $RE(c) = (ag_1^r, by^r)$ where r is randomly chosen from Z_q.
- A ciphertext $c = (a, b)$ is decrypted into b/a^x.
- Product of two ciphertexts $c_1 = (a_1, b_1)$ and $c_2 = (a_2, b_2)$ is $c_1 c_2 = (a_1 a_2, b_1 b_2)$

Suppose the input ciphertexts are $c_i = (a_i, b_i)$ for $i = 1, 2, \ldots, n$ and they are shuffled to $c_i' = RE(c_{\pi(i)}) = (a_i', b_i')$ for $i = 1, 2, \ldots, n$ where $\pi()$ is a random permutation of $\{1, 2, \ldots, n\}$. Random L-bit integers t_i for $i = 1, 2, \ldots, n$ are chosen (e.g. by a verifier or multiple verifiers) where L is a security parameter and $2^L < q$. The shuffling node proves satisfaction of (1).

Note that the setting requiring that p is prime, $p-1 = 2q$, message space is G_1 and $2^L < q$ is a little more strict than in some shuffling schemes. Theorem 1 and a special check-and-adjustment mechanism[2] in Figure 1 demonstrate that such a setting helps to guarantee soundness of shuffling. So it is suggested to be adopted by the shuffling schemes depending on (1). If message G_1 is not suitable for an application (e.g. requiring a message space in the form of Z_ρ), it is suggested to employ an additive homomorphic encryption algorithm and use the technique in Section 2.2.

---

[2] This check-and-adjustment mechanism is necessary for soundness of shuffling although it is sometimes ignored (e.g. in [10]).

Theorem 1. *When $a'_1, b_1, a'_2, b'_2, \ldots, a'_n, b'_n$ are in G_1, the probability that (1) is successfully proved and verified but $D(c'_1), D(c'_2), \ldots, D(c'_n)$ is not a permutation of $D(c_1), D(c_2), \ldots, D(c_n)$ is a negligible concrete probability.*

To prove Theorem 1, a lemma is proved first.

Lemma 1. *Suppose $y_i, z_i \in G_1$ for $i = 1, 2, \ldots, n$. Let t_i for $i = 1, 2, \ldots, n$ be random integers such that $t_i < 2^L$. If $Pr\ [\ t_1, t_2, \ldots, t_n \in \{0, 1, \ldots, 2^L - 1\}\ |\ \log_{g_1} \prod_{i=1}^n y_i^{t_i} = \log_y \prod_{i=1}^n z_i^{t_i}\ ] > 2^{-L}$, then $\log_{g_1} y_i = \log_y z_i$ for $i = 1, 2, \ldots, n$.*

Proof: $Pr\ [\ t_1, t_2, \ldots, t_n \in \{0, 1, \ldots, 2^L - 1\}\ |\ \log_{g_1} \prod_{i=1}^n y_i^{t_i} = \log_y \prod_{i=1}^n z_i^{t_i}\ ] > 2^{-L}$ implies that for any given integer v in $\{1, 2, \ldots, n\}$ there must exist integers $t_1, t_2, \ldots, t_n$ and t'_v in $\{0, 1, \ldots, 2^L - 1\}$ such that

$$\log_{g_1} \prod_{i=1}^n y_i^{t_i} = \log_y \prod_{i=1}^n z_i^{t_i} \qquad (2)$$

$$\log_{g_1} ((\prod_{i=1}^{v-1} y_i^{t_i}) y_v^{t'_v} \prod_{i=v+1}^n y_i^{t_i}) = \log_y ((\prod_{i=1}^{v-1} z_i^{t_i}) z_v^{t'_v} \prod_{i=v+1}^n z_i^{t_i}) \qquad (3)$$

Otherwise, for any $(t_1, t_2, \ldots, t_{v-1}, t_{v+1}, \ldots, t_n)$, there is at most one t_v to satisfy $\log_{g_1} \prod_{i=1}^n y_i^{t_i} = \log_y \prod_{i=1}^n z_i^{t_i}$. This implies that among the 2^{nL} possible choices for $(t_1, t_2, \ldots, t_n)$ (combination of $2^{(n-1)L}$ possible choices for $(t_1, t_2, \ldots, t_{v-1}, t_{v+1}, \ldots, t_n)$ and 2^L possible choices for t_v) there is at most $2^{(n-1)L}$ choices to satisfy $\log_{g_1} \prod_{i=1}^n y_i^{t_i} = \log_y \prod_{i=1}^n z_i^{t_i}$, which is a contradiction to the assumption that $Pr\ [\ t_1, t_2, \ldots, t_n \in \{0, 1, \ldots, 2^L - 1\}\ |\ \log_{g_1} \prod_{i=1}^n y_i^{t_i} = \log_y \prod_{i=1}^n z_i^{t_i}\ ] > 2^{-L}$.

(2) divided by (3) yields

$$log_{g_1} y_v^{t_v - t'_v} = log_y z_v^{t_v - t'_v}$$

Namely

$$(t_v - t'_v) log_{g_1} y_v = (t_v - t'_v) log_y z_v \bmod q$$

Note that $t_v \neq t'_v$ and $t_v, t'_v < 2^L < q$. So $t_v - t'_v \neq 0 \bmod q$ and

$$log_{g_1} y_v = log_y z_v$$

Therefore, $\log_{g_1} y_i = \log_y z_i$ for $i = 1, 2, \ldots, n$ as v can be any integer in $\{1, 2, \ldots, n\}$. $\qquad \square$

Proof of Theorem 1: Let A_1 be the event that $D(c'_1), D(c'_2), \ldots, D(c'_n)$ is a permutation of $D(c_1), D(c_2), \ldots, D(c_n)$; A_2 be the event that (1) is correct; A_3 be the event that the shuffling passes the verification of (1); $P(A)$ denote the probability of event A.

$$P(A_3/\bar{A}_1) = P((A_3 \wedge A_2)/\bar{A}_1) + P((A_3 \wedge \bar{A}_2)/\bar{A}_1)$$
$$= P(A_3 \wedge A_2 \wedge \bar{A}_1)/P(\bar{A}_1) + P(A_3 \wedge \bar{A}_2 \wedge \bar{A}_1)/P(\bar{A}_1)$$
$$= P(\bar{A}_1 \wedge A_2)P(A_3/\bar{A}_1 \wedge A_2)/P(\bar{A}_1) +$$

$$P(A_3 \wedge \bar{A}_2 \wedge \bar{A}_1)P(\bar{A}_2 \wedge \bar{A}_1)/(P(\bar{A}_1)P(\bar{A}_2 \wedge \bar{A}_1))$$
$$= P(A_2/\bar{A}_1)P(A_3/\bar{A}_1 \wedge A_2) +$$
$$P(\bar{A}_2/\bar{A}_1)P(A_3 \wedge \bar{A}_2 \wedge \bar{A}_1)/P(\bar{A}_2 \wedge \bar{A}_1)$$
$$= P(A_2/\bar{A}_1)P(A_3/\bar{A}_1 \wedge A_2) +$$
$$P(\bar{A}_2/\bar{A}_1)P(A_3 \wedge \bar{A}_2 \wedge \bar{A}_1)/(P(\bar{A}_2)P(\bar{A}_1/\bar{A}_2))$$

$P(\bar{A}_1/\bar{A}_2) = 1$ as $P(A_2/A_1) = 1$. So

$$P(A_3/\bar{A}_1) = P(A_2/\bar{A}_1)P(A_3/\bar{A}_1 \wedge A_2) +$$
$$P(\bar{A}_2/\bar{A}_1)P(A_3 \wedge \bar{A}_2 \wedge \bar{A}_1)/P(\bar{A}_2)$$
$$\leq P(A_2/\bar{A}_1)P(A_3/\bar{A}_1 \wedge A_2) + P(\bar{A}_2/\bar{A}_1)P(A_3 \wedge \bar{A}_2)/P(\bar{A}_2)$$
$$\leq P(A_2/\bar{A}_1)P(A_3/\bar{A}_1 \wedge A_2) + P(\bar{A}_2/\bar{A}_1)P(A_3/\bar{A}_2)$$
$$\leq P(A_2/\bar{A}_1)P(A_3/\bar{A}_1 \wedge A_2) + P(A_3/\bar{A}_2)$$

If $P(A_2/\bar{A}_1) > 2^{-L}$, then when $\bar{A}_1$ happens the probability that (1) is correct is larger than 2^{-L}. Namely, when $\bar{A}_1$ happens,

$$RE(\textstyle\prod_{i=1}^{n} c_i^{t_i}) = \prod_{i=1}^{n} c'^{t_{\pi(i)}}_i$$

with a probability larger than 2^{-L} where $\pi()$ is a permutation of $\{1, 2, \ldots, n\}$. Namely, when $\bar{A}_1$ happens,

$$RE(\textstyle\prod_{i=1}^{n} c_i^{t_i}) = \prod_{i=1}^{n} c'^{t_i}_{\pi^{-1}(i)}$$

with a probability larger than 2^{-L} .

According to multiplicative homomorphism of the employed encryption algorithm, when $\bar{A}_1$ happens,

$$\textstyle\prod_{i=1}^{n}(c_i/c'_{\pi^{-1}(i)})^{t_i} = E(1)$$

with a probability larger than 2^{-L}. Namely, when $\bar{A}_1$ happens

$$\log_{g_1} \textstyle\prod_{i=1}^{n}(a_i/a'_{\pi^{-1}(i)})^{t_i} = \log_y \prod_{i=1}^{n}(b_i/b'_{\pi^{-1}(i)})^{t_i}$$

with a probability larger than 2^{-L}.

So, according to Lemma 1, when $\bar{A}_1$ happens,

$$\log_{g_1}(a_i/a'_{\pi^{-1}(i)}) = \log_y(b_i/b'_{\pi^{-1}(i)}) \text{ for } i = 1, 2, \ldots, n$$

and thus $D(c'_1), D(c'_2), \ldots, D(c'_n)$ is a permutation of $D(c_1), D(c_2), \ldots, D(c_n)$, which is a contradiction. So $P(A_2/\bar{A}_1) \leq 2^{-L}$ must be true to avoid the contradiction.

As with multiplicative homomorphic encryption algorithm (1) is proved using a standard Chaum-Pedersen proof of equality of discrete logarithms [4], $P(A_3/\bar{A}_1 \wedge A_2) = 1$ and $P(A_3/\bar{A}_2) < 2^{-L'}$ where L' is the bit length of the challenge in the Chaum-Pedersen proof of equality of logarithms. Therefore,

$$P(A_3/\bar{A}_1) \leq P(A_2/\bar{A}_1) + P(A_3/\bar{A}_2) = 2^{-L} + 2^{-L'} \qquad \square$$

---

1. Any one can publicly calculate Legendre symbols of $a_1', b_1, a_2', b_2', \ldots, a_n', b_n'$ to check validity of the output ciphertexts.
2. c_i' is valid iff both a_i' and b_i' have Legendre symbols 1 as they are only valid when they are quadratic residues.
3. Any invalid ciphertext c_i' is adjusted to $-c_i'$.

Fig. 1. Checking and adjusting the output ciphertexts

2.2 Shuffling Employing Additive Homomorphic Encryption Algorithm

Let's recall the parameter setting of shuffling schemes employing Paillier encryption. Other factorization based homomorphic encryption algorithms like [15] can be employed in the same way. Suppose Paillier encryption [16] or Paillier encryption with distributed decryption [5] is employed. The latter may be more suitable as in shuffling applications like e-voting it is usually desired that the private key is shared by multiple parties.

- The multiplication modulus is N^2 where $N = p'q'$ and p', q' are large primes.
- A message m is encrypted into $c = g^m r^N$ where g is a public integer generated by the key generation algorithm (see [5] for more details) and r is randomly chosen from Z_N^*.
- A ciphertext c is re-encrypted into $c' = RE(c) = cr^N$ where r is randomly chosen from Z_N^*.

Suppose the input ciphertexts are c_i for $i = 1, 2, \ldots, n$ and they are shuffled to $c_i' = RE(c_{\pi(i)})$ for $i = 1, 2, \ldots, n$ where $\pi()$ is a random permutation of $\{1, 2, \ldots, n\}$. Random L-bit integers t_i for $i = 1, 2, \ldots, n$ are chosen (e.g. by a verifier or multiple verifiers) where L is a security parameter and $2^L < min(p', q')$. The shuffling node proves satisfaction of (1). Theorem 2 formally and precisely guarantees soundness of shuffling with Paillier encryption.

Theorem 2. *With Paillier encryption, the probability that (1) is successfully proved and verified but $D(c_1'), D(c_2'), \ldots, D(c_n')$ is not a permutation of $D(c_1), D(c_2), \ldots, D(c_n)$ is a negligible concrete probability.*

To prove Theorem 2, a lemma is proved first.

Lemma 2. *If $\prod_{i=1}^n y_i^{t_i}$ is an Nth residue with a probability larger than 2^{-L} where $t_1, t_2, \ldots, t_n$ are randomly chosen from $\{0, 1, \ldots, 2^L - 1\}$, then $y_1, y_2, \ldots, y_n$ are N^{th} residues.*

Proof: $\prod_{i=1}^n y_i^{t_i}$ is an Nth residue with a probability larger than 2^{-L} implies that for any given integer v in $\{1, 2, \ldots, n\}$ there must exist integers $t_1, t_2, \ldots, t_n$ and t_v' in $\{0, 1, \ldots, 2^L - 1\}$, x and x' such that

$$\prod_{i=1}^n y_i^{t_i} = x^N \tag{4}$$

$$(\prod_{i=1}^{v-1} y_i^{t_i}) y_v^{t_v'} \prod_{i=v+1}^n y_i^{t_i} = x'^N \tag{5}$$

Otherwise, for any $(t_1, t_2, \ldots, t_{v-1}, t_{v+1}, \ldots, t_n)$ in $\{0, 1, \ldots, 2^L - 1\}^{n-1}$, there is at most one t_v in $\{1, 2, \ldots, 2^L - 1\}$ such that $\prod_{i=1}^n y_i^{t_i}$ is an Nth residue. This implies that among the 2^{nL} possible choices for $(t_1, t_2, \ldots, t_n)$ (combination of $2^{(n-1)L}$ possible choices for $(t_1, t_2, \ldots, t_{v-1}, t_{v+1}, \ldots, t_n)$ and 2^L possible choices for t_v) there is at most $2^{(n-1)L}$ choices to construct N^{th} residue $\prod_{i=1}^n y_i^{t_i}$, which is a contradiction to the assumption that $\prod_{i=1}^n y_i^{t_i}$ is an Nth residue with a probability larger than 2^{-L}.

(4) and (5) implies $y_v^{t_v - \hat{t}_v}$ is an Nth residue. According to Euclidean algorithm there exist integers α and β to satisfy $\beta(t_v - \hat{t}_v) = \alpha N + GCD(N, t_v - \hat{t}_v)$. $GCD(N, t_v - \hat{t}_v) = 1$ as $t_v, \hat{t}_v < 2^L < min(p', q')$. So $y_v^{\beta(t_v - \hat{t}_v)} = y_v^{\alpha N} y_v$. Thus,

$$y_v = y_v^{\beta(t_v - \hat{t}_v)} / y_v^{\alpha N} = (y_v^{(t_v - \hat{t}_v)})^\beta / y_v^{\alpha N} = (x/x')^{N\beta} / (y_v^\alpha)^N = ((x/x')^\beta / y_v^\alpha)^N$$

So y_v is an Nth residue. Therefore, $y_1, y_2, \ldots, y_n$ are N^{th} residues as v can be any integer in $\{1, 2, \ldots, n\}$.   □

Proof of Theorem 2: Let A_1 be the event that $D(c_1'), D(c_2'), \ldots, D(c_n')$ is a permutation of $D(c_1), D(c_2), \ldots, D(c_n)$; A_2 be the event that (1) is correct; A_3 be the event that the shuffling node successfully proves (1); $P(A)$ denote the probability of event A.

$$P(A_3/\bar{A}_1) = P((A_3 \wedge A_2)/\bar{A}_1) + P((A_3 \wedge \bar{A}_2)/\bar{A}_1)$$
$$= P(A_3 \wedge A_2 \wedge \bar{A}_1)/P(\bar{A}_1) + P(A_3 \wedge \bar{A}_2 \wedge \bar{A}_1)/P(\bar{A}_1)$$
$$= P(\bar{A}_1 \wedge A_2)P(A_3/\bar{A}_1 \wedge A_2)/P(\bar{A}_1) +$$
$$P(A_3 \wedge \bar{A}_2 \wedge \bar{A}_1)P(\bar{A}_2 \wedge \bar{A}_1)/(P(\bar{A}_1)P(\bar{A}_2 \wedge \bar{A}_1))$$
$$= P(A_2/\bar{A}_1)P(A_3/\bar{A}_1 \wedge A_2) +$$
$$P(\bar{A}_2/\bar{A}_1)P(A_3 \wedge \bar{A}_2 \wedge \bar{A}_1)/P(\bar{A}_2 \wedge \bar{A}_1)$$
$$= P(A_2/\bar{A}_1)P(A_3/\bar{A}_1 \wedge A_2) +$$
$$P(\bar{A}_2/\bar{A}_1)P(A_3 \wedge \bar{A}_2 \wedge \bar{A}_1)/(P(\bar{A}_2)P(\bar{A}_1/\bar{A}_2))$$

$P(\bar{A}_1/\bar{A}_2) = 1$ as $P(A_2/A_1) = 1$. So

$$P(A_3/\bar{A}_1) = P(A_2/\bar{A}_1)P(A_3/\bar{A}_1 \wedge A_2) +$$
$$P(\bar{A}_2/\bar{A}_1)P(A_3 \wedge \bar{A}_2 \wedge \bar{A}_1)/P(\bar{A}_2)$$
$$\leq P(A_2/\bar{A}_1)P(A_3/\bar{A}_1 \wedge A_2) +$$
$$P(\bar{A}_2/\bar{A}_1)P(A_3 \wedge \bar{A}_2)/P(\bar{A}_2)$$
$$\leq P(A_2/\bar{A}_1)P(A_3/\bar{A}_1 \wedge A_2) + P(\bar{A}_2/\bar{A}_1)P(A_3/\bar{A}_2)$$
$$\leq P(A_2/\bar{A}_1)P(A_3/\bar{A}_1 \wedge A_2) + P(A_3/\bar{A}_2)$$

If $P(A_2/\bar{A}_1) > 2^{-L}$, then when $\bar{A}_1$ happens the probability that (1) is correct is larger than 2^{-L}. Namely, when $\bar{A}_1$ happens,

$$RE(\prod_{i=1}^n c_i^{t_i}) = \prod_{i=1}^n c_i'^{t_{\pi(i)}}$$

with a probability larger than 2^{-L} where $\pi()$ is a permutation of $\{1, 2, \ldots, n\}$. Namely, when $\bar{A}_1$ happens,

$$RE(\textstyle\prod_{i=1}^{n} c_i^{t_i}) = \prod_{i=1}^{n} c'^{t_i}_{\pi^{-1}(i)}$$

with a probability larger than 2^{-L}.

According to additive homomorphism of the employed encryption algorithm, when $\bar{A}_1$ happens,

$$\textstyle\prod_{i=1}^{n}(c_i/c'_{\pi^{-1}(i)})^{t_i} = E(0)$$

with a probability larger than 2^{-L}. Namely, when $\bar{A}_1$ happens, $\prod_{i=1}^{n}(c_i/c'_{\pi^{-1}(i)})^{t_i}$ is an Nth residue with a probability larger than 2^{-L}.

So, according to Lemma 2, when $\bar{A}_1$ happens $c_i/c'_{\pi^{-1}(i)}$ is an Nth residue for $i = 1, 2, \ldots, n$, and thus $D(c'_1), D(c'_2), \ldots, D(c'_n)$ is a permutation of $D(c_1), D(c_2), \ldots, D(c_n)$, which is a contradiction. So $P(A_2/\bar{A}_1) \leq 2^{-L}$ must be true to avoid the contradiction.

As with Paillier encryption (1) is proved using a standard proof of knowledge of root [11], $P(A_3/\bar{A}_1 \wedge A_2) = 1$ and $P(A_3/\bar{A}_2) < 2^{-L'}$ where L' is the bit length of the challenge in the proof of knowledge of root. Therefore,

$$P(A_3/\bar{A}_1) \leq P(A_2/\bar{A}_1) + P(A_3/\bar{A}_2) = 2^{-L} + 2^{-L'} \qquad \square$$

3   Failure of Soundness in [21]

The analysis in this paper has formally illustrated that it is important and necessary to satisfy (1) where $t'_1, t'_2, \ldots, t'_n$ must be a permutation of $t_1, t_2, \ldots, t_n$. It is proved in [21]

$$\prod_{i=1}^{n} t_i = \prod_{i=1}^{n} t'_i \qquad (6)$$
$$\sum_{i=1}^{n} t_i = \sum_{i=1}^{n} t'_i \qquad (7)$$

Obviously, only (6) and (7) are not enough to guarantee that $t'_1, t'_2, \ldots, t'_n$ is a permutation of $t_1, t_2, \ldots, t_n$. A simple counter example is $n = 10, t_1 = t_2 = \ldots = t_{10} = 2$ while $t'_1 = t'_2 = t'_3 = t'_4 = 4, t'_5 = t'_6 = 2, t'_7 = t'_8 = 1$ and $t'_9 = t'_{10} = -1$. Although t_i and t'_i must be in certain ranges to guatantee that $t'_1, t'_2, \ldots, t'_n$ is a permutation of $t_1, t_2, \ldots, t_n$, no range proof is specified in protocol description nor included in cost estimation in [21]. So it has a serious problem in soundness.

4   Conclusion

Lack of formal and precise proof for soundness in some shuffling schemes is noticed. Formal proof techniques are proposed to guarantee soundness of the schemes with a precise analysis of the probability of failure of soundness, which is demonstrated to be a negligible concrete probability. As our soundness analysis is precise, appropriate trade-off can be made between soundness and efficiency to improve efficiency of the shuffling schemes. Moreover, an existing shuffling scheme is shown to fail in soundness.

References

1. Abe, M.: Mix-networks on permutation networks. In: Lam, K.-Y., Okamoto, E., Xing, C. (eds.) ASIACRYPT 1999. LNCS, vol. 1716, pp. 258–273. Springer, Heidelberg (1999)
2. Abe, M., Hoshino, F.: Remarks on mix-network based on permutation networks. In: Kim, K.-c. (ed.) PKC 2001. LNCS, vol. 1992, pp. 317–324. Springer, Heidelberg (2001)
3. Chaum, D.: Untraceable electronic mail, return address and digital pseudonym. Communications of the ACM 24(2), 84–88 (1981)
4. Chaum, D., Pedersen, T.: Wallet databases with observers. In: Brickell, E.F. (ed.) CRYPTO 1992. LNCS, vol. 740, pp. 89–105. Springer, Heidelberg (1993)
5. Fouque, P.-A., Poupard, G., Stern, J.: Sharing decryption in the context of voting or lotteries. In: Frankel, Y. (ed.) FC 2000. LNCS, vol. 1962, pp. 90–104. Springer, Heidelberg (2001)
6. Furukawa, J., Sako, K.: An efficient scheme for proving a shuffle. In: Kilian, J. (ed.) CRYPTO 2001. LNCS, vol. 2139, pp. 368–387. Springer, Heidelberg (2001)
7. Gabber, E., Gibbons, P.B., Matias, Y., Mayer, A.: How to make personalized web browsing simple, secure, and anonymous. In: Luby, M., Rolim, J.D.P., Serna, M. (eds.) FC 1997. LNCS, vol. 1318, pp. 17–31. Springer, Heidelberg (1997)
8. Groth, J., Ishai, Y.: Sub-linear zero-knowledge argument for correctness of a shuffle. In: Smart, N.P. (ed.) EUROCRYPT 2008. LNCS, vol. 4965, pp. 379–396. Springer, Heidelberg (2008)
9. Groth, J., Lu, S.: Verifiable shuffle of large size ciphertexts. In: Okamoto, T., Wang, X. (eds.) PKC 2007. LNCS, vol. 4450, pp. 377–392. Springer, Heidelberg (2007)
10. Groth, J.: A verifiable secret shuffle of homomorphic encryptions. In: Desmedt, Y.G. (ed.) PKC 2003. LNCS, vol. 2567, pp. 145–160. Springer, Heidelberg (2002)
11. Guillou, L.C., Quisquater, J.J.: A "paradoxical" identity-based signature scheme resulting from zero-knowledge. In: Goldwasser, S. (ed.) CRYPTO 1988. LNCS, vol. 403, pp. 216–231. Springer, Heidelberg (1990)
12. Furukawa, J.: Efficient and verifiable shuffling and shuffle-decryption. IEICE Transactions 88-A(1), 172–188 (2005)
13. Andrew Neff, C.: A verifiable secret shuffle and its application to e-voting. In: ACM Conference on Computer and Communications Security 2001, pp. 116–125 (2001)
14. Andrew Neff, C.: Verifiable mixing (shuffling) of elgamal pairs (2004), http://theory.lcs.mit.edu/~rivest/voting/papers/ Neff-2004-04-21-ElGamalShuffles.pdf
15. Okamoto, T., Uchiyama, S.: A new public-key encyptosystem as secure as factoring. In: Nyberg, K. (ed.) EUROCRYPT 1998. LNCS, vol. 1403, pp. 308–318. Springer, Heidelberg (1998)
16. Paillier, P.: Public key cryptosystem based on composite degree residuosity classes. In: Stern, J. (ed.) EUROCRYPT 1999. LNCS, vol. 1592, pp. 223–238. Springer, Heidelberg (1999)
17. Peng, K.: A secure and efficient batched shuffling scheme. In: Qing, S., Imai, H., Wang, G. (eds.) ICICS 2007. LNCS, vol. 4861, Springer, Heidelberg (2007)

18. Peng, K., Bao, F.: An shuffling scheme with strict and strong security. To Appear at SecureWare 2010 (2010)
19. Peng, K., Boyd, C., Dawson, E.: Simple and efficient shuffling with provable correctness and ZK privacy. In: Shoup, V. (ed.) CRYPTO 2005. LNCS, vol. 3621, pp. 188–204. Springer, Heidelberg (2005)
20. Peng, K., Boyd, C., Dawson, E., Viswanathan, K.: A correct, private and efficient mix network. In: Bao, F., Deng, R., Zhou, J. (eds.) PKC 2004. LNCS, vol. 2947, pp. 439–454. Springer, Heidelberg (2004)
21. Wikstrom, D.: A sender verifiable mix-net and a new proof of a shuffle. In: Roy, B. (ed.) ASIACRYPT 2005. LNCS, vol. 3788, pp. 273–292. Springer, Heidelberg (2005)

Distinguishing Distributions Using Chernoff Information

Thomas Baignères[1], Pouyan Sepehrdad[2], and Serge Vaudenay[2]

[1] CryptoExperts, Paris, France
[2] EPFL, Switzerland
thomas.baigneres@cryptoexperts.com,
{pouyan.sepehrdad, serge.vaudenay}@epfl.ch

Abstract. In this paper, we study the soundness amplification by repetition of cryptographic protocols. As a tool, we use the Chernoff Information. We specify the number of attempts or samples required to distinguish two distributions efficiently in various protocols. This includes weakly verifiable puzzles such as CAPTCHA-like challenge-response protocols, interactive arguments in sequential composition scenario and cryptanalysis of block ciphers. As our main contribution, we revisit computational soundness amplification by sequential repetition in the threshold case, i.e when completeness is not perfect. Moreover, we outline applications to the Leftover Hash Lemma and iterative attacks on block ciphers.

Keywords: distinguishing distributions, Chernoff Information, proof systems, block ciphers.

1 Introduction

In many occasions in cryptography we encounter the challenge of distinguishing distributions such as pseudorandom number generators, symmetric key cryptanalysis or challenge-response puzzles. We consider protocols in which one distribution (null) is usually associated with the probability distribution of an adversary winning a game. The other distribution (alternate) corresponds to the probability of success of a legitimate party. For instance, challenge-response puzzles are often deployed to distinguish between a real and a fake solver. Differentiation is obtained by the probability of them solving a randomly chosen challenge. What we focus on in this paper is the application of such distinguishers in weakly verifiable puzzle protocols, sequential repetition of arguments and the Leftover Hash lemma.

Initially, we concentrate on interactive protocols, where there always exist a number of false negative and false positive responses by the verifier. They correspond to the completeness and soundness probability of the protocol. One might think of a method to reduce the error associated with the relevant distinguisher. One straightforward strategy to decrease the probability of error in both cases is to provoke the protocol iteratively and output "accept" if all instances accept (non-threshold case). Assuming the passing probability of non-authentic (vs. authentic) parties is b (vs. a), one would like to obtain error probability of b^q after q iterations, but it makes the success probability of authentic parties go down to a^q. To solve this bottleneck, what we investigate in this paper is

S.-H. Heng and K. Kurosawa (Eds.): ProvSec 2010, LNCS 6402, pp. 144–165, 2010.

the general scenario of threshold repetition, i.e we accept if the number of accepting repetitions is larger than a given threshold m. We can find an optimal m in which it makes the error probabilities of the protocol arbitrary close to zero. This strategy can be deployed in other similar interactive protocols like weakly verifiable puzzle protocols in which a verifier sends a puzzle to the solver and depends on the solver's response, he outputs *accept* or *reject*. In one section, we principally study CAPTCHA-like protocols as an example of such puzzles. We offer q puzzles to the solver and accept if she replies correctly to at least a threshold m of instances.

The problem of soundness amplification and the previous results. In interactive systems, the soundness probability of the protocol corresponds to upper bounding the probability of success of a malicious party. We always assume that the verifier is computationally bounded, but depending on computational capability of the prover we can define *argument* or *proof* systems, where the former corresponds to polynomial time provers and the latter to computationally unbounded provers (see section 3.1). We refer to the soundness probability of proof systems as *statistical* soundness versus the *computational* soundness in argument systems. To decrease the soundness error of such protocols, making a problem harder by repetition can be performed using two distinct approaches, namely *sequential* and *parallel* repetition. By sequential repetition we mean repeating the protocol several times, beginning the next run after the previous one terminates. Conversely, in the parallel case, all the instances are yielded to the prover at the same time without waiting for any arbitrary instance to terminate. It is well-known that sequential and parallel repetition of interactive proof systems reduce the error (statistical soundness) with an exponential rate (see [15]) in the non-threshold case (i.e, when there are no false rejections). In fact, [13] has given the proof that sequential repetition of computationally sound proof systems improves their security with an exponential rate in the "non-uniform model" under non-threshold approach, but it seems there is no explicit proof for the error reduction in the threshold case.

For a long period, it was assumed by the community that there is no distinction between error reduction of interactive arguments (computational soundness) when the protocol is iterated sequentially or in parallel. Finally, Bellare et al. [4] disproved this argument by providing a 4-round protocol in which q iterations does not reduce the computational soundness error probability of the protocol at all. In fact, they showed that there is no "black box" error reduction for such protocols when parallel repetition is concerned. On the other hand, they proved the surprising result that error reduction in parallel case depends fundamentally on the number rounds of the protocol. They proved that error decreases exponentially fast with the increase in the number of iterations if the number of rounds is less than 4. The computation complexity of each instance of their counter-example grows linearly with the number of repetitions and for such protocols the error does not even decrease for some types of interactive proofs. They constructed an artificial oracle to solve this problem. To discard the effect of this oracle, using universal arguments of Barak and Goldreich [3], Pietrzak et al. [27] provided an 8-round protocol in which the q-fold parallel repetition does not decrease the error probability below some constant for any polynomial q (where the communication complexity does not depend on q). As an extension, multi-prover systems were examined in multiple articles such as [14,28].

Weakly verifiable puzzles. As another application, we study weakly verifiable puzzles. These are interactive protocols in which the verifier sends a puzzle to the solver and outputs 0 or 1 depending the solver's response. They are *weakly verifiable* in the sense that only the puzzle generator can check the correctness of the responses, either because the challenge may have multiple correct responses and the verifier seeks a particular one of those or because the solver is computationally constrained, for instance in CAPTCHA puzzles [1]. CAPTCHA is a fuzzy challenge response protocol for distinguishing humans from programs (bots) mostly based on a distorted text with extraneous lines [1]. The current vision protocols are not able to pass CAPTCHA efficiently and the probability that a human can pass is much higher than the programs. This is thankful of the non-efficiency of the current image recognition systems not being able to identify distorted texts efficiently, but their passing success rate is still non-negligible. Moreover, many humans (including us) fail a non-negligible fraction of puzzles. This implies that it might not be desirable to consider the non-threshold scenario for such protocols. Previously, Canetti et al. [8] proved that the parallel repetition of weakly verifiable puzzle protocols decreases the error with an exponential rate. In fact, they found a tighter bound than [4]. Their proof is restricted to the non-threshold case which might not be appropriate for CAPTCHAs since their completeness are not perfect. This result can be extended to parallel repetition of interactive arguments. As the pioneers in threshold parallel repetition of such protocols, Impagliazzo et al. [17,18] have introduced two distinct bounds on the maximum success probability of a malicious algorithm for the parallel repetition of such protocols in the threshold case. The authors observed that the authentic party is on average expect to solve $a.q$ puzzles and if a Chernoff like bound holds, then the probability of fake parties solving $a.q$ puzzles may drop exponentially and they gave an exponential bound. The complication in reducing a single puzzle instance to a direct product puzzle instance originates from the fact that the given single puzzle instance is required to be incorporated in all simulated direct product puzzle instances and thus they are not independent. However, the bound they obtained has a weak constant in the exponent and although their results apply to the parallel composition scenario, they provided values which are irrelevant in practice, CAPTCHA for instance (see section 3.2). This was noticed by the authors themselves motivating to find better bounds as an open problem. Jutla [21] deployed a uniformized parallel solver, who first permutes his given first q-puzzles randomly, solves them as before and permutes the results back. Deploying this strategy, he improved the aforementioned bound and then he plugged it into "trust reduction" strategy in [17] and considered a linearly weighted metric and derived a more optimal bound. In fact, we show by a concrete example that his bound is still not applicable in practice since it asks for solving a huge number of CAPTCHAs in parallel.

Our contribution. The fundamental issue in this area is an approximation on the number of iterations required to effectively tune the probability of false acceptance or false rejection optimally. In fact, we find the optimal threshold m for the best distinguisher in section 3. We show that soundness amplification in the threshold case works as expected for statistical soundness and works with a small gap for computational soundness when the number of repetitions is logarithmic. We find a practical bound restricted to sequential repetition of such protocols. Notice that our bounds might not work in the parallel composition scenario but it provides figures which can be deployed in practice. It seems more logical for practical applications like CAPTCHAs (see section 3.2).

We also consider the Leftover-Hash lemma. Let assume we have a secret key $\mathcal{K}$ that has t uniform random bits. If ℓ bits of the key are leaked, but it is not clear which one, the Leftover-Hash Lemma [19] tells us that we can produce a key of almost $m = t - \ell$ bits that is ε-indistinguishable from uniform distribution over the key space. We define a distinguisher given n samples in Luby-Rackoff model which distinguishes between a universal hash function and a uniform distribution. We derive the same bound as in [11] by deploying Chernoff Information which turns out to be optimal by introducing the Multi-Session Leftover-Hash Lemma when more than one such key generations are of interest.

In Appendix, we present iterative attacks on block ciphers with applications in linear and differential cryptanalysis and show that we can recover the number of plaintext/ciphertext pairs required to obtain a significant advantage.

Structure of this paper. First, we mention some preliminaries regarding the facts and previous results on hypothesis testing problem and statistical distinguishers. Then, we model our distinguishing games as a challenge of distinguishing two random Boolean sources in section 3. In section 3.1, we focus on sequential repetition of interactive arguments in the threshold case and derive better bounds to strengthen them. In section 3.2, we investigate the sequential repetition of weakly verifiable puzzles and we compare 7 distinct bounds. Furthermore, in section 5 we derive a useful bound which we use to investigate the Leftover Hash Lemma. In Appendix, we revisit iterative attack on block ciphers.

2 Preliminaries

Notations. In this paper, we let $\mathcal{Z}$ denote a finite set and $P_0, P_1, \ldots, P_k$ be $k + 1$ probability distributions over $\mathcal{Z}$. The support of a distribution P over $\mathcal{Z}$ is the set $\text{supp}(P) = \{z \in \mathcal{Z} : P[z] > 0\}$. The distribution P is of full-support when $\text{supp}(P) = \mathcal{Z}$. When considering the two distributions P_0, P_1 we will usually denote $\mathcal{Z}' = \text{supp}(P_0) \cap \text{supp}(P_1)$ and have $\mathcal{Z} = \text{supp}(P_0) \cup \text{supp}(P_1)$. The natural and base 2 logarithms will respectively be denoted by $\ln$ and $\log$. The *Kullback-Leibler divergence* [22] and the *Chernoff Information* [9] between P_0 and P_1 are respectively defined by

$$D(P_0\|P_1) = \sum_{z \in \text{supp}(P_0)} P_0[z] \log \frac{P_0[z]}{P_1[z]} \qquad C(P_0, P_1) = -\inf_{0 < \lambda < 1} \log \sum_{z \in \mathcal{Z}'} P_0[z]^{1-\lambda} P_1[z]^{\lambda}$$

When $\text{supp}(P_0) \not\subseteq \text{supp}(P_1)$ then $D(P_0\|P_1) = +\infty$. A sequence of q elements $z_1, \ldots, z_q \in \mathcal{Z}$ and a sequence of random variables $Z_1, \ldots, Z_q \in \mathcal{Z}$ are respectively denoted by $\mathbf{z}^q$ and $\mathbf{Z}^q$. Finally, we say that two functions f and g are asymptotically equivalent when $\lim_{q \to \infty} \frac{1}{q} \ln \frac{f(q)}{g(q)} = 0$ or equivalently when $f(q) = g(q)e^{o(q)}$. This is denoted by $f(q) \overset{\bullet}{=} g(q)$.

Essential Definitions on Hypothesis Testing. Cryptographic problems we consider can all be formalized as a hypothesis testing problem in which a distinguisher A distinguishes between the hypotheses $H_0 : P = P_0$ and $H_1 : P \in \mathcal{D} = \{P_1, \ldots, P_k\}$ on the basis of knowledge of the P_i's and of $q > 0$ elements $Z_1, \ldots, Z_q \in \mathcal{Z}$ sampled according to the distribution P. It is assumed that one of the hypotheses is true, the q samples are independent and identically distributed (iid), the distinguisher A eventually outputs 0 or 1 to indicate its guess and that this distinguisher is computationally unbounded (so that we can assume it is deterministic); for this last reason, A is referred to as a *q-limited distinguisher*. In fact, we are following Luby-Rackoff model of indistinguishability [24] where the only adversarial limitation is the number of queries. In the particular case where $k = 1$, we will refer to the previous problem as a *simple* hypothesis test, whereas when $k > 1$ we call it a *composite* hypothesis test. A q-limited distinguisher A which is given q samples $\mathbf{Z}^q = Z_1, \ldots, Z_q$ is denoted as $A_q(\mathbf{Z}^q)$. The effectiveness of A is mathematically formulated by its *advantage*.

Definition 1. *The* advantage *of a q-limited distinguisher A_q between the hypotheses H_0 and H_1, based on the q samples $\mathbf{Z}^q = Z_1, \ldots, Z_q$, is defined by*

$$\mathrm{Adv}_{A_q}(H_0, H_1) = \Pr[A_q(\mathbf{Z}^q) = 1 | H_0] - \Pr[A_q(\mathbf{Z}^q) = 1 | H_1]$$

The hypotheses H_0 and H_1 are (q, ε)-indistinguishable if for any q-limited distinguisher A_q we have $|\mathrm{Adv}_{A_q}(H_0, H_1)| \leq \varepsilon$.

Existence of an Optimal Distinguisher. Since the samples are assumed to be iid, their particular *order* must be irrelevant. What really matters is the number of occurrences of each symbol of $\mathcal{Z}$ in the string $Z^q = Z_1, \ldots, Z_q$ or equivalently the *type* (or *empirical probability distribution*) of this sequence, defined by

$$P_{\mathbf{Z}^q}[z] = \frac{\#\{i : Z_i = z\}}{q}$$

Consequently, a distinguisher can be thoroughly specified by the set Π of all types for which it will output 1, i.e., $A_q(\mathbf{Z}^q) = 1 \Leftrightarrow P_{\mathbf{Z}^q} \in \Pi$. The set Π is called the *acceptance region* of A. Since q is fixed, the number of possible types is finite and thus we can assume wlog that Π is finite. Consequently, there is also a finite number of potential adversaries so that there must be at least one which maximizes the advantage. We call them *best distinguishers* and denote by $\mathrm{BestAdv}_q(H_0, H_1)$ (or simply by $\mathrm{BestAdv}_q$) their advantage.

The Optimal Adversary in the Simple Hypothesis Testing Case. We consider the simple case where A distinguish between $H_0 : P = P_0$ and $H_1 : P = P_1$. In that case, we call A a distinguisher between P_0 and P_1 and denote its advantage by $\mathrm{Adv}_{A_q}(P_0, P_1)$. The best advantage is obtained by *likelihood ratio test*, where the acceptance region of the distinguisher is such that

$$A_q(\mathbf{Z}^q) = 1 \iff \frac{P_{\mathbf{Z}^q | P_0}}{P_{\mathbf{Z}^q | P_1}} \leq 1 \tag{1}$$

where $P_{\mathbf{Z}^q | P_i}$ is the type of the sequence given the distribution P_i has happened. It can be shown [2] that the distinguisher $A^\star$ defined by the acceptance region

$$\Pi^* = \{P_{\mathbf{Z}^q} : D(P_{\mathbf{Z}^q} \| P_1) \le D(P_{\mathbf{Z}^q} \| P_0)\} \tag{2}$$

is a best distinguisher.

The following essential theorem allows to relate the advantage of the best distinguisher between P_0 and P_1 to the Chernoff Information[1] [9].

Theorem 2. *Let* P_0, P_1 *be two probability distributions. We have*

$$1 - \text{BestAdv}_q(P_0, P_1) \overset{\bullet}{=} 2^{-qC(P_0, P_1)} \tag{3}$$

This result verifies **asymptotically** that having access to $q \approx \frac{1}{C(P_0, P_1)}$ samples we can distinguish P_0 from P_1 with a significant advantage.

3   Application to Boolean Cases

In this paper, we concentrate on applications of distinguishers in scenarios such as soundness amplification and weakly verifiable puzzles. In all these relevant applications, we are trying to differentiate between a legitimate and a malicious party. One strategy is to model this scenario as a distinguishing game between two Boolean random sources. We consider the problem of distinguishing two Boolean random sources with expected values a and b respectively. Suppose P_0, P_1 be two probability distributions over the set $\mathcal{Z} = \{0, 1\}$. Let

$$P_0[X] = \begin{cases} a & X = 1 \\ 1 - a & X = 0 \end{cases} \quad \text{and} \quad P_1[X] = \begin{cases} b & X = 1 \\ 1 - b & X = 0 \end{cases}$$

We define a distinguisher which outputs 1 *iff* $n_1 \le m$, where $bq < m < aq$ and n_1 is the number of occurrences of 1 in the sample set. Intuitively, a refers to the probability that a legitimate user or a program can pass a single challenge successfully and b refers to which of a malicious user or program. As a matter of fact, we mostly investigate the protocols which are distinguishing a legitimate and a malicious user or program offering them q times to try and then if they can pass with a particular minimum threshold, algorithm outputs *accept* otherwise it *rejects*.It can be shown using (2) that

$$m = \frac{q}{1 - \dfrac{\ln \frac{b}{a}}{\ln \frac{1-b}{1-a}}} \tag{4}$$

defines the best distinguisher using q samples to distinguish P_0 from P_1 (Note that if $a \approx b$, we have $m \approx q\frac{a+b}{2}$ which is a pretty intuitive threshold). Then, employing the Chernoff Information, Theorem 2 gives $1 - \text{Adv}_q \overset{\bullet}{=} 2^{-qC(P_0, P_1)}$. More precisely, having access to q samples and using the binomial distribution

$$
\begin{aligned}
1 - \text{Adv}_q &= \sum_{i \le m} \binom{q}{i} a^i (1-a)^{q-i} + \sum_{i > m} \binom{q}{i} b^i (1-b)^{q-i} \\
&= 1 - \sum_{i \le m} \binom{q}{i} \left(b^i (1-b)^{q-i} - a^i (1-a)^{q-i} \right)
\end{aligned} \tag{5}
$$

---

[1] A proof of this result can be found in [12] asymptotically, where it is implicitly assumed that $\text{supp}(P_0) = \text{supp}(P_1)$. The general case is treated in [2].

which is expressed as the *concrete* expression for computing the advantage of the best distinguisher. It might be assumed that this bound only works when the adversary's responses are independent, but we will show in Theorem 6 that it is true even if the adversary's responses are not independent, the only difference is an additive factor of $2^q \varepsilon$. In fact, the adversary may decide to answer identically to all challenges or decide to respond to the following challenge as a function of the previous response. The fundamental question is that whether she gains anything by following this approach. What we prove is that she gains an additive factor of $2^q \varepsilon$ which can be made arbitrary small for constant values of m and q (see 3.1). The effect of ε would be canceled out in the case of statistical soundness when proof systems are of interest since the prover is supposed to be computationally unbounded.

A theorem by *Hoeffding* [16] called *Chernoff-Hoeffding* theorem gives an upper bound on the probability of the addition of q identically independent Boolean random variables referred to as *Chernoff-Hoeffding bound* which can be used as a bound in our distinguishing game.

Theorem 3. (Chernoff-Hoeffding Theorem) *Let $\{X_1, \ldots, X_q\} \in \{0,1\}^q$ be q identically independent random variables with $E[X_i] = a$, for $(1 \le i \le q)$. Then, for $\forall b > a$, we have*

$$\Pr\left[\frac{1}{q}\sum_{i=1}^{q} X_i \ge b\right] \le \left(\left(\frac{a}{b}\right)^b \left(\frac{1-a}{1-b}\right)^{1-b}\right)^q = 2^{-q\mathrm{D}(b\|a)}$$

where $\mathrm{D}(b\|a)$ is the Kullback-Leibler divergence of Boolean random variables of expected values b and a.

As another representation, we can rewrite the Chernoff-Hoeffding bound as

$$\sum_{i=\lceil bq \rceil}^{q} \binom{q}{i} a^i (1-a)^{q-i} \le 2^{-q\mathrm{D}(b\|a)}$$

Using the above representation of Chernoff-Hoeffding bound, we obtain

$$1 - \mathrm{Adv}_q \le 2^{-q\mathrm{D}\left(\frac{m}{q}\|a\right)} + 2^{-q\mathrm{D}\left(\frac{m}{q}\|b\right)} \tag{6}$$

We will compare these bounds in section 3.2.

3.1 Soundness Amplification

As an application to the distinguisher in section 3, we consider interactive argument protocols. In fact, we analyze the sequential composition of interactive arguments where the algorithm repeats q times sequentially and if the number of successes is more than a specific threshold, the protocol outputs *accept* otherwise *reject*. First, we define the notion of proof and argument systems.

Definition 4. *Given a language L over an alphabet Z, an interactive proof system (resp. a computationally proof system or an argument) for L is a pair $(\mathcal{P}, \mathcal{V})$ of interactive machines, where $\mathcal{P}$ is computationally unbounded (resp. $\mathcal{P}$ is computationally bounded) and $\mathcal{V}$ is polynomial-time such that there exist a polynomial P and a, b, where $0 \le b < a \le 1$ and*

- **Termination:** *for any $x, \omega, r_{\mathcal{P}}, r_{\mathcal{V}}$, the total complexity of $\mathcal{V}$ (until termination) in $\mathcal{P}(\omega; r_{\mathcal{P}}) \overset{x}{\leftrightarrow} \mathcal{V}(r_{\mathcal{V}})$ is bounded by $P(|x|)$, where x is the security parameter.*
- *a-**completeness:** for any $x \in L$, there exists a string ω, such that*

$$\Pr_{r_{\mathcal{P}}, r_{\mathcal{V}}} \left(Out_{\mathcal{V}}(\mathcal{P}(\omega; r_{\mathcal{P}}) \overset{x}{\leftrightarrow} \mathcal{V}(r_{\mathcal{V}})) = accept \right) \geq a(|x|)$$

- *b-**statistical soundness (resp. b-computational soundness):** for any $x \notin L$ and any computationally unbounded (resp. polynomial-time) interactive machine $\mathcal{P}^\star$*

$$\Pr_{r_{\mathcal{P}}, r_{\mathcal{V}}} \left(Out_{\mathcal{V}}(\mathcal{P}^\star(r_{\mathcal{P}}) \overset{x}{\leftrightarrow} \mathcal{V}(r_{\mathcal{V}})) = accept \right) \leq b(|x|)$$

Given an interactive proof system $(\mathcal{P}, \mathcal{V})$ for L which is a-complete and b-sound, we define a new proof system $(\mathcal{P}^q, \mathcal{V}_m^q)$ with threshold m as follows

- *$\mathcal{P}^q$ (resp. $\mathcal{V}_m^q$) simulates $\mathcal{P}$ (resp. $\mathcal{V}$), but have no terminal message until $q(|x|)$ sequential iterations with the same input x are made.*
- *after an iteration completes, they restart the entire protocol with fresh random coins.*
- *$\mathcal{V}_m^q$ accepts if at least $m(|x|)$ iterations of $\mathcal{V}$ are accepted out of $q(|x|)$.*

We use the following Lemma to prove our main theorem.

Lemma 5. *Assume that $(\mathcal{P}, \mathcal{V})$ is a b-sound argument for L. Given q and ε such that $q\varepsilon^{-1}$ is polynomially bounded in terms of $|x|$, we consider $(\mathcal{P}^q, \mathcal{V}_m^q)$ and a polynomially bounded malicious $\mathcal{P}^\star$. For $I \subseteq \{1, \ldots, q\}$ we let p_I be the probability that $\mathcal{P}^\star$ succeeds in every iteration i for $i \in I$. Given $J \subseteq \{1, \ldots, i-1\}$ and $I = J \cup \{i\}$, we have $p_I \leq \max(bp_J, \varepsilon)$.*

More precisely, if for some I this inequality is not satisfied, then there is a malicious prover for $(\mathcal{P}, \mathcal{V})$ with complexity $q\varepsilon^{-1}$ times the one by $\mathcal{P}^\star$ to break b-soundness.

Proof. If $p_J \leq \varepsilon$, the result is clear since $p_I \leq p_J$. Otherwise, we have $p_J > \varepsilon$. We construct a malicious prover for $(\mathcal{P}, \mathcal{V})$ who simply simulates $i - 1$ iterations for the verifier to $\mathcal{P}^\star$. It repeats the simulation until every iteration j for $j \in J$ succeeds. The number of iterations is expected to be p_J^{-1} which is dominated by ε^{-1}. Then it runs an extra simulation with the real verifier in the $(\mathcal{P}, \mathcal{V})$ protocol. The complexity of this malicious prover is bounded by $q\varepsilon^{-1}$ which is a polynomial. So, it is polynomially bounded and the probability that the last iteration succeeds is bounded by b. Clearly, this is the conditional probability of success given that every iteration j for $j \in J$ succeeds. Hence, $p_I \leq bp_J$. □

Using this lemma, we prove that soundness amplification in the threshold case behaves as expected for statistical soundness in proof systems. Furthermore, there is only a small gap between the expected value in statistical soundness and computational soundness when the number of repetitions is logarithmic.

Theorem 6. *For any computationally sound proof system $(\mathcal{P}, \mathcal{V})$ and for a language L and any q, m and ε such that $q\varepsilon^{-1}$ is polynomially bounded in terms of $|x|$, we consider*

$(\mathcal{P}^q, \mathcal{V}_m^q)$ with threshold m. If $(\mathcal{P}, \mathcal{V})$ is a-complete and b-sound, then $(\mathcal{P}^q, \mathcal{V}_m^q)$ is a'-complete and b'-sound where

$$a' = \sum_{i=m}^{q} \binom{q}{i} a^i (1-a)^{q-i} \qquad \text{and} \qquad b' = \sum_{i=m}^{q} \binom{q}{i} b^i (1-b)^{q-i} + 2^q \varepsilon$$

and the time reduction factor is of $q \varepsilon^{-1}$.

Note that if we know $bq < m < aq$ and if we consider the optimal m by equation (4), the above theorem shows that the completeness of the protocol increases and the soundness probability of the protocol declines by q iterations. *Since the reduction factor is $q\varepsilon^{-1}$, for constants m and q, the value ε can be fixed to an arbitrary low constant,* so we achieve

$$b' = \sum_{i=m}^{q} \binom{q}{i} b^i (1-b)^{q-i}$$

More generally, let $\varepsilon = |x|^{-c}$, where c is a constant and set m to equation (4) and q be logarithmic in terms of $|x|$, hence we obtain $a' = 1 - O(|x|^{-\alpha})$ and $b' = O(|x|^{-\beta})$ with polynomial reduction factor. We conclude that with a logarithmic number of repetitions we can make a', b' tend toward 1 and 0 respectively at a polynomial speed.

Proof. The proof for the a'-completeness is trivial using binomial distribution and considering that repetitions are independent. For b'-soundness the prover may decide to evaluate iterations dependently. In fact, we show that even if the prover does not consider each iteration independently, he may not achieve anything better than responding to each iteration independently except with a gap of $2^q \varepsilon$. We define p_I as in the Lemma 5. Let X_j be a 0 or 1 random variable associated with the success of a malicious protocol $\mathcal{P}^*$ in the j_{th} iteration. We define $p_{x_1 \ldots x_i}$ to be a pattern probability in i iterations as

$$p_{x_1 \ldots x_i} = \Pr\left[\bigwedge_{j=1}^{i} X_j = x_j \right]$$

and T as a random variable enumerating the number of times $\mathcal{P}^*$ passes the protocol and $P = \Pr(T \geq m)$. Note that p_x can be recursively defined from the set of p_I's, then P can be computed. Due to Lemma 5, p_I's are subject to inequalities. We define an arbitrary $\varepsilon > 0$ and we first show that P is lower than a new P called P' defined by a set of p_I''s, where the inequalities in the Lemma 5 are replaced by equalities. Next, we show that for this new set of p_I's we have

$$P \leq \sum_{i \geq m} \binom{q}{i} b^i (1-b)^{q-i} + 2^q \varepsilon$$

to obtain b'-soundness.

For the first step, we use a rewriting procedure on the set of p_I's. In the same time we verify that the new set is still consistent with the law of probabilities, with the inequalities from the Lemma 5, and that P only increases. By iterating the rewriting procedure we eventually obtain a new set of p_I's satisfying $p_I = \max(b p_J, \varepsilon)$ for all $I = J \cup \{i\}$ with $i > \max J$. The rewriting procedure works as follows.

Initially, we identify $I = J \cup \{i\}$ with $i > \max J$, such that $p_I < \max(bp_J, \varepsilon)$, then for any $K \subseteq \{i+1, \ldots, q\}$, we have $p'_{I \cup K} = (1-\lambda)p_{I \cup K} + \lambda p_{J \cup K}$ with λ such that $p'_I = \max(bp'_J, \varepsilon)$. Subsequently, we get $\lambda = \frac{\max(bp_J, \varepsilon) - p_I}{p_J - p_I}$. All other p_J's are left unchanged. This is equivalent to rewriting $p'_{x0y} = (1-\lambda)p_{x0y}$ and $p'_{x1y} = p_{x1y} + \lambda p_{x0y}$ for $x \in \{0,1\}^{i-1}$ such that $x_j = 1$ for all $j \in I$. It can be shown that p' only updates a subtree starting at position I such that $p'_I = \max(bp'_J, \varepsilon)$. Ultimately, all the equalities are reached. To check

$$\sum_{x : x_1 + \cdots + x_q \geq m} p_x \leq \sum_{x : x_1 + \cdots + x_q \geq m} p'_x$$

we split the sum depending on x:

- for the set of y in which $y_j = 0$ for some $j \in J$, we observe $p'_y = p_y$.
- for the set of y of the form $y = x\beta z$ with the cumulated weight of x and z be at least m and $x_j = 1$ for all $j \in J$, we group by the same x and z, since $p'_{x0z} + p'_{x1z} = p_{x0z} + p_{x1z}$.
- for the set of y of the form $y = x1z$ with the weight m and $x_j = 1$ for all $j \in J$, we observe that $p'_{x1z} \geq p_{x1z}$.

We now assume that the p_I's satisfy $p_I = \max(bp_J, \varepsilon)$ for all $I = J \cup \{i\}$ with $i > \max J$ and we want to upper bound P'. Clearly, we have $p'_I = \max(b^{\#I}, \varepsilon)$. When turned into p'_x's we have

$$p'_x = \begin{cases} b^{w(x)}(1-b)^{q-w(x)} & \text{if } w(x) \leq \tau \\ \varepsilon(1-b)^{q-w(x)} & \text{if } w(x) > \tau \text{ and } x_{q-w(x)+\tau+1} = \cdots = x_q = 1 \\ 0 & \text{otherwise} \end{cases}$$

for all I, where $w(x) = x_1 + \cdots + x_q$ and $\tau = \lfloor \frac{\ln \varepsilon}{\ln b} \rfloor$. We have

$$\begin{aligned} P' &= \sum_{x : w(x) \geq m} p'_x \\ &= \sum_{x : m \leq w(x) \leq \tau} p'_x + \sum_{x : w(x) > \tau} p'_x \\ &\leq \sum_{i \geq m} \binom{q}{i} b^i (1-b)^{q-i} + \varepsilon \sum_{x : w(x) > \tau} 1_{x_{q-w(x)+\tau+1} = \cdots = x_q = 1}(1-b)^{q-w(x)} \\ &= \sum_{i \geq m} \binom{q}{i} b^i (1-b)^{q-i} + \varepsilon \sum_{x : w(x) > \tau} \binom{q-w(x)+\tau}{\tau}(1-b)^{q-w(x)} \\ &\leq \sum_{i \geq m} \binom{q}{i} b^i (1-b)^{q-i} + 2^q \varepsilon \end{aligned}$$

$\square$

3.2 Application to Weakly Verifiable Puzzles

A weakly verifiable puzzle protocol is a game $P = (\mathcal{D}, R)$ between a solver and a verifier consisting of a set of distributions $\mathcal{D} = \{\mathcal{D}_1, \ldots, \mathcal{D}_k\}$ of cardinality k (the security parameter) which are defined on pairs (p_i, c_i) [8]. In fact, p_i is called a *puzzle* which is associated with a challenge from the verifier being sent to the solver and we refer to c_i as the *check string*. The second component is a *relation* $R[(p, c), r]$ where r is a string of a fixed length, which can be assumed as the solver's response. The verifier is aware of p_i and c_i and so he can inspect the response r of the solver. If $R[(p,c),r]$ holds, we say that the solver *passes*, otherwise we say that he *fails*. We define a direct product for P. That is, since q and $m \in [0,q]$, we define $P_m^q = (\mathcal{D}^{\otimes q}, R_m^q)$, where

$$R_m^q[((p_1,\ldots,p_q),(c_1,\ldots,c_q)),r_1,\ldots,r_q] \Leftrightarrow \#\{i \in [0,q]; R[(p_i,c_i),r_i]\} \geq m$$

CAPTCHA is an example of such protocols. The prominent issue is to find the best method to distinguish a human from a program using q attempts[2]. This can be translated to a hypothesis testing problem, involved is a random variable *accept* with an expected value a (resp. b) associated with hypothesis H_0 (resp. H_1). We can use the results on the previous distinguisher with an application to such puzzles. We use the theorem by *Impagliazzo et al.* [17] to estimate the total probability of error the threshold-based distinguisher attains which can be used for the parallel repetition of such protocols. This was the first bound found on upper bounding the success probability of an adversary in the parallel composition of weakly verifiable puzzles in the threshold case. They also introduced a bound for the corresponding probability distribution in [18]. We consider a pretty good CAPTCHA for which humans pass with probability $a = 90\%$ and such that there exist attacks solving them with probability $b = 33\%$. For instance, we can consider Gimpy. (see [26,30]).

Theorem 7. (*Impagliazzo-Jaiswal-Kabanets* 2007, 2009) *If all malicious algorithms can pass a challenge with probability at most b, then the probability that a malicious algorithm passes the challenge at most m times out of q parallel instances is lower than*
$\beta = 2e^{-\frac{(m-bq)^2}{64q}}$ (*resp.* $\beta = \frac{100q}{m-bq}e^{-\frac{(m-bq)^2}{40q(1-b)}}$).

Equivalently, if "pass", b and m are replaced by "fail", $1-a$ and $q-m$ respectively, it leads to the expression that legitimate people succeed less than m times out of q with probability lower than $\alpha = 2e^{-\frac{(m-aq)^2}{64q}}$ (*resp.* $\frac{100q}{aq-m}e^{-\frac{(m-aq)^2}{40qa}}$). Hence, the advantage of a distinguisher which distinguishes the legitimate users from malicious programs using the threshold m can be computed as

$$1 - \text{Adv}_q \leq \alpha + \beta = 2e^{-\frac{(m-bq)^2}{64q}} + 2e^{-\frac{(m-aq)^2}{64q}} \tag{7}$$

$$1 - \text{Adv}_q \leq \alpha + \beta = \frac{100q}{m-bq}e^{-\frac{(m-bq)^2}{40q(1-b)}} + \frac{100q}{aq-m}e^{-\frac{(m-aq)^2}{40qa}} \tag{8}$$

Recently, Jutla in [21,20] improved the above bounds and derived tighter bounds to the Chernoff bound, but as illustrated in the following table, the results are still non-relevant in practice. It is because all four bounds still ask for a huge number of CAPTCHAs which can not be used in real life. Using the same notations, he derived the follwoing error probabilities in two seperate papers:

$$1 - \text{Adv}_q \leq \frac{2(q-bq)^3}{(q-m)^2(m-bq)} \cdot e^{-\left(\frac{q-m}{2}\right)\left(\frac{m-bq}{q-bq}\right)^2} + \frac{2(aq)^3}{m^2(aq-m)} \cdot e^{-\left(\frac{m}{2}\right)\left(\frac{aq-m}{aq}\right)^2} \tag{9}$$

---

[2] Intuitive solution is to ask for many independent challenges.

$$1 - \mathrm{Adv}_q \leq \frac{4q^2(1-b)^2}{(m-bq)(q-m)} \cdot e^{-\frac{(m-bq)^2}{2q(1-b)}} + \frac{4a^2q^2}{m((1-b)q-m)} \cdot e^{-\frac{((1-b)q-m)^2}{2aq}} \quad (10)$$

where $bq < \min\{m, q-1\}$.

We compare the seven distinct bounds already discussed with the concrete value extracted in equation (5). As a summary, the table of advantage bounds we already computed together with the concrete value for the advantage of the distinguisher in section 3 is depicted in Table 1.

Table 1. $[1 - \mathrm{Adv}_q]$ (total error) comparison for 7 distinct bounds with respect to q for $a = 90\%$ and $b = 33\%$, the exact advantage is given by (5)

q	m	Parallel Repetition				Sequential Repetition		
		IJK07 (7)	IJK09 (8)	J10 (9)	J10$_2$ (10)	asymptotic (3)	concrete (5)	Chernoff (6)
1	0	> 1	> 1	N/A	N/A	0.803	0.430	1.606
3	1	> 1	> 1	> 1	> 1	0.517	0.283	1.035
4	2	> 1	> 1	> 1	> 1	0.415	0.160	0.831
5	3	> 1	> 1	> 1	> 1	0.333	0.125	0.667
7	4	> 1	> 1	> 1	> 1	0.215	0.069	0.430
100	65	> 1	> 1	> 1	> 1	$2^{-31.68}$	$2^{-34.95}$	$2^{-30.68}$
5000	3273	0.019	0.095	≈ 0	> 1	≈ 0	≈ 0	≈ 0

As the figures represent, for all the range of q the asymptotic value is the closest one to the concrete value. Clearly, solving 4 CAPTCHAs in at most 7 sequential attempts provides an error probability below 10% using parameters $a = 90\%$ and $b = 33\%$. "(7), (8) bounds are quite weak when applied to concrete problems such as actual CAPTCHA protocol with reasonable numbers of repetitions" [17,18], which can be verified by the result in the table above. Although we are comparing sequential with parallel composition, it makes more sense to ask for 7 CAPTCHAs attempts sequentially than requiring to solve 5000 CAPTCHAs (as (7) bound recommends) at the same time. It still remains an open problem to find a better bound which works for the case of parallel repetition. Moreover, from the above table the value of the concrete error is always less than the asymptotic value which is the implication of Theorem 8.

4   Useful Bounds

In this section, we derive two bounds which we use one in the ongoing section and one which argues that the total error probability in the general case is bounded by its asymptotic value and as was shown in the example in section 3.2, this provides a better bound than (6).

Theorem 8. *Let $\mathcal{Z}$ be a finite set and P_0 and P_1 be two distributions with support of union $\mathcal{Z}$ and intersection $\mathcal{Z}'$. Let $\mathrm{BestAdv}_q(\mathsf{P}_0, \mathsf{P}_1)$ be the best advantage for distinguishing P_0 from P_1 using q samples. We have*

$$1 - \mathrm{BestAdv}_q \leq 2^{-qC(\mathsf{P}_0, \mathsf{P}_1)}$$

This result yields an upper bound on the probability of error of the best distinguisher. In fact, this result can be verified by the comparison between the concrete value of the error and asymptotic bound derived above.

Proof. Using (1), we have

$$1 - \text{BestAdv}_q(P_0, P_1) = \sum_{\substack{\mathbf{z}^q \\ \Pr[\mathbf{z}^q|P_0] > \Pr[\mathbf{z}^q|P_1]}} \Pr[\mathbf{z}^q|P_1] + \sum_{\substack{\mathbf{z}^q \\ \Pr[\mathbf{z}^q|P_0] < \Pr[\mathbf{z}^q|P_1]}} \Pr[\mathbf{z}^q|P_0]$$

$$= \sum_{\mathbf{z}^q \in Z^{\prime q}} \min\left(\Pr[\mathbf{z}^q|P_0], \Pr[\mathbf{z}^q|P_1]\right)$$

Since for $\forall a, b > 0 : \min(a,b) \leq a^{1-\lambda}b^\lambda$ and $0 \leq \lambda \leq 1$, we have

$$1 - \text{BestAdv}_q(P_0, P_1) \leq \inf_{0 < \lambda < 1} \sum_{\mathbf{z}^q \in Z^{\prime q}} \Pr[\mathbf{z}^q|P_0]^{1-\lambda}\Pr[\mathbf{z}_q|P_1]^\lambda$$

$$= \inf_{0 < \lambda < 1} \sum_{\mathbf{z}^q \in Z^{\prime q}} \prod_{i=1}^q P_0[z_i]^{1-\lambda}P_1[z_i]^\lambda$$

$$= \inf_{0 < \lambda < 1} \left(\sum_{z \in Z'} P_0^{1-\lambda}[z]P_1^\lambda[z]\right)^q = 2^{-qC(P_0, P_1)} \qquad \square$$

Theorem 9. *Let* P_0 *and* P_1 *be distributions of support* Z, *We have*

$$\frac{1}{8}\sum_{x \in Z} P_0[x]\left(\frac{P_1[x] - P_0[x]}{\max(P_0[x], P_1[x])}\right)^2 \leq 1 - 2^{-C(P_0,P_1)} \leq \frac{1}{8}\sum_{x \in Z} P_0[x]\left(\frac{P_1[x] - P_0[x]}{\min(P_0[x], P_1[x])}\right)^2$$

As a result, for P_0 be the uniform distribution over a domain of size N, since $P_0[x] - \|P_1 - P_0\|_2 \leq P_1[x] \leq P_0[x] + \|P_1 - P_0\|_2$, we can rewrite the bound as

$$\frac{1}{8}\frac{N\|P_1 - P_0\|_2^2}{(1 + N\|P_1 - P_0\|_2)^2} \leq 1 - 2^{-C(P_0,P_1)} \leq \frac{1}{8}\frac{N\|P_1 - P_0\|_2^2}{(1 - N\|P_1 - P_0\|_2)^2}$$

where $\|P_0 - P_1\|$ states the Euclidean distance between distribution P_0, P_1.

Proof. Let λ be such that

$$F(\lambda) = \sum_{x \in Z} P_0[x]^{1-\lambda}P_1[x]^\lambda$$

and let $P_1[x] = P_0[x](1 + \varepsilon_x)$ with $\varepsilon_x \leq B_x$, where $B_x = \frac{1}{P_0[x]} - 1$, We have

$$F(\lambda) = \sum_{x \in Z} P_0[x](1 + \varepsilon_x)^\lambda$$

Thanks to the *Taylor Theorem*, for any ε there exists $\theta \in [0, 1]$, such that

$$(1 + \varepsilon)^\lambda - (1 + \lambda\varepsilon) = \frac{\lambda(\lambda - 1)}{2}\varepsilon^2(1 + \theta\varepsilon)^{\lambda-2}$$

Since $\sum_x P_0[x](1 + \lambda \varepsilon_x) = 1$, we obtain

$$1 - F(\lambda) = \frac{\lambda(1-\lambda)}{2} \sum_x P_0[x] \varepsilon_x^2 (1 + \theta_x \varepsilon_x)^{\lambda-2}$$

$$= \frac{\lambda(1-\lambda)}{2} \sum_x P_0[x] \frac{(P_1[x] - P_0[x])^2}{P_0[x]^2} (1 + \theta_x \varepsilon_x)^{\lambda-2}$$

If $\varepsilon_x \geq 0$, then $(1 + \theta_x \varepsilon_x)^{\lambda-2} \leq 1$ and $P_0[x] \leq P_1[x]$. Otherwise, $(1 + \theta_x \varepsilon_x)^{\lambda-2} \leq \left(\frac{P_0[x]}{P_1[x]}\right)^2$ and $P_1[x] \leq P_0[x]$. Ultimately,

$$1 - \inf_{0 < \lambda < 1} F(\lambda) \leq \frac{1}{8} \sum_{x \in \mathcal{Z}} P_0[x] \left(\frac{P_1[x] - P_0[x]}{\min(P_0[x], P_1[x])}\right)^2$$

The other inequality can be shown similarly. □

5 Multi-session Leftover-Hash Lemma

Let X be a random variable over a finite set $\mathcal{Z}$, the minimum entropy of X is defined as

$$H_\infty[X] = -\log\left(\max_x \Pr[X = z]\right)$$

The *Rényi entropy* [29] of order α, where $\alpha \geq 0$, is defined as

$$H_\alpha[X] = \frac{1}{1-\alpha} \log\left(\sum_x \Pr[X = z]^\alpha\right)$$

Notice that $2^{-H_2[X]}$ is the collision probability and $2^{-H_2[X]} \leq 2^{-H_\infty[X]}$.

If X is a random variable over a set $\mathcal{Z}$ of order N, the square of Euclidean distance between the distribution of X called $P_1[X]$ and the uniform distribution $P_0[X]$ can be expressed as $\|P_1[X] - P_0[X]\|_2^2 = 2^{-H_2[X]} - \frac{1}{N}$. Let $d(P_1, P_0)$ be the statistical distance between the distribution P_1 and the uniform distribution P_0, the expression $d(P_1[X], P_0[X]) \leq \sqrt{N}\|P_1[X], P_0[X]\|_2$ shows the link between statistical and Euclidean distance of distributions.

Definition 10. *Let $H = \{H_N\} : D \to \{0,1\}^m$ be a family of functions, where $N \in \mathcal{N}$. H_N is a universal hash function if for any $x, y \in \{0,1\}^m$ such that $x \neq y$, we have*

$$\Pr(H_N[x] = H_N[y]) = 2^{-m}$$

where N is uniformly distributed.

Lemma 11. *(Leftover Hash Lemma [19]: Impagliazzo-Levin-Luby 1989) If h is a universal hash function with a range of size 2^m and X, N, U are independent random variables where N, U are uniformly distributed and $m \leq H_\infty[X] - 2\log\frac{1}{\varepsilon}$, then the distributions of $(h_N[X], N)$ and (U, N) are ε-indistinguishable.*

Proof. We define P_0 and P_1 as two distributions and compute the Euclidean distance

$$
\begin{aligned}
\|P_1 - P_2\|^2 &= \sum_{k,n} \left(\Pr_{X,N}[h_n[X] = k, N = n] - \frac{1}{2^m \# \mathcal{N}} \right)^2 \\
&= \frac{1}{(\# \mathcal{N})^2} \sum_{k,n} \Pr_{X,X'}[h_n[X] \\
&= h_n[X'] = k] - \frac{1}{2^m \# \mathcal{N}} \\
&= \frac{1}{\# \mathcal{N}} \sum_{x,x'} \Pr[X = x, X' = x', h_N[x] = h_N[x']] - \frac{1}{2^m \# \mathcal{N}} \\
&= \frac{1 - 2^{-m}}{\# \mathcal{N}} \sum_x \Pr[X = x]^2 \\
&\leq \frac{1 - 2^{-m}}{\# \mathcal{N}} 2^{-H_\infty[X]} \leq \frac{1}{2^m \# \mathcal{N}} \varepsilon^2
\end{aligned}
$$

Applying the link between the statistical distance and Euclidean distance, we obtain $d(P_1, P_2) \leq \varepsilon$.   □

We recall an application of the above Lemma in ElGamal encryption from Boneh [7]. Let $\langle g \rangle$ be a subgroup generated by some g of prime order q in $\mathbb{Z}_p^*$. Consider a scenario in which party A encrypts a message m using the party B's public key e. A picks a random value $r \in \mathbb{Z}_q^*$ and computes the pair $\text{Enc}[e, m; r] = (g^r, me^r) = (c_1, c_2)$ and sends it to B. At the other end based on the fact that $e^r = c_1^d$ where d is B's private key (secret key), B decrypts the message by computing $\text{Dec}[d, (c_1, c_2)] = m = c_2 / (c_1)^d$.

Key recovery in ElGamal encryption is equivalent to the discrete logarithm problem, likewise, the decryption is equivalent to Diffie-Hellman problem [7]. On the other hand, ElGamal is **not** a semantically secure cryptosystem, because $q | \frac{(p-1)}{2}$ and so $g^{\frac{p-1}{2}} = 1$. Let $(\frac{a}{b})$ be the *Legendre symbol* for integers a and b, then $(\frac{g}{p}) = 1$. We deduce that $(\frac{me^r}{p}) = (\frac{m}{p})$. So, if for $b = \{0, 1\} : (\frac{m_b}{p}) = (-1)^b$, a distinguisher can distinguish $\text{Enc}[e, m_0; r]$ and $\text{Enc}[e, m_1; r]$ with advantage 1.

We define a scheme based on ElGamal encryption which is argued to be $(\varepsilon_{\text{DDH}} + \varepsilon)$-IND-CPA secure. Let $\langle g \rangle$ be a group generated by some g of prime order q. Following a similar approach as ElGamal, define the triple $\text{Enc}[e, m; N, r] = (g^r, m \oplus h_N[e^r], N) = (c_1', c_2', N)$ where $r \in \mathbb{Z}_q^*$ and N is uniformly distributed. Similarly, A sends this triple to B and B decrypts it using $\text{Dec}[d, (c_1', c_2', N)] = c_2' \oplus h_N[c_1'^d]$.

Due to the Decisional Diffie-Hellman assumption [7], we have $(g, g^r, m \oplus h_N[e^r], N)$ is ε_{DDH}-indistinguishable from $(g, g^r, m \oplus h_N[g^{r'}], N)$. According to Lemma 11, we have $(g, g^r, m \oplus h_N[g^{r'}], N)$ is ε-indistinguishable from $(g, g^r, m \oplus U, N)$, where U is the uniform distribution. Furthermore, $(g, g^r, m \oplus U, N)$ is perfectly indistinguishable from (g, g^r, U, N). Consequently, $(g, g^r, m \oplus h_N[e^r], N)$ is $(\varepsilon_{\text{DDH}} + \varepsilon)$-indistinguishable from something independent from m which leads the scheme to be $(\varepsilon_{\text{DDH}} + \varepsilon)$-IND-CPA secure.

As another application to the Lemma 11, consider the Diffie-Hellman key exchange protocol. Let $\langle g \rangle$ be a group generated by some g of prime order q. In a key exchange between two parties A and B, the party A picks a random $x \in \mathbb{Z}_q^*$ and computes $X \leftarrow g^x$ and sends it to B. The party B aborts if $X \notin \langle g \rangle \setminus \{1\}$, otherwise he picks a random value $y \in \mathbb{Z}_q^*$ and computes $Y \leftarrow g^y$ and sends it to A. The party A aborts if $Y \notin \langle g \rangle \setminus \{1\}$, otherwise $K_{ses} = g^{xy}$ is computed and is shared between two parties as their session key. Since $\mathbb{Z}_q^*$ is cyclic, K_{ses} is a uniformly distributed non-neutral element of $\langle g \rangle$ (even locally under active attacks). Assume a non-ambiguous representation format for values which may be in $\langle g \rangle$ or not

$$\Pr(K_{ses} = x) = \begin{cases} \frac{1}{q-1} & x \in \langle g \rangle \setminus \{1\} \\ 0 & \text{otherwise} \end{cases}$$

Thus, $H_\infty[K_{ses}] = \log(q-1)$. Now, consider the protocol that exchanges a random number N and derives the key $K = h_N[K_{ses}]$. Let $\varepsilon = \sqrt{2^m/(q-1)}$ by Leftover Hash Lemma, K is indistinguishable from a random key. Moreover, a protocol using n such key generations is $n\varepsilon$-indistinguishable from the same protocol where K is truly random (thanks to the hybrid arguments) implying that it is safe to generate the key n times using the same protocol until n is of order $\sqrt{q.2^{-m}}$. This result is originating from the trivial bound, which can be improved employing a *Multi-Sample Leftover Hash Lemma*.

Lemma 12. (Multi-Sample Leftover Hash Lemma) *Assume h is a universal hash function with a range of size 2^m and key space $\mathcal{N}$. Let $N \in_U \mathcal{N}$ and $U \in_U \{0,1\}^m$ and X be independent random variables. If $\varepsilon = \sqrt{(2^m-1)2^{-H_2[X]}}$ and $\varepsilon' = \varepsilon\sqrt{2^m\#\mathcal{N}}$, the best advantage for distinguishing $(h_N[X],N)$ from (U,N) using n samples is such that*

$$1 - \text{BestAdv}_n \overset{\bullet}{=} 2^{-nC}$$

where C is bounded by $-\log\left(1 - \frac{\varepsilon^2}{8(1+\varepsilon')^2}\right) \le C \le -\log\left(1 - \frac{\varepsilon^2}{8(1-\varepsilon')^2}\right)$.

Although this result is not so precise, it already suggests that we can find a better bound. In the above example, we have $H_2(X) = \log(q-1)$. Therefore, if we take $\varepsilon = \sqrt{(2^m-1)/(q-1)}$ and $\#\mathcal{N} \ll q.2^{-2m}$, we obtain that the minimal n for distinguishing is at least within the order of magnitude of ε^{-2} which is $q.2^{-m}$.

Proof. Let P_0, P_1 be two distributions, we proved in Lemma 11 that $\|P_1 - P_0\|_2^2 = 2^{-H_2[X]}(1 - 2^{-m})/\#\mathcal{N}$, where the domain size is $2^m\#\mathcal{N}$. Deploying Theorem 9, we get

$$1 - 2^{-C(P_0,P_1)} \le \frac{(2^m-1)2^{-H_2[X]}}{8\left(1-\sqrt{(2^m-1)2^{m-H_2[X]}\#\mathcal{N}}\right)^2}$$

$$= \frac{\varepsilon^2}{8(1-\varepsilon')^2}$$

Similar procedure can be shown for the lower bound. $\square$

It has been shown that the min-entropy $H_\infty(X) = m + 2\log(\frac{1}{\varepsilon}) + 2\log n$ suffices for the joint distribution to be ε-close to the uniform distribution (see [10,19,31]). Furthermore, recently Chung et al. [11] improved the previous bound by reducing $2\log n$ to $\log n$ and they proved that it is optimal for 2-universal hashing by using *Hellinger distance* to evaluate the error accumulation over each hashed instance. In fact they showed that

$$\varepsilon = \sqrt{\frac{n}{q.2^{-m}}}$$

Therefore, the minimal n for distinguishing efficiently is of magnitude $q.2^{-m}$ which is the same bound we found by another approach, that is Chernoff Information and asymptotic q-limited distinguisher.

6   Conclusion

We mentioned various applications of distinguishers in cryptography. We evaluated their efficiency using the Chernoff Information. We revisited the interactive argument systems and relying on sequential repetition, we derived new bounds for the soundness property of such protocols (computational soundness) even in the case of dependent responses. Moreover, we compared seven distinct bounds for the error probability of the best distinguisher in weakly verifiable puzzle protocols when q samples are given. We introduced an application to the Leftover Hash Lemma and by introducing the Multi-Sample Leftover Hash Lemma we derived the same optimal bound as [11] with another approach (Chernoff Information) when the number of iterations is more than unity. We specified the number of samples to obtain a significant advantage in block ciphers cryptanalysis using Chernoff Information approach.

References

1. Ahn, L.V., Blum, M., Hopper, N.J., Langford, J.: CAPTCHA: Using Hard AI Problems for Security. In: Biham, E. (ed.) EUROCRYPT 2003. LNCS, vol. 2656, pp. 294–311. Springer, Heidelberg (2003)
2. Baignères, T.: Quantitative Security of Block Ciphers: Designs and Cryptanalysis Tools. PhD thesis, EPFL (2008)
3. Barak, B., Goldreich, O.: Universal arguments and their applications. In: Electronic Colloquium on Computational Complexity (2001)
4. Bellare, M., Impagliazzo, R., Naor, M.: Does Parallel Repetition Lower the Error in Computationally Sound Protocols. In: Proceedings of the Thirty-Eighth Annual IEEE Symposium on Foundations of Computer Science, pp. 374–383 (1997)
5. Biham, E., Shamir, A.: Differential Cryptanalysis of DES-like Cryptosystems. Journal of Cryptology 4(1), 3–72 (1991)
6. Blondeau, C., Gérard, B.: On the Data Complexity of Statistical Attacks Against Block Ciphers. In: Cryptology ePrint (2009)
7. Boneh, D.: The Decision Diffie-Hellman Problem. In: Buhler, J.P. (ed.) ANTS 1998. LNCS, vol. 1423, pp. 48–63. Springer, Heidelberg (1998)
8. Canetti, R., Halevi, S., Steiner, M.: Hardness Amplification of Weakly Verifiable Puzzles. In: Kilian, J. (ed.) TCC 2005. LNCS, vol. 3378, pp. 17–33. Springer, Heidelberg (2005)
9. Chernoff, H.: Sequential Analysis and Optimal Design. CBMS-NSF Regional Conference Series in Applied Mathematics, vol. 8. SIAM, Philadelphia (1972)
10. Chor, B., Goldreich, O.: Unbiased bits from sources of weak randomness and probabilistic communication complexity. SIAM Journal on Computing 17(2), 230–261 (1988)
11. Chung, K., Vadhan, S.: Tight Bounds for Hashing Block Sources. In: Goel, A., Jansen, K., Rolim, J.D.P., Rubinfeld, R. (eds.) APPROX and RANDOM 2008. LNCS, vol. 5171, pp. 357–370. Springer, Heidelberg (2008)
12. Cover, T.M., Thomas, J.A.: Elements of Information Theory. Wiley Series in Telecommunications. John Wiley & Sons, Chichester (1991)
13. Damgård, I., Pfitzmann, B.: Sequential Iteration of Interactive Arguments and an Efficient Zero-knowledge Argument for NP. Technical report, BRICS Report Series, Department of Computer Science, University of Aarhus (1997)
14. Feige, U., Verbitsky, O.: Error Reduction by Parallel Repetition - A Negative Result. Combinatorica 22, 461–478 (2001)

15. Goldreich, O.: Modern Cryptography, Probabilistic Proofs and Pseudo-randomness. Algorithms and Combinatorics. Springer, Heidelberg (1999)
16. Hoeffding, W.: Probability Inequalities for Sums of Bounded Random Variables. Journal of the American Statistical Association 58(301), 13–30 (1963)
17. Impagliazzo, R., Jaiswal, R., Kabanets, V.: Chernoff-Type Direct Product Theorems. In: Menezes, A. (ed.) CRYPTO 2007. LNCS, vol. 4622, pp. 500–516. Springer, Heidelberg (2007)
18. Impagliazzo, R., Jaiswal, R., Kabanets, V.: Chernoff-Type Direct Product Theorems. Journal of Cryptology 22(1), 75–92 (2009)
19. Impagliazzo, R., Levin, L.A., Luby, M.: Pseudo-random Generation from One-way Functions. In: Proceedings of the 21st Annual ACM Symposium on Theory of Computing, pp. 12–24. ACM Press, New York (1989)
20. Juta, C.S.: Almost Optimal Bounds for Direct Product Threshold Theorem. Technical report, ECCC (2010)
21. Jutla, C.S.: Almost Optimal Bounds for Direct Product Threshold Theorem. In: Theory of Cryptography Conference. Springer, Heidelberg (2010)
22. Kullback, S., Leibler, R.A.: On Information and Sufficiency. The Annals of Mathematical Statistics 22(1), 79–86 (1951)
23. Lai, X., Massey, J.L., Murphy, S.: Markov Ciphers and Differential Cryptanalysis. In: Davies, D.W. (ed.) EUROCRYPT 1991. LNCS, vol. 547, pp. 17–38. Springer, Heidelberg (1991)
24. Luby, M., Rackoff, C.: How to Construct Pseudorandom Permutations from Pseudorandom Functions. SIAM Journal of Computing 17, 373–386 (1988)
25. Matsui, M.: Linear Cryptanalysis Method for DES Cipher. In: Helleseth, T. (ed.) EUROCRYPT 1993. LNCS, vol. 765, pp. 386–397. Springer, Heidelberg (1994)
26. Mori, G., Malik, J.: Recognising Objects in Adversarial Clutter: Breaking a Visual CAPTCHA. In: IEEE Conference Compurt Vision and Pattern Recognition, pp. 134–141. IEEE CS Press, Los Alamitos (2003)
27. Pietrzak, K., Wikström, D.: Parallel Repetition of Computationally Sound Protocols Revisited. In: Vadhan, S.P. (ed.) TCC 2007. LNCS, vol. 4392, pp. 86–102. Springer, Heidelberg (2007)
28. Raz, R.: A parallel repetition theorem. SIAM Journal on Computing 27, 763–803 (1998)
29. Rényi, A.: On Measures of Information and Entropy. In: Proceedings of the 4th Berkeley Symposium on Mathematics, Statistics and Probability, pp. 547–561 (1960)
30. Yan, J., Salah, A.: CAPTCHA Security: A Case Study. Journal of IEEE Security and Privacy 7, 22–28 (2009)
31. Zuckerman, D.: Simulating BPP using a general weak random source. Algorithmica 16(4-5), 367–391 (1996)

A   Iterative Attacks on Block Ciphers

We now apply the results regarding simple hypothesis testing to block cipher analysis. We consider a statistical distinguisher who has access to an oracle implementing either an instance c of a block cipher C or an instance c of $C^\star$, a theoretical ideal scheme (sometimes called the *perfect cipher*) which corresponds to the set of *all* possible permutations over the same text space as C. Viewing both C and $C^\star$ as *sets* of permutations, the objective of the distinguisher is to choose between the hypotheses[3] $H_0 : c \in C^\star$ and $H_1 : c \in C$.

---

[3] Note that the fact that the hypotheses are not disjoint is not a problem here, since all our previous results hold in that case too.

Oracle: a permutation c
1: **for** i from 1 to q **do**
2:     pick $(X_1, \ldots, X_d)$ according to the distribution D
3:     for all $1 \leq j \leq d$, query the oracle for $Y_j = c(X_j)$
4:     set $Z_i = h(X_1, \ldots, X_d, Y_1, \ldots, Y_d)$
5: **end for**
6: return $A^\star(Z_1, \ldots Z_q)$

Fig. 1. A q-limited iterative h-distinguisher of order d

Most statistical distinguishers against block ciphers can be seen as q-limited itera-tive h-distinguishers of order d given some parameters q, h, d. These distinguishers are formalized in Figure 1. At each of the q iterations, the d-tuple $(X_1, \ldots, X_d)$ is chosen according to a certain distribution D. The function h returns at each iteration a value in a finite set $\mathcal{Z}$. Under a hypothesis similar to that of the hypothesis of stochastic equiv-alence [23], we can assume that the Z_i's follow a distribution P_0 under hypothesis H_0 (when c is an instance of the perfect cipher) or a distribution P_1 under hypothesis H_1 (when c is an instance of the block cipher considered). The two hypotheses can be refor-mulated as $H_0 : P = P_0$ and $H_1 : P = P_1$, where P is the distribution according to which the Z_i's are sampled. Letting $A^\star$ be the best distinguisher between P_0 and P_1, the iter-ated distinguisher finally outputs $A^\star(\mathbf{Z}^q)$. From Theorem 2 we know that its advantage Adv_q to distinguish H_0 from H_1 (i.e., the block cipher C from the perfect cipher $C^\star$) verifies $1 - Adv_q(H_0, H_1) = 1 - BestAdv_q(P_0, P_1) \overset{\bullet}{=} 2^{-qC(P_0, P_1)}$. This result verifies asymptotically that having access to

$$q \approx \frac{1}{C(P_0, P_1)} \tag{11}$$

samples derived from the plaintext/ciphertext pairs allows to distinguish C from $C^\star$ with a significant advantage. As an illustration, we propose to revisit various classical iter-ated distinguishers, compute their complexity based on (11) and derive their strategy from that of $A^\star$. We focus on the case of differential distinguishers, impossible differ-entials and linear distinguishers. We attain estimate on q which are similar as in [6]. (see equations (15), (16) and (17)).

In the current application, the two distributions P_0 and P_1 are very close. In that case, it is possible to derive an approximation of the Chernoff Information that is easier to deal with. More formally, considering the case where both distributions are of full support and letting $\varepsilon_z = (P_1[z] - P_0[z])/P_0[z]$ be such that $\varepsilon_z = o(1)$ for all $z \in \mathcal{Z}$, then it can be shown (see [2, p.50]) that $C(P_0, P_1) = \frac{1}{8 \ln 2} \sum_z P_0[z] \varepsilon_z^2 + o(\|\varepsilon\|_2^2)$, where $\varepsilon = (\varepsilon_z)_{z \in \mathcal{Z}}$. Approximating the Chernoff Information by the right-hand side of the previous equation leads to

$$C(P_0, P_1) \approx \frac{1}{8 \ln 2} \sum_{z \in \mathcal{Z}} \frac{(P_1[z] - P_0[z])^2}{P_0[z]}. \tag{12}$$

A.1   Differential Distinguishers

Differential distinguishers [5] are iterated h-distinguishers of order $d = 2$ in which $h(x_1, x_2, y_1, y_2) = y_1 \oplus y_2$ and for which the distribution D is such that X_1 is chosen uniformly at random and $X_2 = X_1 \oplus a$ for some fixed a. Typically, we expect the function $h(X_1, X_2, Y_1, Y_2) = Y_1 \oplus Y_2$ to be biased under H_1 and uniformly distributed under H_0. Under H_1, we expect in practice for a well chosen b to have $Y_1 \oplus Y_2 = b$ with probability p and $Y_1 \oplus Y_2 = b' \neq b$ with probability $\frac{1-p}{n-1}$, where n is the cardinality of the text space, such that[4] $\frac{1}{n} = o(p)$ and $p = o(1)$. Accordingly, we have that P_0 is the uniform distribution and that

$$P_1[z] = \begin{cases} p & \text{when } z = b, \\ \frac{1-p}{n-1} = \beta & \text{when } z \neq b \end{cases} \tag{13}$$

Under these notations, we now evaluate $C(P_0, P_1)$ to approximate the number of plaintext/ciphertext pairs required by a differential distinguisher to choose between C and $C^\star$ with a significant advantage. Letting

$$C(P_0, P_1) = - \inf_{0 < \lambda < 1} \log F(\lambda)$$

where $F(\lambda) = \sum_z P_0[z]^{1-\lambda} P_1[z]^\lambda$, we have

$$F(\lambda) = \frac{p}{(np)^\lambda} + \frac{1-p}{(n\beta)^\lambda}$$

We also have $F(0) = F(1) = 1$ and $F'(0) \leq 0$, so that we know that F is minimum for a λ_0 such that $F'(\lambda_0) = 0$. We get

$$\lambda_0 = \frac{\ln\left(\frac{p \ln(np)}{(1-p) \ln \frac{1-1/n}{1-p}}\right)}{\ln\left(np \frac{1-1/n}{1-p}\right)} \sim \frac{\ln \ln(np)}{\ln(np)} \tag{14}$$

Consequently, $(np)^{\lambda_0} \sim \ln(np)$ and $(n\beta)^{\lambda_0} = 1 + o(p)$ and thus $F(\lambda_0) = 1 - p + o(p)$. The Chernoff Information verifies $C(P_0, P_1) = -\log F(\lambda_0) \sim \frac{p}{\ln 2}$. We conclude from (11) that a differential distinguisher approximately needs

$$q \approx \frac{\ln 2}{p} \tag{15}$$

samples to achieve a significant advantage.

It is also possible to find the practical (and optimal) strategy of a differential distinguisher. We know that the best distinguisher $A^\star$ should yield 1 iff $D(P_{\mathbf{Z}^q} \| P_1) \leq D(P_{\mathbf{Z}^q} \| P_0)$ (see (2)). Since this is equivalent to yielding 1 when

$$2^{q(D(P_{\mathbf{Z}^q} \| P_1) - D(P_{\mathbf{Z}^q} \| P_0))} \leq 1$$

and also

$$D(P_{\mathbf{Z}^q} \| P_1) - D(P_{\mathbf{Z}^q} \| P_0) = \sum_z P_{\mathbf{Z}^q}[z] \log \frac{P_0[z]}{P_1[z]} = \frac{1}{q} \log \frac{(\beta/p)^{n_b}}{(n\beta)^q}$$

---

[4] These assumptions simply express the fact that we expect p to be small (otherwise the cipher would be trivial to break), but much larger than $\frac{1}{n}$ (otherwise the cipher would be impossible to break for the chosen a and b).

n_b denotes the number of times, where $Y_1 \oplus Y_2 = b$. The optimal strategy is to output 1 when $\frac{n_b}{q} \geq \frac{\ln(n\beta)}{\ln(\beta/p)} \sim \frac{p}{\ln(np)}$. Since we take $q \approx \frac{\ln 2}{p}$, this condition is equivalent to $n_b > 0$. Subsequently, we can formalize a differential distinguisher as in Figure 2.

Oracle: a permutation c
   for i from 1 to q **do**
      pick a uniformly distributed random X
      query the oracle for $c(X)$ and $c(X \oplus a)$
      if $c(X \oplus a) \oplus c(X) = b$, output 1 and stop
   end for
   output 0

Fig. 2. A differential distinguisher based on the input difference a and output difference b

A.2   Impossible Differential

The scenario is similar to that considered in the case of differential distinguishers, except that the particular difference b in the ciphertexts can never occur under H_1, i.e., we have $p = 0$. Using the same notations as in Section A.1, we now have $F(\lambda) = (1 - 1/n)^\lambda$ and so $C(P_0, P_1) = -\log(1 - 1/n) \sim \frac{1}{n\ln 2}$. Using (11) we conclude that an iterative distinguisher based on an impossible differential requires

$$q \approx n \ln 2 \tag{16}$$

samples to reach a significant advantage. It is easy to see that this distinguisher should output 1 iff $n_b = 0$.

A.3   Linear Distinguisher

Linear distinguishers [25] are iterated h-distinguishers of order $d = 1$ where $h(x,y) = a \cdot x \oplus b \cdot y \in \{0,1\}$ (where $\cdot$ denotes the bit-wise xor) for some fixed input mask a and output mask b and for which the distribution D is the uniform distribution. We expect $h(x,y)$ to be biased under H_1 and uniformly distributed under H_0, so that P_0 is assumed to be uniform and $P_1^\pm$ is such that $P_1^\pm[0] = \frac{1}{2}(1 \mp \varepsilon)$ and $P_1^\pm[1] = \frac{1}{2}(1 \pm \varepsilon)$ for some positive real value ε. In this case, we have a composite hypothesis testing problem $H_0 : P = P_0$ and $H_1 : P \in \{P_1^+, P_1^-\}$. In such a case (see [2]), we have a best distinguisher which its acceptance region and advantage can be specified by

$$\Pi^\star = \{P \; : \; \min_{1 \leq i \leq k} D(P \| P_i) \leq D(P \| P_0)\} \quad 1 - \mathrm{BestAdv}_q(P_0, \mathcal{D}) \doteq \max_{1 \leq i \leq k} 2^{-qC(P_0, P_i)}$$

Assuming that $\varepsilon = o(1)$, we have from (12) that $C(P_0, P_1^\pm) \approx \frac{\varepsilon^2}{8\ln 2}$ from which we conclude (using (11)) that a linear distinguisher requires

$$q \approx \frac{8 \ln 2}{\varepsilon^2} \qquad (17)$$

samples to reach a non-negligible advantage. It is easy to see that this linear distinguisher should output 1 iff $\left| 2\frac{n_0}{q} - 1 \right| \geq \frac{|\varepsilon|}{2}$ (where n_0 denotes the number of 0's in the Z_i's), so that we can formalize a linear distinguisher as in Figure 3.

Oracle: a permutation c
  initialize a counter m to 0
  for i from 1 to q **do**
    pick a uniformly distributed random X
    query the oracle for $c(X)$
    if $a \cdot X = b \cdot c(X)$, increment the counter m
  end for
  output 1 if $\left| 2\frac{m}{q} - 1 \right| \geq \frac{|\varepsilon|}{2}$, otherwise output 0.

Fig. 3. A linear distinguisher based on the input mask a and output mask b

A Suite of Non-pairing ID-Based Threshold Ring Signature Schemes with Different Levels of Anonymity (Extended Abstract)[*]

Patrick P. Tsang[1], Man Ho Au[2], Joseph K. Liu[3],
Willy Susilo[2], and Duncan S. Wong[4]

[1] Department of Computer Science
Dartmouth College
Hanover NH 03755, USA
patrick@cs.dartmouth.edu
[2] Centre for Computer and Information Security Research
School of Computer Science and Software Engineering
University of Wollongong, Australia
{aau,wsusilo}@uow.edu.au
[3] Cryptography and Security Department
Institute for Infocomm Research, Singapore
ksliu@i2r.a-star.edu.sg
[4] Department of Computer Science
City University of Hong Kong, Hong Kong
duncan@cityu.edu.hk

Abstract. Since the introduction of Identity-based (ID-based) cryptography by Shamir in 1984, numerous ID-based signature schemes have been proposed. In 2001, Rivest et al. introduced ring signature that provides irrevocable signer anonymity and spontaneous group formation. In recent years, ID-based ring signature schemes have been proposed and almost all of them are based on bilinear pairings. In this paper, we propose the first ID-based threshold ring signature scheme that is not based on bilinear pairings. We also propose the first ID-based threshold 'linkable' ring signature scheme. We emphasize that the anonymity of the actual signers is maintained even against the private key generator (PKG) of the ID-based system. Finally we show how to add identity escrow to the two schemes. Due to the different levels of signer anonymity they support, the schemes proposed in this paper actually form a suite of ID-based threshold ring signature schemes which is applicable to many real-world applications with varied anonymity requirements.

1 Introduction

As the number of applications on the Internet continues to grow, more and more traditional human interactions have been converted to their electronic counterparts: messaging, voting, payments, commerce, etc. The increase in reliance on

---

[*] A full version of the paper can be found at [55].

S.-H. Heng and K. Kurosawa (Eds.): ProvSec 2010, LNCS 6402, pp. 166–183, 2010.

the Internet potentially erodes personal privacy, the right of the individual to be let alone [58], or the right to determine the amount of personal information which should be available to others [59]. Privacy is important for many reasons, such as impersonation and fraud. As more identity information is collected, correlated, and sold, it becomes easier for criminals to commit fraud. But privacy is more than that, it also concerns about the secrecy of which websites we visited, the candidates we voted for, etc.

Anonymity is one important form of privacy protection. In practice, anonymity diversifies into various forms with different levels of anonymity. For example, look at how anonymous remailers [35] have evolved over time – from type 0 to type I to type II, every successor provides a higher level of anonymity, at the cost of lower efficiency and higher resource consumption. On the other side, for some applications, too high a level of anonymity can do more harm than good. For example, while unconditional anonymity provides maximum protection to users which can be useful for scenarios such as secret leaking [52]. However, unconditional anonymity may not be desirable for some other applications. For instance, in some scenarios one would like to have a trusted third party to have the capability to trace users after the fact that the users have misbehaved, such as tracing double-spenders in an e-cash system.

Designing secure cryptographic schemes with unconditional anonymity is undoubtedly challenging. However, designing schemes with a carefully adjusted level of anonymity is sometimes even more challenging. It is also very rewarding due to the fact that these schemes find many applications in practice. For example, a ring signature scheme [52] allows a signer to generate a signature on behalf of a group of signers such that everyone can be sure that the signature is generated by one of the group members yet no one can tell who the real signer is. Different from group signature, there is no group manager, no member revocation, and it is spontaneous (setup-free). While a *linkable* ring signature [46] allows anyone to tell whether two signatures are generated by the same signer while still maintaining the anonymity of the real signer as a conventional ring signature scheme in the way that no one can revoke the real signer's anonymity.

1.1   Background and Related Work

Identity-based Cryptography. In 1984, Shamir [54] introduced the notion of Identity-based (ID-based) cryptography to simplify certificate management. The unique feature of ID-based cryptography is that a user's public key can be any arbitrary string. Since then, many other ID-based signature schemes have been proposed, despite the fact that the first practical ID-based encryption appeared only until 2001 [13]. In 2004, Bellare et al. [10] developed a framework to analyze the security of ID-based signature schemes and they proved the security (or insecurity) of 14 schemes found in the literature. As in the case of standard signature, there are also blind signature [63], proxy signature [61], proxy blind signature [32], proxy ring signature [6,63], and proxy signcryption [44] in the paradigm of ID-based cryptography.

Group-oriented Cryptography. This type of schemes has a group of users involved, e.g. secret sharing schemes, group signature schemes, etc. In some of them, group members participate equally well in all the processes and therefore, there is no concern of anonymity. In some other schemes, however, the participation of only one or a proper subset of members is required to complete a process, while the remaining members are not involved in (and are possibly unaware of) the process. Such a distinction between participants and non-participants gives anonymity a meaning. Specifically, a participant may prefer to be indistinguishable from the whole group of members, thus maintaining his privacy in participating the process. According to the level of anonymity the group-oriented cryptographic schemes provide, they can be categorized as follows.

NO ANONYMITY means the identities of the participating users are known to everyone. Privacy is simply not a concern here. For example, in a multi-signature scheme [41,48], everyone can identify who has contributed in the signing process.

ANONYMITY means not everyone should be able to identify participating users. A good example is ring signature [52], in which besides the actual signer, no one can identify the actual signer of a signature among a group of possible signers. There have been many different schemes proposed [1,31,53,21] since the first appearance of ring signature in 1994 [30] and the formal introduction of it in 2001 [52]. The first ID-based ring signature was proposed in 2002 [62]. Two constructions in the standard model were proposed [5]. Their first construction was discovered to be flawed [33], while the second construction is only proven secure in a weaker model, namely, selective-ID model. The first scheme claimed to be secure in the standard model is [39] under the trusted setup assumption. However, their proof is wrong and it is unknown whether their scheme is secure or not.[1] Other existing ID-based ring signatures includes [23,7,64,28,26,50,40]. Threshold variant of ID-based ring signatures includes [24,29,39]. To the best of the authors' knowledge, all the existing ID-based ring signature schemes are pairing-based except the one in [40] which is RSA-based.

REVOCABLE ANONYMITY can be summarized as "no anonymity to an authority, but anonymity to anybody else". In schemes with revocable anonymity, there is always an authority who is capable of revoking the anonymity, e.g., under dispute or court order. The authority is often assumed to be trusted not to abuse power. Users are anonymous to everybody other than this authority. Group signature schemes [22,9,12] provide revocable anonymity. Many credential systems [16,17,18] also provide revocable anonymity.

LINKABLE ANONYMITY is "anonymity with a condition". Schemes with linkable anonymity give maximal anonymity to users who succeeded in satisfying the condition and take away a certain degree of anonymity from users who failed as a punishment. Let us illustrate the idea using a linkable ring signature scheme. In this scheme, users are assumed to sign only once, in which case they enjoy anonymity in full. However, if a user signs twice (or k times, in general), anyone can tell if two signatures are produced by the same user or not, thus resulting

---

[1] We explicitly point out the flaw in Appendix A.

in a reduced level of anonymity. Linkable ring signature was introduced in [46]. [57] gave a separable construction that supports threshold. The first constant-size linkable ring signature was proposed in [56]. Linkable group signature first appeared in [49]. Escrowed linkable ring signature was proposed in [27]. The first constant-size linkable ring signature (and revocable if and only if linked variant) was proposed in [4]. The construction, however, was flawed as shown in [42]. A practical application of linkable ring signature is e-voting [25].

A technical difficulty in constructing an ID-based linkable ring signature is that there exists a Private Key Generator (PKG) in the system responsible for issuing users' secret keys yet linkable anonymity should be maintained, even against the PKG. Our construction solves this by modifying the key extraction algorithm such that user's secret key is co-generated by the PKG and the user. This idea is reminiscent to the idea of self-certified keys [37]. It also allows the users in our ID-based linkable signature scheme to refute any framing attacks launched by the PKG through generating another signature which is unlinked to the forged signature.

1.2   Our Contributions and Motivations

- We propose the first ID-based threshold ring signature scheme that is *not* based on bilinear pairings. We show its security under the Strong RSA and DDH Assumption, in the random oracle model [11]. In particular, anonymity of the ring signers is maintained even against the PKG.
- By extending on our basic construction, we propose the first ID-based *linkable* threshold ring signature scheme. All previously proposed linkable ring signature schemes except [27] are not ID-based.[2]
- We show the method of adding identity escrow in both of our schemes. With identity escrow, some trusted authority can revoke the anonymity of a ring signature when it becomes necessary. The ability of revoking the real signer can help prevent the signature scheme from being abused by misbehaving users. The schemes, plus their identity-escrowed counterparts, form a suite of ID-based signature schemes applicable to a wide variety of scenarios with different anonymity requirements. Note that even with identity escrow, the scheme is not the same as a group signature scheme due to the spontaneity property of the ring signature scheme.

Our Motivations. As we have seen many constructions of threshold ring signature schemes [30,14,60,45,47,57,24,29,39] proposed recently, there are only few of them [24,29,39] under the setting of ID-based cryptography. ID-based ring signature schemes have similar applications to that of conventional public key setting, but with the key escrow property. Applications include whistle-blowing [52] and ad hoc group authentication [14]. All ID-based threshold ring signature schemes proposed are pairing based. Also it is obvious to further extend them

---

[2] We note that although the linkable ring signature scheme in [4] is ID-based, it is later proven insecure in [42].

to a **linkable** variant, especially it needs to be secure under the security models we define in this paper. Therefore, the work presented in this paper is mainly motivated by the following two aspects.

1. As of theoretical interest, we target to propose an identity-based scheme which does not rely on security assumptions related to pairings, for example, Gap Diffie-Hellman Problem.
2. All current ID-based threshold ring signature schemes do not allow us to extend it to an ID-based **linkable** threshold ring signature scheme. We target to construct a scheme which can be extended so that we can construct a linkable variant.

1.3   Comparison

We compare our scheme with other ID-based threshold ring signature schemes [24,29,39] in Table 1.

Table 1. Comparison of different ID-based threshold ring signature schemes

	Signature size (group elements)	Number of pairing in verification	Mathematical Assumption	Security model	Extend to linkable
[24]	$\mathcal{O}(n)$	$\mathcal{O}(n)$	GDH	ROM	No
[29]	$\mathcal{O}(n^2)$	$\mathcal{O}(n^2)$	ECDL, BPI	ROM	No
[39]	$\mathcal{O}(n)$	$\mathcal{O}(n)$	SGH, CDH	Unknown	No
Our schemes	$\mathcal{O}(n)$	0	Strong RSA, DDH	ROM	Yes

In the table, n is the number of users included in the ring. The assumptions mentioned include:

- GDH: Gap Diffie-Hellman problem
- ECDL: Elliptic Curve Discrete Logarithm problem
- BPI: Bilinear Pairings Identity problem
- SGH: Subgroup Decision problem
- DDH: Decisional Diffie-Hellman problem

Note that each group element of our scheme is about 1024 bits, while a group element of other pairing-based schemes is about 160 bits.

We also note that although the authors of the scheme in [39] claimed that their scheme is secure in the standard model, we find out a flaw in the proof. It is unknown whether their scheme is secure or not, at least in the standard model. We present the flaw in Appendix A.

Paper Organization. We give some preliminaries in Sec. 2 and define a security model in Sec. 3. We then propose an ID-based threshold ring signature scheme in Sec. 4 and an ID-based linkable variant in Sec. 5. In Sec. 6, we show how to add identity escrow to our schemes.

2   Preliminaries

A safe prime p is a prime such that $(p-1)/2$ is also prime[3]. Denote by $QR(N)$ the group of quadratic residues modulo the safe prime product N. For positive real numbers $a \leq b$, $\lfloor a \rfloor$ denotes the greatest integer less than or equal to a; $[a, b]$ denotes the set $\{x \in \mathbb{Z} | \lfloor a \rfloor \leq x \leq \lfloor b \rfloor\}$ and $S(a, b)$ denotes $[\lfloor a \rfloor - \lfloor b \rfloor + 1, \lfloor a \rfloor + \lfloor b \rfloor - 1]$. If S is a set, $\wp(S)$ denotes the power set of S and $\wp_t(S)$ denotes the set of elements in $\wp(S)$ of size t, i.e. $\wp_t(S) \doteq \{s \in \wp(S) | \; |s| = t\}$. A *negligible* function $\nu(\lambda)$ is a function such that for all polynomial poly and sufficiently large λ, $\nu(\lambda) < 1/\text{poly}(\lambda)$. When G is a finite cyclic group, define $\mathcal{G}(G)$ to be the set of generators of G, i.e. $\{g \in G | \langle g \rangle = G\}$.

2.1   Mathematical Assumptions

Definition 1 (Strong RSA [8,36]). *Let $n = pq$ be an RSA modulus. Let G be a cyclic subgroup of $\mathbb{Z}_n^*$ of order u. Given n and $z \in_R G$, the Strong RSA Problem is to find $x \in G$ and $e \in \mathbb{Z}_{>1}$ such that $z = x^e \mod n$. The Strong RSA Assumption says that there exists no PPT algorithm that can solve the Strong RSA Problem, in time polynomial in the size of $|u|$.*

In our schemes, we need to make restriction to safe primes for p and q in the Strong RSA assumption. However, it is easy to see that the Strong RSA assumption without this restriction implies the Strong RSA assumption with this restriction, assuming that safe primes are sufficiently dense.

Definition 2 (Decisional Diffie-Hellman (DDH) [11]). *Let G be a cyclic group generated by g of order u. The DDH Problem is to distinguish between the distributions (g, g^a, g^b, g^c) and (g, g^a, g^b, g^{ab}), with $a, b, c \in_R \mathbb{Z}_u$. The DDH Assumption says there exists no PPT algorithm solve the DDH Problem, in time polynomial in the size of $|u|$.*

2.2   Signature of Knowledge

A Σ-protocol for an **NP**-relation R is a 3-round two-party protocol, such that for every input $(x, y) \in R$ to a prover $\mathcal{P}$ and y to a verifier $\mathcal{V}$, the first $\mathcal{P}$-round yields a commitment t, the subsequent $\mathcal{V}$-round replies with a challenge c, and the last $\mathcal{P}$-round concludes by sending a response s. At the end of a run, $\mathcal{V}$ outputs a 0/1 value, functionally dependent on y and the transcript $\pi \doteq (t, c, s)$ only. A transcript is valid if the output of the honest verifier is 1. Additionally, we require a Σ-protocol to satisfy:

- *(Special Soundness.)* There exists a computable function $\mathcal{K}$ (Knowledge Extractor) that on input y in the domain of the second component of R and a pair of valid transcripts (t, c, s) and (t, c', s'), with the same commitment, outputs x such that $(x, y) \in R$.

---

[3] Although it has never been proven, it is widely conjectured and amply supported by empirical evidence, that safe primes are sufficiently dense.

- *(Special Honest-Verifier Zero-Knowledge (Special HVZK).)* There exists an efficient algorithm $\mathcal{S}$ (Simulator) that on input y in the domain of the second component of R and a challenge c, outputs a pair of commitment/response messages t, s, such that the transcript $\pi \doteq (t, c, s)$ is valid, and it is distributed according to the distribution $(\mathcal{P}(x, y) \leftrightarrow \mathcal{V}(y))$.

A signature of knowledge allows a signer to prove the knowledge of a secret with respect to some public information non-interactively. Following [20], we call this type of signatures "a signature based on proofs of knowledge", SPK for short. A HVZK Σ-protocol can be turned into a SPK by setting the challenge to the hash value of the commitment together with the message to be signed [34]. Such schemes can be proven secure against existential forgery under chosen-message attack [38] in the random oracle model using the proofing technique introduced in [51].

3   Definitions and Security Models

3.1   ID-TRS (ID-based Threshold Ring Signature)

An ID-Based Threshold Ring Signature (ID-TRS) scheme is defined as a tuple of four probabilistic polynomial-time (PPT) algorithms:

- ID-TRS.Setup. On input 1^λ where $\lambda \in \mathbb{N}$ is a security parameter, it outputs a master secret key s and a system parameter set $\mathsf{param} = (1^\lambda, \mathcal{S}, \mathcal{M}, \Psi)$, where $\mathcal{S}$ is the user secret key space, $\mathcal{M}$ the message space, and Ψ the signature space.
- ID-TRS.Extract. On input param, an identity $\mathsf{ID}_i \in \{0,1\}^*$ for a user and the master secret key s, it outputs a user secret key $s_i \in \mathcal{S}$ for the user.
- ID-TRS.Sign. On input param, an integer n as the ring size, a threshold $t \in [1, n]$, an identity set $\{\mathsf{ID}_i \in \{0,1\}^* \mid i \in [1, n]\}$, a message $m \in \mathcal{M}$, and a t-element user secret key set $\{s_j \in \mathcal{S} \mid j \in \Pi\}$ where $\Pi \in \wp_t([1, n])$, it outputs an ID-based (t, n)-threshold ring signature $\sigma \in \Psi$.
- ID-TRS.Verify. On input param, ring size n, threshold t, identity set $\{\mathsf{ID}_i \in \{0,1\}^* \mid i \in [1, n]\}$, message $m \in \mathcal{M}$ and signature $\sigma \in \Psi$, it outputs either valid or invalid.

Correctness. An ID-TRS scheme defined above satisfies **verification correctness** if for any $(s, \mathsf{param}) \leftarrow \mathtt{ID\text{-}TRS.Setup}(1^\lambda)$, $n \in \mathbb{N}$, $t \in [1, n]$, $L = \{\mathsf{ID}_i \in \{0,1\}^* \mid i \in [1, n]\}$, $\Pi \in \wp_t([1, n])$, $\{s_i \leftarrow \mathtt{ID\text{-}TRS.Extract}(\mathsf{param}, \mathsf{ID}_i, s) \mid i \in [1, n]\}$ and $m \in \mathcal{M}$, if $\sigma \leftarrow \mathtt{ID\text{-}TRS.Sign}(\mathsf{param}, n, t, L, m, \{s_j \mid j \in \Pi\})$, then $\mathsf{valid} \leftarrow \mathtt{ID\text{-}TRS.Verify}(\mathsf{param}, n, t, L, m, \sigma)$.

A secure ID-TRS scheme should be **unforgeable** and **anonymous**. Specific to ID-based setting, our security model captures the *adaptive chosen ID attacks*. Due to page limitation, please refer to the full version of the paper for formal definitions.

3.2 ID-LTRS (ID-based Linkable Threshold Ring Signature)

As introduced at the beginning of this paper, ID-LTRS (ID-based **Linkable** Threshold Ring Signature) scheme is a variant of ID-TRS. In the following, we give the formal definition and specify the security requirements.

- ID-LTRS.Setup. Same as ID-TRS.Setup, except: (1) it has an additional input $k \in \mathbb{N}$ which represents the maximum number of events that the system supports, and (2) param additionally includes an event-ID space $\mathcal{E}$. We have $|\mathcal{E}| = k$.
- ID-LTRS.Extract Protocol. User with identity ID_i engage with PKG in the protocol with common input param. After the protocol, the user is obtained a user secret key $s_i \in \mathcal{S}$.
- ID-LTRS.Sign,Verify. Same as ID-TRS.Sign,Verify, except they both additionally have an input event-ID $e \in \mathcal{E}$.
- ID-LTRS.Link. On input param, $e \in \mathcal{E}$, two ring sizes n_1, n_2, two thresholds $t_1 \in [1, n_1]$ and $t_2 \in [1, n_2]$, two identity sets $\mathcal{Y}_j = \{\mathsf{ID}_i^{(j)} \mid i \in [1, n_j]\}$ for $j = 1, 2$, two messages $m_1, m_2 \in \mathcal{M}$, and two signatures $\sigma_1, \sigma_2 \in \Psi$ such that valid $\leftarrow$ ID-LTRS.Verify(param, $e, n_j, t_j, \mathcal{Y}_j, m_j, \sigma_j$) for $j = 1, 2$, the algorithm returns either linked or unlinked.

Note that we require an interactive extract protocol (between the PKG and user) instead of the normal extract algorithm here. The purpose is to prevent the PKG from learning the identity of the actual signer from the additional linking tag.

Correctness. Besides **verification correctness** (which is defined similarly to that for ID-TRS), an ID-LTRS scheme also satisfies **linking correctness** if

$$\text{linked} \leftarrow \text{ID-LTRS.Link}(\text{param}, e, n_1, n_2, t_1, t_2, \mathcal{Y}_1, \mathcal{Y}_2, m_1, m_2, \sigma_1, \sigma_2)$$

for any $(s, \text{param}) \leftarrow \text{ID-LTRS.Setup}(1^\lambda, k)$, $n_1, n_2 \in \mathbb{N}$, $t_j \in [1, n_j]$, $\mathcal{Y}_j = \{\mathsf{ID}_i^{(j)} \mid i \in [1, n_j]\}$, $\Pi_j \in \wp_{t_j}([1, n_j])$, $\{s_i^{(j)} \leftarrow \text{ID-LTRS.Extract Protocol} \mid i \in [1, n_j]\}$, $m_1, m_2 \in \mathcal{M}$ such that $\sigma_j \leftarrow \text{ID-LTRS.Sign}(\text{param}, n_j, t_j, \mathcal{Y}_j, m_j, \{s_i^{(j)} \mid i \in \Pi_j\})$, for $j = 1, 2$ and $\Pi_1 \cap \Pi_2 \neq \emptyset$.

Remark: According to [56], linkability for threshold ring signatures is diversified into *individual-linkability* and *coalition-linkability*, our definition belongs to the former type. That is, two signatures are linked if they share at least one common signer even though the two identity sets are different. The definition of linkability affects directly the level of anonymity due to the additional access to ID-LTRS.Link by the adversary.

The security requirements of ID-LTRS schemes include **Unforgeability**, **Anonymity**, **Linkability** and **Non-slanderability**, whose formal definitions can be found in the full version of the paper. *Note that we do not model the case of a **malicious PKG** [3] where the adversary acts as a malicious PKG who generates all public parameters instead of just given the secret key.*

4   Our ID-TRS Scheme

We first give an overview of our construction. For an identity ID, the corresponding secret key is (a, x), with $x > 1$, such that $a^x \equiv H_{id}(\text{ID}) \pmod{N}$, where $H_{id} : \{0,1\}^* \to QR(N)$ is some hash function. The modulus N is a product of two equal-length safe primes with factorization only known to the PKG.

A user proves the knowledge of his secret key by running the Σ-protocol given by:

$$PK\{(a, x) : y \equiv a^x \wedge x \in \Gamma\}$$

for $y = H_{id}(\text{ID})$ and some suitable range Γ. An ID-based signature scheme is readily available after carrying out the Fiat-Shamir transformation on the Σ-protocol:

$$SPK_1\{(a, x) : y \equiv a^x \wedge x \in \Gamma\}(m). \tag{1}$$

Now, to extend the IBS scheme construction above into a threshold ring setting, we implement the following signature of knowledge (SPK):

$$SPK_2\left\{(\alpha_i, \chi_i)_{i=1}^n : \bigvee_{\mathcal{J} \in \wp_t([1,n])} \bigwedge_{i \in \mathcal{J}} y_i \equiv \alpha_i^{\chi_i} \wedge \chi_i \in \Gamma\right\}(m) \tag{2}$$

with $y_i = H_{id}(\text{ID}_i)$ for all $i \in [1, n]$. This SPK proves that there exists d identities in $\{\text{ID}_1, \cdots, \text{ID}_n\}$ such that the prover knows the secret keys corresponding to these identities. To implement SPK_2, we incorporate the polynomial interpolation technique [30] into SPK_1.

We now describe the details of our ID-based (t, n)-threshold ring signature scheme.

- ID-TRS.Setup. On input a security parameter λ, the algorithm randomly generates a safe prime product $N = pq = (2p' + 1)(2q' + 1)$, where $|p'| = |q'| = \lambda$. It then selects two cryptographic hash functions $H_{id} : \{0,1\}^* \to QR(N)$ and $H_{sig} : \{0,1\}^* \to \mathbb{Z}_{2^\kappa}$. For security analysis, we consider them to behave as random oracles. It also randomly picks $g_1, g_2, g_3 \in QR(N)$ that are generators of $QR(N)$.

  To implement H_{id} using a conventional string-based hash function, we need to randomly choose another generator g of $QR(N)$ and define H_{id} as ID $\to$ g$^{h(\text{ID})}$ mod N, where h $: \{0,1\}^* \to \{0,1\}^{2\lambda+\theta}$ is a hash function. The parameter $\theta > 0$ defines the quality of the hash output of H_{id}. A good construction of H_{id} should have the hash value distributed uniformly on $QR(N)$. It can be seen that the construction above can yield a good distribution when θ is large enough. In practice, we may consider setting θ to 8.

  Let $\kappa, \gamma_1, \gamma_2 \in \mathbb{N}$ and $1 < \epsilon \in \mathbb{R}$ be further security parameters such that $\gamma_1 - 2 > \epsilon(\gamma_2 + \kappa) > 2\lambda$. Define $\Gamma' \doteq S(2^{\gamma_1}, 2^{\gamma_2})$, and $\Gamma \doteq S(2^{\gamma_1}, 2^{\epsilon(\gamma_2+\kappa)})$. The master secret key is set to msk $:= (p, q)$. The list of system parameters is param $:= (\lambda, \kappa, \epsilon, N, H_{id}, H_{sig}, g_1, g_2, g_3, \Gamma', \Gamma)$.

  To achieve security comparable to the standard 1024-bit RSA signature, $\lambda = 512$, $\kappa = 160$, $\epsilon = 1.1$, $\gamma_1 = 1080$, $\gamma_2 = 800$ can be used as the security parameters. For security analysis, we require that all these security parameters to be sufficiently large. It is also important for the generators g, g_1, g_2, g_3 are generated independently, that is, their relative discrete logarithm should not be known to anyone. This is to prevent the secret keys of users from being known from the auxiliary commitments which is defined below and make sure that the proper implementation of H_{id} described above.

- ID-TRS.Extract. On input a new user ID ID_i, the algorithm computes $y_i := H_{id}(ID_i)$, picks a prime $x_i \in_R \Gamma'$, and then solves $a_i^{x_i} \equiv y_i \pmod{N}$ for a_i using the master secret key msk. It finally returns the user's secret key $sk_i := (a_i, x_i)$. An entry $\langle ID_i, y_i, a_i, x_i \rangle$ is recorded. On input an old user ID, the algorithm retrieve the corresponding entry to maintain consistency.

- ID-TRS.Sign. On input the list of system parameters param, a group size $n \in \mathbb{N}$ of size polynomial in λ, a threshold $t \in [1, n]$, a set of n IDs $\mathcal{Y} = \{ID_1, \cdots, ID_n\}$, a list of t secret keys $\mathcal{X} = \{sk_{\pi_1}, \cdots, sk_{\pi_t}\}$ such that the corresponding public key ID_{π_i} of each $sk_{\pi_i} = (a_{\pi_i}, x_{\pi_i})$ is contained in $\mathcal{Y}$, a message $m \in \{0, 1\}^*$, the algorithm first sets $\Pi := \{\pi_1, \cdots, \pi_t\} \subseteq [1, n]$, computes $y_i := H_{id}(ID_i)$ for all $i \in [1, n]$ and then does the following:

1. *(Auxiliary commitment.)* For all $i \in \Pi$, pick $u_i \in_R \pm\{0, 1\}^{2\lambda}$ and compute $w_i := u_i x_i$. Compute in modulo N:

$$A_{i,1} := g_1^{u_i}, \quad A_{i,2} := a_i g_2^{u_i}, \quad A_{i,3} := g_1^{x_i} g_3^{u_i}.$$

For all $i \in [1, n] \backslash \Pi$, pick $A_{i,1}, A_{i,2}, A_{i,3} \in_R QR(N)$.

2. *(Commitment.)* For all $i \in \Pi$, pick $r_{i,x} \in_R \pm\{0, 1\}^{\epsilon(\gamma_2+\kappa)}$, $r_{i,u} \in_R \pm\{0, 1\}^{\epsilon(2\lambda+\kappa)}$, $r_{i,w} \in_R \pm\{0, 1\}^{\epsilon(\gamma_1+2\lambda+\kappa+1)}$. Compute in modulo N:

$$T_{i,1} := g_1^{r_{i,u}}, \quad T_{i,2} := g_1^{r_{i,x}} g_3^{r_{i,u}}, \quad T_{i,3} := A_{i,1}^{r_{i,x}} g_1^{-r_{i,w}}, \quad T_{i,4} := A_{i,2}^{r_{i,x}} g_2^{-r_{i,w}}.$$

For all $i \in [1, n] \backslash \Pi$, pick $c_i \in_R \mathbb{Z}_{2^\kappa}$, $s_{i,u} \in_R \pm\{0, 1\}^{\epsilon(2\lambda+\kappa)}$, $s_{i,x} \in_R \pm\{0, 1\}^{\epsilon(\gamma_2+\kappa)}$, $s_{i,w} \in_R \pm\{0, 1\}^{\epsilon(\gamma_1+2\lambda+\kappa+1)}$. Compute in modulo N:

$$T_{i,1} := g_1^{s_{i,u}} A_{i,1}^{c_i}, \qquad T_{i,2} := g_1^{s_{i,x}-c_i 2^{\gamma_1}} g_3^{s_{i,u}} A_{i,3}^{c_i},$$
$$T_{i,3} := A_{i,1}^{s_{i,x}-c_i 2^{\gamma_1}} g_1^{-s_{i,w}}, \quad T_{i,4} := A_{i,2}^{s_{i,x}-c_i 2^{\gamma_1}} g_2^{-s_{i,w}} y_i^{c_i}.$$

3. *(Challenge.)* Compute

$$c_0 := H_{sig}(\text{param}, n, d, (y_i, A_{i,1}, A_{i,2}, A_{i,3})_{i=1}^n, (T_{i,1}, \cdots, T_{i,4})_{i=1}^n, m).$$

4. *(Response.)* Generate a polynomial f over $GF(2^\kappa)$ of degree at most $(n - t)$ such that $c_0 = f(0)$ and $c_i = f(i)$ for all $i \in [1, n] \backslash \Pi$. For all $i \in \Pi$, compute $c_i := f(i)$, and compute in $\mathbb{Z}$:

$$s_{i,u} := r_{i,u} - c_i u_i, \quad s_{i,x} := r_{i,x} - c_i (x_i - 2^{\gamma_1}), \quad s_{i,w} := r_{i,w} - c_i w_i.$$

5. *(Signature.)* Set $\sigma' := (f, (s_{i,u}, s_{i,x}, s_{i,w})_{i=1}^n)$.

6. *(Output.)* Return the signature as: $\sigma := ((A_{i,1}, A_{i,2}, A_{i,3})_{i=1}^n, \sigma')$.
   Remark: step 2 to 4 together contribute to the signing algorithm of:

$$SPK_3 \left\{ \begin{pmatrix} u_i, \\ x_i, \\ w_i \end{pmatrix}_{i=1}^n : \bigvee_{\mathcal{J} \in \wp_t([1,n])} \bigwedge_{i \in \mathcal{J}} \begin{matrix} A_{i,1} \equiv g_1^{u_i} \wedge A_{i,3} \equiv g_1^{x_i} g_3^{u_i} \wedge \\ A_{i,1}^{x_i} \equiv g_1^{w_i} \wedge A_{i,2}^{x_i} \equiv g_2^{w_i} y_i \wedge \\ x_i \in \Gamma \end{matrix} \right\} (m),$$

(3)

which is an instantiation of SPK_2. The signature of SPK_3 is σ' in step 5.

- ID-TRS.Verify. On input param, a group size n of length polynomial in λ, a threshold $t \in [1,n]$, a set $\{ID_i \in \{0,1\}^* | i \in [1,n]\}$ of n user identities, a message $m \in \mathcal{M}$, a signature $\sigma \in \Psi$, the algorithm computes $y_i := H_{id}(ID_i)$ for all $i \in [1,n]$ and then does the following.

  1. Check if f is a polynomial over $GF(2^\kappa)$ of degree at most $(n-t)$.
  2. For all $i \in [1,n]$, compute $c_i := f(i)$ and compute in modulo N:

$$T'_{i,1} := g_1^{s_{i,u}} A_{i,1}^{c_i}, \qquad T'_{i,2} := g_1^{s_{i,x} - c_i 2^{\gamma_1}} g_3^{s_{i,u}} A_{i,3}^{c_i},$$
$$T'_{i,3} := A_{i,1}^{s_{i,x} - c_i 2^{\gamma_1}} g_1^{-s_{i,w}}, \quad T'_{i,4} := A_{i,2}^{s_{i,x} - c_i 2^{\gamma_1}} g_2^{-s_{i,w}} y_i^{c_i}.$$

  3. Check if the following statements hold: $s_{i,u} \stackrel{?}{\in} \{0,1\}^{\epsilon(2\lambda+\kappa)+1}$, $s_{i,x} \stackrel{?}{\in} \{0,1\}^{\epsilon(\gamma_2+\kappa)+1}$, $s_{i,w} \stackrel{?}{\in} \{0,1\}^{\epsilon(\gamma_1+2\lambda+\kappa+1)+1}$, for all $i \in [1,n]$, and

$$f(0) \stackrel{?}{=} H_{sig}(\text{param}, n, t, (y_i, A_{i,1}, A_{i,2}, A_{i,3})_{i=1}^n, (T'_{i,1}, \cdots, T'_{i,4})_{i=1}^n, m).$$

  4. Accept if all checks pass and reject otherwise.
  Remark: The above verification actually verifies SPK_3.

The proof for correctness is straightforward. We show its security in the full version of the paper.

5   ID-Based Linkable Threshold Ring Signature

In this section, we propose the *first* ID-based linkable threshold ring signature (ID-LTRS) and present its security analysis.

5.1   Our Proposed Construction

The key idea is to include a tag to the original ID-TRS signature for the purpose of linking. Such a tag is a one-way and unique image of the signer's secret signing key. To prevent PKG from learning the signer identity from the tag, we modify the extract protocol so that the secret signing key is co-generated by signer and PKG. The signature, besides proving the knowledge of a secret signing key, now also proves that the tag is formed correctly. To test whether two signatures are linked, one simply checks if the two signatures contain the same tag. Below is our construction.

- ID-LTRS.Setup. Same as ID-TRS.Setup, except it additionally picks $e_i \in_R \mathcal{G}(QR(N))$ for all $i \in [1, k]$ and sets $\mathcal{E} := \{e_i | i \in [1, k]\}$. It also picks one more generator $h \in_R \mathcal{G}(QR(N))$. Define λ_1, λ_2 such that $\gamma_2 > \lambda_1 + 2, \lambda_1 > \epsilon(\lambda_2 + \kappa)$ and $\lambda_2 > 2\lambda$. Define $\tilde{\Lambda}' =]0, 2^{\lambda_2}[, \Lambda' = S(2^{\lambda_1}, 2^{\lambda_2})$ and $\Lambda = S(2^{\lambda_1}, 2^{\epsilon(\lambda_2 + \kappa)})$
- ID-LTRS.Extract Protocol. User i with ID ID_i engage with PKG in the following protocol.
  1. User randomly generates $\tilde{d}_i \in_R \tilde{\Lambda}'$, a random $\tilde{r} \in_R \pm\{0,1\}^{2\lambda}$ and sends $C_1 = g_1^{\tilde{d}_i} g_2^{\tilde{r}}$, together with knowledge of representation of C_1 with respect to g_1 and g_2 to PKG. It also sends ID_i together.
  2. PKG checks that the proof is valid and randomly selects $\alpha, \beta \in_R \tilde{\Lambda}'$ and sends α, β to user.
  3. User computes $d_i = 2^{\lambda_1} + (\alpha\tilde{d}_i + \beta \bmod 2^{\lambda_2})$ and sends $C_2 = h^{d_i}$ together with the proof of validity to PKG. This can be done by $SPK\{(u, v, w) : C_1^\alpha g_1^\beta = g_1^u g_1^{2^{\lambda_2} v} g_2^w \wedge C_2 = h^u \wedge u \in \Lambda'\}(m)$
  4. PKG checks if the proof is valid, and picks a prime $x_i \in_R \Gamma'$, and then solves $a_i^{x_i} \equiv y_i C_2 \pmod{N}$ for a_i using the master secret key msk, where $y_i = H(\mathsf{ID}_i)$. Return (a_i, x_i) to user and record the entry $\langle \mathsf{ID}_i, y_i, a_i, x_i \rangle$.
  5. User checks if $a_i^{x_i} = y_i h^{d_i} \pmod{N}$

We remark that this structure is used by the ACJT group signature [2].

- ID-LTRS.Sign. For an event with event-ID $e \in \mathcal{E}$, compute $\tau_i := e^{d_i} \bmod N$ for all $i \in \Pi$ and $\tau_i := e^{t_i} \bmod N$ with $t_i \in_R \Lambda'$ for all $i \in [1, n] \backslash \Pi$. The algorithm is subsequently modified from ID-TRS.Sign to also prove that the τ_i's are correctly formed. Specifically, the algorithm now implements:

$$SPK_4 \left\{ (a_i, x_i, d_i)_{i=1}^n : \bigvee_{\mathcal{J} \in \wp_t([1,n])} \bigwedge_{i \in \mathcal{J}} y_i h^{d_i} \equiv a_i^{x_i} \wedge \tau_i \equiv e^{d_i} \wedge d_i \in \Lambda, x_i \in \Gamma \right\} (m) \tag{4}$$

which is instantiated as:

$$SPK_5 \left\{ (u_i, x_i, w_i)_{i=1}^n : \bigvee_{\mathcal{J} \in \wp_t([1,n])} \bigwedge_{i \in \mathcal{J}} \begin{array}{ll} A_{i,1} \equiv g_1^{u_i} \wedge & A_{i,3} \equiv g_1^{x_i} g_3^{u_i} \wedge \\ A_{i,1}^{x_i} \equiv g_1^{w_i} \wedge & A_{i,2}^{x_i} \equiv g_2^{w_i} y_i h^{d_i} \wedge \\ \tau_i \equiv e^{d_i} \wedge x_i \in \Gamma \wedge d_i \in \Lambda \end{array} \right\} (m). \tag{5}$$

The actual steps implementing the SPK_5 above follow closely those implementing SPK_3 in ID-TRS.Sign and are thus not verbosely enumerated. Denote by σ_5 the signature output of SPK_5. Note that it includes $\tau_1, \cdots, \tau_n$. In addition, generate a signature σ_6 for the following SPK using the knowledge of x_i's for $i \in \Pi$ and t_i's for $i \in [1, n] \backslash \Pi$:

$$SPK_6 \left\{ (\alpha_i)_{i=1}^n : \bigwedge_{i=1}^n \tau_i \equiv e^{\alpha_i} \right\} (m). \tag{6}$$

The detailed implementation of the above SPK is given in the full version of the paper.

Finally the signature is output as $\sigma := (\sigma_5, \sigma_6)$.

- ID-LTRS.Verify. Given a signature $\sigma = (\sigma_5, \sigma_6)$, verify the validity of σ_5 with respect to SPK_5 and that of σ_6 with respect to SPK_6. Again we omit the verification algorithm for SPK_5 as it can be adapted in a straightforward manner from ID-TRS.Verify. Verification for SPK_6 is given in the full version of the paper.

- ID-LTRS.Link. On input the list of system parameters param, an event-ID $e \in \mathcal{E}$, two group sizes $n_1, n_2 \in \mathbb{N}$ of length polynomial in the security parameter λ, two thresholds $t_1 \in [1, n_1]$ and $t_2 \in [1, n_2]$, two identity sets $\mathcal{Y}_j = \{ \mathsf{ID}_i^{(j)} \in \{0,1\}^* | i \in [1, n_j] \}$ for $j = 1, 2$, two messages $m_1, m_2 \in \mathcal{M}$, and two signatures $\sigma_1, \sigma_2 \in \Psi$ such that valid $\leftarrow$ Verify(param, e, n_j, t_j, $\mathcal{Y}_j$, m_j, σ_j) for $j = 1, 2$, the algorithm parses σ_1 for the tags $(\tau_1^{(1)}, \cdots, \tau_{n_1}^{(1)})$ and σ_2 for the tags $(\tau_1^{(2)}, \cdots, \tau_{n_2}^{(2)})$. If there exists a tag from the first set and a tag from the second set such that the two tags are equal in value, the algorithm outputs linked. Otherwise it returns unlinked.

Correctness of our scheme is straightforward and we show its security in the full version of the paper.

6   Identity Escrow

As mentioned earlier, the anonymity provided by ring signatures can be undesirably strong in some situations. Authorities prefer providing only revocable anonymity to their users. Their ability of revocation serves as a mechanism that prevents them from being suffered from the presence of misbehaving users. Introducing a trusted authority who can reveal the true identity of the user under certain circumstances is formally known as identity escrow [43].

To add identity escrow to ring signature schemes, one could variably encrypt any information sufficient for identifying the signer, and then include in the signature the resulting ciphertext plus a proof that it is correctly formed. In fact, verifiable encryption [15,19] has been frequently used (though sometimes implicitly) to achieve revocable anonymity. For instance, the generic constructions of group signatures [9,12]. As a concrete example, in [2], part of the user's secret key[4] is ElGamal encrypted under the public key of an authority. The unforgeability of the signature scheme implies that valid signatures are actually proofs of the fact that encryption was done according to specification.

Our Construction. We use the same technique as in [2] to add identity escrow to the two schemes proposed above. The resulting schemes are virtually the same as their respective original schemes without identity escrow, except that in Setup, g_2 is not generated randomly. Instead it is generated in a way such that the revocation manager knows the discrete logarithm of g_2 in base g_1, i.e. he knows an integer s such that $g_2 \equiv g_1^s \pmod{N}$. Assume the revocation manager is trusted not to abuse his knowledge of s in the sense that he does not collude with any adversary and only uses s when trying to revoke the anonymity of a

---

[4] Also known as the user's signing certificate in the context of group signatures.

signature with eligible reasons, e.g. under court orders. Then the two schemes with identity escrow still enjoy all the security notions we proved for original schemes.

To see how the anonymity can be revoked, the revocation manager can compute from a signature a part of the secret key (a_i, x_i), namely a_i, of all participating users by computing $A_{i,2}/A_{i,1}^s \mod N$ for all $i \in [1, n]$. The unforgeability of the signature scheme forces at least d pairs of $A_{i,1}$ and $A_{i,2}$ to be formed correctly. These pairs are exactly those belonging to the participating users. The remaining a_i could just be some random numbers. All n a_i's are passed to the key issuing manager, whom can then look up in his database the identity of the user possessing a_i as a part of his secret key, for each $i \in [1, n]$. In this way, the d actual signers can be identified.

The revocation manager cannot frame a user if he is required to prove (in zero-knowledge of s) the statement $g_2 \equiv g_1^s \wedge A_{i,2} \equiv a_i A_{i,1}^s$. The key issuing manager cannot frame a user as well if he is required to prove (in zero-knowledge of x_i) the statement $a_i^{x_i} \equiv y_i$, where $y_i = H_{id}(\mathsf{ID}_i)$.

7   Performance and Conclusion

The computation complexity and the signature size of our construction are both linear to the ring size. This is the major tradeoff of our schemes as they achieve different levels of anonymity. To improve their efficiency, especially on constructing an efficient ID-based linkable threshold ring signature scheme, will be our next research work.

In this paper, we proposed the first ID-based threshold ring signature construction that is *not* based on bilinear pairings. We formally proved the security of the construction under well-known mathematical assumptions in the RO model. Based on the construction, we then proposed the first ID-based linkable (threshold) ring signature scheme. We argued the security of all the constructions. Finally we showed how to add identity escrow to the two schemes. All the ID-based threshold ring signature schemes proposed in this paper form a suite of schemes applicable to many real world applications with varied anonymity requirements.

Memorial

This paper is dedicated to the first author, Patrick P. Tsang, who was a PhD student in the Computer Science program at Dartmouth College, has passed away on October 27, 2009 as a victim to cancer. He was 28 years old.

References

1. Abe, M., Ohkubo, M., Suzuki, K.: 1-out-of-n signatures from a variety of keys. In: Zheng, Y. (ed.) ASIACRYPT 2002. LNCS, vol. 2501, pp. 415–432. Springer, Heidelberg (2002)

2. Ateniese, G., Camenisch, J., Joye, M., Tsudik, G.: A practical and provably secure coalition-resistant group signature scheme. In: Bellare, M. (ed.) CRYPTO 2000. LNCS, vol. 1880, pp. 255–270. Springer, Heidelberg (2000)
3. Au, M., Chen, J., Liu, J., Mu, Y., Wong, D., Yang, G.: Malicious KGC attacks in certificateless cryptography. In: ASIACCS 2007, pp. 302–311. ACM Press, New York (2007)
4. Au, M.H., Liu, J.K., Susilo, W., Yuen, T.H.: Constant-size id-based linkable and revocable-iff-linked ring signature. In: Barua, R., Lange, T. (eds.) INDOCRYPT 2006. LNCS, vol. 4329, pp. 364–378. Springer, Heidelberg (2006)
5. Au, M.H., Liu, J.K., Yuen, T.H., Wong, D.S.: Id-based ring signature scheme secure in the standard model. In: Yoshiura, H., Sakurai, K., Rannenberg, K., Murayama, Y., Kawamura, S.-i. (eds.) IWSEC 2006. LNCS, vol. 4266, pp. 1–16. Springer, Heidelberg (2006)
6. Awasthi, A.K., Lal, S.: Id-based ring signature and proxy ring signature schemes from bilinear pairings. Cryptology ePrint Archive, Report 2004/184 (2004), http://eprint.iacr.org/
7. Awasthi, A.K., Lal, S.: Id-based ring signature and proxy ring signature schemes from bilinear pairings. CoRR, abs/cs/0504097 (2005)
8. Barić, N., Pfitzmann, B.: Collision-free accumulators and fail-stop signature schemes without trees. In: Fumy, W. (ed.) EUROCRYPT 1997. LNCS, vol. 1233, pp. 480–494. Springer, Heidelberg (1997)
9. Bellare, M., Micciancio, D., Warinschi, B.: Foundations of group signatures: Formal definitions, simplified requirements, and a construction based on general assumptions. In: Biham, E. (ed.) EUROCRYPT 2003. LNCS, vol. 2656, pp. 614–629. Springer, Heidelberg (2003)
10. Bellare, M., Namprempre, C., Neven, G.: Security proofs for identity-based identification and signature schemes. In: Cachin, C., Camenisch, J.L. (eds.) EUROCRYPT 2004. LNCS, vol. 3027, pp. 268–286. Springer, Heidelberg (2004)
11. Bellare, M., Rogaway, P.: Random oracles are practical: a paradigm for designing efficient protocols. In: Proc. of the 1st ACM Conference on Computer and Communications Security, pp. 62–73. ACM Press, New York (1993)
12. Bellare, M., Shi, H., Zhang, C.: Foundations of group signatures: The case of dynamic groups. In: Menezes, A. (ed.) CT-RSA 2005. LNCS, vol. 3376, pp. 136–153. Springer, Heidelberg (2005)
13. Boneh, D., Franklin, M.K.: Identity-based encryption from the weil pairing. In: Kilian, J. (ed.) CRYPTO 2001. LNCS, vol. 2139, pp. 213–229. Springer, Heidelberg (2001)
14. Bresson, E., Stern, J., Szydlo, M.: Threshold ring signatures and applications to ad-hoc groups. In: Yung, M. (ed.) CRYPTO 2002. LNCS, vol. 2442, pp. 465–480. Springer, Heidelberg (2002)
15. Camenisch, J., Damgård, I.: Verifiable encryption, group encryption, and their applications to separable group signatures and signature sharing schemes. In: Okamoto, T. (ed.) ASIACRYPT 2000. LNCS, vol. 1976, pp. 331–345. Springer, Heidelberg (2000)
16. Camenisch, J., Lysyanskaya, A.: An efficient system for non-transferable anonymous credentials with optional anonymity revocation. In: Pfitzmann, B. (ed.) EUROCRYPT 2001. LNCS, vol. 2045, pp. 93–118. Springer, Heidelberg (2001)
17. Camenisch, J., Lysyanskaya, A.: Dynamic accumulators and application to efficient revocation of anonymous credentials. In: Yung, M. (ed.) CRYPTO 2002. LNCS, vol. 2442, pp. 61–76. Springer, Heidelberg (2002)

18. Camenisch, J., Lysyanskaya, A.: Signature schemes and anonymous credentials from bilinear maps. In: Franklin, M. (ed.) CRYPTO 2004. LNCS, vol. 3152, pp. 56–72. Springer, Heidelberg (2004)
19. Camenisch, J., Shoup, V.: Practical verifiable encryption and decryption of discrete logarithms. In: Boneh, D. (ed.) CRYPTO 2003. LNCS, vol. 2729, pp. 126–144. Springer, Heidelberg (2003)
20. Camenisch, J., Stadler, M.: Efficient group signature schemes for large groups (extended abstract). In: Kaliski Jr., B.S. (ed.) CRYPTO 1997. LNCS, vol. 1294, pp. 410–424. Springer, Heidelberg (1997)
21. Chandran, N., Groth, J., Sahai, A.: Ring signatures of sub-linear size without random oracles. In: Arge, L., Cachin, C., Jurdziński, T., Tarlecki, A. (eds.) ICALP 2007. LNCS, vol. 4596, pp. 423–434. Springer, Heidelberg (2007)
22. Chaum, D., van Heyst, E.: Group signatures. In: Davies, D.W. (ed.) EUROCRYPT 1991. LNCS, vol. 547, pp. 257–265. Springer, Heidelberg (1991)
23. Chien, H.-Y.: Highly efficient id-based ring signature from pairings. In: APSCC, pp. 829–834 (2008)
24. Chow, S.S.M., Hui, L.C.K., Yiu, S.-M.: Identity based threshold ring signature. In: Park, C.-s., Chee, S. (eds.) ICISC 2004. LNCS, vol. 3506, pp. 218–232. Springer, Heidelberg (2005)
25. Chow, S.S.M., Liu, J.K., Wong, D.S.: Robust receipt-free election system with ballot secrecy and verifiability. In: NDSS. The Internet Society (2008)
26. Chow, S.S.M., Lui, R.W.C., Hui, L.C.K., Yiu, S.-M.: Identity based ring signature: Why, how and what next. In: Chadwick, D., Zhao, G. (eds.) EuroPKI 2005. LNCS, vol. 3545, pp. 144–161. Springer, Heidelberg (2005)
27. Chow, S.S.M., Susilo, W., Yuen, T.H.: Escrowed linkability of ring signatures and its applications. In: Nguyên, P.Q. (ed.) VIETCRYPT 2006. LNCS, vol. 4341, pp. 175–192. Springer, Heidelberg (2006)
28. Chow, S.S.M., Yiu, S.-M., Hui, L.C.K.: Efficient identity based ring signature. In: Ioannidis, J., Keromytis, A.D., Yung, M. (eds.) ACNS 2005. LNCS, vol. 3531, pp. 499–512. Springer, Heidelberg (2005)
29. Chung, Y.-F., Wu, Z.Y., Lai, F., Chen, T.-S.: A novel id-based threshold ring signature scheme competent for anonymity and anti-forgery. In: Wang, Y., Cheung, Y.-m., Liu, H. (eds.) CIS 2006. LNCS (LNAI), vol. 4456, pp. 502–512. Springer, Heidelberg (2007)
30. Cramer, R., Damgård, I., Schoenmakers, B.: Proofs of partial knowledge and simplified design of witness hiding protocols. In: Desmedt, Y.G. (ed.) CRYPTO 1994. LNCS, vol. 839, pp. 174–187. Springer, Heidelberg (1994)
31. Dodis, Y., Kiayias, A., Nicolosi, A., Shoup, V.: Anonymous identification in ad hoc groups. In: Cachin, C., Camenisch, J.L. (eds.) EUROCRYPT 2004. LNCS, vol. 3027, pp. 609–626. Springer, Heidelberg (2004)
32. Dong, Z., Zheng, H., Chen, K., Kou, W.: ID-based proxy blind signature. In: AINA (2), pp. 380–383 (2004)
33. Ferrara, A.L., Green, M., Hohenberger, S., Pedersen, M.Ø.: Practical short signature batch verification. In: Fischlin, M. (ed.) CT-RSA 2009. LNCS, vol. 5473, pp. 309–324. Springer, Heidelberg (2009), http://eprint.iacr.org/2008/015
34. Fiat, A., Shamir, A.: How to prove yourself: Practical solutions to identification and signature problems. In: Odlyzko, A.M. (ed.) CRYPTO 1986. LNCS, vol. 263, pp. 186–194. Springer, Heidelberg (1987)
35. Fischer-Hübner, S.: IT-Security and Privacy - Design and Use of Privacy-Enhancing Security Mechanisms. LNCS, vol. 1958. Springer, Heidelberg (2001)

36. Fujisaki, E., Okamoto, T.: Statistical zero knowledge protocols to prove modular polynomial relations. In: Kaliski Jr., B.S. (ed.) CRYPTO 1997. LNCS, vol. 1294, pp. 16–30. Springer, Heidelberg (1997)
37. Girault, M.: Self-certified public keys. In: Davies, D.W. (ed.) EUROCRYPT 1991. LNCS, vol. 547, pp. 490–497. Springer, Heidelberg (1991)
38. Goldwasser, S., Micali, S., Rivest, R.L.: A digital signature scheme secure against adaptive chosen-message attacks. SIAM J. Comput. 17(2), 281–308 (1988)
39. Han, J., Xu, Q., Chen, G.: Efficient id-based threshold ring signature scheme. In: EUC (2), pp. 437–442. IEEE Computer Society, Los Alamitos (2008)
40. Herranz, J.: Identity-based ring signatures from RSA. Theor. Comput. Sci. 389(1-2), 100–117 (2007)
41. Itakura, K., Nakamura, K.: A public key cryptosystem suitable for digital multisignatures. NEC Research & Development 71, 1–8 (1983)
42. Jeong, I.R., Kwon, J.O., Lee, D.H.: Analysis of revocable-iff-linked ring signature scheme. IEICE Transactions 92-A(1), 322–325 (2009)
43. Kilian, J., Petrank, E.: Identity escrow. In: Krawczyk, H. (ed.) CRYPTO 1998. LNCS, vol. 1462, pp. 169–185. Springer, Heidelberg (1998)
44. Li, X., Chen, K.: Identity based proxy-signcryption scheme from pairings. In: IEEE SCC, pp. 494–497 (2004)
45. Liu, J.K., Wei, V.K., Wong, D.S.: A separable threshold ring signature scheme. In: Lim, J.-I., Lee, D.-H. (eds.) ICISC 2003. LNCS, vol. 2971, pp. 12–26. Springer, Heidelberg (2004)
46. Liu, J.K., Wei, V.K., Wong, D.S.: Linkable spontaneous anonymous group signature for ad hoc groups (extended abstract). In: Wang, H., Pieprzyk, J., Varadharajan, V. (eds.) ACISP 2004. LNCS, vol. 3108, pp. 325–335. Springer, Heidelberg (2004)
47. Liu, J.K., Wong, D.S.: On the security models of (threshold) ring signature schemes. In: Park, C.-s., Chee, S. (eds.) ICISC 2004. LNCS, vol. 3506, pp. 204–217. Springer, Heidelberg (2005)
48. Micali, S., Ohta, K., Reyzin, L.: Accountable-subgroup multisignatures: extended abstract. In: CCS 2001: Proc. of the 8th ACM conf. on Computer and Communications Security, pp. 245–254. ACM Press, New York (2001)
49. Nakanishi, T., Fujiwara, T., Watanabe, H.: A linkable group signature and its application to secret voting. Trans. of Information Processing Society of Japan 40(7), 3085–3096 (1999)
50. Nguyen, L.: Accumulators from bilinear pairings and applications. In: Menezes, A. (ed.) CT-RSA 2005. LNCS, vol. 3376, pp. 275–292. Springer, Heidelberg (2005)
51. Pointcheval, D., Stern, J.: Security proofs for signature schemes. In: Maurer, U.M. (ed.) EUROCRYPT 1996. LNCS, vol. 1070, pp. 387–398. Springer, Heidelberg (1996)
52. Rivest, R.L., Shamir, A., Tauman, Y.: How to leak a secret. In: Boyd, C. (ed.) ASIACRYPT 2001. LNCS, vol. 2248, pp. 552–565. Springer, Heidelberg (2001)
53. Shacham, H., Waters, B.: Efficient ring signatures without random oracles. In: Okamoto, T., Wang, X. (eds.) PKC 2007. LNCS, vol. 4450, pp. 166–180. Springer, Heidelberg (2007)
54. Shamir, A.: Identity-based cryptosystems and signature schemes. In: Blakely, G.R., Chaum, D. (eds.) CRYPTO 1984. LNCS, vol. 196, pp. 47–53. Springer, Heidelberg (1985)
55. Tsang, P.P., Au, M.H., Liu, J.K., Susilo, W., Wong, D.S.: A suite of non-pairing id-based threshold ring signature schemes with different levels of anonymity. Cryptology ePrint Archive, Report 2005/326 (2005), http://eprint.iacr.org/

56. Tsang, P.P., Wei, V.K.: Short linkable ring signatures for e-voting, e-cash and attestation. In: Deng, R.H., Bao, F., Pang, H., Zhou, J. (eds.) ISPEC 2005. LNCS, vol. 3439, pp. 48–60. Springer, Heidelberg (2005)
57. Tsang, P.P., Wei, V.K., Chan, T.K., Au, M.H., Liu, J.K., Wong, D.S.: Separable linkable threshold ring signatures. In: Canteaut, A., Viswanathan, K. (eds.) INDOCRYPT 2004. LNCS, vol. 3348, pp. 384–398. Springer, Heidelberg (2004)
58. Warren, S.D., Brandeis, L.D.: The right to privacy. Harvard Law Review IV(5), 193–220 (1890)
59. Westin, A.F.: Privacy and freedom. Atheneum (1970)
60. Wong, D.S., Fung, K., Liu, J.K., Wei, V.K.: On the RS-code construction of ring signature schemes and a threshold setting of RST. In: Qing, S., Gollmann, D., Zhou, J. (eds.) ICICS 2003. LNCS, vol. 2836, pp. 34–46. Springer, Heidelberg (2003)
61. Xu, J., Zhang, Z., Feng, D.: Id-based proxy signature using bilinear pairings. Cryptology ePrint Archive, Report 2004/206 (2004), http://eprint.iacr.org/
62. Zhang, F., Kim, K.: Id-based blind signature and ring signature from pairings. In: Zheng, Y. (ed.) ASIACRYPT 2002. LNCS, vol. 2501, pp. 533–547. Springer, Heidelberg (2002)
63. Zhang, F., Kim, K.: Efficient id-based blind signature and proxy signature from bilinear pairings. In: Safavi-Naini, R., Seberry, J. (eds.) ACISP 2003. LNCS, vol. 2727, pp. 312–323. Springer, Heidelberg (2003)
64. Zhang, J.: An efficient identity-based ring signature scheme and its extension. In: Gervasi, O., Gavrilova, M.L. (eds.) ICCSA 2007, Part II. LNCS, vol. 4706, pp. 63–74. Springer, Heidelberg (2007)

A   Analysis of the Proof of [39]

We point out a flaw in the security proof of [39]. While in the security model, the attacker is allowed to query secret key of any identity of his choice (private key query), However, in the security proof of anonymity and unforgeability, no description is given on how this query is handled.

Indeed, this flaw in the security proof leads to the following theoretical error. Recalled that the secret key of an identity ID is $H(ID)^a$, where H is some collision-resistant hash function and a is the master secret key of the PKG. This is in fact a very common key structure in identity-based encryption or signature [13], and is well-known to be secure under the CDH assumption in the random oracle model.

However, in the standard model where the hash function is only required to be collision-resistant, it is entirely possible for an attacker to obtain the secret key of identity ID_1 by issuing private key queries on a set of identities $\{ID_2, \ldots, ID_k\}$ such that $H(ID_1) = \prod H(ID_i)$.

Thus, it is very doubtful, to say the least, that [39] can be proven secure in the standard model when H is only modelled as collision-resistant hash function. The claim that the scheme in [39] is secure *in the standard model* is not accurate. One could, however, possibly simulates the ID query in the random oracle model.

An Anonymous Designated Verifier Signature Scheme with Revocation: How to Protect a Company's Reputation

Keita Emura[1], Atsuko Miyaji[2], and Kazumasa Omote[2]

[1] Center for Highly Dependable Embedded Systems Technology
[2] School of Information Science
Japan Advanced Institute of Science and Technology, 1-1, Asahidai, Nomi, Ishikawa, 923-1292, Japan
{k-emura,miyaji,omote}@jaist.ac.jp

Abstract. There are many cryptographic schemes with anonymity, such as group signatures. As one important property, anonymity revocation has been introduced. In such schemes, the fact of *whether a signer's rights have been revoked or not* is important additional information. For example, if a third party knows that there are many revoked members in a company, then the company's reputation may be damaged in many ways. People may think that *there might be many problematic employees (who have bad behavior-s) in this company, there might be many people who have quit, i.e., the labor environment may not be good,* and so on. To avoid such harmful rumors, in this paper, we propose an Anonymous Designated Verifier Signature (ADVS) scheme with revocation. In ADVS, a designated verifier can only verify a signature anonymously, and a third party cannot identify whether the rights of the signer have been revoked or not. We show two security-enhanced schemes as applications of our scheme: a biometric-based remote authentication scheme, and an identity management scheme.

1 Introduction

Back Ground: There are many cryptographic schemes with anonymity, such as group signatures [6]. Anonymous schemes are useful to protect a signer's privacy, and therefore many applications of group signature have been proposed such as the BCPZ (Bringer, Chabanne, Pointcheval, and Zimmer) biometric-based authentication scheme [5], the IMSTY (Isshiki, Mori, Sako, Teranishi, and Yonezawa) identity management scheme [11], and so on. As one important property, anonymity revocation has been introduced [3,4,15,17,18]. In these revocable group signature schemes, revocation check can be executed by *any entity*. Actually, the fact of *whether a signer's rights have been revoked or not* is important additional information. Let a signatory group of a group signature scheme be a company. If a third party knows that there are many revoked members in this company, then the company's reputation may be damaged in many ways. For example, someone may think that:

S.-H. Heng and K. Kurosawa (Eds.): ProvSec 2010, LNCS 6402, pp. 184–198, 2010.

- There might be many problematic employees (who have bad behavior) in this company.
- There might be many people who have quit, i.e., the labor environment may not be good.

In addition, there are possibilities of user privacy exposure, for example:

- If the third party knows an employee who left the company three days ago, and also knows a signer was revoked three days ago, then the signer may be this employee.

Actually, the third party can detect whether a signer was revoked or not by checking whether a value was added to a revocation list RL or not. In this example, the third party can link signatures made by this employee who has left by executing the revocation check, even if a group signature scheme with backward unlinkability (such as [15,18]) is used[1]. This scenario can occur, since (revocable) group signatures are applied in many applications. As a solution for protecting against damage caused by rumors, we consider to apply a crypto-graphic primitive with a property that a third party cannot check whether a signer's rights have already been revoked or not. Someone may think that group signature schemes with Verifier-Local Revocation (VLR) [4,15,18] can be applied for this purpose. By hiding a revocation list RL from the third party[2], the third party can be prevented from executing the revocation check. However, there is a problem in this scenario: a revoked user can make a *valid group signature* which is verified by the third party, since the third party can verify the valid-ity of this signature by using a group public key gpk only (RL is used for the revocation check only). Therefore, VLR group signature schemes are not useful in protecting the company's reputation. This suggests that it is not enough to restrict the revocation check. As another solution for protecting against damage caused by rumors, we need to apply a cryptographic primitive with properties that not only the third party cannot check whether a signer's rights have already been revoked or not, but also the third party cannot check whether a signature is valid or not. As a candidate for this purpose, Designated Verifier Signature (DVS) [7,10,13,14,16,20,21,22] is nominated, since a signer can indicate a desig-nated verifier. Especially, strong DVS has been proposed [13,14] which enables protection of the signer's anonymity from a third party. However, in the verifica-tion phase of strong DVS, a designated verifier verifies a signature with *the public key of a signer* and the secret key of the designated verifier. This means that these schemes do not provide the signer anonymity from the designated verifier, and this is a difference between DVS and group signatures. In addition, DVS does not have the revocation property. To sum up, no previous group signature and DVS schemes can be applied to protect the company's reputation.

---

[1] Note that backward unlinkability means that even after a signer's rights are revoked, signatures made by the signer before the revocation remain anonymous.

[2] In VLR schemes, a verifier verifies a group signature by using a group public key gpk, and checks whether the rights of the signer have been revoked or not by using RL. A signer does not have to obtain RL to sign.

Our Contribution: In this paper, by applying the designated verification property of DVS, we propose a way to protect the company's reputation. By indicating a designated verifier, (1) a third party cannot check whether a signature is valid or not, and (2) the third party cannot check whether a signer's rights have already been revoked or not, and (3) no entity (except the opening manager OM, which is defined later) can determine who a signer is. We call this signature primitive Anonymous Designated Verifier Signature (ADVS) scheme with revocation. We compare these functions with other primitives in Table 1.

Table 1. Function Comparisons

	Signer Anonymity	Designated Verification	Designated Revocation Check
DVS [12]	no	yes	no
Strong DVS [13, 14]	yes*	yes	no
Revocable Group Signature [3, 4, 15, 17, 18]	yes	no	no
Our ADVS	yes	yes	yes

∗ From a third party only.

The property (1) is the same concept as in DVS schemes. The property (2) is a difference between revocable group signatures and our scheme. As a difference between strong DVS and our signer-anonymous DVS scheme, our scheme protects the signer anonymity from the designated verifier (property (3)). We provide formal definitions of ADVS, and prove our scheme along with these definitions. Our ADVS scheme can be applied to *protecting company's reputation* scenario.

Related works: The concept of designated verifier proof was introduced in Jakobsson, Sako, and Impagliazzo [12] (called JSI scheme), where a specific designated verifier can only verify the validity of proofs made by a prover's secret key and a verifier's public key. In the JSI scheme, although any entity can verify the validity of a proof, this entity cannot distinguish whether the proof was made by a prover or not. The designated verifier can make the same proof, and only the prover and the designated verifier know who is the actual prover. The JSI scheme uses the *or proof technique* [8], namely, the actual signer knows the secret key of the signer *or* the secret key of the designated verifier. A DVS signature can be achieved [7] by using the ring signature scheme with a two-person group (namely, members are the signer and the designated verifier only). From the viewpoint of a third party, nobody knows who the actual signer is, although the third party can verify the signature. There are DVS schemes such that the validity of a signature can only be verified by a designated verifier by using his/her secret key (e.g., [10,13,22]). In these schemes, a third party cannot verify the validity of a signature. Designated revocation check property has been considered in [9]. However, that paper did not define formal security requirements, and there is a flaw whereby a designated verifier can link two signatures by using his/her secret key. A designated group signature scheme, which enables both signer anonymity and designated verifier property[3], has not been proposed yet.

Organization : The paper is organized as follows: Security definitions of ADVS are presented in Section 3. Our proposed ADVS scheme is described in Section 4. The security proofs are presented in Section 5. Applications of our ADVS scheme to the BCPZ biometric-based authentication scheme [5] and the IMSTY identity management scheme [11] are presented in Section 6.

2 Preliminary

In this section, we show definitions of bilinear groups and complexity assumptions. Note that $x \in_R S$ means x is randomly chosen for a set S.

2.1 Bilinear Groups

Definition 1. (Bilinear Groups) *Bilinear groups and a bilinear map are defined as follows:*

1. $\mathbb{G}$ *and* $\mathbb{G}_T$ *are cyclic groups of prime order* p.
2. g *is a generator of* $\mathbb{G}$.
3. e *is an efficiently computable bilinear map* $e : \mathbb{G} \times \mathbb{G} \to \mathbb{G}_T$ *with the following properties.*
   - *Bilinearity : for all* $u, u', v, v' \in \mathbb{G}$, $e(uu', v) = e(u, v)e(u', v)$ *and* $e(u, vv') = e(u, v)e(u, v')$.
   - *Non-degeneracy :* $e(g, g) \neq 1_{\mathbb{G}_T}$ ($1_{\mathbb{G}_T}$ *is the* $\mathbb{G}_T$*'s unit*).

2.2 Complexity Assumptions

Definition 2. (DLIN assumption) *[3] The Decision Linear (DLIN) problem in* $\mathbb{G}$ *is a problem, for input of a tuple* $(u, v, h, u^\alpha, v^\beta, Z) \in \mathbb{G}^6$ *where* $\alpha, \beta \in \mathbb{Z}_p$ *are random values, to decide whether* $Z = h^{\alpha+\beta}$ *or not. An algorithm* $\mathcal{A}$ *has advantage* ϵ *in solving DLIN problem in* $\mathbb{G}$ *if* $Adv_{DLIN}(\mathcal{A}) := |\Pr[\mathcal{A}(u, v, h, u^\alpha, v^\beta, h^{\alpha+\beta}) = 0] - \Pr[\mathcal{A}(u, v, h, u^\alpha, v^\beta, h^z) = 0]| \geq \epsilon(\kappa)$, *where* $h^z \in \mathbb{G} \setminus \{h^{\alpha+\beta}\}$. *We say that the DLIN assumption holds in* $\mathbb{G}$ *if no PPT algorithm has an advantage of at least* ϵ *in solving the DLIN problem in* $\mathbb{G}$.

Definition 3. (q-SDH assumption) *[2,3] The q-Strong Diffie-Hellman (q-SDH) problem in* $\mathbb{G}$ *is a problem, for input of a* $(q + 1)$ *tuple* $(g, g^\gamma, \cdots, g^{\gamma^q}) \in \mathbb{G}^{q+1}$ *where* $\gamma \in \mathbb{Z}_p$ *is a random value, to compute a tuple* $(x, g^{1/(\gamma+x)}) \in \mathbb{Z}_p \times \mathbb{G}$. *An algorithm* $\mathcal{A}$ *has an advantage* ϵ *in solving the q-SDH problem in* $\mathbb{G}$ *if* $\Pr[\mathcal{A}(g, g^\gamma, \cdots, g^{\gamma^q}) = (x, g^{1/(\gamma+x)})] \geq \epsilon$. *We say that the q-SDH assumption holds in* $\mathbb{G}$ *if no PPT algorithm has an advantage of at least* ϵ *in solving the q-SDH problem in* $\mathbb{G}$.

---

[3] Note that the concept of designated group signature (called ML scheme) proposed in [16] is different from this concept: the ML scheme enables the verifier anonymity, where designated verifiers are indicated.

3   Definitions of ADVS

In this section, we define ADVS and its security requirements. The ADVS scheme consists of six algorithms, Setup, KeyGen$_S$, KeyGen$_V$, Sign, Verify, and Revoke. The group public key gpk and the group secret key gsk are obtained by executing Setup(1^κ), where κ is the security parameter. A signer public key spk and a signer secret key (which is also called a membership certificate) ssk are obtained by executing KeyGen$_S$(gpk, gsk). A verifier public key vpk and a verifier secret key vsk are obtained by executing KeyGen$_V$(1^κ). For a message M, a designated signature σ is obtained by executing Sign(gpk, ssk, vpk, M). σ is verified by executing Verify(gpk, vsk, M, σ). If both (1) σ is a valid signature, and (2) σ was made by using vpk (corresponding to vsk), then 1 is output, and 0, otherwise. A designated signature is *valid* means that (1) a signer has a membership certificate ssk issued by GM, and (2) the rights of the signer have not been revoked. Membership revocation is done by executing Revoke(gpk, gsk, ssk, RL), where RL is the revocation list. The Revoke algorithm outputs the updated RL. We assume three entities, the group manager GM, a signer, and a designated verifier, which runs (Setup, KeyGen$_S$, Revoke), Sign, and (KeyGen$_V$, Verify), respectively.

Next, we define the security requirements: *Unforgeability, Non-transferability*, and *Signer anonymity*. The DVS scheme is said to be unforgeable if the advantage is negligible for any probabilistic polynomial time (PPT) adversary $\mathcal{A}$ in the following experiment. In this experiment, $\mathcal{A}$ can access the signing oracle $\mathcal{O}_{\text{Sign}(ssk^*, vpk)}$, where for an input message M, the signing oracle returns a signature σ made by ssk^* and designated to vpk, and appends (M, σ) to the set of signatures SigSet. In addition, $\mathcal{A}$ can access the verification oracle $\mathcal{O}_{\text{Verify}(vsk)}$. For the input of the message/signature pair (M, σ), $\mathcal{O}_{\text{Verify}(vsk)}$ returns the result of Verify(gpk, vsk, M, σ). In addition, $\mathcal{A}$ can access the corruption oracle $\mathcal{O}_{\text{corr}}$. For the input of the identity of signer i, $\mathcal{O}_{\text{corr}}$ returns ssk_i, and appends i to the set of corrupted users CU. Note that $\mathcal{A}$ cannot query i^* to the corruption oracle, where i^* is the target signer (who manages ssk^*). In addition, $\mathcal{A}$ can access the revocation oracle $\mathcal{O}_{\text{revoke}}$. For the input of the identity of signer i, $\mathcal{O}_{\text{revoke}}$ runs Revoke(gpk, gsk, ssk_i, RL). Note that $\mathcal{A}$ cannot query i^* to the revocation oracle. Finally, $\mathcal{A}$ outputs $(M^*, \sigma^*) \notin$ SigSet. To guarantee that no ssk_i ($i \in$ CU) were used to compute (M^*, σ^*), Revoke(gpk, gsk, ssk_i, RL) is executed for all corrupted users i.

Definition 4.   *Unforgeability*

$$Adv_{\mathcal{A}}^{UF}(\kappa) = \Pr\big[(gpk, gsk) \leftarrow \text{Setup}(1^\kappa);\ \text{CU} \rightarrow \emptyset;\ \text{SigSet} \rightarrow \emptyset;\ (vpk, vsk) \leftarrow \text{KeyGen}_V(1^\kappa);$$

$$(i^*, State) \leftarrow \mathcal{A}^{\mathcal{O}_{\text{Verify}(vsk)}(\cdot), \mathcal{O}_{\text{corr}}(\cdot), \mathcal{O}_{\text{revoke}}(\cdot)}(gpk, vpk);$$

$$(spk^*, ssk^*) \leftarrow \text{KeyGen}_S(gpk, gsk);$$

$$(M^*, \sigma^*) \leftarrow \mathcal{A}^{\mathcal{O}_{\text{Sign}(ssk^*, vpk)}(\cdot), \mathcal{O}_{\text{Verify}(vsk)}(\cdot), \mathcal{O}_{\text{corr}}(\cdot), \mathcal{O}_{\text{revoke}}(\cdot)}(gpk, spk^*, vpk, State);$$

$$\forall i \in \text{CU},\ \text{Revoke}(gpk, gsk, ssk_i, RL);\ (M^*, \sigma^*) \notin \text{SigSet};$$

$$\text{Verify}(gpk, vsk, M^*, \sigma^*) = 1\big]$$

Next, we define Non-transferability. Non-transferability means that a designated verifier cannot produce evidence which convinces a third party that a signature was *actually* computed by the signer. The ADVS scheme is said to be non-transferable if the advantage is negligible for any PPT adversary $\mathcal{A}$ in the following experiment. Intuitively, there exists a simulated signing algorithm Sign' for which the distribution of $(M, \mathsf{Sign}(gpk, ssk, vpk, M))$ and the distribution of $(M, \mathsf{Sign}'(gpk, spk, vsk, M))$ are indistinguishable.

Definition 5. *Non-transferability*

$$
\begin{aligned}
Adv_{\mathcal{A}}^{Non\text{-}Trans}(\kappa) = \Big| \Pr \big[& (gpk, gsk) \leftarrow \mathsf{Setup}(1^\kappa); \ (spk, ssk) \leftarrow \mathsf{KeyGen_S}(gpk, gsk); \\
& (vpk, vsk) \leftarrow \mathsf{KeyGen_V}(1^\kappa); \\
& (M^*, State) \leftarrow \mathcal{A}(gpk, spk, ssk, vpk, vsk); \mu \in_R \{0,1\}; \\
& \sigma_0 \leftarrow \mathsf{Sign}(gpk, ssk, vpk, M^*); \ \sigma_1 \leftarrow \mathsf{Sign}'(gpk, spk, vsk, M^*); \\
& \mu' \leftarrow \mathcal{A}(\sigma_\mu, State); \mu = \mu' \big] - 1/2 \Big|
\end{aligned}
$$

Next, we define Signer anonymity. The ADVS scheme is said to be signer-anonymous if the advantage is negligible for any PPT adversary $\mathcal{A}$ in the following experiment. Intuitively, Signer anonymity means that $\mathcal{A}$ with vsk cannot determine who the actual signer is. This suggests that even if a malicious designated verifier opens its own secret key vsk, Signer anonymity is still effective.

Definition 6. *Signer anonymity*

$$
\begin{aligned}
Adv_{\mathcal{A}}^{Sign\text{-}Anon}(\kappa) = \Big| \Pr \big[& (gpk, gsk) \leftarrow \mathsf{Setup}(1^\kappa); \ (spk_0, ssk_0) \leftarrow \mathsf{KeyGen_S}(gpk, gsk); \\
& (spk_1, ssk_1) \leftarrow \mathsf{KeyGen_S}(gpk, gsk); \ (vpk, vsk) \leftarrow \mathsf{KeyGen_V}(1^\kappa); \\
& (M^*, State) \leftarrow \mathcal{A}(gpk, spk_0, ssk_0, spk_1, ssk_1, vpk, vsk) \\
& \mu \in_R \{0,1\}; \sigma_\mu \leftarrow \mathsf{Sign}(gpk, ssk_\mu, vpk, M^*); \\
& \mu' \leftarrow \mathcal{A}(\sigma_\mu, State); \mu = \mu' \big] - 1/2 \Big|
\end{aligned}
$$

4   The Proposed Scheme

In this section, we propose an Anonymous Designated Verifier Signature (ADVS) scheme with revocation. Let SPK be a Signature based on a Proof of Knowledge and $DSig(sigkey, M)$ be a digital signature of a message M under a signing key $sigkey$. $DSig(sigkey, M)$ is verified by using a verification key, $verkey$. We use $DSig(sigkey, M)$ to guarantee that GM updates RL. Intuitively, our construction is as follows: A signer computes an "or proof", namely, SPK with knowledge of either part-1: an actual signer knows the secret key of the signer (this is the short group signature proposed by Boneh et al. [3]), or part-2: the actual signer knows the secret key of a designated verifier. This construction is needed to achieve Non-transferability. In addition, the signer encrypts a part of the part-1 SPK using the public key of the designated verifier. We improve the revocation algorithm of the Nakanishi-Funabiki group signature [18] to satisfy the property that a third party cannot check whether a signer has already been revoked or not.

Protocol 1. *Our ADVS scheme*

Setup(1^κ): *Choose a prime number p, a bilinear group $(\mathbb{G}, \mathbb{G}_T)$ with order p, generators $g, h, u, v, f \in_R \mathbb{G}$, and $\gamma \in_R \mathbb{Z}_p$, and compute $\omega = g^\gamma$. Output $gpk = (e, (\mathbb{G}, \mathbb{G}_T), g, h, u, v, f, \omega, H, verkey)$ and $gsk = (\gamma, sigkey)$, where H is a cryptographic hash function from $\{0,1\}^*$ to $\mathbb{Z}_p$.*

KeyGen$_S$(gpk, gsk) *Choose $x \in_R \mathbb{Z}_p$, and compute $A = g^{\frac{1}{x+\gamma}}$. Output $spk = \emptyset$ and $ssk = (A, x)$.*

KeyGen$_V$(1^κ): *Choose $x_v, y_v, z_v, r_v \in_R \mathbb{Z}_p$, and compute $h_d = g^{x_v y_v r_v}$, $u_d = g^{y_v r_v}$, $v_d = g^{x_v r_v}$, and $t_d = v^{z_v}$. Output $vpk = (h_d, u_d, v_d, t_d)$ and $vsk = (x_v, y_v, z_v)$.*

Sign(gpk, ssk, vpk, M): *Choose $a, b, \alpha, \beta, \delta \in_R \mathbb{Z}_p$, and compute $T_1 = A \cdot h^{\alpha+\beta}$, $T_2 = u^\alpha$, $T_3 = v^\beta$, $D_1 = T_1 \cdot h_d^{a+b}$, $D_2 = u_d^a$, $D_3 = v_d^b$, $S_1 = f^{x_i+\delta}$, and $S_2 = t_d^\delta$. Let $\tau = \alpha x$ and $\lambda = \beta x$. Compute SPK as follows:*

  - *Choose $r_x, r_\alpha, r_\beta, r_\delta, r_\tau, r_\lambda, s_{z_v}, c_v \in_R \mathbb{Z}_p$.*

  - *Compute $R_v = v^{s_{z_v}} t_d^{-c_v}$, $R_{s,1} = u^{r_\alpha}$, $R_{s,2} = v^{r_\beta}$, $R_{s,3} = e(T_1, g)^{r_x} \cdot e(h, \omega)^{-r_\alpha - r_\beta} \cdot e(h, g)^{-r_\tau - r_\lambda}$, $R_{s,4} = T_2^{r_x} \cdot u^{-r_\tau}$, $R_{s,5} = T_3^{r_x} \cdot v^{-r_\lambda}$, $R_{s,6} = f^{r_x + r_\delta}$, and $R_{s,7} = t_d^{r_\delta}$. Compute $c = H(T_1, T_2, T_3, D_1, D_2, D_3, S_1, S_2, R_v, R_{s,1}, \ldots, R_{s,7}, M)$, $c_s = c - c_v \bmod p$, $s_x = r_x + c_s x$, $s_\alpha = r_\alpha + c_s \alpha$, $s_\beta = r_\beta + c_s \beta$, $s_\delta = r_\delta + c_s \delta$, $s_\tau = r_\tau + c_s \tau$, and $s_\lambda = r_\lambda + c_s \lambda$.*

  - *Output $\sigma = (T_2, T_3, D_1, D_2, D_3, S_1, S_2, c_s, c_v, s_x, s_\alpha, s_\beta, s_\delta, s_\tau, s_\lambda, s_{z_v})$.*

Revoke(gpk, gsk, ssk, RL): *Let $ssk = (A, x)$. Compute v^x and $Cert_{A,x} = DSig(sigkey, v^x)$. Output the updated list $RL \cup (v^x, Cert_{A,x})$.*

Verify(gpk, vsk, M, σ, RL): *Output 1 if both the following verification check and revocation check algorithms output 1, and output 0, otherwise.*

  Verification check: *Compute $T_1' = D_1/(D_2^{x_v} D_3^{y_v})$, $R_v' = v^{s_{z_v}} t_d^{-c_v}$, $R_{s,1}' = u^{s_\alpha} T_2^{-c_s}$, $R_{s,2}' = v^{s_\beta} T_3^{-c_s}$, $R_{s,3}' = e(T_1', g)^{s_x} \cdot e(h, \omega)^{-s_\alpha - s_\beta} \cdot e(h, g)^{-s_\tau - s_\lambda} (\frac{e(T_1', \omega)}{e(g,g)})^{c_s}$, $R_{s,4}' = T_2^{s_x} \cdot u^{-s_\tau}$, $R_{s,5}' = T_3^{s_x} \cdot v^{-s_\lambda}$, $R_{s,6}' = g^{s_x + s_\delta} S_1^{-c_s}$, and $R_{s,7}' = t_d^{s_\delta} S_2^{-c_s}$. Output 1, if $c_s + c_v = H(T_1', T_2, T_3, D_1, D_2, D_3, S_1, S_2, R_v', R_{s,1}', \ldots, R_{s,7}', M)$ holds, and output 0, otherwise.*

  Revocation check: *For all $(v^x, Cert_{A,x}) \in RL$, verify $Cert_{A,x}$ by using verkey, and check $e(S_1, t_d) \stackrel{?}{=} e((v^x)^{z_v} S_2, f)$. If there exists a pair $(v^x, Cert_{A,x}) \in RL$, where $Cert_{A,x}$ is a valid certificate and the above condition holds, then output 1. Otherwise, output 0.*

Note that $e(S_1, t_d) = e(f^{x+\delta}, v^{z_v}) = e(f, v)^{z_v(x+\delta)}$ and $e((v^x)^{z_v} S_2, f) = e(v^{z_v x} v^{z_v \delta}, f) = e(v, f)^{z_v(x+\delta)}$ hold, and $e((v^x)^{z_v} S_2, f)$ can only be computed by the designated verifier (who has z_v).

Next, we describe the simulated signing algorithm as follows:

Protocol 2. *The simulated signing algorithm*

$\mathsf{Sign}'(gpk, spk, vsk, M)$: *Choose* $T_2, T_3, D_1, D_2, D_3, S_1, S_2 \in_R \mathbb{G}$. *Compute SPK as follows:*

- *Choose* $s_x, s_\alpha, s_\beta, s_\delta, s_\tau, s_\lambda, r_{z_v}, c_s \in_R \mathbb{Z}_p$.
- *Compute* $R_v = v^{r_{z_v}}$, $R_{s,1} = u^{s_\alpha} T_2^{-c_s}$, $R_{s,2} = v^{s_\beta} T_3^{-c_s}$, $R_{s,3} = e(T_1, g)^{s_x} \cdot$
  $e(h, \omega)^{-s_\alpha - s_\beta} \cdot e(h, g)^{-s_\tau - s_\lambda} \left(\frac{e(T_1, \omega)}{e(g,g)} \right)^{c_s}$, $R_{s,4} = T_2^{s_x} \cdot u^{-s_\tau}$, $R_{s,5} = T_3^{s_x} \cdot$
  v^{-s_λ}, $R_{s,6} = g^{s_x + s_\delta} S_1^{-c_s}$, *and* $R_{s,7} = t_d^{s_\delta} S_2^{-c_s}$. *Compute* $c = H(T_1, T_2,$
  $T_3, D_1, D_2, D_3, S_1, S_2, R_v, R_{s,1}, \ldots, R_{s,7}, M)$, $c_v = c - c_s \mod p$, *and*
  $s_{z_v} = r_{z_v} + c_v z_v$.
- *Output* $\sigma = (T_2, T_3, D_1, D_2, D_3, S_1, S_2, c_s, c_v, s_x, s_\alpha, s_\beta, s_\delta, s_\tau, s_\lambda, s_{z_v})$.

Obviously, a signature generated by the Sign' algorithm is a valid signature. Therefore, our ADVS scheme satisfies Non-transferability.

Can $\mathbf{RL}$ be publicly opened?: In our scheme, RL is used to execute the Verify algorithm. Therefore, RL is given to verifiers only. Even if RL is given to a third party, the third party cannot execute the revocation check. However, a different problem occurs. If RL is publicly opened, then the third party can obtain the number of revoked signers. To prevent this, in a natural way, dummy certificates can be used as follows: Let N be the number of group members. Then GM chooses $v_i' \in_R \mathbb{G}$, where $i = 1, 2, \ldots, N - |RL|$. Note that this procedure can deal with a dynamic update of RL, namely, dummy certificates are chosen for each revocation. Although the cost of revocation check and updating the list are increased, $\mathbf{RL}$ can be opened. However, as with VLR schemes, a signer does not need RL to make a signature. Therefore, practically, we can assume that RL is given to verifiers only. In this setting, we can prevent a revoked user from making a valid signature that is verified by the third party, since the third party cannot verify the validity of a signature by using only gpk. However, in VLR schemes, the third party can verify the validity of a signature by using gpk only, since RL is used for the revocation check only. Therefore, VLR group signature schemes are not used (under the assumption that RL is given to verifiers only), since a revoked user could make a valid group signature which could be verified by the third party. This is a superior point of our scheme compared with VLR schemes.

The Open algorithm: The Open algorithm is described as follows: $A \leftarrow$ $\mathsf{Open}(gpk, gsk, (M, \sigma))$, where A is a signer secret key. Let $\xi_1 := \log_u h$ and $\xi_2 := \log_v h$. By adding (ξ_1, ξ_2) to gsk, GM can compute $T_1 / (T_2^{\xi_1} T_3^{\xi_2})$ if T_1 is given. Therefore, the designated verifier needs to send (T_1', T_2, T_3) to GM to request the Open procedure. If the opening and issuing roles need to be separated, then only the opening key $osk = (\xi_1, \xi_2)$ is given to the Opening Manager OM. A designated verifier sends (T_1', T_2, T_3) to OM. If (T_1', T_2, T_3) is included in a signature computed by the simulated signing algorithm Sign', then the Open algorithm does not work, since (T_1', T_2, T_3) is not a valid ciphertext of a membership certificate A (T_2 and T_3 are randomly chosen). Therefore, Non-transferability is not satisfied from the viewpoint of OM. This suggests OM can reveal not only the identity of a signer, but also information about who the actual signer is.

5   Security Analysis

In this section, we prove that our scheme satisfies security requirements defined in Section 3.

Theorem 1. *Our scheme satisfies Unforgeability under the q-SDH assumption.*

Proof. Let $\mathcal{A}$ be an adversary to break Unforgeability of our scheme. We construct an algorithm $\mathcal{B}$ to break the q-SDH problem: Let $(g_1, g_1^\gamma, \cdots, g_1^{\gamma^q})$ be an instance of q-SDH problem. Let q_n be the number of signers ($q_n \leq q$). W.l.o.g., we assume that $q_n = q$. $\mathcal{B}$ chooses distinct $x_1, \ldots, x_{q-1} \in_R \mathbb{Z}_p$, and sets $f(X) := \prod_{i=1}^{q-1}(X + x_i) := \sum_{i=0}^{q-1} \alpha_i X^i$, where $\alpha_0, \ldots, \alpha_{q-1} \in \mathbb{Z}_p$ are the coefficients of the polynomial f. $\mathcal{B}$ chooses $\theta \in_R \mathbb{Z}_p$, and computes $g' := \prod_{i=0}^{q-1}(g_1^{\gamma^i})^{\alpha_i \theta} = g_1^{\theta f(\gamma)}$ and $g'' := \prod_{i=1}^{q}(g_1^{\gamma^i})^{\alpha_{i-1}\theta} = g_1^{\theta \gamma f(\gamma)} = (g')^\gamma$. Let $f_i(X) := f(X)/(\gamma + x_i) = \prod_{j=1, j \neq i}^{q-1}(X + x_j) := \sum_{j=0}^{q-2} \beta_i X^j$, where $\beta_0, \ldots, \beta_{q-2} \in \mathbb{Z}_p$ are the coefficients of the polynomial f_i. Then $A_i = \prod_{j=0}^{q-2}(g_1^{\gamma^j})^{\beta_j \theta} = g_1^{\theta f_i(\gamma)} = (g')^{1/(\gamma+x_i)}$ is a signer public key. $\mathcal{B}$ sets $g := g'$ and $\omega := g'' = g^\gamma$. $\mathcal{B}$ chooses $h, u, v, f \in_R \mathbb{G}$, $x_v, y_v, z_v, r_v \in_R \mathbb{Z}_p$, and computes $h_d = g^{x_v y_v r_v}$, $u_d = g^{y_v r_v}$, $v_d = g^{x_v r_v}$, and $t_d = v^{z_v}$. $\mathcal{B}$ gives $gpk = (e, (\mathbb{G}, \mathbb{G}_T), g, h, u, v, f, \omega, H)$ and $vpk = (h_d, u_d, v_d, t_d)$ to $\mathcal{A}$, where $H : \{0,1\}^* \rightarrow \mathbb{Z}_p$ is a random oracle. In addition, $\mathcal{B}$ selects a signing key of DSig $sigkey$, and opens a corresponding verification key $verkey$. For verification queries and signing queries issued by $\mathcal{A}$, $\mathcal{B}$ can answer these queries perfectly, since $\mathcal{B}$ has $vsk = (x_v, y_v, z_v)$, and can execute the simulated signing algorithm Sign$'$. For a corruption query i, $\mathcal{B}$ returns (A_i, x_i) to $\mathcal{A}$. For a revocation query i, $\mathcal{B}$ computes v^{x_i} and $Cert_{A_i, x_i} = \mathsf{DSig}(sigkey, v^{x_i})$, and outputs updated list $RL \cup (v^{x_i}, Cert_{A_i, x_i})$. $\mathcal{A}$ outputs (M^*, σ^*). Let $\sigma^* = (T_2, T_3, D_1, D_2, D_3, S_1, S_2, c_s, c_v, s_x, s_\alpha, s_\beta, s_\delta, s_\tau, s_\lambda, s_{z_v})$. $\mathcal{B}$ computes $T_1 = D_1/(D_2^{x_v} D_3^{y_v})$, and can obtain $(T_1, T_2, T_3, c_s, s_\alpha, s_\beta, s_\tau, s_\lambda)$. By using the Forking Lemma [19], $\mathcal{B}$ can obtain $(T_1, T_2, T_3, c'_s, s'_\alpha, s'_\beta, s'_\tau, s'_\lambda)$, where $c_s \neq c'_s$, with non-negligible probability. By using Lemma 4.4 of [3], we can extract a new SDH tuple $(\tilde{A}, \tilde{x})$ as follows: Let $\Delta c_s := c_s - c'_s$, $\Delta s_\alpha := s_\alpha - s'_\alpha$, $\Delta s_\beta := s_\beta - s'_\beta$, $\Delta s_x := s_x - s'_x$, $\Delta s_\tau := s - s'_\tau$, $\Delta s_\lambda := s_\lambda - s'_\lambda$, $\tilde{\alpha} := \Delta s_\alpha/\Delta c_s$, $\tilde{\beta} := \Delta s_\beta/\Delta c_s$, $\tilde{x} := \Delta s_x/\Delta c_s$, and $\tilde{A} := T_1 \cdot h^{-\tilde{\alpha}-\tilde{\beta}}$. Therefore, $\mathcal{B}$ can solve q-SDH problem.   □

Theorem 2. *Our scheme satisfies Signer anonymity under the DLIN assumption in the random oracle model.*

To prove Theorem 2, we apply the BBS short group signature scheme and CPA-full anonymity experiment. For the sake of clarity, we introduce the BBS scheme and the definition of CPA-full anonymity in Appendices A.1 and A.2, respectively.

Proof. Let $\mathcal{A}$ be an adversary to break Signer anonymity of our scheme. We construct an algorithm $\mathcal{B}$ to break CPA-full-anonymity of the BBS short group signature scheme with 2-person group as follows: First, the challenger $\mathcal{C}$ sends $(e, (\mathbb{G}, \mathbb{G}_T), g, \omega, H)$, ssk_0, and ssk_1 to $\mathcal{B}$. $\mathcal{B}$ chooses $h, u, v, f \in_R \mathbb{G}$, $x_v, y_v, z_v, r_v \in_R \mathbb{Z}_p$, and computes $h_d = g^{x_v y_v r_v}$, $u_d = g^{y_v r_v}$, $v_d = g^{x_v r_v}$, and $t_d = v^{z_v}$. $\mathcal{B}$ gives $gpk = (e, (\mathbb{G}, \mathbb{G}_T), g, h, u, v, f, \omega, H)$, $vpk = (h_d, u_d, v_d, t_d)$, $vsk = (x_v, y_v, z_v)$, ssk_0, and ssk_1, where $H : \{0, 1\}^* \rightarrow \mathbb{Z}_p$ is a hash function. In addition, $\mathcal{B}$ selects a signing key of DSig *sigkey*, and opens a corresponding verification key *verkey*. $\mathcal{A}$ sends M^* to $\mathcal{B}$. $\mathcal{B}$ forwards M^* to $\mathcal{C}$, and obtains $\sigma^* = (T_1, T_2, T_3, c_s, s_x, s_\alpha, s_\beta, s_\tau, s_\lambda)$. $\mathcal{B}$ chooses $s_\delta, r_{z_v}, c_v \in_R \mathbb{Z}_p$ and $S_1, S_2 \in_R \mathbb{G}$. $\mathcal{B}$ computes $R_v = v^{r_{z_v}} t_d^{-c_v}$, $R_{s,1} = u^{s_\alpha} T_2^{-c_s}$, $R_{s,2} = v^{s_\beta} T_3^{-c_s}$, $R_{s,3} = e(T_1, g)^{s_x} \cdot e(h, \omega)^{-s_\alpha - s_\beta} \cdot e(h, g)^{-s_\tau - s_\lambda} \left(\frac{e(T_1, \omega)}{e(g, g)}\right)^{c_s}$, $R_{s,4} = T_2^{s_x} \cdot u^{-s_\tau}$, $R_{s,5} = T_3^{s_x} \cdot v^{-s_\lambda}$, $R_{s,6} = g^{s_x + s_\delta} S_1^{-c_s}$, and $R_{s,7} = t_d^{s_\delta} S_2^{-c_s}$. $\mathcal{B}$ also computes $s_{z_v} = r_{z_v} + c_v z_v$, and sets $c := H(T_1, T_2, T_3, D_1, D_2, D_3, S_1, S_2, R_v, R_{s,1}, \ldots, R_{s,7}, M^*)$, where $c = c_v + c_s \bmod p$. $\mathcal{B}$ sends the challenge signature $(T_2, T_3, D_1, D_2, D_3, S_1, S_2, c_s, c_v, s_x, s_\alpha, s_\beta, s_\delta, s_\tau, s_\lambda, s_{z_v})$ to $\mathcal{A}$. $\mathcal{A}$ outputs μ'. Finally, $\mathcal{B}$ outputs μ' as the answer to the anonymity game of the BBS group signature scheme. Therefore, our scheme satisfies Signer anonymity under the DLIN assumption, since the BBS group signature scheme satisfies anonymity under the DLIN assumption in the random oracle model.   □

The following theorem clearly holds, since there exists the simulated signing algorithm Sign', and OM with a linear encryption secret key (ξ_1, ξ_2) can reveal information about who the actual signer is.

Theorem 3. *Our scheme satisfies Non-transferability under the DLIN assumption.*

6   Applications of Our ADVS Scheme

In this section, we show the applications of our scheme to a biometric-based remote authentication scheme (the BCPZ scheme [5]) and an identity management scheme (the IMSTY scheme [11]).

6.1   Biometric Authentication

The BCPZ scheme [5] is based on the Boneh and Shacham VLR group signature [4]. $\mathcal{H}$ is a human user (who authenticates himself/herself to a service provider $\mathcal{P}$ by using his/her biometric data b preserved on a plastic card). A sensor client $\mathcal{S}$ extracts human user's biometric trait (e.g., iris is used in the BCPZ scheme), and communicates with $\mathcal{P}$, so that the user will be authenticated by $\mathcal{P}$. $\mathcal{P}$ executes KeyGen_V, and obtains vpk and vsk. A card issuer $\mathcal{I}$ (with a group secret key γ) issues a card to a human user, and $(A = g^{\frac{1}{x+\gamma}}, b)$ is preserved in the card, where b is biometric data of the user and $x = Hash(b)$. In addition, $\mathcal{I}$ generates RL if malicious behavior occurs or a user loses his/her cards. First, $\mathcal{P}$ sends the challenge M to $\mathcal{S}$. $\mathcal{S}$ gets (A, b) and the *fresh* biometric trait b' from a human user (with a card), confirms $b' \sim b$ (which indicates that b' and b are acquired from the same biometric source), and computes $x = Hash(b)$ and a group signature σ by using a secret x and vpk. $\mathcal{P}$ verifies (M, σ), and checks whether the user is a malicious user or not, by using RL. In the (original) BCPZ scheme, a third party (with RL) may think that:

- There might be many malicious behaviors in this company.
- There might be many lost cards, i.e., goods management may deteriorate in this company.

and so on. This is where our ADVS scheme comes into effect. We illustrate a modified BCPZ scheme in Fig.1.

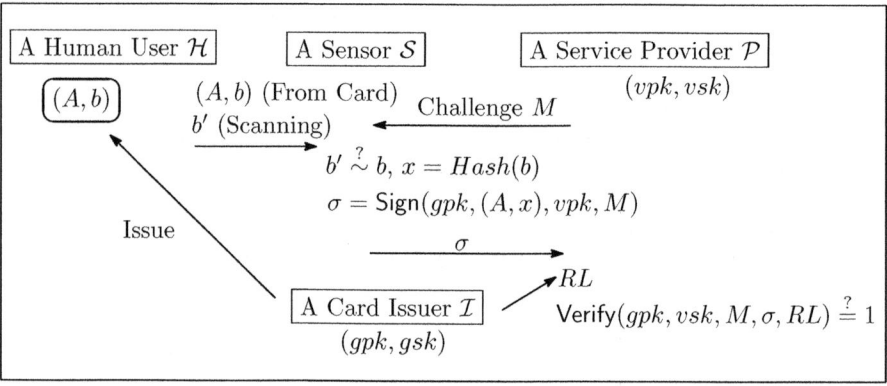

Fig. 1. Modified BCPZ scheme

We assume that RL is given to $\mathcal{P}$ only, or that RL is opened with dummy certificates. The service provider $\mathcal{P}$ does not have to manage the identity of each user. Users do not have to manage any extra values (e.g., passwords), since they only use their own biometric traits and their cards.

6.2   Identity Management

An outsourcing business using group signature has been proposed in [11] (called the IMSTY scheme). In existing systems (which do not apply group signature), authentication servers store the list of identities of users. In group signature settings, authentication servers only have to verify users by using the group public key gpk, and do not have to manage the list of identities of users ID-$list$. Therefore, the risk of leaking user information (i.e., the list of identities of users) can be minimized, and this is the merit of using group signature in identity management. In the IMSTY scheme, the role of Group Manager GM is separated into three roles: Issuing Manager IM, User-Revocation Manager RM, and Opening

Manager OM. IM issues membership certificates for users. When a user requests the service, the user makes a group signature σ, and sends it to Outsourcee who is in charge of providing the service to legitimate users. Outsourcee verifies σ, provides the service if this signature is valid, and stores σ into the usage log $ULog$. After a certain interval, Outsourcee sends $ULog$ to OM who can open group signatures. OM charges the users who have already used the service. If a user does not pay a fee, then OM announces the identity of this user to RM. RM updates the revocation list RL when a user wants to leave the group, or when a user does not pay a fee. ID-$list$ is managed by IM, and it is updated when a new user joins. IM sends ID-$list = \{(A, x), UserID\}$ to OM, namely Outsourcee does not have to manage ID-$list$. In the (original) IMSTY scheme, a third party may think that:

- There might be many seceders, i.e., this service may not be interesting.
- Signer's rights have been revoked, maybe, he/she did not pay the service fee. That is to say, the service fee may be expensive.

and so on. This is where our ADVS scheme comes into effect. GM of our ADVS scheme also can be separated into three roles, since γ (which is used to issue membership certificates) is not used for executing the Revoke algorithm, and the Open algorithm is independent of other procedures. We illustrate a modified IMSTY scheme in Fig.2.

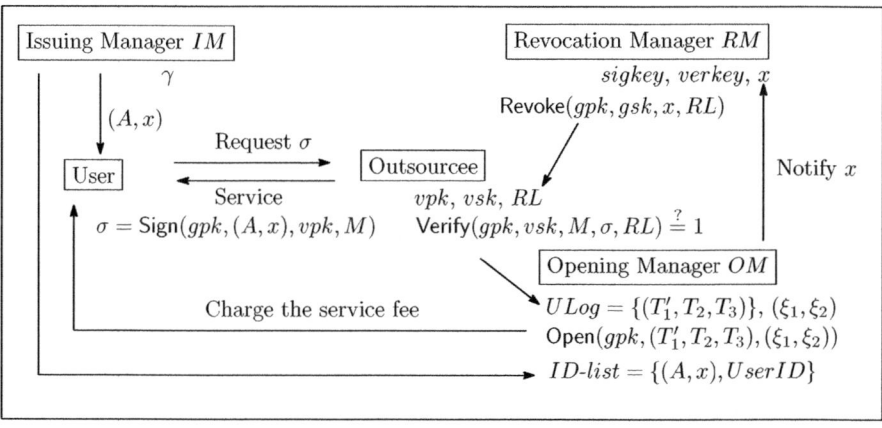

Fig. 2. Modified IMSTY scheme

We assume that RL is given to Outsourcee only, or that RL is opened with dummy certificates, and all entities know the group public key gpk. In the modified IMSTY scheme, (T'_1, T_2, T_3) is stored into $ULog$, since the signature validity has already been checked by Outsourcee, and OM needs (T'_1, T_2, T_3) only to execute the Open procedure. After a certain interval, Outsourcee sends $ULog$ to OM, and OM charges the users who have already used the service. If a user does not pay a fee, then OM notifies x of this user to RM. RM updates the revocation list RL, and sends it to Outsourcee, or opens RL with dummy certificates $v_i' \in \mathbb{G}$ $(i = 1, 2, \ldots, N - |RL|)$, where N is the number of group members.

7   Conclusion

In this paper, we propose an ADVS scheme with revocation. Our ADVS scheme satisfies not only designated verification and Signer anonymity, but also designated revocation check. To the best of our knowledge, our scheme is the first provably secure scheme with designated revocation check. Our scheme can be applied to the *protecting company's reputation* scenario. Neither strong DVS nor revocable group signature schemes can be used in this situation. Our ADVS scheme can be directly and easily applied to the BCPZ scheme and the IMSTY scheme. From this fact, our ADVS scheme can be directly and easily applied to many cryptographic schemes based on (revocable) group signatures, when designated property is required.

Acknowledgements

The authors would like to thank anonymous reviewers of ProvSec 2010 for their invaluable comments. The first author Keita Emura is supported by the Center for Highly Dependable Embedded Systems Technology as a Postdoc researcher.

References

1. Bellare, M., Micciancio, D., Warinschi, B.: Foundations of group signatures: Formal definitions, simplified requirements, and a construction based on general assumptions. In: Biham, E. (ed.) EUROCRYPT 2003. LNCS, vol. 2656, pp. 614–629. Springer, Heidelberg (2003)
2. Boneh, D., Boyen, X.: Short signatures without random oracles and the SDH assumption in bilinear groups. J. Cryptology 21(2), 149–177 (2008)
3. Boneh, D., Boyen, X., Shacham, H.: Short group signatures. In: Franklin, M. (ed.) CRYPTO 2004. LNCS, vol. 3152, pp. 41–55. Springer, Heidelberg (2004)
4. Boneh, D., Shacham, H.: Group signatures with verifier-local revocation. In: ACM Conference on Computer and Communications Security, pp. 168–177 (2004)
5. Bringer, J., Chabanne, H., Pointcheval, D., Zimmer, S.: An application of the Boneh and Shacham group signature scheme to biometric authentication. In: Matsuura, K., Fujisaki, E. (eds.) IWSEC 2008. LNCS, vol. 5312, pp. 219–230. Springer, Heidelberg (2008)
6. Chaum, D., van Heyst, E.: Group signatures. In: Davies, D.W. (ed.) EUROCRYPT 1991. LNCS, vol. 547, pp. 257–265. Springer, Heidelberg (1991)
7. Chow, S.S.M., Wong, D.S.: Anonymous identification and designated-verifiers signatures from insecure batch verification. In: López, J., Samarati, P., Ferrer, J.L. (eds.) EuroPKI 2007. LNCS, vol. 4582, pp. 203–219. Springer, Heidelberg (2007)
8. Cramer, R., Damgård, I.B., Schoenmakers, B.: Proofs of partial knowledge and simplified design of witness hiding protocols. In: Desmedt, Y.G. (ed.) CRYPTO 1994. LNCS, vol. 839, pp. 174–187. Springer, Heidelberg (1994)

9. Emura, K., Miyaji, A., Omote, K.: A certificate revocable anonymous authentication scheme with designated verifier. In: ARES, pp. 769–773 (2009)
10. Huang, X., Susilo, W., Mu, Y., Zhang, F.: Short (identity-based) strong designated verifier signature schemes. In: Chen, K., Deng, R., Lai, X., Zhou, J. (eds.) ISPEC 2006. LNCS, vol. 3903, pp. 214–225. Springer, Heidelberg (2006)
11. Isshiki, T., Mori, K., Sako, K., Teranishi, I., Yonezawa, S.: Using group signatures for identity management and its implementation. In: Digital Identity Management, pp. 73–78 (2006)
12. Jakobsson, M., Sako, K., Impagliazzo, R.: Designated verifier proofs and their applications. In: Maurer, U.M. (ed.) EUROCRYPT 1996. LNCS, vol. 1070, pp. 143–154. Springer, Heidelberg (1996)
13. Laguillaumie, F., Vergnaud, D.: Designated verifier signatures: Anonymity and efficient construction from any bilinear map. In: SCN, pp. 105–119 (2004)
14. Laguillaumie, F., Vergnaud, D.: Multi-designated verifiers signatures: anonymity without encryption. Inf. Process. Lett. 102(2-3), 127–132 (2007)
15. Libert, B., Vergnaud, D.: Group signatures with verifier-local revocation and backward unlinkability in the standard model. In: CANS, pp. 498–517 (2009)
16. Ma, C., Li, J.: Adaptable designated group signature. In: ICIC (1), pp. 1053–1061 (2006)
17. Nakanishi, T., Fujii, H., Hira, Y., Funabiki, N.: Revocable group signature schemes with constant costs for signing and verifying. In: Public Key Cryptography, pp. 463–480 (2009)
18. Nakanishi, T., Funabiki, N.: A short verifier-local revocation group signature scheme with backward unlinkability. IEICE Transactions 90-A(9), 1793–1802 (2007)
19. Pointcheval, D., Stern, J.: Security arguments for digital signatures and blind signatures. J. Cryptology 13(3), 361–396 (2000)
20. Shahandashti, S.F., Safavi-Naini, R.: Construction of universal designated-verifier signatures and identity-based signatures from standard signatures. In: Cramer, R. (ed.) PKC 2008. LNCS, vol. 4939, pp. 121–140. Springer, Heidelberg (2008)
21. Steinfeld, R., Wang, H., Pieprzyk, J.: Efficient extension of standard schnorr/RSA signatures into universal designated-verifier signatures. In: Bao, F., Deng, R., Zhou, J. (eds.) PKC 2004. LNCS, vol. 2947, pp. 86–100. Springer, Heidelberg (2004)
22. Zhang, Y., Zhang, J., Zhang, Y.: Multi-signers strong designated verifier signature scheme. In: SNPD, pp. 324–328 (2008)

Appendix

A.1 BBS Short Group Signature

In this appendix, we introduce the BBS short group signature [3]. Let $(\mathbb{G}, \mathbb{G}_T)$ be a bilinear group with pairing $e : \mathbb{G} \times \mathbb{G} \to \mathbb{G}_T$, and $\mathcal{P} = \{U_1, \ldots, U_n\}$ be a set of participants.

Protocol 3. *BBS Short Group Signature [3]*

KeyGen(1^κ): *Choose $g, h \in \mathbb{G}$ and $\gamma, \xi_1, \xi_2 \in \mathbb{Z}_p$, and set $u = h^{\xi_1}$, $v = h^{\xi_2}$, and $\omega = g^\gamma$. For a user $U_i \in \mathcal{P}$, choose $x_i \in_R \mathbb{Z}_p$, and compute $A_i = g^{\frac{1}{x_i+\gamma}}$. Output the group public key gpk $= (e, (\mathbb{G}, \mathbb{G}_T), g, \omega, H)$, the group secret* key gsk $= \gamma$, and user secret keys $\{ssk_i = (x_i, A_i)\}_{U_i \in \mathcal{P}}$, where H is a cryptographic hash function from $\{0,1\}^*$ to $\mathbb{Z}_p$.

GSig(gpk, ssk_i, M): Choose $\alpha, \beta, r_x, r_\alpha, r_\beta, r_\tau, r_\lambda \in_R \mathbb{Z}_p$, and compute $T_1 = A_i \cdot h^{\alpha+\beta}$, $T_2 = u^\alpha$, $T_3 = v^\beta$, $R_1 = u^{r_\alpha}$, $R_2 = v^{r_\beta}$, $R_3 = e(T_1, g)^{r_x} \cdot e(h, \omega)^{-r_\alpha - r_\beta} \cdot e(h, g)^{-r_\tau - r_\lambda}$, $R_4 = T_2^{r_x} u^{-r_\tau}$, $R_5 = T_3^{r_x} v^{-r_\lambda}$, $c = H(M, T_1, T_2, T_3, R_1, \ldots, R_5)$, $s_x = r_x + c_s x$, $s_\alpha = r_\alpha + c_s \alpha$, $s_\beta = r_\beta + c_s \beta$, $s_\tau = r_\tau + c_s \tau$, and $s_\lambda = r_\lambda + c_s \lambda$. Output $\sigma = (T_1, T_2, T_3, s_x, s_\alpha, s_\beta, s_\tau, s_\lambda)$.

GVer(gpk, σ, M): Compute $R_1' = u^{s_\alpha} T_2^{-c}$, $R_2' = v^{s_\beta} T_3^{-c}$, $R_3' = e(T_1, g)^{s_x} \cdot e(h, \omega)^{-s_\alpha - s_\beta} \cdot e(h, g)^{-s_\tau - s_\lambda} \left(\frac{e(T_1, \omega)}{e(g, g)} \right)^c$, $R_4' = T_2^{s_x} u^{-s_\tau}$, and $R_5' = T_3^{s_x} v^{-s_\lambda}$, and check $c \stackrel{?}{=} H(M, T_1, T_2, T_3, R_1', \ldots, R_5')$. If checking condition holds, then output 1, and 0, otherwise.

Open(gpk, gsk, σ, M): Verify that σ is a valid signature on M to execute Verify(gpk, σ, M). Next, compute $A_i = T_1 / (T_2^{\xi_1} T_3^{\xi_2})$, and return the signer's identity i.

A.2 CPA-Anonymity

In this appendix, we introduce the definition of full-anonymity [1]. Note that the BBS short group signature is proven under CPA-full-anonymity, where an adversary cannot issue the Open oracle. Therefore, we introduce this weaker security notion as follows:

Definition 7. *CPA-Anonymity*

$$Adv_{\mathcal{A}}^{Anon}(\kappa) = \Big| \Pr \Big[(gpk, gsk, \{ssk_i\}_{U_i \in \mathcal{P}}) \leftarrow \mathsf{KeyGen}(1^\kappa);$$
$$(M^*, i_0, i_1, State) \leftarrow \mathcal{A}(gpk, \{ssk_i\}_{U_i \in \mathcal{P}})$$
$$\mu \in_R \{0,1\}; \sigma_\mu \leftarrow \mathsf{GSig}(gpk, ssk_{i_\mu}, M^*);$$
$$\mu' \leftarrow \mathcal{A}(\sigma_\mu, State); \mu = \mu' \Big] - \frac{1}{2} \Big|$$

The BBS short signature satisfies CPA-full-anonymity under the DLIN assumption in the random oracle model (Theorem 5.2 of [3]).

Cryptographic Protocols from Lattices

Eike Kiltz

CWI, Amsterdam
kiltz@cwi.nl

Abstract. In this talk, we will introduce abstract tools and techniques for working with lattices from the perspective of a cryptographic protocol designer. We will also show how to apply these tools to yield a number of provably secure public-key primitives ranging from digital signatures and public-key encryption, to more advanced protocols such as (hierarchical) identity-based encryption.

S.-H. Heng and K. Kurosawa (Eds.): ProvSec 2010, LNCS 6402, p. 199, 2010.
© Springer-Verlag Berlin Heidelberg 2010

A Timed-Release Proxy Re-encryption Scheme and Its Application to Fairly-Opened Multicast Communication

Keita Emura[1], Atsuko Miyaji[2], and Kazumasa Omote[2]

[1] Center for Highly Dependable Embedded Systems Technology
[2] School of Information Science
Japan Advanced Institute of Science and Technology, 1-1, Asahidai, Nomi, Ishikawa, 923-1292, Japan
{k-emura,miyaji,omote}@jaist.ac.jp

Abstract. Timed-Release Encryption (TRE) (proposed by May in 1993) prevents even a legitimate recipient decrypting a ciphertext before a semi-trusted Time Server (TS) sends trapdoor s_T assigned with a release time T of the encryptor's choice. Cathalo et al. (ICICS2005) and Chalkias et al. (ESORICS2007) have already considered encrypting a message intended to multiple recipients with the same release time. These schemes are efficient compared with previous TRE schemes with recipient-to-recipient encryption, since the most costly part (especially pairing computation) has only to be computed once, and this element is used commonly. One drawback of these schemes is the ciphertext size and computational complexity, which depend on the number of recipients N. In this paper, for the first time we propose Timed-Release Proxy Re-Encryption (TR-PRE) scheme. As in PRE, a semi-trusted proxy transforms a ciphertext under a particular public key (this can be regarded as a mailing list) into re-encrypted ciphertexts under each recipient (who can be regarded as mailing list members). *Even if the proxy transformation is applied to a TRE ciphertext, the release time is still effective.* An encryptor can transfer N-dependent computation parts to the proxy. This function can be applied to multicast communication with a release time indication. For example, in an on-line examination, an examiner sends encrypted e-mails to each examinee, and each examination can be fairly opened at the same time. Our TR-PRE scheme is provably secure under both chosen-time period chosen-ciphertext attack (IND-CTCA) and replayable chosen-ciphertext attack (IND-RCCA) without random oracles.

1 Introduction

Timed-Release Encryption (TRE) was proposed by May [26], where even a legitimate recipient cannot decrypt a ciphertext before a semi-trusted Time Server (TS) sends (or broadcasts) trapdoor s_T assigned with release time T of the encryptor's choice. Several kinds of TRE schemes have been proposed, e.g., TRE with Pre-open Capability (TRE-PC) [15,16,21], some generic constrictions [12,13,14,28],

S.-H. Heng and K. Kurosawa (Eds.): ProvSec 2010, LNCS 6402, pp. 200–213, 2010.

and so on. Points worthy of special mention are Cathalo et al. [10] and Chalkias et al. [11][1], who have already considered encrypting a message intended to several recipients with the same release time. As in Cathalo et al. [10], we do not consider encrypting with distinct release times, since colluding receivers could decrypt the message without having the appropriate trapdoor. Schemes by Cathalo et al. and Chalkias et al. are efficient compared with previous TRE schemes with recipient-to-recipient encryption, since the most costly part (especially pairing computation $e(\cdot, \cdot)$) has only to be computed once, and this element is used commonly. Informally, for a common release time T and number of recipients N, the form of a ciphertext in the Cathalo et al. scheme is: $(C_1, C_2, \ldots, C_N, (M\|\text{random nonce}) \oplus K), RecipientList, T)$, where $K = Hash(e(\cdot, \cdot))$ is a commonly used ephemeral key computed by both C_i and a user U_i's secret key. One drawback of this scheme is the ciphertext size, namely, the length of the ciphertext depends on the number of recipients N (See Fig.1). If each ciphertext (for a user U_i) is represented as $(C_i, (M\|\text{random nonce}) \oplus K, T)$, then actual transferred ciphertext size is constant. Nevertheless, there is still a remaining problem, where computational complexity also depends on N. This can be a serious problem when N becomes large.

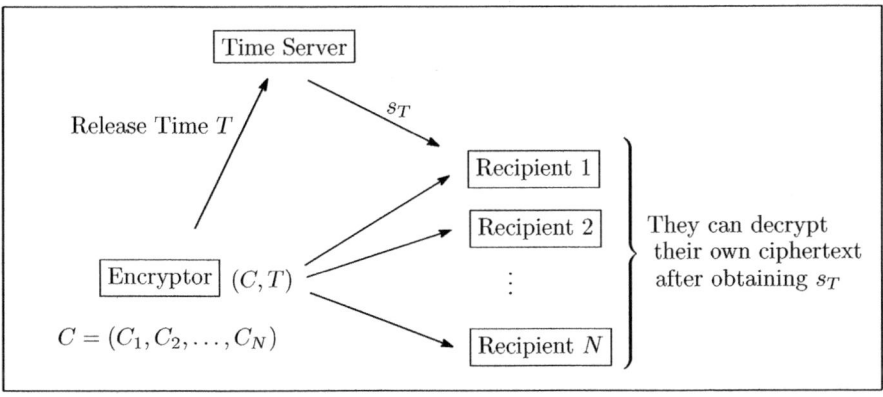

Fig. 1. Previous TRE for Multiple Recipients

Proxy Re-Encryption (PRE) was proposed in [4] by Blaze, Bleumer, and Stauss, where a semi-trusted proxy transforms a ciphertext encrypted by a delegator Alice's public key into a re-encrypted ciphertext that can be decrypted using a delegatee Bob's secret key. As application of PRE schemes, e-mail systems based on PRE have been proposed, such as [5,22,23,24].

In cloud computing environments [30], users do not have to consider the actual data storage of some services, and therefore data management becomes more and more difficult. Usually, *access control of data* and *encryption of data* are different technologies. Therefore, TRE (attribute-based encryption [3,20,27] is

---

[1] Note that Chow et al. [15] showed that the Chalkias et al. scheme is vulnerable under the CCA attack.

also another example) is suitable in cloud computing environments, since the access control function is included in the encrypted data itself. In PRE, access control (namely, who has decryption rights) may be complicated and difficult to manage, when the number of users becomes large.

Our contribution: In this paper, for the first time we propose a Timed-Release Proxy Re-Encryption (TR-PRE) scheme. An encryptor computes a TRE ciphertext under a particular public key (this can be regarded as a mailing list), and a proxy translates this ciphertext into re-encrypted ciphertexts under each recipient (who can be regarded as mailing list members). *Even if the proxy transformation is applied to a TRE ciphertext, the release time is still effective.* To the best of our knowledge, no TR-PRE have considered this release time property, although there are several research papers on TRE and PRE. We illustrate our TR-PRE in Fig.2. In this situation, from the viewpoint of an encryptor, the number of ciphertexts (and computational complexity also) does not depend on the number of recipients N. In other words, the encryptor can transfer these N-dependent parts to the proxy. As in PRE, the proxy cannot decrypt ciphertexts.

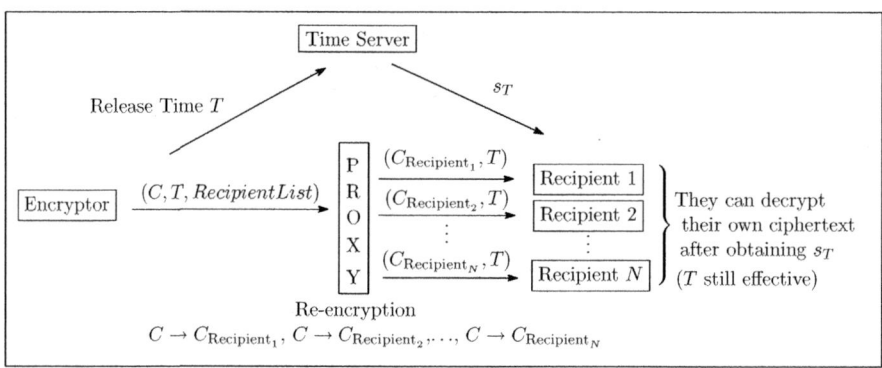

Fig. 2. Our TR-PRE with Multiple Recipients

Our TR-PRE can be applied to multicast communication with a release time indication. For example, in an on-line examination, an examiner sends encrypted e-mails to each examinee, and each examination can be opened at the same time. As another application, by using our scheme as a building tool for e-mail systems based on PRE [5,22,23,24], we can achieve e-mail systems with release time indication. Our work is valuable in adding an access control function into encrypted (and re-encrypted) data itself.

The difficulty: The construction of TR-PRE is not trivial, even if a generic construction of TRE is given. For example, in Nakai et al.'s construction [28][2]

---

[2] This construction also handles pre-open capability. A recipient can decrypt a ciphertext by using a pre-open key before the release time has not been passed. We omit the explanation of this property.

(based on Identity-Based Encryption (IBE), Public Key Encryption (PKE), and Strongly Existential Unforgeable (SEU) one-time signature), a ciphertext is represented as $(K_v, T, c_1, c_2, \sigma)$, where K_v is a signature verification key (paired with a signing key K_s), T is a release time, $c_1 = \mathsf{PKE.Enc}(upk, (K_v||r))$, r is a random number chosen from the message space, upk is a user's public key, $c_2 = \mathsf{IBE.Enc}(T, (K_v||(M \oplus r)))$, and $\sigma = \mathsf{Sign}(K_s, (T||c_1||c_2))$. In this construction, T is regarded as the "identity" of IBE scheme. When simply exchanging underlying PKE scheme to a CCA-secure proxy re-encryption scheme (such as [25]), σ cannot work after the proxy translates c_1 into c_1' (which can be decrypted by another user), since a "signed-message" c_1 has already been changed. Other generic constructions [12,13] require random oracles, since these constructions apply the Fujisaki-Okamoto transformation [18]. In [14], a general construction of TRE based on Security-Mediated Certificateless Encryption (SMCLE) was proposed. However, SMCLE is not a primitive tool (such as PKE, IBE, digital signatures, hash functions, and so on), and therefore "TRE combines PRE" is similar to "SMCLE combines PRE". From the above considerations, we need another structure to combine TRE and PRE schemes without random oracles.

Organization: The paper is organized as follows: Security definitions of TR-PRE are presented in Section 3. Our scheme is described in Section 4. The security analyses are presented in Section 5.

2   Preliminaries

Note that $x \xleftarrow{\$} S$ means that x is chosen uniformly from a set S. $y \leftarrow A(x)$ means that y is an output of an algorithm A under an input x.

2.1   Bilinear Groups and Complexity Assumption

Definition 1. (Bilinear Groups) *Bilinear groups and a bilinear map are defined as follows:*

1. $\mathbb{G}_1$ *and* $\mathbb{G}_2$ *are cyclic groups of prime order* p.
2. g *is a generator of* $\mathbb{G}_1$.
3. e *is an efficiently computable bilinear map* $e : \mathbb{G}_1 \times \mathbb{G}_1 \rightarrow \mathbb{G}_2$ *with the following properties.*
   - *Bilinearity : for all* $u, u', v, v' \in \mathbb{G}_1$, $e(uu', v) = e(u, v)e(u', v)$ *and* $e(u, vv') = e(u, v)e(u, v')$.
   - *Non-degeneracy :* $e(g, g) \neq 1_{\mathbb{G}_2}$ ($1_{\mathbb{G}_2}$ *is the* $\mathbb{G}_2$ *unit*).

Definition 2. (3-QDBDH assumption) *[25] The 3-Quotient Decision Bilinear Diffie-Hellman (3-QDBDH) problem is a problem, for input of a tuple* $(g, g^a, g^{a^2}, g^{a^3}, g^b, Z) \in \mathbb{G}_1^5 \times \mathbb{G}_2$ *to decide whether* $Z = e(g, g)^{b/a}$ *or not. An algorithm* $\mathcal{A}$ *has advantage* ϵ *in solving 3-QDBDH problem in* $\mathbb{G}_1$ *if* $Adv_{3\text{-}QDBDH}(\mathcal{A}) := |\Pr[\mathcal{A}(g, g^a, g^{a^2}, g^{a^3}, g^b, e(g, g)^{b/a}) = 0] - \Pr[\mathcal{A}(g, g^a, g^{a^2}, g^{a^3}, g^b, e(g, g)^z) = 0]| \geq \epsilon(k)$, *where* $e(g, g)^z \in \mathbb{G}_2 \setminus \{e(g, g)^{b/a}\}$. *We say that the 3-QDBDH assumption holds in* $\mathbb{G}_1$ *if no PPT algorithm has an advantage of at least* ϵ *in solving the 3-QDBDH problem.*

The hardness of the 3-QDBDH problem was discussed in [25], where the 3-QDBDH problem is not easier than the q–Decisional Bilinear Diffie-Hellman Inversion (q-DBDHI) problem [6]. The difficulty of q-DBDHI problem in generic groups was shown in [17], and this result implies the difficulty of the 3-QDBDH problem in generic groups. As in [25], we use the modified version of the 3-QDBDH (modified 3-QDBDH) problem, where for input of a tuple $(g, g^{1/a}, g^a, g^{a^2}, g^b, Z) \in \mathbb{G}_1^5 \times \mathbb{G}_2$ to decide whether $Z = e(g,g)^{b/a^2}$ or not. This modified 3-QDBDH problem is equivalent to the 3-QDBDH problem (See [25] Lemma 1).

Definition 3. (Truncated decisional q-ABDHE assumption) *[19] The truncated decisional q-Augmented Bilinear Diffie-Hellman (q-ABDHE) problem is a problem, for input of a tuple $(g', g'^{(\alpha^{q+2})}, g, g^\alpha, g^{\alpha^2}, \ldots, g^{\alpha^q}, Z) \in \mathbb{G}_1^{q+3} \times \mathbb{G}_2$ to decide whether $Z = e(g, g')^{\alpha^{q+1}}$ or not. An algorithm $\mathcal{A}$ has advantage ϵ in solving truncated decisional q-ABDHE problem in $\mathbb{G}_1$ if $Adv_{q\text{-}ABDHE}(\mathcal{A}) := |\Pr[\mathcal{A}(g', g'^{(\alpha^{q+2})}, g, g^\alpha, g^{\alpha^2}, \ldots, g^{\alpha^q}, e(g, g')^{\alpha^{q+1}}) = 0] - \Pr[\mathcal{A}(g', g'^{(\alpha^{q+2})}, g, g^\alpha, g^{\alpha^2}, \ldots, g^{\alpha^q}, e(g, g')^z) = 0]| \geq \epsilon(k)$, where $e(g, g')^z \in \mathbb{G}_2 \setminus \{e(g, g')^{\alpha^{q+1}}\}$. We say that the truncated decisional q-ABDHE assumption holds in $\mathbb{G}_1$ if no PPT algorithm has an advantage of at least ϵ in solving the truncated decisional q-ABDHE problem.*

2.2   Strongly Existential Unforgeable One-Time Signatures

We apply the Libert-Vergnaud PRE [25], which applies the CHK transformation [8] to satisfy CCA security. Therefore, we also use an SEU one-time signature [2,7,29]. An SEU one-time signature Π consists of three algorithms, Sig.KeyGen, Sign and Verify. Sig.KeyGen is a probabilistic algorithm which outputs a signing/verification key pair (K_s, K_v). Sign is a probabilistic algorithm which outputs a signature σ from K_s, and a message $M \in \mathcal{M}_{Sig}$, where $\mathcal{M}_{Sig}$ is the message space of a signature scheme. Verify is a deterministic algorithm which outputs a bit from σ, K_v and M. "Verify outputs 1" indicates that σ is a valid signature of M, and 0, otherwise. The security experiment of SEU one-time signature under an adaptive Chosen Message Attack (one-time CMA-SEU) is defined as follows:

Definition 4.   *one-time CMA-SEU*

$$Adv_{\Pi,\mathcal{A}}^{one\text{-}time\ CMA\text{-}SEU}(k) = |\Pr[(K_s, K_v) \leftarrow \mathsf{Sig.KeyGen}(1^k);$$
$$(M, State) \leftarrow \mathcal{A}(K_v); \sigma \leftarrow \mathsf{Sign}(K_s, M); (M^*, \sigma^*) \leftarrow \mathcal{A}(K_v, \sigma, State);$$
$$(M^*, \sigma^*) \neq (M, \sigma); \mathsf{Verify}(K_v, \sigma^*, M^*) = 1|$$

We say that a signature scheme is one-time CMA-SEU secure if the advantage $Adv_{\Pi,\mathcal{A}}^{one\text{-}time\ CMA\text{-}SEU}(k)$ is negligible for any polynomial-time adversary $\mathcal{A}$. Intuitively, an SEU one-time signature scheme is secure when an adversary $\mathcal{A}$ cannot issue a pair (M^*, σ^*) even if $\mathcal{A}$ has already obtained a signature of M^*.

3   Definitions of TR-PRE

3.1   System Operations of TR-PRE

First, we define encryption levels (refer to [1]) as follows: A "first-level" cipher-text is a ciphertext which cannot be re-encrypted for another user. A "second-level" ciphertext is a ciphertext which can be re-encrypted into a first-level ciphertext using an appropriate re-encryption key. In this paper, we consider a single-hop scheme (such as [25]). A TR-PRE scheme Π consists of seven algorithms (Setup, KeyGen, Encrypt, TS-Release, RKGen, Re-Encrypt, Decrypt):

Setup(1^k) : This algorithm takes as input the security parameter k, and returns the master public parameters $params$, the time server's public key TS_{pub}, and the time server's secret key ts_{priv}. We assume that $params$ includes TS_{pub}.

KeyGen($params$) : This algorithm takes as input $params$, and returns a pub-lic/secret key pair (upk, usk).

TS-Release($params, ts_{\text{priv}}, T$) : This algorithm takes as input $params$, ts_{priv}, and a release time T, and returns a trapdoor s_T.

Encrypt($params, upk, M, T$) : This algorithm takes as input $params$, a user's public key upk, a plaintext M, and T, and returns a second-level ciphertext C which can be transformed into a first-level ciphertext using an appropriate re-encryption key.

RKGen($params, usk_i, upk_j$) : This algorithm takes as input $params$, a user U_i's secret key usk_i, and a user U_j's public key upk_j, and returns a re-encryption key R_{ij}.

Re-Encrypt($params, R_{ij}, upk_i, C$) : This algorithm takes as input $params$, R_{ij}, and upk_i, and a second-level ciphertext C encrypted by upk_i, and returns a first-level re-encrypted ciphertext C which can be decrypted by usk_j.

Decrypt($params, usk, s_T, C, T$) : This algorithm takes as input $params$, usk, s_T and C, and returns M or $\bot$.

3.2   Security Requirements

We define the chosen-ciphertext security of TR-PRE. This is naturally defined from the security definitions of TRE [10] and PRE [25]. Let (upk^*, usk^*) be the challenge public/secret key. For other honest parties, keys are subscripted by h or h'. For corrupted parties, keys are subscripted by c or c'. As in [25], an adversary is given all re-encryption keys, except from the target user to a corrupted user.

Oracles: $\mathcal{A}$ can issue re-encryption queries to the re-encryption oracle $\mathcal{O}_{RE\text{-}ENC}$, where for an input (upk_i, upk_j, C), if either "C is a first-level ciphertext" or "upk_j is a corrupted user and $C = C^*$", then $\mathcal{O}_{RE\text{-}ENC}$ returns $\bot$. Otherwise, $\mathcal{O}_{RE\text{-}ENC}$ returns a re-encrypted ciphertext C'. $\mathcal{A}$ can issue decryption queries to the decryp-tion oracle $\mathcal{O}_{DEC}$, where for an input (upk, C, T), if either "upk was not produced by KeyGen" or "$(upk, C, T) = (upk^*, C^*, T^*)$", then $\mathcal{O}_{DEC}$ returns $\bot$. In addition, if C is a first-level ciphertext derived from C^*, and $upk \in \{upk_h, upk_{h'}\}$, then $\mathcal{O}_{DEC}$ returns $\bot$. Otherwise, $\mathcal{O}_{DEC}$ returns a decryption result M. We assume that C is a first-level ciphertext, since a second-level decryption oracle is useless. More precisely, $\mathcal{A}$ with R_{hc} and R_{*h} (these are defined in the following experiment) can re-encrypt second-level ciphertexts.

We say that a (single-hop) TR-PRE scheme is *replayable chosen-ciphertext* (IND-RCCA) secure if the advantage is negligible for any polynomial-time adversary $\mathcal{A}$ in the following experiment.

Definition 5. *IND-RCCA*

$$Adv_{\Pi,\mathcal{A}}^{IND\text{-}RCCA}(k) = \big| \Pr \big[(params, ts_{priv}) \leftarrow \mathsf{Setup}(1^k); (upk^*, usk^*) \leftarrow \mathsf{KeyGen}(params);$$
$$(upk_h, usk_h) \leftarrow \mathsf{KeyGen}(params); (upk_{h'}, usk_{h'}) \leftarrow \mathsf{KeyGen}(params);$$
$$(upk_c, usk_c) \leftarrow \mathsf{KeyGen}(params); (upk_{c'}, usk_{c'}) \leftarrow \mathsf{KeyGen}(params);$$
$$Set\ Keys := \{upk^*, upk_h, upk_{h'}, (upk_c, usk_c), (upk_{c'}, usk_{c'})\};$$
$$R_{c*} \leftarrow \mathsf{RKGen}(params, usk_c, upk^*); R_{h*} \leftarrow \mathsf{RKGen}(params, usk_h, upk^*);$$
$$R_{*h} \leftarrow \mathsf{RKGen}(params, usk^*, upk_h); R_{hc} \leftarrow \mathsf{RKGen}(params, usk_h, upk_c);$$
$$R_{ch} \leftarrow \mathsf{RKGen}(params, usk_c, upk_h); R_{cc'} \leftarrow \mathsf{RKGen}(params, usk_c, upk_{c'});$$
$$R_{hh'} \leftarrow \mathsf{RKGen}(params, usk_h, upk_{h'});$$
$$Set\ ReKeys := \{R_{c*}, R_{h*}, R_{*h}, R_{hc}, R_{ch}, R_{cc'}, R_{hh'}\};$$
$$(M_0^*, M_1^*, T^*, State) \leftarrow \mathcal{A}^{\mathcal{O}_{RE\text{-}ENC}, \mathcal{O}_{DEC}}(params, Keys, ReKeys, ts_{priv});$$
$$\mu \xleftarrow{\$} \{0,1\}; C^* \leftarrow \mathsf{Encrypt}(params, upk^*, M_\mu^*, T^*);$$
$$\mu' \leftarrow \mathcal{A}^{\mathcal{O}_{RE\text{-}ENC}, \mathcal{O}_{DEC}}(C^*, State); \mu = \mu' \big] - 1/2 \big|$$

In this experiment, $\mathcal{A}$ does not have to access the timed-release trapdoor extraction oracle $\mathcal{O}_{TS\text{-}Release}$ (defined in the IND-CTCA experiment), since $\mathcal{A}$ is given ts_{priv}. IND-RCCA security guarantees that even if the appropriate trapdoor is given, non-legitimate users (who do not have an appropriate secret key) cannot decrypt a ciphertext. This suggests $\mathcal{A}$ is an "honest but curious" time server. As in [9,25], we assume a static corruption model, which does not capture a scenario in which an adversary generates public/secret keys for all parties.

Next, we define *chosen-time period chosen-ciphertext* (IND-CTCA) security. $\mathcal{A}$ can issue key generation queries to the key generation oracle $\mathcal{O}_{KeyGen}$, where $\mathcal{O}_{KeyGen}$ returns (upk, usk). $\mathcal{A}$ can issue re-encryption queries to the re-encryption key generation oracle $\mathcal{O}_{RKGen}$, where for an input (usk_i, upk_j), $\mathcal{O}_{RKGen}$ returns R_{ij}. $\mathcal{A}$ can issue trapdoor extraction queries $\mathcal{O}_{TS\text{-}Release}$, where for an input time T, $\mathcal{O}_{TS\text{-}Release}$ returns a trapdoor s_T. Note that $\mathcal{A}$ cannot query T^* to $\mathcal{O}_{TS\text{-}Release}$, where T^* is the challenge time. $\mathcal{A}$ can issue decryption queries to the decryption oracle $\mathcal{O}_{DEC}$, where for an input (upk, C, T), if either "upk was not produced by KeyGen" or "$(upk, C, T) = (upk^*, C^*, T^*)$", then $\mathcal{O}_{DEC}$ returns $\bot$. Note that if C is a first-level ciphertext derived from C^*, then the decryption oracle $\mathcal{O}_{DEC}$ returns $\bot$. In our scheme, we can detect whether a first-level ciphertext C is derived from C^* or not, since a part of the ciphertext $(C_1^*, C_3^*, C_4^*, C_5^*, \sigma^*, T^*)$ is also included in C. We say that a (single-hop) TR-PRE scheme is IND-CTCA-secure if the advantage is negligible for any polynomial-time adversary $\mathcal{A}$ in the following experiment.

Definition 6. *IND-CTCA*

$$Adv_{\Pi,\mathcal{A}}^{IND\text{-}CTCA}(k) = \Big| \Pr \Big[(params, ts_{priv}) \leftarrow \mathsf{Setup}(1^k);$$
$$Set\ \mathcal{O} := \{\mathcal{O}_{KeyGen}, \mathcal{O}_{RE\text{-}ENC}, \mathcal{O}_{RKGen}, \mathcal{O}_{DEC}, \mathcal{O}_{TS\text{-}Release}\}$$
$$(M_0^*, M_1^*, T^*, upk^*, State) \leftarrow \mathcal{A}^{\mathcal{O}}(params);$$
$$\mu \xleftarrow{\$} \{0,1\}; C^* \leftarrow \mathsf{Encrypt}(params, upk^*, M_\mu^*, T^*);$$
$$\mu' \leftarrow \mathcal{A}^{\mathcal{O}}(C^*, State); \mu = \mu' \Big] - 1/2 \Big|$$

IND-CTCA security guarantees that even if the appropriate secret key is given, $\mathcal{A}$ cannot decrypt a ciphertext before the appropriate trapdoor is released. This suggests $\mathcal{A}$ is a malicious user in this experiment.

The above two definitions are secure for a second-level ciphertext, since the challenge ciphertext is a second-level one. We can define experiments for a first-level ciphertext in an orthogonal manner. We omit the details of definitions, since they are similar to the Libert-Vergnaud definitions [25].

4   Proposed Scheme

In this section, we propose our TR-PRE scheme. Our TR-PRE is based on the Libert-Vergnaud PRE [25], and the Gentry IBE [19].

Protocol 1. *The proposed TR-PRE scheme*

$\mathsf{Setup}(1^k)$: *Let n and m be polynomials in the security parameter k. Let $(\mathbb{G}_1, \mathbb{G}_2)$ be a bilinear group with prime order p, $e : \mathbb{G}_1 \times \mathbb{G}_1 \rightarrow \mathbb{G}_2$ a bilinear map, $g, u, v, h_1, h_2, h_3 \in \mathbb{G}_1$ generators, $\mathcal{M} = \{0,1\}^n$ a message space, and $\mathcal{T} = \{0,1\}^m$ a release time space. Select $s \xleftarrow{\$} \mathbb{Z}_p^*$, compute $TS_{pub} = g^s$, and output $ts_{priv} = s$ and $params = (g, u, v, h_1, h_2, h_3, TS_{pub}, H_1, H_2)$, where $H_1 : \{0,1\}^m \rightarrow \mathbb{Z}_p$ and $H_2 : \{0,1\}^* \rightarrow \mathbb{Z}_p$ are cryptographic hash functions.*

$\mathsf{KeyGen}(params)$: *For a user U_i, choose $x_i \xleftarrow{\$} \mathbb{Z}_p$, compute $X_i = g^{x_i}$, and output $(upk_i, usk_i) = (X_i, x_i)$.*

$\mathsf{TS\text{-}Release}(params, ts_{priv}, T)$: *For a release time $T \in \mathcal{T}$, choose $r_{T,1}, r_{T,2}, r_{T,3} \xleftarrow{\$} \mathbb{Z}_p^*$, compute $s_T = \big((r_{T,1}, (h_1 \cdot g^{-r_{T,1}})^{\frac{1}{s - H_1(T)}}), (r_{T,2}, (h_2 \cdot g^{-r_{T,2}})^{\frac{1}{s - H_1(T)}}), (r_{T,3}, (h_3 \cdot g^{-r_{T,3}})^{\frac{1}{s - H_1(T)}}) \big)$, and output s_T.*

$\mathsf{Encrypt}(params, upk_i, M, T)$: *Let $upk_i = X_i$. For $M \in \mathcal{M}$ and $T \in \mathcal{T}$, choose $r_1, r_2 \xleftarrow{\$} \mathbb{Z}_p$ and a one-time signature key pair $(K_s, K_v) \leftarrow \mathsf{Sig.KeyGen}(1^k)$, set $C_1 := K_v$, compute $C_2 = X_i^{r_1}$, $C_3 = M \cdot e(g,g)^{r_1} \cdot e(g, h_1)^{r_2}$, $C_4 = (u^{K_v} \cdot v)^{r_1}$, $C_5 = (g^{-H_1(T)} \cdot TS_{pub})^{r_2}$, $C_6 = e(g,g)^{r_2}$, $C_7 = (e(g, h_2) \cdot e(g, h_3)^\beta)^{r_2}$, where $\beta = H_2(C_3, C_5, C_6)$, and $\sigma = \mathsf{Sign}(K_s, (C_3, C_4, C_5, C_6, C_7, T))$, and output a second-level ciphertext $C = (C_1, C_2, C_3, C_4, C_5, C_6, C_7, \sigma, T)$.*

RKGen$(params, usk_i, upk_j)$: Let $usk_i = x_i$ and $upk_j = X_j$. Compute $R_{ij} = X_j^{\frac{1}{x_i}} = g^{\frac{x_j}{x_i}}$, and output R_{ij}.

Re-Encrypt$(params, R_{ij}, upk_i, C)$: Let $upk_i = X_i$. From a second-level ciphertext C, a first-level ciphertext C' is computed as follows: Let $C = (C_1, C_2, C_3, C_4, C_5, C_6, C_7, \sigma, T)$. Check $e(C_2, u^{C_1} \cdot v) \overset{?}{=} e(X_i, C_4)$ and Verify$(C_1, (C_3, C_4, C_5, C_6, C_7, T)) \overset{?}{=} 1$. If well-formed, choose $t \overset{\$}{\leftarrow} \mathbb{Z}_p$, compute $C_2' = X_i^t$, $C_2'' = R_{ij}^{\frac{1}{t}}$, and $C_2''' = C_2^t$, and output a first-level ciphertext $C' = (C_1, C_2', C_2'', C_2''', C_3, C_4, C_5, C_6, C_7, \sigma, T)$.

Decrypt$(params, usk, C, s_T)$:

In the case of first-level ciphertext : Let $(C_1, C_2', C_2'', C_2''', C_3, C_4, C_5, C_6, C_7, \sigma, T)$ be a first-level ciphertext, and $s_T = ((r_{T,1}, h_{T,1}), (r_{T,2}, h_{T,2}), (r_{T,3}, h_{T,3}))$ be the trapdoor of T. Check $e(C_2', C_2'') \overset{?}{=} e(X_j, g)$, $e(C_2''', u^{C_1} \cdot v) \overset{?}{=} e(C_2', C_4)$, $C_7 \overset{?}{=} e(C_5, h_{T,2}h_{T,3}^\beta) \cdot C_6^{r_{T,2}+r_{T,3}\beta}$, where $\beta = H_2(C_3, C_5, C_6)$, and Verify$(C_1, (C_3, C_4, C_5, C_6, C_7, T)) \overset{?}{=} 1$. If well-formed, compute

$$e(C_2'', C_2''')^{\frac{1}{x_j}} = e(g^{\frac{x_j}{tx_i}}, g^{tx_i r_1})^{\frac{1}{x_j}} = e(g, g)^{r_1},$$

$$e(C_5, h_{T,1}) \cdot C_6^{r_{T,1}} = e((g^{-H_1(T)} \cdot TS_{pub})^{r_2}, (h_1 \cdot g^{-r_{T,1}})^{\frac{1}{s-H_1(T)}}) \cdot e(g, g)^{r_{T,1}r_2}$$
$$= e(g, h_1)^{r_2}, \text{ and}$$

$$C_3/\{e(g, g)^{r_1} \cdot e(g, h_1)^{r_2}\} = M, \text{ and output } M.$$

In the case of second-level ciphertext : Let $(C_1, C_2, C_3, C_4, C_5, C_6, C_7, \sigma, T)$ be a second-level ciphertext, and $s_T = ((r_{T,1}, h_{T,1}), (r_{T,2}, h_{T,2}), (r_{T,3}, h_{T,3}))$ be the trapdoor of T. Check $e(C_2, u^{C_1} \cdot v) \overset{?}{=} e(X_i, C_4)$, $C_7 \overset{?}{=} e(C_5, h_{T,2}h_{T,3}^\beta) \cdot C_6^{r_{T,2}+r_{T,3}\beta}$, where $\beta = H_2(C_3, C_5, C_6)$, and Verify$(C_1, (C_3, C_4, C_5, C_6, C_7, T)) \overset{?}{=} 1$. If well-formed, compute

$$e(C_2, g)^{\frac{1}{x_i}} = e(X_i^{r_1}, g)^{\frac{1}{x_i}} = e(g, g)^{r_1},$$

$$e(C_5, h_{T,1}) \cdot C_6^{r_{T,1}} = e((g^{-H_1(T)} \cdot TS_{pub})^{r_2}, (h_1 \cdot g^{-r_{T,1}})^{\frac{1}{s-H_1(T)}}) \cdot e(g, g)^{r_{T,1}r_2}$$
$$= e(g, h_1)^{r_2}, \text{ and}$$

$$C_3/\{e(g, g)^{r_1} \cdot e(g, h_1)^{r_2}\} = M, \text{ and output } M.$$

A first-level ciphertext can be computed directly: for an input $(param, upk_j = X_j, M, T)$, choose $t, r_1, r_2 \overset{\$}{\leftarrow} \mathbb{Z}_p^*$, and a one-time signature key pair $(K_s, K_v) \leftarrow$ Sig.KeyGen(1^k), set $C_1 := K_v$, and compute $C_2 = X_j^t$, $C_2'' = g^{1/t}$, $C_2''' = X_j^{r_1 t}$, $C_3 = M \cdot e(g, g)^{r_1} \cdot e(g, h_1)^{r_2}$, $C_4 = (u^{K_v} \cdot v)^{r_1}$, $C_5 = (g^{-H_1(T)} \cdot TS_{pub})^{r_2}$, $C_6 = e(g, g)^{r_2}$, $C_7 = (e(g, h_2) \cdot e(g, h_3)^\beta)^{r_2}$, where $\beta = H_2(C_3, C_5, C_6)$, and $\sigma = $ Sign$(K_s, (C_3, C_4, C_5, C_6, C_7, T))$. Then $C' = (C_1, C_2', C_2'', C_2''', C_3, C_4, C_5, C_6, C_7, \sigma, T)$ is a valid second-level ciphertext under

U_j. We call this encryption "direct encryption method" (we use this in the proof of Theorem 1).

Intuitively, $e(g,g)^{r_1}$ is computed from a PRE section, and $e(g,h_1)^{r_2}$ is computed from a TRE section constructed by the Gentry IBE. Together with these elements, the cancel element $e(g,g)^{r_1} \cdot e(g,g)^{r_2}$ can be computed. (C_3, C_5, C_6, C_7) is a ciphertext for a message M' of the Gentry IBE scheme, where $M' := M \cdot e(g,g)^{r_1}$, and (C_1, C_2, C_3, C_4) is a (part of) ciphertext for a message M'' of the Libert-Vergnaud PRE scheme [25], where $M'' := M \cdot e(g,h_1)^{r_2}$.

5   Security Analysis

Theorem 1. *Our TR-PRE scheme is IND-RCCA-secure if the modified 3-QDBDH assumption holds, and the underlying one-time signature scheme is SEU.*

Proof. This proof is similar to that of the Libert-Vergnaud PRE scheme. However, we cannot directly use the challenger of the Libert-Vergnaud PRE scheme in a black-box manner, since the signature part of our scheme is different from that of the Libert-Vergnaud PRE scheme. Therefore, we have to write down the detailed proof: Let $(g, A_{-1} = g^{1/a}, A_1 = g^a, A_2 = g^{a^2}, B = g^b, Z)$ be a modified 3-QDBDH instance. We construct an algorithm $\mathcal{B}$ that can decide whether $Z = e(g,g)^{b/a^2}$ or not, by using an adversary $\mathcal{A}$ to break our TR-PRE scheme.

Before constructing $\mathcal{B}$, we explain two cases, in which we can break SEU of underlying one-time signature scheme: Let $C^* = (C_1^* = K_v^*, C_2^*, C_3^*, C_4^*, C_5^*, C_6^*, C_7^*, \sigma^*, T^*)$ be the challenge ciphertext. Let event_1 be the event that $\mathcal{A}$ issues a decryption query $(K_v^*, C_2', C_2'', C_2''', C_3, C_4, C_5, C_6, C_7, T)$, where $\mathsf{Verify}(K_v^*, (C_3, C_4, C_5, C_6, C_7, T)) = 1$. Let event_2 be the event that $\mathcal{A}$ issues a re-encryption query $(K_v^*, C_2, C_3, C_4, C_5, C_6, C_7, T)$, where $\mathsf{Verify}(K_v^*, (C_3, C_4, C_5, C_6, C_7, T)) = 1$. If either event_1 or event_2 occurs, then we can construct an algorithm that breaks SEU of the underlying one-time signature scheme.

From now, we construct an algorithm $\mathcal{B}$ that outputs a random bit and aborts when either event_1 or event_2 occurs. $\mathcal{B}$ computes $(K_s^*, K_v^*) \leftarrow \mathsf{Sig.KeyGen}(1^k)$, chooses $\alpha_1, \alpha_2 \xleftarrow{\$} \mathbb{Z}_p^*$, and computes $u := A_1^{\alpha_1} = g^{a\alpha_1}$ and $v := A_1^{-\alpha_1 \cdot K_v^*} \cdot A_2^{\alpha_2} = g^{-a\alpha_1 K_v^* + a^2\alpha_2}$. $u^{K_v} \cdot v = A_1^{\alpha_1(K_v - K_v^*)} \cdot A_2^{\alpha_2}$ will appear in a part of a ciphertext. $\mathcal{B}$ chooses $s \xleftarrow{\$} \mathbb{Z}_p$ as ts_{priv}, and $h_1, h_2, h_3 \xleftarrow{\$} \mathbb{Z}_p$, and computes $TS_{\mathrm{pub}} = g^s$.

Public/Secret Key Generation: For the target user, $\mathcal{B}$ chooses $x^* \xleftarrow{\$} \mathbb{Z}_p$, and computes $upk^* = X^* := A_2^{x^*}$. For an honest user U_h (also in the case of $U_{h'}$), $\mathcal{B}$ chooses $x_h \xleftarrow{\$} \mathbb{Z}_p$, and computes $upk_h = X_h := A_1^{x_h}$. For a corrupted user U_c (also in the case of $U_{c'}$), $\mathcal{B}$ chooses $x_c \xleftarrow{\$} \mathbb{Z}_p$ as usk_c, and computes $upk_c = X_c := g^{x_c}$.

Re-encryption Key Generation: For R_{c*}, $\mathcal{B}$ can compute $R_{c*} = (X^*)^{1/x_c}$, since $\mathcal{B}$ knows $usk_c = x_c$. For R_{h*}, $\mathcal{B}$ can compute $R_{h*} = A_1^{x^*/x_h} = g^{x^*a^2/(x_h a)}$. For R_{*h}, $\mathcal{B}$ can compute $R_{*h} = A_{-1}^{x_h/x^*} = g^{x_h a/(x^* a^2)}$. Note that R_{h*} and R_{*h}

are valid re-encryption keys, since $usk^* = x^* a^2$ and $usk_h = x_h a$. For R_{hc}, $\mathcal{B}$ can compute $R_{hc} = A_{-1}^{x_c/x_h} = g^{x_c/(x_h a)}$. For R_{ch}, $\mathcal{B}$ can compute $R_{ch} = A_1^{x_h/x_c} = g^{x_h a/x_c}$. For $R_{cc'}$, $\mathcal{B}$ can compute $R_{cc'} = g^{x_c/x_{c'}}$, since $\mathcal{B}$ knows $usk_c = x_c$ and $usk_{c'} = x_{c'}$. For $R_{hh'}$, $\mathcal{B}$ can compute $R_{hh'} = g^{x_{h'}/x_h} = g^{x_{h'} a/(x_h a)}$.

From the above considerations, $\mathcal{B}$ can send $params = (g, u, v, h_1, h_2, h_3, TS_{\mathrm{pub}}, H_1, H_2)$, $Keys$, $ReKeys$, and ts_{priv} to $\mathcal{A}$, where $Keys := \{upk^*, upk_h, upk_{h'}, (upk_c, usk_c), (upk_{c'}, usk_{c'})\}$ and $ReKeys := \{R_{c*}, R_{h*}, R_{*h}, R_{hc}, R_{ch}, R_{cc'}, R_{hh'}\}$.

- If $\mathcal{A}$ issues $\mathcal{O}_{RE\text{-}ENC}$ with an input (upk_i, upk_j, C), where $C = (C_1, C_2, C_3, C_4, C_5, C_6, C_7, \sigma, T)$ is a second-level ciphertext, we consider the following three cases:

  - **i is the target user and j is an honest user** : $\mathcal{B}$ simply re-encrypts C by using R_{*h}.
  - **i is not the target user and j is an honest user** : $\mathcal{B}$ simply re-encrypts C by using $R_{hh'}$ or R_{ch}.
  - **i is the target user and j is a corrupted user** : If $C_1 = K_v^*$ (event$_2$), then $\mathcal{B}$ outputs a random bit, and aborts. Otherwise, $\mathcal{B}$ computes $C_2^{1/x^*} = ((X^*)^{r_1})^{1/x^*} = A_2^{r_1}$. Now $C_4 = (u^{K_v} \cdot v)^{r_1} = (A_1^{\alpha_1(K_v - K_v^*)} \cdot A_2^{\alpha_2})^{r_1}$. Therefore, $A_1^{r_1} = g^{a r_1} = (C_4/(C_2^{1/x^*})^{\alpha_2})^{1/(\alpha_1(K_v - K_v^*))}$ holds. $\mathcal{B}$ chooses $t, r_2 \xleftarrow{\$} \mathbb{Z}_p$, sets $\tilde{t} := at/x_c$, and computes $C_2' = A_1^t = g^{at} = g^{x_c \cdot at/x_c} = g^{x_c \tilde{t}} = X_c^{\tilde{t}}$, $C_2'' = A_{-1}^{x_c/t} = g^{x_c/at} = g^{1/\tilde{t}}$, and $C_2''' = \{(C_4/(C_2^{1/x^*})^{\alpha_2})^{1/(\alpha_1(K_v - K_v^*))}\}^t = g^{a r_1 t} = g^{r_1 x_c \tilde{t}} = (X_c^{r_1})^t$. Note that we use the direct encryption method.

- When $\mathcal{A}$ issues $\mathcal{O}_{DEC}$ with an input (upk_j, C, T), where C is a first-level ciphertext under upk_j, then if C is ill-formed, $\mathcal{B}$ returns $\perp$. If $upk_j = upk_c$, then $\mathcal{B}$ can decrypt C, since $\mathcal{B}$ knows usk_c. We consider the remaining two cases as follows:

  - **j is an honest user** : Since $X_j = g^{a x_j}$, $e(C_2'', C_2''') = e(X_j, g)^{r_1} = e(g, g)^{a r_1 x_j}$ hold. In addition, $C_4 = (u^{K_v} \cdot v)^{r_1} = (A_1^{\alpha_1(K_v - K_v^*)} \cdot A_2^{\alpha_2})^{r_1} = g^{a \alpha_1 r_1(K_v - K_v^*)} \cdot g^{a^2 \alpha_2 r_1}$ holds. Therefore $\left(\frac{e(C_4, A_{-1})}{e(C_2'', C_2''')^{\alpha_2/x_j}}\right)^{\frac{1}{\alpha_1(K_v - K_v^*)}} = e(g, g)^{r_1}$ holds. By using x_j, $\mathcal{B}$ can compute $e(g, g)^{r_1}$. In addition, $\mathcal{B}$ can compute s_T, and $e(g, h_1)^{r_2}$ from (C_5, C_6, C_7). $\mathcal{B}$ returns $M = C_3/\{e(g, g)^{r_1} \cdot e(g, h_1)^{r_2}\}$ to $\mathcal{A}$.

  - **j is the target user** : If $C_1 = K_v^*$ (event$_1$), then $\mathcal{B}$ outputs a random bit, and aborts. Now $X_j = g^{x^* a^2}$. Therefore, $e(C_2'', C_2''') = (e, X_j, g)^{r_1} = e(g, g)^{a^2 r_1 x^*}$ hold. Since $C_4 = g^{a \alpha_1 r_1(K_v - K_v^*)} \cdot g^{a^2 \alpha_2 r_1}$ holds, $e(C_4, g) = e(g, g)^{a \alpha_1 r_1(K_v - K_v^*)} \cdot e(g, g)^{a^2 \alpha_2 r_1}$ holds. Therefore $\left(\frac{e(C_4, g)}{e(C'', C_2''')^{\alpha_2/x_j}}\right)^{\frac{1}{\alpha_1(K_v - K_v^*)}} = e(g, g)^{a r_1}$ holds. In addition, $e(C_4, A_{-1}) = e(g, g)^{\alpha_1 r_1(K_v - K_v^*)} \cdot e(g, g)^{a \alpha_2 r_1}$ holds. $\mathcal{B}$ computes $\left(\frac{e(g,g)^{\alpha_1 r_1(K_v - K_v^*)} \cdot e(g,g)^{a \alpha_2 r_1}}{(e(g,g)^{a r_1})^{\alpha_2}}\right)^{\frac{1}{\alpha_1(K_v - K_v^*)}} = e(g, g)^{r_1}$. In addition,

$\mathcal{B}$ can compute s_T, and $e(g, h_1)^{r_2}$ from (C_5, C_6, C_7). $\mathcal{B}$ returns $M = C_3/\{e(g, g)^{r_1} \cdot e(g, h_1)^{r_2}\}$ to $\mathcal{A}$.

Challenge: $\mathcal{A}$ sends (M_0^*, M_1^*, T^*) to $\mathcal{B}$. $\mathcal{B}$ chooses $r_2^* \xleftarrow{\$} \mathbb{Z}_p$, sets $C_1^* = K_v^*$, and computes $C_2^* = B^{x^*}$, $C_3 = M_\mu^* \cdot Z \cdot e(g, h_1)^{r_2^*}$, $C_4^* = B^{\alpha_2}$, $C_5^* = (g^{-H_1(T^*)} \cdot TS_{\mathrm{pub}})^{r_2^*}$, $C_6 = e(g, g)^{r_2^*}$, and $C_7 = e(g, h_2)^{r_2^*} \cdot e(g, h_3)^{r_2^* \beta}$, where $\beta = H_2(C_3^*, C_5^*, C_6^*)$, and $\sigma^* = \mathrm{Sign}(K_s^*, (C_3^*, C_4^*, C_5^*, C_6^*, C_7^*, T^*))$. When $Z = e(g, g)^{b/a^2}$, $C^* = (C_1^*, C_2^*, C_3^*, C_4^*, C_5^*, C_6^*, C_7^*, \sigma^*, T^*)$ is a valid ciphertext of M_μ^* with $r_1^* := b/a^2$. Otherwise, if Z is a random value, M_μ^* is perfectly hidden by Z. Therefore, $\mathcal{B}$ decides $Z = e(g, g)^{b/a^2}$ when $\mu' = \mu$, and Z is a random value, otherwise. $\square$

Theorem 2. *Our TR-PRE scheme is IND-CTCA-secure if the truncated decisional q-ABDHE assumption holds.*

Proof. This proof clearly holds, since we can use the challenger of the Gentry IBE scheme $\mathcal{C}$ in a black-box manner, and the Gentry IBE scheme is secure under the truncated decisional q-ABDHE assumption. More precisely, the simulator $\mathcal{B}$ chooses all PRE-related parameters (incl. all user's secret keys), and can use $\mathcal{C}$ when $\mathcal{O}_{TS\text{-}Release}$ and $\mathcal{O}_{DEC}$ are issued by $\mathcal{A}$. Note that $\mathcal{B}$ can decrypt (C, T) if an element (canceled by the TRE section) $e(g, h_1)^{r_2}$ is computed by $\mathcal{C}$, since $\mathcal{B}$ knows all user's secret keys. For the challenge phase, $\mathcal{B}$ can set $((M_0')^*, (M_1')^*) := (M_0^* \cdot e(g, g)^{r_1^*}, M_1^* \cdot e(g, g)^{r_1^*})$ as the challenge message, and sends this to $\mathcal{C}$. $\mathcal{B}$ can compute the challenge ciphertext C^* to add the PRE section into the challenge ciphertext of the IBE scheme given by $\mathcal{C}$. Note that $\mathcal{B}$ cannot decrypt the challenge ciphertext C^*, since the TRE part of the C^* is the challenge ciphertext of the Gentry IBE scheme. $\mathcal{B}$ outputs μ' to $\mathcal{C}$ as the guessing bit, where μ' is the output result of the IND-CTCA adversary $\mathcal{A}$. $\square$

Note that the above proofs only cover a second-level ciphertext, since the challenge ciphertext is a second-level one. As in [25], we can prove the security of the first-level ciphertext in the IND-RCCA (resp. IND-CTCA) experiment in the same manner as the proof of Theorem 1 (resp. Theorem 2).

6 Conclusion

In this paper, for the first time we propose a TR-PRE scheme. Even if the proxy transformation is applied to a TRE ciphertext, the release time is still effective. Our construction is based on the Libert-Vergnaud PRE [25] and the Gentry IBE [19]. We modified Nakai et al.'s construction [28] (which is a generic construction of TRE) to combine PRE and TRE. Our work is valuable in adding an access control function into encrypted (and re-encrypted) data itself. This feature is suitable for data management in cloud computing environments.

Acknowledgements

The authors would like to thank anonymous reviewers of ProvSec 2010 for their invaluable comments. The first author Keita Emura is supported by the Center for Highly Dependable Embedded Systems Technology as a Postdoc researcher.

References

1. Ateniese, G., Fu, K., Green, M., Hohenberger, S.: Improved proxy re-encryption schemes with applications to secure distributed storage. ACM Trans. Inf. Syst. Secur. 9(1), 1–30 (2006)
2. Bellare, M., Shoup, S.: Two-tier signatures, strongly unforgeable signatures, and fiat-shamir without random oracles. In: Public Key Cryptography, pp. 201–216 (2007)
3. Bethencourt, J., Sahai, A., Waters, B.: Ciphertext-policy attribute-based encryption. In: IEEE Symposium on Security and Privacy, pp. 321–334 (2007)
4. Blaze, M., Bleumer, G., Strauss, M.: Divertible protocols and atomic proxy cryptography. In: Nyberg, K. (ed.) EUROCRYPT 1998. LNCS, vol. 1403, pp. 127–144. Springer, Heidelberg (1998)
5. Bobba, R., Muggli, J., Pant, M., Basney, J., Khurana, H.: Usable secure mailing lists with untrusted servers. In: IDtrust, pp. 103–116 (2009)
6. Boneh, D., Boyen, X.: Efficient selective-ID secure identity-based encryption without random oracles. In: Cachin, C., Camenisch, J.L. (eds.) EUROCRYPT 2004. LNCS, vol. 3027, pp. 223–238. Springer, Heidelberg (2004)
7. Boneh, D., Boyen, X.: Short signatures without random oracles and the SDH assumption in bilinear groups. J. Cryptology 21(2), 149–177 (2008)
8. Canetti, R., Halevi, S., Katz, J.: Chosen-ciphertext security from identity-based encryption. In: Cachin, C., Camenisch, J.L. (eds.) EUROCRYPT 2004. LNCS, vol. 3027, pp. 207–222. Springer, Heidelberg (2004)
9. Canetti, R., Hohenberger, S.: Chosen-ciphertext secure proxy re-encryption. In: ACM Conference on Computer and Communications Security, pp. 185–194 (2007)
10. Cathalo, J., Libert, B., Quisquater, J.-J.: Efficient and non-interactive timed-release encryption. In: Qing, S., Mao, W., López, J., Wang, G. (eds.) ICICS 2005. LNCS, vol. 3783, pp. 291–303. Springer, Heidelberg (2005)
11. Chalkias, K., Hristu-Varsakelis, D., Stephanides, G.: Improved anonymous timed-release encryption. In: Biskup, J., López, J. (eds.) ESORICS 2007. LNCS, vol. 4734, pp. 311–326. Springer, Heidelberg (2007)
12. Cheon, J.H., Hopper, N., Kim, Y., Osipkov, I.: Timed-release and key-insulated public key encryption. In: Di Crescenzo, G., Rubin, A. (eds.) FC 2006. LNCS, vol. 4107, pp. 191–205. Springer, Heidelberg (2006)
13. Cheon, J.H., Hopper, N., Kim, Y., Osipkov, I.: Provably secure timed-release public key encryption. ACM Trans. Inf. Syst. Secur. 11(2) (2008)
14. Chow, S.S.M., Roth, V., Rieffel, E.G.: General certificateless encryption and timed-release encryption. In: SCN, pp. 126–143 (2008)
15. Chow, S.S.M., Yiu, S.-M.: Timed-release encryption revisited. In: Baek, J., Bao, F., Chen, K., Lai, X. (eds.) ProvSec 2008. LNCS, vol. 5324, pp. 38–51. Springer, Heidelberg (2008)
16. Dent, A.W., Tang, Q.: Revisiting the security model for timed-release encryption with pre-open capability. In: ISC, pp. 158–174 (2007)

17. Dodis, Y., Yampolskiy, A.: A verifiable random function with short proofs and keys. In: Vaudenay, S. (ed.) PKC 2005. LNCS, vol. 3386, pp. 416–431. Springer, Heidelberg (2005)
18. Fujisaki, E., Okamoto, T.: Secure integration of asymmetric and symmetric encryption schemes. In: Wiener, M. (ed.) CRYPTO 1999. LNCS, vol. 1666, pp. 537–554. Springer, Heidelberg (1999)
19. Gentry, C.: Practical identity-based encryption without random oracles. In: Vaudenay, S. (ed.) EUROCRYPT 2006. LNCS, vol. 4004, pp. 445–464. Springer, Heidelberg (2006)
20. Goyal, V., Pandey, O., Sahai, A., Waters, B.: Attribute-based encryption for fine-grained access control of encrypted data. In: ACM Conference on Computer and Communications Security, pp. 89–98 (2006)
21. Hwang, Y.H., Yum, D.H., Lee, P.J.: Timed-release encryption with pre-open capability and its application to certified e-mail system. In: Zhou, J., López, J., Deng, R.H., Bao, F. (eds.) ISC 2005. LNCS, vol. 3650, pp. 344–358. Springer, Heidelberg (2005)
22. Khurana, H., Hahm, H.-S.: Certified mailing lists. In: ASIACCS, pp. 46–58 (2006)
23. Khurana, H., Heo, J., Pant, M.: From proxy encryption primitives to a deployable secure-mailing-list solution. In: Ning, P., Qing, S., Li, N. (eds.) ICICS 2006. LNCS, vol. 4307, pp. 260–281. Springer, Heidelberg (2006)
24. Khurana, H., Slagell, A.J., Bonilla, R.: SELS: a secure e-mail list service. In: SAC 2005, pp. 306–313 (2005)
25. Libert, B., Vergnaud, D.: Unidirectional chosen-ciphertext secure proxy re-encryption. In: Cramer, R. (ed.) PKC 2008. LNCS, vol. 4939, pp. 360–379. Springer, Heidelberg (2008)
26. May, T.C.: Time-release crypto. Unpublished manuscript (1993)
27. Mizuno, T., Doi, H.: Hybrid proxy re-encryption scheme for attribute-based encryption. In: INSCRYPT, pp. 385–399 (2009)
28. Nakai, Y., Matsuda, T., Kitada, W., Matsuura, K.: A generic construction of timed-release encryption with pre-open capability. In: Takagi, T., Echizen, I. (eds.) IWSEC 2009. LNCS, vol. 5824, pp. 53–70. Springer, Heidelberg (2009)
29. Teranishi, I., Oyama, T., Ogata, W.: General conversion for obtaining strongly existentially unforgeable signatures. IEICE Transactions 91-A(1), 94–106 (2008)
30. Wikipedia. Cloud computing, http://en.wikipedia.org/wiki/Cloud_computing

Efficient Broadcast Encryption
with Personalized Messages

Go Ohtake[1], Goichiro Hanaoka[2], and Kazuto Ogawa[1]

[1] Japan Broadcasting Corporation
1-10-11 Kinuta, Setagaya-ku, Tokyo 157-8510, Japan
{ohtake.g-fw,ogawa.k-cm}@nhk.or.jp
[2] National Institute of Advanced Industrial Science and Technology
1102 Akihabara Daibiru, 1-18-13 Sotokanda, Chiyoda-ku, Tokyo 101-0021, Japan
hanaoka-goichiro@aist.go.jp

Abstract. Broadcasters transmit not only encrypted content but also encrypted personalized messages to individual users. The current broadcasting services employ an inefficient encryption scheme based on a symmetric key. On the other hand, several broadcast encryption schemes using a public key have been proposed in which the broadcaster encrypts a message for some subset S of users with a public key and any user in S can decrypt the broadcast with his/her private key. However, it is difficult to encrypt a personalized message and transmit it to every user efficiently. In this paper, we propose a broadcast encryption scheme that has a personalized message encryption function. We show that our scheme is efficient in terms of the ciphertext size.

Keywords: digital broadcasting, copyright protection, Conditional Access System (CAS), broadcast encryption.

1 Introduction

1.1 Background

Broadcasters transmit not only broadcast content but also personalized messages such as contract information to individual users. The broadcast content should be encrypted for copyright protection and the personalized messages should be encrypted to ensure the user's privacy. Moreover, a broadcaster would naturally want to minimize the key management cost. Therefore, the encryption scheme of a broadcasting service should be such that (i) the broadcaster can encrypt both common messages and personalized messages, (ii) it can transmit them to every user efficiently, and (iii) it must bear only a low key management cost. Unfortunately, as yet, there is no encryption scheme satisfying such requirements.

Japanese digital broadcasting employs a Conditional Access System (CAS) [1] that uses only symmetric key encryption. The broadcaster can transmit two kinds of encrypted messages to each user: an Entitlement Control Message (ECM), which is common information to all users, and an Entitlement Management Message (EMM), which includes contract information for a particular

S.-H. Heng and K. Kurosawa (Eds.): ProvSec 2010, LNCS 6402, pp. 214–228, 2010.

user. The user's receiver decrypts content by using these messages. Note that the user's secret key is used for encrypting EMM and the broadcaster must manage all of the users' secret keys. Hence, the key management cost is huge.

On the other hand, several broadcast encryption schemes [4,5,6,8,9] have been proposed in which a broadcaster encrypts a message for some subset S of users and any user in S can use his/her private key to decrypt the broadcast. Such a scheme provides one-to-many secure communication; the broadcaster can encrypt content by using only one public key, which does not have to be managed securely, and therefore, its key management cost is very small. However, such a scheme cannot be used by the broadcaster to transmit personalized messages to individual users.

The multi-recipient public key encryption scheme [10] can be used to encrypt all of the personalized messages and transmit them to users efficiently. However, if only this scheme is used, the broadcaster must transmit a common message to each user individually, so it is not efficient.

1.2   Our Contributions

We propose a broadcast encryption scheme with personalized messages (BEPM), whereby a broadcaster can encrypt not only the content but also a personalized message and transmit them to each user efficiently. To construct this BEPM, we extend the broadcast encryption scheme proposed by Boneh, Gentry, and Waters [4] and make use of the idea of the multi-recipient public key encryption scheme proposed by Kurosawa [10]. In particular, in our scheme, the broadcaster transmits only one random element g^r as part of the ciphertext to each user, whereas in a trivial scheme, the broadcaster transmits all of the random elements $g^{r_1}, g^{r_2}, ..., g^{r_n}$ as part of the ciphertext to each user. We show that our scheme is IND-CPA secure under the decision BDHE assumption and that it is efficient in terms of the ciphertext size.

1.3   Related Work

Fiat and Naor [7] were the first to advocate a broadcast encryption scheme. Their scheme is secure against a collusion of t users, and its ciphertext size is dependent on the threshold t and the number of users. Several other broadcast encryption schemes have been proposed [5,6,8,9,12] since then, but the ciphertext of each typically grows linearly with either the number of privileged users or the number of revoked users on the condition that the schemes are fully collusion resistant. Boneh, Gentry, and Waters [4] proposed a fully collusion resistant broadcast encryption scheme with a short ciphertext (only two group elements).

Naor and Reingold [14] proposed the construction of pseudorandom synthesizers to get a parallel construction of a pseudorandom function. Using this idea, Kurosawa [10] proposed the multi-recipient public key encryption scheme that reuses randomness for efficiency. In the trivial n-recipient public key encryption scheme, a ciphertext is a concatenation of independently encrypted messages for n recipients. Kurosawa scheme has a "shortened ciphertext" property, wherein the length of the ciphertext is half (or less) that of the trivial scheme and the security is almost the same as the underlying single-recipient scheme. Bellare, Boldyreva, and Staddon [3] proposed the multi-recipient encryption scheme which is extended Kurosawa construction to fit a stronger adversarial model. Peikert and Waters [15] proposed the construction of lossy trapdoor function which are technically similar to the ElGamal-like cryptosystems of Bellare et al. [3] and to constructions of pseudorandom synthesizers by Naor et al. [14].

2   Requirements

The broadcaster may transmit not only content but also personalized messages. In Japanese digital broadcasting, the broadcaster transmits contract information for distinguishing subscribers from others. Moreover, certain user terminals cannot connect to a communications network so the broadcaster needs to transmit both the content and personalized messages simultaneously via radio wave. Furthermore, the broadcast content should be encrypted for copyright protection and the personalized message should be encrypted for the sake of the user's privacy. These considerations lead us to the following requirements for the encryption scheme:

(1) A broadcaster should be able to encrypt a common message containing broadcast content and efficiently transmit it to all users.
(2) A broadcaster should be able to encrypt personalized messages and efficiently transmit them to individual user.
(3) The key management cost borne by the broadcaster should be low.

Unfortunately, there is no encryption scheme satisfying all of the above requirements. Several public key encryption schemes, for example, a broadcast encryption scheme and a multi-recipient public key encryption scheme, have been proposed for one-to-many secure communication, and we shall describe them briefly below. However, each of these schemes fails to meet the requirements in some way.

Broadcast encryption scheme [4]. The broadcaster encrypts a content decryption key by using one public key and transmits it to users. Only the users specified by the broadcaster can decrypt and play the content. Boneh, Gentry, and Waters proposed an efficient broadcast encryption scheme [4]. The header for transmitting the content decryption key is as follows:

$$\text{Hdr} = \left(g^t, (g^\gamma \cdot \prod_{j \in S} g_{n+1-j})^t \right)$$

where t, γ, and α are random numbers, g is a generator of a bilinear group $\mathbb{G}$, $g_i = g^{(\alpha^i)}$, n denotes the total number of users, and S denotes a set of users who the broadcaster specified. The header has only two elements in $\mathbb{G}$, and its size is independent of the number of users. Let M be a message to be broadcast to S, and let C_M be the encryption of M under a message encryption key K. The broadcast message to users in S consists of (S, Hdr, C_M). Only users in S can decrypt Hdr by using his/her private key and obtain K, which in turn can be used to decrypt C_M and obtain the message M.

This scheme is a public key encryption scheme, and the broadcaster does not have to manage the users' secret keys. Hence, requirement (3) is satisfied. In addition, the broadcast message (S, Hdr, C_M) is a common message to all users, and hence, requirement (1) is satisfied. However, this scheme does not have a function for transmitting a personalized message for each user. Thus, its does *not* satisfy requirement (2).

Multi-recipient public key encryption [10]. The broadcaster encrypts messages M_1, M_2, ..., M_n, where M_i is a message for user i, and transmits them to users: The most trivial scheme is that the broadcaster encrypts M_i by using the public key pk_i for user i, concatenates all encrypted messages, and transmits them to the users.

$$C = (\text{Enc}_{pk_1}(M_1)||\text{Enc}_{pk_2}(M_2)||\cdots||\text{Enc}_{pk_n}(M_n))$$

where $\text{Enc}_{pk_i}(M_i)$ denotes encrypting the message M_i with the public key pk_i. For example, the ciphertext is as follows when using the ElGamal encryption scheme:

$$C = ((g^{r_1}, M_1 X_1^{r_1})||(g^{r_2}, M_2 X_2^{r_2})||\cdots||(g^{r_n}, M_n X_n^{r_n}))$$

where r_i $(i = 1, ..., n)$ is a random number that the broadcaster selects, g is a generator of a group $\mathbb{G}$, $X_i = g^{x_i}$ is the public key for user i, and x_i is his/her private key.

Kurosawa proposed multi-recipient public-key encryption [10] in which the ciphertext size can be reduced by using a same random number for encryption. The ciphertext is as follows when using the ElGamal encryption scheme:

$$C = (g^r, M_1 X_1^r, M_2 X_2^r, ..., M_n X_n^r)$$

Note that the ciphertext has $n + 1$ elements in $\mathbb{G}$.

The above is a public key encryption scheme, and the broadcaster does *not* have to manage the users' secret keys. Thus, requirement (3) is satisfied. The ciphertext has a personalized message for each user, and the ciphertext size of the scheme is about half that of the above trivial scheme. Hence, requirement (2) is satisfied. However, the broadcaster must transmit the common message to each user individually, and thus, requirement (1) is *not* satisfied.

3 Preliminaries

3.1 Bilinear Maps

Let $\mathbb{G}$, $\mathbb{G}_1$ be multiplicative cyclic groups of prime order p and g be a generator of $\mathbb{G}$. A bilinear map is a map $e : \mathbb{G} \times \mathbb{G} \to \mathbb{G}_1$ with the following properties:

- Bilinear: $e(g^a, g^b) = e(g, g)^{ab}$ $\forall a, b \in \mathbb{Z}_p$
- Non-degenerate: $e(g, g) \neq 1$

We say that $\mathbb{G}$ is a bilinear group if the group action in $\mathbb{G}$ can be computed efficiently and there exists a group $\mathbb{G}_1$ and an efficiently computable bilinear map $e : \mathbb{G} \times \mathbb{G} \to \mathbb{G}_1$, as above. Note that $e(\cdot, \cdot)$ is symmetric since $e(g^a, g^b) = e(g, g)^{ab} = e(g^b, g^a)$.

3.2   Decision BDHE Assumption [2]

Let $\mathbb{G}$ be a bilinear group of prime order p. The ℓ-BDHE problem in $\mathbb{G}$ can be stated as follows: given a vector of $2\ell + 1$ elements

$$\left(h, g, g^\alpha, g^{(\alpha^2)}, ..., g^{(\alpha^\ell)}, g^{(\alpha^{\ell+2})}, ..., g^{(\alpha^{2\ell})} \right) \in \mathbb{G}^{2\ell+1}$$

as input, output $e(g, h)^{(\alpha^{\ell+1})} \in \mathbb{G}_1$.

Let $g_i = g^{(\alpha^i)} \in \mathbb{G}_1$ and $\boldsymbol{y}_{g,\alpha,\ell} = (g_1, ..., g_\ell, g_{\ell+2}, ..., g_{2\ell})$. An algorithm $\mathcal{A}$ which outputs $b \in \{0, 1\}$ has advantage ϵ in solving the decision ℓ-BDHE problem in $\mathbb{G}$ if

$$\left| \Pr[\mathcal{A}(g, h, \boldsymbol{y}_{g,\alpha,\ell}, e(g_{\ell+1}, h)) = 0] - \Pr[\mathcal{A}(g, h, \boldsymbol{y}_{g,\alpha,\ell}, T)) = 0] \right| \geq \epsilon$$

where the probability is over a random selection of generators g, h in $\mathbb{G}$, a random selection of α in $\mathbb{Z}_p$, a random selection of $T \in \mathbb{G}_1$, and random bits consumed by $\mathcal{A}$.

Definition 1. *We say that the decision* (τ, ϵ, ℓ)*-BDHE assumption holds in* $\mathbb{G}$ *if no τ-time algorithm has advantage of at least ϵ in solving the decision ℓ-BDHE problem in* $\mathbb{G}$.

4   Proposed Scheme

4.1   Model

The broadcast encryption scheme with personalized messages (BEPM) consists of three polynomial time algorithms: (Setup, Encrypt, Decrypt).

Setup(n): This is a probabilistic algorithm that takes as input the number of users n. It returns a public key PK and n private keys $\{sk_i\}_{1 \leq i \leq n}$.

Encrypt(S, PK): This is a probabilistic algorithm that takes as inputs a subset $S \subseteq \{1, ..., n\}$ and a public key PK. It returns a pair (Hdr, K, $\{K_i'\}_{i \in S}$), where Hdr is called the header, $K \in \mathcal{K}$ is a common message encryption key, and $\{K_i'\}_{i \in S} \in \mathcal{K}'$ is a personalized message encryption key.

Let M be a common message to be broadcast to the set S, and let $C(M)$ be the encryption of M under the symmetric key K. Let M_i be a personalized message for user i, and let $C(M_i)$ be the encryption of M_i under the symmetric key K_i'. The broadcast message to users in S consists of $(S,$ Hdr, $C(M), \{C(M_i)\}_{i \in S})$.

Decrypt(S, i, sk_i, Hdr, PK): This is a deterministic algorithm that takes as
inputs a subset S, a user ID $i \in \{1, ..., n\}$, the private key sk_i for user i,
a header Hdr, and the public key PK. If $i \in S$, the algorithm returns the
common message encryption key K and the personalized message encryption
key K_i'. The key K can be used to decrypt $C(M)$ and obtain the common
message M. The key K_i' can be used to decrypt $C(M_i)$ and obtain the
personalized message M_i for user i.

4.2 Security Definition

We shall now define the chosen plaintext security of a broadcast encryption
scheme against a static adversary by using the following game between an ad-
versary $\mathcal{A}$ and a challenger $\mathcal{C}$. Both $\mathcal{C}$ and $\mathcal{A}$ are given n, the total number of
users, as input.

Init. $\mathcal{A}$ outputs a set $S^* \subseteq \{1, ..., n\}$ of users that it wants to attack.
Setup. $\mathcal{C}$ runs Setup(n) to obtain a public key PK and private keys $\{sk_i\}_{1 \leq i \leq n}$.
  It gives $\mathcal{A}$ the public key PK and all private keys sk_j for which $j \notin S^*$.
Challenge. $\mathcal{C}$ runs algorithm Encrypt(S^*, PK) to obtain (Hdr*, K, $\{K_i'\}_{i \in S^*}$)
  where $K \in \mathcal{K}$ and $\{K_i'\}_{i \in S} \in \mathcal{K}'$. $\mathcal{C}$ then picks a random bit $b_0 \in \{0, 1\}$. If
  $b_0 = 0$, it sets $K^* = K$. Otherwise, it sets $K^* \leftarrow_R \mathcal{K}$. $\mathcal{C}$ then picks a random
  bit $b_i \in \{0, 1\}$ for all $i \in S^*$. If $b_i = 0$, it sets $K_i^* = K_i'$. Otherwise, it sets
  $K_i^* \leftarrow_R \mathcal{K}'$. $\mathcal{C}$ gives (Hdr$^*, K^*, \{K_i^*\}_{i \in S^*}$) to $\mathcal{A}$.
Guess. $\mathcal{A}$ outputs its guess b_0' and $\{b_i'\}_{i \in S^*}$ for b_0 and $\{b_i\}_{i \in S^*}$. It wins the
  game if $b_0 = b_0'$ and $b_i = b_i'$ for all $i \in S^*$

The security of a BEPM is defined as follows:

Definition 2. *We say that a BEPM is (τ, ϵ, n) IND-CPA secure if*

$$\left| \Pr[(b_0' = b_0) \wedge (b_i' = b_i)_{\forall i \in S^*}] - \frac{1}{2^{|S^*|+1}} \right| < \epsilon$$

is satisfied for all τ-time adversaries $\mathcal{A}$ in the above game.

4.3 Our Construction

To construct BEPM, we extend the broadcast encryption scheme proposed by
Boneh-Gentry-Waters [4] and borrow the idea of multi-recipient public key encryption proposed by Kurosawa [10].

Setup(n): Let n be the number of users and $\mathbb{G}$ be a bilinear map of prime
  order p. The algorithm first picks a random generator $g \in \mathbb{G}$ and a random
  $\alpha, \beta_1, ..., \beta_n \in \mathbb{Z}_p$. It computes $g_i = g^{(\alpha^i)} \in \mathbb{G}$ for $i = 1, 2, ..., n, n+2, ..., 2n$.
  Next, it picks a random $\gamma_1, \gamma_2 \in \mathbb{Z}_p$ and sets $v_1 = g^{\gamma_1}$ and $v_2 = g^{\gamma_2} \in \mathbb{G}$.
  The public key is:

$$PK = (g, g_1, ..., g_n, g_{n+2}, ..., g_{2n}, g^{\beta_1}, ..., g^{\beta_n}, v_1, v_2) \in \mathbb{G}^{3n+2}$$

The private key for user $i \in \{1, ..., n\}$ is set as:

$$sk_i = (sk_i[1], sk_i[2]) = (g_i^{\gamma_1}, (g^{\beta_i})^{\gamma_2}) \in \mathbb{G}^2$$

Note that $sk_i = (v_1^{(\alpha^i)}, v_2^{\beta_i})$. The algorithm outputs the public key PK and n private keys $sk_1, ..., sk_n$.

Encrypt(S, PK): Pick a random $t \in \mathbb{Z}_p$ and set a common message encryption key $K = e(g_{n+1}, g)^t = e(g_n, g_1)^t \in \mathbb{G}$. Next, set a personalized message encryption key $K_i' = e(g^{\beta_i}, v_2)^t$ for all $i \in S$. Then, set

$$\text{Hdr} = \left(g^t, (v_1 \cdot \prod_{j \in S} g_{n+1-j})^t \right) \in \mathbb{G}^2$$

and output the pair (Hdr, K, $\{K_i'\}_{i \in S}$).

Decrypt(S, i, sk_i, Hdr, PK): Let $\text{Hdr} = (C_0, C_1)$. If $i \in S$, output the common message encryption key:

$$K = e(g_i, C_1) / e(sk_i[1] \cdot \prod_{j \in S, j \neq i} g_{n+1-j+i}, C_0)$$

and the personalized message encryption key:

$$K_i' = e(g^t, sk_i[2]) = e(g^t, v_2^{\beta_i}) = e(g^{\beta_i}, v_2)^t$$

for all $i \in S$.

Remark 1. *Our scheme exploits the idea of multi-recipient public key encryption [10]. That is, g^t, part of the header Hdr, is used to make a personalized message encryption key $K_i' = e(g^t, sk_i[2])$ in the algorithm of* Decrypt. *Accordingly, a new random number does not have to be added to* Hdr, *and it makes our scheme efficient in terms of the ciphertext size.*

The broadcaster in BEPM needs to generate only one header when it simultaneously transmits a common message encryption key and $|S|$ personalized message encryption keys. That is, it requires two elements in $\mathbb{G}$. In contrast, the broadcaster in a broadcast encryption scheme has to generate $|S| + 1$ headers: one for a common message encryption key and $|S|$ headers for $|S|$ personalized message encryption keys. That is, $2 \cdot |S| + 2$ elements are required in total. Moreover, the broadcaster in a multi-recipient public key encryption scheme has to generate two ciphertexts: one for a common message encryption key and the other for $|S|$ personalized message encryption keys. That is, $2 \cdot |S| + 2$ elements are required in total. Our scheme is thus the most efficient among these schemes.

Remark 2. *BEPM is constructed by extending the "special case" of the broadcast encryption scheme in [4], where the ciphertext size and the private key size are fixed and the public key size depends on the number of users. It is also possible to construct BEPM by extending the "general construction" of the broadcast encryption scheme in [4]; this enables us to trade off the public key size for the ciphertext size.*

4.4 Security Proof

Theorem 1. *Let $\mathbb{G}$ be a bilinear group of prime order p. For any positive integers n, our scheme is (τ, ϵ, n) IND-CPA secure under the assumption that the decision $(\tau + 4(n+1)\tau_M + |S^*|\tau_P, \frac{\epsilon}{2}, n)$-BDHE assumption holds in $\mathbb{G}$, where τ_M denotes the processing time for modulo exponentiation, τ_P denotes the processing time for the pairing computation, and $|S^*|$ denotes the number of users who the adversary wants to attack.*

Proof. Suppose there exists a τ-time adversary $\mathcal{A}$ that has advantage ϵ in breaking our scheme. We build an algorithm $\mathcal{B}$ that solves the decision n-BDHE problem in $\mathbb{G}$ by using $\mathcal{A}$. $\mathcal{B}$ takes as inputs $(g, h, \mathbf{y}_{g,\alpha,n}, Z)$, where $\mathbf{y}_{g,\alpha,n} = (g_1, ..., g_n, g_{n+2}, ..., g_{2n})$ and Z is either $e(g_{n+1}, h)$ or T, a random element of $\mathbb{G}_1$. $\mathcal{B}$ proceeds as follows:

Init. $\mathcal{B}$ runs $\mathcal{A}$ and receives the set S^* of users that $\mathcal{A}$ wishes to be challenged on.

Setup. $\mathcal{B}$ chooses random $u_1, u_2, \beta'_1, ..., \beta'_n, \gamma_1, ..., \gamma_n \in \mathbb{Z}_p$ and sets

$$g^{\beta_i} = \begin{cases} g_1^{\beta'_i} g^{\gamma_i} & (i \in S^*) \\ g^{\beta'_i} & (i \notin S^*) \end{cases}$$

$$v_1 = g^{u_1} \Big(\prod_{j \in S^*} g_{n+1-j} \Big)^{-1}, v_2 = g_n^{u_2}$$

It gives $\mathcal{A}$ the public key

$$PK = (g, g_1, ..., g_n, g_{n+2}, ..., g_{2n}, g^{\beta_1}, ..., g^{\beta_n}, v_1, v_2) \in \mathbb{G}^{3n+2}$$

Note that since $g, \alpha, u_1, u_2, \beta'_1, ..., \beta'_n, \gamma_1, ...,\gamma_n$ are chosen uniformly at random, this public key has an identical distribution to that of the actual construction. Next, $\mathcal{B}$ computes all private keys that are not in the target set S.

$$sk_i = (sk_i[1], sk_i[2]) = (g_i^{u_1} \prod_{j \in S^*} (g_{n+1-j+i})^{-1}, g_n^{u_2 \beta'_i})$$

Note that $sk_i[1] = (g^{u_1} \prod_{j \in S^*} (g_{n+1-j})^{-1})^{(\alpha^i)} = v_1^{(\alpha^i)}$, $sk_i[2] = g_n^{u_2 \beta'_i} = v_2^{\beta_i}$. $\mathcal{B}$ gives $\mathcal{A}$ all private keys sk_i $(i \notin S^*)$.

Challenge. $\mathcal{B}$ computes $\text{Hdr}^* = (h, h^{u_1})$. It then randomly chooses a bit $b_0 \in \{0, 1\}$. If $b_0 = 0$, it sets $K^* = Z$. Otherwise, it picks a random K^* in $\mathbb{G}_1$. Moreover, $\mathcal{B}$ randomly chooses $b_i \in \{0, 1\}$ for all $i \in S^*$. If $b_i = 0$, it sets $K_i^* = Z^{\beta'_i u_2} \cdot e(h, v_2)^{\gamma_i}$. Otherwise, it picks a random K_i^* in $\mathbb{G}_1$. $\mathcal{B}$ gives $(\text{Hdr}^*, K^*, \{K_i^*\}_{i \in S^*})$ as the challenge to $\mathcal{A}$.

We claim that when $Z = e(g_{n+1}, h)$ (i.e. the input to $\mathcal{B}$ is a n-BDHE tuple), then $(\text{Hdr}^*, K^*, \{K_i^*\}_{i \in S^*})$ is a valid challenge to $\mathcal{A}$, as in a real attack. To see this, write $h = g^t$ for some $t \in \mathbb{Z}_p$. Then, we have

$$h^{u_1} = (g^{u_1})^t = (g^{u_1} \Big(\prod_{j \in S^*} g_{n+1-j} \Big)^{-1} \Big(\prod_{j \in S^*} g_{n+1-j} \Big))^t = (v_1 \prod_{j \in S^*} g_{n+1-j})^t$$

Therefore, $\text{Hdr}^* = (h, h^{u_1})$ is a valid encryption of the common message encryption key $K = e(g_{n+1}, g)^t$. Furthermore,

$$
\begin{aligned}
K^* &= Z = e(g_{n+1}, h) = e(g_{n+1}, g)^t \\
K_i^* &= Z^{\beta_i' u_2} \cdot e(h, v_2)^{\gamma_i} = e(g_{n+1}, h)^{\beta_i' u_2} \cdot e(h, v_2)^{\gamma_i} \\
&= e(g_{n+1}, g^t)^{\beta_i' u_2} \cdot e(g^t, v_2)^{\gamma_i} = e(g_n, g_1)^{\beta_i' u_2 t} \cdot e(g^{\gamma_i}, v_2)^t \\
&= e(g_1^{\beta_i'}, v_2)^t \cdot e(g^{\gamma_i}, v_2)^t = e(g^{\beta_i}, v_2)^t
\end{aligned}
$$

and hence, $(\text{Hdr}^*, K^*, \{K_i^*\}_{i \in S^*})$ is a valid challenge to $\mathcal{A}$.

Guess. $\mathcal{A}$ outputs a guess b_0' of b_0 and $\{b_i'\}_{i \in S^*}$ of $\{b_i\}_{i \in S^*}$. If $b_0 = b_0'$ and $(b_i' = b_i)_{\forall i \in S^*}$, $\mathcal{B}$ outputs 0 (indicating that $Z = e(g_{n+1}, h)$). Otherwise, it outputs 1 (indicating that $Z = T$ is random in $\mathbb{G}_1$).

We refer to the case of $Z = e(g_{n+1}, h)$ as Z_{real} and the case of $Z = T$ as Z_{rand}. Furthermore, we refer to the event that $b_0 = b_0'$ and $(b_i' = b_i)_{\forall i \in S^*}$ as $\mathcal{A}_{win}$ and the event that $\mathcal{B}$ outputs 0 (indicating $Z = e(g_{n+1}, h)$) as $\mathcal{B}_{real}$. Then, we have

$$
\Pr[\mathcal{A}_{win} | Z_{real}] = \frac{1}{2^{|S^*|+1}} + \epsilon
$$

$$
\Pr[\bar{\mathcal{A}}_{win} | Z_{real}] = 1 - \left(\frac{1}{2^{|S^*|+1}} + \epsilon \right)
$$

Therefore,

$$
\begin{aligned}
\Pr[\mathcal{B}_{real} | Z_{real}] &= \Pr[\mathcal{B}_{real} | \mathcal{A}_{win}, Z_{real}] \cdot \Pr[\mathcal{A}_{win} | Z_{real}] \\
&\quad + \Pr[\mathcal{B}_{real} | \bar{\mathcal{A}}_{win}, Z_{real}] \cdot \Pr[\bar{\mathcal{A}}_{win} | Z_{real}] \\
&= 1 \cdot \left(\frac{1}{2^{|S^*|+1}} + \epsilon \right) + \frac{1}{2} \cdot \left\{ 1 - \left(\frac{1}{2^{|S^*|+1}} + \epsilon \right) \right\} \\
&= \frac{1}{2^{|S^*|+2}} + \frac{1}{2} + \frac{\epsilon}{2}
\end{aligned}
$$

In the case of $Z = T$, the random number γ_i, which is used for constructing $K_i^* = Z^{\beta_i' u_2} \cdot e(h, v_2)^{\gamma_i}$, is independent of Z. γ_i is also used for constructing g^{β_i} for $i \in S^*$, one of the elements of PK. However, even if the adversary $\mathcal{A}$ can get g^{β_i} and $g_1 = g^{\alpha}$ and then it can solve their discrete logarithm problems and obtain β_i and α, it cannot obtain β_i'. $g^{\beta_i} = g_1^{\beta_i'} g^{\gamma_i} = g^{\alpha \beta_i' + \gamma_i}$ results in $\gamma_i = \beta_i - \alpha \beta_i'$. Therefore, there exist p candidates for the value of γ_i, and they are uniformly distributed. Hence, from $\mathcal{A}$'s view, K_i^*, which is constructed from the random element $Z = T$ of $\mathbb{G}_1$, is uniformly distributed. That is, $\mathcal{A}$ can get no information about b_i from K^* and K_i^*, and it outputs b_i' randomly. Therefore,

$$
\Pr[\mathcal{A}_{win} | Z_{rand}] = \frac{1}{2^{|S^*|+1}}
$$

$$
\Pr[\bar{\mathcal{A}}_{win} | Z_{rand}] = 1 - \frac{1}{2^{|S^*|+1}}
$$

Hence,

$$\begin{aligned}
\Pr[\mathcal{B}_{real}|Z_{rand}] &= \Pr[\mathcal{B}_{real}|\mathcal{A}_{win}, Z_{rand}] \cdot \Pr[\mathcal{A}_{win}|Z_{rand}] \\
&\quad + \Pr[\mathcal{B}_{real}|\bar{\mathcal{A}}_{win}, Z_{rand}] \cdot \Pr[\bar{\mathcal{A}}_{win}|Z_{rand}] \\
&= 1 \cdot \frac{1}{2^{|S^*|+1}} + \frac{1}{2} \cdot \left(1 - \frac{1}{2^{|S^*|+1}}\right) = \frac{1}{2} + \frac{1}{2^{|S^*|+2}}
\end{aligned}$$

The advantage of $\mathcal{B}$ is:

$$|\Pr[\mathcal{B}_{real}|Z_{real}] - \Pr[\mathcal{B}_{real}|Z_{rand}]| = \frac{1}{2^{|S^*|+2}} + \frac{1}{2} + \frac{\epsilon}{2} - \left(\frac{1}{2} + \frac{1}{2^{|S^*|+2}}\right) = \frac{\epsilon}{2}$$

Since the construction of $\mathcal{B}$ needs $4(n+1)$ modulo exponentiations and $|S^*|$ pairing computations, $\mathcal{B}$'s total processing time for solving the decision BDHE problem is $\tau + 4(n+1)\tau_M + |S^*|\tau_P$. $\square$

4.5   Performance Evaluation

We show that our scheme satisfies all the requirements of Section 2. First, our scheme is a public key encryption scheme, and the broadcaster does not have to manage the users' secret keys. Hence, requirement (3) is satisfied. The broadcast message $(S, \text{Hdr}, C(M), \{C(M_i)\}_{i \in S})$ includes both a common message for all users and a personalized message for each user. Using our scheme, the broadcaster can transmit those messages to each user efficiently. Therefore, requirements (1) and (2) are satisfied.

In the Boneh-Gentry-Waters broadcast encryption scheme [4], it is difficult to encrypt personalized messages and transmit them to each user efficiently since a broadcaster must transmit the following header to each user.

$$\text{Hdr} = \left(g^t, \{g^{t_j}\}_{j \in S}, (v_1 \cdot \prod_{j \in S} g_{n+1-j})^t\right) \in \mathbb{G}^{|S|+2}$$

In contrast, in our scheme, a broadcaster transmits the following header to each user.

$$\text{Hdr} = \left(g^t, (v_1 \cdot \prod_{j \in S} g_{n+1-j})^t\right) \in \mathbb{G}^2$$

The most trivial scheme using Kurosawa multi-recipient public key encryption scheme [10] is as follows: let K be a common message encryption key, and let K_i' be a personalized message encryption key. The header for transmitting K and K_i' using ElGamal encryption is:

$$\text{Hdr} = (g^r, KX_1^r, K_1'X_1^r, KX_2^r, K_2'X_2^r, ..., KX_s^r, K_s'X_s^r)$$

Table 1 lists the comparison of header sizes, public key sizes, and private key sizes of the Boneh-Gentry-Waters scheme, Kurosawa scheme, and our scheme. Each

Table 1. Comparison of header sizes, public key sizes, and private key sizes of Boneh-Gentry-Waters broadcast encryption [4] (BGW05), Kurosawa multi-recipient public key encryption [10] (Kur02), and our scheme. Each size denotes the number of elements in $\mathbb{G}$.

	BGW05	Kur02	Our scheme
Header size	$|S| + 2$	$2 \cdot |S| + 1$	2
Public key size	$2n + 1$	n	$3n + 2$
Private key size	1	1	2

size denotes the number of elements in $\mathbb{G}$. The header sizes of Boneh-Gentry-Waters scheme, Kurosawa scheme, and our scheme number $|S| + 2$, $2 \cdot |S| + 1$, and 2, respectively. The public key sizes of Boneh-Gentry-Waters scheme, Kurosawa scheme, and our scheme number $2n + 1$, n, and $3n + 2$, respectively. The private key sizes of Boneh-Gentry-Waters scheme, Kurosawa scheme, and our scheme number 1, 1, and 2, respectively. Our scheme is more efficient than the others in terms of the ciphertext size, although the public key size of our scheme is larger than that of the others.

5   Application

As described in Section 4.3, BEPM has the following features: (i) the broadcaster can encrypt common messages and a personalized messages, and (ii) the broadcaster can efficiently transmit a common message and a personalized message to each user. Here, we shall describe a conditional access system for a broadcasting service as an application of our scheme.

5.1   Conventional Conditional Access System

Japanese digital broadcasting uses the Conditional Access System (CAS) [1] for access control and copyright protection. CAS prevents broadcast content from being illegally used, and only the subscribers can receive the content that it protects.

Figure 1 shows a block diagram of CAS. Content is scrambled (encrypted using a symmetric encryption, MULTI-2 [1,11]). A scramble key (K_s), which is used for encrypting content, is updated every few seconds, and content information such as program type, date/time, recording control, MAC, etc., is transmitted to each user's terminal. A broadcaster encrypts K_s and the information by using a work key K_w. The encrypted information is called an *Entitlement Control Message (ECM)* and is common to all users. The broadcaster encrypts K_w and the contract information about each user, including subscribed channel, expire date, etc., by using the user's master key K_m, which differs from those of other users. The encrypted information is called an *Entitlement Management Message (EMM)*, and it includes all of the personalized messages for each user. The scrambled content, ECM, and EMM are transmitted to all user terminals. The user

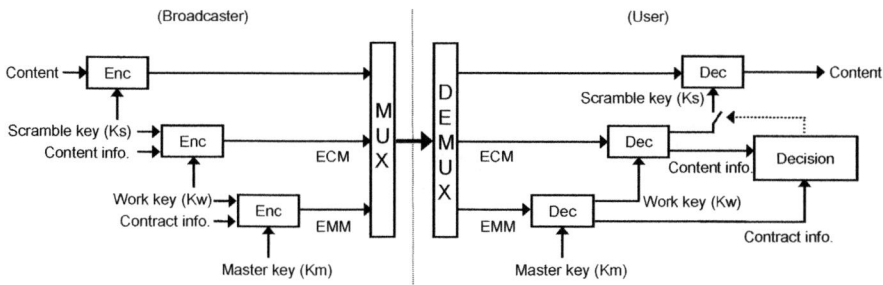

Fig. 1. Conditional Access System (CAS)

terminal receives them and picks up its EMM. K_w and the contract information are obtained by decrypting EMM using K_m. K_s and the content information are obtained by decrypting ECM using K_w. The decision upon descrambling the content is made by checking the content information and contract information. That is, the content can be descrambled (decrypted) by using K_s only if the user subscribes to the content.

As mentioned above, CAS has a function for transmitting the common message to all users as well as a function for transmitting personalized messages to each user. However, CAS is based on symmetric key encryption, and the broadcaster must securely manage all of the user's master key K_m. Hence, CAS entails a huge key management costD

5.2 Proposed Conditional Access System

Figure 2 shows a conditional access system based on our scheme. The broadcaster first runs Encrypt(S, PK) using a set S of subscriber's ID and a public key PK, and it obtains a header Hdr, a common message encryption key K, and personalized message encryption keys $\{K_i'\}_{i \in S}$. Next, it encrypts the content M using K after which it encrypts a personalized message M_i using K_i' for $i \in S$. It transmits the encrypted content $C(M)$, the pair (S, Hdr), which corresponds to ECM in CAS, and the encrypted personalized message $C(M_i)$, which corresponds to EMM in CAS. User i runs Decrypt($S, i, sk_i, \text{Hdr}, PK$) by using his/her private key sk_i, a public key PK, and (S, Hdr). If $i \in S$, he/she can obtain K and K_i'. User i then decrypts $C(M_i)$ by using K_i' and obtains personalized message M_i. Moreover, he/she decrypts $C(M)$ by using K and obtains content M.

The conditional access system based on our scheme (Figure 2) has the following strong points:

(1) *Low-cost key management*

 The broadcaster can encrypt messages by using a public key PK. Therefore, it does not have to manage all the users' secret keys, and its key management cost is very low. A symmetric key encryption scheme is used for encrypting

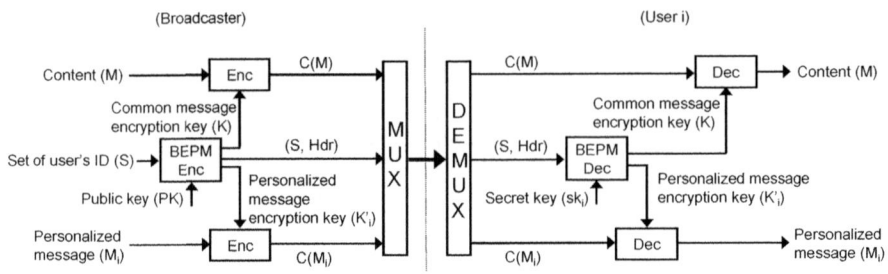

Fig. 2. Conditional access system using our scheme

the content and the personalized messages. However, a broadcaster does not have to manage a common message encryption key K and a personalized message encryption key $\{K'_i\}_{i \in S}$, since K and $\{K'_i\}_{i \in S}$ can be altered whenever it wants.

(2) *Easy access control*

The broadcaster can specify a set S of users who can decrypt its content. For example, a pay-TV service can be realized by specifying S to be subscribers. When the broadcaster wants to revoke a user or to register a new user with its service, the broadcaster simply reconstructs S; hence, access control is easy.

(3) *Transmission of personalized messages*

The broadcaster can encrypt personalized messages and transmit them to each user efficiently.

The system using a conventional broadcast encryption scheme has strong points (1) and (2), whereas the system using our scheme has all three strong points. In addition, the personalized message can include any information in our scheme. For example, a broadcaster can analyze preferences according to the individual contracts and create personalized content recommendation messages for each user.

Table 2 compares our scheme with the conventional schemes. "CAS" denotes the conditional access system (CAS) of Japanese digital broadcasting, "BGW" denotes the conditional access system using the Boneh-Gentry-Waters scheme [4], and "Ours" denotes a conditional access system using our scheme. The table shows that our system is the most effective one since it has three strong points.

In CAS, the broadcaster must manage all of the master keys K_m securely. The key management cost is accordingly huge. The broadcaster transmits content information and contract information to each user. The decision upon descrambling the content is made by checking the content information and contract information. Therefore, the access control scheme is somewhat complicated.

In CAS, the bandwidth required to transmit contract information for all users is about 300 kbps. The bandwidth required to transmit a scramble key K_s is 32 bps, assuming that K_s is updated every two seconds and $|K_s| = 64$ bits.

Table 2. Comparison of our scheme and conventional schemes: the conditional access system of Japanese digital broadcasting (CAS), a conditional access system using the Boneh-Gentry-Waters scheme [4] (BGW), and a conditional access system using BEPM (Ours). ($\star$: bad, $\star\star$: good, $\star\star\star$: excellent)

	CAS	BGW	Ours
Low-cost key management	$\star$	$\star\star\star$	$\star\star\star$
Easy access control	$\star\star$	$\star\star\star$	$\star\star\star$
Transmission of personalized messages	$\star\star\star$	$\star$	$\star\star\star$

Therefore, the total bandwidth for access control is about 300 kbps. Our scheme also uses symmetric key encryption on the personalized information. Thus, the bandwidth required to transmit personalized information for all users is about 300 kbps, the same as in CAS. Moreover, in our scheme, the bandwidth required to transmit a header is 160 bps, assuming that K is updated every two seconds, and the size of element of $\mathbb{G}$ is 160 bits. Hence, the total bandwidth for access control in our system is about 300 kbps. More precisely, the difference between total bandwidths of CAS and our system is only $128(= 160 - 32)$ bps, which is negligibly small.

As described in Section 4.5, our scheme is more efficient than the conventional ones in terms of the ciphertext size. Assuming that the representation of $\mathbb{G}$ is 160 bits and 10,000 users can decrypt a piece of content ($|S| = 10,000$), the header sizes in BGW and our system are 1.6 Mbits and 320 bits, respectively. As this calculation illustrates, our system is much more efficient than BGW in terms of the ciphertext size.

5.3 Discussion for CCA Security

As described in Section 4.4, our scheme of BEPM is IND-CPA secure under the decision BDHE assumption. Japanese digital broadcasting uses the CAS, where a security module (smart card) is distributed to each user and inserted into a user's terminal. A broadcaster encrypts user's contract information and transmit it to each user. However, this personalized message can be decrypted only in a security module since it is used for decision upon descrambling the content. That is, no one can get a personalized message as a plaintext in CAS, which means that there exists no decryption oracle. Therefore, we do not need to consider CCA security of our scheme.

References

1. Association of Radio Industries and Businesses, Conditional Access System Specifications for Digital Broadcasting ARIB STD-B25
2. Boneh, D., Boyen, X., Goh, E.: Hierarchical identity based encryption with constant size ciphertext. In: Cramer, R. (ed.) EUROCRYPT 2005. LNCS, vol. 3494, pp. 440–456. Springer, Heidelberg (2005)

3. Bellare, M., Boldyreva, A., Staddon, J.: Randomness Re-Use in Multi-Recipient Encryption Schemes. In: Desmedt, Y.G. (ed.) PKC 2003. LNCS, vol. 2567, pp. 85–99. Springer, Heidelberg (2002)
4. Boneh, D., Gentry, C., Waters, B.: Collusion Resistant Broadcast Encryption With Short Ciphertexts and Private Keys. In: Shoup, V. (ed.) CRYPTO 2005. LNCS, vol. 3621, pp. 258–275. Springer, Heidelberg (2005)
5. Dodis, Y., Fazio, N.: Public key broadcast encryption for stateless receivers. In: Proc. of the DRM Workshop 2002, pp. 61–80 (2002)
6. Dodis, Y., Fazio, N.: Public key broadcast encryption secure against adaptive chosen ciphertext attack. In: Desmedt, Y.G. (ed.) PKC 2003. LNCS, vol. 2567, Springer, Heidelberg (2002)
7. Fiat, A., Naor, M.: Broadcast encryption. In: Stinson, D.R. (ed.) CRYPTO 1993. LNCS, vol. 773, pp. 480–491. Springer, Heidelberg (1994)
8. Goodrich, M.T., Sun, J.Z., Tamassia, R.: Efficient tree-based revocation in groups of low-state devices. In: Franklin, M. (ed.) CRYPTO 2004. LNCS, vol. 3152, pp. 511–527. Springer, Heidelberg (2004)
9. Halevy, D., Shamir, A.: The LSD Broadcast Encryption Scheme. In: Yung, M. (ed.) CRYPTO 2002. LNCS, vol. 2442, pp. 47–60. Springer, Heidelberg (2002)
10. Kurosawa, K.: Multi-recipient Public-Key Encryption with Shortened Ciphertext. In: Naccache, D., Paillier, P. (eds.) PKC 2002. LNCS, vol. 2274, pp. 48–63. Springer, Heidelberg (2002)
11. ISO/IEC. Algorithm registry entry 9979/0009 (1994)
12. Naor, D., Naor, M., Lotspiech, J.: Revocation and tracing schemes for stateless receivers. In: Kilian, J. (ed.) CRYPTO 2001. LNCS, vol. 2139, pp. 41–62. Springer, Heidelberg (2001)
13. Naor, M., Pinkas, B.: Efficient trace and revoke schemes. In: Proc. of Financial cryptography 2000, pp. 1–20 (2000)
14. Naor, M., Reingold, O.: Synthesizers and Their Application to the Parallel Construction of Pseudo-Random Functions. In: Proc. of FOCS 1995, pp. 170–181 (1995)
15. Peikert, C., Waters, B.: Lossy Trapdoor Functions and Their Applications. In: Proc. of STOC 2008, pp. 187–196 (2008)

Toward an Easy-to-Understand Structure for Achieving Chosen Ciphertext Security from the Decisional Diffie-Hellman Assumption

Shota Yamada[1], Goichiro Hanaoka[2], and Noboru Kunihiro[3]

[1] The University of Tokyo
yamada@it.k.u-tokyo.ac.jp
[2] National Institute of Advanced Industrial Science and Technology (AIST)
hanaoka-goichiro@aist.go.jp
[3] The University of Tokyo
kunihiro@k.u-tokyo.ac.jp

Abstract. In this paper, we present a new public key encryption scheme which is proven chosen-ciphertext (CCA) secure under the decisional Diffie-Hellman (DDH) assumption. The main motivation behind this scheme is to clarify the essential mechanism for yielding CCA-security from the DDH assumption. The structure and security proof of our scheme is simple, and it is likely that even non-experts can immediately understand them with ease. We consider that our scheme is helpful for convincing a wide range of users (including developers and students who are just starting to study CCA-secure encryption) how the Cramer-Shoup cryptosystem and its variants work.

Keywords: public key encryption, CCA security, the decisional Diffie-Hellman assumption.

1 Introduction

1.1 Background

For practical communication systems, chosen-ciphertext (CCA) security [20,8] is considered as the de facto standard security notion for public key encryption (PKE) schemes, and there is no doubt about its importance. However, in contrast to its importance, we also notice that the essential mechanisms of CCA-secure PKE schemes are not generally easy to understand except for experts, and thus, for example, this often makes developers pause to implement newly-invented useful schemes. Especially, the Cramer-Shoup scheme [7] is recognized as one of the most basic CCA-secure PKE schemes, but its mechanism for yielding provable CCA-security under the decisional Diffie-Hellman (DDH) assumption seems not very intuitive. Therefore, for further activating research and development of CCA-secure PKE schemes, it is important to present the essential mechanism for handling CCA-security in a more easy-to-understand manner.

S.-H. Heng and K. Kurosawa (Eds.): ProvSec 2010, LNCS 6402, pp. 229–243, 2010.

1.2 Our Contribution

In this paper, we propose a novel PKE scheme which is designed by pursuing a more easy-to-understand structure for handling CCA-security under the DDH assumption. Our proposed scheme is constructed based on Hanaoka et al.'s scheme [10] which was also designed for providing an easy-to-understand security proof for CCA-security. Since Hanaoka et al.'s scheme requires the gap Diffie-Hellman assumption, we modify it to be provably secure under the DDH assumption. This modification yields clearer intuition how CCA-security is handled under the DDH assumption, and would be helpful for understanding the essential mechanism of the existing DDH-based PKE schemes. We further slightly modify our proposed scheme with enhanced efficiency and less intuitive security proof. Interestingly, the resulting scheme becomes very similar to the hash free variant of the Cramer-Shoup scheme (which is mentioned in Sec. 5.3 in [7]). This implies that our proposed scheme well explains the essential mechanism of the existing DDH-based schemes.

1.3 Related Works

In the beginning of nineties, the first CCA-secure PKE scheme was proposed by Dolev, Dwork, and Naor [8] by extending the Naor-Yung paradigm [17]. However, it took seven years until the first practical CCA-secure scheme was proposed by Cramer and Shoup [7] under the DDH assumption. Moreover, it further took another six years until its significantly improved (but very simple) variant was discovered by Kurosawa and Desmedt [13]. This fact implies that the mechanism for handling CCA-security is not generally easy. Later, Cash, Kiltz, and Shoup [5] introduced the notion of twin Diffie-Hellman problem and proposed a variant of the Cramer-Shoup scheme with a much simpler security proof. Hanaoka and Kurosawa [11] also proposed another scheme and explained its CCA-security via the Lagrange interpolation. Security of these schemes can be proven under even weaker assumption, i.e. the computational Diffie-Hellman assumption, and descriptions of their security proofs are fairly short. However, both schemes still require non-intuitive calculations (e.g. the Boneh-Boyen technique [2]) in the security proofs, and therefore, these are not considered very easy-to-understand for starters to grasp the essential mechanism. Of course, for those who naturally understand those techniques, schemes in [5] and [11] are already easy-to-understand.

In [10], Hanaoka, Imai, Ogawa, and Watanabe presented a PKE scheme whose security proof is very short without using any non-intuitive calculation. However, their scheme requires the gap Diffie-Hellman assumption. Later, Cramer, Hofheinz, and Kiltz [6] showed a generic method for constructing CCA-secure PKE schemes from a class of computational assumptions, and [10] (and thus our proposed scheme) can be regarded as a special case of their framework.

Recently, Peikert and Waters [19] advocated another methodology for constructing CCA-secure PKE schemes from a special kind of trapdoor functions called *lossy trapdoor functions*. Rosen and Segev [21] relaxed its requirement, and showed that *correlation secure trapdoor functions* are sufficient. Kiltz, Mohassel, and O'Neill [14] further showed that *adaptive trapdoor functions*, which are weaker than correlation secure trapdoor functions are also sufficient.

2   Definitions

Here, we give definitions for CCA-security of Key Encapsulation Mechanism and the Decisional Diffie-Hellman assumption which is the number theoretic assumption that we use. For other number theoretic assumptions, see Appendix A. See also Appendix B.2 for data encapsulation mechanisms (DEMs).

2.1   Key Encapsulation Mechanism (KEM)

For simplicity, we define PKE schemes as key encapsulation mechanisms (KEM). It is well-known that by combining a CCA-secure KEM and a CCA-secure data encryption mechanism (DEM), a CCA-secure PKE scheme is generically obtained [22], and furthermore, there exist some other flexible methods for hybrid encryption as well [1,12]. It is also known that a CCA-secure DEM can be generically constructed from any pseudorandom functions without redundancy [15]. Therefore, we concentrate on constructions of CCA-secure KEMs.

The Model. Let $\mathcal{K}$ denote the key space of the key encapsulation mechanism (KEM). A KEM scheme consists of the following three algorithms:

Setup(1^k). Takes as input the security parameter 1^k and outputs a decryption key dk and a public key PK.

Encapsulate(PK). Takes as input a public key PK, and outputs a ciphertext ψ and corresponding session key $K \in \mathcal{K}$.

Decapsulate(dk, ψ, PK). Takes as input the decryption key dk, a ciphertext ψ, and the public key PK, and outputs the session key $K \in \mathcal{K}$ or a special symbol "$\perp$".

We require that if $(dk, PK) \xleftarrow{R} \textbf{Setup}(1^k)$ and $(\psi, K) \xleftarrow{R} \textbf{Encapsulate}(PK)$ then **Decapsulate**$(dk, \psi, PK) = K$.

Chosen-Ciphertext Security. CCA-security of a KEM scheme is defined using the following game (which we call IND-CCA game) between an attack algorithm A and a challenger. Both the challenger and A are given 1^k as input.

Setup. The challenger runs **Setup**(1^k) to obtain a decryption key dk and a public key PK, and gives PK to A.

Challenge. The challenger runs algorithm **Encapsulate** to obtain the challenge ciphertext and its session key as $(\psi^\star, K^\star) \xleftarrow{R} \textbf{Encapsulate}(PK)$ and sets $K_0 = K^\star$. Next, the challenger obtain random key $K_1 \xleftarrow{R} \mathcal{K}$. Then the challenger picks a random $b \in \{0, 1\}$ and give $(\psi^\star, K_b)$ to A.

Query. Algorithm A adaptively issues decryption queries $\psi_1, \ldots, \psi_{q_D}$. For query ψ_i, the challenger responds with **Decapsulate**(dk, ψ_i, PK). A is not allowed to submit $\psi^\star$.

Guess. Algorithm A outputs its guess $b' \in \{0, 1\}$ for b and wins the game if $b = b'$.

Let $\mathsf{AdvKEM_A}$ denote the probability that A wins the game.

Definition 1. We say that a KEM scheme is (τ, ϵ, q_D) CCA-secure if for all τ-time algorithms A who make a total of q_D decryption queries, we have that $|\mathsf{AdvKEM_A} - 1/2| < \epsilon$.

2.2   The Decisional Diffie-Hellman Assumption

Let $\mathbb{G}$ be a multiplicative group with prime order p. Then, the *Decisional Diffie-Hellman* (DDH) problem in $\mathbb{G}$ is stated as follows. Let A be an algorithm, and we say that A has advantage ϵ in solving the DDH problem in $\mathbb{G}$ if

$$\frac{1}{2} \cdot | \Pr[\mathsf{A}(g, Z, g^{r^\star}, Z^{r^\star}) = 0] - \Pr[\mathsf{A}(g, Z, g^{r^\star}, T) = 0]| \geq \epsilon,$$

where the probability is over the random choice of random elements g, Z, and T in $\mathbb{G}$, the random choice of $r^\star$ in $\mathbb{Z}_p$, and the random bits consumed by A.

Definition 2. *We say that the (τ, ϵ)-DDH assumption holds in $\mathbb{G}$ if no τ-time algorithm has advantage at least ϵ in solving the DDH problem in $\mathbb{G}$.*

Occasionally we drop the τ and ϵ and refer to the DDH in $\mathbb{G}$.

3   The Proposed Scheme

3.1   High Level Overview

Our proposed scheme is almost the same as the Hanaoka-Imai-Ogawa-Watanabe scheme [10] except that in our scheme we add more redundant components in a ciphertext. This redundancy removes necessity of the DDH oracle in the security proof of the Hanaoka-Imai-Ogawa-Watanabe scheme, and consequently, security of the resulting scheme can be proven under the standard DDH assumption. This technique is similar to the twinning technique in [5].

3.2   The Construction

Let $\mathbb{G}$ be a multiplicative group with prime order p, and $g \in \mathbb{G}$ be a generator. We assume that a group element of $\mathbb{G}$ is k-bit long where 1^k is the security parameter. Then, the construction of our proposed KEM scheme is as follows:

Setup(1^k): Pick $dk = ((x_i, \bar{x}_i, y_i, \bar{y}_i)_{1 \leq i \leq k}, z) \in \mathbb{Z}_p^{4k+1}$ randomly, and compute $(X_i, \bar{X}_i, Y_i, \bar{Y}_i) = (g^{x_i}, g^{\bar{x}_i}, g^{y_i}, g^{\bar{y}_i})$, and $Z = g^z$ for $i = 1, \ldots, k$. The decryption key is dk, and the public key is $PK = (\mathbb{G}, g, (X_i, \bar{X}_i, Y_i, \bar{Y}_i)_{1 \leq i \leq k}, Z)$.

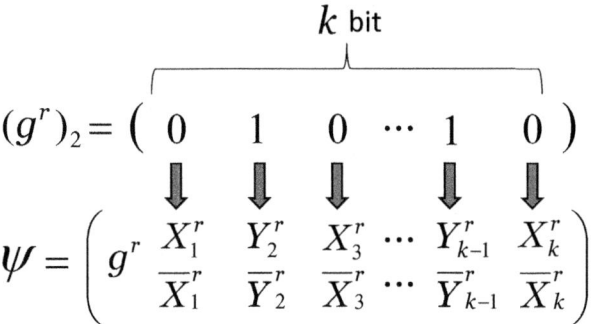

Fig. 1. The structure of a ciphertext

Encapsulate(PK): Pick a random $r \xleftarrow{R} \mathbb{Z}_p$, and compute

$$\psi = (g^r, (U_i^r, \bar{U}_i^r)_{1 \leq i \leq k}),$$
$$K = Z^r,$$

where $(U_i, \bar{U}_i) = (X_i, \bar{X}_i)$ if $v_i = 0$, or $(U_i, \bar{U}_i) = (Y_i, \bar{Y}_i)$ if $v_i = 1$, v_i is i-th bit of $(g^r)_2$, and $(W)_2$ denotes the binary representation of $W \in \mathbb{G}$. The ciphertext is ψ. The corresponding session key is K. Fig. 1 illustrates the structure of the ciphertext.

Decapsulate(dk, ψ, PK): For a ciphertext $\psi = (C_0, (C_i, \bar{C}_i)_{1 \leq i \leq k})$, check whether for all $i = 1, \ldots, k$, $(C_0^{u_i}, C_0^{\bar{u}_i}) \stackrel{?}{=} (C_i, \bar{C}_i)$ where $(u_i, \bar{u}_i) = (x_i, \bar{x}_i)$ if $v_i = 0$, or $(u_i, \bar{u}_i) = (y_i, \bar{y}_i)$ if $v_i = 1$ where v_i is i-th bit of $(C_0)_2$. If not, output $\bot$. Otherwise, output $K = C_0^z$.

The required operation for encryption in the proposed scheme is only exponentiations with a common exponent r under fixed bases (which are contained in PK).

3.3 Security

Theorem 1. *Let $\mathbb{G}$ be a multiplicative group with prime order p. Then, the above scheme is $(\tau - o(\tau), \epsilon_{ddh} + q_D/p, q_D)$ CCA-secure assuming the (τ, ϵ_{ddh}) DDH assumption holds in $\mathbb{G}$.*

Overview of the Security Proof. Before going into the formal proof, we explain its strategy briefly. For proving the above theorem, we construct an algorithm B which for a given DDH instance (g, Z, g^{r^*}, R), distinguishes whether R is Z^{r^*} or random group element T of $\mathbb{G}$. B may interact with A which breaks the CCA-security of our proposed scheme. By setting public key and challenge ciphertext as $PK = (\cdots, Z)$ and $\psi^* = (g^{r^*}, \cdots)$, respectively, B can enforce A to solve the given DDH problem since the corresponding session key of ψ^*

is Z^{r^*}. However, this idea does not immediately work since B has to respond to A's decryption queries without knowing $z = \log_g Z$. To solve this problem, B also sets redundant component X_i (or Y_i) as $X_i = Z^c$ (or $Y_i = Z^c$) in PK where c is a random blind factor. Then, A's decryption query always forms as $\psi = (g^r, \cdots, U_i^r, \cdots)$ if it is valid, and therefore, B can compute the correct answer $Z^r = (U_i^r)^{\frac{1}{c}}$ and respond it to A. Furthermore, by introducing the *test function* (which will be explained later), B can distinguish invalid decryption queries from valid ones.

Proof. Assume we are given an adversary A which breaks the CCA-security of the above scheme with running time τ, advantage ϵ, and q_D decryption queries. We use A to construct another adversary B distinguishes Z^{r^*} from random element in $\mathbb{G}$. Define adversary B as follows:

1. For a given DDH instance (g, Z, g^{r^*}, R), B picks random $(a_i, b_i, c_i, d_i, e_i)_{1 \le i \le k} \in \mathbb{Z}_p^{5k}$ and sets a test function $test_i$ such that $test_i(x, y) = x^{d_i} y^{e_i}$. Let v_i^* be i-th bit of $(g^{r^*})_2$ for $1 \le i \le k$.
2. B sets $T_i = test_i(Z^{c_i}, g)$ and $(X_i, \bar{X}_i, Y_i, \bar{Y}_i) = (g^{a_i}, g^{b_i}, Z^{c_i}, T_i)$ if $v_i^* = 0$, or $(X_i, \bar{X}_i, Y_i, \bar{Y}_i) = (Z^{c_i}, T_i, g^{a_i}, g^{b_i})$ if $v_i^* = 1$, for $i = 1, \ldots, k$. B inputs public key $PK = (\mathbb{G}, g, (X_i, \bar{X}_i, Y_i, \bar{Y}_i)_{1 \le i \le k}, Z)$, challenge ciphertext $\psi^* = (g^{r^*}, ((g^{r^*})^{a_i}, (g^{r^*})^{b_i})_{1 \le i \le k})$, and real/random key R to A. Fig. 2 illustrates the structure of PK and ψ^*.

   Functionality of $test_i$. We note that the test function $test_i$ has the following property: Let $\bar{U}$ be $\bar{U} = test_i(U, g)$ where U is randomly chosen from $\mathbb{G}$. For given U and $\bar{U}$ (and nothing else), it is hard to evaluate the value of $test_i(U^r, g^{r+r'})$ for any r and $r' \in \mathbb{Z}_p$ unless $r' = 0$. Namely, if $r' = 0$, $test_i(U^r, g^{r+r'}) = \bar{U}^r$, and otherwise, $test_i(U^r, g^{r+r'}) = \bar{U}^r \cdot (g^{r'})^{e_i}$ which cannot be computed without knowing e_i. We also note that U and $\bar{U}$ do not leak any information on e_i. By using this property, B can detect invalid ciphertexts with overwhelming probability (as shown in Step 3). This is due to the fact that a valid ciphertext forms as $\psi = (g^r, (U_i^r, \bar{U}_i^r)_{1 \le i \le k})$ for a common exponent r.

3. When A makes decryption query $\psi = (C_0, (C_i, \bar{C}_i)_{1 \le i \le k}) \in \mathbb{G}^{2k+1}$ (if a query is not in this form, then B simply rejects it), B determines a binary string $(C_0)_2 = (v_i)_{1 \le i \le k}$ and proceeds as follows:
   (a) For all i such that $v_i = v_i^*$, B checks whether $(C_i, \bar{C}_i) \overset{?}{=} (C_0^{a_i}, C_0^{b_i})$. If not so, B rejects ψ. Notice that if $v_i = v_i^*$, then $(U_i, \bar{U}_i) = (g^{a_i}, g^{b_i})$, and thus a valid ciphertext always satisfies the above equality.
   (b) For all i such that $v_i \ne v_i^*$, B checks whether

   $$\bar{C}_i \overset{?}{=} test_i(C_i, C_0). \tag{1}$$

   If not so, B rejects ψ. If ψ is valid, then Eq. (1) always holds since $(U_i, \bar{U}_i) = (Z^{c_i}, T_i)$.
   (c) If ψ is not rejected, then B picks (one of) i such that $v_i \ne v_i^*$. We note that there always exists at least one such i if $\psi \ne \psi^*$. B also calculates $K' = C_i^{1/c_i}$, and responds it to A.

$$(g^{r^*})_2 = \begin{pmatrix} 0 & 1 & \cdots & 0 \end{pmatrix}$$

$$PK = \begin{pmatrix} X_1 = g^{a_1} & X_2 = Z^{c_2} & \cdots & X_k = g^{a_k} \\ \overline{X}_1 = g^{b_1} & \overline{X}_2 = T_2 & \cdots & \overline{X}_k = g^{b_k} \\ Y_1 = Z^{c_1} & Y_2 = g^{a_2} & \cdots & Y_k = Z^{c_k} \\ \overline{Y}_1 = T_1 & \overline{Y}_2 = g^{b_2} & \cdots & \overline{Y}_k = T_k \end{pmatrix} Z$$

$$\psi^* = \begin{pmatrix} g^{r^*} & (g^{r^*})^{a_1} & (g^{r^*})^{a_2} & \cdots & (g^{r^*})^{a_k} \\ & (g^{r^*})^{b_1} & (g^{r^*})^{b_2} & \cdots & (g^{r^*})^{b_k} \end{pmatrix}$$

$$= \begin{pmatrix} g^{r^*} & X_1^{r^*} & Y_2^{r^*} & \cdots & X_k^{r^*} \\ & \overline{X}_1^{r^*} & \overline{Y}_2^{r^*} & \cdots & \overline{X}_k^{r^*} \end{pmatrix}$$

Fig. 2. The structure of PK and ψ^* in the simulation

4. Finally, when A outputs his guess b', B also outputs b' as his guess.

Let Win denote the event that A succeeds to guess b in IND-CCA game, Invalid denote the event that A submits an invalid ciphertext which satisfies equality of Eq. (1). B's simulation is perfect if the event Invalid does not occur. B's advantage is estimated as follows.

$$\frac{1}{2}|Pr[\mathsf{B}(g, Z, g^{r^*}, Z^{r^*}) = 0] - Pr[\mathsf{B}(g, Z, g^{r^*}, T) = 0]|$$

$$\geq |Pr[\mathsf{Win} \wedge \overline{\mathsf{Invalid}}] - \frac{1}{2}|$$

$$\geq |Pr[\mathsf{Win}] - Pr[\mathsf{Invalid}] - \frac{1}{2}|$$

$$\geq |Pr[\mathsf{Win}] - \frac{1}{2}| - Pr[\mathsf{Invalid}]$$

The proof completes by proving the following lemma.

Lemma 1. $Pr[\mathsf{Invalid}] \leq q_D/p.$

Proof. Since there are at most q_D decryption queries, it is sufficient to prove that for one query, the probability that B fails to reject an invalid ciphertext is at most $1/p$.

Without loss of generality, for an invalid decryption query $\psi = (C_0, (C_i, \bar{C}_i)_{1 \leq i \leq k})$, we can assume that for some r and $r'(\neq 0)$ there exists index j such that $C_0 = g^{r+r'}$ and $C_j = U_j^r$. Note that $test_j(C_j, C_0) = \bar{U}_j^r \cdot (g^{r'})^{e_j}$. However, since e_j is information theoretically hidden from A's view, and $\bar{U}_j^r \cdot (g^{r'})^{e_j}$ takes p different values according to p different values of e_j, A can predict the value of $\bar{U}_j^r \cdot (g^{r'})^{e_j}$ with at most probability $1/p$. This implies that A cannot submit an invalid ciphertext which satisfies equality of Eq. (1) with probability more than $1/p$.

3.4   HDH-Based and CDH-Based Variants

We can obtain another PKE scheme by changing session key from K to $h(K)$, and adding h to public key, where $h : \mathbb{G} \to \mathcal{K}$ is hash function. This scheme is CCA-secure under the HDH assumption (see Appendix A.2), which is a weaker assumption than the DDH assumption. Especially, if h is hardcore bit function of Diffie-Hellman key [3,4,9], then this scheme is CCA-secure under the CDH assumption (see Appendix A.1). Regarding the CDH-based scheme, we directly construct PKE without the KEM/DEM framework [22] by using a technique in [10]. This scheme yields only one-bit plaintext space, but it can be extended to be many-bit plaintext space by the result of Myers and Shelat [16].

3.5   Compressing Keys

It is possible to compress the size of keys by using target collision resistant hash functions (see Appendix B.1). Specifically, by replacing the vector $(v_i)_{1 \le i \le k} = ((C_0)_2)$ with another vector $(v_i')_{1 \le i \le \ell} = \mathsf{TCR}(C_0)$ where $\mathsf{TCR} : \mathbb{G} \to \{0,1\}^\ell$ is a target collision resistant hash function, sizes for both decryption and public key are reduced by approximately $\ell/k \simeq 1/2$.[1]

4   A Comparison

In this section, we discuss "easiness-to-understand" of our proposed scheme by comparing it with the Cramer-Shoup scheme [7] and the Hanaoka-Imai-Ogawa-Watanabe scheme [10] by focusing on their techniques for responding to decryption queries.

   In the proof of our scheme, the simulator has to check the validity of a queried ciphertext by the simulator itself, whereas in the proof of the Hanaoka-Imai-Ogawa-Watanabe scheme, validity of a queried ciphertext is very easy to check by using the DDH oracle. Cost of this easiness is necessity of a rather unnatural assumption, i.e. the gap Diffie-Hellman assumption [18]. Although the Hanaoka-Imai-Ogawa-Watanabe scheme is very good introduction to starters who want to know how to respond to decryption queries without knowing a decryption key, but the security proof of their scheme does not well explain the technique for rejecting invalid ciphertexts.

   In contrast to the Hanaoka-Imai-Ogawa-Watanabe scheme, our scheme well explains how to check the validity of a ciphertext without any complicated computation while in the security proof of the Cramer-Shoup scheme, a determinant of a matrix with rank four has to be computed. By introducing the twin Diffie-Hellman assumption, it can be significantly simplified [5]. The reduction from

---

[1] For ℓ-bit security, the size of a group element is required to be at least 2ℓ-bit long, while the size of an output of TCR is required to be at least ℓ-bit long.

the DDH problem to the twin Diffie-Hellman problem needs the Boneh-Boyen technique [2], and if one can naturally understand this technique, the scheme in [5] is already easy-to-understand. However, it is not generally intuitive for starters and non-experts.

Hence, we consider that our scheme and its security proof are good help for understanding the essential mechanism of existing DDH-based schemes.

5 Bridging to the Cramer-Shoup Scheme

In this section, we show the relationship between the Cramer-Shoup scheme and our proposed scheme. Specifically, we demonstrate that it is possible to significantly shorten the ciphertext length of our scheme in a straightforward manner. Though the security proof becomes less intuitive, its essential mechanism is still the same as of the original one. Interestingly, the resulting scheme is very similar to the hash free variant of the Cramer-Shoup scheme which is mentioned in Sec. 5.3 in [7]. This implies that our scheme is a redundant version of the Cramer-Shoup scheme, and thus, the mechanisms for handling CCA-security under the DDH assumption are essentially common in these two schemes.

5.1 The Modified Scheme with Compressed Ciphertext

Here, we give a concrete construction of the modified version of our proposed scheme. Let $\mathbb{G}$ be a multiplicative group with prime order p, and $g \in \mathbb{G}$ be a generator. We assume that a group element of $\mathbb{G}$ is k-bit long where 1^k is the security parameter. Then, the construction is as follows:

Setup(1^k): The same as our scheme in Sec. 3.2.
Encapsulate(PK): Compute $(g^r, (U_i^r, \bar{U}_i^{\,r})_{1 \leq i \leq k})$ as our scheme in Sec. 3.2, and calculate

$$\psi = (g^r, \left(\prod_{i=1}^{k} U_i\right)^r, \left(\prod_{i=1}^{k} \bar{U}_i\right)^r),$$
$$K = Z^r.$$

The ciphertext is ψ. The corresponding session key is K.
Decapsulate(dk, ψ, PK): For a ciphertext $\psi = (C_0, C_1, C_2)$, choose $(u_i, \bar{u}_i)_{1 \leq i \leq k}$ as the same as our scheme in Sec. 3.2, and check whether $(C_0^{\sum_{i=1}^{k} u_i}, C_0^{\sum_{i=1}^{k} \bar{u}_i}) \stackrel{?}{=} (C_1, C_2)$. If not, output $\bot$. Otherwise, output $K = C_0^z$.

Theorem 2. *Let $\mathbb{G}$ be a multiplicative group with prime order p. Then, the above PKE scheme is $(\tau - o(\tau), \epsilon_{ddh} + 2q_D/p, q_D)$ CCA-secure assuming the (τ, ϵ_{ddh}) DDH assumption holds in $\mathbb{G}$.*

Proof. Assume we are given an adversary A which breaks CCA-security of the above scheme with running time τ, advantage ϵ, and q_D decryption queries. We use A to construct another adversary B which for a given DDH instance (g, Z, g^{r^*}, R), distinguishes whether R is Z^{r^*} or random group element T of $\mathbb{G}$. Define adversary B as follows:

1. For a given DDH instance (g, Z, g^{r^*}, R), B picks random $(d, (\alpha_i, a_i, b_i, c_i, e_i)_{1 \le i \le k}) \in \mathbb{Z}_p^{4k+1}$. Let v_i^* be i-th bit of $(g^{r^*})_2$ for $1 \le i \le k$.

2. B sets $(X_i, \bar{X}_i, Y_i, \bar{Y}_i) = (g^{a_i}, g^{b_i}, g^{\alpha_i} Z^{c_i}, (g^{\alpha_i} Z^{c_i})^d g^{e_i})$ if $v_i^* = 0$, or $(X_i, \bar{X}_i, Y_i, \bar{Y}_i) = (g^{\alpha_i} Z^{c_i}, (g^{\alpha_i} Z^{c_i})^d g^{e_i}, g^{a_i}, g^{b_i})$ if $v_i^* = 1$, for $i = 1, \ldots, k$. B inputs public key $PK = (\mathbb{G}, g, (X_i, \bar{X}_i, Y_i, \bar{Y}_i)_{1 \le i \le k}, Z)$, challenge ciphertext

$$\psi^* = (g^{r^*}, (g^{r^*})^{\sum_{i=1}^k a_i}, (g^{r^*})^{\sum_{i=1}^k b_i}),$$

and real or random key R to A.

3. When A makes decryption query $\psi = (C_0, C_1, C_2) \in \mathbb{G}^3$ (if a query is not in this form, then B simply rejects it), B determines a binary string $(C_0)_2 = (v_i)_{1 \le i \le k}$ and proceeds as follows:

(a) B checks whether

$$\left(\frac{C_1}{C_0^{\sum_{v_i^* = v_i} a_i}} \right)^d \cdot C_0^{\sum_{v_i^* \ne v_i} e_i + \sum_{v_i^* = v_i} b_i} \overset{?}{=} C_2. \tag{2}$$

If Eq. (2) does not hold, then B responds $\perp$.

(b) If Eq. (2) holds, then B computes $\sum_{v_i^* \ne v_i} c_i$, if it is 0, then B aborts. Otherwise, B computes

$$K' = \left(\frac{C_1}{C_0^{\sum_{v_i^* = v_i} a_i + \sum_{v_i^* \ne v_i} \alpha_i}} \right)^{\frac{1}{\sum_{v_i^* \ne v_i} c_i}},$$

and responds K' to A.

4. Finally, A outputs his guess b', and B outputs the same bit b' as his guess on R.

Let Win denote the event that A succeeds to guess b in IND-CCA game, Invalid denote the event that B fails to reject an invalid ciphertext, and Abort denote the event that A queries a ciphertext that $\sum_{v_i^* \ne v_i} c_i = 0$ and B aborts. Then, B's advantage in solving the DDH problem is estimated as follows:

$$\frac{1}{2} |Pr[\mathsf{B}(g, Z, g^{r^*}, Z^{r^*}) = 0] - Pr[\mathsf{B}(g, Z, g^{r^*}, T) = 0]|$$

$$\ge |Pr[\mathsf{Win} \wedge \overline{\mathsf{Invalid}} \wedge \overline{\mathsf{Abort}}] - \frac{1}{2}|$$

$$\geq |Pr[\mathsf{Win}] - Pr[\mathsf{Invalid}] - Pr[\mathsf{Abort}] - \frac{1}{2}|$$

$$\geq |Pr[\mathsf{Win}] - \frac{1}{2}| - Pr[\mathsf{Invalid}] - Pr[\mathsf{Abort}]$$

We can complete the proof by showing the lemmas below.

Lemma 2. $Pr[\mathsf{Invalid}] \leq q_D/p$.

Proof. Since there are at most q_D decryption queries, it is sufficient to prove that for one query, the probability that B fails to reject an invalid ciphertext is at most $1/p$.

Without loss of generality, for an invalid decryption query $\psi = (C_0, C_1, C_2)$, we can assume that for some r and $r'(\neq 0)$, $C_0 = g^r$ and $C_1 = \left(\prod_{i=1}^{k} U_i\right)^r \cdot g^{r'}$. Note that the left side of Eq. (2) is $\left(\prod_{i=1}^{k} \bar{U}_i\right)^r \cdot (g^{r'})^d$. However, since d is information theoretically hidden from A's view, and $\left(\prod_{i=1}^{k} \bar{U}_i\right)^r \cdot (g^{r'})^d$ takes p different values according to p different values of d, A can predict the value of $\left(\prod_{i=1}^{k} \bar{U}_i\right)^r \cdot (g^{r'})^d$ with at most probability $1/p$. This implies that A cannot submit an invalid ciphertext which satisfies equality of Eq. (2) with probability more than $1/p$.

Lemma 3. $Pr[\mathsf{Abort}] \leq q_D/p$.

Proof. Since there are at most q_D decryption queries, it is sufficient to prove that for one query, the probability that $\sum_{v_i^* \neq v_i} c_i = 0$ occurs is at most $1/p$.

Since each c_i is information theoretically hidden, so $\sum_{v_i^* \neq v_i} c_i$ is uniformly distributed over $\mathbb{Z}_p$ for any $(C_0)_2 \neq (g^{r^*})_2$ from the view of A. So A cannot submit a ciphertext such that $\sum_{v_i^* \neq v_i} c_i = 0$ holds with probability more than $1/p$.

5.2 Relation to the Cramer-Shoup Scheme

Here we discuss similarity between the Cramer-Shoup scheme and our proposed scheme. More specifically, we compare the structure of the hash free variant of the Cramer-Shoup (HF-CS) scheme (Sec. 5.3 in [7]) with the modified version of our scheme (Sec. 5.1 in this paper). We first review the HF-CS scheme[2]: Let $\mathbb{G}$ be a multiplicative group with prime order p, and g and h be generator of $\mathbb{G}$. We assume that a group element of $\mathbb{G}$ is k-bit long where 1^k is the security parameter. Then, the construction of the hash free variant of the Cramer-Shoup KEM is as follows:

Setup(1^k): Pick $dk = ((x_i, \bar{x}_i, y_i, \bar{y}_i)_{1 \leq i \leq 2k}, z) \in \mathbb{Z}_p^{8k+1}$, and compute $(X_i, Y_i) = (g^{x_i} h^{\bar{x}_i}, g^{y_i} h^{\bar{y}_i})$ and $Z = g^z$ for $i = 1, \ldots, 2k$. The decryption key is dk, and the public key is $PK = (\mathbb{G}, g, h, (X_i, Y_i)_{1 \leq i \leq 2k}, Z)$.

---

[2] The description of this scheme in this paper is different from that in [7]. However, they are essentially identical.

Encapsulate(PK): Pick a random $r \xleftarrow{R} \mathbb{Z}_p$, and compute

$$\psi = (g^r, h^r, \left(\prod_{i=1}^{2k} U_i\right)^r),$$

$$K = Z^r,$$

where $U_i = X_i$ if $v_i = 0$, or $U_i = Y_i$ if $v_i = 1$, v_i is i-th bit of $((g^r)_2||(h^r)_2)$. The ciphertext is ψ, the corresponding session key is K.

Decapsulate(dk, ψ, PK): For a ciphertext $\psi = (C_0, C_1, C_2)$, check whether

$$C_0^{\sum_{i=1}^{2k} u_i} \cdot C_1^{\sum_{i=1}^{2k} \bar{u}_i} \overset{?}{=} C_2,$$

where $(u_i, \bar{u}_i) = (x_i, \bar{x}_i)$ if $v_i = 0$, or $(u_i, \bar{u}_i) = (y_i, \bar{y}_i)$ if $v_i = 1$. If not, output $\bot$. Otherwise, output $K = C_0^z$.

As seen above, a ciphertext in the HF-CS scheme forms as $\psi = (g^r, h^r, \left(\prod_{i=1}^{2k} U_i\right)^r)$ while that in our scheme in Sec. 5.1 forms as $\psi = (g^r, \left(\prod_{i=1}^{k} U_i\right)^r, \left(\prod_{i=1}^{k} \bar{U}_i\right)^r)$. Furthermore, in the HF-CS scheme, the formula for checking validity of a ciphertext is $C_0^{\sum_{i=1}^{2k} u_i} \cdot C_1^{\sum_{i=1}^{2k} \bar{u}_i} \overset{?}{=} C_2$, and on the other hand, that in our scheme in Sec. 5.1 is $(C_0^{\sum_{i=1}^{k} u_i}, C_0^{\sum_{i=1}^{k} \bar{u}_i}) \overset{?}{=} (C_1, C_2)$. Therefore, we see that these two schemes are very similar to each other with only slight difference. This fact implies that the essential mechanism of the Cramer-Shoup scheme and our proposed scheme is considered common, and hence, our scheme would be helpful for understanding the existing DDH-based schemes.

Acknowledgement

The authors would like to thank Bagus Santoso, Yutaka Kawai and Yusuke Sakai for their helpful comments and suggestions. The authors also would like to thank anonymous reviewers for their invaluable comments.

References

1. Abe, M., Gennaro, R., Kurosawa, K., Shoup, V.: Tag-KEM/DEM: a new framework for hybrid encryption and a new analysis of Kurosawa-Desmedt KEM. In: Cramer, R. (ed.) EUROCRYPT 2005. LNCS, vol. 3494, pp. 128–146. Springer, Heidelberg (2005)
2. Boneh, D., Boyen, X.: Efficient selective-ID secure identity-based encryption without random oracles. In: Cachin, C., Camenisch, J.L. (eds.) EUROCRYPT 2004. LNCS, vol. 3027, pp. 223–238. Springer, Heidelberg (2004)
3. Boneh, D., Shparlinski, I.: On the unpredictability of bits of the elliptic curve Diffie-Hellman scheme. In: Kilian, J. (ed.) CRYPTO 2001. LNCS, vol. 2139, pp. 201–212. Springer, Heidelberg (2001)

4. Boneh, D., Venkatesan, R.: Hardness of computing the most significant bits of secret keys in Diffie-Hellman and related schemes. In: Koblitz, N. (ed.) CRYPTO 1996. LNCS, vol. 1109, pp. 129–142. Springer, Heidelberg (1996)
5. Cash, D., Kiltz, E., Shoup, V.: The twin Diffie-Hellman problem and applications. In: Smart, N.P. (ed.) EUROCRYPT 2008. LNCS, vol. 4965, pp. 127–145. Springer, Heidelberg (2008)
6. Cramer, R., Hofheinz, D., Kiltz, E.: A twist on the Naor-Yung paradigm and its application to efficient CCA-secure encryption from hard search problems. In: Micciancio, D. (ed.) TCC 2010. LNCS, vol. 5978, pp. 146–164. Springer, Heidelberg (2010)
7. Cramer, R., Shoup, V.: A practical public key cryptosystem provably secure against adaptive chosen ciphertext attack. In: Krawczyk, H. (ed.) CRYPTO 1998. LNCS, vol. 1462, pp. 13–25. Springer, Heidelberg (1998)
8. Dolev, D., Dwork, C., Naor, M.: Non-malleable cryptography. In: Proc. of STOC 1991, pp. 542–552 (1991)
9. Goldreich, O., Levin, L.A.: A hard-core predicate for all one-way functions. In: Proc. of STOC 1989, pp. 25–32 (1989)
10. Hanaoka, G., Imai, H., Ogawa, K., Watanabe, H.: Chosen ciphertext secure public key encryption with a simple structure. In: Matsuura, K., Fujisaki, E. (eds.) IWSEC 2008. LNCS, vol. 5312, pp. 20–33. Springer, Heidelberg (2008)
11. Hanaoka, G., Kurosawa, K.: Efficient chosen ciphertext secure public key encryption under the computational Diffie-Hellman assumption. In: Pieprzyk, J. (ed.) ASIACRYPT 2008. LNCS, vol. 5350, pp. 308–325. Springer, Heidelberg (2008)
12. Hofheinz, D., Kiltz, E.: Secure hybrid encryption from weakened key encapsulation. In: Menezes, A. (ed.) CRYPTO 2007. LNCS, vol. 4622, pp. 553–571. Springer, Heidelberg (2007)
13. Kurosawa, K., Desmed, Y.: A new paradigm of hybrid encryption scheme. In: Franklin, M. (ed.) CRYPTO 2004. LNCS, vol. 3152, pp. 426–442. Springer, Heidelberg (2004)
14. Kiltz, E., Mohassel, P., O'Neill, A.: Adaptive trapdoor functions and chosen-ciphertext security. In: Eurocrypt 2010. LNCS, vol. 6110, pp. 673–692. Springer, Heidelberg (2010)
15. Luby, M., Rackoff, C.: How to construct pseudorandom permutations from pseudorandom functions. SIAM J. Comput. 17(2), 373–386 (1988)
16. Myers, S., Shelat, A.: Bit encryption is complete. In: Proc. of FOCS 2009, pp. 607–616 (2009)
17. Naor, M., Yung, M.: Public-key cryptosystems provably secure against chosen ciphertext attacks. In: Proc. of STOC 1990, pp. 427–437 (1990)
18. Okamoto, T., Pointcheval, D.: The gap-problems: a new class of problems for the security of cryptographic schemes. In: Kim, K.-c. (ed.) PKC 2001. LNCS, vol. 1992, pp. 104–118. Springer, Heidelberg (2001)
19. Peikert, C., Waters, B.: Lossy trapdoor functions and their applications. In: Proc. of STOC 2008, pp. 187–196 (2008)
20. Rackoff, C., Simon, D.R.: Non-interactive zero-knowledge proof of knowledge and chosen ciphertext attack. In: Feigenbaum, J. (ed.) CRYPTO 1991. LNCS, vol. 576, pp. 433–444. Springer, Heidelberg (1992)

21. Rosen, A., Segev, G.: Chosen-ciphertext security via correlated products. In: Reingold, O. (ed.) TCC 2009. LNCS, vol. 5444, pp. 419–436. Springer, Heidelberg (2009)
22. Shoup, V.: Using hash functions as a hedge against chosen ciphertext attack. In: Preneel, B. (ed.) EUROCRYPT 2000. LNCS, vol. 1807, pp. 275–288. Springer, Heidelberg (2000)

A   Number Theoretic Assumptions

A.1   The Computational Diffie-Hellman Assumption

Let $\mathbb{G}$ be a multiplicative group with prime order p. Then, the *Computational Diffie-Hellman* (CDH) problem in $\mathbb{G}$ is stated as follows. Let A be an algorithm, and we say that A has advantage ϵ in solving the CDH problem in $\mathbb{G}$ if

$$\Pr[\mathsf{A}(g, Z, g^{r^\star}) = Z^{r^\star}] \geq \epsilon,$$

where the probability is over the random choice of generators g, Z in $\mathbb{G}$, the random choice of $r^\star$ in $\mathbb{Z}_p$, and the random bits consumed by A.

Definition 3. *If for all PPT A, A's advantage is negligible in security parameter 1^k, then we call the CDH assumption holds on $\mathbb{G}$.*

Occasionally we drop the τ and ϵ and refer to the CDH in $\mathbb{G}$.

A.2   The Hashed Diffie-Hellman Assumption

The *hashed Diffie-Hellman* (HDH) problem in $\mathbb{G}$ and function $h : \mathbb{G} \rightarrow \mathcal{K}$ is stated as follows. Let A be an algorithm, and we say that A has advantage ϵ in solving the HDH problem in $\mathbb{G}$ and h if

$$\frac{1}{2} \cdot |\Pr[\mathsf{A}(g, Z, g^{r^\star}, h(Z^{r^\star})) = 0] - \Pr[\mathsf{A}(g, Z, g^{r^\star}, T) = 0]| \geq \epsilon,$$

where the probability is over the random choice of generators g and Z in $\mathbb{G}$, the random choice of $r^\star$ in $\mathbb{Z}_p$, the random choice of $T \in \mathcal{K}$, and the random bits consumed by A.

Definition 4. *If for all PPT A, A's advantage is negligible in security parameter 1^k, then we call the HDH assumption holds on $\mathbb{G}$ and h.*

B   Cryptographic Tools

B.1   Target Collision Resistant Hash Functions

Let $\mathsf{TCR} : \mathcal{X} \rightarrow \mathcal{Y}$ be a hash function, A be an algorithm, and A's advantage $\mathsf{AdvTCR_A}$ be

$$\mathsf{AdvTCR_A} = \Pr[\mathsf{TCR}(x') = \mathsf{TCR}(x) \in \mathcal{Y} \wedge x' \neq x|\; x \xleftarrow{R} \mathcal{X};\; x' \xleftarrow{R} \mathsf{A}(x)].$$

Definition 5. We say that TCR is a (τ, ϵ) *target collision resistant hash function* if for all τ-time algorithm A, we have that $\mathsf{AdvTCR_A} < \epsilon$.

It is obvious that any injective mapping can be used as a perfectly secure target collision resistant hash function.

B.2   Data Encapsulation Mechanism

The Model. Let $\mathcal{K}$ denote the key space and $\mathcal{M}$ denote the plaintext space. A data encapsulation mechanism (DEM) scheme consists of the following two algorithms:

$\mathsf{E}(K, M)$ Takes as input a data encryption key $K \in \mathcal{K}$ and a plaintext $M \in \mathcal{M}$, and outputs a ciphertext ψ.

$\mathsf{D}(K, \psi)$ Takes as input a data encryption key $K \in \mathcal{K}$ and a ciphertext ψ, and outputs the plaintext $M \in \mathcal{M}$.

We require that if $\psi \leftarrow \mathsf{E}(K, M)$ then $\mathsf{D}(K, \psi) = M$.

Chosen-Ciphertext Security. CCA-security of a DEM is defined using the following game between an attack algorithm A and a challenger. Both the challenger and A are given 1^k as input.

Setup. The challenger chooses a data encryption key $K \in \{0, 1\}^k$.

Query I. Algorithm A adaptively issues decryption queries $\psi_1, \ldots, \psi_m$. For query ψ_i, the challenger responds with $\mathsf{D}(K, \psi_i)$.

Challenge. At some point, A submits a pair of plaintexts $(M_0, M_1) \in \mathcal{M}^2$. Then, the challenger picks a random $b \in \{0, 1\}$, runs algorithm E to obtain the challenge ciphertext $\psi^\star \leftarrow \mathsf{E}(K, M_b)$, and give $\psi^\star$ to A.

Query II. Algorithm A continues to adaptively issue decryption queries $\psi_{m+1}, \ldots, \psi_{q_D}$. For query $\psi_i (\neq \psi^\star)$, the challenger responds as **Query I**.

Guess. Algorithm A outputs its guess $b' \in \{0, 1\}$ for b and wins the game if $b = b'$.

Let $\mathsf{AdvDEM_A}$ denote the probability that A wins the game.

Definition 6. We say that a DEM is *CCA-secure* if for all PPT A who make a polynomial time of decryption queries, we have that $|\mathsf{AdvDEM_A} - 1/2|$ is negligible.

Identity Based Public Verifiable Signcryption Scheme

S. Sharmila Deva Selvi, S. Sree Vivek*, and C. Pandu Rangan*

Theoretical Computer Science Lab,
Department of Computer Science and Engineering,
Indian Institute of Technology Madras, India
{sharmila,svivek,prangan}@cse.iitm.ac.in

Abstract. Signcryption as a cryptographic primitive that offers both confidentiality and authentication simultaneously. Generally, in signcryption schemes, the message is hidden and thus the validity of the signcryption can be verified only after the unsigncryption process. Thus, a third party will not be able to verify whether the signcryption is valid or not. Signcryption schemes that allow any one to verify the validity of signcryption without the knowledge of the message are called public verifiable signcryption schemes. Third party verifiable signcryption schemes allow the receiver of a signcryption, to convince a third party that the signcryption is valid, by providing some additional information along with the signcryption. This information can be anything other than the receiver's private key and the verification may or may not require the exposure of the corresponding message.

This paper shows the security weaknesses in two such existing schemes namely [14] and [4]. The scheme in [14] is Public Key Infrastructure (PKI) based scheme and the scheme in [4] is an identity based scheme. More specifically, [14] is based on elliptic curve digital signature algorithm (ECDSA). We also, provide a new identity based signcryption scheme that provides both public verifiability and third party verification. We formally prove the security of the newly proposed scheme in the random oracle model.

Keywords: Signcryption, Public verifiable Signcryption, Cryptanalysis, Identity Based, Bilinear Pairing, Random Oracle Model.

1 Introduction

Secure communication through an insecure channel requires both confidentiality and authenticity as security goals. Encryption schemes are used to achieve confidentiality and digital signature schemes offer unforgeability. Signcryption scheme is a cryptographic primitive that provides both these properties together in an

---

* Work supported by Project No. CSE/05-06/076/DITX/CPAN on Protocols for Secure Communication and Computation sponsored by Department of Information Technology, Government of India.

S.-H. Heng and K. Kurosawa (Eds.): ProvSec 2010, LNCS 6402, pp. 244–260, 2010.

efficient way. Zheng, in [17] proposed the first digital signcryption scheme that offers both confidentiality and authentication in a single logical step with lower computational cost and communication overhead than sign then encrypt (StE) or encrypt then sign (EtS) approach. Since then, many signcryption schemes were proposed. Baek et al. [1] gave the formal security model for digital signcryption schemes and provided the security proof for Zheng's scheme [17] in the random oracle model.

Adi Shamir [11] introduced the concept of identity based cryptography and proposed the first identity based signature scheme. The idea of identity based cryptography is to enable a user to use any arbitrary string, that uniquely identifies him, as his public key. Identity based cryptography serves as an efficient alternative to Public Key Infrastructure (PKI) based systems. Digital signcryption in the identity based setting was first studied by Malone-Lee et al. [8]. Later, Libert et al. [7] pointed out that the scheme proposed by Malone-Lee [8] is not semantically secure, since the signature of the message is visible in the signcryption and thus cannot achieve CCA2 security. Following that many signcryption schemes were proposed in both PKI as well as identity based settings [10,2,9,13,15,3,4,6].

Normally, in a signcryption scheme, the message is hidden and thus the validity of the signcryption can be verified only after the unsigncryption process. Thus, a third party (who is unaware of the receiver's private key) will not be able to verify whether a signcryption is valid or not. Public verifiable signcryption scheme is well motivated in the following scenarios.

Secure e-mail: One of the main applications of signcryption scheme is secure e-mail systems. Public verifiable signcryption schemes are applicable in filtering out the spams in secure e-mail systems. The spam filter should be able to verify the authenticity of the signcrypted e-mail without knowing the message (i.e., check whether the signcryption is generated from the claimed sender or not). Here, if the signcryption does not satisfy the public verifiability, it can be considered as spam and can be filtered out.

Private Contract Signing: Moreover, in applications such as private contract signing, made between two parties, the receiver of the signcryption should be able to convince the third party that indeed the sender has signed the corresponding message hidden in the signcryption. In this case, the receiver should not reveal his secret key in order to convince the third party, instead he reveals the message and some information computable with his private key required for the signature verification.

In literature, signcryption schemes in which a third party can verify the validity of the signcryption without the knowledge of the hidden message, or without knowing the receiver private key are called third party verifiable signcryption schemes.

Related Work: To the best of out knowledge, Bao et al. [2] proposed the first public verifiable signcryption scheme in the PKI based setting. Following that, a number of schemes [14,16,12,5] were proposed in the PKI based setting.

However, the scheme in [2] did not withstand CCA2 attacks and it was shown in [12]. Chow et al. [4] proposed an identity based signcryption scheme that provides both public verifiability and forward security and to the best of our knowledge the scheme in [4] is the only identity based scheme providing public verifiability and third party verification.

Our Contribution: In this paper, we have upgraded the security model for public verifiable and third party verifiable identity based signcryption scheme by providing additional power to the adversary. The additional power the adversary gains is due to the access given to the third party verify oracle, which provides the information necessary for the third party verification. Next, we show that the scheme in [4] is not secure by demonstrating a CCA2 attack and a forgery on it. We show a CCA2 attack on the forward security of [14] in the next section and finally, we propose a new identity based signcryption scheme that offers both public verifiability and third party verification. We formally prove the security of the new scheme in the newly proposed improved security model. Our scheme offers forward secrecy in addition to confidentiality and authenticity.

2   Formal Model for Identity Based Signcryption Schemes with Public Verifiability

In this section, we give the generic framework for identity based signcryption scheme which supports both public verifiability and third party verification. We also give the formal security model for this scheme.

2.1   Generic Scheme

An identity based signcryption scheme consists of the following algorithms.

Setup(1^κ)**:** *Given the security parameter κ, the Private Key Generator (PKG) generates the master private key msk and public parameters Params. Params is made public while msk is kept secret by the PKG.*

Extract(ID_i)**:** *Given an identity ID_i as input, the PKG executes this algorithm to generate the private key D_i corresponding to ID_i and sends D_i to the user with identity ID_i through a secure channel.*

Signcrypt(m, ID_A, D_A, ID_B)**:** *A sender with identity ID_A and private key D_A in order to signcrypt a message m to a receiver whose identity is ID_B, runs this algorithm to generate the corresponding signcryption σ.*

Unsigncrypt$(\sigma, ID_A, ID_B, D_B)$**:** *On receiving the signcryption σ from sender with identity ID_A, receiver with identity ID_B and the private key D_B of the receiver, the receiver executes this algorithm to obtain the message m, if σ is a valid signcryption of m from ID_A to ID_B or "Invalid" indicating that the signcryption is not valid.*

Public-Verify(σ, ID_A, ID_B)**:** *This algorithm allows any third party to verify the authenticity of the signcryption σ without knowing the message used for the generation of the signcryption σ. It takes the signcryption σ, the sender identity*

ID_A and the receiver identity ID_B as input and outputs "Valid", if σ is a valid signcryption or "Invalid", otherwise.

TP-Verify(ϕ, ID_A, ID_B): This algorithm allows the receiver ID_B to prove the authenticity of the signcryption σ to third party by providing additional information needed (other than the private key D_B). This algorithm run by the third party takes as input ϕ (σ and additional information provided by ID_B), the sender identity ID_A and receiver identity ID_B, and outputs "Valid", if σ is a valid signcryption from ID_A to ID_B or "Invalid", otherwise. Here, it should be noted that $TP - Verify$ has two types. First type, is to prove the validity without exposing the message (similar to Public-Verify but receiver concern is involved) and the second type, is to prove that the signcryption is indeed a valid signcryption of the message (done by exposing the message being signcrypted).

2.2 Security Notions

Definition 1: *An ID-Based signcryption scheme is said to be indistinguishable against adaptive chosen ciphertext attacks (IND-IBSC-CCA2) if no polynomially bounded adversary has non-negligible advantage in the following game:*

Setup: The challenger $\mathcal{C}$ runs the *Setup* algorithm with a security parameter κ and obtains public parameters *Params* and the master private key *msk*. $\mathcal{C}$ sends *Params* to the adversary $\mathcal{A}$ and keeps *msk* secret.

Phase I: The adversary $\mathcal{A}$ performs a polynomially bounded number of queries to $\mathcal{C}$. The queries made by $\mathcal{A}$ may be adaptive, i.e. current query may depend on the answers to the previous queries. The various oracles and the queries made to these oracles are defined below:

- *Key extraction queries(Oracle $\mathcal{O}_{Extract}(ID_i)$):* $\mathcal{A}$ produces an identity ID_i and receives the private key D_i.
- *Signcryption queries(Oracle $\mathcal{O}_{Signcrypt}(m, ID_A, ID_B)$):* $\mathcal{A}$ produces two identities ID_A, ID_B and a plaintext m. $\mathcal{C}$ computes $D_A = \mathcal{O}_{Extract}(ID_A)$ and generates the signcryption σ of the message m using D_A following the signcryption protocol and sends σ to $\mathcal{A}$.
- *Unsigncryption queries(Oracle $\mathcal{O}_{Unsigncrypt}(\sigma, ID_A, ID_B)$):* $\mathcal{A}$ produces the sender identity ID_A, the receiver identity ID_B and the signcryption σ as input to this algorithm and requests the unsigncryption of σ. $\mathcal{C}$ generates the private key D_B and performs the unsigncryption of σ using D_B and sends the result to $\mathcal{A}$. The result of unsigncryption will be "Invalid" if σ is not a valid signcryption. It returns the message m if σ is a valid signcryption.
- *TP-Verify queries(Oracle $\mathcal{O}_{TP-Verify}(\sigma, ID_A, ID_B)$):* $\mathcal{A}$ submits the information ϕ, the sender identity ID_A and the receiver identity ID_B. $\mathcal{C}$ generates the private key D_B corresponding to ID_B, unsigncrypts σ using D_B and returns the information required for TP-verify corresponding to σ, if σ is a valid signcryption returns "Valid" if σ is a proper and correct signcryption and "Invalid" otherwise.

Challenge: $\mathcal{A}$ chooses two plaintexts, m_0 and m_1 of equal length, the sender identity $ID_\mathbb{S}$, the receiver identity $ID_\mathbb{R}$ and submits them to $\mathcal{C}$. However, $\mathcal{A}$

should not have queried the private key corresponding to $ID_{\mathbb{R}}$ in Phase I. $\mathcal{C}$ now chooses $\delta \in_R \{0, 1\}$ and computes $\sigma^* = \mathcal{O}_{Signcrypt}(m_\delta, ID_{\mathbb{S}}, ID_{\mathbb{R}})$ and sends σ^* to $\mathcal{A}$. (It is to be noted that the private key $D_{\mathbb{S}}$ corresponding to the sender $ID_{\mathbb{S}}$ can be queried by $\mathcal{A}$.)

Phase II: $\mathcal{A}$ is allowed to interact with $\mathcal{C}$ as in **Phase-I** with the following restrictions.

- $\mathcal{A}$ should not query the extract oracle for the private key corresponding to the receiver identity $ID_{\mathbb{R}}$.
- $\mathcal{A}$ should not query the unsigncrypt oracle with $(\sigma^*, ID_{\mathbb{S}}, ID_{\mathbb{R}})$ as input, i.e. a query of the form $\mathcal{O}_{Unsigncrypt}(\sigma^*, ID_{\mathbb{S}}, ID_{\mathbb{R}})$ is not allowed.

Guess: Finally, $\mathcal{A}$ produces a bit δ' and wins the game if $\delta' = \delta$.
The advantage of $\mathcal{A}$ in the above game is defined by

$$Adv(\mathcal{A}) = 2 \left| Pr \left[\delta' = \delta \right] - 1 \right| \ where \ Pr \left[\delta' = \delta \right]$$

denotes the probability that $\delta' = \delta$.

The confidentiality game described above deals with insider security since the adversary is given access to the private key of the sender $ID_{\mathbb{S}}$ used for the challenge phase.

Definition 2: *An ID-Based signcryption scheme is said to be existentially unforgeable against adaptive chosen message attacks (EUF-IBSC-CMA) if no polynomially bounded adversary has a non-negligible advantage in the following game.*
Setup: The challenger $\mathcal{C}$ runs the Setup algorithm with security parameter κ and obtains public parameters *Params* and the master private key *msk*. $\mathcal{C}$ sends *Params* to the adversary $\mathcal{A}$ and keeps *msk* secret.
Training Phase: The adversary $\mathcal{A}$ performs a polynomially bounded number of queries adaptively as in Phase I of confidentiality game (IND-IDSC-CCA).
Forgery: After a sufficient amount of training, $\mathcal{A}$ produces a signcryption $(\sigma, ID_{\mathbb{S}}, ID_{\mathbb{R}})$ to $\mathcal{C}$. Here, $\mathcal{A}$ should not have queried the private key of $ID_{\mathbb{S}}$ during the training phase and σ is not the output of signcrypt oracle with $(m, ID_{\mathbb{S}}, ID_{\mathbb{R}})$ as input $(m=\mathcal{O}_{Unsigncrypt}(\sigma, ID_{\mathbb{S}}, ID_{\mathbb{R}}))$. $\mathcal{A}$ wins the game, if $Unsigncrypt(\sigma, ID_{\mathbb{S}}, ID_{\mathbb{R}}, D_{\mathbb{R}})$ is valid. (It is to be noted that the private key $D_{\mathbb{R}}$ corresponding to the receiver $ID_{\mathbb{R}}$ can be queried by $\mathcal{A}$.)
The security model discussed above captures the notion of insider security since the adversary is provided access to the private key of receiver with identity $ID_{\mathbb{R}}$, used for generating the signcryption σ during the forgery phase.

3   Review and Attacks of the Signcryption Scheme in [4]

Chow et al. [4] have proposed the first identity based signcryption scheme which offers public verifiability. [4] claims to be insider secure during both confidentiality and unforgeability proof, which is the strongest notion of security for signcryption schemes. In this section, we review the identity based signcryption scheme proposed in [4] and demonstrate attacks on both CCA2 security as well as the existential unforgeability of the scheme. As the scheme was claimed to be insider secure we demonstrate the attack on confidentiality in the security model that captures insider security for signcryption schemes. However, the attack on unforgeability does not require the private key corresponding to the receiver associated with the forgery generated.

3.1   Review of Scheme in [4]

Let $\mathbb{G}_1, \mathbb{G}_2$ be two cyclic groups of prime order q and $\hat{e} : \mathbb{G}_1 \times \mathbb{G}_1 \to \mathbb{G}_2$ be the bilinear pairing. Let $\mathcal{H}_1 : \{0,1\}^{\bar{n}} \to \mathbb{G}_1, \mathcal{H}_2 : \mathbb{G}_2 \to \{0,1\}^{\bar{n}}$ and $\mathcal{H}_3 : \{0,1\}^{\bar{n}} \times \mathbb{G}_2 \to \mathbb{F}_q^*$ be three cryptographic hash functions. Let $(\mathcal{E}, \mathcal{D})$ be the encryption and decryption algorithms of a secure symmetric cipher which takes a plaintext / ciphertext of length n respectively, and also a key of length $\bar{n}$.

Setup(1^κ):

- $P \in_R \mathbb{G}_1$
- $s \in_R \mathbb{F}_q^*$
- $P_{Pub} = sP$
- $Params = \langle \mathbb{G}_1, \mathbb{G}_2, q, n, P, P_{pub}, \hat{e}(.,.), \mathcal{H}_1, \mathcal{H}_2, \mathcal{H}_3, (\mathcal{E}, \mathcal{D}) \rangle$

Extract(ID_A)

- $Q_A = \mathcal{H}_1(ID_A)$
- $S_A = s^{-1} Q_A$
- $D_A = s Q_A$

Signcrypt(m, ID_A, S_A, ID_B)

- $x \in_R \mathbb{F}_q^*$
- $X_A \leftarrow x Q_A$
- $k_1 = \hat{e}(X_A, P)$
- $k_2 = \mathcal{H}_2(\hat{e}(X_A, Q_B))$
- $c = \mathcal{E}_{k_2}(m)$
- $r = \mathcal{H}_3(c, k_1)$
- $S = (x - r) S_A$

- Signcryption $\sigma = \langle c, r, S \rangle$

Unsigncrypt(σ, ID_A, ID_B, D_B)

- $X_A' = r Q_A$
- $k_1' = \hat{e}(S, P_{pub}) \hat{e}(X_A', P)$
- $k_2' = \mathcal{H}_2(\hat{e}(S, D_B) \hat{e}(X_A', Q_B))$
- $m' = \mathcal{D}_{k_2'}(c)$
- $r' = \mathcal{H}_3(c, k_1')$
- Output $\sigma' = \langle k_2', m, \sigma \rangle$ if and only if $r = r'$ else, return "*Invalid*"

TP-Verify(σ', ID_A, ID_B)

- $k_1' = \hat{e}(S, P_{pub}) \hat{e}(X_A', P)$
- $r' = \mathcal{H}_3(c, k_1')$
- Accept σ if and only if $r = r'$
- Accept authenticity of m if and only if $m = \mathcal{D}_{k_2'}(c)$
- Return "*Valid*" if and only if the above two test holds, else return "*Invalid*"

3.2   Attack on Scheme in [4]

We show the attacks on [4] with respect to the confidentiality and unforgeability in this section.

Attack on Confidentiality: This scheme does not provide insider security during the confidentiality game due to the following fact, stated informally: During the confidentiality game, the attacker knows the private key corresponding to the sender identity used for generating the challenge signcryption. The attacker can make use of this information, alter the challenge signcryption in a meaningful manner and get the unsigncryption of the altered signcryption during the second phase (Phase-II) of interaction with the challenger during the confidentiality game. This reveals the message used for generation of challenge signcryption. The details of the attack follows:

- During the challenge phase the attacker $\mathcal{A}$ chooses two message (m_0, m_1) of equal length, the sender identity $ID_\mathbb{S}$ and the receiver identity $ID_\mathbb{R}$, and submits them to the challenger $\mathcal{C}$.
- $\mathcal{C}$ chooses a random bit $\delta \in \{0, 1\}$ and generates the signcryption $\sigma^* = \langle c^*, r^*, S^* \rangle = \mathcal{O}_{Signcrypt}(m_\delta, ID_\mathbb{S}, ID_\mathbb{R})$
- $\mathcal{C}$ issues σ^* as the challenge signcryption to $\mathcal{A}$.
- On receiving σ^*, $\mathcal{A}$ generates the signcryption $\widehat{\sigma} \neq \sigma^*$ by performing the following computations :
  - Let $ID_A \neq ID_\mathbb{S}$ be any user identity for which $\mathcal{A}$ knows the signcryption key S_A.
  - According to the definition of confidentiality with insider security, $\mathcal{A}$ also knows the signcryption key $S_\mathbb{S}$ of $ID_\mathbb{S}$
  - Set $\widehat{c} = c^*$, $\widehat{r} = r^*$
  - $\widehat{S} = S^* + r^* S_\mathbb{S} - r^* S_A = x^* S_\mathbb{S} - r^* S_A$. Here $r^* \in \sigma^*$ and $S^* \in \sigma^*$
  - $\widehat{\sigma}$ is the signcryption of m_δ from ID_A to $ID_\mathbb{R}$
- Now, $\mathcal{A}$ queries the unsigncryption oracle for the unsigncryption of $\widehat{\sigma}$ i.e. $\mathcal{O}_{Unsigncrypt}(\widehat{\sigma}, ID_A, ID_\mathbb{R})$

The unsigncryption of σ^* (the signcryption of m_δ from $ID_\mathbb{S}$ to $ID_\mathbb{R}$) and the unsigncryption of $\widehat{\sigma}$ (the signcryption from ID_A to $ID_\mathbb{R}$ derived from σ^*) yields the same output m_δ. This can be shown by the following :

$$
\begin{aligned}
\widehat{k}_1 &= \widehat{e}(\widehat{S}, P_{pub})\widehat{e}(\widehat{r}Q_A, P) \\
&= \widehat{e}(x^* S_\mathbb{S} - r^* S_A, P_{pub})\widehat{e}(\widehat{r}Q_A, P) \\
&= \widehat{e}(s^{-1}(x^* Q_\mathbb{S} - r^* Q_A), sP)\widehat{e}(\widehat{r}Q_A, P) \\
&= \widehat{e}(x^* Q_\mathbb{S} - r^* Q_A, P)\widehat{e}(\widehat{r}Q_A, P) \\
&= \widehat{e}(x^* Q_\mathbb{S}, P)\widehat{e}(r^* Q_A, P)^{-1}\widehat{e}(\widehat{r}Q_A, P) \\
&= \widehat{e}(x^* Q_\mathbb{S}, P) \\
&= k_1^*.
\end{aligned}
$$

$$
\begin{aligned}
\widehat{k}_2 &= \mathcal{H}_2(\widehat{e}(\widehat{S}, D_\mathbb{R})\widehat{e}(\widehat{r}Q_A, Q_\mathbb{R})) \\
&= \mathcal{H}_2(\widehat{e}(s^{-1}(x^* Q_\mathbb{S} - r^* Q_A), sQ_\mathbb{R}) \\
&\quad \widehat{e}(\widehat{r}Q_A, Q_\mathbb{R}))(\text{Since } \widehat{S} = x^* S_\mathbb{S} - r^* S_A) \\
&= \mathcal{H}_2(\widehat{e}(x^* Q_\mathbb{S} - r^* Q_A, Q_\mathbb{R})\widehat{e}(\widehat{r}Q_A, Q_\mathbb{R})) \\
&= \mathcal{H}_2(\widehat{e}(x^* Q_\mathbb{S}, Q_\mathbb{R})\widehat{e}(r^* Q_A, Q_\mathbb{R})^{-1} \\
&\quad \widehat{e}(\widehat{r}Q_A, Q_\mathbb{R})) \\
&= \mathcal{H}_2(\widehat{e}(x^* Q_\mathbb{S}, Q_\mathbb{R})) = k_2^*
\end{aligned}
$$

This clearly shows that, the key k_2^* of σ^* and $\widehat{k}_2$ of $\widehat{\sigma}$ are the same.

From this, it is clear that the value k_1^* of σ^* and $\widehat{k}_1$ of $\widehat{\sigma}$ are the same.

According to the computations done by $\mathcal{A}$ it is clear that $c^* = \widehat{c}$. When $c^* = \widehat{c}$, $k_1^* = \widehat{k}_1$ and $k_2^* = \widehat{k}_2$, we see that $r^* = \widehat{r}$. This clearly shows that irrespective of the modifications done to $\widehat{\sigma}$ with few components unaltered (sender $ID_\mathbb{S}$ of σ^* changed to sender ID_A of $\widehat{\sigma}$ and $S^* \neq \widehat{S}$), the unsigncryption of σ^* and $\widehat{\sigma}$ will output the same message. This allows $\mathcal{A}$ to know the message m_δ by making use of the unsigncrypt oracle during Phase-II of the confidentiality game by querying the unsigncryption of $\widehat{\sigma}$. Hence $\mathcal{C}$ will not be able to gain any advantage, if $\mathcal{A}$ responds with the correct $\delta' = \delta$.

Attack on Unforgeability: During the training phase of unforgeability game, $\mathcal{A}$ queries the signcrypt oracle for the signcryption of message $\hat{m}$ from sender $ID_\mathbb{S}$ to receiver ID_B. Here, it should be noted that $\mathcal{A}$ does not know the private key (both signcryption key and unsigncryption key) of $ID_\mathbb{S}$. Let this signcryption be $\sigma = \langle c, r, S \rangle$. Now, $\mathcal{A}$ submits $\sigma^* = \sigma$(i.e. $c^* = c, r^* = r$ and $S^* = S$) as forgery with $ID_\mathbb{S}$ as sender and $ID_\mathbb{R}$ as receiver to $\mathcal{C}$. σ^* is a valid signcryption of some message m^*. It should be noted that, even $\mathcal{A}$ is not aware of the message m^*. The correctness and validity of $\sigma^* = \langle c^*, r^*, S^* \rangle$(signcryption of m^* from sender $ID_\mathbb{S}$ to receiver $ID_\mathbb{R}$) is shown below:

$$
\begin{aligned}
k_1^* &= \hat{e}(S^*, P_{pub})\hat{e}(r^*Q_\mathbb{S}, P) \\
&= \hat{e}(S, P_{pub})\hat{e}(rQ_\mathbb{S}, P) \\
&\qquad \text{(since } S^* = S) \\
&= \hat{e}((x - r)S_\mathbb{S}, sP)\hat{e}(rQ_\mathbb{S}, P) \\
&= \hat{e}((x - r)s^{-1}Q_\mathbb{S}, sP)\hat{e}(rQ_\mathbb{S}, P) \\
&= \hat{e}((x - r)Q_\mathbb{S}, P)\hat{e}(rQ_\mathbb{S}, P) \\
&= \hat{e}(xQ_\mathbb{S}, P)\hat{e}(rQ_\mathbb{S}, P)^{-1}\hat{e}(rQ_\mathbb{S}, P) \\
&= \hat{e}(xQ_\mathbb{S}, P) \\
&= k_1
\end{aligned}
$$

(Therefore, k_1^* of $\sigma^* = k_1$ of σ).

$$
\begin{aligned}
k_2^* &= \mathcal{H}_2(\hat{e}(S^*, D_\mathbb{R})\hat{e}(r^*Q_\mathbb{S}, Q_\mathbb{R})) \\
&= \mathcal{H}_2(\hat{e}(S, D_\mathbb{R})\hat{e}(rQ_\mathbb{S}, Q_\mathbb{R})) \\
&\qquad \text{(Since } S^* = S) \\
&= \mathcal{H}_2(\hat{e}((x - r)S_\mathbb{S}, sQ_\mathbb{R})\hat{e}(rQ_\mathbb{S}, Q_\mathbb{R})) \\
&= \mathcal{H}_2(\hat{e}((x - r)s^{-1}Q_\mathbb{S}, sQ_\mathbb{R})\hat{e}(rQ_\mathbb{S}, Q_\mathbb{R})) \\
&= \mathcal{H}_2(\hat{e}((x - r)Q_\mathbb{S}, Q_\mathbb{R})\hat{e}(rQ_\mathbb{S}, Q_\mathbb{R})) \\
&= \mathcal{H}_2(\hat{e}(xQ_\mathbb{S}, Q_\mathbb{R})\hat{e}(rQ_\mathbb{S}, Q_\mathbb{R})^{-1}\hat{e}(rQ_\mathbb{S}, Q_\mathbb{R})) \\
&= \mathcal{H}_2(\hat{e}(xQ_\mathbb{S}, Q_\mathbb{R})) \\
&\neq k_2 \text{ (since } k_2 = \mathcal{H}_2(\hat{e}(xQ_\mathbb{S}, Q_B)))
\end{aligned}
$$

(Therefore, k_2^* of $\sigma^* \neq k_2$ of σ).

From the above computation it is clear that $k_1^* = k_1$ and $c^* = c$ (from the definition of σ^*). Hence the check $r^* = r$ holds. Since $k_2 \neq k_2^*$, c^* will get decrypted to some message m^* and not to message m (used for the generation of σ). Now, this clearly shows that the $\mathcal{C}$ will accept σ^* as a valid signcryption of m^* from sender $ID_\mathbb{S}$ to receiver $ID_\mathbb{R}$. Also, it does not violate the definition of unforgeability game that the forgery generated by $\mathcal{A}$ (σ^*) is not the output of signcrypt oracle for message m^* with $ID_\mathbb{S}$ as sender and $ID_\mathbb{R}$ as receiver. Thus, $\mathcal{A}$ can successfully forge the signcryption on some message m^* (not known to $\mathcal{A}$) without doing any computation or breaking any hard problem assumption.

4   Review and Attack of Signcryption Scheme in [14]

Tso et al. in [14] proposed a PKI based signcryption scheme that offers forward security and public verifiability. The scheme offers public verifiability, in the sense that, a receiver can prove the authenticity of the signcryption from a sender by providing some additional information other than his private key and the message being signcrypted. They have formally proved the confidentiality and unforgeability, and informally argued that their schemes offers forward secrecy, even if the additional information required for third party verification and private key of the sender are known to the adversary. We have reviewed the scheme in [14] and showed that the scheme does not provide confidentiality when the private key of sender and the information required for third party verification are known to the adversary.

4.1   Review of the Scheme[14]

Public Parameters(κ):

- q: a large prime $> 2^{160}$.
- $\mathbb{F}_q$: finite field.
- $\mathbb{E}(\mathbb{F}_q)$: Elliptic curve defined over $\mathbb{F}_q$.
- P: a point on $\mathbb{E}(\mathbb{F}_q)$, $|P| = n$.
- $\mathcal{H}$: a cryptographic one-way hash function.
- $\mathcal{T}$: a secure hash function.
- $bind_{A,B}$: concatenation of identities of A and B.
- $PointComp()$: point compress function.
- $PointDecomp()$: point decompress function.
- $(\mathcal{E}, \mathcal{D})$: the encryption and decryption algorithms of a symmetric key cryptosystem (CPA secure).
- $params = \langle q, P, n, (\mathcal{E}, \mathcal{D}), \mathcal{H}, \mathcal{T} \rangle$

User Key:

- A: Sender.
- B: receiver.
- x_A: private key of sender A.
- x_B: private key of receiver B.
- Y_A: public key of sender A ($Y_A = x_A P$).
- Y_B: public key receiver B. ($Y_B = x_B P$).

Signcrypt(m, Y_A, x_A, Y_B)

- $k \in_R \{1, \ldots, (n-1)\}$.
- $R = kP = (\hat{x}_1, \hat{y}_1)$.
- $(\hat{x}_1, \alpha_1) = PointComp(\mathbb{E}(\mathbb{F}_q), R)$.

- $r = \hat{x}_1 \bmod n$. If $r = 0$ goto the first step.
- $K = kY_B = (\hat{x}_2, \hat{y}_2)$.
- $\alpha_2 = \mathcal{H}(\hat{x}_2)$.
- $(\alpha_e, u) = \mathcal{T}(\alpha_2)$, where $u \in \{1, \ldots, (n-1)\}$.
- $U = uR$.
- $\hat{c} = \mathcal{E}_{\alpha_e}(m)$ and $c = \hat{c} \| \alpha_1$.
- $h = \mathcal{H}(c \| bind_{A,B}, \hat{x}_1 \| U)$.
- $v = (ku)^{-1}(h + rx_A) \bmod n$.
- Output $\sigma = \langle c, \hat{x}_1, v \rangle$

Unsigncrypt(σ, Y_A, Y_B, x_B)

- $R' = PointDecomp(\mathbb{E}(\mathbb{F}_q), \hat{x}_1, \alpha_1)$.
- $K' = x_B R = (\hat{x}_2', \hat{y}_2')$ and $\alpha_2' = \mathcal{H}(\hat{x}_2')$.
- $(\alpha_e', u') = \mathcal{T}(\alpha_2')$.
- $U' = u'R$ and $h' = \mathcal{H}(c \| bind_{A,B} \| \hat{x}_1 \| U')$.
- $r' = \hat{x}_1 \bmod n$.
- $e_1' = h'/v \bmod n$ and $e_1 = e_1'(u')^{-1}$.
- $e_2' = r'/v \bmod n$ and $e_1 = e_2'(u')^{-1}$.
- $\hat{R} = e_1 P + e_2 Y_A = (\hat{x}_1', \hat{y}_1')$.
- Accept σ iff $\hat{x}_1 = \hat{x}_1'$, otherwise, output "*Invalid*"
- Output $m' = \mathcal{D}_{\alpha_e'}(\hat{c})$.

Public-Verify(σ, h, Y_A, Y_B)

- $\bar{r} = \hat{x}_1 \bmod n$.
- $\bar{e}_1 = h/v \bmod n$ and $\bar{e}_2 = \bar{r}/v \bmod n$.
- $\bar{U} = \bar{e}_1 P + \bar{e}_2 Y_A$.
- Accept and output "*Valid* iff $h = \mathcal{H}(c \| bind_{A,B} \| \hat{x}_1 \| \bar{U})$. Otherwise, output "*Invalid*"

4.2   Attack on the Scheme [14]

In [14], Tso et al. have proposed a signcryption scheme which offers non-repudiation, public verifiability and forward security in addition to the security properties provided by the signcryption primitive. The forward secrecy property of the scheme is not formally proved in [14]. Instead, it was informally stated that the signcryption generated between sender $\mathbb{S}$ with public key $Y_{\mathbb{S}}$ and receiver $\mathbb{R}$ with public key $Y_{\mathbb{R}}$ is confidential even if the private key $(x_{\mathbb{S}})$ of $\mathbb{S}$ is compromised (known to the adversary). This is equivalent to the insider security notion of confidentiality game in signcryption. We show that, the scheme in [14] does not provide confidentiality when sender private key is compromised.

- Let (m_0, m_1) be the two messages chosen by the adversary $\mathcal{A}$ and, $\mathbb{S}$ be the sender and $\mathbb{R}$ be the receiver chosen by adversary during the challenge phase.
- Let σ^* be the challenge signcryption generated by the challenger $\mathcal{C}$ on message m_δ (where $\delta \in \{0,1\}$) from sender $\mathbb{S}$ to receiver $\mathbb{R}$.
- Now, $\mathcal{A}$ cooks up a signcryption $\tilde{\sigma}$ from σ^* on message m_b (chosen by $\mathcal{C}$ for generation of σ^*) from sender C to receiver $\mathbb{R}$ as follows :
  - Obtain h^* from $\mathcal{C}$ by requesting third party signature verification (as mentioned in their discussion).
  - Computes $(k^*u^*) = (v^{*-1}(r^* + h^*x_{\mathbb{S}}))$.
  - Computes $\check{U} = k^*u^*P$.
  - Computes $\tilde{h} = \mathcal{H}(c\|bind_{C,\mathbb{S}}\|\hat{x}_1^*\|\check{U})$
  - Computes $\tilde{v} = (k^*u^*)^{-1}(r^* + \tilde{h}x_C)$
  - Sets $\tilde{c} = c^*$ and $\hat{x}_1' = \hat{x}_1^*$
- $\mathcal{A}$ now submits $\tilde{\sigma} = \langle \tilde{c}, \hat{x}_1', \tilde{v} \rangle$ to the unsigncrypt oracle as if $\tilde{\sigma}$ is a signcryption from sender C to receiver $\mathbb{R}$ during Phase-II. It should be noted that unsigncryption of $\tilde{\sigma}$ will output the message m_δ(used for generation of σ^*) and it will pass the signature verification.

5 Identity Based Signcryption Scheme with Public Verifiability(IDPVS)

In this section, we propose a new identity based signcryption that offers public verifiability, third party verification (proving the binding of message to the signcryption with the help of additional information provided by the receiver) and forward security. We have formally proved the security of our scheme in the newly proposed security model. Our security model captures insider notion for the security of signcryption schemes.

Let $\mathbb{G}_1$, $\mathbb{G}_2$ be two cyclic groups of prime order q and $\hat{e} : \mathbb{G}_1 \times \mathbb{G}_1 \to \mathbb{G}_2$ be a bilinear map. Let $\mathcal{M}$ be the message space and $\mathfrak{I}$ be the ciphertext space and $\mathcal{H}_i$ (i=1 to 4) be four cryptographic hash functions.

5.1 IDPVS Scheme

Setup(1^κ):

- $P \in_R \mathbb{G}_1$
- $s \in_R \mathbb{Z}_q^*$
- $P_{pub} = sP$
- $(\mathcal{E}, \mathcal{D})\rangle$ be the CPA secure symmetric key cipher.

- $\mathcal{H}_1 : \{0,1\}^* \to \mathbb{G}_1$.
- $\mathcal{H}_2 : \mathbb{G}_2 \to \{0,1\}^{|\mathfrak{I}|}$.
- $\mathcal{H}_3 : \{0,1\}^{|\mathfrak{I}|} \times \mathbb{G}_1^3 \to \mathbb{G}_1$.
- $\mathcal{H}_4 : \{0,1\}^{|\mathcal{M}|} \times \mathbb{G}_1 \times \mathbb{G}_2 \times \mathbb{G}_1^2 \to \{0,1\}^{\hat{n}}$.
- $Params = \langle \mathbb{G}_1, \mathbb{G}_2, q, n, P,$
  $P_{pub}, \hat{e}(.,.), (\mathcal{E}, \mathcal{D}), \mathcal{H}_1, \mathcal{H}_2, \mathcal{H}_3, \mathcal{H}_4 \rangle$

Extract(ID_A)

- $Q_A = \mathcal{H}_1(ID_A)$
- $D_A = sQ_A$

Signcrypt(m, ID_A, D_A, ID_B)

- $x \in_R \mathbb{Z}_q^*$
- $U = xP$
- $\hat{\alpha} = \hat{e}(P_{pub}, Q_B)^x$
- $\alpha_2 = \mathcal{H}_2(\hat{\alpha})$
- $r = \mathcal{H}_4(m, \hat{\alpha}, U, Q_A, Q_B)$
- $c = \mathcal{E}_{\alpha_2}(m\|r)$
- $R = \mathcal{H}_3(c, U, Q_A, Q_B)$
- $V = xR + D_A$
- Signcryption $\sigma = \langle U, V, c \rangle$

Public-Verify(σ, ID_A, ID_B)

- $\bar{R} = \mathcal{H}_3(c, U, Q_A, Q_B)$
- If $\hat{e}(V, P) = \hat{e}(U, \bar{R})\,\hat{e}(Q_A, P_{pub})$, then return "$Valid$". Otherwise, return "$Invalid$"

Unsigncrypt$(\sigma, ID_A, ID_B, D_B)$

- If Public-Verify$(\sigma, ID_A, ID_B) \neq$ "$Valid$", output "$Invalid$"
- $\hat{\alpha}' = \hat{e}(U, D_B)$
- $\alpha_2' = \mathcal{H}_2(\hat{\alpha}')$
- $m'\|r' = \mathcal{D}_{\alpha_2'}(c)$
- Output $\phi = \langle m', r', \hat{\alpha}', \sigma \rangle$ iff $r' = \mathcal{H}_4(m', \hat{\alpha}', U, Q_A, Q_B)$ else, return "$Invalid$"

TP-Verify(ϕ, ID_A, ID_B)

- If Public-Verify$(\sigma, ID_A, ID_B) \neq$ "$Valid$", output "$Invalid$"
- $\bar{\alpha}_2 = \mathcal{H}_2(\hat{\alpha}')$
- $\bar{m}\|\bar{r} = \mathcal{D}_{\bar{\alpha}_2}(c)$
- Accept σ and output "$Valid$" iff $\bar{r} = \mathcal{H}_4(\bar{m}, \hat{\alpha}', U, Q_A, Q_B)$ and $\bar{r} = r'$. Otherwise, output "$Invalid$"

Proof of Correctness of IDPVS: The correctness of signature verification and the consistency of signcrypt and unsigncrypt algorithm are shown below:

Correctness of signature verification:

$$\begin{aligned}
\text{LHS} = \hat{e}(V, P) &= \hat{e}(xR + D_A, P) \\
&= \hat{e}(xR, P)\hat{e}(D_A, P) \\
&= \hat{e}(R, P)^x \hat{e}(sQ_A, P) \\
&= \hat{e}(\bar{R}, U)Q_A, \hat{P}_{pub} \\
&= \text{RHS}
\end{aligned}$$

Correctness of $\hat{\alpha}'$:

$$\begin{aligned}
\hat{\alpha}' = \hat{e}(U, D_B) &= \hat{e}(xP, sQ_B) \\
&= \hat{e}(P_{pub}, Q_B)^x = \hat{\alpha}
\end{aligned}$$

(Therefore, $\hat{\alpha}'$ of $Unsigncrypt$ is same as $\hat{\alpha}$ of $Signcrypt$).

5.2   Security Analysis of IDPVS

Proof for Unforgeability of IDPVS Scheme

Theorem 1. *If there exists an adversary $\mathcal{A}$ who can break the EUF-CMA$_{IDPVS}$ security of IDPVS scheme with advantage ϵ then there exists another algorithm which can break the CDHP with advantage $\epsilon' \geq \epsilon$.*

Proof: The interaction between $\mathcal{A}$ and $\mathcal{C}$ can be viewed as a game given in section 2. Assume that the challenger $\mathcal{C}$ is provided with the CDHP instance $P, \tilde{a}P, \tilde{b}P$ from $\mathbb{G}_1$ and is supposed to generate the solution $\tilde{a}\tilde{b}P$. Let $\mathcal{A}$ be an adversary who is capable of breaking the $EUF - CMA$ security of $IDPVS$ scheme in polynomial time with advantage ϵ. $\mathcal{C}$ makes use of $\mathcal{A}$ to break the CDHP instance with a non-negligible advantage ϵ'.

Setup: For having the game with $\mathcal{A}$, $\mathcal{C}$ cooks up the system parameters as follows :

- Sets $\mathbb{G}_1$, $\mathbb{G}_2$ as the underlying group, P as the generator of $\mathbb{G}_1$
- Sets $P_{pub} = \tilde{a}P$.
- Publishes $\langle \mathbb{G}_1, \mathbb{G}_2, q, P, P_{pub} \rangle$.

$\mathcal{C}$ also maintains lists $\mathcal{L}_1, \mathcal{L}_2, \mathcal{L}_3, \mathcal{L}_4, \mathcal{L}_{Sign}$ consistency in giving the responses to the queries made by $\mathcal{A}$ to various oracles. The format of various lists maintained by $\mathcal{C}$ are :

- $\mathcal{L}_1 = \langle i, q_i, Q_i \rangle = \langle Ind, \mathbb{Z}_q^*, \mathbb{G}_1 \rangle$. Here $Ind = \{1, \ldots, q_{H_1}\}$ and q_{H_1} is the maximum number of queries allowed to $\mathcal{O}_{\mathcal{H}_1}$ oracle.
- $\mathcal{L}_2 = \langle \hat{\alpha}, \alpha_2 \rangle = \langle \mathbb{Z}_q^*, \mathbb{Z}_q^* \rangle$.
- $\mathcal{L}_3 = \langle c, U, Q_A, Q_B, \hat{r}, R \rangle = \langle \{0,1\}^{|c|}, \mathbb{G}_1, \mathbb{G}_1, \mathbb{Z}_q^* \mathbb{G}_1 \rangle$.
- $\mathcal{L}_4 = \langle m, U, \hat{\alpha}, Q_A, Q_B \rangle = \langle \{0,1\}^{|m|}, \mathbb{G}_1, \mathbb{G}_2, \mathbb{G}_1, \mathbb{G}_1 \rangle$.

Training Phase: During training phase, the adversary $\mathcal{A}$ is allowed to access the various oracles provided by $\mathcal{C}$. $\mathcal{A}$ can get sufficient training before generating the forgery. The various oracles provided by $\mathcal{C}$ to $\mathcal{A}$ during training are as follows:

- **Hash Oracle Queries:**
  - $\mathcal{H}_1$ **Oracle Queries** ($\mathcal{O}_{\mathcal{H}_1}(ID_i)$)**:** When this oracle is queried with ID_i as input by $\mathcal{A}$, $\mathcal{C}$ responds as follows:
    * If $i = \gamma$, Sets $Q_i = \tilde{b}P$, stores $\langle i,' -', Q_i \rangle$ in list $\mathcal{L}_1$.
    * If $i \neq \gamma$, Picks a new $q_i \in_R \mathbb{Z}_q^*$, stores $\langle i, q_i, Q_i \rangle$ in list $\mathcal{L}_1$

    Now, returns Q_i to $\mathcal{A}$.
  - $\mathcal{H}_2$ **Oracle Queries**($\mathcal{O}_{\mathcal{H}_2}(\hat{\alpha})$)**:** When $\mathcal{A}$ makes a query with input $(\hat{\alpha})$, $\mathcal{C}$ performs the following:
    * If $\langle \hat{\alpha}, \alpha_2 \rangle$ is available in list $\mathcal{L}_2$, then $\mathcal{C}$ retrieves α_2 from $\mathcal{L}_2$.
    * Else, picks a new random $\alpha_2 \in \mathbb{Z}_q^*$, stores the tuple $\langle \hat{\alpha}, \alpha_2 \rangle$ in list $\mathcal{L}_2$.

    Then, $\mathcal{C}$ returns α_2 to $\mathcal{A}$
  - $\mathcal{H}_3$ **Oracle Queries**($\mathcal{O}_{\mathcal{H}_3}(c, U, Q_A, Q_B)$)**:** When $\mathcal{A}$ queries the $\mathcal{O}_{\mathcal{H}_3}$ oracle with input of the form (c, U, Q_A, Q_B), $\mathcal{C}$ responds as follows :
    * If $\langle c, U, Q_A, Q_B, R \rangle$ is available in list $\mathcal{L}_3$, then $\mathcal{C}$ retrieves R corresponding to the input from list $\mathcal{L}_3$.
    * Else,
      · If $B \neq \gamma$, $\mathcal{C}$ picks a new random $\hat{r} \in \mathbb{Z}_q^*$ and sets $R = \hat{r}P$.
      · Otherwise, If $B = \gamma$, $\mathcal{C}$ randomly picks a new $\hat{r} \in_R \mathbb{Z}_q^*$ and sets $R = \hat{r}Q_B$.
      · $\mathcal{C}$ stores the tuple $\langle c, U, Q_A, Q_B, \hat{r}, R \rangle$ in list $\mathcal{L}_3$.

    Challenger $\mathcal{C}$ returns R to $\mathcal{A}$.
  - $\mathcal{H}_4$ **Oracle Queries**($\mathcal{O}_{\mathcal{H}_4}(m, U, \hat{\alpha}, Q_A, Q_B)$)**:** When $\mathcal{A}$ queries the $\mathcal{O}_{\mathcal{H}_4}$ oracle with input of the form $(m, U, \hat{\alpha}, Q_A, Q_B)$, $\mathcal{C}$ responds as follows :
    * If the tuple $\langle m, U, \hat{\alpha}, Q_A, Q_B, r \rangle$ corresponding to input is available in list $\mathcal{L}_4$, $\mathcal{C}$ retrieves r from $\mathcal{L}_4$.
    * Otherwise, $\mathcal{C}$ picks a new random $r \in_R \mathbb{Z}_q^*$ and stores the tuple $\langle m, U, \hat{\alpha}, Q_A, Q_B, r \rangle$ in $\mathcal{L}_4$.

    $\mathcal{C}$ outputs r to $\mathcal{A}$.

- **Signcrypt Oracle Queries($\mathcal{O}_{Signcrypt}(m, ID_A, ID_B)$):** When a query is made by $\mathcal{A}$ with message m, sender ID_A, receiver ID_B as input to this oracle, $\mathcal{C}$ will generate the response as follows :
  - If $A \neq \gamma$, $\mathcal{C}$ knows the private key D_A of sender A and hence generates the signcryption σ by using the signcrypt protocol.
  - If $A = \gamma$, $\mathcal{C}$ generate the signcryption σ by doing the following computations:
    * Picks $\hat{r}, x \in_R \mathbb{Z}_q^*$.
    * Sets $U = (xP - \hat{r}^{-1}Q_A)$
    * Sets $\alpha_2 = \mathcal{O}_{\mathcal{H}_2}(\hat{\alpha} = \hat{e}(U, D_B))$ and $r = \mathcal{O}_{\mathcal{H}_4}(m, U, \hat{\alpha}, Q_A, Q_B)$.
    * Computes $c = \mathcal{E}_{\alpha_2}(m\|r)$.
    * Sets $R = \hat{r}P_{pub}$ and $V = \hat{r}xP_{pub}$ and stores $\langle c, U, Q_A, Q_B, \hat{r}, R \rangle$ to list $\mathcal{L}_3$. Here it should be noted that if a similar entry exists in $\mathcal{L}_3$, repeat the procedure by choosing different $\hat{r}$.
    * correctness of V can be shown by :

$$\begin{aligned} RHS &= \hat{e}(R, U)\hat{e}(Q_A, P_{pub}) \\ &= \hat{e}(\hat{r}P_{pub}, (xP - \hat{r}^{-1}Q_A))\hat{e}(Q_A, P_{pub}) \\ &= \hat{e}(\hat{r}P_{pub}, xP)\hat{e}(\hat{r}P_{pub}, \hat{r}^{-1}Q_A))^{-1}\hat{e}(Q_A, P_{pub}) \\ &= \hat{e}(\hat{r}xP_{pub}, P)\hat{e}(P_{pub}, Q_A))^{-1}\hat{e}(Q_A, P_{pub}) \\ &= \hat{e}(\hat{r}xP_{pub}, P) \\ &= \hat{e}(V, P) = LHS \end{aligned}$$

    From this it is clear that the signcryption $\sigma = \langle c, U, V \rangle$ will pass the verification test of V.

- **Unsigncrypt Oracle Queries($\mathcal{O}_{Unsigncrypt}(\sigma, ID_A, ID_B)$):** For an unsigncrypt query made to this oracle by $\mathcal{A}$, $\mathcal{C}$ does the following computations :
  - If $B \neq \gamma$, $\mathcal{C}$ knows the private key D_B of ID_B and can unsigncrypt σ using the computations in $Unsigncrypt$ algorithm and returns the corresponding output.
  - Otherwise, $\mathcal{C}$ does the following :
    * Here, $\mathcal{C}$ knows the private key D_A corresponding to ID_A (sender).
    * If $Public-Verify(\sigma, ID_A, ID_B) = $ "$Invalid$" return "$Invalid$", Else, Proceed with the next step.
    * Performs $R = \mathcal{O}_{\mathcal{H}_3}(c, U, Q_A, Q_B)$ and retrieves the corresponding $\hat{r}$ from list $\mathcal{L}_3$.
    * Checks $\hat{e}(U, Q_B) \stackrel{?}{=} \hat{e}(\hat{r}^{-1}R, P)$. If not, returns "$Invalid$". Else, proceeds with the next step.
    * Computes $\hat{\alpha}' = \hat{e}(\hat{r}^{-1}R, P_{pub})$ and $\alpha_2' = \mathcal{O}_{\mathcal{H}_2}(\hat{\alpha}')$.
    * Retrieves $(m'\|r') = \mathcal{D}_{\alpha_2'}(c)$.
    * If $r' = \mathcal{O}_{\mathcal{H}_4}(m', U, \hat{\alpha}', Q_A, Q_B)$, then returns m'.
    * Otherwise, returns "$Invalid$"

- **TP-Verify Oracle Queries($\mathcal{O}_{TP-Verify}(\sigma, ID_A, ID_B)$):** When $\mathcal{C}$ receives a query from $\mathcal{A}$ with σ as input, $\mathcal{C}$ performs the following :
  - If $B \neq \gamma$, knows the private key D_B of ID_B and can unsigncrypt σ using the computations in $Unsigncrypt$ algorithm and returns ϕ if σ is valid, else, returns "$Invalid$"

- if $B = \gamma$, $\mathcal{C}$ does the computations as given in $\mathcal{O}_{Unsigncrypt}$ oracle and returns $\phi = \langle \sigma, m', \hat{\alpha}', Q_A, Q_B \rangle$ if σ is valid, else, returns *"Invalid"*

Forgery Phase: After getting sufficient training, $\mathcal{A}$ submits the signcryption $\langle \sigma^*, ID_{\mathbb{S}}, ID_{\mathbb{R}} \rangle$. If $\mathbb{S} = \gamma$ and σ^* is valid, $\mathcal{C}$ does the following:

- Retrieves $\hat{r}$ corresponding to $(c, U, Q_{\mathbb{S}}, Q_{\mathbb{R}})$ from list $\mathcal{L}_3$.
- Computes $D_{\mathbb{S}} = V - \hat{r}U$.
- The computation $V - \hat{r}U$ gives the private key $D_{\mathbb{S}}$ corresponding to $ID_{\mathbb{S}}$. This can be shown as follows:

$$
\begin{aligned}
V - \hat{r}U &= xR + D_{\mathbb{S}} - \hat{r}U \\
&= x\hat{r}P + D_{\mathbb{S}} - \hat{r}U \\
&= \hat{r}U + D_{\mathbb{S}} - \hat{r}U \\
&= D_{\mathbb{S}}
\end{aligned}
$$

- Since $\mathbb{S} = \gamma$, $D_{\mathbb{S}} = D_\gamma = \tilde{a}Q_\gamma = \tilde{a}\tilde{b}P$

Thus, $\mathcal{C}$ obtains the solution to the CDHP instance.   □

Probability Analysis: The probability of success of $\mathcal{C}$ can be measured by analyzing the various events that happen during the simulation :

Assume, $q_{H_1}, q_{H_2}, q_{H_3}, q_{H_4}, q_e$ are the maximum polynomial number of queries allowed to the oracles $\mathcal{O}_{H_1}, \mathcal{O}_{H_2}, \mathcal{O}_{H_3}, \mathcal{O}_{H_4}, \mathcal{O}_{Extract}$ oracles respectively. The events in which $\mathcal{C}$ aborts the $EUF - IBSC - CMA$ game are,

1. E_1 - *when $\mathcal{A}$ queries the private key of the target identity ID_γ and $Pr[E_1] = \frac{q_e}{q_{H_1}}$.*
2. E_2 - *when $\mathcal{A}$ does not choose the target identity ID_γ as the receiver during the challenge and $Pr[E_2] = 1 - \frac{1}{q_{H_1} - q_e}$.*

The probability that $\mathcal{C}$ does not abort in the EUF-IBSC-CMA game is given by,

$$
Pr[\neg E_1 \wedge \neg E_2] = \left(1 - \frac{q_e}{q_{H_1}}\right)\left(\frac{1}{q_{H_1} - q_e}\right) = \frac{1}{q_{H_1}}.
$$

The probability of $\mathcal{C}$ solving the CDHP is given by,

$$
Pr[\mathcal{A}(P, \tilde{a}P, \tilde{b}P | \tilde{a}, \tilde{b} \in \mathbb{G}_2) = \hat{e}(P, P)^{\tilde{a}\tilde{b}\tilde{c}}] = \epsilon\left(\frac{1}{q_{H_1}}\right)
$$

Here, ϵ is non-negligible and hence the probability of $\mathcal{C}$ solving CDHP is also non-negligible.

Proof for Confidentiality of IDPVS Scheme

Theorem 2. *If there exists an adversary $\mathcal{A}$ who can break the IND-IBSC-CCA2 security of IDPVS scheme with advantage ϵ then there exists another algorithm which can break the CBDHP with advantage $\epsilon' \geq \epsilon$.*

Proof: For proving the confidentiality of IDPVS, $\mathcal{A}$ is allowed to interact with $\mathcal{C}$, as given in section 2. Assume that the challenger $\mathcal{C}$ is provided with the

CBDHP instance $P, \tilde{a}P, \hat{b}P, \tilde{c}P$ from $\mathbb{G}_1$ and is supposed to generate the solution $\hat{e}(P, P)^{\tilde{a}\hat{b}\tilde{c}} \in \mathbb{G}_2$. Assume there exists an algorithm $\mathcal{A}$(adversary), capable of breaking the $IND - IBSC - CCA2$ security of $IDPVS$ scheme in polynomial time with advantage ϵ. $\mathcal{C}$ can makes use of $\mathcal{A}$ to find the solution for the CBDHP instance.

Setup: In order to provide the system parameters to $\mathcal{A}$, $\mathcal{C}$ uses the $CBDHP$ instance to cook up the system parameters as given below :
- Sets $\mathbb{G}_1$, $\mathbb{G}_2$ as the underlying group, P as the generator of $\mathbb{G}_1$
- Sets $P_{pub} = \tilde{a}P$.
- Publishes $\langle \mathbb{G}_1, \mathbb{G}_2, q, P, P_{pub} \rangle$.

$\mathcal{C}$ also maintains lists $\mathcal{L}_1, \mathcal{L}_2, \mathcal{L}_3, \mathcal{L}_4, \mathcal{L}_{Sign}$ consistency in giving the responses to the queries made by $\mathcal{A}$ to various oracles. The format of various lists maintained by $\mathcal{C}$ are :
- $\mathcal{L}_1 = \langle i, q_i, Q_i \rangle = Ind, \mathbb{Z}_q^*, \mathbb{G}_1$. Here $Ind = \{1, \ldots, q_{H_1}\}$ and q_{H_1} is the maximum number of queries allowed to $\mathcal{O}_{\mathcal{H}_1}$ oracle.
- $\mathcal{L}_2 = \langle \hat{\alpha}, \alpha_2 \rangle = \langle \mathbb{Z}_q^*, \mathbb{Z}_q^* \rangle$.
- $\mathcal{L}_3 = \langle c, U, Q_A, Q_B, \hat{r}, R \rangle = \langle \{0,1\}^{|c|}, \mathbb{G}_1, \mathbb{G}_1, \mathbb{G}_1 \rangle$.
- $\mathcal{L}_4 = \langle m, U, \hat{a}, Q_A, Q_B \rangle = \langle \{0,1\}^{|m|}, \mathbb{G}_1, \mathbb{G}_2, \mathbb{G}_1, \mathbb{G}_1 \rangle$.

Phase-I: During **Phase-I** of training, the adversary $\mathcal{A}$ is allowed to access the various oracles provided by $\mathcal{C}$. $\mathcal{A}$ can get sufficient training before taking up the challenge. The various oracles provided by $\mathcal{C}$ to $\mathcal{A}$ during **Phase-I** are similar to the oracles described in training phase of the unforgeability proof.

Challenge Phase: At the end of **Phase-I** interaction, $\mathcal{A}$ picks two messages (m_0, m_1) of equal length, the sender identity $ID_\mathbb{S}$ and the receiver identity $ID_\mathbb{R}$, and submits to $\mathcal{C}$. On getting this, $\mathcal{C}$ checks whether $\mathbb{R} = \gamma$. If $\mathbb{R} \neq \gamma$, then $\mathcal{C}$ aborts. Otherwise, $\mathcal{C}$ chooses a random bit $\delta \in \{0,1\}$ and generates the signcryption of m_δ as follows:
- Chooses a random $\hat{r} \in_R \mathbb{Z}_q^*$.
- Sets $U^* = \tilde{c}P$ and $R^* = \hat{r}P$.
- Picks a random $c^* \in_R \{0,1\}^{|\Im|}$.
- Stores the tuple $\langle c^*, U^*, Q_\mathbb{S}, Q_\mathbb{R}, R^* \rangle$
- Computes $V^* = \hat{r}\tilde{c}P + D_\mathbb{S}$. This is equal to $V^* = \tilde{c}R^* + D_\mathbb{S}$. (Also, $D_\mathbb{S}$ is known to $\mathcal{C}$).
- Sets $\sigma^* = \langle c^*, U^*, V^* \rangle$

$\mathcal{C}$ provides σ^* as the challenge signcryption to $\mathcal{A}$.

Phase-II: Now, $\mathcal{A}$ interacts with $\mathcal{C}$ as in **Phase-I**, but with the following restrictions :
- $\mathcal{A}$ should not query the private key corresponding to $ID_\mathbb{R}$ to the extract oracle i.e. $\mathcal{O}_{Extract}(ID_\mathbb{R})$.
- $\mathcal{A}$ should not query the unsigncryption of σ^* with $ID_\mathbb{S}$ as sender and $ID_\mathbb{R}$ as receiver i.e. $\mathcal{O}_{Unsigncrypt}(\sigma^*, ID_\mathbb{S}, ID_\mathbb{R})$
- $\mathcal{A}$ should not query for the third party verification of σ^* with $ID_\mathbb{S}$ as sender and $ID_\mathbb{R}$ as receiver i.e.$\mathcal{O}_{TP-Verify}(\sigma^*, ID_\mathbb{S}, ID_\mathbb{R})$.

Here, it should be noted that for getting the message m_δ from σ^*, $\mathcal{A}$ should have queried $\mathcal{O}_{\mathcal{H}_2}$ or $\mathcal{O}_{\mathcal{H}_4}$ oracle. If $\mathcal{A}$ has queried $\mathcal{O}_{\mathcal{H}_2}$ or $\mathcal{O}_{\mathcal{H}_4}$ oracle, then it leaves an entry $\langle \hat{\alpha}^*, \alpha_2 \rangle$ in list $\mathcal{L}_2$, where $\hat{\alpha}^* = \hat{e}(U, D_{\mathbb{R}}) = \hat{e}(\tilde{c}P, \tilde{a}\tilde{b}P) = \hat{e}(P,P)^{\tilde{a}\tilde{b}\tilde{c}}$. If $\mathcal{A}$ has queried the $\mathcal{O}_{\mathcal{H}_4}$ oracle, then $\mathcal{A}$ should have computed $\hat{\alpha}^* = \hat{e}(P,P)^{\tilde{a}\tilde{b}\tilde{c}}$. This leaves an entry $\langle m, U, \hat{\alpha}^*, Q_A, Q_B, r \rangle$ in the list $\mathcal{L}_4$. Therefore, on receiving $\mathcal{A}$'s response, $\mathcal{C}$ ignores the result and picks an $\hat{\alpha}$ from the list $\mathcal{O}_{\mathcal{H}_2}$ or $\mathcal{O}_{\mathcal{H}_4}$ and returns it as the solution to the CBDHP instance. With probability $1/(q_{H_2} + q_{H_4})$ this will be valid solution to the CBDHP instance provided to $\mathcal{C}$. □

Probability Analysis: The probability of success of $\mathcal{C}$ can be measured by analyzing the various events that happen during the simulation :

Assume $q_{H_1}, q_{H_2}, q_{H_3}, q_{H_4}, q_e$ are the maximum polynomial number of queries allowed to the oracles $\mathcal{O}_{H_1}, \mathcal{O}_{H_2}, \mathcal{O}_{H_3}, \mathcal{O}_{H_4}, \mathcal{O}_{Extract}$ respectively. The events in which $\mathcal{C}$ aborts the IND-IBSC-CCA2 game are,

1. E_1 - *when $\mathcal{A}$ queries the private key of the target identity ID_γ and* $Pr[E_1] = \frac{q_e}{q_{H_1}}$.
2. E_2 - *when $\mathcal{A}$ does not choose the target identity ID_γ as the receiver during the challenge and $Pr[E_2] = 1 - \frac{1}{q_{H_1} - q_e}$.*

The probability that $\mathcal{C}$ does not abort in the IND-IBSC-CCA2 game is given by,

$$Pr[\neg E_1 \wedge \neg E_2] = \left(1 - \frac{q_e}{q_{H_1}}\right)\left(\frac{1}{q_{H_1} - q_e}\right) = \frac{1}{q_{H_1}}.$$

The probability that the random entry chosen by $\mathcal{C}$ from the list $\mathcal{L}_2$ or $\mathcal{L}_4$ being the solution to the CBDHP is $\left(\dfrac{1}{q_{H_2} + q_{H_4}}\right)$. Therefore the probability of $\mathcal{C}$ solving the CBDHP is given by,

$$Pr[\mathcal{A}(P, \tilde{a}P, \tilde{b}P, \tilde{c}P | \tilde{a}, \tilde{b}, \tilde{c} \in \mathbb{G}_2) = \hat{e}(P,P)^{\tilde{a}\tilde{b}\tilde{c}}] = \epsilon\left(\frac{1}{q_{H_1}(q_{H_2} + q_{H_4})}\right)$$

As ϵ is non-negligible, the probability of $\mathcal{C}$ solving CBDHP is also non-negligible.

Note: Security proofs will be available soon.

6 Conclusion

In this paper, we showed the security weaknesses in two existing public verifiable signcryption schemes that appear in [14] and [4]. The scheme in [14] is Public Key Infrastructure (PKI) based and the scheme in [4] is an identity based scheme. We have also provided a new identity based signcryption scheme that provides public verifiability and third party verification. We have formally proved the security of the newly proposed scheme in the random oracle model.

References

1. Baek, J., Steinfeld, R., Zheng, Y.: Formal proofs for the security of signcryption. In: Naccache, D., Paillier, P. (eds.) PKC 2002. LNCS, vol. 2274, pp. 80–98. Springer, Heidelberg (2002)
2. Bao, F., Deng, R.H.: A signcryption scheme with signature directly verifiable by public key. In: Imai, H., Zheng, Y. (eds.) PKC 1998. LNCS, vol. 1431, pp. 55–59. Springer, Heidelberg (1998)
3. Boyen, X.: Multipurpose identity-based signcryption (a swiss army knife for identity-based cryptography). In: Boneh, D. (ed.) CRYPTO 2003. LNCS, vol. 2729, pp. 383–399. Springer, Heidelberg (2003)
4. Chow, S.S.M., Yiu, S.-M., Hui, L.C.K., Chow, K.P.: Efficient forward and provably secure id-based signcryption scheme with public verifiability and public ciphertext authenticity. In: Lim, J.-I., Lee, D.-H. (eds.) ICISC 2003. LNCS, vol. 2971, pp. 352–369. Springer, Heidelberg (2004)
5. Gamage, C., Leiwo, J., Zheng, Y.: Encrypted message authentication by firewalls. In: Imai, H., Zheng, Y. (eds.) PKC 1999. LNCS, vol. 1560, pp. 69–81. Springer, Heidelberg (1999)
6. Libert, B., Quisquater, J.-J.: Efficient signcryption with key privacy from gap diffie-hellman groups. In: Bao, F., Deng, R., Zhou, J. (eds.) PKC 2004. LNCS, vol. 2947, pp. 187–200. Springer, Heidelberg (2004)
7. Libert, B., Quisquater, J.-J.: A new identity based signcryption scheme from pairings. In: IEEE Information Theory Workshop, pp. 155–158 (2003)
8. Malone-Lee, J.: Identity-based signcryption. Cryptology ePrint Archive, Report 2002/098 (2002)
9. Mu, Y., Varadharajan, V.: Distributed signcryption. In: Roy, B., Okamoto, E. (eds.) INDOCRYPT 2000. LNCS, vol. 1977, pp. 155–164. Springer, Heidelberg (2000)
10. Pieprzyk, J., Pointcheval, D.: Parallel authentication and public-key encryption. In: Safavi-Naini, R., Seberry, J. (eds.) ACISP 2003. LNCS, vol. 2727, pp. 387–401. Springer, Heidelberg (2003)
11. Shamir, A.: Identity-based cryptosystems and signature schemes. In: Blakely, G.R., Chaum, D. (eds.) CRYPTO 1984. LNCS, vol. 196, pp. 47–53. Springer, Heidelberg (1985)
12. Shin, J.-B., Lee, K., Shim, K.: New dsa-verifiable signcryption schemes. In: Lee, P.J., Lim, C.H. (eds.) ICISC 2002. LNCS, vol. 2587, pp. 35–47. Springer, Heidelberg (2003)
13. Steinfeld, R., Zheng, Y.: A signcryption scheme based on integer factorization. In: Okamoto, E., Pieprzyk, J.P., Seberry, J. (eds.) ISW 2000. LNCS, vol. 1975, pp. 308–322. Springer, Heidelberg (2000)
14. Tso, R., Okamoto, T., Okamoto, E.: Ecdsa-verifiable signcryption scheme with signature verification on the signcrypted message. In: Pei, D., Yung, M., Lin, D., Wu, C. (eds.) Inscrypt 2007. LNCS, vol. 4990, pp. 11–24. Springer, Heidelberg (2008)
15. Yang, G., Wong, D.S., Deng, X.: Analysis and improvement of a signcryption scheme with key privacy. In: Zhou, J., López, J., Deng, R.H., Bao, F. (eds.) ISC 2005. LNCS, vol. 3650, pp. 218–232. Springer, Heidelberg (2005)
16. Yum, D.H., Lee, P.J.: New signcryption schemes based on kcdsa. In: Kim, K.-c. (ed.) ICISC 2001. LNCS, vol. 2288, pp. 305–317. Springer, Heidelberg (2002)
17. Zheng, Y.: Digital signcryption or how to achieve cost(signature & encryption) < < cost(signature) + cost(encryption). In: Kaliski Jr., B.S. (ed.) CRYPTO 1997. LNCS, vol. 1294, pp. 165–179. Springer, Heidelberg (1997)

Fully Secure Threshold Unsigncryption

Javier Herranz, Alexandre Ruiz, and Germán Sáez

Dept. Matemàtica Aplicada IV, Universitat Politècnica de Catalunya,
C. Jordi Girona 1-3, Mòdul C3, 08034, Barcelona, Spain
{jherranz,aruiz,german}@ma4.upc.edu

Abstract. Signcryption is a very studied primitive in cryptography, which simultaneously performs the functionalities of encryption and signature, in a more efficient way than encrypting and signing separately. The variant of signcryption where the unsigncryption power is distributed among a group of users, through a (t, n) threshold process, has received very few attention (maybe surprisingly).

In this work we consider this task of threshold unsigncryption. First we describe the (strong) security requirements that such a protocol should satisfy: existential unforgeability and indistinguishability, under insider chosen message/ciphertext attacks, in a multi-user setting. We then show that the existing threshold unsigncryption protocols in the literature (including generic constructions obtained by composing a signature scheme and a threshold decryption scheme) do not achieve this strong level of full security. Finally, we propose a new protocol for threshold unsigncryption, which we prove to be fully secure -as described above- in the random oracle model.

1 Introduction

Threshold cryptography deals with situations where the power to do a secret cryptographic task (typically signing or decrypting) is shared among a group of n users. The cooperation of at least t of them is necessary to successfully finish the task. This kind of situations are very common in real-life applications, where giving too much power to a single user may be delicate, both for security (because corruption of this user can compromise the whole system) and for reliability (because a technical problem at this user can lead to important delays in the life of the system) reasons. A typical example is key escrow: a trusted entity stores encrypted versions of the secret key material of all the users in a system or community. If a user loses his secret key, he can ask it to the entity. Also if a judge decides that the secret communications involving a malicious user must be revealed, he can ask the secret key of that user to the key escrow entity. A good solution is to distribute the power of this trusted entity among a set of n entities, through a threshold process.

Regarding either threshold signatures or threshold decryption, a lot of papers have been published in the last 15-20 years, dealing with (strong) security properties, proposing new protocols, proving security under different computational assumptions (RSA, factoring, discrete logarithm, Diffie-Hellman, quadratic residuosity, etc.). In particular, designing secure threshold decryption schemes has been proved to be a quite hard problem.

S.-H. Heng and K. Kurosawa (Eds.): ProvSec 2010, LNCS 6402, pp. 261–278, 2010.

When a digital communication system requires all the properties that encryption and signature offer (confidentiality, authentication, non-repudiation), then there are more efficient solutions than signing and encrypting each message separately. Protocols that provide the same properties than encryption and signature together receive the name of *signcryption* protocols [24] (or also *authenticated encryption* protocols [4]). Since the invention of this concept in 1997, many papers discussing different security properties and proposing new signcryption schemes have appeared.

What happens if we put the two concepts we have talked about (threshold cryptography and signcryption) together? This question makes perfect sense, because for example many of the real uses of threshold decryption (key escrow, e-voting systems, etc.) may require the encrypted information to be authenticated, as well. For example, in a digital auction system, bidders may send their authenticated private bids, encrypted with the public key of a set of servers. In this way, even if some dishonest servers collude, they will not be able to obtain information about the bids. At the end of the auction, a large enough number of servers will cooperate to decrypt the bids and determine the winner of the auction and the price to pay.

Since signcryption involves two secret tasks, signcryption and unsigncryption, two possible combinations with the concept of threshold cryptography can be considered. The first one leads to the concept of threshold signcryption [15]: the sender entity A is now a group of n users, and t or more of them must cooperate to correctly signcrypt a message to an entity B. The second one leads to the concept of threshold unsigncryption [10]: the receiver entity B is a group of n users, and t or more of them must cooperate to correctly unsigncrypt a ciphertext sent by an entity A. Of course, the two concepts can be combined, which results in a fully distributed signcryption protocol where the tasks of both signcryption and unsigncryption require the cooperation of a number of members in the corresponding groups.

These concepts have not received a lot of attention from the cryptographic community. For the concept of threshold signcryption, this may be due to the intuition that designing a threshold signcryption variant of an ordinary signcryption scheme may be reasonably easy, for example if the signcryption scheme works in the Discrete Logarithm framework. This is something similar to what happens with the transition from a standard signature scheme to a threshold signature scheme.

For the concept of threshold unsigncryption, however, the reason of the lack of activity must be a different one, because distributing a decryption task in a secure way has been proved to be a hard problem, and for example very few fully secure threshold decryption schemes exist. In this case, due to the hardness of designing threshold decryption protocols, maybe people just believe that the most efficient and fully secure threshold unsigncryption schemes are those which combine in some way a standard signature scheme with a secure threshold decryption scheme. One of the conclusions that the reader will draw from this paper is that, contrary to that popular belief, such combinations do not lead to fully secure threshold unsigncryption schemes.

Our contribution. We focus on the task of threshold unsigncryption, because it seems harder to realize than that of threshold signcryption. First of all, we will describe in detail the sub-protocols that take part in a threshold unsigncryption scheme, and the two strong security properties that should be required from such a scheme. The first one is unforgeability of new and valid signcryptions, even against attackers who have adaptive access to a signcryption oracle, in a multi-user setting where the attacker knows all the secret keys but that of the target sender. The second one is indistinguishability of plaintexts, against attackers who know the secret information of at most $t - 1$ members of a target set B and the secret information of all users out of B, and have adaptive access to a threshold unsigncryption oracle for the set B.

After formalizing this security model, we discuss why the (few) threshold unsigncryption protocols that exist in the literature fail to achieve these strong levels of security. This includes generic constructions of threshold unsigncryption schemes that are obtained by combining a fully secure standard signature scheme and a fully secure threshold decryption scheme.

The previous negative result motivates the necessity to design a threshold unsigncryption scheme with full security. We do this by modifying the secure threshold decryption scheme by Shoup and Gennaro [20], so that a ciphertext contains also some (unforgeable) authentication information. Both unforgeability and confidentiality are formally proved in the random oracle model; the proofs follow quite standard techniques [16,20]. In terms of efficiency, the new scheme is equivalent to a combination of using Schnorr signature scheme [17] and Shoup-Gennaro threshold decryption scheme. However, as we have already mentioned, generic combinations of these two schemes do not lead to fully secure threshold unsigncryption, whereas our new tailor-made scheme achieves full security.

Organization of the paper. The rest of the paper is organized as follows. In Section 2 we give the syntactic definition of a protocol for threshold unsigncryption and of the two basic security properties (unforgeability and indistinguishability) that such a protocol must satisfy. We argue in Section 3 that all the previously proposed (explicitly or implicitly) threshold unsigncryption schemes do not satisfy the maximum level of security (specifically, the indistinguishability property does not hold). As a more detailed example, we include in Appendix A the description of an attack against the indistinguishability of the scheme in [12]. Then we describe our new threshold unsigncryption scheme in Section 4, where we also prove that this scheme enjoys the required level of security. The work is concluded with some remarks and possible lines of future work in Section 5.

2   Signcryption with Threshold Unsigncryption

In a signcryption scheme, a user A sends a message to an intended receiver B, in a confidential and authenticated way: only B can obtain the original message, and B is convinced that the message comes from A. In a scenario where the role of B is distributed among a set of users, the cooperation of some authorized subset of these users will be necessary to perform the unsigncryption phase. Each user in the set B will have a share of the secret information of B, and will use it to perform his part of the unsigncryption process. In this paper we will focus on threshold families of authorized subsets: the cooperation of at least t users in B will be necessary to successfully run the unsigncryption protocol. Both our formal definitions and our concrete scheme can be extended to more general families of authorized subsets, by replacing threshold secret sharing techniques (i.e. Shamir's scheme [18]) with more general secret sharing schemes.

2.1   Syntactic Definition

A *signcryption scheme with threshold unsigncryption* $\Sigma = (\Sigma.\mathsf{St}, \Sigma.\mathsf{KG}, \Sigma.\mathsf{Sign}, \Sigma.\mathsf{Uns})$ consists of four probabilistic polynomial-time algorithms:

- The randomized *setup* algorithm $\Sigma.\mathsf{St}$ takes a security parameter λ and outputs some public parameters params that will be common to all the users in the system: the mathematical groups, generators, hash functions, etc. We write params $\leftarrow \Sigma.\mathsf{St}(1^\lambda)$ to denote an execution of this algorithm.
- The *key generation* algorithm $\Sigma.\mathsf{KG}$ is different for an individual sender A than for a collective B of receivers. A single user A will get a pair $(\mathsf{sk}_A, \mathsf{pk}_A)$ of secret and public keys. In contrast, for a collective $B = \{B_1, \ldots, B_n\}$ of n users, the output will be a single public key pk_B for the group, and then a threshold secret share $\mathsf{sk}_{B,j}$ for each user B_j, for $j = 1, \ldots, n$, and for some threshold t such that $1 \leq t \leq n$. The key generation process for the collective B can be either run by a trusted third party, or by the users in B themselves. We will write $(\mathsf{sk}_A, \mathsf{pk}_A) \leftarrow \Sigma.\mathsf{KG}(\mathsf{params}, A, \text{'single'})$ and $(\{\mathsf{sk}_{B,j}\}_{1 \leq j \leq n}, \mathsf{pk}_B) \leftarrow \Sigma.\mathsf{KG}(\mathsf{params}, B, n, t, \text{'collective'})$ to refer to these two key generation protocols.
- The *signcryption* algorithm $\Sigma.\mathsf{Sign}$ takes as input params, a message m, the public key pk_B of the intended receiver group B, and the secret key sk_A of the sender. The output is a ciphertext C. We denote an execution of this algorithm as $C \leftarrow \Sigma.\mathsf{Sign}(\mathsf{params}, m, \mathsf{pk}_B, \mathsf{sk}_A)$.
- The *threshold unsigncryption* algorithm $\Sigma.\mathsf{Uns}$ is an interactive protocol run by some subset of users $B' \subset B$. The common inputs are a ciphertext C and the public key pk_A of the sender, whereas each user $B_j \in B'$ has as secret input his secret share $\mathsf{sk}_{B,j}$. The output is a message $\widetilde{m}$, which can eventually be the special symbol $\bot$, meaning that the ciphertext C is invalid. We write $\widetilde{m} \leftarrow \Sigma.\mathsf{Uns}(\mathsf{params}, C, \mathsf{pk}_A, B', \{\mathsf{sk}_{B,j}\}_{B_j \in B'})$ to refer to an execution of this protocol.

For correctness, $\Sigma.\mathsf{Uns}(\mathsf{params}, \Sigma.\mathsf{Sign}(\mathsf{params}, m, \mathsf{pk}_B, \mathsf{sk}_A), \mathsf{pk}_A, B', \{\mathsf{sk}_{B,j}\}_{B_j \in B'}) = m$ is required, whenever B' contains at least t honest users and the values $\mathsf{params}, \mathsf{sk}_A, \mathsf{pk}_A, \{\mathsf{sk}_{B,j}\}_{1 \leq j \leq n}, \mathsf{pk}_B$ have been obtained by properly executing the protocols $\Sigma.\mathsf{St}$ and $\Sigma.\mathsf{KG}$.

A different property that can be required is that of *robustness*, which informally means that dishonest receivers in B who do not follow the threshold unsigncryption protocol correctly can be detected and discarded.

2.2   Security Model

A correct signcryption scheme must satisfy the security properties that are required for both encryption and signatures: confidentiality and unforgeability. In the threshold setting for unsigncryption, confidentiality must hold even if an attacker corrupts $t-1$ members of a collective of receivers. Different models for the unforgeability and confidentiality of signcryption have been proposed [5,2,13], but our goal is to consider here the strongest security notions. For this, we consider a multi-user setting where an adversary is allowed to corrupt the maximum possible number of users (all except the target one), and where he can make queries to signcryption and unsigncryption queries for different users, messages and ciphertexts. In particular, unforgeability must hold even if the adversary knows the secret keys of all the possible collectives of receivers, and confidentiality must hold even if the adversary knows the secret keys of all the possible senders (*insider security*).

Unforgeability. *Unforgeability under chosen message attacks* is the standard security notion for signature schemes and in general for any cryptographic primitive which pretends to provide some kind of authentication or non-repudiation. The idea is that an attacker who does not know the secret key of a user A and who can ask A for some valid signatures (or, in our case, signcryptions) for messages of his choice must not be able to produce a different valid signature (signcryption) on behalf of A. For a security parameter $\lambda \in \mathbb{N}$, this notion is formalized by describing the following game that an attacker $\mathcal{A}_{\mathsf{UNF}}$ plays against a challenger:

1. The challenger runs params $\leftarrow \Sigma.\mathsf{St}(1^\lambda)$ and gives params to $\mathcal{A}_{\mathsf{UNF}}$.
2. $\mathcal{A}_{\mathsf{UNF}}$ chooses a target user $A^\star$. The challenger runs $(\mathsf{sk}_{A^\star}, \mathsf{pk}_{A^\star}) \leftarrow \Sigma.\mathsf{KG}(\mathsf{params}, A^\star, \text{'single'})$, keeps $\mathsf{sk}_{A^\star}$ private and gives $\mathsf{pk}_{A^\star}$ to $\mathcal{A}_{\mathsf{UNF}}$.
3. [**Queries**] $\mathcal{A}_{\mathsf{UNF}}$ can make adaptive queries to a signcryption oracle for sender $A^\star$: $\mathcal{A}_{\mathsf{UNF}}$ sends a tuple (m, pk_B) for some collective B of his choice, and obtains as answer $C \leftarrow \Sigma.\mathsf{Sign}(\mathsf{params}, m, \mathsf{pk}_B, \mathsf{sk}_{A^\star})$.
   Note that other kinds of queries (such as unsigncryption queries or signcryption queries for senders different from $A^\star$) make no sense because $\mathcal{A}_{\mathsf{UNF}}$ can reply such queries by himself.
4. [**Forgery**] Eventually, the attacker $\mathcal{A}_{\mathsf{UNF}}$ outputs a tuple $(\mathsf{pk}_{A^\star}, \mathsf{pk}_{B^\star}, \{\mathsf{sk}_{B^\star,j}\}_{B_j \in B^\star}, C^\star)$.

We say that $\mathcal{A}_{\mathsf{UNF}}$ wins the game if:

- the protocol $\Sigma.\mathsf{Uns}(\mathsf{params}, C^\star, \mathsf{pk}_{A^\star}, B^\star, \{\mathsf{sk}_{B^\star,j}\}_{B_j \in B^\star})$ outputs a message $m^\star \neq \perp$,
- the tuple $(\mathsf{pk}_{A^\star}, m^\star, \mathsf{pk}_{B^\star}, C^\star)$ has not been obtained by $\mathcal{A}_{\mathsf{UNF}}$ through a signcryption query,

The *advantage* of such an adversary $\mathcal{A}_{\mathsf{UNF}}$ in breaking the unforgeability of the signcryption scheme is defined as

$$\mathsf{Adv}_{\mathcal{A}_{\mathsf{UNF}}}(\lambda) = \Pr[\mathcal{A}_{\mathsf{UNF}} \text{ wins}].$$

A signcryption scheme Σ (with threshold unsigncryption) is said to be unforgeable if, for any polynomial time adversary $\mathcal{A}_{\mathsf{UNF}}$, the value $\mathsf{Adv}_{\mathcal{A}_{\mathsf{UNF}}}(\lambda)$ is negligible with respect to the security parameter λ, meaning that it decreases (when λ increases, asymptotically) faster than the inverse of any polynomial.

Indistinguishability. The confidentiality requirement for a signcryption scheme Σ with (t, n)-threshold unsigncryption (i.e. the fact that a signcryption on the message m addressed to B leaks no information on m to an attacker who only knows $t - 1$ secret shares of sk_B) is ensured if the scheme enjoys the property of *indistinguishability under chosen ciphertext attacks* (IND-CCAsecurity, for short). For a security parameter $\lambda \in \mathbb{N}$, this property is defined by considering the following game that an attacker $\mathcal{A}_{\mathsf{IND\text{-}CCA}}$ plays against a challenger:

1. The challenger runs $\mathsf{params} \leftarrow \Sigma.\mathsf{St}(1^\lambda)$ and gives params to $\mathcal{A}_{\mathsf{IND\text{-}CCA}}$.
2. $\mathcal{A}_{\mathsf{IND\text{-}CCA}}$ chooses a target set $B^\star$ of n users and a subset $\widetilde{B} \subset B^\star$ of $t - 1$ users, to be corrupted. The challenger runs $(\{\mathsf{sk}_{B^\star,j}\}_{1 \leq j \leq n}, \mathsf{pk}_{B^\star}) \leftarrow \Sigma.\mathsf{KG}(\mathsf{params}, B^\star, n, t, \text{'collective'})$ and gives to $\mathcal{A}_{\mathsf{IND\text{-}CCA}}$ the values $\mathsf{pk}_{B^\star}$ and $\{\mathsf{sk}_{B^\star,j}\}_{B_j \in \widetilde{B}}$. Without loss of generality, we can assume $B^\star = \{B_1, \ldots, B_n\}$ and $\widetilde{B} = \{B_1, \ldots, B_{t-1}\}$.

   Note that we are considering only *static* adversaries who choose the subset $\widetilde{B}$ of corrupted users at the beginning of the attack. Considering security against *adaptive* adversaries is an interesting problem for future research.
3. [**Queries**] $\mathcal{A}_{\mathsf{IND\text{-}CCA}}$ can make adaptive queries to a threshold unsigncryption oracle for the target set $B^\star$: $\mathcal{A}_{\mathsf{IND\text{-}CCA}}$ sends a tuple (pk_A, C) for some public key pk_A of his choice. The challenger runs $\widetilde{m} \leftarrow \Sigma.\mathsf{Uns}(\mathsf{params}, C, \mathsf{pk}_A, B^\star, \{\mathsf{sk}_{B^\star,j}\}_{B_j \in B^\star})$. The attacker $\mathcal{A}_{\mathsf{IND\text{-}CCA}}$ must be given all the information that is broadcast during the execution of this protocol $\Sigma.\mathsf{Uns}$.

   Note that other kinds of queries (such as unsigncryption queries for other collectives $B \neq B^\star$ or signcryption queries) make no sense because $\mathcal{A}_{\mathsf{UNF}}$ can reply such queries by himself.
4. $\mathcal{A}_{\mathsf{IND\text{-}CCA}}$ chooses two messages m_0, m_1 of the same length, and a sender $A^\star$ along with $(\mathsf{sk}_{A^\star}, \mathsf{pk}_{A^\star})$.
5. [**Challenge**] The challenger picks a random bit $b \in \{0, 1\}$, runs $C^\star \leftarrow \Sigma.\mathsf{Sign}(\mathsf{params}, m_b, \mathsf{pk}_{B^\star}, \mathsf{sk}_{A^\star})$ and gives $C^\star$ to $\mathcal{A}_{\mathsf{IND\text{-}CCA}}$.
6. Step 3 is repeated, with the restriction that the tuple $(\mathsf{pk}_{A^\star}, C^\star, B^\star)$ cannot be queried to the threshold unsigncryption oracle.
7. Finally, $\mathcal{A}_{\mathsf{IND\text{-}CCA}}$ outputs a bit b'.

The advantage of such a (static) adversary $\mathcal{A}_{\mathsf{IND\text{-}CCA}}$ in breaking the IND-CCAsecurity of the signcryption scheme is defined as

$$\mathsf{Adv}_{\mathcal{A}_{\mathsf{IND\text{-}CCA}}}(\lambda) = |2\Pr[b' = b] - 1|.$$

A signcryption scheme Σ with threshold unsigncryption is said to be IND-CCA secure if $\mathsf{Adv}_{\mathcal{A}_{\mathsf{IND\text{-}CCA}}}(\lambda)$ is negligible with respect to the security parameter λ, for any polynomial time (static) adversary $\mathcal{A}_{\mathsf{IND\text{-}CCA}}$.

3   Existing Threshold Unsigncryption Schemes Are Not Fully Secure

There are very few papers proposing explicit signcryption schemes with threshold unsigncryption. We are only aware of two proposals [10,23] in the traditional PKI setting, and three proposals [11,12,22] in the identity-based setting.

It turns out that none of these schemes achieves the full level of security described in the previous section. The security weakness is always related to the indistinguishability property. For the two schemes in the PKI setting (which do not contain any formal security definitions or analysis), simple IND-CCA attacks can be mounted without assuming multiple users or insider attackers. The schemes proposed for the identity-based scenario are analyzed more formally, but IND-CCA attacks against them exist anyway. Specifically, the scheme in [22] has the same security problems than the two schemes in the PKI setting: the verification step is performed at the end of the protocol, once all the receivers have broadcast their partial decryption shares. This means that an attacker can take the challenge ciphertext $C^\star$ and modify only the "signature" part of it, obtaining an invalid ciphertext $C \neq C^\star$ that will be queried to the threshold unsigncryption oracle. As answer, the attacker will obtain the final value $\perp$, but also the partial decryption values broadcast by all the receivers, which will allow the attacker to decrypt the (valid) challenge ciphertext.

The scheme in [11] does not resist insider attacks: knowing the secret key of the sender $A^\star$, one can immediately obtain the plaintext from the challenge ciphertext. Finally, the scheme in [12] is also insecure against insider attacks. We describe this scheme and such an attack in Appendix A as an illustrative example.

3.1   What about Generic Constructions?

Since the existing threshold unsigncryption schemes are not fully secure, one could wonder if such fully secure schemes actually exist. The first attempt could / should be to think of possible generic constructions like the threshold versions of the well-known approaches Sign_then_Encrypt and Encrypt_then_Sign, that have been deeply analyzed in [1] for the case of ordinary signcryption. There, it is proved that both generic constructions achieve full security (against insider attackers in a multi-user setting) if the underlying signature and encryption schemes have full security. Thus, one could expect that the same happens in the scenario with threshold unsigncryption. But unfortunately this is not the case, as we argue below.

Let $\Omega = (\Omega.\mathsf{KG}, \Omega.\mathsf{Sign}, \Omega.\mathsf{Vfy})$ be a signature scheme, and $\Pi = (\Pi.\mathsf{KG}, \Pi.\mathsf{Enc}, \Pi.\mathsf{ThrDec})$ be a public encryption scheme with threshold decryption. For the keys of the generic signcryption schemes with threshold unsigncryption, an individual sender will run $(\mathsf{sk}_A, \mathsf{pk}_A) \leftarrow \Omega.\mathsf{KG}$ and a collective of receivers B will run $(\{\mathsf{sk}_{B,j}\}_{1 \leq j \leq n}, \mathsf{pk}_B) \leftarrow \Pi.\mathsf{KG}$.

Let us consider for example the ThresholdEncrypt_then_Sign approach. To signcrypt a message m for the collective B, a sender A first computes

$c \leftarrow \Pi.\mathsf{Enc}(\mathsf{pk}_B, m||\mathsf{pk}_A)$ and then signs $c||\mathsf{pk}_B$ to obtain $\omega \leftarrow \Omega.\mathsf{Sign}(\mathsf{sk}_A, c||\mathsf{pk}_B)$. The final ciphertext is $C = (c, \omega)$. To unsigncrypt such a ciphertext, members of B first verify the correctness of signature ω by running $\Omega.\mathsf{Vfy}(\mathsf{pk}_A, c||\mathsf{pk}_B, \omega)$. If the signature is not correct, the symbol $\bot$ is output. Otherwise, a subset $\tilde{B} \subset B$ of at least t members of B run $\Pi.\mathsf{ThrDec}(\{\mathsf{sk}_{B,j}\}_{B_j \in \tilde{B}}, c)$ to recover the message $m||\mathsf{pk}_A$. If the public key pk_A corresponds with that of the sender A, then m is the output of the protocol. If not, the output is $\bot$.

The IND-CCA security of this generic construction can be broken by an insider attacker $\mathcal{A}_{\mathsf{IND\text{-}CCA}}$ in a multi-user scenario. $\mathcal{A}_{\mathsf{IND\text{-}CCA}}$ receives a challenge ciphertext $C^\star = (c^\star, \omega^\star)$ for a challenge sender $A^\star$ and a challenge collective $B^\star$ of receivers. After that, $\mathcal{A}_{\mathsf{IND\text{-}CCA}}$ can generate keys $(\mathsf{sk}_A, \mathsf{pk}_A)$ for another user $A \neq A^\star$, compute a valid signature ω for $c^\star||\mathsf{pk}_{B^\star}$ using sk_A, and send $C = (c^\star, \omega)$ as a threshold unsigncryption query for sender A and collective $B^\star$ of receivers. As answer to this query, since the signature ω is valid, $\mathcal{A}_{\mathsf{IND\text{-}CCA}}$ must receive all the information that the members of $B^\star$ would broadcast in the execution of the threshold decryption of $c^\star$. Even if the final output of this query is $\bot$, because the public key pk_A does not match the public key $\mathsf{pk}_{A^\star}$ which is encrypted in $c^\star$, the attacker $\mathcal{A}_{\mathsf{IND\text{-}CCA}}$ has obtained enough information to recover the whole plaintext encrypted in $c^\star$, and therefore succeeds in breaking the indistinguishability of the scheme. We stress that this same attack is valid against relaxed IND-CCA (see [7]), because the decryption of C (which is $\bot$) is different from the decryption of $C^\star$.

Regarding the Sign_then_ThresholdEncrypt approach, the attack is even simpler. Once $\mathcal{A}_{\mathsf{IND\text{-}CCA}}$ gets a challenge ciphertext $C^\star = c^\star$ for $A^\star$ and $B^\star$, where $c^\star$ is an encryption under Π of $(m, \omega^\star, \mathsf{pk}_{A^\star})$ and $\omega^\star$ is a signature on $m||\mathsf{pk}_{B^\star}$, all that $\mathcal{A}_{\mathsf{IND\text{-}CCA}}$ has to do is to make an unsigncryption query for the tuple $(C^\star, \mathsf{pk}_A, \mathsf{pk}_{B^\star})$, where $A \neq A^\star$. Even if the output of the protocol is again $\bot$, the attacker $\mathcal{A}_{\mathsf{IND\text{-}CCA}}$ gets all the partial information broadcast by the members of $B^\star$ in the execution of the threshold decryption of $c^\star$, which allows $\mathcal{A}_{\mathsf{IND\text{-}CCA}}$ to directly obtain the plaintext m.

4   New Threshold Unsigncryption with Full Security

This section is dedicated to the description and analysis of a new signcryption scheme with (t, n)-threshold unsigncryption, achieving full security. Attempts to design such a scheme starting from an existing (individual) signcryption scheme do not seem to work, either because many signcryption schemes are not secure against insider attacks [24,4,3] or because the verification process is placed at the very end, after the decryption process has been done [14,21,5,13], which makes it impossible to extend them securely to threshold unsigncryption scenarios.

Our approach has been to take a secure public key encryption scheme with threshold decryption and modify it in order to accommodate also the authentication process. In particular, we have considered the scheme TDH1 of Shoup and Gennaro [20]. The idea of that scheme, to encrypt a message m for a collective B with public key pk_B, is to first compute a hashed ElGamal encryption

(R, c) of m. That is, assuming that we have fixed a cyclic group $\mathbb{G} = \langle g \rangle$ of prime order q, along with a hash function H_0, the sender computes $R = g^r$ and $c = m \oplus H_0((pk_B)^r)$. After that, he adds to the ciphertext another element $\bar{g} \in \mathbb{G}$ and the value $\bar{R} = \bar{g}^r$, and finally a zero-knowledge proof that $\mathsf{DiscLog}_g(R) = \mathsf{DiscLog}_{\bar{g}}(\bar{R})$. Members of B will start the real decryption process only if the proof of knowledge is valid.

Our signcryption scheme follows the same principle, but the sender A will compute a zero-knowledge proof that $\mathsf{DiscLog}_g(R) = \mathsf{DiscLog}_{\bar{g}}(\bar{R})$ holds and that he knows sk_A such that $pk_A = g^{sk_A}$. We will prove that the resulting signcryption scheme (with threshold unsigncryption) enjoys the strong notions of unforgeability and indistinguishability. We consider for simplicity a scenario where the receivers follow the threshold unsigncryption protocol correctly. A simple modification of our scheme, by including appropriate non-interactive zero-knowledge proofs of the equality of two discrete logarithms, allows to provide robustness to the scheme against the action of malicious receivers. We do not detail the efficiency of the scheme; this is usually done when a cryptographic scheme is designed to improve the efficiency of previous equivalent proposals. But this is not the case here: previous proposals of threshold unsigncryption protocols do not achieve the level of security achieved by this new scheme, so it would not be fair to compare, for instance, the efficiency of this scheme with the efficiency of some generic construction such as ThresholdEncrypt_then_Sign.

The protocols of the scheme are described below.

Setup: $\Sigma.\mathsf{St}(1^\lambda)$.
Given a security parameter λ, a cyclic group $\mathbb{G} = \langle g \rangle$ of prime order q, such that q is λ bits long, is chosen. A length ℓ, which must be polynomial in λ, is defined for the maximum number of bits of the messages to be sent by the system. Three hash functions $H_0 : \{0,1\}^* \rightarrow \{0,1\}^\ell$, $H_1 : \{0,1\}^* \rightarrow \mathbb{G}$ and $H_2 : \{0,1\}^* \rightarrow \mathbb{Z}_q$ are chosen. The output of the protocol is $\mathsf{params} = (q, \mathbb{G}, g, H_0, \ell, H_1, H_2)$.

Key Generation: $\Sigma.\mathsf{KG}(\mathsf{params}, A, \text{'single'})$ and $\Sigma.\mathsf{KG}(\mathsf{params}, B, n, t, \text{'collective'})$.
For an individual user A, the secret key sk_A is a random element in $\mathbb{Z}_q^*$, whereas the corresponding public key is $pk_A = g^{sk_A}$. The public output of this protocol is pk_A, and the secret output that is privately stored by A is sk_A.

For a collective $B = \{B_1, \ldots, B_n\}$ of n users, the common public key is computed as $pk_B = g^{sk_B}$ for some random value $sk_B \in \mathbb{Z}_q^*$ that will remain unknown to the members of B. Each user $B_j \in B$ will receive a (t, n)-threshold share $sk_{B,j}$ of sk_B, computed by using Shamir's secret sharing scheme [18]. This means that, for every subset $B' \subset B$ containing exactly t users, there exist values $\lambda_j^{B'} \in \mathbb{Z}_q^*$ such that $sk_B = \sum_{B_j \in B'} \lambda_j^{B'} sk_{B,j}$. The public output of this protocol is pk_B, whereas each user $B_j \in B$ receives a secret output $sk_{B,j}$.

The key generation process for a collective B can be performed by a trusted dealer, or by the members of B themselves, by using some well-known techniques [9]. Both solutions permit that the values $D_{B,j} = g^{sk_{B,j}}$ are made public, for

$j = 1, \ldots, n$. These values would be necessary to provide robustness to the threshold unsigncryption process.

We assume that both pk_A and pk_B include descriptions of the identities of A and members of B.

Signcryption: $\Sigma.\mathsf{Sign}(\mathsf{params}, m, \mathsf{pk}_B, \mathsf{sk}_A)$.

1. Choose at random $r \in \mathbb{Z}_q^*$ and compute $R = g^r$.
2. Compute $k = H_0(R, \mathsf{pk}_B, (\mathsf{pk}_B)^r, \mathsf{pk}_A)$ and $c = m \oplus k$.
3. Choose at random $\alpha_1, \alpha_2 \in \mathbb{Z}_q^*$ and compute $Y_1 = g^{\alpha_1}$ and $Y_2 = g^{\alpha_2}$.
4. Compute $\bar{g} = H_1(c, R, Y_1, Y_2, \mathsf{pk}_A, \mathsf{pk}_B) \in \mathbb{G}$, and then $\bar{R} = \bar{g}^r$ and $\bar{Y}_1 = \bar{g}^{\alpha_1}$.
5. Compute $h = H_2(c, R, \bar{g}, \bar{R}, Y_1, Y_2, \bar{Y}_1, \mathsf{pk}_A, \mathsf{pk}_B)$.
6. Compute $s_1 = \alpha_1 - h \cdot r \bmod q$.
7. Compute $s_2 = \alpha_2 - h \cdot \mathsf{sk}_A \bmod q$.
8. Return the signcryption $C = (c, R, \bar{R}, h, s_1, s_2)$.

Threshold Unsigncryption: $\Sigma.\mathsf{Uns}(\mathsf{params}, C, \mathsf{pk}_A, B', \{\mathsf{sk}_{B,j}\}_{B_j \in B'})$.
Let $B' \subset B$ be a subset of users in B that want to cooperate to unsigncrypt a signcryption $C = (c, R, \bar{R}, h, s_1, s_2)$. They proceed as follows.

1. Each $B_j \in B'$ computes $\bar{g} = H_1(c, R, g^{s_1} \cdot R^h, g^{s_2} \cdot (\mathsf{pk}_A)^h, \mathsf{pk}_A, \mathsf{pk}_B)$ and then checks if the following equality holds:

$$h = H_2(c, R, \bar{g}, \bar{R}, g^{s_1} \cdot R^h, g^{s_2} \cdot (\mathsf{pk}_A)^h, \bar{g}^{s_1} \cdot \bar{R}^h, \mathsf{pk}_A, \mathsf{pk}_B)$$

2. If the equality does not hold, B_j broadcasts $(j, \perp)$.
3. Otherwise, $B_j \in B'$ broadcasts the value $T_j = R^{\mathsf{sk}_{B,j}}$.
   [If robustness was required, then B_j should also provide a non-interactive zero-knowledge proof that $\mathsf{DiscLog}_g(D_{B,j}) = \mathsf{DiscLog}_R(T_j)$.]
4. From t valid values T_j, different from $(j, \perp)$, recover the value R^{sk_B} by interpolation in the exponent: $R^{\mathsf{sk}_B} = \prod_{B_j \in B'} T_j^{\lambda_j^{B'}}$, where $\lambda_j^{B'} \in \mathbb{Z}_q$ are the Lagrange interpolation coefficients. If there are not t valid shares, then stop and output $\perp$.
5. Compute $k = H_0(R, \mathsf{pk}_B, R^{\mathsf{sk}_B}, \mathsf{pk}_A)$.
6. Return the value $m = c \oplus k$.

4.1 Security Analysis

Necessary Computational Assumptions. Given a security parameter λ, let $\mathbb{G} = \langle g \rangle$ be a cyclic group of prime order q, such that q is λ bits long.

The *Diffie-Hellman (DH, for short) problem* consists of computing the value g^{ab} from the values g, g^a, g^b, for random elements $a, b \in \mathbb{Z}_q^*$. The *Diffie-Hellman Assumption* states that the DH problem is hard to solve. A bit more formally, for any polynomial-time algorithm $\mathcal{A}^{DH}$ that receives as input $\mathbb{G}, g^a, g^b$, for random elements $a, b \in \mathbb{Z}_q^*$, we can define as $\mathsf{Adv}_{\mathcal{A}^{DH}}(\lambda)$ the probability that $\mathcal{A}$

outputs the value g^{ab}. The Diffie-Hellman Assumption states that $\mathrm{Adv}_{\mathcal{A}_{DH}}(\lambda)$ is negligible in λ.

The Diffie-Hellman problem is easier to solve than the *Discrete Logarithm (DL, for short) problem*: the input is $(\mathbb{G}, y)$, where $y \in \mathbb{G}$, and the goal for a solver $\mathcal{A}^{DL}$ is to find the integer $x \in \mathbb{Z}_q^*$ such that $y = g^x$. We can define $\mathrm{Adv}_{\mathcal{A}_{DL}}(\lambda)$ and the *Discrete Logarithm Assumption* analogously to the Diffie-Hellman case. The unforgeability of our signcryption scheme will be reduced to the hardness of the DL problem, whereas its indistinguishability will be reduced to the hardness of the DH problem.

Unforgeability. We are going to prove that our scheme enjoys unforgeability as long as the Discrete Logarithm problem is hard to solve. The proof is in the random oracle model for the hash function H_2.

Theorem 1. *Let λ be an integer. For any polynomial-time attacker $\mathcal{A}_{\mathsf{UNF}}$ against the unforgeability of the new signcryption scheme, in the random oracle model, there exists a solver $\mathcal{A}^{DL}$ of the Discrete Logarithm problem such that*

$$Adv_{\mathcal{A}_{DL}}(\lambda) \geq \mathcal{O}\left(Adv_{\mathcal{A}_{\mathsf{UNF}}}(\lambda)^2\right).$$

Proof. Assuming the existence of an adversary $\mathcal{A}_{\mathsf{UNF}}$ that has advantage $\mathrm{Adv}_{\mathcal{A}_{\mathsf{UNF}}}(\lambda)$ in breaking the unforgeability of our scheme, and assuming that the hash function H_2 behaves as a random oracle, we are going to construct an algorithm $\mathcal{A}^{DL}$ that solves the Discrete Logarithm problem in $\mathbb{G}$.

Let $(\mathbb{G}, y)$ be the instance of the Discrete Logarithm problem in $\mathbb{G} = \langle g \rangle$ that $\mathcal{A}^{DL}$ receives. The goal of $\mathcal{A}^{DL}$ is to find the integer $x \in \mathbb{Z}_q$ such that $y = g^x$. The algorithm $\mathcal{A}^{DL}$ initializes the attacker $\mathcal{A}_{\mathsf{UNF}}$ by giving params $= (q, \mathbb{G}, g, H_0, \ell, H_1, H_2)$ to him. Here the hash functions $H_0 : \{0,1\}^* \to \{0,1\}^\ell$ and $H_1 : \{0,1\}^* \to \mathbb{G}$ are arbitrarily chosen by $\mathcal{A}^{DL}$. However, H_2 is modeled as a random oracle and so $\mathcal{A}^{DL}$ will maintain a table TAB_2 to answer the hash queries from $\mathcal{A}_{\mathsf{UNF}}$.

Key generation. $\mathcal{A}_{\mathsf{UNF}}$ chooses a target sender $A^\star$ and requests the execution of the key generation protocol for this user. $\mathcal{A}^{DL}$ defines the public key of $A^\star$ as $\mathsf{pk}_{A^\star} = y$ and sends it to $\mathcal{A}_{\mathsf{UNF}}$. Note that the corresponding secret key $\mathsf{sk}_{A^\star}$, which is unknown to $\mathcal{A}^{DL}$, is precisely the solution to the given instance of the DL problem.

Hash queries. Since H_2 is assumed to behave as a random function, $\mathcal{A}_{\mathsf{UNF}}$ can make queries $(c, R, \bar{g}, \bar{R}, Y_1, Y_2, \bar{Y}_1, \mathsf{pk}_A, \mathsf{pk}_B)$ to the random oracle model for H_2. $\mathcal{A}^{DL}$ maintains a table TAB_2 to reply to these queries. TAB_2 contains two columns, one for the inputs and one for the corresponding outputs h of H_2. To reply the query $(c, R, \bar{g}, \bar{R}, Y_1, Y_2, \bar{Y}_1, \mathsf{pk}_A, \mathsf{pk}_B)$, the algorithm $\mathcal{A}^{DL}$ checks if this input is already in TAB_2. If so, the matching output h is answered. If not, a random value $h \in \mathbb{Z}_q$ is chosen and answered to $\mathcal{A}_{\mathsf{UNF}}$, and the entry $H_2(c, R, \bar{g}, \bar{R}, Y_1, Y_2, \bar{Y}_1, \mathsf{pk}_A, \mathsf{pk}_B) = h$ is added to TAB_2.

Signcryption queries. $\mathcal{A}_{\mathsf{UNF}}$ can make signcryption queries for the sender $A^\star$, for pairs (m, pk_B) of his choice, where m is a message and B is a collective of receivers with public key pk_B. To reply to such queries, $\mathcal{A}^{DL}$ chooses at random a value $r \in \mathbb{Z}_q^*$ and computes $R = g^r$, $k = H_0(R, \mathsf{pk}_B, (\mathsf{pk}_B)^r, \mathsf{pk}_{A^\star})$ and $c = m \oplus k$. Then, $\mathcal{A}^{DL}$ must simulate a valid proof of knowledge to complete the rest of the ciphertext. To do this, $\mathcal{A}^{DL}$ acts as follows:

1. Choose at random $h, s_1, s_2 \in \mathbb{Z}_q$ and compute the values $Y_1 = g^{s_1} \cdot R^h$ and $Y_2 = g^{s_2} \cdot (\mathsf{pk}_{A^\star})^h$.
2. Compute $\bar{g} = H_1(c, R, Y_1, Y_2, \mathsf{pk}_{A^\star}, \mathsf{pk}_B)$, and then the values $\bar{R} = \bar{g}^r$ and $\bar{Y}_1 = \bar{g}^{s_1} \cdot \bar{R}^h$.
3. If the input $(c, R, \bar{g}, \bar{R}, Y_1, Y_2, \bar{Y}_1, \mathsf{pk}_{A^\star}, \mathsf{pk}_B)$ is already in TAB_2 (which happens with negligible probability), go back to Step 1.
4. Otherwise, 'falsely' add the relation $h = H_2(c, R, \bar{g}, \bar{R}, Y_1, Y_2, \bar{Y}_1, \mathsf{pk}_{A^\star}, \mathsf{pk}_B)$ to TAB_2.

The final signcryption that $\mathcal{A}^{DL}$ sends to $\mathcal{A}_{\mathsf{UNF}}$ is $C = (c, R, \bar{R}, h, s_1, s_2)$.

Forgery. At some point, $\mathcal{A}_{\mathsf{UNF}}$ outputs a successful forgery; that is, a public key $\mathsf{pk}_{B^\star}$ and a signcryption $C^\star = (c^\star, R^\star, \bar{R}^\star, h^\star, s_1^\star, s_2^\star)$ such that:

- the protocol $\Sigma.\mathsf{Uns}(\mathsf{params}, C^\star, \mathsf{pk}_{A^\star}, B^\star, \{\mathsf{sk}_{B^\star,j}\}_{B_j \in B^\star})$ outputs $m^\star \neq \bot$,
- $(\mathsf{pk}_{A^\star}, m^\star, \mathsf{pk}_{B^\star}, C^\star)$ has not been obtained by $\mathcal{A}_{\mathsf{UNF}}$ during a signcryption query.

Since the forgery is valid, we must have $h^\star = H_2(c^\star, R^\star, \bar{g}^\star, \bar{R}^\star, Y_1^\star, Y_2^\star, \bar{Y}_1^\star, \mathsf{pk}_{A^\star}, \mathsf{pk}_{B^\star})$, where $Y_1^\star = g^{s_1^\star} \cdot (R^\star)^{h^\star}$, $Y_2^\star = g^{s_2^\star} \cdot (\mathsf{pk}_{A^\star})^{h^\star}$ and $\bar{Y}_1^\star = (\bar{g}^\star)^{s_1^\star} \cdot (\bar{R}^\star)^{h^\star}$.

Furthermore, since the forgery is different from the ciphertexts obtained during the signcryption queries, we can be sure that the input $\mathsf{query}^\star = (c^\star, R^\star, \bar{g}^\star, \bar{R}^\star, Y_1^\star, Y_2^\star, \bar{Y}_1^\star, \mathsf{pk}_{A^\star}, \mathsf{pk}_{B^\star})$ for H_2 has not been 'falsely' added by $\mathcal{A}^{DL}$ to TAB_2.

Replying the attack. Now the idea is to use the reply techniques introduced by Pointcheval and Stern in [16]. Without going into the details, $\mathcal{A}^{DL}$ will repeat the execution of the attacker $\mathcal{A}_{\mathsf{UNF}}$, with the same randomness but changing the values output by the random oracle H_2 from the query $\mathsf{query}^\star$ on.

With non-negligible probability (quadratic on the probability $\mathsf{Adv}_{\mathcal{A}_{\mathsf{UNF}}}(\lambda)$ of the first successful forgery), the whole process run by $\mathcal{A}^{DL}$ would lead to two different successful forgeries $C^\star$ and $C'^\star$, for the same values of $c^\star, R^\star, \bar{g}^\star, \bar{R}^\star, Y_1^\star, Y_2^\star, \bar{Y}_1^\star, \mathsf{pk}_{A^\star}, \mathsf{pk}_{B^\star}$ (the input values for H_2), but with different H_2 outputs $h^\star \neq h'^\star$, and therefore (possibly different) values $s_1^\star, s_2^\star, s_1'^\star, s_2'^\star$.

We thus have

$$g^{s_2^\star} \cdot (\mathsf{pk}_{A^\star})^{h^\star} = Y_2^\star = g^{s_2'^\star} \cdot (\mathsf{pk}_{A^\star})^{h'^\star},$$

which leads to the relation $y = \mathsf{pk}_{A^\star} = \left(g^{s_2^\star - s_2'^\star} \right)^{1/(h'^\star - h^\star)}$.

Summing up, $\mathcal{A}^{DL}$ can output the value $x = \frac{s_2^\star - s_2'^\star}{h'^\star - h^\star} \bmod q$ as the solution to the given instance of the DL problem. $\qquad \square$

Indistinguishability. We reduce the IND-CCA security of the scheme to the hardness of solving the DH problem. The proof is in the random oracle model for the three hash functions H_0, H_1, H_2. The conclusion is that, under the Diffie Hellman Assumption for our group $\mathbb{G} = \langle g \rangle$, the new signcryption scheme has IND-CCA security.

Theorem 2. *Let λ be an integer. For any polynomial-time attacker $\mathcal{A}_{\text{IND-CCA}}$ against the IND-CCA security of the new signcryption scheme, in the random oracle model, there exists a solver $\mathcal{A}^{DH}$ of the Diffie-Hellman problem such that*

$$\text{Adv}_{\mathcal{A}^{DH}}(\lambda) \geq \text{Adv}_{\mathcal{A}_{\text{IND-CCA}}}(\lambda)/2.$$

Proof. Assuming the existence of an adversary $\mathcal{A}_{\text{IND-CCA}}$ that has advantage $\text{Adv}_{\mathcal{A}_{\text{IND-CCA}}}(\lambda)$ in breaking the IND-CCA security of our scheme, and assuming that hash functions H_0, H_1, H_2 behave as random oracles, we are going to construct an algorithm $\mathcal{A}^{DH}$ that solves the Diffie-Hellman problem.

$\mathcal{A}^{DH}$ receives as input $\mathbb{G}, g^a, g^b$, where $\mathbb{G} = \langle g \rangle$ is a cyclic group of prime order q. The goal of $\mathcal{A}^{DH}$ is to compute g^{ab}. $\mathcal{A}^{DH}$ initializes the attacker $\mathcal{A}_{\text{IND-CCA}}$ by giving $\text{params} = (q, \mathbb{G}, g, H_0, \ell, H_1, H_2)$ to him. Here the hash functions H_0, H_1 and H_2 will be modeled as random oracles; therefore, $\mathcal{A}^{DH}$ will maintain three tables TAB_0, TAB_1 and TAB_2 to answer the hash queries from $\mathcal{A}_{\text{IND-CCA}}$.

Let $B^* = \{B_1, \ldots, B_n\}$ be the target collective, and $\widetilde{B} = \{B_1, \ldots, B_{t-1}\} \subset B^*$ be the subset of corrupted members of B^*. The algorithm $\mathcal{A}^{DH}$ defines the public key of B^* as $\text{pk}_{B^*} = g^b$. This means that sk_{B^*} is implicitly defined as b. For the corrupted members of B^*, the shares $\{\text{sk}_{B^*,j}\}_{B_j \in \widetilde{B}}$ are chosen randomly and independently in $\mathbb{Z}_q$. Using interpolation in the exponent, all the values $D_{B^*,j} = g^{\text{sk}_{B^*,j}}$ can be computed, for all the members $B_j \in B^*$, corrupted or not.

Hash queries. $\mathcal{A}^{DH}$ creates and maintains three tables TAB_0, TAB_1 and TAB_2 to reply the hash queries from $\mathcal{A}_{\text{IND-CCA}}$. All the hash queries are processed by $\mathcal{A}^{DH}$ in the same way: given the input for a hash query, the algorithm $\mathcal{A}^{DH}$ checks if there already exists an entry in the corresponding table for that input. If this is the case, the existing output is answered. If this is not the case, a new output is chosen at random and answered to $\mathcal{A}_{\text{IND-CCA}}$, and the new relation between input and output is added to the corresponding table.

For the particular case of H_1 queries, the corresponding outputs $\bar{g}$ are chosen as random powers of g^b. That is, $\mathcal{A}^{DH}$ chooses at random a fresh value $\beta \in \mathbb{Z}_q^*$ and computes the new output of H_1 as $\bar{g} = (g^b)^\beta$. The value β is stored as an additional value of the new entry in table TAB_1.

Whenever $\mathcal{A}^{DH}$ receives a H_0 query whose two first elements are g^a and g^b, the third element of the query is added to a different output table TAB^*, which will be the final output of $\mathcal{A}^{DH}$.

Unsigncryption queries. For an unsigncryption query (pk_A, C) sent for the target collective B^*, where $C = (c, R, \bar{R}, h, s_1, s_2)$, the first thing to do is to check the validity of the zero-knowledge proof (h, s_1, s_2); that is, to check if $h = H_2(c, R, \bar{g}, \bar{R}, g^{s_1} \cdot R^h, g^{s_2} \cdot (\mathsf{pk}_A)^h, \bar{g}^{s_1} \cdot \bar{R}^h, \mathsf{pk}_A, \mathsf{pk}_{B^\star})$, where $\bar{g} = H_1(c, R, g^{s_1} \cdot R^h, g^{s_2} \cdot (\mathsf{pk}_A)^h, \mathsf{pk}_A, \mathsf{pk}_{B^\star}) = (g^b)^\beta$, for some value β known by $\mathcal{A}^{DH}$. If this equation does not hold, then the answer to the query is $\bot$.

Otherwise, $\mathcal{A}^{DH}$ has to give to $\mathcal{A}_{\mathsf{IND\text{-}CCA}}$ the values $R^{\mathsf{sk}_{B^\star,j}}$, for all $B_j \in B^\star$. For the corrupted members B_j, $j = 1, \ldots, t-1$, such values can be easily computed by $\mathcal{A}^{DH}$, because it knows $\mathsf{sk}_{B^\star,j}$. Note now that the value $R^{\mathsf{sk}_{B^\star}}$ can be computed by $\mathcal{A}^{DH}$ as $\bar{R}^{1/\beta}$. In effect, since the zero-knowledge proof is valid, this means that $\mathsf{DiscLog}_g(R) = \mathsf{DiscLog}_{\bar{g}}(\bar{R})$, where $\bar{g} = g^{b\beta}$, and so $R^{b\beta} = \bar{R}$. Now, knowing $R^{\mathsf{sk}_{B^\star}}$ and $R^{\mathsf{sk}_{B^\star,j}}$ for $j = 1, \ldots, t-1$, the algorithm $\mathcal{A}^{DH}$ can compute the rest of values $R^{\mathsf{sk}_{B^\star,j}}$, for $j = t, t+1, \ldots, n$, by interpolation in the exponent. Once this is done, the rest of the unsigncryption process can be easily completed by $\mathcal{A}^{DH}$, who obtains a message m and sends all this information to $\mathcal{A}_{\mathsf{IND\text{-}CCA}}$.

Challenge. At some point, $\mathcal{A}_{\mathsf{IND\text{-}CCA}}$ outputs two messages m_0, m_1 of the same length, along with a key pair $(\mathsf{sk}_{A^\star}, \mathsf{pk}_{A^\star})$ for a sender $A^\star$. To produce the challenge ciphertext $C^\star$, the algorithm $\mathcal{A}^{DH}$ defines $R^\star = g^a$ and then chooses at random the values $c^\star \in \{0,1\}^\ell$, $h^\star, s_1^\star, s_2^\star \in \mathbb{Z}_q$ and $\beta^\star \in \mathbb{Z}_q^\star$. After that, $\mathcal{A}^{DH}$ defines $\bar{g}^\star = g^{\beta^\star}$, $\bar{R}^\star = (g^a)^{\beta^\star}$, $Y_1^\star = g^{s_1^\star} \cdot (R^\star)^{h^\star}$, $Y_2^\star = g^{s_2^\star} \cdot (\mathsf{pk}_{A^\star})^{h^\star}$ and $\bar{Y}_1^\star = \bar{g}^{s_1^\star} \cdot (\bar{R}^\star)^{h^\star}$.

If either the input $(c^\star, R^\star, Y_1^\star, Y_2^\star, \mathsf{pk}_{A^\star}, \mathsf{pk}_{B^\star})$ already exists in TAB_1, or the input $(c^\star, R^\star, \bar{g}^\star, \bar{R}^\star, Y_1^\star, Y_2^\star, \bar{Y}_1^\star, \mathsf{pk}_{A^\star}, \mathsf{pk}_{B^\star})$ already exists in TAB_2, the algorithm $\mathcal{A}^{DH}$ goes back to choose at random other values for $c^\star, h^\star$, etc. Finally, the relation $\bar{g}^\star = H_1(c^\star, R^\star, Y_1^\star, Y_2^\star, \mathsf{pk}_{A^\star}, \mathsf{pk}_{B^\star})$ is added to TAB_1 and the relation $h^\star = H_2(c^\star, R^\star, \bar{g}^\star, \bar{R}^\star, Y_1^\star, Y_2^\star, \bar{Y}_1^\star, \mathsf{pk}_{A^\star}, \mathsf{pk}_{B^\star})$ is added to TAB_2.

The challenge ciphertext that $\mathcal{A}^{DH}$ sends to $\mathcal{A}_{\mathsf{IND\text{-}CCA}}$ is $C^\star = (c^\star, R^\star, \bar{R}^\star, h^\star, s_1^\star, s_2^\star)$.

More unsigncryption queries. $\mathcal{A}_{\mathsf{IND\text{-}CCA}}$ can make more hash and unsigncryption queries, which are answered exactly in the same way as described before the challenge phase. The only delicate point is that $\mathcal{A}^{DH}$ could not answer to a valid unsigncryption query $C = (c, R, \bar{R}, h, s_1, s_2)$ for which the value of $\bar{g} = H_1(c, R, g^{s_1} \cdot R^h, g^{s_2} \cdot (\mathsf{pk}_A)^h, \mathsf{pk}_A, \mathsf{pk}_{B^\star}) = \bar{g}^\star$, because this value does not have the necessary form $(g^b)^\beta$. But this happens only if the two inputs of H_1, in both the challenge ciphertext and in this queried ciphertext, are the same. Since both zero-knowledge proofs are valid, we would also have that the value of $\bar{R}$ is equal in both cases, and therefore the values of $h, s_1, s_2, \mathsf{pk}_A$ would also be equal. The conclusion is that the unsigncryption query C would be exactly the challenge ciphertext, and this query is prohibited to $\mathcal{A}_{\mathsf{IND\text{-}CCA}}$.

Final analysis. Finally, $\mathcal{A}_{\mathsf{IND\text{-}CCA}}$ outputs a guess bit b'. We are assuming that $\mathcal{A}_{\mathsf{IND\text{-}CCA}}$ succeeds with probability significantly greater than $1/2$ (random guess). Since H_0 is assumed to behave as a random function, this can happen only if $\mathcal{A}_{\mathsf{IND\text{-}CCA}}$ has asked to the random oracle H_0 the input corresponding to the challenge $C^\star$. This input is $(g^a, g^b, g^{ab}, \mathsf{pk}_{A^\star})$. Therefore, with non-negligible probability $\mathsf{Adv}_{\mathcal{A}_{\mathsf{IND\text{-}CCA}}}(\lambda)/2$, the value g^{ab} is in the table $\mathsf{TAB}^\star$ constructed by $\mathcal{A}^{DH}$, and therefore the output of $\mathcal{A}^{DH}$ contains the correct answer for the given instance of the DH problem. As the authors of [20] indicate, we could use the Diffie-Hellman self-corrector described in [19] to transform this algorithm $\mathcal{A}^{DH}$ into an algorithm that only outputs the single and correct solution to the DH problem.   □

5   Conclusion

We have considered in this paper the strong security properties that one could (or should) require for a signcryption scheme with threshold unsigncryption: existential unforgeability and indistinguishability under insider chosen message / ciphertext attacks, in a multi-user setting. We have shown that none of the (few) existing threshold unsigncryption protocols, either in the traditional PKI or in the identity-based scenario, achieves this level of security. This includes generic constructions obtained by composing a fully secure signature scheme and a fully secure threshold decryption scheme.

After that, we have constructed a threshold unsigncryption scheme which achieves those strong security properties. It is a modification of the threshold decryption scheme by Shoup and Gennaro [20]. Its security is proved in the random oracle model. As future work, one could investigate if other secure threshold decryption schemes can be modified to obtain more fully secure threshold unsigncryption schemes, maybe without random oracles (see for example [6]).

Acknowledgments

The work of Javier Herranz is partially supported by Spanish program CONSOLIDER-INGENIO 2010, under project ARES (CSD2007-00004). Javier Herranz enjoys a *Ramón y Cajal* grant, partially funded by the European Social Fund (ESF), from Spanish MICINN Ministry. Finally, the work of the three authors is partially supported by Spanish MICINN Ministry, under project MTM2009-07694.

References

1. An, J.H., Dodis, Y., Rabin, T.: On the security of joint signature and encryption. In: Knudsen, L.R. (ed.) EUROCRYPT 2002. LNCS, vol. 2332, pp. 83–107. Springer, Heidelberg (2002)
2. Baek, J., Steinfeld, R., Zheng, Y.: Formal proofs for the security of signcryption. Journal of Cryptology 20(2), 203–235 (2007)
3. Bao, F., Deng, R.H.: A signcryption scheme with signature directly verifiable by public key. In: Imai, H., Zheng, Y. (eds.) PKC 1998. LNCS, vol. 1431, pp. 55–59. Springer, Heidelberg (1998)
4. Bellare, M., Rogaway, P.: Minimizing the use of random oracles in authenticated encryption schemes. In: Han, Y., Quing, S. (eds.) ICICS 1997. LNCS, vol. 1334, pp. 1–16. Springer, Heidelberg (1997)

5. Bjørstad, T.E., Dent, A.W.: Building better signcryption schemes with Tag-KEMs. In: Yung, M., Dodis, Y., Kiayias, A., Malkin, T.G. (eds.) PKC 2006. LNCS, vol. 3958, pp. 491–507. Springer, Heidelberg (2006)
6. Boneh, D., Boyen, X., Halevi, S.: Chosen ciphertext secure public key threshold encryption without random oracles. In: Pointcheval, D. (ed.) CT-RSA 2006. LNCS, vol. 3860, pp. 226–243. Springer, Heidelberg (2006)
7. Canetti, R., Krawczyk, H., Nielsen, J.B.: Relaxing chosen-ciphertext security. In: Boneh, D. (ed.) CRYPTO 2003. LNCS, vol. 2729, pp. 565–582. Springer, Heidelberg (2003)
8. Chow, S.M., Yiu, S.M., Hui, L.K., Chow, K.P.: Efficient forward and provably secure ID-based signcryption scheme with public verifiability and public ciphertext authenticity. In: Lim, J.-I., Lee, D.-H. (eds.) ICISC 2003. LNCS, vol. 2971, pp. 352–369. Springer, Heidelberg (2004)
9. Gennaro, R., Jarecki, S., Krawczyk, H., Rabin, T.: Secure distributed key generation for Discrete-Log based cryptosystems. Journal of Cryptology 20(1), 51–83 (2007)
10. Koo, J.H., Kim, H.J., Jeong, I.R., Lee, D.H., Lim, J.I.: Jointly unsigncryptable signcryption schemes. In: Proceedings of WISA 2001, vol. 2, pp. 397–407 (2001)
11. Li, F., Gao, J., Hu, Y.: ID-based threshold unsigncryption scheme from pairings. In: Feng, D., Lin, D., Yung, M. (eds.) CISC 2005. LNCS, vol. 3822, pp. 242–253. Springer, Heidelberg (2005)
12. Li, F., Xin, X., Hu, Y.: ID-based signcryption scheme with (t,n) shared unsigncryption. International Journal of Network Security 3(2), 155–159 (2006)
13. Li, C.K., Yang, G., Wong, D.S., Deng, X., Chow, S.M.: An efficient signcryption scheme with key privacy. In: López, J., Samarati, P., Ferrer, J.L. (eds.) EuroPKI 2007. LNCS, vol. 4582, pp. 78–93. Springer, Heidelberg (2007)
14. Libert, B., Quisquater, J.J.: Efficient signcryption with key privacy from Gap Diffie-Hellman groups. In: Bao, F., Deng, R., Zhou, J. (eds.) PKC 2004. LNCS, vol. 2947, pp. 187–200. Springer, Heidelberg (2004)
15. Ma, C., Chen, K., Zheng, D., Liu, S.: Efficient and proactive threshold signcryption. In: Zhou, J., López, J., Deng, R.H., Bao, F. (eds.) ISC 2005. LNCS, vol. 3650, pp. 233–243. Springer, Heidelberg (2005)
16. Pointcheval, D., Stern, J.: Security arguments for digital signatures and blind signatures. Journal of Cryptology 13(3), 361–396 (2000)
17. Schnorr, C.P.: Efficient signature generation by smart cards. Journal of Cryptology 4, 161–174 (1991)
18. Shamir, A.: How to share a secret. Communications of the ACM 22, 612–613 (1979)
19. Shoup, V.: Lower bounds for discrete logarithms and related problems. In: Fumy, W. (ed.) EUROCRYPT 1997. LNCS, vol. 1233, pp. 256–266. Springer, Heidelberg (1997)
20. Shoup, V., Gennaro, R.: Securing threshold cryptosystems against chosen ciphertext attack. Journal of Cryptology 15(2), 75–96 (2002)
21. Yang, G., Wong, D.S., Deng, X.: Analysis and improvement of a signcryption scheme with key privacy. In: Zhou, J., López, J., Deng, R.H., Bao, F. (eds.) ISC 2005. LNCS, vol. 3650, pp. 218–232. Springer, Heidelberg (2005)
22. Yang, B., Yu, Y., Li, F., Sun, Y.: Provably secure identity-based threshold unsigncryption scheme. In: Xiao, B., Yang, L.T., Ma, J., Muller-Schloer, C., Hua, Y. (eds.) ATC 2007. LNCS, vol. 4610, pp. 114–122. Springer, Heidelberg (2007)
23. Zhang, Z., Mian, C., Jin, Q.: Signcryption scheme with threshold shared unsigncryption preventing malicious receivers. In: Proceedings of TENCON 2002, vol. 2, pp. 196–199. IEEE Computer Society, Los Alamitos (2002)

24. Zheng, Y.: Digital signcryption or How to achieve cost (signature & encryption) $<<$ cost(signature) + cost(encryption). In: Kaliski Jr., B.S. (ed.) CRYPTO 1997. LNCS, vol. 1294, pp. 165–179. Springer, Heidelberg (1997)

A   Analysis of an ID-Based Threshold Unsigncryption Scheme

The identity-based threshold unsigncryption scheme proposed in [12] works for groups $\mathbb{G}_1 = \langle P \rangle$ (additive) and $\mathbb{G}_2$ (multiplicative), both with prime order q, which admit a bilinear pairing $e : \mathbb{G}_1 \times \mathbb{G}_1 \to \mathbb{G}_2$. The main property of e is that $e(aP, bP) = e(P, P)^{ab}$ for any pair of values $a, b \in \mathbb{Z}_q$.

A.1   Description of the Scheme

We describe for simplicity the variant of the scheme in [12] which does not provide robustness to the threshold unsigncryption process. The attack that we describe later applies also to the robust variant.

The Setup of the scheme is run by a master entity, who chooses hash functions $H_1 : \{0,1\}^* \to \mathbb{G}_1$, $H_2 : \mathbb{G}_2 \to \{0,1\}^\ell$ and $H_3 : \{0,1\}^* \times \mathbb{G}_2 \to \mathbb{Z}_q^*$. The master entity chooses her secret key at random as $\alpha \in \mathbb{Z}_q^*$, and computes $P_{pub} = \alpha P$. The public parameters are $(q, \mathbb{G}_1, P, \mathbb{G}_2, e, H_1, H_2, H_3, \ell, P_{pub})$.

Let us define for each identity ID the value $Q_{ID} = H_1(ID) \in \mathbb{G}_1$. The secret key for a sender with identity ID_A is $\mathsf{SK}_A = \alpha^{-1} Q_{ID_A} \in \mathbb{G}_1$. For a collective of receivers ID_B, the master entity computes the secret key $\mathsf{SK}_B = \alpha Q_{ID_B} \in \mathbb{G}_1$ and then computes a (t, n) sharing of SK_B. That is, each member $B_j \in B$ will receive a share $\mathsf{SK}_{B,j} \in \mathbb{G}_1$ such that t or more shares allow to recover, by interpolation, the value SK_B.

To signcrypt a message $m \in \{0,1\}^\ell$ for the collective of receivers B, a sender A acts as follows.

1. Choose $x \in \mathbb{Z}_q^*$ at random.
2. Compute $R = e(P, Q_{ID_A})^x$.
3. Compute $k = H_2(\, e(Q_{ID_A}, Q_{ID_B})^x \,)$.
4. Compute $c = m \oplus k$.
5. Compute $h = H_3(c, R)$.
6. Compute $S = (x - h)\mathsf{SK}_A$.
7. Return the ciphertext $C = (c, h, S)$.

To jointly unsigncrypt a ciphertext $C = (c, h, s)$ coming from a sender A, each member of B first computes $R = e(S, P_{pub}) \cdot e(Q_{ID_A}, P)^h$ and then checks if $h = H_3(c, R)$. If this is not the case, the symbol $\perp$ is the output of the unsigncryption process. Otherwise, each $B_j \in B$ broadcasts the partial information $T_j = e(S, \mathsf{SK}_{B,j})$. From t or more values T_j, the value $T = e(S, \mathsf{SK}_B)$ can be interpolated, which is then multiplied with $e(Q_{ID_A}, Q_{ID_B})^h$, to result in

$$e(S, \mathsf{SK}_B) \cdot e(Q_{ID_A}, H_2(ID_B))^h = e(Q_{ID_A}, Q_{ID_B})^{x-h} \cdot e(Q_{ID_A}, Q_{ID_B})^h = e(Q_{ID_A}, Q_{ID_B})^x.$$

This value is injected into H_2, and the resulting output k is combined with c to obtain the plaintext $m = c \oplus k$.

278   J. Herranz, A. Ruiz, and G. Sáez

A.2   Description of the Attack

Actually, this threshold unsigncryption protocol [12] is a distributed variant of the ordinary signcryption scheme of [8], which is proved to achieve IND-CCA security even against insider attacks. The authors of [12] claim that the security of their scheme infers from the security of that in [8]. However, as we have seen for example for the generic constructions in Section 3.1, security of threshold unsigncryption protocols is much more subtle than security of ordinary signcryption schemes.

This is another example of that fact. An insider attacker $\mathcal{A}_{\text{IND-CCA}}$ against the indistinguishability property of this threshold unsigncryption scheme can be designed as follows.

1. $\mathcal{A}_{\text{IND-CCA}}$ receives a challenge ciphertext $C^* = (c^*, h^*, S^*)$ for sender A^* and collective of receivers B^*. We assume that $\mathcal{A}_{\text{IND-CCA}}$ knows the secret key $\text{SK}_{A^*} = \alpha^{-1} H_1(ID_{A^*})$.
   [The idea is that, if the randomness employed in the challenge ciphertext C^* is x^*, then $\mathcal{A}_{\text{IND-CCA}}$ will produce a valid ciphertext $C \neq C^*$ whose randomness is $2x^*$.]
2. $\mathcal{A}_{\text{IND-CCA}}$ first computes $R^* = e(S^*, P_{pub}) \cdot e(H_1(ID_{A^*}), P)^{h^*}$.
3. $\mathcal{A}_{\text{IND-CCA}}$ defines $R = (R^*)^2$ and computes $h = H_3(c^*, R) \neq h^*$.
4. $\mathcal{A}_{\text{IND-CCA}}$ computes $S = 2S^* + 2h^*\text{SK}_{A^*} - h\text{SK}_{A^*}$.
5. $\mathcal{A}_{\text{IND-CCA}}$ sends (ID_{A^*}, ID_{B^*}, C) to the threshold unsigncryption oracle, where $C = (c^*, h, S)$.
6. Since the ciphertext C is consistent, the attacker $\mathcal{A}_{\text{IND-CCA}}$ will obtain the values $T_j = e(S, \text{SK}_{B^*,j})$ broadcast by the members of B^*.
7. From these values, $\mathcal{A}_{\text{IND-CCA}}$ can interpolate these values T_j to obtain

$$e(S, \text{SK}_{B^*}) = e(2S^*, \text{SK}_{B^*}) \cdot e(\text{SK}_{A^*}, \text{SK}_{B^*})^{2h^*-h} = e(2S^*, \text{SK}_{B^*}) \cdot e(Q_{ID_{A^*}}, Q_{ID_{B^*}})^{2h^*-h}.$$

8. From the previous value, $\mathcal{A}_{\text{IND-CCA}}$ can easily recover the value $T^* = e(S^*, \text{SK}_{B^*})$ and complete the decryption of the challenge C^* by himself, breaking in this way the IND-CCA security of the scheme.

Author Index

GPSR Compliance

The European Union's (EU) General Product Safety Regulation (GPSR)
is a set of rules that requires consumer products to be safe and our
obligations to ensure this.

If you have any concerns about our products, you can contact us on
ProductSafety@springernature.com

In case Publisher is established outside the EU, the EU authorized
representative is:

Springer Nature Customer Service Center GmbH
Europaplatz 3
69115 Heidelberg, Germany

Batch number: 09490872

Printed by Printforce, the Netherlands